SIR PAUL PRESTON CBE is Pro[...] London School of Economics [...] University of Reading and Pro[...] of Modern History at Queen Mary University of London. He is a Fellow of the British Academy and holds the Marcel Proust Chair of the European Academy of Yuste. He has been awarded honorary doctorates by universities in Spain and the UK. In 2006, he was awarded the International Ramon Llull Prize by the Catalan Government and, in 2018, the Guernica Peace Prize. Among his many works are *Franco: A Biography*, *Comrades*, *Doves of War: Four Women of Spain*, *Juan Carlos*, *The Spanish Civil War*, *The Spanish Holocaust*, *The Last Stalinist*, *The Last Days of the Spanish Republic* and *A People Betrayed*. In Spain, he was appointed a Comendador de la Orden del Mérito Civil in 1986 and awarded, in 2007, the Gran Cruz de la Orden de Isabel la Católica. He lives in London.

'Deeply researched and revealing ... Preston's study is based on both profound knowledge and shrewd human understanding'
Daily Telegraph, five-star review

'Preston's great skill lies in carefully dissecting these vile characters ... This book reveals Preston at the peak of his powers; he's an enormous intellect and a great storyteller'
The Times

'Rightly acclaimed as one of today's pre-eminent historians of mid-twentieth-century Spain ... in his new book *Architects of Terror*, intense specialisation and high-level gossip come together ... Powerfully recounted by Preston, the details are so outrageous that they would be funny if the topic weren't so grave'
TLS

'A revealing account of the shocking antisemitism that formed the intellectual (I use the word loosely) underpinning of the 1936 nationalist uprising led by General Franco ... With his customary meticulous research, Professor Preston shows how fake news is certainly not an invention of the twenty-first century, and that its consequences can be far-reaching and frequently lethal'
Jewish Chronicle

'Shocking and fascinating … Using his mastery of this highly complicated period of Spanish history, Preston shows how the massacres,
brutality and dehumanisation of the enemy for which the period is
remembered were built on a tissue of lies and invented plots …
Preston's book moves at great pace and is filled with telling details. He
has an eye for an anecdote, but always keeps the bigger picture in
mind … Preston's original and frightening book is about Spain in the
1930s and 1940s, but it is also about the world we live in today'

Literary Review

'Preston's book – a thorough dismantling of any attempt to rehabili-
tate the Fascist right – provides useful ammunition to critics of the
Right's convenient forgetting of history. The only shame is how timely
it is'   *Jacobin*

'This was a book I devoured. Paul Preston's *Architects of Terror* is a
chilling read, not just for what it tells us about Franco and his
murderers, but because it carries a warning from history that cannot
be ignored'   *Counterfire*

BY THE SAME AUTHOR

The Coming of the Spanish Civil War
The Triumph of Democracy in Spain
The Politics of Revenge
Franco: A Biography
¡Comrades! Portraits from the Spanish Civil War
Doves of War: Four Women of Spain
Juan Carlos: Steering Spain from Dictatorship to Democracy
The Spanish Civil War: Reaction, Revolution and Revenge
*We Saw Spain Die: Foreign Correspondents in
the Spanish Civil War*
*The Spanish Holocaust: Inquisition and Extermination in
Twentieth-Century Spain*
The Last Stalinist: The Life of Santiago Carrillo
*A People Betrayed: A History of Corruption, Political
Incompetence and Social Division in Modern Spain
1874–2018*

ARCHITECTS OF TERROR

Paranoia, Conspiracy and Anti-Semitism
in Franco's Spain

Paul Preston

WILLIAM
COLLINS

William Collins
An imprint of HarperCollins*Publishers*
1 London Bridge Street
London SE1 9GF

WilliamCollinsBooks.com

HarperCollins*Publishers*
Macken House, 39/40 Mayor Street Upper
Dublin 1, D01 C9W8, Ireland

First published in Great Britain in 2023 by William Collins
This William Collins paperback edition published in 2024

1

A catalogue record for this book is
available from the British Library

ISBN 978-0-00-852215-5

Set in Minion Pro
Printed and bound in the UK using 100%
renewable electricity at CPI Group (UK) Ltd

MIX
Paper | Supporting
responsible forestry
FSC
www.fsc.org   FSC™ C007454

This book contains FSC™ certified paper and other controlled
sources to ensure responsible forest management.

For more information visit: www.harpercollins.co.uk/green

For Helen Graham

Contents

Preface

Broadly speaking, this book is about how fake news contributed to the coming of a civil war. It returns to issues raised in an earlier volume, *The Spanish Holocaust*, expanding particularly on its fourth chapter, 'Theorists of Extermination'. A further element of contemporary relevance is the centrality of the theme of anti-Semitism. In a country with a tiny minority of Jews, perhaps fewer than 6,000 in 1936, and a similar number of freemasons, it is astonishing that a central justification for the civil war that took the lives of around 500,000 Spaniards, should have been the alleged plans for world domination of the so-called Jewish–masonic–Bolshevik conspiracy. The term used in Spanish by its propagators, *contubernio judeo-masónico-bolchevique*, has a stronger connotation than the English. It should properly be rendered as 'the filthy Jewish–masonic–Bolshevik concubinage'.

The war was actually fought to overturn the educational and social reforms of the democratic Second Republic and to combat its cultural challenges to the established order. In that sense, it was fought in the interests of the landowners, industrialists, bankers, clerics and army officers whose privileges were threatened, and directed against the liberals and leftists who were promulgating the reforms and cultural challenges. Yet, during the years of the Republic from 1931 to 1936, throughout the war itself and for many decades after it ended, the myth continued to be fostered in Spain that the defeated enemy in the war was the Jewish–masonic–Bolshevik Conspiracy.

The book is not a history of either anti-Semitism or anti-freemasonry in Spain. Rather, it takes the form of biographical studies of key individuals who propagated the anti-Semitic and anti-

masonic myth and of the central figures who implemented the
horrors that it justified. There are six chapters dedicated to these men
and two framing chapters dealing more broadly with Franco and his
circle and their belief in the existence of, and need to annihilate, the
so-called *contubernio*.

The first chapter, 'Fake News and Civil War', examines the relationship between Francisco Franco and the *contubernio*. It analyses the
personal, professional and political motives that explain his fervent
embrace, and subsequent implementation, of the idea. It looks at the
reading, the friendships and the collaborations that consolidated his
use of the myth. Key figures are his brother-in-law and political
mentor Ramón Serrano Suñer, the psychiatrist Antonio Vallejo
Nágera and the paediatrician and educationalist Professor Enrique
Suñer Ordóñez.

The second chapter, 'The Policeman', is about Mauricio Carlavilla,
one of the most unsavoury propagandists of the *contubernio*. The
material that he collected as an undercover agent in the late 1920s
was the basis of the first of many best-sellers on the *contubernio*. One
of his books actually sold 100,000 copies. He was personally corrupt
and was a central element in an attempt to assassinate the Republican
Prime Minister Manuel Azaña. His multiple publications included
scurrilous tomes on sodomy and on Satanism.

The third chapter, 'The Priest', is about the extraordinary life of
Father Joan Tusquets. As a prominent cleric, his many publications
on the Jewish–masonic–Bolshevik conspiracy were immensely influential. Among his celebrity readers were Generals Franco and Mola.
Despite his ecclesiastical vocation, he engaged in criminal activity to
spy on masonic lodges. He was an active propagandist for, and a
participant in, the preparation of the 1936 military uprising. Before
the war, he compiled huge lists of the names of freemasons. During
the war, he was the effective head of the Jewish–Masonic Section of
Franco's military intelligence service. The unit collected material that
swelled his lists and provided a crucial part of the infrastructure of
repression. After the civil war, he made considerable efforts to deny
his activities.

The protagonist of the fourth chapter is 'The Poet', José María
Pemán, a wealthy landowner and popular poet and dramatist. A

fervent monarchist, Pemán was a key propagandist of the military dictatorship of General Primo de Rivera between 1923 and 1930. Appalled by the coming of the democratic Republic in 1931, he became an important civilian advocate and sponsor of the military uprising of 1936. When it took place, he put himself forward as the official public orator on behalf of the military rebels. In hundreds of articles and public speeches, he peddled virulently anti-Semitic ideas in order to justify the bloody repression of the Republican enemy. After the defeat of Hitler, he transformed himself into the moderate face of the Franco regime. He assiduously rewrote his extremist past and was honoured by King Juan Carlos.

The fifth chapter, entitled 'The Messenger', focuses on an aristo-cratic landowner, Gonzalo Aguilera, the Conde de Alba de Yeltes. Unlike the other protagonists, he was not an advocate of the Jewish–masonic conspiracy nor was he involved in mass terror. However, he played an important role in justifying the atrocities of the military rebels. His mother was English, he was educated in England and Germany and he served as a liaison officer with the German army on the Eastern Front during the First World War. He had considerable linguistic abilities and, during the Spanish Civil War, he was employed as a liaison with the foreign press correspondents. Those in his charge were entranced by his notion that the repression was merely a necessary periodic culling of the working class. He had so internalized the brutality he experienced in the Moroccan colonies that he ended up murdering his two sons and trying unsuccessfully to do the same to his wife. With access to large tranches of his personal correspondence, it has been possible to build a fascinating psychological portrait.

The sixth chapter concerns 'The Killer in the North', General Emilio Mola. He served as an officer in the African wars. His memoirs of his experiences reveal that he delighted in their savagery. After the fall of the Primo de Rivera dictatorship, he served as head of the national security apparatus, vainly trying to hold back the Republican tide. At that time, he was Carlavilla's superior officer and shared his hatred of Jews, freemasons and leftists, all of whom were painted as Communists. He was a fervent believer in the notorious fabrication about the alleged global domination of the Jews, *The Protocols of the*

Elders of Zion, and an avid reader of the works of Tusquets. His commitment to the idea of the *contubernio* underlay the enthusiasm with which he oversaw the murders of tens of thousands of civilians as head of the Army of the North.

The seventh chapter, 'The Psychopath in the South', deals with General Gonzalo Queipo de Llano. He served in the colonial wars in Cuba and Morocco and was notorious for the violence of his temper as well as for his unlimited ambition, which he pursued with endless political flexibility. Initially a monarchist, perceiving himself to have been spurned by the King and the Dictator Primo de Rivera his resentment saw him join the Republican cause. Despite lavish preferment from the Republic, a similar personal resentment in 1936 provoked another change of allegiance. He took part in the military uprising and conquered Seville for the rebels, an achievement about which he concocted heroic myths. As a kind of viceroy of the south, he oversaw the savage repression in Western Andalusia and Extremadura, which involved the deaths of over 40,000 men and women. He also prospered from corruption.

The eighth chapter, 'The Never-Ending War', recounts how Franco and his closest collaborators – Ramón Serrano Suñer, his lifelong collaborator and political chief of staff Luis Carrero Blanco and the surrealist and co-founder of Spanish fascism Ernesto Giménez Caballero – continued to propagate the notion of the *contubernio*. Their anti-Semitism was a key component of Franco's relationship with Hitler. It survived the defeat of the Third Reich. Franco published articles and a book denouncing the Jewish–masonic conspiracy and was still referring to it in his last speech a few weeks before he died in 1975.

Various factors united the protagonists. The most striking is their unanimous conviction of the factual veracity of *The Protocols of the Elders of Zion* and of the idea that freemasonry was responsible for Spain's loss of empire. Several – Francisco Franco, Emilio Mola, Gonzalo Queipo de Llano, Gonzalo Aguilera, Mauricio Carlavilla, Antonio Vallejo Nágera, Luis Carrero Blanco and Ernesto Giménez Caballero – were brutalized by their experiences in the colonial wars in North Africa. Those eight and the four who avoided service in Africa, Ramón Serrano Suñer, Juan Tusquets, Jose María Pemán and

Enrique Suñer, all celebrated the bloodshed of the civil war. After the civil war, with the exception of Mola who was killed in 1937 and Carlavilla and Franco who never wavered in their anti-Semitism, most employed considerable mendacity and invention to rewrite their past behaviour. The deconstruction of their untruths has been one of the central preoccupations of the book.

1

Fake News and Civil War

In the spring of 1937, a book was published in the zone controlled by the military rebels commanded by General Franco. Its subject was the progress of the Spanish Civil War to date and it was entitled *War in Spain against Bolshevik Judaism*.[1] This was curious because there is no mention of Jews or Bolsheviks on any of its pages. Moreover, there were no more than 6,000 Jews in Spain in 1936, of whom around 30 per cent had fled from Nazism and found refuge in the Republic after 1934.[2] Furthermore, the Communist Party of Spain was tiny. How then could this be a war against Jews and Bolsheviks? Yet many supporters of the military coup of July 1936 that provoked the civil war believed this to be so. That was testimony to the success of a massive campaign mounted during the years of the Republic to convince Spaniards, particularly Catholic Spaniards, that their country was threatened by a cabal of Jews, freemasons and Bolsheviks. Behind this fraudulent notion of a nation in mortal peril, the military uprising in fact had the less apocalyptic, and more materially profitable, aim of reversing the many reforms with which the Second Republic had planned to modernize Spain. In power for two and a half years from 14 April 1931, the Republican–Socialist coalition had challenged the Catholic Church, the military, the landowning elite, bankers and industrialists with an ambitious programme of social, economic and educational reform.

Across the right, there was outrage at these challenges to conservative values and economic interests. In consequence, the right-wing press and propaganda apparatus mounted a major campaign to delegitimize the Republic. Deep-rooted historical prejudices were conjured up in order to pinpoint the 'other' against whom blame, fear and hatred could be directed. This 'other' came to be called the Jewish–masonic–Bolshevik conspiracy (*el contubernio judeo-masónico-bolchevique*). This fictitious notion portrayed the Second Republic as aiming to destroy Christian civilization and its faithful guardian Spain. This assault was allegedly masterminded by the Jews and carried out by their puppets, freemasons and leftists. The generation of mass conservative belief in the conspiracy was the work of many. However, the conversion of the belief into enmity towards the Republic was most successfully implemented by the writings and lectures of its three persuasive propagandists, the Catalan theologian Juan Tusquets, the policeman Mauricio Carlavilla and the poet José María Pemán. Tusquets revealed the purpose of the simplistic campaigns against Jews and freemasons. Claiming that the objective of the conspiracy was to divide, he made it clear that his efforts were directed at creating unity against them.[3] His aim was to use easily digestible propaganda to unify opposition against an imaginary enemy: 'All for one, without groups, without personality cults … The truth attractively presented is all-powerful.'[4] That ambition was shared by Carlavilla and Pemán.

Thus, although the Francoist forces did not fight in the Spanish Civil War in order to annihilate Jews, anti-Semitic and anti-masonic propaganda had served to unify and to intensify enmity against the Republic. Inevitably, the latent anti-Semitism of the right in Spain fed into approval for the activities of Hitler and the Nazis. A comparison was made between the influence that the Nazis accused the Jews of having in Weimar Germany and the influence that they allegedly enjoyed in medieval Spain. Similarly, the activities of the Nazis were presented as a twentieth-century emulation of the expulsion of the Jews by the so-called Catholic Kings Isabel de Castilla and Fernando de Aragón in 1492. Both were presented as necessary measures to protect national values and interests.[5]

Anti-Semitism and the idea of a plot masterminded by the Jews to destroy Christian civilization and its self-proclaimed champion, Spain, had proliferated in clerical and right-wing circles for centuries. However, it was only after the foundation of the Second Republic in April 1931 that they began to play a key role in day-to-day politics. The extreme right was determined to destroy the new regime and its reformist agenda. To justify its efforts, the cover was used that this was a life-or-death struggle to defend Spain's traditional values against attack by a coordinated force of leftists and freemasons masterminded by the Jews. The bogeyman of the Jewish–masonic–Bolshevik conspiracy provided a convenient label for a huge range of leftists and liberals bundled into an 'other' that needed to be exterminated. Its apocalyptic and yet simplistic language provided an inspiring justification for what were narrow sectional objectives. There were numerous 'theorists' of the conspiracy who were able to propagate their views through several newspapers. The more vehement among them, such as *El Siglo Futuro* and *El Correo Catalán*, were those that supported the extreme rightist dissident Carlist dynasty. However, diatribes against the Jewish–masonic–Bolshevik conspiracy could often be found in more mainstream conservative dailies such as the monarchist *ABC* and the Catholic *El Debate*.

Condemnation of freemasonry and simmering anti-Semitism were common within the Catholic Church and right-wing political circles in Spain long before the fall of the monarchy of Alfonso XIII and the advent of a reforming Republic in April 1931. The rejection of what was condemned as a revolution, despite the moderate ambitions of the Republican–Socialist government, was all the more virulent because several of its senior politicians were freemasons. From early 1932 onwards, the four principal right-wing groups of the opposition to the new regime acquired an ever more marked anti-Semitic veneer. Two of the four were the militant monarchist groups, the Carlist Comunión Tradicionalista and the Alfonsist Acción Española group, made up of wealthy landowners, bankers and industrialists, many of whom were prominent aristocrats.[6] Together with the tiny nascent fascist groups that would coalesce into the Falange, they wished to overthrow the Republic by violence and were thus known collectively as 'catastrophists'. The fourth group coalesced under the intellectual leadership of the Catholic intellectual Ángel Herrera Oria in the coalition Acción Popular. They were known as 'accidentalists' because Herrera argued that forms of government, republican or monarchical, were 'accidental' whereas what was 'fundamental' was the social and economic content of a regime. Although there was considerable overlap in the membership of all of these groups, Acción Popular has been regarded as the 'moderate' right.

The intensification of anti-Semitism within all these groups can be attributed to the appearance in Spain from 1932 of numerous translations of the fiercely anti-Semitic fiction *The Protocols of the Elders of Zion* and a commercially successful and immensely influential book, *Origins of the Spanish Revolution*, by Juan Tusquets, a Catalan priest of Carlist sympathies.[7] The first and commercially most successful of the editions of the *Protocols* was the Duque de la Victoria's translation of the French version by Monsignor Ernest Jouin.[8] Prior to the civil war, there were five subsequent editions of this translation. In addition, there were six other translations, one of which was published by Tusquets.[9] Another was produced by Onésimo Redondo, a disciple of Ángel Herrera's brother, Enrique, and founder of one of the component groups that would eventually unite as the Falange. Redondo affirmed the authenticity of the *Protocols*, arguing that they had been translated into Russian from Hebrew. He claimed that world Jewry had frantically tried to prevent their diffusion by buying up copies in order to destroy them.[10] None of these editions was translated from the Russian original by Sergei Aleksandrovich Nilus.[11] Tusquets's own *Orígenes de la revolución española* had done much to popularize the allegations of the *Protocols* that the Jews aimed at world domination through their puppets, freemasonry and left-wing movements. As late as 1963, one of the major protagonists of this book, Mauricio Carlavilla, published an annotated edition of the *Protocols*.

Of the three leaders of the fascist groups that would fuse as the Falange, Onésimo Redondo was the only one actively committed to anti-Semitism. Although an enthusiast for Nazism and the translator of the Spanish edition of *Mein Kampf*, his influences were the traditional Catholic ones associated with Tusquets and Enrique Herrera. The second, Ramiro Ledesma Ramos, was more influenced by Italian fascism. He regarded anti-Semitism as having relevance only in Germany because, unlike Spain, where the Jewish threat was a 'mere abstraction', Hitler faced 'real enemies, enemies of Germany as a nation'. Among those enemies of Germany, the internal ones were 'the Jew and his finance capital'.[12] The third Spanish fascist, the leader of the Falange José Antonio Primo de Rivera, son of the Dictator, had relatively little interest in 'the Jewish problem' except when it came to the Jewish–Marxist influence over the working class. Nevertheless, the Falangist daily *Arriba* claimed that 'the Judaic–Masonic International is the creator of the two great evils that have afflicted humanity: capitalism and Marxism'. After a bishop had recommended in December 1934 that Catholics should not use the Jewish-owned SEPU department store in Madrid, José Antonio Primo de Rivera approved attacks by Falangists on it the following spring.[13] If he was not actively anti-Semitic, he shared the belief of the more conservative advocates that it was legitimate to annihilate the Jewish–masonic–Bolshevik conspiracy by violence.[14] It was during the civil war and the Second World War that anti-Semitism became a major element of Falangist discourse by way of emulating and currying favour with the Nazis.

The influence of both Tusquets and the *Protocols* could be seen in the language used by contributors to the monarchist journal *Acción Española*, the mouthpiece of the ultra-right-wing conspiratorial group of the same name. Among subscribers to the journal was General Franco. The founder and first editor of the journal was the major landowner Fernando Gallego de Chaves, the Marqués de Quintanar. At an event at the Ritz in Madrid held in his honour by fellow members of the group, Quintanar praised the *Protocols*. He declared that the disaster of the fall of the monarchy came about because 'The great worldwide Jewish–masonic conspiracy injected the autocratic Monarchies with the virus of democracy to defeat them, after turning them into liberal Monarchies.'[15]

In the same issue of the journal that reported Quintanar's speech, there was an article by another owner of huge estates, the Marqués de la Eliseda. It was an adulatory review of a new edition of the most frequently translated French version of *The Protocols of the Elders of Zion*, by Monsignor Ernest Jouin, first published in 1920. Eliseda followed Jouin in asserting the factual validity of the *Protocols* on the flimsy grounds that there was a copy of the Russian original in the British Museum. Eliseda started from the premise – almost certainly influenced by Tusquets's book – that the 'Spanish revolution', that is to say, the fall of the monarchy, had been the work of freemasonry and Judaism. He hailed the *Protocols* for providing both a 'collection of powerful arguments against the false principles of democracy' and 'abundant material for an analytical study of Judaic psychology, of its special concept of things and its racial characteristics'. He affirmed that 'the Jews boast of having spread the liberal and democratic poison through the world so that anarchy and chaos will ensue and allow them to take control of it'. He managed to insinuate, with a veiled reference to the Jewish deputy for Badajoz, Margarita Nelken, that the bloody events at Castilblanco were the result of Jewish involvement. In that village on 31 December 1931, in an outburst of collective rage at systematic oppression, and the shooting of peaceful strikers, the villagers turned on the four Civil Guards responsible and beat them to death. Similarly, he followed Jouin in blaming the Jews for both the assassination of the Archduke Franz Ferdinand in Sarajevo and the Russian revolution. The article was replete with anti-Semitic clichés. He claimed that, through the *Protocols*, it was possible to understand 'Judaic thought, the contempt that they have for Christians – whom they call Goim while referring to themselves as Israelites and never as Jews – and the concept that they have of honour, a sentiment that they neither possess nor understand'. He claimed, allegedly on the basis of personal observation in Palestine, that 'The Jews are true parasites who profit from what they are incapable of producing themselves.'[16] Eliseda's admiration for the book, and the fact that his article was published in the society's journal, was revealing of the attitudes of mainstream monarchist thinking.

Another subscriber to the journal *Acción Española*, Julián Cortés Cavanillas, cited *The Protocols of the Elders of Zion* as proof that, through prominent freemasons, the Jews controlled the anarchist, socialist and communist hordes. Freemasonry was the 'evil offspring of Israel'. He took the fact that the new Republican–Socialist government contained freemasons, Socialists and men accused of being Jewish as proof that the alliance of Marx and Rothschild was behind the demise of the monarchy.[17]

Among other contributors to *Acción Española* were Dr Francisco Murillo Palacios and Wenceslao González Oliveros, both of whom wrote approvingly of the early achievements of the Third Reich. For Murillo these included the efforts made to prevent the German race being undermined by its blood being mixed with that of Jews and

Slavs. In admiring terms, he explained Hitler's views on the Jews and their relationship with Marxism. He wrote:

> The Jew, says Hitler, is the exponent of the most crass egotism, except when presented with shared plunder or shared danger. Even if the Jews could be isolated in the world, this would not cleanse them of the dirt and filth in which they drown, nor would it put an end to the hateful struggle between themselves to exploit and exterminate each other, nor would they abandon their cowardice and absolute lack of a spirit of sacrifice.[18]

Acción Española was only one of the many influences on Franco's anti-Semitism and his fervent belief in the Jewish–masonic–Bolshevik conspiracy. Even more important in the development of his political thinking was a gift from the Dictator General Miguel Primo de Rivera. Shortly before leaving Madrid to take up his appointment at the Academia Militar in Zaragoza in 1927, Primo had arranged for Franco, and several other senior officers, including Generals Emilio Mola and Gonzalo Queipo de Llano, a subscription to the Geneva-based *Bulletin de L'Entente Internationale contre la Troisième Internationale*, a journal opposed to the Moscow-based Communist International (Comintern). The Entente, founded by the Swiss rightist Théodore Aubert and the White Russian émigré Georges Lodygensky, was vehemently anti-Bolshevik and praised the achievements of fascism and military dictatorships as bulwarks against communism. An emissary from the Entente, its deputy chairman, Colonel Odier of the Swiss army, had visited Madrid and arranged with General Primo de Rivera for several subscriptions to be purchased by the Ministry of War and to be distributed to a few key officers. Primo appointed Lieutenant Colonel José Ungría de Jiménez as his liaison with Geneva. Ungría was appointed secretary of the Centro Español Antibolchevique, the Spanish branch of the Entente. Interestingly, during the civil war Ungría would be chief of Franco's intelligence service, the Servicio de Información y Policía Militar.[19]

The gift of this subscription clinched what was to be Franco's life-long obsession with the threat of the Jewish–masonic–Bolshevik conspiracy. Several factors account for the virulence of Franco's hatred of freemasonry. Some predate his introduction to the *Bulletin* from Geneva and his readings of the works of Juan Tusquets. One persuasive reason was his resentment of the sympathy for freemasonry expressed by his father, Nicolás Franco Salgado-Araujo. Francisco Franco despised his father because of his womanizing and the fact that he had abandoned his wife, Pilar Bahamonde, in 1907. In 1962, Franco inadvertently revealed this when he wrote a bizarre interpretation of the fall of Alfonso XIII in his draft memoirs. He alleged that the monarchy had been brought down by a group of 'historic republicans, freemasons, separatists and Socialists'. In terms that were unconsciously about his father, he went on to describe the freemasons as 'atheistic traitors in exile, delinquents, swindlers, men who betrayed their wives'.[20]

The dislike was mutual. Nicolás Franco Salgado-Araujo found his son's obsession with the 'Jewish–masonic conspiracy' laughable, saying, 'what could my son possibly know about freemasonry? It is an association full of illustrious and honourable men, certainly his superiors in knowledge and openness of spirit.'[21] Franco's obsession may also relate to the fact that his unconventional younger brother Ramón was a freemason whose wild behaviour, in both political and personal terms, had caused him considerable embarrassment. Besides the genesis of hostility to freemasonry within his family, it is also probable that he was seeking revenge for the rejection of his own efforts to become a freemason. He had applied to join the Lixus lodge of Larache in 1924 and was turned down because, some months earlier, he had accepted promotion to lieutenant colonel on merit grounds when most fellow officers in Morocco had sworn to abide by the rule of promotion only by strict seniority.[22]

Thus, already deeply hostile to freemasonry, he was especially susceptible to the claims of the Geneva *Bulletin* whose issues he received uninterruptedly until 1936. Thanks to them, but also to *Acción Española* and the works of Tusquets and Carlavilla, he came to see the threat of the Jewish–masonic–Bolshevik conspiracy everywhere and to believe that the entire Spanish left was wittingly or unwittingly working in its interests. In interviews given in 1965, Franco revealed to two biographers, Brian Crozier and George Hills, the influence that the Entente had had over him. He told Hills:

It was while I was director of the Zaragoza Military Academy that I began regularly to receive a Review of Comintern Affairs from Geneva. Later, I discovered that Primo de Rivera had taken out several subscriptions and thought I might be interested in it. I was. It gave me an insight into international communism – into its ends, its strategy and its tactics. I could see communism at work in Spain, undermining the country's morale, as in France.[23]

As will be seen in the later chapter on Mauricio Carlavilla, some of the material that Franco read as an objective external report had actually been generated within Spain by an agent provocateur in the service of General Mola when he was Director General of Security, effectively national police chief. It is not known whether Mola realized that what he was reading thanks to the subscription taken out by Primo de Rivera came from within his own security apparatus. The agent in question, Mauricio Carlavilla, infiltrated the Spanish Communist Party and his exaggerated report on its activities was forwarded to the Entente. Again, as will be seen in the chapter on Mola, the vehemence of the General's hatred of Jews and freemasons was, on his own admission, inflamed by the *Bulletin* of the Entente, the writings of Tusquets and the reports of Carlavilla.

At roughly the same period that he was interviewed by Hills, Franco told Brian Crozier that in 1928 he 'began a systematic study of communism' on the basis of his subscription to the *Bulletin de l'Entente Internationale contre la Troisième Internationale*. His study of the *Bulletin*, he claimed, had alerted him to the murky activities of the Spanish Communists. Moreover, he asserted that, until 1936, he never missed an issue of the *Bulletin* and had persuaded other officers to read it. Indeed, he left Crozier with the impression that contact with the Entente's work was a life-changing experience. The information from Geneva carried by the *Bulletin*, which he read avidly from 1928 to 1936, brought only 'knowledge and a spur to action – the knowledge of an enemy, and the ambition to defeat him'. Given his pre-existing susceptibility to the Entente's message it is not surprising that Franco believed every word published in the *Bulletin*.[24]

In fact, Franco's receptiveness to the various anti-masonic messages was intensified by the coming of the Second Republic. After

his meteoric rise through the ranks prior to 1931, especially his prestigious appointment in 1927 as Director of the Academia General
Militar in Zaragoza, the obstacles that he encountered after the establishment of the new regime provoked intense resentment. The biggest
blow was the closure of the academy in the summer of 1931.
Inevitably, ignoring the financial reasons behind the decision, he
attributed this affront to the fact that the politician responsible, the
Minister of War Manuel Azaña, was a freemason, as indeed were
many other members of the government. Doubting his loyalty to the
Republic, Azaña left Franco without a posting for eight months
which gave him plenty of time to absorb anti-masonic and anti-
Semitic literature. In early 1932, Franco began to read the first of
Tusquets's books. Eaten up with envy of those officers who received
the preferment of the Republic, he came to see them as lackeys of
freemasonry and communism. In 1932, he tried again to recover lost
ground by trying to join a masonic lodge in Madrid but again his
application was turned down by officers of indubitable Republican
convictions, among them his brother Ramón. Even when Franco was
given senior postings, he believed that he was being spied on by
officers who were freemasons.[25]

During the Republic, the ever cautious Franco was careful to
distance himself from those generals who were active in monarchist
conspiracies. Nevertheless, he certainly shared their prejudices and
preoccupations. After all, he was a subscriber to *Acción Española*
which was devoted to justifying an uprising against what its organizers saw as an illegitimate Republic. His thinking on political, social
and economic issues was further influenced by reading the right-
wing press and, as he later revealed, the works of Tusquets. Among
other key influences on the political thinking of Franco, one of the
most important was the brilliant lawyer Ramón Serrano Suñer,
whom he met in 1929 in Zaragoza when he was Director of the
Academia General Militar there. They established a close friendship
that soon led to family links. As a frequent lunch and dinner guest of
the Franco family, Serrano Suñer came to know Franco's sister-in-
law, Zita. When they married in February 1931, Serrano's friend José
Antonio Primo de Rivera, future founder of the Falange, acted as his
witness. Franco did the honours for the bride.[26] So close was this

friendship that Serrano Suñer gradually became a kind of political mentor to Franco. At the time, and until the spring of 1936, Serrano Suñer was an adherent of Ángel Herrera's Acción Popular and, in both the 1933 and 1936 elections, was a candidate for its political party, the Confederación Española de Derechas Autónomas (Confederation of Autonomous Right-wing Groups). For obvious reasons, his newspaper of choice was Herrera's *El Debate*, and Franco followed suit.

This brought him into contact with the ideas of Francisco de Luis who, from early 1933, had succeeded Ángel Herrero as editor of *El Debate*. De Luis was a fierce proponent of the Jewish–masonic–Bolshevik conspiracy theory. His magnum opus on the subject was published in 1935 with an ecclesiastical imprimatur. He embraced the *Protocols* as factual documentary proof of the evil schemes of the Jews: 'In the famous secret programme of the Jews, written in 1896, providentially discovered and published since 1902 with the title *Protocols of the Elders of Zion*, we find clearly expressed the Jewish control of freemasonry.'[27] In his book, enthusiastically quoting the work of Joan Tusquets, the *Protocols*, the Carlist press and General Mola, De Luis argued that the purpose of freemasonry was to corrupt Christian civilization with oriental values. His premise was that 'the Jews, progenitors of freemasonry, having no fatherland of their own, want no man to have one'. Having freed the masses of patriotic and moral impulses, the Jews could then recruit them for the assault on Christian values. In his interpretation, Catholics faced a struggle to the death because 'in every Jew there is a freemason: cunning, deceitful, secretive, hating Christ and his civilization, thirsting for extermination. Freemasons and Jews are the begetters and controllers of socialism and Bolshevism.'[28]

The ostensibly moderate Confederación Española de Derechas Autónomas (CEDA) was led by a brilliant Catholic lawyer, José María Gil Robles, who had been imbued with Carlist ideas by his father. A close collaborator of Gil Robles was José María Fernández Ladreda, the Conde de San Pedro, who had been Mayor of Oviedo during the Primo de Rivera dictatorship. As a major in the artillery, he had left the army in protest against the military reforms of Manuel Azaña. It was logical that, as a soldier and an aristocrat, he would also be part of the Acción Española group. In August 1933, as leader of the powerful Asturian section of Acción Popular, he called for 'a Catholic united front against freemasonry and Judaism that together want to destroy Christian civilization'.[29] The Manichaean rhetoric propagated by Tusquets, Carlavilla, De Luis and the *Protocols* that underlay much of the rhetoric of the CEDA implied a determination to annihilate the left physically.

During the CEDA campaign for the November 1933 elections, shortly after returning from a study tour of Nazi Germany, Gil Robles declared belligerently, 'We must found a new state, purge the Fatherland of judaizing freemasons ... We must proceed to a new state and this imposes duties and sacrifices. What does it matter if we have to shed blood!'[30] Gil Robles's manifesto for the elections consisted of a diatribe against the agrarian and religious reforms of the Republican–Socialist coalition and the disorders for which it was held responsible. In relation to the Republic's alleged destruction of property and the Church, he spoke of 'the pain of the Fatherland as it writhes in the anguish of the tragic agony caused by the crimes and outrages of the maniacs in the pay and service of the masonic lodges and international Jewry and supported by Marxist sectarianism'.[31] A CEDA electoral poster portrayed the four monstrous and sinister powers that were invading Spain: a Bolshevik, a separatist, a freemason and a Jew.[32]

The climax of Gil Robles's campaign came in a speech given on 15 October in the Monumental Cinema of Madrid. His tone could only make the left wonder what a CEDA victory would mean for them: 'We must reconquer Spain ... We must give Spain a true unity, a new spirit, a totalitarian polity ... For me there is only one tactic today: to form an anti-Marxist front and the wider the better. It is necessary now to defeat socialism inexorably.' Gil Robles's language was indistinguishable from that of the extreme conspiratorial right: 'We need full power and that is what we demand ... To realize this ideal we are not going to waste time with archaic forms. Democracy is not an end but a means to the conquest of the new state. When the time comes, either parliament submits or we will eliminate it.'[33]

This speech, described by *El Socialista* as an 'authentic fascist harangue', was regarded by the left as the clearest statement of the threat posed by the CEDA. Certainly, every sentence was greeted by ecstatic applause. Fernando De los Rios, a moderate Socialist and a distinguished professor of law, pointed out with horror that Gil Robles's call for a purge of Jews and freemasons was a denial of the juridical and political postulates of the regime.[34] There was something ominous about the way Gil Robles ended a plea for financial assistance for the party by threatening 'a black list of bad patriots' who did not contribute. The tenor of the speech was carried over to election posters, which emphasized the need to save Spain from 'Marxists, freemasons, separatists and Jews'.[35]

In March 1934, José María Pérez Laborda, Secretary General of the CEDA, declared in an interview quoted by the London *Jewish Chronicle*, 'Jewry as an international power is the principal enemy of the Catholic Church and thus of our party, whose programme is based on the principles of Catholicism. In this general sense Gil Robles is an anti-Semite.' He went on to say that the party's anti-Semitism was directed at international Jewry because there were few real Jews in Spain. Not reassured, the paper commented, 'The grave ideological, if not practical, menace therefore that it presents to Jewry, not only in Spain but the world over, is not to be under-estimated.'[36] One month later, on 22 April, a crowd of 20,000 gathered at El Escorial in driving sleet in a close replica of the Nazi rallies. In the now obligatory Manichaean terms, speaker after speaker declared that the true Spain had to be defended against what they condemned as the anti-Spain. For Luciano de la Calzada, CEDA deputy for Valladolid, the true Spain consisted of those who embraced Spanish tradition and Catholic values. 'All the rest – Jews, arch-heretics, Protestants, Communists, Moors, Encyclopaedists, Francophiles, freemasons, Krausists, liberals, Marxists – were and are a dissenting minority beyond nationality. Outside and against the Fatherland is the anti-Fatherland.'[37]

In the first months of 1934, a series of meetings optimistically heralded the 'new state' that would be installed when Gil Robles reached power. This was accompanied by nightmarish warnings of the growing threat from freemasonry and Judaism. A rally held at Uclés (Cuenca) by the CEDA youth organization, the Juventud de Acción Popular, was organized with a great panoply of preparatory meetings, special trains and buses. One of the speakers, Dimas de Madariaga, was a CEDA deputy for Toledo and a representative of landowners threatened by the Republic's proposed agrarian reforms. The defence of traditional values and property rights would, he announced, be undertaken by the 'new state'. This would not be based on 'decadent liberalism in which there circulates the poison of Marxism and separatism and which is infiltrated by freemasons, Jews and Judaizers'.[38]

In the spring of 1934, the subscriptions financed by Primo de Rivera to the *Bulletin de L'Entente Internationale contre la Troisième Internationale* lapsed. Now military commander in the Balearic Islands, Franco did not hesitate to take out a new one at his own expense. From his headquarters in Mallorca he wrote to Geneva, in French, on 16 May:

> I have learned of the great work which you are carrying out for the defence of all nations against communism, and I should like to receive, each month, your highly interesting bulletins of information, so well documented and so efficacious. I wish to cooperate, in our country, with your greatest enterprise and to be informed about such questions. I shall be grateful if you will let me know the conditions under which I may receive your bulletins each month. Please accept, Sir, my admiration for your great enterprise and my gratitude.

The Entente replied immediately with a packet of their publications. On 23 June, he sent a cheque for fifty Swiss francs to cover the cost of a subscription for 1935.[39]

By now, the Entente was collaborating with Dr Goebbels's Antikomintern. It skilfully targeted and linked up influential people convinced of the need to prepare for the struggle against communism, freemasons and the Jews. Subscribers were sent reports on alleged plans for imminent offensives by all three. When seen through the prism of these reports, the many strikes that took place during 1934 convinced Franco that a major Communist assault on Spain was under way.[40] Similarly, his reaction to the revolutionary events in Asturias of that October reflected how his thinking, fed by the material he received from the Entente and his reading of *El Debate* and the works of Tusquets, had been influenced. He wrote later that the workers' uprising had been 'deliberately prepared by the agents of Moscow'. It was all part of a conspiracy (*contubernio*) of the Republicans (freemasons), Catalan separatists and Socialists. The use of the word *contubernio* suggested his identification with those who denounced the alleged Jewish–masonic–Bolshevik conspiracy. He claimed that 'the freemasons planned to take power by using the workers as cannon fodder', with the collaboration of the Socialists. These elements, he claimed, 'thought they were going to be able to install a dictatorship with technical instructions from the Communists'.[41]

In February 1935, the CEDA–Radical coalition government made Franco Commander-in-Chief of the Spanish armed forces in Morocco. Shortly after arriving there, anxious not to miss any issues of the *Bulletin*, he wrote, this time in Spanish, on 18 March 1935, to inform the Entente Internationale contre la Troisième Internationale of his change of posting. He wrote again on 5 June to confirm his new address.[42] Not long afterwards, he was recalled to mainland Spain to become Chief of the General Staff. Comintern approval of the Popular Front strategy, ratified at its VII Congress on 2 August 1935, was used by the Entente in November, just as Popular Fronts were being assembled in France and Spain, to convince its subscribers, including Franco, that Moscow planned revolution in those countries.[43] Franco's papers contain a Spanish text of a long report about the VII Congress sent to him by the Entente.[44] In his conversation with George Hills, Franco discussed how he had been affected by this report:

Developments in Spain towards the end of 1935 were disturbing. There was growing violence and disorder. What worried me however was not so much what was happening *within* Spain as outside and the relations between people in Spain and Moscow. I had had a full report of the proceedings of the VIIth Congress of the Comintern. I had however to be certain that what had been decided upon in Moscow was in fact going to be carried out in Spain.[45]

Franco's frantic efforts to set off a military coup in the wake of the elections of February 1936 make sense only as confirmation of his belief in the Entente's apocalyptic predictions of an imminent Communist take-over. In that regard, they constitute implicit indications of his readiness to swallow Entente propaganda wholesale.[46]

The intensity and malevolence of the CEDA campaign in the Popular Front elections of February 1936 were as bellicose as those of the monarchists and Carlists who were declared enemies of the Republic. A central plank of its propaganda was that Judaism, Marxism and freemasonry were the enemy to be defeated. Thus *El Debate* presented the election as a fight to the death between Spain and anti-Spain, between civilization and barbarism. The Juventud de Acción Popular, which took the lead in the CEDA campaign, was more explicit and declared that the battle was between Gil Robles and the triangle (freemasonry), the sickle and the solitary star (of David).[47]

The publisher of *El Debate*, Editorial Católica, also published the immensely popular and virulently anti-Semitic and anti-masonic magazine *Gracia y Justicia*. Financed by elements of the CEDA and scurrilously satirical, *Gracia y Justicia* was edited by Manuel Delgado Barreto, a close collaborator of General Primo de Rivera. Its weekly circulation of 200,000 copies made it the most influential weekly of the extreme right.[48] An article on 7 December 1935 was headed 'Freemasons, Jews, Marxists and other bugs'. It complained that 'we've got Jews, freemasons and comrades by the ton and they want to destroy Spain'. It ended with the threat that they would soon all be blown up. Other issues called for the expulsion of the Jews from Spain. In its edition for Christmas 1935, it suggested that the crib should have freemasonry, Judaism and Marxism as the camels of the three kings.[49]

An even more ferociously anti-Semitic newspaper was *Informaciones* which distributed around 50,000 copies each day. It belonged to the millionaire Juan March who threw in his lot with the military conspirators. He guaranteed the financial future of the coup leaders in the event of its failing and would bankroll much of their war effort. *Informaciones*, which received subsidies from the German Embassy, was edited by another subscriber to *Acción Española*, Juan

Pujol, a crony of Juan March. He was a CEDA deputy for Madrid from 1933 to 1935, during which time he wrote an anti-Semitic novel.[50] During the campaign for the February 1936 elections, *Informaciones* declared that 'German Jewish émigrés have made Spain the international centre for boycotting Hitler's Germany which is saving Europe from the Asiatic red hordes.'[51]

Anti-Semitism abounded in the clandestine leaflets circulated by the Unión Militar Española, the organization at the heart of preparations for the coup. This reflected the fact that many of the texts were drafted by Mauricio Carlavilla. In mid-July 1936, last-minute UME proclamations claimed that Spain was 'shackled by a Republican government of traitors in the pay of freemasonry and Judaism'. The UME programme for the coup included the 'expulsion from Spain of Jews and freemasons, and the dissolution of political parties and trade unions'.[52]

Collusion between the anti-Semitic press and the military conspirators was undeniable. Within days of the coup, the population of Seville was told by *ABC*:

> The moment has arrived for everyone without exception to help the military authorities and the army that is fighting to save the Fatherland from falling into the clutches of the anti-Spain made up of the Jewish banks and their henchmen of the secret societies of freemasons and the Marxist groups controlled from Moscow. We must strain every sinew to combat these international swine.[53]

It was no coincidence that a fervent anti-Semite like Juan Pujol should be appointed as head of the rebel Oficina de Prensa y Propaganda service in August 1936 and was free to give vent to his virulent hatred of the Jews.[54] Typical of his views was an article of December 1936 in which he wrote that the left-wing volunteers from around the world who joined the International Brigades, 'the flea-ridden hordes of the slums of Europe', were controlled by 'the secret Israelite Committee that governs the Jews of the world. It is determined more than ever to dominate the world. Spain is at war with universal Jewry which already controls Russia and now wants to take over our country'. Among the Jews that he denounced was Margarita

Nelken: 'Stinking Jewess and heartless vermin is Margarita Nelken, brought here from a German ghetto by her pedlar father. Another Jew is Companys [the president of the Catalan autonomous government, the Generalitat] – descendant of converted Jews, and you only have to see his snout to understand this without the need for more research into his family tree.'[55] Such remarks, like those quoted earlier from *Acción Española*, belie the oft-repeated Francoist claim that Spanish anti-Semitism was not racist but only religious. Ironically, the references to the Inquisition in support of this assertion forgot that, after the expulsion of the Jews in 1492, the *estatutos de limpiezas* (statutes of blood purity) had been enacted to prevent anyone with Jewish blood from occupying high office.[56] When Pujol became head of the rebel Oficina de Prensa y Propaganda service, he wrote in *Domingo*, a weekly he had founded, that the Spanish Civil War was 'the holy war' of the Jews who had sent the International Brigades to Spain 'to plunder'.[57]

Despite the open anti-Semitism emanating from the press ruled over by Pujol, there was clearly concern about its impact abroad. In February 1937, one of his press officers, Laureano de Armas, wrote from Franco's headquarters to the editor of the *Jewish Chronicle* in London:

> Sir, I have been informed of the rumour which is being spread in England that the Spanish National Movement has an anti-Jewish character. I have been authorised to state that this is entirely untrue and would in consequence be very obliged if you were to inform your readers of the true facts. An anti-Jewish policy in Spain presumes the existence of a Jewish problem, which, as you are certainly aware, does not exist in this country. Besides which, a mere glance at General Franco's speeches of the 1st of October, 1936, and the 19th of January, 1937, will show you that there is but one exclusion in the programme of the New Spain: Bolshevism.[58]

This ingenuous missive managed to ignore the much trumpeted rebel association of Judaism and Bolshevism while inadvertently implying that only a shortage of Jews prevented a more anti-Semitic policy. Contrary to the assertions of Laureano de Armas that there was no anti-Semitism to be found in Franco's new state, Falangist posters were displayed with fiercely anti-Jewish cartoons taken from the scurrilous Nazi weekly *Der Stürmer*.[59] The *Jewish Chronicle* responded by citing the virulently anti-Jewish propaganda in the broadcasts of General Queipo de Llano and in the press of the rebel zone. The paper asked Laureano de Armas how such incessant proclamations could be reconciled with the claim that there was no anti-Semitism in Franco's Spain. The paper also reported the admiration for *Der Stürmer* expressed in the rebel media.[60]

Anti-Semitism clinched the alliance between the military rebels and the Catholic Church. This was highlighted on 28 September 1936 in a broadcast by Cardinal Isidro Gomá, Archbishop of Toledo and Primate of All Spain, directed at the defenders of the recently liberated Alcázar. He described the war as the 'clash of civilization with barbarism, of Hell against Christ', and directed his venom against 'the bastard soul of the sons of Moscow'. He dated Spain's disasters from the day on which Spanish blood was mixed with that of 'Jews and the freemasons who poisoned the nation's soul with absurd doctrines, Tartar and Mongol tales dressed up, in the murky societies controlled by the Semite International, as a political and social system'.[61] Three years later, Franco himself would speak in similar terms at another ceremony in Toledo to commemorate the liberation of the Alcázar. He declared that the crimes of the 'red hordes' were inspired by 'the limitless cruelty of an accursed race'.[62]

It was hardly surprising that Franco's admiration for the writings of Tusquets ensured that, when he reached the rebel base in Burgos in September 1936, the Catalan propagandist was welcomed on to his staff. This was to be the basis of a close relationship during the civil war.[63] Needless to say they encouraged each other's prejudices about the Jews and freemasons. Tusquets also served as a liaison between Franco and Cardinal Gomá. On 10 May 1937, Franco asked Gomá to persuade the Vatican to denounce the Basques for siding with the Republic. He complained bitterly to Gomá about what he alleged was the hostility to the rebels of the international Catholic press, particularly in Britain, France and Belgium. He denounced as equally damaging the lukewarm support of senior ecclesiastical authorities in some countries. In his report to Rome about the conversation, Gomá

wrote, 'The General attributed the phenomenon to traditional malevolence, to a fear of dictatorships, to the influence of Judaism and
masonry and especially to the bribery of certain proprietors and
editors of newspapers who – this is a proven fact – had accepted large
sums for carrying on the hate campaign.'[64] That the issue remained an
obsession was revealed on 25 July 1937 at the ceremony of offering
(*ofrenda*) to Santiago in the cathedral of Santiago de Compostela.
Franco's speech was read out by General Fidel Dávila. He hailed the
patron saint of Spain as a guide for the re-establishment of the traditional unity of Spain which 'had been torn apart through the
conspiracies of secret revolutionary forces concealed in atheistic
laicism and in Judaizing freemasonry.'[65]

Among the believers in the Jewish–masonic–Bolshevik conspiracy
given prominence by Franco was Jose María Pemán. As will be seen,
from October 1936 Pemán headed the Comisión de Cultura which
was effectively the ministry of education in the improvised government set up in October 1936. Pemán's task was to purge the teaching
profession of Jews, freemasons and Communists. An even more
fervent believer in the conspiracy was Pemán's deputy, Dr Enrique
Suñer Ordóñez. When Pemán departed to devote himself to propaganda tours, Franco named Suñer Ordóñez in July 1937 to succeed
him at the head of the Comisión. Suñer would carry out his mission
with such zeal that Franco later chose him to be president of one of
the great instruments of the repression, the Tribunal Nacional de
Responsabilidades Políticas.

Suñer Ordóñez had made his name as professor of paediatric
medicine at Madrid University. During the dictatorship of Primo de
Rivera he had held an important post in the Ministry of Education.
Shortly before the coming of the Republic, he made many enemies
on the left. The harsh reaction of the Civil Guard to student demonstrations in support of amnesty for political prisoners on 25 March
1931 had seen the deaths of a student and a Civil Guard, as well as
sixteen people badly hurt. Outraged, Suñer gave vent to what he
called his 'holy fury' in a virulent article published in *El Debate* on 27
March. Entitled 'La Puericultura de la Revolución' (The Paediatrics of
the Revolution), it claimed that bullets fired through the windows of
a children's ward in the University hospital had come from the guns

of students. This provoked fierce reactions within the academic board of the Faculty of Medicine and he was suspended from his chair. His hatred of the Republic saw him become an active member of the Acción Española group.[66]

Not long after being made Pemán's deputy, in 1937, Suñer published his denunciation of the teachers and intellectuals whom he held responsible for the blood shed during the war. His explanation was that General Miguel Primo de Rivera had been too tolerant of opposition:

> One of his most serious errors was, in my view, not to have reacted, when opportunities presented themselves, with 'dictatorial' methods in which a justified repression would be applied on the necessary scale. Despite the system of fines, dismissals and the like, the noble heart of Primo de Rivera was shown to be too weak to shed blood. All that was needed for the rule of law and sacred respect for the authorities to have been felt was as many deaths as now take place in one day. With a few dozen death penalties imposed on the leaders and some deportations, most of the maniacs, agitators and revolutionary cowards responsible for our present misfortunes would have shut up totally.[67]

Suñer distinguished two kinds of blood. On the Republican side, there was that 'of deliberate criminals, authors of the blood sacrifices that we suffer, of vile brutes, with worse instincts than those of wild beasts'. On the side of the military rebels, blood flowed 'from noble Spanish breasts – soldiers and militiamen – generous youth, full of an abnegation and a heroism so immense that their wounds lift them to the status of the demigods of Greek myth'. Then, in justification of what he and Pemán were doing in the Comisión, he asked:

> And all this horrific death toll, must it go without its just punishment? Our spirit rebels against the possibility of impunity for the pitiless individuals who caused our tragedy. It is just not possible that Providence and man do not punish so many murders, rapes and cruelties, so much pillage and destruction of artistic wealth and the means of production. It is necessary to swear before our

beloved dead that the well-deserved sanctions will be executed with the most holy of violence.[68]

Sharing the ideas of Pemán, Suñer denounced all Republican politicians as:

> horrific, truly devilish men. Sadists and madmen working with professional thieves, fraudsters, armed robbers and murderers have occupied the posts of ministers, under-secretaries, senior civil servants and all kinds of important jobs ... Wild boars and cloven-hoofed beasts running through what was once the Cortes, in search of sacrificial victims to bite with their fangs or smash with their hooves ... Monsters in the style of Nero, leaders of sects and their agents, murdered the greatest hope of the Fatherland: Calvo Sotelo [leader of the Alfonsist monarchists] ... Behind them stand the freemasons, the Socialists, the Communists, the Azañistas, the anarchists, all the Jewish leaders of the black Marxism that has Russia for its mother and the destruction of European civilization for its motto. Spain has been before and is once again the theatre of an epic cyclopean combat, the action of Titans against apocalyptic monsters. The programmes laid out in the 'Protocols of the Elders of Zion' are becoming reality.[69]

What was needed was 'profound, austere, quiet, diligent work, like that carried out by those two great men, geniuses for today and for tomorrow, called Mussolini and Hitler'.[70] The aim of the war, wrote Suñer, was 'to strengthen the race for which it is necessary to bring about the total extirpation of our enemies, of those front-line intellectuals who brought about the catastrophe'.[71] His position as Pemán's deputy allowed him to take untrammelled revenge for his perceived persecution. Determined to eliminate any intellectuals who had contributed to the liberal culture of the Republic, Suñer sent numerous denunciations to the rebel intelligence service, the Servicio de Información Militar, including conservative figures such as the distinguished medievalist and philologist Ramón Menéndez Pidal.[72]

Among the members of the *Acción Española* who found berths alongside Franco, Pemán, Enrique Suñer and other anti-Semites was the eminent psychiatrist Dr Antonio Vallejo Nágera. Vallejo shared their ideas and, during the civil war, when he was head of Franco's military Psychiatric Services, had the opportunity to put them into practice. He was obsessed with the need for racial cleansing. In a book published in 1934, he had advocated the castration of psychopaths.[73] Vallejo received official authorization to implement his theories thanks to his personal contacts both with Franco (his wife was a close friend of Franco's wife, Carmen Polo) and with senior figures of the Falange.[74] He clinched his relationship with Franco by means of sycophancy. His book on the psychopathology of war incorporated his work on the links between Marxism and mental deficiency. It was dedicated to Franco 'in respectful and admiring homage to the undefeated Imperial Caudillo'. Vallejo saw his mission as 'this transcendent work of cleansing our race'. He took as his model the Inquisition because he believed, as did Franco, that in the past it had safeguarded Spain from poisonous doctrines. From the premise that 'the racist spirit has always been latent in Spain as was revealed by the Inquisition's proceedings on the cleansing of the blood, applied to Jews and Moors', Vallejo advocated 'a modernized Inquisition with other emphases, ends, means and organization but an Inquisition none the less'.[75]

In August 1938, Franco authorized the necessary funds for Vallejo Nágera to set up the Laboratory of Psychological Investigations with which he proposed to pathologize left-wing ideas. Vallejo set out to identify the environmental factors that fostered the 'red gene' and the links between Marxism and mental deficiency by means of psychological tests carried out on vulnerable Republican prisoners already physically exhausted and mentally anguished. The investigating team consisted of two physicians, a criminologist and two German scientific advisers. His subjects were captured International Brigaders in San Pedro de Cardeña and fifty Republican women prisoners in Malaga, thirty of whom had been sentenced to death. Starting from the premise that the women were degenerate and thus prone to Marxist criminality, he explained 'female revolutionary criminality' by reference to the animal nature of the female psyche and the 'marked sadistic nature' unleashed when political circumstances allowed females to 'satisfy their latent sexual appetites'.[76] His underly-

ing premise was that the 'red gene' polluted the pure Spanish race
with Jewish strains. His work 'confirmed' the prejudices already
absorbed from the works of Tusquets, Carlavilla and Pemán by the
military high command by providing 'scientific' arguments to justify
their views on the subhuman nature of their adversaries. He was
rewarded with promotion to colonel.[77]

Franco's closest collaborators, his brother-in-law and successively
Minister of the Interior and of Foreign Affairs Ramón Serrano Suñer
and his lifelong crony Luis Carrero Blanco, were both believers in *The
Protocols of the Elders of Zion*. Serrano Suñer, as Minister of the
Interior, had given a speech on 19 June 1938 celebrating the first
anniversary of the fall of Bilbao. In a lengthy diatribe against French
Catholics such as François Mauriac and Jacques Maritain who had
suggested that there was nothing sacred about the Francoist cause, he
made remarks that would have flown over the heads of many in his
audience. The main target of his insults was the liberal Catholic
philosopher Jacques Maritain whose views were summed up in his
declaration: 'Let them kill in the name of the social order or the
nation, which is horrible enough but they must not kill in the name
of Christ the King, who is not a military chieftain but a king of grace
and charity who died for all men and whose kingdom is not of this
world.'[78] Even more infuriating for the Francoist faithful were
Maritain's comments about Franco and the war in the Basque
Country. He had written that 'If in Spain any one man has worked
effectively for international communism, that man, without doubt, is
Señor Largo Caballero who wanted it. But it is also General Franco
who wanted the opposite.' Francisco Largo Caballero was leader of
the Socialist Party and, at this time, Republican Prime Minister.
Especially annoying for Serrano Suñer was Maritain's sympathy for
the Catholic population of the Basque Country, the 'bleeding victim'
of the civil war unleashed by the rebels.[79]

Serrano described Maritain as 'that converted Jew who commits
the infamy of broadcasting to the four winds the lie that Franco is a
killer and the sheer idiocy of proclaiming that the government of
Barcelona is legitimate'. Twisting the fact that Maritain was a
Protestant convert to Catholicism and happened to be married to a
Jewish woman, Serrano attacked him as if he were a Jew:

Spain, which did the Church of Christ the great service of combating the Protestant heresy, today comes into the world to renew that service. In that context, what do the ideas of Jacques Maritain matter to us? The ideas of Jacques Maritain have accents that recall the thinking of the Elders of Zion and he has the false style of Jewish democrats. We know that he is on course to receive, or has already received, the tributes of the masonic lodges and the synagogues. We have every right to doubt the sincerity of his conversion and to denounce to the whole Catholic world the tremendous danger posed by his treachery.[80]

A delighted editorial in *ABC* applauded his attack on 'that vile campaign to which certain elements in France, in many cases dishonouring their Catholicism and the cassocks they wear, have devoted themselves, like Maritain, the Jew who pretends to be a convert. They are just agents of the lodges cleverly infiltrated into certain circles.'[81] This set off a deluge of anti-Semitic attacks on Maritain throughout the press of the rebel zone. Serrano Suñer's attacks on Maritain were seconded by Juan Tusquets.[82]

While Franco was concerned primarily with military matters, political issues were the province of Serrano Suñer. As Minister of the Interior and effective head of the Falange in his role as deputy head of the Junta Política of which Franco was the symbolic chief, he had total control of the regime's propaganda apparatus. His influence could be seen in the enthusiasm of the tightly controlled rebel press for the anti-Semitic measures of the Third Reich and Fascist Italy. At the end of January 1938, an article in *El Ideal Gallego* under the headline 'In Praise of Nazism' declared, 'In five years, Germany has freed itself of its most fearful enemies, Marxism and Judaism. In five years, Germany has again scaled the highest peak of progress and greatness.'[83]

José Pemartín, like his cousin José María Pemán and his close friend Eugenio Vegas Latapie, had been an energetic supporter of the Primo de Rivera dictatorship and an active member of Acción Española. In February 1938, Pemartín was named Chief of the National University and Secondary Education Service by the newly appointed Minister of Education, Pedro Sainz Rodríguez. Shortly afterwards, he published a densely detailed programme for the future

Francoist state, *Qué es 'lo nuevo'* which was a curious amalgam of the ideas of Acción Española and the Falange. In it, Pemartín wrote that 'Hitler had to seek out the mysticism of racism to awaken in Germanic veins the heroic spirit of the warriors of the North ... It is not only mysticism but a defence against a terrible historical reality: "the satanic destructiveness of the Jewish people", felt more in Germany than elsewhere.'[84]

Towards the end of his book, Pemartín confessed:

> Our programme for the total Catholicization of Spain cannot be achieved without determined and timely action against the anti-Catholic sects; against freemasonry and Judaism. We do not want to end this book without firmly pointing out that freemasonry and Judaism are the two great, most powerful enemies of the fascist movements in the regeneration of Europe; particularly in the regeneration of Spain, in the totally Catholic way that we advocate ... Hitler is thoroughly right in his anti-Jewish fight.[85]

As Herbert Southworth wrote at the time, the book 'must be considered official and authoritative, not only because of the author's prominent position in the Burgos set-up, but because no book is printed in Rebel territory that does not reflect official opinion'.[86] Copies of the book were still on sale in Madrid in 1970 when I found several on the shelves of La Casa del Libro. Needless to say, at the time the book was published, coverage of events in Nazi Germany did not mention the increasing persecution of the Jews.[87]

In Franco's Spain, sweeping statements directed against the Jews, denominated by collective nouns such as 'Israel' or 'the Sanhedrin' or 'the Rabbinate', were, as could be seen in the writings of Pujol, Pemán and others, accompanied by reference to physical stereotypes. The differentiation often made between religious and racist motivation was just sophistry where extermination was concerned. Of course, the consequences of anti-Semitism in Spain were not the same as in Germany and across most of continental Europe. The tens of thousands of liberals and leftists who were murdered in the smaller geographical confines of Spain were fewer than the victims of the Third Reich and few of them were actually Jews. Nevertheless, the justification for the killing was that those executed were the puppets of the Jewish–masonic–Bolshevik conspiracy. In those Spanish territories where there was a Jewish community, such as Spanish Morocco, there was an explicitly anti-Semitic repression. This was most vicious in respect to Jews who were supporters of the Republic. Twenty-two of 100 Jews who took refuge in Tangier were shot. In Ceuta, thirty of the city's 300 Jews were executed. In Melilla, with a much larger Jewish population, around eleven were tried by summary court martial and executed. Some Jews had their hair shaved in the shape of a cross and many were imprisoned in forced-labour camps. The Jews of the Spanish protectorate were subjected to crippling financial extortion. In addition, as part of the rebel need to recruit Moorish mercenaries, the Arab population was targeted with anti-Semitic propaganda. This campaign was intensified by the powerful local branch of the Nazi Auslands-Organisation which had been instrumental in arranging German support for Franco.[88]

During the civil war, the underlying anti-Semitism of the press associated with Acción Popular became increasingly explicit. The Acción Popular organ in Segovia, *La Ciudad y los Campos*, ran seven major articles on the 'La Bestia Judía' (Jewish Beast) throughout the first three months of 1937. They argued that the 'ruin of great nations' had been the work of the Jews who must be fought 'to the death' and that the civil war was a twentieth-century crusade, a reconquest of Spain, an imperial mission and a purifying apocalypse.[89]

This was the constant theme right until the end of the war. In his triumphal speech at the spectacular victory parade in Madrid on 19 May 1939, Franco provided more evidence that his thinking ran along the same lines as that of Tusquets, Carlavilla, Pemán, Enrique Suñer and other fellow subscribers to *Accion Española*. Now, as he celebrated his victory, Franco justified the past, ongoing and future repression and managed to link it to the eternal struggle against the Jews. He declared:

The Victory would be wasted if we did not stay on the alert and maintain the concerns of the heroic days, if we left eternal dissidents, the embittered, the egoists, the defenders of liberal economics free to act ... Let us have no illusions: we cannot extin-

guish in one day the Jewish spirit that facilitated the alliance of big
capital with Marxism, that knows all about deals with the
anti-Spanish revolution. That spirit still flutters in many hearts.[90]

The real objectives were about privilege, yet the theme of a racial and
religious enemy was always there to mask them.

Franco's triumphal theme was echoed in the innumerable ceremonies that celebrated the victory. One of the most significant was held
on 18 July 1939, at the hill known as the Cerro de los Ángeles in
Getafe, south of Madrid. It was a spectacular ceremony of *desagravio*
(amendment or restitution) to Jesus Christ for a Republican sacrile-
gious transgression. On 28 July 1936, a firing squad of Republican
militiamen had symbolically shot the statue that towered over the
monument to the Sacred Heart of Jesus. The post-war event inaugu-
rated the construction works to rebuild the monument. In addition
to private cars and crowded buses and trains, more than 100 trucks
had been laid on to take people from the centre of Madrid to the
Cerro. Dozens of barefoot pilgrims made their way to hear the
sermon of the Bishop of Alcalá-Madrid, Leopoldo Eijo Garay, who
arrived flanked by units of the army and the Falange. In his passionate sermon to the assembled throng, he portrayed the defeated as the
'satanic spirit of evil' and 'modern-day Jews'.[91]

These post-war events seemed to justify Jorge Villarín's presenta-
tion of the conflict as a war against Jews and Bolsheviks. Yet the rebel
war effort had been directed against the Second Republic, its social
and education reforms and its supporters, among whom Jews and
Bolsheviks were a tiny minority. It goes without saying that the plans
of the military conspirators and their civilian backers found some
justification in the disorder associated with localized anarchist insur-
rections in 1932 and 1933 and the revolutionary general strike in
Asturias in October 1934. Yet they too had nothing to do with Jews,
freemasons or Bolsheviks. Overall, however, the intention of the
military coup and the consequent war was to protect the privileges of
property owners, the Catholic Church and the military. Nevertheless,
these sweeping objectives were obscured and spurred on by the
underlying anti-Semitic rhetoric which was both a conscience-salv-
ing excuse and a religious justification.

2

The Policeman: Mauricio Carlavilla

Extreme denunciations of the imagined Jewish–masonic–Bolshevik conspiracy abounded in the right-wing press before the civil war. The anti-Semitic fantasies of *The Protocols of the Elders of Zion* were assumed to be factual by many commentators and their readers. In this respect, there was little difference between the pronouncements of the fascist Onésimo Redondo, the professor of paediatric medicine at Madrid University Enrique Suñer, the newspaper editor Francisco de Luis, the priest Juan Tusquets and a one-time subordinate of General Mola, the policeman Julián Mauricio Carlavilla del Barrio. However, Carlavilla far outdid his fellow 'theorists' in the extreme nature of his hatred of Jews and freemasons, whom he denominated 'ersatz Jews' (*judíos ersatz*) and in the sheer volume of his book sales, as well as in the corruption and criminality of his personal and professional life.[1]

He was born on 13 February 1896 into a poor rural family in a tiny village in New Castile, Valparaíso de Arriba, in the province of Cuenca. His father, Manuel Carlavilla, was a farmer and his mother, Juliana del Barrio Martínez, a village schoolteacher. He had four brothers and two sisters. The young Carlavilla worked as an agricultural labourer, as an olive harvester and as a shepherd, and did rudimentary training as a schoolteacher.[2] Aged twenty-one, he was called up to do military service and spent three years as a conscript soldier in Morocco 'because I couldn't buy myself out'. While still in Melilla in late October 1920, awaiting his demobilization on 31 December, he successfully applied to take the entrance examination for the police. He chose to become a police officer because the application fee was cheap and the entrance examination easy. As he wrote later, 'if I became a policeman, it was because it cost me only 150 pesetas and 45 days of study'.[3] A more important question is how a poorly educated man from his rural background became a famous and highly successful pedlar of conspiracy theories about the left. The answer lies in his early experiences in the police force.

After approximately eight weeks' work, he passed the examinations and joined the Cuerpo General de Policía. On 24 June 1921, aged twenty-five, he was posted to Valencia as an *agente de vigilancia* second class, the second-lowest rung on the promotion ladder. Only eleven months later, he was transferred to Zaragoza after complaints from the Civil Governor of Valencia to the Director General of Security that Carlavilla's behaviour was bringing the police into disrepute.[4] It was while in Zaragoza that he met and worked under a detective inspector of police, Santiago Martín Báguenas, who became his mentor and friend. The thirty-eight-year-old Martín Báguenas was quite senior, five ranks higher than Carlavilla.[5] Their experience in Zaragoza was the beginning of their shared hatred of the left and collaboration over the next decade and a half. They were involved in a violent campaign against the extremists active in the Aragonese capital. A savage wave of repression of the anarchist movement in Catalonia by General Severiano Martínez Anido had seen mass arrests and a terror campaign involving the murder of key leaders including Francesc Layret, Salvador Seguí and Francesc Comes. In response, in late 1922 Buenaventura Durruti, Ricardo Sanz, Francisco Ascaso and Aurelio Fernández formed a group called Los Solidarios. On 4 June the following year, Los Solidarios assassinated the deeply unpopular and fiercely reactionary Cardinal of Zaragoza, José Soldevila Romero. Soldevila was believed in anarchist circles to finance gunmen from the scab union the Sindicatos Libres, and to have helped set up the murder of Seguí. It was the first step by the Solidarios to create a revolutionary group – the Federación Anarquista Ibérica (FAI). To finance it, they embarked on a series of daring robberies.[6] While in Zaragoza, there were credible threats to Carlavilla's life which were said to have been the work of 'anarcho-syndicalist elements'. As another report put it, the threats were the result of his prominent role in the pursuit and prosecution of anti-anarchist policing. For his own security, in

THE POLICEMAN 31

March 1923, he was sent in rapid succession to Segovia and then Bilbao.[7]

In Bilbao, his hostility towards the left was intensified.[8] According to his own account, his experience replicated what he had seen in Zaragoza. He continued his work against leftist subversion, albeit against the Communists rather than the anarchists. He claimed that, on 23 September 1923, he had frustrated an attempt on the life of Indalecio Prieto. A group of Communists led by Óscar Pérez Solís planned to blow up the offices of Prieto's newspaper *El Liberal* with him inside. Fortuitously, Carlavilla just happened to be passing in a tram when he saw the would-be assassins outside the building and alerted the Civil Guard. Forgetting, or unaware of, the identity of his alleged saviour, Prieto did not acknowledge this intervention, for which Carlavilla bore against him a lifelong grudge.[9] In October 1923, Carlavilla requested a transfer to Madrid to a unit commanded by Martín Báguenas. In December 1924, the unit was commended for its role in the repression of anarchists and Communists.[10] At some point in this cycle of transfers, he was demoted to *agente de vigilancia* third class. The reasons are not known but it was almost certainly related to his propensity to corruption and abusive treatment of prisoners. In November 1925, he accepted a posting to Morocco, where the pay was higher. There he made contacts with military figures that would stand him in good stead later in his career.[11]

While serving in North Africa, he was still being investigated for his activities in Bilbao. Before those investigations were completed, the head of the police where was working in Morocco requested that he be relieved of his post at the police station in Alcazarquivir (now Ksar el-Kebir) for failing to fulfil his duties with the requisite dedication and propriety. The report stated that his behaviour was not only reprehensible but also punishable. The abuses and irregularities of which he was accused included pocketing fines, acting as a pimp and selling protection for prostitutes. His activities were so notorious that they had been denounced in the local press. He was dismissed from his post in Alcazarquivir and returned to Spain, where he found himself effectively unemployed.

He applied for a posting but, given the gravity of his offences, he was regarded as having been expelled and so he was required to apply

to be readmitted to the service. Accordingly, the Director General of
Security, General Pedro Bazán Esteban, requested the case file from
the High Commissioner in Morocco. Bazán's team included, as head
of the political police, the Brigada de Investigación Social, Santiago
Martín Báguenas, who had been promoted in April 1927 to inspector
second class.[12] Accordingly, there was every possibility that Carlavilla's
case would be examined sympathetically. Moreover, there was an
intercession on his behalf from the Marqués de Magaz, the Spanish
Ambassador to the Vatican, which had been arranged by his uncle,
Ángel del Barrio Martínez, a canon in the cathedral of Tarazona in
the province of Zaragoza.[13] The request for documentation met with
the response that there was no concrete proof of criminal behaviour
by Carlavilla but that, given that his activities had been reported in
the press, it was convenient that he be transferred back to Spain. It
was recommended that such a transfer be regarded as sufficient
punishment. Finally, at the end of June 1927, he was given a post in
Madrid. On arrival, he applied for back pay for the months without a
posting. His request was denied on the grounds that his dismissal
had been 'the penalty for his questionable conduct in the police headquarters of Alcazarquivir'.[14]

After a brief period in Madrid, he was transferred on 1 January
1928 to the railway police. There he worked with the flying squad.[15]
He was part of a team that scored some notable successes. Together
with Francisco Horacio Iglesias Sánchez, with whom he would work
frequently over the next few years, the squad garnered considerable
publicity for catching a gang of jewel thieves and for breaking up a
gang that specialized in forging the necessary documents and organizing transport for fugitives from the law to escape to North and South
America.[16] His work with the railway police consolidated his growing
obsession with communism and freemasonry. He was part of the
team that arrested the Conservative politician José Sánchez Guerra
when he had landed in Valencia to lead an abortive coup against the
dictatorship at the end of January 1929.[17] He wrote later that his investigations into the case led him to the conclusion that Spain was under
siege from freemasonry, communism and anarchism.

He claimed further to have been deeply alarmed by the lack of
official concern about this alleged threat. That perception led to him

undertaking his own private intelligence operation to expose these enemies. 'After the rebellions of Ciudad Real and Valencia in January 1929, I found myself faced with an unassailable wall of incomprehension. Personally, I was heavily involved in the investigation into those frustrated revolutionary attempts, as far as my personal means permitted and as far as my superiors allowed me. What did all that mean for me? In a word, I can say that it was the first bolt of lightning of the distant storm, still not visible, of the Communist–masonic assassination of Spain.' In fact, the incidents in question were attempts by senior military officers to overthrow the corrupt military dictatorship of General Primo de Rivera. Justifying his prescience, Carlavilla fancifully portrayed the movement's profoundly conservative monarchist figurehead, José Sánchez Guerra, arriving in Valencia 'with all the requisites of a professional revolutionary', surrounded by 'freemasons, republicans and anarchists'. He claimed that the poorly organized plot, whose objective was the restoration of the 1876 Constitution, was financed by international – by which he implied Jewish – capital and aimed at the imposition of communism in Spain.[18]

I must have had powerful patriotic reasons in 1929, immediately after the Sánchez Guerra affair, to infiltrate the conspiracy, using skill and cunning to gain the total confidence of the revolutionary leadership. I did this on my own initiative. For my own safety, I did not inform the security authorities, given the proven feebleness of the upper reaches of the police, a reflection of the King's own state of mind. I hope that it will be seen that my readiness to take a double risk, of disciplinary action from those that I was defending and, obviously, from the conspirators, reflected the highest imperative. That imperative drove me to try by every possible means to save my Fatherland from the catastrophe that I foresaw, without stopping to reflect on the fact that, at my personal risk, I was saving the life and the crown of the King, who was ever more determined, through his own mistakes and the suggestions of others, to lose both his life and his crown.[19]

This self-appointed role as undercover agent, while still a member of the railway police, took the form of infiltrating left-wing groups where he would then act as an agent provocateur. This involved both creating a network of informers and himself adopting disguises to gain entry to clandestine meetings. He claimed that he did so on his own initiative, without informing his superior officers. However, by early 1930, the head of the railway police was none other than Santiago Martín Báguenas. It is difficult to believe that he did not know about, and approve of, Carlavilla's participation in plotting, and then later frustrating, two assassination attempts against both Alfonso XIII and General Miguel Primo de Rivera during the opening of the great exhibition in Seville in May 1929.[20] There is no evidence for this beyond Carlavilla's own boasts. It is certainly the case that he did infiltrate a later scheme to kidnap, but certainly not to assassinate, the Dictator. That plan was hatched by a group of opponents of the dictatorship, one of whom was a prominent freemason and member of the Socialist Party, Juan Simeón Vidarte.

Their plan, worthy of an operetta, was to drug and snatch Primo while he was in bed with one of his lovers. Neutralizing him was to be the trigger for a coup by liberal army officers. In the event, on the night chosen for the deed, Primo did not appear. Instead, he sent an emissary with a bouquet of flowers to inform the woman that the relationship was over because he was about to get married. Unless Primo made a habit of using this excuse to rid himself of his lovers, this would probably date the kidnap plot to June 1928. This was when he had broken his engagement to the aristocratic Mercedes 'Nini' Castellanos. At the time, Primo's mistress was Inés Luna, the one-time lover of Gonzalo Aguilera. The details about the kidnap plan were omitted from Carlavilla's own fictitious account, as was the fact that his own offer to murder Primo for a substantial sum of money had been dismissed out of hand.[21]

It was only later that Carlavilla revealed to his superior officers what he was doing in his spare time. 'When General Mola arrived I judged that I was no longer running any risk from the police top-brass and I let him know about my role as catalyst within the highest circle of the revolutionaries.'[22] In fact, far from simply present-ing himself directly to General Mola, when he became Director

General of Security in early 1930, it is far more likely that Carlavilla was gradually brought into his secret services by Martín Báguenas. In fact, now an inspector first class, Martín Báguenas had been made head of the Brigada Social of the Dirección General de Seguridad on 27 December 1930.[23] In that position, he was notorious for his brutality. On one occasion in 1930, the beating that he gave the young Communist Enrique Castro Delgado, including kicking him in the testicles, left him infertile.[24]

Shortly after the promotion of his mentor, Carlavilla too moved from the railway police, formally joining the political police on 6 January 1930. He acted as secretary to Martín Báguenas in compiling the prosecution case against the civilians involved in the failed Republican uprising in Jaca.[25] Finally informed of Carlavilla's clandestine activities as a provocateur, Mola was happy to use him as an agent provocateur. In his memoirs, Mola makes two references to this. He mentioned 'the book *El comunismo en España*, by Mauricio Karl – a pseudonym behind which are hidden the names of two people whom I know well'. This could refer only to Martín Báguenas and Carlavilla. It suggests that any commissions given by Mola to Carlavilla came via Martín Báguenas. Mola later describes the work of an unnamed undercover policeman who was enmeshed in tentative plots to assassinate the King. Carlavilla subsequently boasted that this was a reference to his own role in thwarting plots against the life of the King.[26]

One of the tasks undertaken by Carlavilla was the surveillance of the activities of the Republican opposition. His prejudices were revealed when he claimed that his police activities had furnished proof that Manuel Azaña was homosexual:

As a result of being a policeman on active service, the author had to spy on the conspiratorial activities of Azaña throughout 1930 when, recently elected as President of the Ateneo [de Madrid, the highly prestigious debating society], he began to acquire a degree of political celebrity ... Not only are there clues to the homosexual nature of the man who would become the principal figure of the Second Republic. One day in the autumn of 1930, there was a major scandal in a small office in the Ateneo. Azaña went too far with a young man, at the time a revolutionary. He had made a mistake. The scandalized young man thumped him and left calling him the vulgar word that his actions deserved.[27]

In late 1930, Carlavilla was set a more enduring task by Mola. This was to compile a dossier on the supposed activities of the Communist Party in Spain. What Carlavilla produced was a wild mixture of fantasy and paranoia. He claimed that Mola had commissioned this document on behalf of the Entente Internationale contre la Troisième Internationale. When he had read and approved its contents, Mola forwarded it to Geneva. It would not be unreasonable to surmise that its contents were fed into the bulletins that the Entente sent to its subscribers in Spain, including General Franco.[28]

The report formed the basis of Carlavilla's first book *El comunismo en España*. He perceived the arrival of the Second Republic as a disaster and proof of his prophecies about the Jewish–masonic–Bolshevik conspiracy. Its arrival saw the dismissal of his two admired superiors, Mola and Martín Báguenas. He was posted to a Madrid police station. There, using constant claims of ill-health, he took much time off, presumably spent writing the book. He claimed that, as a necessary precaution to preserve his undercover identity, he had been obliged to publish it under the pseudonym Mauricio Karl. Since the book criticized the government and the Republic, he may also have been protecting himself from possible sanction by his superiors in the police force. Later still again, he claimed that the use of the pseudonym was the work of his publisher who was deceived by the Germanic sound of the name 'Karl'. The jacket blurb described the author as being an agent of 'the International Secret Service'. Both untruths were Carlavilla's own invention and the denials typical of the feeble lies that littered his career. In his prologue to the book, the lawyer Luis Fernando Saavedra Núñez claimed to have met 'Mauricio Karl, German and professional tourist' in an hotel in Nice. He went on to 'explain' that, because 'Karl' was about to depart on a mission to Manchuria, he had left the manuscript with him.[29] The book was widely and favourably reviewed across the Spanish press, although several reviewers were suspicious about the real identity of the author. In *Mundo Gráfico*, the investigative journalist José Luis Barberán commented shrewdly, 'This work, which appears under the foreign name Mauricio Karl, was written without a shadow of a doubt by a high-ranking Spanish policeman, whose complete command of serious social problems shows that he must have spent some considerable time studying them.' Barberán's conclusion was that the book was so interesting that 'a copy should be owned and consulted on a daily basis by the entire police force from the Director General of Security down to the lowest functionary'. In *ABC*, Álvaro Alcalá Galiano shared Barberán's suspicions.[30]

Another reviewer pointed out that, in the preface, the author was described as 'a German who has spent five years in our country working as a secret agent of the International Service against Communism'. The reviewer doubted the existence of any such entity. However, since Carlavilla's original report had been sent to the Entente Internationale contre la Troisième Internationale, it is entirely probable that he fantasized about himself as an agent of that organization.[31] Another reviewer, intrigued by the anonymity of the author, wrote, 'there are those who think that he is a confidant of Stalin. There are even those who think that it is Trotsky himself.'[32] Inevitably, the most laudatory reviews of the book appeared in the right-wing press. In one case, it was recommended as a book that had to be read alongside an edition of *The Protocols of the Elders of Zion*.[33] In November 1933, Barberán suggested that Mauricio Karl was actually Santiago Martín Báguenas, much to the latter's annoyance. He immediately wrote a letter to *ABC* denying it. Barberán's presumption was understandable. According to Carlavilla, since Martín Báguenas was short of money, the pair had decided that he could pretend to be the author of the book. In this version, Martín Báguenas managed to sell several hundred copies to members of the police force, for which he received a commission of 40 per cent on the cover price.[34]

Intriguingly, one review questioned the veracity of Carlavilla's account of having foiled attempts on the lives of the King and General Primo de Rivera.[35] The allegation that this was fiction came from the pen of the retired artillery Captain Jorge Vigón Suerodíaz. Vigón was one of the most prominent and influential monarchist conspirators against the Republic who would shortly be using the services of both Carlavilla and his friend Santiago Martín Báguenas.

Carlavilla claimed later that fear of reprisals obliged him to destroy the documentation that certified his role as an undercover agent when it became clear that the monarchy was about to fall.[36] Soon after the establishment of the Republic, in punishment for his anti-republican efforts, Santiago Martín Báguenas had been put on forced leave of absence, on half-pay, accused of negligence and ineptitude during the disorders associated with the burning of churches in Madrid on 11–13 May 1931 and also accused of brutally mistreating detainees while interrogating them. Effectively, this was a punishment for his role under Mola of combating the Republican conspiracies against the dictatorship.[37] Carlavilla later claimed that he arranged for Martín Báguenas to work for the conspirators who were preparing the coup that would be headed by General Sanjurjo in August 1932. Given his habitual mendacity, it is more likely that it was the other way around and he was taking advantage of the fact that Martín Báguenas, who was killed in 1936, was in no position to contradict him. He and Martín Báguenas worked together providing Sanjurjo's collaborators with information about the units of the security services that were shadowing the nascent conspiracy. According to the monarchist Juan Antonio Ansaldo, for this work Martín Báguenas received a substantial monthly salary.[38] However, with the right-wing Radical–CEDA coalition in power, in 1934 the then Prime Minister, Alejandro Lerroux, recalled him to active service and promoted him vertiginously to a number of important positions. Martín Báguenas headed Lerroux's security detachment, rising to be Chief of Police in Madrid (Jefe Superior) on 1 June 1935, as well as head of the detective branch of the police (Comisario General de Vigilancia). One month later, he was posted to Barcelona to be Chief of Police there and, within three months, head of public order in Catalonia. In what was to be his last cabinet meeting, Lerroux even proposed that Martín Báguenas be made Director General of Security. The proposal was accepted by the President, Niceto Alcalá-Zamora, but was not implemented after Lerroux's government fell. Martín Báguenas repaid Lerroux's patronage by saving his life. He warned him, on 17 July 1936, that the military rising would begin that night and that he should leave Madrid. Lerroux began his long trek into exile.[39]

Carlavilla was a conspiracy theorist who argued that freemasons, Jews, leftists and homosexuals plotted to undermine Spain. Between 1932 and 1936, again using the pseudonym Mauricio Karl, he wrote a number of sensationalist best-sellers.[40] The first, *El comunismo en España*, described the various Socialist, anarchist and Communist elements of the working-class movement as the enemy of Spain that would have to be defeated. The second and third, *El enemigo* and *Asesinos de España*, argued that the enemies masterminding the left-wing assassins of Spain were the Jews. This was done through freemasonry, 'their first army'; then Socialists and Communists, 'the mercenary army of Israel, the Marxist army'; and world capitalism. Spanish greatness in the sixteenth and seventeenth centuries was the fruit of the expulsion of the Jews. The loss of empire was the fault of Jews and freemasons. To rebuild a great empire would require repeating the policies being implemented by German Nazism and Italian Fascism. Indeed, his admiration for both Hitler and Mussolini was explicit. The only hope of stopping the destruction of Christian civilization and the establishment of the empire of Israel lay in defeating the 'sectarians of masonic Jewry'. Since there were hardly any Jews in Spain, that meant their lackeys, the freemasons and the left.[41] Nevertheless, he alleged that the Spanish Socialist Party had many Jewish members even though the only one that he could name was Margarita Nelken. His 'proof' was a series of favourable quotations from Hitler's *Mein Kampf*. 'Only knowledge of freemasonry, the slave of Judaism, provides the key to real aims of Socialism.'[42]

Carlavilla asserted that General Primo de Rivera, who had died of natural causes, probably deriving from inadequately treated diabetes, had been poisoned by a Jewish freemason. He claimed that masonic assassins despatched to kill Primo de Rivera had been sent by the Catalan financier, Francesc Cambó, 'the 100% Jew'. Cambó was neither Jewish nor a freemason. Carlavilla's calumnies led, in 1934, to an abortive attempt by Cambó to have him prosecuted for libel. Since his real identity was unknown, Carlavilla managed to avoid appearing before the courts.[43] However, in early September 1934, *El enemigo* was banned. When orders were issued for it to be confiscated, there remained only four unsold copies. Nevertheless, even when Carlavilla had removed the offending passages, the second edition was not authorized. This reflected both the legal firepower that Cambó was able to mobilize and the fact that Carlavilla had insulted the Minister of the Interior, Rafael Salazar Alonso, accusing him of being 'radiated' by freemasonry. Salazar Alonso had indeed been an active freemason but had subsequently moved to the right. Carlavilla wrote a letter of protest claiming that the bans were the work of freemasons determined to silence him. His complaints were published in the extreme right-wing press.[44]

Nevertheless, he made even more outrageous comments about Cambó in his subsequent book, the virulently anti-Semitic *Asesinos de España. Marxismo. Anarquismo. Masonería*. It was dedicated to the army in gratitude because it had crushed the rebellion of October 1934 in Asturias. Two weeks before the events in Asturias, Carlavilla had been posted to the political intelligence section of the Dirección General de Seguridad.[45] However, after the defeat of the miners' uprising, he was attached to the staff of the forty-four-year-old Civil Guard Major Lisardo Doval Bravo. He participated enthusiastically in the subsequent repression overseen by the notoriously brutal Doval. Carlavilla was employed interrogating prisoners. On 15 November, the Director General of Security, Captain José Valdivia Garci-Borrón, sent one of his subordinates, Inspector Ricardo Adrover, to investigate Doval's atrocities. Adrover was violently expelled from Asturias by Carlavilla who threatened to throw him in jail. Although Carlavilla's main task seems to have been preventing investigation into Doval's excesses, it was alleged that he brought back from Asturias as trophies the ears and noses of several miners.[46]

In January 1936, Carlavilla published a compendium of his first three books. Confusingly, it had the same title as the third, *Asesinos de España*, although it both contained some new material and omitted some from the earlier volumes. In it, he claimed that 100,000 copies, for which he renounced his royalties, were being distributed free to army officers.[47] What he failed to mention was how the cost of this 'generous' gesture had been met. The printing and distribution of this edition was part of the coordinated plans of the civilian infrastructure of the Unión Militar Española to prepare the ground for the coming coup.[48] He claimed later that the police had tried to prevent the book's distribution but had managed to confiscate only 4,000

copies. In fact, accusations were made that he had arranged for
friends in the police to seize most of the copies paid for by his right-
wing patrons so as not to impinge on sales of his books.[49]

That Carlavilla was obsessed by money was revealed in a brazen
note at the end of *Asesinos de España*:

> Dear Reader. If this book has awakened in your soul some sympa-
> thy towards me, help me to live by lending it only to those who
> can't afford to buy a copy. Just think that every copy not sold is a
> peseta that I lose. So do others, the bookseller, the printer, the
> binder etc. Above all, remember that only if you help me can I keep
> on writing in defence of the truth, despite the risks, the unpleas-
> antness and enemies involved in doing so.[50]

In October 1935, just as the book was appearing, a group of his
admirers, monarchists and Falangists expressed their desire to organize a tribute to him. Given the need to protect his identity, the usual
device, a banquet, was ruled out. Instead, they proposed to raise a
subscription for the publication of a luxury edition of his first three
books for the startlingly high price of 50 pesetas (around £100 in
today's money) or of *Asesinos* for 25 pesetas. The money was collected
and, presumably, donated to Carlavilla. The books, however, never
appeared. The announcement appeared in *La Nación*, the newspaper
of one of the signatories, Manuel Delgado Barreto, the extreme right-
wing friend of José Antonio Primo de Rivera. Perhaps because
contributions were slow in materializing, the same announcement
appeared one week later in *La Época*, alongside a virulently anti-
Semitic article. Under the headline 'Israel Commands', it claimed to
prove that *The Protocols of the Elders of Zion* was based on empirical
fact. The author went on to assert that, in order to achieve their ambition of world domination, the Jews had as their principal instrument
the freemasons. Signed only 'M', it is more than likely that the author
was Carlavilla.[51]

The depth of Carlavilla's anti-Semitism was evident in his attack on
Cambó: 'His Jewish features are plain to see and are clear even behind
the curtains of the farce. His presence can be sensed, it can be smelt
like the scent of beasts, identified always in the most subtle

manoeuvres, lurking in the shadows, in blood, in misfortunes. His person gives off a Talmudic stench.' The book ended with a provocative challenge to the right. Describing Jews, left-wingers and freemasons as vultures hovering over the corpse of Spain, he wrote, 'The Enemy howls with laughter while the nations that serve Zion play diplomatic dice for the cadaver's land. Thus might be the real end of Spain who was once feared by a hundred nations. And so it will be because her sons no longer know how to die. Nor how to kill.'[52] The anti-masonic diatribes of Mauricio Karl were amply quoted in the Carlist press as absolute fact.[53]

In mid-1935, Carlavilla revealed the venom underlying his sulphurous temper. In an article about the role of the police, Álvaro de Albornoz, who had served as the Republic's Minister of Justice between 1931 and 1933, made some comment about *El comunismo* and *El enemigo*: 'signed with the pseudonym Mauricio Karl, they show us in full the old-school Spanish police, although adulterated with a baroque and picturesque modern pseudo-culture'. Noting that hatred of freemasonry 'filled the pages of *El enemigo* with rancour and poison', Albornoz commented that 'Not a single one of the major Republicans is safe from his vengeful fury.' He quoted Karl's judgement on Santiago Casares Quiroga, one-time Minister of the Interior: 'Perhaps his destiny should be to be nailed up on a street corner by five bullets from a Mauser like a gob of bloodied spit.' Albornoz revealed his suspicions that Mauricio Karl was the current Chief of Police in Madrid, Santiago Martín Báguenas: 'It is frightening to think that whoever wrote this could have the entire Spanish police force at his command.' A furious Carlavilla replied in *El Siglo Futuro* denying the insinuation that Mauricio Karl was Martín Báguenas. He repeated the denial in *Asesinos de España*. He revealed more than he intended when he stated that, if he were a high-ranking police officer, he would smash freemasonry and implied that Albornoz would be dead.[54]

In February 1935, a biography of General Primo de Rivera by César González Ruano was criticized in the liberal newspaper *La Voz* for asserting that he had been murdered by freemasons. The author of the article, Rufino Blanco Fombona, described the accusation as 'the wild exaggerations of a penny dreadful', asked what González

Ruano's source was and questioned why any freemason would want to assassinate Primo. González Ruano's 'source' was Mauricio Karl's most recent book, *El enemigo*, in which he had insinuated that Primo had been poisoned: 'on the night before his death, the General had dinner with a high-ranking freemason. What is more, this brother was a Sephardic Jew.' This absurd invention implied that the plot was the work of a mysterious 'grupo M.' and had the approval of the Spanish Ambassador to France, the deeply conservative José María Quiñones de León.[55] Carlavilla responded indignantly. He wrote a furious letter to *La Época* containing laughable 'proof' of his account: 'Firstly, I accuse freemasonry because I personally obtained a confession from the culprit. Secondly, I accuse freemasonry because I happened to see at the side of Primo de Rivera, in Paris, a Jewish freemason in a position to get away with committing the murder.' In the highly unlikely event that Carlavilla was present when Primo died in Paris on 16 March 1930, it is odd that he did not intervene to prevent him being poisoned.[56] The Dictator's son, the future founder of the Falange, José Antonio, dismissed Carlavilla's theory out of hand.[57]

Still only an officer second class, Carlavilla was expelled from the police on 27 September 1935, as a result, according to his official record, 'of serious offences'. The authorities already had their eyes on him as a result of accusations in the spring of 1935 that he was involved in a scheme to assassinate several senior Republican politicians. That investigation was dropped. Nevertheless, enquiries were ongoing into the authorship of his books *El comunismo en España* and *El enemigo*. They were initiated on the grounds that these books revealed professional secrets known only to members of the police force. Moreover, suspicion fell on him because of the demand in *El comunismo* that twelve politicians, including Francisco Largo Caballero, Indalecio Prieto and Juan Simeón Vidarte should be hung in the Puerta del Sol. Carlavilla acknowledged that he knew the identity of the author but refused to divulge it. When a series of charges were put to him, he did not deny knowing who Mauricio Karl was. Presumably on his instructions, his secretary, Gustavo Villar de la Riva, declared that he was the author, but his claim was dismissed as implausible. Carlavilla stated that, if he revealed the name, it would simply give information to those who wanted to kill an honest man for his revelations about freemasonry, communism and anarchism. He defended this stance, arguing that those investigating the case were freemasons infiltrated into the apparatus of the state. He also added outrageously insulting comments about senior politicians, including the then Minister of the Interior, Manuel Portela Valladares, and the deputy Director General of Security, Ramón Fernández Mato. He claimed, as he did in his books, that they wanted to know the identity of Mauricio Karl so that they could have him murdered. All of this, together with accumulated disciplinary offences on his record, led to his expulsion. Luis Fernando Saavedra Núñez was interviewed by the police. Despite having stated in his preface to *El comunismo en España* that he had met Mauricio Karl in Nice, he denied knowing his real name.[58] Obviously, Martín Báguenas knew the identity of Mauricio Karl. However, he was either unable, given his post in Catalonia, or unwilling to exercise his authority to save Carlavilla.

In a formal appeal against his expulsion, Carlavilla would later claim that his dismissal was persecution for his anti-masonic revelations or, as he put it, 'for the crime of being Mauricio Karl'. The claim was reiterated in a full-page advertisement for *El comunismo*, *El enemigo* and *Asesinos de España*, which stated, 'For defending the truth, Mauricio Karl has just suffered extremely serious damage.' This was a twisted interpretation of the lengthy investigation by the authorities into the authorship of his subversive anti-Republican works. In his confusingly written appeal against the expulsion, he claimed that, since it was not illegal to criticize Marxism, anarchism or freemasonry, his expulsion was the work of freemasons with authority over the police. This was a clear reference to Manuel Portela Valladares, the Interior Minister. Carlavilla alleged that it was common for freemasons to have their critics murdered, a claim similar to those made by Juan Tusquets. In support of this, he claimed that, when he was working as an agent provocateur in the opposition to the dictatorship, the person who had instructed him to assassinate Alfonso XIII and General Primo de Rivera in 1929 was the prominent member of the Socialist Party Juan Simeón Vidarte.[59]

In addition to his criminal activities, Carlavilla was an active collaborator of the conspiratorial group the Unión Militar Española, which had been founded in December 1933 by army officers outraged by numerous actions of Manuel Azaña. These included his military reforms, the closure of the newspaper *La Correspondencia Militar* and the imprisonment of officers involved in the failed military coup of General Sanjurjo. Finance for their activities came from the Acción Española group. The link was Jorge Vigón, who had already commissioned Santiago Martín Báguenas to organize an intelligence service to ensure that the conspirators were informed of what the government and its security service knew about their activities. The UME's first leader was the Falangist Lieutenant Colonel Emilio Rodríguez Tarduchy. He was soon replaced by a triumvirate consisting of Captain Bartolomé Barba Hernández, who had a visceral hatred of Azaña, the military lawyer Captain Eduardo Pardo Reina and Colonel Valentín Galarza. By late 1934, the UME had close links with the Falange and was increasingly moving towards the preparation of a military coup.[60] In addition to using his position in the police force to forestall actions against the UME, Carlavilla wrote much of the UME's propaganda material, widely distributed among army officers who were members or sympathizers of the organization. These pamphlets and leaflets were produced on the printing press of his brother Jesús, in Guadalajara. He also arranged for the Madrid offices of his own publishing business to be used as the headquarters of the UME in the capital.[61]

In May 1936, a communiqué from the Dirección General de Seguridad revealed the supposed implication of Carlavilla, Pardo Reina and other key elements of the UME, together with several police officers in plots to kill Azaña, Francisco Largo Caballero and Diego Martínez Barrio. The assassination of Manuel Azaña, the first of those proposed, had been in the making since March 1935. Carlavilla was financing the operation from the offices of his prosperous publishing operation. In April 1935, the plot had been revealed to the police intelligence unit in which Carlavilla worked, the Oficina de Información y Enlace, by a paid informer of that same department, Emiliano Carmelo Ruano Sánchez Seco. Ruano had served in the Spanish Foreign Legion under the notorious Captain Manuel

Díaz Criado and subsequently worked for him in Madrid. Díaz Criado had instigated the shootings in the Parque de María Luisa in Seville in July 1931.[62] Ruano claimed that he had been approached by Díaz Criado, Eduardo Pardo Reina and Julián Carlavilla. They told him implausibly that the Dirección General de Seguridad had instructed them to assemble a team capable of assassinating Azaña, Largo Caballero and Martínez Barrio. Under the supervision of Díaz Criado, with cash provided by Carlavilla, Ruano then set about recruiting a team.

In preparation for the attacks, Carlavilla bought two rifles and two pistols and paid for the purchase of a car to be used in the operation. He also bought a false moustache, glasses and a big hat to disguise himself when interviewing the potential assassins. The payments ceased when Carlavilla decided that he wanted committed volunteers who would act out of ideological conviction and not for money. The man chosen to shoot Azaña was a young Falangist, Cipriano Eroles Roda. The assault on Azaña was planned to take place when he was en route to address a public meeting at Alcázar de San Juan in the province of Ciudad Real. Members of his escort were supposed to fake a breakdown at which point Eroles, following in the recently purchased car, would shoot him. In the event, Azaña could not attend and the meeting did not take place. Eroles abandoned the car and the guns in a Madrid street where they were found by the police. Carlavilla was tipped off that the case was being investigated and the plan was abandoned.

Officially, for want of hard documentary evidence, the investigation was shelved. Nevertheless, there were ample suspicions that this was because the perpetrators, especially Pardo Reina and Carlavilla, could count on the protection of friends and sympathizers in high places. The head of the investigation division of the police, Captain Vicente Santiago Hodsson of the Civil Guard, had worked with Carlavilla and Martín Báguenas in the political police created back in the day when General Mola was Director General of Security. The current Director General, Captain José Valdivia Garci-Borrón, a crony of Alejandro Lerroux, was equally reactionary. He was dismissed in June 1935 for his involvement in the Estraperlo corruption scandal, a scam involving a rigged roulette wheel that led to the downfall of Lerroux (Estraperlo was an amalgam of the names of the three main protagonists). At best, he took little or no action in the case regarding the assassination project of Carlavilla. The left Socialist daily, *Claridad*, pointed the finger at Santiago Hodsson and Martín Báguenas as the principal protectors of Carlavilla and Pardo Reina. At the time of the plot to kill Azaña, Díaz Criado had worked in the intelligence service of the Ministry of War while Gil Robles was Minister.

After the victory of the Popular Front in the elections of February 1936, the case was reopened. A large number of people were questioned, including Carlavilla's secretary and bagman Gustavo Villar, Díaz Criado and Pardo Reina; the latter two both claimed that they knew nothing about the assassination scheme. Warrants were issued for the arrest of Carlavilla. However, warned that this was about to happen, on 18 February he had been able to flee to Portugal helped by two fellow officers, Juan Antonio Escobar Raggio and his long-term partner Francisco Horacio Iglesias Sánchez. Allegedly, he was able to cross the frontier by using the identity badge of Iglesias.[63] Proceedings were begun against Carlavilla, Díaz Criado, Pardo Reina, Gustavo Villar, Carmelo Ruano, Horacio Iglesias and Escobar Raggio. However, in the absence of Carlavilla, the denials of the other participants in the plot and the lack of concrete evidence led to the case being dismissed.[64]

Since his expulsion from the police in September, Carlavilla's main activity had been the preparation of two new books together with his work gathering information on behalf of the military plotters. This largely consisted of warning them about the progress of investigations into their activities gleaned from his cronies in the police. He also provided Bartolomé Barba with lists of names of 'untrustworthy' liberal officers for elimination from the UME. The books were provisionally titled *Hispanismo* and *La homosexualidad de un gobernante*. Neither was ever published, although material from the latter, clearly a diatribe against Azaña, appeared in his later book *Sodomitas*.[65] In the wake of the Popular Front elections, his work on the books was overtaken by the tasks of the writing and distribution of propaganda in favour of a military coup. He played an active role in the unofficial intelligence operation mounted for Mola by his crony Inspector

Santiago Martín Báguenas. All these plans seem to have been masterminded by Martín Báguenas, who had been working since September
1932 for the monarchist–military plotters.[66] In Lisbon, Carlavilla
linked up with the exiled General Sanjurjo and remained on the
fringes of the military plot.

Shortly after the outbreak of war, Carlavilla joined the volunteer
column of exiled rightists set up by Comandante Lisardo Doval. In
Salamanca, Carlavilla helped Doval organize and recruit for his
column, as well as briefly participating in it as a rank-and-file soldier.
Doval sent him back to Portugal to arrange the purchasing of arms
and supplies for the column. There he made contact with Nicolás
Franco, who was acting on behalf of his brother. On his return to
Salamanca, Carlavilla collaborated briefly with Father Joan Tusquets
compiling information about suspected freemasons, but increasingly
he worked as an agent for Nicolás Franco, who was effectively his
brother's political factotum under the title of Secretario General del
Estado. One of his schemes was to domesticate the Falange and eventually bring it under his brother's control. To this end, the undercover
skills that Carlavilla had used to infiltrate left-wing groups in the late
1920s and early 1930s were now put to use within the Falange. With
initial success, Carlavilla masqueraded as a Falangist. As was later
confirmed by Felipe Ximénez de Sandoval, Carlavilla was involved in
one of several efforts to free José Antonio Primo de Rivera from the
Republican prison in Alicante, where he was being held following his
arrest for his alleged involvement in an assassination attempt on a
Socialist parliamentary deputy.[67]

One of the possibilities was to exchange the Falangist leader for
the son of the then Republican Prime Minister, Francisco Largo
Caballero. His son, Francisco Largo Calvo, had been doing his military service when the military uprising took place and had been
detained by rebel officers. In September 1936, Largo Calvo was a
prisoner in Segovia. The proposed prisoner exchange came to naught
but, years later in exile in Mexico, Largo Calvo recalled that Carlavilla
would visit him in prison to try to force him to write to his father and
get him to agree to the exchange. Presenting himself as Mauricio
Karl, he would delight in taunting the young man cruelly. He told
him that he would be shot if his father did not accept. The young man

wrote as asked in what, given the pressure he was under, were digni-
fied terms. In any case, after lengthy debate, the Republican cabinet
rejected the prisoner exchange. In an interview given years later in
Mexico, Largo Calvo recounted that:

> On another occasion, there appeared a Falangist who said that his
> name was Mauricio Karl. I found out later that he had been a
> police inspector in the Dirección General de Seguridad in Madrid.
> He said that he had been commissioned to arrange my exchange
> for José Antonio Primo de Rivera, the founder of the Falange, who
> was being held in the Provincial Prison in Alicante. This individ-
> ual, who visited me often for a while, used to take much pleasure
> in sadistically repeating that my life depended on the survival of
> Primo de Rivera which, given the situation in which he said the
> fascist chief found himself, was just a way of saying that my days
> were numbered. I wrote a letter to my father, more than anything
> else just to give him some news about my situation since, as was
> only to be expected, and as I confirmed later, both he and the rest
> of my family assumed that I had been shot. Indeed, my sisters were
> wearing mourning. I wrote the letter convinced that my father
> would never agree to a prisoner exchange and I told Mauricio Karl
> that that was the case. To this day, I do not know if the letter ever
> arrived since I never had the chance to see my father again.[68]

As an experienced agent provocateur, Carlavilla's main function was
to cause as much dissension as possible in Falangist ranks. Under the
direction of Nicolás Franco, he and Ximénez de Sandoval wrote
the draft of the decree of unification between the Falange and the
Comunión Tradicionalista. He asserted later that, after Franco's
elevation to the position of *generalísimo* and head of state, Nicolás
suspected subversive intentions on the part of some leading elements
of the Falange, the so-called *legitimista* clique, relatives of José
Antonio Primo de Rivera, determined to prevent the Falange falling
under the control of Franco. They consisted of the loutish Agustín
Aznar, head of the Falange militias and fiancé of José Antonio's
cousin Lola, his dour sister Pilar, his ambitious cousin Sancho Dávila,
the head of the Seville Falange, and his one-time law clerk, the

sinuous Rafael Garcerán. Carlavilla seems to have encouraged the ambitions of Aznar with the intention of tempting him into a major indiscretion. He informed Nicolás Franco that the Aznar group had contacts with the Republican government. Nicolás ordered him to investigate the case further.

While working on this in Seville, Carlavilla wrote an article in the local Falangist newspaper celebrating Franco's elevation to the position of head of state. The article, entitled 'El Jefe del Estado. La Unidad', alerted the Aznar group to the fact that he was working for Nicolás Franco. In consequence, Carlavilla was the victim of two efforts to kill him, both in Valladolid, a violent physical assault and an attempted poisoning. Given that the hatred felt towards him by the followers of Agustín Aznar meant that his life was in permanent danger, he took refuge in Portugal. It is impossible to put an exact date on this but it is probable that it was in mid- to late October 1936.[69] Intriguingly, in his sycophantic article about Franco, he coined a phrase, 'the masonic super-state', that was later picked up by the Caudillo.[70]

In an important speech on 11 September 1945 to the religious advisers of the Sección Femenina of the Falange, Franco used phrases that suggested that he had read and was influenced by the works of Carlavilla. He told his audience that the civil war had been undertaken to combat the 'satanic machinations' of freemasons operating secretly. Now, he warned them, Spain was coming under attack from 'the masonic super-state' which controlled the world's press and radio stations as well as the key politicians in the Western democracies. 'Above states, above the very life of governments, there exists a super-state: the masonic super-state, that dictates its laws to its followers to whom it sends its orders and slogans. And there exist those who, out of political ambition and bastardies of all kinds, blindly obey its instructions. And since they are not stupid, bit by bit, they have managed to take control of much of the world's broadcasters and press, the instruments of public opinion.' This monstrous power, he warned, was used to denigrate Spain.[71] In fact, Carlavilla had first alleged that masonic lodges constituted a super-state in his book *Asesinos de España*. Elsewhere in the same volume, he referred to 'the super-state of Israel'. 'Israel' in this context was a generic reference to Judaism. Among several references to the super-state, he defined it, incomprehensibly, as being like a pair of scissors with 'the lever of capitalism and the lever of Marxism articulated by the Jewish pivot'.[72]

Once in Lisbon, Carlavilla worked for a time as an unofficial intelligence agent on the staff of Nicolás Franco, who now was there as acting Ambassador. Carlavilla's file in the Spanish police archives is curiously devoid of detail on his activities in Portugal. They seem initially to have been directed to spying on dissident Falangist and Carlist exiles. However, in collaboration with another 'honorary agent', Antonio Velez y Fernández de la Torre, he soon developed illegal financial activities on the side. The pair eventually attracted the attention of the Portuguese political police, the Polícia de Vigilância e de Defesa do Estado. In the spring of 1939, the head of the PVDE ordered that certain Spanish individuals exercising police functions cease to do so. On 13 April that year, Carlavilla was arrested by the PVDE while enquiries were made. He was detained in the political prison of Cadeia do Aljube in Lisbon but released after four days.

A report from the Spanish Embassy in Lisbon of 19 September 1939 acknowledged that Carlavilla and his partner Antonio Velez were operating with some success as intelligence agents but lamented that the propriety of their public and private conduct left much to be desired. The report was sent to the Dirección General de Seguridad by the police attaché to the Spanish Embassy, Manuel Varela. Varela wrote that Carlavilla was working in 'a private capacity' for the Embassy. While they carried out their intelligence work 'with some success and to the satisfaction of the Ambassador, the same cannot be said, in my view, on the basis of the information I have easily been able to gather, of the moral dimension of both the public and private aspects of their work'.[73]

This prophetic report was written only three days before Carlavilla was arrested again, in company with Velez. This time, more thorough enquiries were conducted into their suspected contraband and illicit currency dealings on the black market. Carlavilla described himself to the Portuguese secret police as a 'teacher and writer', while Velez identified himself as a lawyer. After three months' imprisonment, on

23 December they were both expelled from Portugal. Their files indicate that 'their entry into the country is forbidden for an indefinite period'.[74]

Interestingly, while Carlavilla was in Portugal, there were developments in the organization of the Francoist police that presented tailor-made opportunities for him. In 1937, the regime created a Brigada Anti-Marxista whose purpose was to combat the Jewish–masonic–Bolshevik conspiracy that Carlavilla had done so much to publicize. In the course of 1937, Franco's headquarters included several sections dedicated to the collection and cataloguing of material seized in captured areas from the offices of political parties and trade unions, from masonic lodges and from the homes of leftists. There was the Oficina de Investigación y Propaganda Antimarxista, the Oficina para la Recuperación de Documentos and the Sección Judeo-Masónica of the rebel military intelligence service, the Servicio de Información Militar. The names garnered from material captured by these units went into a huge file-card index of leftists to be arrested, tried and punished. They were merged in April 1938 into the Delegación del Estado para la Recuperación de Documentos under the command of Marcelino de Ulibarri Eguílaz. One of the most influential of Ulibarri's staff was the policeman Eduardo Comín Colomer, a friend of Carlavilla. In August 1938, all security services in the Francoist zone had been unified into the National Security Service headed by Lieutenant Colonel José Medina. At that point, by his own account, Carlavilla was working in Portugal on the orders of Medina.[75] In the meantime, one of the principal departments of the newly created National Security Service was the Investigation and Security Police, which in turn was divided into various sections. One of them, Anti-Marxism, consisted of three sub-sections, Freemasonry, Judaism and Publications. Comín Colomer was the head of both the Freemasonry and Judaism offices, as well as producing the *Boletín de Información Antimarxista*. It was inevitable that Carlavilla would eventually be recruited as a contributor. After all, these developments were what he had been advocating since his first book. Comín Colomer became Marcelino de Ulibarri's deputy and would play a key role in the classification and sifting of the captured material in preparation for its use by the secret police.[76]

It is puzzling that Carlavilla chose to remain in Portugal rather than return to Spain and bask in the success of his ideas. Given his enthusiasm for making money, it is highly probable that he had not returned because, in Portugal, his illicit earnings were far in excess of his salary as a police officer in Spain. The photographs in the files of the Portuguese police show an extremely well-dressed Carlavilla, much smarter than his rank in the police would have permitted. In March 1940, Carlavilla appealed against his September 1935 expulsion on the grounds that he had been the victim of political persecution because of his opposition to communism and freemasonry. His application was supported by the Director General of Security, the Conde de Mayalde, José Finat Escribá de Romaní, who heartily approved of his anti-Semitic, anti-Communist and anti-masonic role. In May, his expulsion was expunged from the records and Carlavilla rejoined the police as officer first class with a posting in Madrid. In December, he applied for his entire back pay since his expulsion in September 1935.[77] However, his return was not, as might have been expected, a triumphant one. His subsequent police career was as notably mediocre as it had been before his expulsion. Mayalde put him in charge of a short-lived unit within the Dirección General de Seguridad that had the mission of controlling Jews resident in Spain. It was created at the request of Himmler. However, Mayalde would soon be going to Berlin as Ambassador.[78]

In any case, Carlavilla now seemed to be more interested in earning a comfortable living. He founded and ran his publishing house Editorial Nos. During the Second World War, considered a celebrity of the extreme right, he was invited to tour Nazi concentration camps where he was especially impressed by the persecution of homosexuals. He wrote approvingly in his book *Sodomitas*, 'The work camps received many thousands of sodomites of all social classes. They were distinguished from other categories of prisoners by the colour of the star sewn on to their uniforms and by the fact that they were the only ones forced to remain upright, marching on the spot, in order to make their work even more tiring.' He then propounded a bizarre explanation for why the homosexuals were treated more harshly than Jews and Communists. He asserted that they were more resistant to anti-aphrodisiac medication and thus their sexual instincts could be restrained only by exhaustion.[79]

In 1940 and 1941, he had several short-term postings in Girona, Palma de Mallorca and Barcelona. Nevertheless, for most of the time after his re-entry into the police force, he had taken leave of absence. When he was posted to Palma de Mallorca in late 1941, he was promoted to inspector second class. However, he applied for a transfer to Madrid. When the application was unsuccessful, he made numerous requests for sick leave in the course of 1942, citing various respiratory problems. Finally, he took leave of absence in October 1942.[80] Carlavilla's records reveal that, in 1943, the political police was investigating a woman called Eloísa Sánchez Sánchez who was in partnership with him in a jewellery business. He had given her 50,000 pesetas to help set up the business and it operated from an apartment that he owned in Madrid's Avenida de José Antonio.[81] Eloísa Sánchez was the widow of Eduardo Barriobero, the corrupt anarchist lawyer who, in the autumn of 1936, ran the so-called Oficina Jurídica, the 'justice system' in revolutionary Catalonia. During that time, Barriobero was accused of using his position to acquire considerable wealth by pocketing huge fines imposed for possession of religious artefacts. Barriobero was imprisoned after it was discovered that he had accumulated substantial sums of money in French banks. In mid-September 1936, seven Falangists had been discovered hiding in the flat that he rented in Madrid for which Eloísa had received substantial sums. It is not clear if the flat was rented from Carlavilla. One of Carlavilla's ventures with Eloísa was a visit to Paris in an unsuccessful effort to recover a cache of the jewels that her husband had taken there before his arrest.[82] It is unlikely to have been coincidence that some of Carlavilla's few successes as a detective had been in tracking down jewel thieves. In one case, according to an article by his partner Francisco Horacio Iglesias, he and Horacio had spent time in Paris trying to locate jewellery stolen in Spain.[83]

While in Barcelona, recovering from illness, although still posted to Palma de Mallorca, he gave private classes to a society called the Asociación Sacerdotal San Antonio María Claret. Women were not allowed to attend his talks about the threats posed by Jews, freemasons and Communists. His audience consisted of priests, Falangists and Carlists. In December 1947, he successfully applied to teach in the police academy in Madrid, the Escuela General de Policía.[84] In 1952, his application to rejoin the regular police force was approved. In October the following year, he finally reached the rank of inspector and was posted to the intelligence service. On reaching the retirement age of sixty in February 1957, he was obliged to leave the police.[85] Throughout these years, he allegedly kept a portrait of Hitler in his office.[86]

In the run-up to, and in the three years after, his retirement from the police, he produced a stream of best-selling books including several that were unauthorized editions of writings by Republican politicians to which he added contentious, not to say offensive, editorial comment. In October 1956, in an advertisement in *ABC*, the Madrid booksellers Rubiños published a list of their seventeen best-selling non-fiction works.[87] Eleven of the seventeen were published by Editorial Nos, six of them written by Carlavilla and five with prefaces by him. Among these works were his most substantial book, a biography of Alfonso XIII and, arguably one of his most ludicrous or demented, *Sodomitas*. Given that the retail price of his books was between 50 and 100 pesetas, significantly in excess of average book prices at the time, it might suggest that, during the 1950s, his financial success was considerable.

Another rather bizarre work, published in 1955, *El dinero de Hitler*, thirteenth on the list, was a translation of a ninety-nine-page booklet that had first appeared in 1933 in Holland as *De geldbronnen van het nationaal-socialisme. Drie gesprekken met Hitler* (The Financial Sources of National Socialism. Three Conversations with Hitler). Its thesis was that Jewish American capitalists financed the Nazi rise to power in the hope that they could profit when the Third Reich ceased making the reparation payments to France imposed by the Versailles Treaty. The purported author, 'Sidney Warburg', ostensibly of the well-known banking dynasty, did not exist. The book was quickly exposed as a fabrication and all copies withdrawn from sale in Holland. Despite the fact that the book was known to be a forgery, Carlavilla advertised it as written by 'the multimillionaire Warburg' and boasted that his commentary revealed how 'a gang of Jewish financiers bankrolled Hitler in 1929 and Lenin and Trotsky in 1917 to provoke the world war'. He claimed that, 'after years of research, he had produced an illuminating documentary report on the authenticity of the work'. His 'historical additions' nearly tripled the size of the book and inflated its central thesis to the claim that American Jews had financed the Nazis in order to provoke a major war as a step to world domination.[88]

Sodomitas would be one of Carlavilla's most successful works. In 1956, it was third in Rubiños's list of best-sellers and, between its first publication and the 1970s, it had a further twelve editions. The book is divided into three sections, dealing respectively with the alleged link between sodomy and communism; what he calls the 'school of sodomy', the allegedly concerted efforts made to propagate homosexuality; and thirdly the apparent connection between sodomy, politics and international espionage. The book's uniquely aberrant combination of lunacy, invention and prejudice is captured in the prologue which takes the form of a warning to parents. Carlavilla describes urban society as a jungle in which there lurk, not ferocious animals, but perverts. He concludes that, if a son is corrupted, 'Better dead!, you will cry in desperation! Yes, better dead. Better devoured by a wild animal. Better for him, better for you and better for God.'

For Carlavilla the link between homosexuality and communism was that both were perversions that led to the destruction of the family, of private property and of the traditional social order. He devoted much space to the enmity between Hitler and the homosexual community, admitting along the way, with a reference to Ernst Röhm (whose name he spelt 'Rhoen'), that the NSDAP had been 'invaded' by homosexuals. On the bizarre grounds that communism is of directly satanic inspiration, he asserts that 'Satanism is the hinge that connects communism and homosexuality.' Unsurprisingly, he saw Jewish influence in both phenomena as, inevitably, he did in his section on the intellectual forces propagating sodomy, a huge group including Spinoza, Marx, Engels, Freud and Einstein. The third section draws on the unpublished psychosexual biography of Azaña that he had been preparing when he had to flee Spain in 1936. Insinuating that most freemasons are homosexuals, traitors to themselves and vulnerable to blackmail, he concludes, in his twisted logic, that they are often traitors in the service of international espionage. He bases this view largely on the experience of the two British spies, Guy Burgess and Donald Maclean.[89]

Sodomitas was followed one year later by *Satanismo*, an equally bizarre essay based on the idea that freemasonry was the brainchild of a Jewish sect in Babylon influenced by the devil. Ludicrously, he associated the distinguished physician and biographer Dr Gregorio Marañón with the sinister sexual consequences of the Kabala. Strangest of all was his claim that millions of ritual crimes had been carried out in Spain by the Jews from the middle ages well into the 1930s.[90]

The Rubiños publicity was followed one month later by a large advertisement placed by Editorial Nos. The inflated descriptions of Carlavilla himself and of the books on offer bordered on megalomania. Of himself, he said that, as Mauricio Karl, he had accurately predicted in 1931, 1934 and 1935 how and when Marxism, anarchism and freemasonry would assassinate Spain. He went on to say that, as Mauricio Carlavilla, he had predicted how these 'assassins of Spain' would destroy Christianity. His biography of Georgy Maximilianovich Malenkov, who enjoyed a short period as successor to Stalin, *Malenkov. Biografiá política y psico-sexual* was presented as 'a true secret history of the USSR through the biography of the eunuch who is still the main man of the Soviet Government'. His book on *Roosevelt* was summed up as 'the treachery of the great freemason in Pearl Harbor, in Teheran and Yalta, handing over half of humanity to Stalin. Documentary proof of this great crime of lèse-Christianity.' *Sinfonía en rojo mayor* was presented as 'the most frightening and marvellous book of the century'. This entirely invented work was described as 'real history that reads like the most riveting novel'.[91]

Carlavilla's hunger for profit was revealed by several blatant acts of piracy. One of the first appeared in 1945 in Guadalajara, produced by his brother's printing business, and was followed by another edition from Editorial Nos in 1947. It was the Spanish translation of the memoirs of the Soviet intelligence agent Walter Krivitsky, which had been published in London and New York in 1939.[92] It was launched with the extravagant title *Yo, jefe del Servicio Secreto Militar Soviético*, Prólogo y notas de Mauricio Carlavilla 'Mauricio Karl', and presented as having been translated from Russian by 'M.B.', who might reasonably be supposed to be Mauricio Carlavilla del Barrio. In fact, Walter Krivitsky was never 'Chief of Soviet Military Intelligence in Western Europe' and the book could not have been translated from Russian because the original text was in English, produced by Krivitsky's ghostwriter, Isaac Don Levine. Far from being a man who had directed Soviet intelligence operations in Spain, Krivitsky knew very little about the civil war since, prior to his defection, he had been an agent in Holland.[93]

In 1952, Carlavilla published another pirated edition, the 'memoirs' of the dissident Communist Valentín González, 'El Campesino', the one-time miner who rose through the ranks of the Republican army, becoming a general and acquiring a reputation for brutality. After the civil war, he went into exile in Russia where he joined the Frunze military academy, only to be expelled for incompetence. He was later imprisoned in a labour camp from which he made a daring escape, walking to the Iran border. It was clear from the prologue that Carlavilla was unaware that the 'memoirs' had been written by Julián Gorkín.[94] This pirate edition was published without the name of a publisher. Astonishingly, advertisements in the press included the pious announcement that 'El Campesino will not profit from the author's royalties in Spain. They will be given to the associations for *Orphans of the Murdered* and *Ex-Prisoners*. As morality and jurisprudence dictate, the profits will go not to the executioner but to his victims.' Since neither association existed, it is highly probable that all the profits went directly to Carlavilla.[95]

The next volume to boost Carlavilla's profits was the memoirs of the Communist Jesús Hernández, who had been Minister of Education during the civil war. The memoirs were published in Mexico in 1953 as *Yo fui un ministro de Stalin*. In 1954, with a slight change of the title to *Yo, ministro de Stalin en España*, Carlavilla published his edition. He omitted Hernández's introduction, in which he had accepted some blame for the repression carried out by the Communist Party during the war, and added a virulent prologue of his own.[96] Two years later he produced a bowdlerized version of

Indalecio Prieto's controversial report to the National Committee of the Socialist Party in which he had denounced the Communist Party. Despite Prieto's evident anti-communism, Carlavilla's twisted account of his career made it seem as if he was somehow responsible for Communist atrocities during the civil war.[97]

The final work in this collection of illegally published memoirs was that of Francisco Largo Caballero. It had been put together in Mexico by Enrique de Francisco in 1954 on the basis of letters that he had received from the veteran Socialist leader after his release from a German concentration camp in 1945. In 1961, Carlavilla published his version with the sensationalist title 'Secret Correspondence'. He added his usual tendentious notes, but omitted the last 100 pages in which Largo wrote of his experiences in exile.[98]

The irresponsibility, not to say lunacy, with which Carlavilla threw out lies and exaggerations was underlined by his book *Borbones masones* which denounced the Spanish royal family as freemasons. He seemed to have forgotten that, just over a decade earlier, he had published his biography of Alfonso XIII, in which every mistake and misfortune of that benighted monarch was attributed to evil Jewish and masonic machinations. The Jews, he insisted, were the enemies of Spain and of Christianity. Their ultimate aim was the total genocide of the Spanish people.[99] He repeated an accusation made twenty years earlier that the assassinations of three of Alfonso XIII's prime ministers, Cánovas, Canalejas and Dato, and of the Dictator Primo de Rivera were the work of freemasons.[100]

He asserted that 'the big secret behind the catastrophes suffered by the Fatherland' was 'the Anglo-Jewish High Command of international freemasonry'. Indicative of his defective, not to say demented, notion of historical chronology was his selection of what he regarded as 'one of the High Command's greatest triumphs in Spain: the treachery that permitted the Muslim invasion and its amazing conquest of Spain almost in its entirety'. The loss of empire from the 1820s onwards was also, he asserted, the work of Jews and freemasons, with pride of place given to Juan de Dios Álvarez Mendizábal. 'Spanish freemasonry, at the behest of the Anglo-Jewish High Command, was behind Basque and Catalan separatism.' He made bizarre insinuations that prime ministers of the Restoration period

(1874–1923) such as Práxedes Mateo Sagasta, José Sánchez Guerra and the Conde de Romanones and intellectuals such as Gregorio Marañón were Jewish freemasons.[101]

Since Franco was about to name as his successor Juan Carlos de Borbón, the grandson of Alfonso XIII, copies of the new book, *Borbones masones*, were confiscated by the authorities.[102] It was during this period that Carlavilla published the best-seller *Sinfonía en rojo mayor*, supposedly by a Russian doctor called Josef Landowsky. It went into many editions, had several translations and is still in print today. The 800-page manuscript was allegedly found on Landowsky's body by a volunteer of the División Azul or Blue Division, which fought with the Germans on the Eastern Front. It is not explained why he was carrying this bulky manuscript in a war zone. The manuscript was presented as having been translated by Carlavilla, despite the fact that he did not know Russian. The ludicrous story involves Landowsky being recruited to help drug and kidnap Lieutenant General Evgenii Karlovich Miller, the head of the organization of the White Russian forces in exile, the Russkii Obshche-Voinskii Soiuz (ROVS, Russian All-Military Union) based in Paris.[103]

Throughout the 1950s, Carlavilla also produced reports on communism and its alleged Jewish–masonic origins for Carrero Blanco's Presidencia de Gobierno (cabinet office). These reports must have reached Franco directly or indirectly. Their content may be surmised from his published works. Some of the most far-fetched of his lies could be found in his book *Anti-España 1959*, which came out at the end of the decade. In this he embellished the chronologically bizarre interpretations of Spanish history to be found in his biography of Alfonso XIII. Denouncing what he called the fallacy of democracy, he alleged that:

From the second decade of the 18th century, from the entry of British–Jewish freemasonry into Spain, democracy and betrayal of the Fatherland were consubstantial. A betrayal dictated, organized and implemented according to the plans of states or super-states for their own benefit, all starting with the Anglo-masonic treachery that imposed upon us masonic monarchs or viceroys with the name of kings who were the servants of foreign states or super-states. And thus there came about the loss of our empire, the permanent decadence of the Fatherland, and finally the attempted murder of the Fatherland frustrated in 1936, frustrated at the cost of one million lives.[104]

Carlavilla's résumé of his vision of the history of Spain from the eighteenth to the twentieth century was an echo of Franco's insistence on the same. The Caudillo made a long speech to the Cortes on 14 May 1946, largely aimed at proving that his regime was not a dicta-torship and owed nothing to the Axis. However, he could not resist a survey of Spanish history as one of the uninterrupted disasters provoked by 'materialist sectarians', a thinly disguised reference to the Jewish–masonic–Bolshevik conspiracy.[105] In May 1948, he spoke of the catastrophe unleashed on Spain by 'freemasonry and the forces of evil'.[106] By freemasonry, Franco understood the flowering of liberal values in Spain or what he called 'the great invasion of evil'. In March 1950, he addressed the Youth Front of the Falange on the 'calamitous centuries' of Spanish history since Felipe II that had brought deca-dence, corruption and freemasonry.[107]

Even more deranged was Carlavilla's boast that he had foreseen as early as 1936 that Franco would never be the military ally of the Third Reich. He went on to claim that he had ample means of reach-ing Hitler to warn him of this because of contacts he had made with senior Nazis while he was trying to secure the release of José Antonio. His personal authority, he said, would ensure that he was believed. This, he asserted with notable amnesia, was because he was the first and most determined person to denounce Marxism, freemasonry and Judaism in Spain. Had he not exercised his discre-tion out of patriotism, he could have provoked the withdrawal of German aid and the downfall of Franco.[108] His anti-Semitism was underlined in 1963 when he published an annotated edition of *The Protocols of the Elders of Zion*. The reason seems to have been that he was appalled by the liberal reforms being introduced into the Catholic doctrine by the Second Vatican Council. He believed that they were the work of occult Jewish–masonic influences. For the notes, however, he used the pseudonym Charles Borough, which suggests that he was wary of falling foul of the Church hierarchy in Spain.[109]

Carlavilla's initiative might have been related to the fact that Franco too had been traumatized by the deliberations of the Vatican Council, which threatened his entire belief system. In notes produced at the time, and written in similar terms to those employed by Carlavilla, Franco confided his conviction that the Curia had been infiltrated by freemasons and Communists. He attributed contemporary political changes in Catholic countries to the subversive actions of freemasons. At the beginning of 1963, he told his cousin Francisco Franco Salgado-Araujo 'Pacón' that he continued to collate information from intelligence sources on what happened in masonic lodges and Socialist and Communist meetings around the world: 'Nothing will catch me by surprise; it is necessary to be prepared for the struggle.' He drew up lengthy notes on the links between the masonic danger and Catholic liberalization.[110]

Throughout the late 1940s and early 1950s, Carlavilla hinted that he worked for the Spanish secret services. If so, this might be linked to the fact that he started to publish work about the Soviet Union. It has been suggested that he had privileged access to CIA intelligence on Russia. This might also be substantiated by the fact that two of his pamphlets were published by Luis Carrero Blanco's Presidencia de Gobierno.[111] He became a great admirer of Senator Joseph McCarthy and dedicated one of his books to him:

To Senator Joseph McCarthy, champion of militant Christianity, in its crusade against the atheist Communism that aims to dominate bodies and kill souls, to impose its universal slavery. Onwards, Senator, the proof of your success and wisdom is the worldwide storm of fury directed against you by the well-known and masked enemy. You should consider its universal and insulting clamour as the biggest and best applause that humanity can offer in tribute to you. May this book be testimony of admiration for your brave struggle, with the wish that it might comfort you in the face of misunderstandings, mistakes and betrayals.[112]

As time wore on, the audience that had devoured Carlavilla's works before the civil war and in the first decades of the Franco dictatorship dwindled. This was evident in the rather disillusioned tone of his final work, the memoirs *Anti-España 1959*. Here he insinuated that he was disillusioned with the regime and spoke dismissively of his career as a police officer:

> I have been, for the minimum period necessary to secure my pension rights, a functionary in the police service, just another functionary, one of many. I was promoted by the strict rules of seniority and, when I reached the requisite age, I retired. That is all there is to it, reader. No one can say that this has given me any distinction, honour, political position, anything to satisfy my vanity, ambition or self-interest. A mediocre profession that I entered by passing a competitive examination in 1921, that was taken from me by the Republic in 1935 and to which I was reinstated by the law in 1940. That, reader, is my past and present relationship with the current regime.

After this apparently humble statement, he went on to state arrogantly that he refrained from revealing his views on the regime because to do so would stain the selfless purity of books written for the sole purpose of defending Spain and Christianity.[113]

The irrelevance of his work in a Spain becoming ever more incorporated within Western consumerist society was reflected in the fact that, in the mid-1970s, he lived in a sordid room in a *pensión* in the Avenida de José Antonio No. 38, sitting around in unwashed underwear, surrounded by piles of dusty books and magazines and obsessing about the Communist menace.[114] His personal situation seems to have improved when he married Yolanda-Hortensia Nicieza González, a nurse who had also been his secretary. His only social life was to meet with his one-time boss in the police Eduardo Comín Colomer, the inveterate Francoist propagandist Tomás Borrás and the young leaders of Spain's fascist fringe, Mariano Sánchez Covisa, Jorge Mora and Santiago Royuela. They convened first in *cafeterías* near the Plaza de Callao and later in the California 47 in Goya, which was to become a centre for neo-fascists. There he would also meet up with Serrano Suñer's one-time protégé Ángel Alcázar de Velasco. Carlavilla became the guru of a number of neo-Nazi groups, such as Jorge Mota's CEDADE (Círculo Español de Amigos de Europa) and Sánchez Covisa's Fuerza Nueva.[115] He died on 24 June 1982.[116]

The Priest: Father Juan Tusquets

Among those who perpetrated the pernicious idea that the Second Republic was the bastard child of the concubinage of Jews and freemasons, the first and arguably the most influential was the Catalan priest Joan Tusquets Terrat. Through his own publications and his 1932 edition of *The Protocols of the Elders of Zion*, he popularized the idea that the Republic had to be annihilated in the interests of Christian civilization. He also assembled the data that would be used during the Spanish Civil War to facilitate the persecution of the alleged members of the so-called Jewish–masonic–Bolshevik conspiracy. Juan Tusquets, who used the Spanish version of his name throughout the 1930s, was the author of the best-seller *Orígenes de la revolución española*. He was born into a wealthy banking family in Barcelona on 31 March 1901. His father was a descendant of Jewish bankers, a committed Catalanist and a friend of the great Catalan politician and banker Francesc Cambó. His mother was a member of the fabulously wealthy Milà family, the patrons of Gaudí. In later life, as part of a concerted effort to sanitize his past as a witchfinder, Tusquets made great play of the fact that, as a teenager, he too had been a militant Catalan nationalist. During the revolutionary disturbances of 1917, he had taken to the streets with his schoolfriends and chanted Catalanist slogans. He had also written nationalist verses with words such as 'Unfurl the flags / Beat your breasts / Frontiers are rising up / Belittled Catalans you have found them too high.' Less truthfully, he claimed never to have reneged on his Catalanist beliefs. This notion of lifelong Catalanist commitment contributed to the favourable image that he enjoyed among Catalan Catholic intellectuals in the last twenty years of his life. However, it deliberately obscured the militant anti-Catalanism of his role throughout the 1930s.[1]

Tusquets's secondary education took place in a Jesuit school. Subsequently, he went to the University of Louvain but his time there was cut short by the death of his father. He transferred to the Pontifical University in Tarragona, where he completed a doctorate on Ramón Llull, the great thirteenth-century Mallorcan mathematician, logician and philosopher. One of Tusquets's teachers and greatest influences was the theologian Lluís Carreras. Tusquets was ordained in 1926 in an accelerated process which enabled him to avoid military service. In 1927, the Capuchin theologian Miquel d'Esplugues, one of his ecclesiastical patrons, described him as 'slim, supple and hyperactive, given to living well and to witticisms of a classical kind, highly intelligent, with a considerable cultural baggage both classical and modern, physically stronger than he seemed, a tireless worker, conceited in small things and, in big things, humble in principle, profoundly pious and polite'. The young scholar was regarded by Father Esplugues as 'one of the brightest and firmest hopes of the Church and of the Fatherland'.[2] Five years later, Father Esplugues had changed his mind about Tusquets as a result of the younger man's murderous denunciations of freemasonry. Indeed, in response to his attacks on the venerable Catalan leader, Francesc Macià, Father Esplugues broke off relations with Tusquets.[3]

On the basis of his ostentatious piety and his enormous culture, in 1926 Tusquets was appointed to a professorship in the seminary of the Catalan capital. While there, he was commissioned by the Archbishop of Tarragona, Cardinal Francesc Vidal i Barraquer, to write a book combating Madame Helena Blavatsky's Theosophy. Its notion of a universal religion based on the principles of brotherhood, freedom of faith, justice and equality had links to, and similarities with, freemasonry. Madame Blavatsky's belief in an ancient brotherhood of spiritual teachers based in Tibet, the 'Masters', evoked the idea of the Elders of Zion. Quite early in his career, Tusquets revealed his suspicions of a wide range of societies out of which would grow his obsessions with freemasonry and the Jews. In his book, he wrote:

There is a neutral area where Protestants and Theosophists often link up. They are the moralizing and altruistic sects: nudism, vegetarianism, anti-alcoholism, sexual education, boy scouts, labour movements, Esperantism, internationalism, Rotary Clubs etc., etc.... An occult force strategically mobilizes these sectors against the Catholic Church. Is this force Judaism? I am almost afraid to say so given how sympathetically many Catholic intellectuals speak of the work of the sons of Israel.[4]

In the course of his researches for the book on Theosophy, Tusquets's interest in secret societies and sects of all kinds, particularly masonic and Jewish, developed into an obsession. There are aspects of the book, the inclusion of the names and addresses of the people whom he suspected, that pointed to his vocation as a spy and an informer. In the wake of the book's success, he continued to work on the subject in conjunction with what he called 'a really solid international Jesuit organization that had a network of informers which they placed at my disposal.'[5]

Despite, or perhaps because of, his own remote Jewish origins, by the time the Second Republic was established his investigations into secret societies had developed into a fierce anti-Semitism and an even fiercer hatred of freemasonry. In a further rejection of his family background, he turned violently against Catalanism. He was perhaps motivated by the desire to be recognized by the anti-Republican right, which was fiercely anti-Catalanist. He gained great notoriety by falsely accusing the piously Catholic President of the Generalitat de Catalunya, Francesc Macià, of being a freemason. He did so on the basis of documents falsified by the French extreme right-wing organization Action Française in the magazine L'Ordre. At the same time, he criticized the Catholic Catalanist newspaper El Matí for its anti-fascist campaigns.[6] Cardinal Francesc Vidal i Barraquer wrote to the Papal Nuncio that one of the articles written by Tusquets in the course of the polemic was 'highly injurious and immensely inopportune'. Vidal had personal knowledge that Macià was not a freemason. Despite the falsification being exposed at the time, Tusquets would maintain his accusations against Macià and El Matí as late as 1939.[7] He began to collaborate with another cleric, Father Joaquim Guiu

Bonastre, the parish priest of the church of Sants Just i Pastor near the cathedral. Together, they built up a network of what Tusquets regarded as their 'informants', mainly freemasons who told them about lodge meetings but also others who shared their obsessions. Despite Tusquets's piety, he was not above spying or even burglary. One of the principal lodges in Barcelona was in the Carrer d'Avinyó next to the Red Cross pharmacy. Since Tusquets's aunt lived above the pharmacy, from her apartment he and Father Guiu were able to spy on the comings and goings of the freemasons. Moreover, he boasted years later to the Catholic intellectual Albert Manent that he had managed to put on his payroll the concierge of the lodge's building. In return for the bribe, she would bring him each day the correspondence sent to the lodge. He became adept at opening envelopes with steam from a kettle. After reading the contents, he would return them to the concierge for delivery. On one occasion, he and Guiu broke into another lodge and started a fire in order, in the ensuing confusion, to steal a series of documents.[8]

These 'researches' and the information gathered were the basis for the regular, and vehemently anti-masonic and anti-Semitic, articles that Tusquets contributed to the Carlist newspaper *El Correo Catalán* and for his book *Orígenes de la revolución española*. He later boasted of the fame that the book gave him: 'It was a best-seller that sold thousands and thousands and thousands of copies, here, in Latin America and everywhere.' He claimed that, when it was published, he received letters of congratulation from the household of the exiled King Alfonso XIII, from Cardinal Vidal i Barraquer, from Francesc Cambó and from Cambó's friend Father Miquel d'Esplugues. When asked years later if he had kept the letters, he said that, after replying to them, he had ripped them up.[9] For a man so obsessed with embellishing his own past, this seems a strange thing to do, particularly in the case of a letter from the exiled King. If indeed he received such letters, their destruction might perhaps be accounted for by the following. Both Cambó and D'Esplugues broke with him around this time in disgust at his extremism. Vidal i Barraquer reprimanded him to the extent of saying that his views should not have been associated with a member of the clergy and that his book should have been published under a pseudonym. If letters had been sent to him by those three, it is unlikely that they would have been written in amicable terms. In the case of Alfonso XIII, as will be seen in his later clashes with Cambó, membership of the Falange was accompanied by a rejection of the monarchy.

The book was indeed immensely successful. Published in January 1932, the first edition of 10,000 copies was sold out by early February. The second edition with a print run of 20,000 copies also flew off the shelves and a third, with a further 25,000 copies, followed.[10] It was notable for its decisive contribution to the popularization of the divisive notion that the Republic was the fruit of the Jewish–masonic–Bolshevik conspiracy. It carried a prologue by Dr Cipriano Montserrat, Professor of Theology in the same Barcelona seminary where Tusquets taught. Writing of 'the sinister masonic sect', Dr Montserrat declared, 'It is beyond doubt that freemasonry in Spain has had secular allies in the form of Jewish capitalism and professional troublemakers.'[11] Dr Montserrat did not deign to explain why Jewish capitalists had tried, by dint of a flight of capital, to destroy the Republic that was allegedly their instrument for the destruction of Spanish Catholicism. Like Tusquets's earlier work, Los orígenes included the names and addresses of many of those he considered to be the most sinister artificers of the Jewish–masonic–Bolshevik conspiracy and the beneficiaries of 'Jewish gold'. The publication of this information could only have been meant as an incitement to violence against them.[12]

Tusquets claimed that his mission was to warn Catholics of the appalling threats posed by the Jews. 'Judaismo, with its firstborn, freemasonry, has spread subversive networks throughout the state. They move with invisible strings their political puppets and have achieved the results that are plain to see and which no sincere Catholic can contemplate without fear or bitterness. In the sects lie the immediate origins of the present revolution.'[13]

In his book, Tusquets cited the Protocols as 'documentary' evidence to prove his essential thesis that there existed 'a secret, international organization of the Jews that aims to destroy the Christian states and substitute them with an international Jewish organisation'. Over the years, he used several shorthand terms for this Jewish international including 'the Sanhedrin' but more often 'Israel'. Israel, he asserted, 'was bent on the ruin of Christian civilization. Its methods would be revolutions, economic catastrophes, ungodly and pornographic propaganda and unlimited liberalism'. He added, 'Judaism and freemasonry, to achieve their sinister ends, use the popular lever of socialism.'[14]

With what was an obvious projection of his own violent feelings, he expressed his fear of revenge attacks by freemasons. In particular, he felt that he might be poisoned by masonic doctors:

> My current undertaking poses more than one risk. I am really afraid that my indiscreet lectures will be punished by the direct or indirect action of the masons. No one should think that I suffer from persecution mania. I remain one of the calmest beings on earth. But I have no reason to hide my sincere and well-founded opinion regarding the revenge of the freemasons. A masonic lodge especially for doctors was recently established in Barcelona – their address is Menéndez Pelayo 10. This is a significant fact especially for those of us who have copious documentation about the methods used by the brotherhood of the masonic apron to achieve its political ambitions. So, if anything disagreeable happens to me, readers should blame it on the secret organizations and strengthen their resolve to combat them.[15]

The reaction of freemasons was far from the sinister threats imagined by Tusquets. They were certainly outraged, but their response was limited to planning a publicity campaign to counteract the more extreme of his accusations. This began with an open letter remonstrating with Tusquets about his erroneous statements.[16] It was followed by two books in reply to him. The first was by Ramón Díaz.[17] The second was by an ex-Catholic missionary priest and theologian turned freemason, Dr Matías Usero Torrente. His book was entitled *Mi respuesta al P. Tusquets* (My reply to Father Tusquets). Among the documents collected by Tusquets, now housed in Salamanca, there survives a publicity sheet for the book along with letters from masonic organizations about its distribution. The leaflet drew attention to the wave of reactionary propaganda attacking the Spanish Republic. It mistakenly assumed that, because Tusquets had been educated at a Jesuit school, he was a Jesuit. That error aside, Usero denounced *Orígenes de la revolución española* as 'A pile of platitudes intended to trick the gullible'. He continued, 'To reply is to provide humanity with a light and a shield with which to combat the parasites. Tusquets, a deliberate swindler and a Jesuit, lies consciously and deliberately.'[18]

The entirely pacific response from freemasons completely gave the lie to the bizarre claims by Tusquets that he wrote his book in fear for his life. Years later, he alleged that, in retaliation for his activities with Joaquim Guiu, the freemasons tried to assassinate them. If there was any truth in his claims, the freemasons in question did not try very hard. In his barely credible account, he described two assassination attempts. In the first incident, a hit squad was waiting for them outside the home of Father Guiu. Tusquets claimed that they cheated death simply by jumping into a taxi as the assassins hesitated in the crowded thoroughfare of the nearby Via Laetana. In the second, he claimed that a group of anarchists from the Confederación Nacional del Trabajo (CNT) newspaper *Solidaridad Obrera* shared his views and admired his writings. To show their appreciation, they had arranged a semi-permanent bodyguard who followed him everywhere on a motorbike. The presence of the bodyguard allegedly forestalled the attack. Such benevolence on the part of the anarchists was utterly improbable given their passionate anti-clericalism. To be aware of Tusquets's writings, any anarchists would have had to be readers of the Carlist newspaper *El Correo Catalán*, which was unlikely in the extreme. The CNT was intensely hostile to the Carlists, who had sponsored the scab unions of the Sindicatos Libres. Moreover, the exiguous finances of the CNT at this time precluded expenditure on a motorcycle.[19]

The book denounced the Second Republic as the child of freemasonry and accused the President, the piously Catholic Niceto Alcalá-Zamora, of being both a Jew and a freemason.[20] The message was clear – Spain and the Catholic Church could be saved only by the destruction of Jews, freemasons and Socialists – in other words, of the entire left of the political spectrum. *Orígenes de la revolución española* not only sold massively but also provoked a noisy national debate which served to give even greater currency to his ideas. On 2

March, in his press conference given in the Generalitat of Catalonia, Macià rebutted in detail Tusquets's totally unfounded accusations. Doing so, of course, gave invaluable publicity to the book.[21] Tusquets's central contention that the Republic was a dictatorship in the hands of 'Judaic freemasonry' was further disseminated through his many articles in *El Correo Catalán* and a highly successful series of fifteen books (advertised as a journal, *Las Sectas*) that he edited with Joaquim Guiu.

The last pages of *Los orígenes* advertised the forthcoming publication of the first volume of *Las Sectas* on 20 March 1932. The advertisement was drafted in the same terms of a warning against an imminent attack by the Jewish–masonic enemy. 'Do you want political developments to catch you unprepared? Do you want a fully documented way of interpreting the way the world is going? Would you like accurate news about the activities of the sectarian elements working in your town, region or state? Subscribe to *Las Sectas*. The reports in this journal will always be based on extremely serious sources and be drafted by very capable people.' The 'accurate news' promised to subscribers would basically consist of allegations that the Second Republic was run by Jewish freemasonry.

Tusquets had revealed his loathing of the Jews in *Los orígenes* and openly acknowledged its basis in his reading of the *Protocols*. The second volume of *Las Sectas* included a complete Spanish translation of the *Protocols* and also repeated his slurs on Macià.[22] The first section, signed 'Fabio' and almost certainly by Tusquets, was an essay on the authenticity of the *Protocols*.[23] The section entitled 'the application to Spain', written by Jesús Lizárraga, asserted that the Jewish assault on Spain had been held back by the expulsion of the Jews in 1492. Thereafter, he claimed, the Jewish determination to destroy Catholic Spain was renewed through freemasonry, 'the hidden mercenary army'. Anti-Spanish feeling fomented in the colonies by freemasons led to the disastrous war with the United States and the loss of Cuba and the Philippines in 1898. Then, the next weapons to be used were the Socialist and anarchist movements, promoted, he said, by promises of plundering the wealth of the rich. This was opposed by the prime ministers Cirilo Cánovas, José Canalejas and Eduardo Dato, for which they were assassinated by the same dark forces that repeatedly tried to murder Antonio Maura. Next, the Jewish-inspired freemasons used the Institución Libre de Enseñanza and the Juntas de Defensa within the army to foment division and revolution. Their nefarious schemes were briefly held back by the dictatorship of General Miguel Primo de Rivera but finally came to fruition in the fall of the monarchy and the establishment of the Second Republic. This, in Lizárraga's narrative, opened the way to a persecution of religion that was an attack on all Spaniards and a series of measures that favoured the Jews, including the construction of many synagogues. He also saw Jewish–masonic manoeuvres in the movement for agrarian reform and the redistribution of the great estates. This he saw as proof of the *Protocols*' claim that the Jews wanted to possess Spanish territory.[24]

The influence of Tusquets's edition of the *Protocols* was considerable, as will be seen in the chapter on José María Pemán in this book. It inspired much of Pemán's wartime oratory, his epic *Poema de la bestia y del ángel* and his policy as President of the Comisión de Cultura y Enseñanza, one of the seven pseudo-ministries of Franco's 'government', the Junta Técnica del Estado. Utterly convinced by Tusquets's book was his brother-in-law, Víctor Guillén, who distributed copies of it to his family and friends. After the Second World War, Víctor would deny the existence of the Holocaust and kept a substantial museum in his house full of photographs of Hitler and Eva Braun and of Nazi flags and artefacts.[25] The book also captivated the young Carlist René Llanas de Niubó, who had been a prominent member of the Unión Patriótica in the 1920s. He became one of Tusquets's principal acolytes. He wrote the fourteenth volume of *Las Sectas, El Judaísmo*, in which he deplored the anti-Catholicism and paganism of the Nazis but declared roundly of Hitler, 'he is entirely justified in his anti-Semitic campaign'. He made a considerable splash in Barcelona with a lecture entitled 'Judaísmo'. In terms inspired by his mentor, he declared that '*Judaísmo*, freemasonry, communism and death, like the four horsemen of the apocalypse, hurl themselves on Spain destroying everything ... The Jews have used first socialism and then communism to wreak destruction throughout the world.' In April 1933, he gave a series of lectures in Madrid including two with the title 'Masonería y judaísmo'.[26] As will be seen, Llanas de Niubó would be one of Tusquets's key collaborators in the efforts to create a civilian infrastructure for the military uprising of July 1936.

So great was the wider impact of his writings that in late 1933 Tusquets was invited by the International Anti-Masonic Association to visit the recently established concentration camp at Dachau. He commented that 'they did it to show us what we had to do in Spain'.[27] Dachau was established as a camp for various groups that the Nazis wished to quarantine: political prisoners (Communist, Socialist, liberal, Catholic and monarchist opponents of the regime) and those that they defined as asocials or deviants (homosexuals, gypsies, vagrants). More than fifty years later, he would claim to have been shocked by what he saw and even that he had campaigned against Nazi anti-Semitism.[28] This is simply not true. Indeed, at the time, the flow and the intensity of his anti-Semitic and anti-masonic publications did not abate. In the tenth volume of *Las Sectas*, in the section on masonic activity, he wrote in praise of Hitler's response to the Jewish problem and of Spandau prison in Berlin.[29]

The eighth volume of *Las Sectas* was written almost in its entirety by Tusquets and Guiu. Tusquets contributed an article about what he claimed were the efforts of freemasonry to combat the victory of the right in the election of November 1933.[30] In a bizarre reversal of their previous attacks on Francesc Macià, Guiu wrote a hymn of praise to the deceased President's piously Catholic death.[31] Thereafter, the bulk of the volume appears to have been compiled jointly. It consisted of a lengthy assertion that Dr José Protasio Rizal Mercado, the Filipino nationalist shot by the Spanish in December 1896, was not the hero proclaimed by freemasons but actually a devout Catholic.[32] It is not clear what interest this would have for the readership of *Las Sectas*. Altogether more likely to appeal to them was the lengthy list of names and addresses of the offices and leading members of the various regional branches of the Grand Orient, the governing body of Spanish freemasonry.[33] It would be of considerable use as part of the documentary infrastructure of the persecution of freemasons during and after the civil war.

Tusquets would come to have enormous influence within the Spanish right in general and specifically over General Franco, who enthusiastically devoured his anti-masonic and anti-Semitic diatribes.[34] Indeed, during the civil war, thanks to the books and lectures of both Tusquets and Pemán, the idea that the war was being fought against the Jewish–masonic–Bolshevik conspiracy dominated the rhetoric of the rebel side. However, Tusquets did more than just develop the ideas that justified violence. He and Joaquim Guiu were active participants in the preparation of the military uprising against the Republic. Through their links with Catalan Carlists, they were an important part of the civilian underpinning of the conspiracy. They formed a secret 'anti-masonic committee' that participated in a group called the Voluntariado Español, which was organized by the Unión Militar Española in Barcelona in 1934. Their committee used the cover name of 'the Order of the Knights of the Immaculate/Legion of St George'. Its members included functionaries, ultra-rightist militants and police, Civil Guard and army officers who provided arms. The overall cover for the Voluntariado Español was the innocuous-sounding España Club.[35] From mid-April 1936 until mid-July, Tusquets and Guiu were active as liaisons between the UME and the various civilian volunteers who aimed to support the uprising in Barcelona.

They also took the lead in the production of anti-Republican propaganda with a policeman, Juan Segura Nieto, a young businessman, Juan Aguasca Bonmati, and the Carlist lawyer René Llanas de Niubó, author, it will be recalled, of a ferociously anti-Semitic volume in *Las Sectas*. Aguasca Bonmati was the secretary of Captain Luis López Varela, the UME member organizing the coup in Barcelona. Since the late summer of 1934, the trio had been compiling a bulletin in both Spanish and Catalan versions, *Cuadernos de Información* and *Quaderns d'Informació*. Originally monthly, after the Popular Front elections of February 1936 some 10,000 to 15,000 copies were cyclostyled and distributed on a daily basis to all the army garrisons, Civil Guard posts and offices of Carlist, Falangist, monarchist and other sympathetic organizations such as the Sindicatos Libres.[36] Franco's brother-in-law and his Minister of the Interior, Ramón Serrano Suñer, praised the impact of the *Cuadernos* on retired army officers who later took part in the coup. He hailed the contribution of the *Cuadernos* to 'creating the atmosphere that facilitated the military uprising'.[37] In the last days before the uprising, Guiu received, from

the police officer Juan Segura Nieto, sealed instructions from López
Varela for the civilian volunteers of the España Club, as well as
armbands to identify them as trusted collaborators of the military
rebels.[38] In addition to these activities, in late May 1936 Tusquets
approached the Catalan plutocrat Francesc Cambó and requested
financial assistance for a journal which may well have been *Cuadernos
de Información*. He may have been emboldened to do so because
Cambó, as a friend of Tusquets's father, had – allegedly – written and
congratulated him on the success of *Orígenes de la revolución
española*. As will be seen, the financial help did not materialize, which
probably accounts for the fact that Tusquets turned viciously against
Cambó.

Despite that minor setback, Tusquets made an important contribution to the rebel cause both before and during the civil war. From
the early 1930s, along with Joaquim Guiu, Tusquets had assiduously
compiled lists of Jews and freemasons partly based on information
provided by a network of what he called 'my faithful and daring
informers'. Some were freemasons. There were others who shared the
obsessions of Tusquets and Guiu and infiltrated masonic lodges or
spied on them. Interrogated by the Francoist authorities in June 1942,
a fellow member of España Club, Firmo Casanova y de Vallés, spoke
about his collaboration with Guiu during the years of the Second
Republic in El Collell (Girona), a village with many connections to
the Guiu family. His testimony both threw revealing light on the scale
of their activities and hinted at how the results were wildly exaggerated.

The fruit of these labours was the compilation of a file-card index
that was kept in Señor Guiu's home and which consisted of innumerable cards which listed the activities and the masonic affiliation
of the individuals referred to. This work was not just about those
listed in the bulletins of the masonic lodges but also about those
individuals whom we had good reason to suppose were freemasons because of how much they helped the lodges. Our
observations, vigilance and collection of data was extended to the
many theosophical, spiritualist, nudist, naturist and pseudo-scien-
tific societies that under these various labels concealed their

masonic origins and affiliation. Such societies were ruled over and inspired by the lodges and even by sympathetic foreign elements that were interested in encouraging their revolutionary activities.

In this regard, Casanova told his interrogators about the British Consul in Barcelona, whose name he could not remember, but who, he claimed, 'at that time had influence on Catalan politics through meetings in his house with the leaders of these groups and societies. All these activities were carefully noted and recorded in Señor Guiu's files.'[39] It is not surprising that Casanova could not bring to mind the name of the British Consul since it is inconceivable that the incumbent at the time would have supported such groups. Between 1926 and 1938, the Consul was Norman King, a fierce opponent of the left and deeply sympathetic to the Francoist cause.[40]

Another of the collaborators of Tusquets and Guiu in the production of the *Cuadernos de Información* was Bartolomé Gali Colli. He claimed in his post-war deposition that all remaining copies were lost when the uprising was defeated in Barcelona. Like Firmo Casanova y de Vallés, he knew that Guiu had hidden duplicates of the files but did not know where. He was particularly interested in the activities of nudist and naturist clubs. Having infiltrated them, he concluded that they were fronts for an operation to snare left-wing men for the Jewish–masonic–Bolshevik conspiracy by using the sexual wiles of naked young women called 'red ladies' (*damas rojas*). In his bizarre scenario, the *damas rojas* seduced young working-class men so that they would become gunmen for the anarchist FAI. Linked to this effort to destroy Christian society were spiritualist and anabaptist societies which 'were manipulated by the hidden strings of freemasonry'.[41]

Altogether more realistic accounts of the work of the collaborators of Tusquets and Guiu were given by a widow who lived with Guiu's family, Carolina Barderi Solé, and by a police officer, Ramón Tubau Coma, who worked closely with him before and during the civil war. Carolina Barderi recounted how their team of collaborators had infiltrated masonic lodges and reported on their membership. The fact that she had also contributed to the compilation of the file-card collection suggests that much of what went into the collection derived from gossip if not from invention. She described how, at the end of July 1936, police of the Generalitat had searched Guiu's house and confiscated the cards. Ramón Tubau revealed just how active both Tusquets and Guiu had been in the preparation of the military uprising. He had collected money from conservative businessmen for arms purchases on behalf of Guiu. Throughout the war, Tubau continued to gather information for Guiu.[42]

In the first days of the coup, Tusquets monitored events in the city centre and received and transmitted information to and from the other members of the Voluntariado Español.[43] With the collapse of the structures of law and order in the immediate aftermath of its defeat, right-wingers of all kinds, industrialists, landowners and clerics, were in serious danger in Republican Spain. This was especially true for Tusquets himself who, given the immense notoriety achieved by his books and the polemic occasioned by his attacks on Macià, had managed to make enemies of the entire spectrum of the left. Tusquets succeeded in escaping from Barcelona, but his faithful collaborator, Joaquim Guiu, remained as an important element within the rebel fifth column. Guiu survived unmolested in Barcelona until 31 May 1937. On that day, a patrol of the Republican security service came to the house but he was absent. They arrested his parents and Carolina Barderi Solé. Father Guiu had gone into hiding in the home of a cousin of Carolina in the village of El Collell. He too was arrested the following May and would eventually be murdered there on 30 January 1939.[44]

Before then, in May 1936 (even before the outbreak of the civil war), Guiu's home had been searched by Republican authorities. What they discovered of his file-card collection was confiscated. According to Firmo Casanova and Carolina Barderi Solé, Guiu had been making copies in preparation for such an eventuality. Tubau claimed that Guiu had three complete copies, one of which might have been in the possession of Tusquets. Casanova estimated that, during the war, Guiu continued to make copies and had reproduced approximately one-third of the files. All of Guiu's collaborators agree that he had hidden a copy in a safe place. Carolina Barderi Solé thought that he had entrusted it to a friendly carpenter who was one of his parishioners. Others among his collaborators believed that the duplicate cards were hidden in the catacombs of his parish church of Sants Just i Pastor. However, a post-war excavation of the cellars of the church did not locate the collection.[45] Accordingly, it is not clear how much, if any, of their collection of file cards Tusquets was able to transport from Barcelona to the rebel zone. He asserted in 1938 that his archive had had to be left behind in Republican Spain.[46] However, given access to copies of his own books and to issues of *Las Sectas*, together with his prodigious memory and his capacity for invention, some at least would have been reconstructed.

Two of Juan Tusquets's brothers, Jaume, a lawyer, and Manuel, a pharmacy student, were among the civilian members of the Voluntariado Español. They supported the military rebellion having been assured by Juan that 'religion was in danger from atheistic Communism'. They both died in the fighting in Barcelona in the early hours of 19 July 1936. Accordingly, Tusquets went into hiding, moving first to the house of Gertrudis Milà, a relative of his mother's, and then to the apartment of another of his brothers, Magí, a doctor and a publisher. Magí was the father of the architect Oscar and the publisher Esther.[47]

The scale of the danger facing Tusquets was further underlined when Emili Blay, the husband of his sister María Teresa, was murdered in Vilafranca del Penedés on 26 July. Three days later, an FAI patrol was about to search the building containing Magí's flat. Despite his claim to have been saved from the murderous intentions of freemasons by sympathetic anarchists, there was every reason to believe that, if the patrol caught him, they would kill him. Magí went out and found a detachment of the middle-class nationalist organiza-tion Estat Català, which obliged the anarchists to move on without searching the building. Finally, through a friend who was Consul of Portugal, Emili Blay's brother Andreu, who was acting Consul of Paraguay, managed to secure a Portuguese passport for Tusquets which stated that he had been born in Guimarães, north of Porto. On 30 July, in a car from the Paraguayan Consulate, he reached the port and was, with the fake passport, able to get aboard a German merchant vessel, the *Uckermark*, bound for Genoa. He later claimed, in yet another implausible story, that, to avoid being thrown over-board, he had to convince the ship's captain that he was not opposed to Nazism. If that story is true, it cannot have been too difficult a task given the anti-Jewish views regularly expressed in his publications. The ship reached Genoa on 31 July and, from there, he went to Rome where he stayed until the end of August. Finally, with permission from the Vatican, he made his way through France and finally reached Pamplona.[48] There, he made contact with Father Luis de Despujol Ricart, whom he knew since the time when Despujol had been a canon of the cathedral of Barcelona. Despujol was the intimate friend and collaborator of Cardinal Isidro Gomá, Archbishop of Toledo and Primate of All Spain. Like Gomá, Despujol had taken up residence in the Navarrese capital. Backed by these eminent clerics, Tusquets soon moved to Burgos to work with the rebel authorities. Initially, he stayed in a *pensión* but soon found himself looking after his bereaved sister and her two children. Among his numerous activities there, he assiduously maintained close links with Gomá.[49]

The Carlist writer Antonio Pérez de Olaguer coincided with Tusquets in the *pensión* and left a surprisingly humorous portrait of him that, in many ways, coincided with the one made some years earlier by Miquel d'Esplugues. 'Blond, always smiling, delicate, mystic, diligent and with a cold, selfless, magnificent courage, obsessed with finding freemasons even under the serviettes.' 'Dr Tusquets pulls out stories like cherries from a basket, one after another, pressing on to tell another one with his graceful wit and his spicy graphic illustrations.' 'And Dr Tusquets who knows the secret of the best way to tell a joke, which consists of starting to laugh just before his listeners get it, doing so with an uninhibited guffaw, with that friendly, rather childish, raucous, but likeable laugh of his.' So agreeable was his company that everyone was hanging on his 'every fluent and stimulating word'. Tusquets was especially keen on word games. On one occasion, he challenged his companions to come up with the only three words in Spanish that contained all five vowels. When no one could answer, he triumphantly produced the three, delightedly defining all three as horrible: 'murciélago, funerario y Republicano' (bat, funereal and Republican).[50]

Highly popular in military circles as the leading Spanish opponent of freemasonry, Tusquets was assured of a warm reception in Burgos.[51] The fact that both Mola and Franco, who were paranoid in their hatred of freemasonry, were known to be enthusiastic readers of his books ensured that he would find preferment within the Nationalist establishment. When he finally began working directly for the rebels there, first for Mola and then for Franco, his knowledge or suspicion of alleged freemasons would provide an important part of the organizational infrastructure of the repression. He worked for a time in Burgos with Mola, alongside one of the most sinister figures to be found on the Nationalist side, the General's friend and one-time subordinate, the policeman Julián Mauricio Carlavilla del Barrio. During the brief time that both Tusquets and Carlavilla worked in Mola's headquarters, they combined in scouring the press for evidence of masonic or Jewish influences. However, that collaboration came to an end when Carlavilla started to work for Nicolás Franco. As a result of his investigations of the followers of Manuel Hedilla, in May 1937 he had been the victim of an attempt on his life in Valladolid, as a result of which he fled to Portugal.[52] In any case, the collaboration between the pious and high-minded Tusquets and the sleazy Carlavilla was not a happy one. In a tone of belated disgust, Tusquets distanced himself from his wartime collaborator in the compilation of lists, telling the historian Jordi Canal that Carlavilla was 'a passionate Nazi who made up more even than Comín Colomer' – a reference to that other policeman who wrote anti-masonic books attacking the left.[53]

After Franco had been installed in Salamanca as Head of the Nationalist State on 1 October 1936, Tusquets's stock rose rapidly. He was helped immensely by the appointment, on 4 October, of Father José María Bulart as chaplain to the Franco family. Bulart, secretary to the Bishop of Salamanca, Enrique Plá i Deniel, was a close friend of Tusquets and one-time fellow student in Barcelona. Father Bulart suggested that, whenever he could not be available, Tusquets go to the Palacio Episcopal to say mass for the General's family. He became a frequent visitor to the Palacio, where the Franco family had taken up residence at the gracious insistence of Bishop Plá i Deniel. In consequence, Tusquets ingratiated himself sufficiently to be appointed tutor (preceptor) to the Dictator's daughter, Carmen. Moving frequently between Salamanca and Burgos, by November Tusquets was also tutor to the two daughters of General Fidel Dávila,

the President of the rebel 'government', the Junta Técnica. He got to
know Serrano Suñer, a relationship reinforced by the fact that they
had both lost two brothers to left-wing actions. Together with his
relationship with Cardinal Gomá, he was so close to the centres of
power that it is hardly surprising that he could write in 1938, 'Since
the military uprising, I have felt more supported than ever. I write on
the basis of suggestions from the ecclesiastical hierarchy. The
Generalísimo himself approves of my campaigns. They have also
been backed by the Minister Serrano Suñer, that man who seems all
logic but has heart and vigour.'[54]

Luis de Despujol, in his capacity as secretary to Cardinal Gomá,
reported to the Archbishop from Salamanca that 'Tusquets is well
placed and highly thought of. His principal activity is the search for
masonic documents and everything related to that subject. The
government has set up an office with this purpose and Tusquets is
employed there and indeed is the very soul of the enterprise.' Tusquets
was also appointed as one of the counsellors of what was effectively
the Junta Técnica del Estado's ministry of education, chaired by José
María Pemán. He advised on matters relating to religious education,
particularly on censorship and books to be removed from circulation. His efforts led to the denunciation of schoolteachers and
university lecturers to be purged. During this time, he liaised closely
with Cardinal Gomá.[55]

What is absolutely not the case, despite Tusquets's inflated claims
to the contrary, is that the idea for a rebel press and propaganda
service was his brainchild and that he had run it.

> I myself was in charge of the press service during the war. That was
> because it was me who suggested to Franco the need to create such
> a service, as long as it remained secret. And, running this service,
> I had considerable influence because it was a daily contact. I did it
> entirely alone apart from the help of a priest who was a friend in
> Burgos. We collected everything that came out, translated it and it
> worked out marvellously.[56]

A press and propaganda service was up and running before he began to work for Franco. It is certainly true, however, that he had duties within the press service, scouring the press for evidence of freemasonry. That could certainly have been at his own suggestion.

Like others who had suffered bereavement at the hands of the other side, Tusquets seems to have felt a mixture of vengefulness and suicidal thoughts. Perhaps that is why this pale and elegant priest established such a close friendship with the similarly traumatized Ramón Serrano Suñer after the Caudillo's brother-in-law arrived in Salamanca in February 1937. Echoing the deranged General José Millán Astray, Tusquests told his Carlist friend Antonio Pérez Olaguer in Burgos, 'I am in love with death. And death is the most disdainful and ungrateful lover. When she realizes that she is desired, that she is idolized, that she is truly loved, she flees, she escapes, she deserts.'[57]

Not long after Franco had established his headquarters in Salamanca, Tusquets's desire for vengeance found an outlet in the office to which Father de Despujol had referred in his report to Cardinal Gomá. In 1937, partly at his own suggestion, and with the encouragement of Franco himself, the Cuartel General (headquarters) had been collecting material seized in captured areas from the offices of political parties and trade unions, in masonic lodges and from the houses of leftists. The scrutiny and cataloguing of this material was carried out principally within the Sección Judeo-Masónica, the anti-Jewish and anti-masonic section of the rebel military intelligence service, the Servicio de Información Militar (SIM). The nominal director was Comandante Antonio Palau but the job of analysing the documentation was carried out by Tusquets, who had inspired its creation. His principal task was the collection and systematization of all information on freemasons both gathered by the intelligence services and published in the Republican and international daily press. From this material, he inflated his existing lists, dossiers and files on freemasons who were assumed to be enemies of the rebel cause. This often inaccurate information would play a crucial role in the repression of liberals and the left. However, Tusquets was equally assiduous in exposing possible freemasons among those who had supported the military uprising.[58] Echoing the words of Pérez Olaguer, the Falangist Maximiano García Venero commented, 'he would seek out traces of freemasonry in the writings, words and private conduct of supporters of the National Movement. Tusquets saw freemasons everywhere.' Tusquets once told Ramón Garriga, a close collaborator of Serrano Suñer in the press service, that he could spot a freemason by the way in which his handkerchief was placed in his top pocket. From this material, he wrote reports about 'our enemies' that were sent both to the army high command and to the ecclesiastical hierarchy.[59]

Cardinal Gomá was delighted and informed Cardinal Pacelli, the Vatican Secretary of State, that the military authorities were now stepping up 'the elimination of freemasonry'. He explained that 'to this end an investigative office has been set up along the lines of the French Deuxième Bureau, directed by specialists and installed within the headquarters of the President of the Government in Burgos'.[60] Tusquets himself described the scrutiny of the Republican press and of captured documentation, the building up of his files on suspected freemasons, as the work of the 'intellectual police' of the new regime.[61]

Father Tusquets complained constantly that his salary from his various jobs was exiguous, 'very, very small'. In February 1937, he wrote in sycophantic terms to Cardinal Gomá, outlining his efforts on behalf of the regime:

> I'm going to explain my current situation in Burgos. We are carrying out a difficult task in several branches of the administration, and it is important that Your Eminence know about this since the information that we are discovering will contribute to undoing the mischief being wreaked abroad by our adversaries against the New Regime, against the Generalísimo and against Your Eminence who is the voice incarnate of the Church in Spain. I would be sorry to leave this work. But I have to maintain my sister, whose husband was barbarously murdered, and her two children, and so as not to run into debt it would be really important for me to enter the Nationalist army's Corps of Military Chaplains as an auxiliary.

This device to increase his income was, he claimed, the idea of General Fidel Dávila, President of the Junta Técnica. As a member of the Junta Técnica's Comisión de Cultura y Enseñanza, and given his

almost daily personal contact with Dávila, it would have been easy
for him to request his support for the scheme. It is certainly more
likely that the suggestion came from Tusquets himself rather than
from Dávila. However, since large numbers of Navarrese Carlist
priests had simply gone to war and abandoned their parishes without
permission, there was a case for Tusquets occasionally being available
to say mass and preach to Falangist and Carlist militias. For this, it
was necessary to seek Gomá's support. After Gomá had granted
permission, Tusquets was given the rank of lieutenant in the army
and worked briefly as a chaplain to units of the Falangist militia. He
joined the Falange, figuring in the lists of the party's Catalan
members.[62] Despite his new post and the additional salary, not to
mention his success as a writer and lecturer, Tusquets was still short
of money and he complained about this to the colonel of his unit.
Unable to authorize a pay increase, the colonel came up with the
solution of giving him a horse. Thereafter, whenever Tusquets needed
money for his sister, he simply put in a request for funds to have the
horse newly shod, the price for which always exactly matched what
he needed for his sister.[63]

As well as his salaries as a member of the Comisión de Cultura y
Educación and as a military chaplain, his income was further
augmented when, in late 1936, Franco's Cuartel General facilitated
the creation of a publishing house. The costs of the enterprise,
Ediciones Antisectarias, seem to have been met largely by Tusquets's
family money. The administrative tasks were assumed by his brother
Carlos. Over the next two years, in a continuation of what he had
done with *Las Sectas*, it would issue twenty volumes denouncing the
sinister machinations of Spain's Jewish and masonic enemies.[64] The
mission statement of the new company read: 'The purpose of these
publications is purely patriotic and in no way partisan. There will be
collaborations by personalities of different ideologies but there will
not be a single author whose commitment to the Regime is in doubt,
nor a single idea that does not contribute to the defence of the norms
being dictated by His Excellency Generalísimo Franco.' Large editions
of between 10,000 and 30,000 copies were sold at extremely low
prices between one and two pesetas.[65] Apart from four titles attributed to Tusquets, another, the rabidly anti-Semitic *El Judaísmo*,

signed by the non-existent 'Barón de Santa Clara', may well have been
by him or possibly René Llanas de Nubió. It was distributed in thousands of copies throughout rebel Spain. Articles signed by 'the Barón
de Santa Clara' were also published in the Sunday newspaper
Domingo in San Sebastián. The titles and the subject matter suggested
that they were the work of Tusquets: 'The Spanish revolution and its
occult forces: the Jews' and 'Israel's demagogic spirit'.[66] At least three
of the series' authors worked alongside Tusquets in the Sección
Judeo-Masónica of the SIM and based their books on its documentation. This suggests that it functioned as the propaganda arm of the
anti-masonic section of the secret services. However, the publishing
house was run as a family business owned jointly by Father Tusquets
and his brother Carlos. Despite Tusquets's claims of penury, the
books he published were massive best-sellers with sales in the tens of
thousands. Serrano Suñer collaborated with him and wrote the eulogistic prologue to his highly contentious tract *Masones y pacifistas*.[67]
He also contributed to the Carlist weekly for children *Pelayos*, spreading his message about the Jewish–masonic enemy to a younger
generation. It has been speculated that it may have been Tusquets
who set up *Pelayos*.[68]

The blond-haired Tusquets was an inspiring public performer and
he made lecture tours propagating his conspiratorial theories to huge
and appreciative audiences. On 1 November 1936, he gave a lecture
in the Teatro Principal of Burgos on 'Freemasonry as a Revolutionary
Force'. The Carlist event included renditions of the traditionalist
hymn 'Oriamendi', accompanied by the band of the Requeté, the
Carlist militia.[69] Tusquets's passionate style was described by Pérez
Olaguer:

> His tall, slim, elegant figure leans gracefully over the table, where
> unpublished documents lie … The spotlights reflect off his blond
> hair and his pale skin. He speaks. His careful and confident oratory
> is energetic, decisive, cutting. He doesn't use images and doesn't
> take pleasure in being colourful. He is bold and goes straight to the
> point. His gestures always are in time with his words. His right
> hand, always raised, sometimes emphasizes a point, sometimes
> smoothing it over. His left hand hangs down motionless until he

makes an accusation or an indisputable affirmation, then it rises and joins the right in a strong, violent gesture that takes his eloquence to the highest level. And he is transfigured.[70]

Antonio Ruiz Vilaplana, a less sympathetic attendee, described how Tusquets's quiet delivery turned into howls of rage as he called for the extermination of all freemasons in Spain. Ruiz Vilaplana, a court official in Burgos, commented that Tusquets's attribution to the freemasons of the various horrors and crimes was instrumental in intensifying the repression in the province. Tusquets denounced Ruiz Vilaplana's comments as calumny because he was alarmed by their possible impact on the rebels' international image. The concern about the publicity being given abroad to Tusquets's exaggerations was shared by Cambó, who had come to loathe him.[71]

The Burgos lecture was subsequently published as *La Francmasonería, crimen de lesa patria* (Freemasonry, Crime of Treachery), which went into several editions and sold 30,000 copies. In it, he repeated his accusations that freemasonry was a Jewish creation, a weapon of English imperialism and responsible for the bloodshed in the Mexican and Russian revolutions. He blamed it for the Semana Trágica of 1909, for the revolutionary events of 1917, for the coming of the Republic and for the insurrection of Asturias in October 1934. It was the axle from which radiated subordinate branches such as Rotary Clubs and the Pen Club. He described it as a cancer in the body and a poison in the veins of the nation. He claimed that among the instruments of freemasonry were nudism, Esperantism and vegetarianism – accusations that would lead to police persecution for the practitioners of such innocuous activities. He accused freemasons of the sexual abuse of children and of propagating incest. Freemasonry had, Tusquets absurdly alleged, directly organized the murder and mutilation of José Calvo Sotelo.[72]

Another of his rabble-rousing lectures, entitled 'Masonería y separatismo', was given in the Teatro Principal of San Sebastián on 28 February 1937 and quickly published as the equally best-selling volume IV of Ediciones Antisectarias. Among several puzzling statements, he declared, 'It is not true that the freemasons have tried more than four times to assassinate me.' He often referred to, and gave contradictory versions of, alleged attempts to murder him by freema-sons.[73] Even more surprisingly, he acknowledged that the *Protocols* might be fake, referring to 'the famous *Protocols of the Elders of Zion* which, if they are not authentic, deserve to be since all of their predic-tions have come true'. Two years later, he wrote, 'The authenticity of *The Protocols of Zion* has been questioned. It is a minor issue. Authentic or not, they demonstrate the objectives and the methods of Judaism. Moreover, all their substantial paragraphs can be confirmed with texts of indubitable Israelite origin.' Given his tenu-ous relationship with the truth, these statements raise important doubts about whether he knew that the *Protocols* was a fabrication when he published it and made damaging statements based on it throughout the 1930s.[74]

In his lecture in San Sebastián, he blamed freemasonry for the loss of Spain's empire and for the birth of Catalan and Basque national-isms. He also 'revealed' the masonic origins of the innocent poetry contests in Barcelona known as the Jocs Florals. He produced an intensely partisan interpretation of the recent history of Catalonia, with harsh criticisms of the Catholic newspaper *El Matí* and of Cambó's conservative political party, the Lliga Regionalista, which he accused of being under masonic influence. He also criticized Basque separatism although, speaking in San Sebastián, did so in slightly less aggressive terms than those in which he had denounced Catalanism. He attributed Basque separatism to the 'Judaizing' schemes of free-masons.[75]

Not long after Tusquets's lecture in San Sebastián, Francesc Cambó wrote to Joan Ventosa i Calvell, his deputy in the Lliga Regionalista who organized his financial contributions to the rebel cause:[76]

That Monsignor Tusquets, a combination of imbecile, intriguer and swine, began to publish a series of interviews in the Milanese Catholic daily *Italia*. He had to stop because the Archbishop of Milan issued categoric orders that nothing more by Tusquets be published. You should know how this individual devotes himself to attacking both us and all the Catalan clerics that sympathize with the Lliga, especially Capuchins and Benedictines. This Monsignor Tusquets, in the first months of the Republic, was an ardent supporter of Macià, an extreme separatist, and specialized in defaming you and me, calling us 'the last pillars of the monarchy'. About a year ago, he came to my home, pretending to be a fervent Catalanist, to request my financial support for a journal that he wanted to publish. Anyway, this individual has said the things that you can read in his two interviews in *Italia* of which I include the text. Can't you get Dr Gomá to shut him up or get him out of Spain?[77]

It is probable that the journal for which Tusquets sought funding was actually *Cuadernos de Información*. The idea that Ventosa could influence Gomá derived from the fact that the Cardinal's right-hand man, Luis de Despujol, was Ventosa's brother-in-law.

In a lecture entitled 'La masonería y el obrero', given in Zaragoza on 21 March 1937, Tusquets took his anti-Semitism to new heights. According to the local Falangist daily *Amanecer*, he emphasized the subordination of freemasonry to the Jews. He argued that the workers' movement in Spain was the puppet of Jewish revolutionaries on the basis that the most prominent Russian revolutionaries were Jews. He made an unconvincing distinction between the 'Judaic nation' and the individual Jewish members of the conspiracy. Given his regular collective references to 'Israel' and the 'Sanhedrin', this was hypocritical. The lecture was advertised for imminent publication in Ediciones Antisectarias but never appeared.[78] A regular feature of these lectures was a spine-chilling recitation of the crimes which he attributed to the freemasons. The impact of these lectures and their later publication inevitably led to an intensification of the repression of freemasonry.[79]

Between the money made by Ediciones Antisectarias, his salary as a chaplain, the deceit about the cost of keeping a horse and his work in the SIM, Tusquets, for all his family commitments, cannot have been as poor as he made out. The information-collecting operation in the Sección Judeo-Masónica was extended, on 20 April 1937, with the creation of the Oficina de Investigación y Propaganda Antimarxista, staffed by army officers and volunteers. Its duties were essentially to do what Tusquets had been doing since 1930, 'to collect, analyse and catalogue all types of propaganda material that has been used by communism and its puppet organizations for its campaigns in our Fatherland, with a view to organizing counter-propaganda, both in Spain and abroad'. As well as captured printed material produced by all the organizations of the left from conservative Republicans to anarchists, including freemasons, pacifists and feminists, correspondence and membership and subscription lists of parties and societies were scoured for the creation of a great file-card index of leftists to be arrested and tried.

Barely one month later, Franco had named the Carlist Marcelino de Ulibarri Eguílaz as head of the Delegación de Servicios Especiales. Its brief was to 'recover all documentation related to secret sects and their activities in Spain found in the possession of individuals or official entities, storing it carefully in a place far removed from danger where it can be catalogued and classified in order to create an archive which will permit the exposure and punishment of the enemies of the Fatherland'.[80]

The dynamic and overbearing Ulibarri enjoyed considerable influence through long-standing friendships with both Franco and Serrano Suñer. A great admirer of Tusquets, he even excelled him in his own obsessive hatred of freemasons and Jews. Indeed, Ulibarri was known among his Carlist comrades as 'the hammer of freemasonry'.[81] Within weeks, Ulibarri had set up the Oficina para la Recuperación de Documentos. In early June, the Basque Country was about to fall into Francoist hands and Ulibarri saw the ORD's purpose as the systematic seizure and subsequent classification of documentation belonging to the defeated. He was soon calling for the merger of his Oficina para la Recuperación de Documentos and the Oficina de Investigación y Propaganda Antimarxista. In the summer of 1937, with the prospect of the capture of Santander and Asturias following on that of the Basque Country, Ulibarri called for the collection of the documentation to be speeded up to expedite the subsequent repression. He stated explicitly that, in the wake of each victory, the rebel authorities needed 'the documents that indicate the guilt of people who must be tried immediately'. After the Francoist victory at Teruel in February 1938 and the subsequent drive through Aragon towards the Mediterranean, huge opportunities were opening up in terms of the seizure of left-wing documentation. Ulibarri's desired departmental merger was formalized on 26 April 1938, when Serrano Suñer, as Minister of the Interior, issued a decree creating the Delegación del Estado para la Recuperación de Documentos (DERD). Its purpose was to gather, store and classify all documents emanating from political parties, organizations and individuals 'hostile to or even out of sympathy with the National Movement' in order to facilitate their location and punishment.[82]

Given the scale of the centralized activities, it was hardly surprising that the overbearing Ulibarri would eventually clash with Tusquets. On 10 May 1938, Ulibarri wrote from Salamanca to Tusquets requesting that he hand over his personal archive. That this was not entirely to the liking of Tusquets can be seen in his curt reply from Burgos in which he expressed surprise at the request and, ignoring the reference to his personal collection, stated that the SIM had already delivered all its masonic material. Ulibarri wrote back coldly to the effect that the SIM's holdings were not the issue and he reiterated his request for Tusquets's own archive. He also added that he believed that Tusquets had been given a large body of masonic material captured by the Falange in Toledo. In reply, Tusquets denied having the Toledo material, stated that his personal archives were not in rebel Spain and snootily informed Ulibarri that his books were available for purchase in bookshops. It may be, given the difficulties that Tusquets must have had in getting any of his material out of Barcelona, that he was telling the truth. Certainly, Ulibarri appears to have accepted the claims made by Tusquets, who eventually did collaborate with the DERD.[83] In an oblique reference to this interchange, Tusquets wrote that, in response to the request for all of his information, he had said that 'to give you all of my information would require me to have a trepanning operation'.[84] This would substantiate the possibility that he had arrived in rebel Spain without his file-card collection and relied on his prodigious memory.

The last of Tusquets's books in the series published by Ediciones Antisectarias was the virulently anti-Semitic *Masones y pacifistas*. The book was a scurrilous interpretation of the origins, rites and ceremonies of freemasonry and a mendacious account of its role in the decades leading up to the civil war. It was larded with accusations about 'the secret ambitions of Israel' and 'the mysterious Jewish power' behind all the secret societies in the world.[85] Tusquets blamed the civil war and left-wing violence on Jewish machinations. The church-burnings of the war were attributed to what he called 'the blind arrogance of a Deicidal race': 'The determination to multiply the number of masonic temples in Spain and turn Spain into the slave of Judaism has led to the burning of the most beautiful altars and has destroyed thousand-year-old churches.' 'The Devil and free-masonry are motivated by the same purpose: to destroy Christian civilization, to build on its ruins the materialistic and despotic temple of Judaism.'[86]

The sections of the book dealing with Spain's recent history were a blend of blatant mendacity and arrogant assertions of his own prophetic role. In his account of the revolutionary events of 6 October 1934 in Catalonia, he claimed that in August he had published an article that foretold exactly what would happen and so provoked yet another masonic attempt on his life. Given the sheer complexity of the local and national political developments that led to the declaration of Catalan independence on that day, it was utterly impossible for him to have foreseen how events would play out. Nevertheless, he wrote, 'I had the luck to stir up hostility to such an extent that the lodges ordered an attempt on my life. It was thwarted in an almost grotesque fashion. To avoid further consequences, I took refuge in Andorra for a fortnight.' Regarding the events in both Asturias and Catalonia, he complained of the culpable weakness demonstrated in the subsequent repression, a weakness that he attributed to masonic machinations.[87] When his recital reached the assassination of José Calvo Sotelo, his imagination was unrestrained. A deplorable event that took place as a result of a spontaneous improvisation he described as being the result of meticulous prior planning. Needless to say, he attributed the destruction of Guernica by German bombing to the work of left-wing militiamen.[88]

Until the occupation of Catalonia in January 1939, Tusquets continued to work in a much reduced Sección Judeo-Masónica within the SIM. In Barcelona, as in other provinces, the contents of bookshops, publishers' warehouses and private collections were confiscated and collected in the provincial Delegación Territorial para la Recuperación de Documentos. Where there were large numbers of copies, these were pulped to help resolve the post-war paper shortage.[89] Once classified, copies were sent to the Delegación Central para la Recuperación de Documentos in Salamanca. There, they were used as one of the key sources of evidence for the work of the Tribunal Especial para la Represión de la Masonería y el Comunismo created in February 1940. Tusquets arrived with the occupying forces and, for a short period at least, took part in the classification of the Catalan material. It is highly ironic that Tusquets was instrumental in the removal of that material to Salamanca. The campaign for its return, sixty years later, was one of the most important Catalan undertakings within the movement for recuperation of historical memory. In 1941, a proposal was made that he be rewarded for his services by the granting of two medals, the Medalla de Campaña con Distintivo de Campaña and the Cruz Roja de Mérito Militar.[90]

Despite the disappointment of the clash with Ulibarri, Tusquets had become an immensely influential figure within the Nationalist zone. He had always put tremendous effort into creating links with those in power. His assiduous links with Cardinal Gomá and Generals Franco and Dávila demonstrated his readiness to take full advantage in terms of jobs and preferment. In July 1937, for instance, he wrote a sycophantic letter congratulating Pedro Sainz Rodríguez on his recent appointment as Jefe Nacional de Educación within the Junta Técnica and offering his services.[91] He had also successfully established a relationship with Ramón Serrano Suñer. The opportunity arose in March 1938 when the distinguished French Catholic philosopher Jacques Maritain criticized the Nationalist bombing raids on Barcelona, which he described as 'the most violent bombing carried out since air forces came into being'. He wrote that 'if humanitarian reasons alone are enough to condemn such a massacre of non-combatants, this massacre is all the more repugnant if such a thing is possible given that those responsible for the operations claim to be defending Christian civilization'. Maritain, who was a convert to Catholicism married to a Jewish woman, was denounced as 'this converted Jew' by Ramón Serrano Suñer on 12 May and again on 19 June 1938, in a speech commemorating the fall of Bilbao. Claiming that the words of Maritain echoed the rhetoric of the Elders of Zion

as denounced by the *Protocols*, he described him as the darling of
masonic lodges and synagogues. A week after Serrano Suñer's first
declaration, Juan Tusquets came out in support of the Minister,
publishing an article attacking Maritain for his links with Jews, freemasons and Catalan nationalists.[92] Cambó was thoroughly appalled
because these attacks confirmed his view that Tusquets's various
declarations were so exaggerated and demagogic as to be counterpro-
ductive in terms of the international image of the regime. For that
reason, the press and propaganda office that he had established in
Paris never gave any publicity to Tusquets.[93]

Tusquets's support for Serrano Suñer paid off, in early 1938, when
the Minister created the Servicio Nacional de Propaganda, and gave
Tusquets the job of selecting material that the Catholic Church would
wish to see published in the regime press. Serrano wrote to the papal
envoy Ildebrando Antoniutti to inform him of this.[94] As has been
seen, Tusquets had boasted to Franco and Serrano Suñer of his
connections with the ecclesiastical hierarchy. This specific task was
inflated by him in later interviews into his being in charge of the
entire Francoist press and propaganda operation.[95] In late 1938, with
the great Nationalist offensive against Catalonia well advanced,
Franco and Serrano Suñer asked Tusquets to suggest names to head
the institutions that would be set up by the occupying forces. On the
basis of his advice, he claimed, Franco selected the future Mayor of
Barcelona, Miquel Mateu, and other important appointees. He also
alleged that he had advised Franco to ensure that his policy regarding
the region respected the Catalan language and culture. If that is true,
which is highly unlikely, Franco paid no heed.[96] Throughout the
autumn of 1938, as Franco's troops massed for their final assault on
Catalonia, Tusquets went to extraordinary lengths to organize a ferocious campaign against international mediation in the war. In terms
used also by Mauricio Carlavilla and by Franco, he denounced the
League of Nations as a step towards 'the Jewish super-state'.[97]

As soon as Barcelona was occupied by Franco's troops at the end
of January 1939, Father Tusquets returned to Barcelona where, once
freemasonry had been eliminated from Spanish life, and perhaps
traumatized by the activities of the occupying forces in Catalonia, he
gradually turned his back on the possibility of preferment. He

claimed that, at the end of the war, Serrano Suñer had offered him the post of Director General of Press and Propaganda. Recalling that he had no wish to spend his time checking the entire daily press, imposing the editorial line of each newspaper and suggesting articles, he allegedly refused, telling Serrano Suñer that he wished to return to his ecclesiastical duties.[98] Similarly, when Franco later offered him the position of religious adviser to the Consejo Superior de Investigaciones Científicas, he declined, alleging that he did not want to live in Madrid and be separated from his widowed sister and his niece and nephew. Given that in previous years Tusquets had revelled in his closeness to the epicentres of power and had, on the grounds of penury, shamelessly sought to accumulate salaries, the refusal of two such important and well-paid posts is noteworthy.

It is possible that he was shocked by the brutality of the occupying Francoist forces in Catalonia and perhaps felt some guilt for his part in fomenting the hatreds that drove it. However, there is nothing in his invariably self-justificatory interviews to suggest that this was the case. Certainly, he claimed later that he had made a special effort to get people of his acquaintance out of concentration camps. This may be true, but no evidence has come to light. Moreover, in several interviews, he asserted that he prevented major Catalan treasures such as the Archive of the Crown of Aragon and the Biblioteca de Catalunya from suffering the fate of so many other Catalan institutions whose books, documents and papers were seized and sent to Salamanca, a process which he had encouraged. He may have had the power to do so since the official posts that he had accepted by February 1939 included those of 'cultural adviser' and delegate of the Ministry of the Interior to the provincial council. However, he soon returned to his specialization in pedagogy and catechesis.[99] Having contributed so substantially to the mentality of hatred that lay behind the repression of Catalonia, it is conceivable that he was alarmed by the practical consequences of his anti-masonic and anti-Jewish campaigns.

What is more likely is that he regarded the Francoist victory in the civil war as a vindication of his campaign against what he saw as the Jewish–masonic–Bolshevik conspiracy. He accepted only minimal official preferment because, with his mission accomplished, he felt able to return to religious education. It may also be the case that he was persuaded by ecclesiastical pressure from on high. Cardinal Gomá was uncomfortable with the involvement of some militant clergy in the Falange. The Vatican was not happy with the association of the clergy with the ferocity of the repression that was coming under international scrutiny nor indeed with Franco's ever closer links with Nazi Germany. The official role of Tusquets as head of the Jewish–masonic section of the military intelligence service was no longer acceptable.[100] Increasingly, therefore, he moved back to religious education as his principal preoccupation. He founded the journals *Formación Catequista* and *Perpectivas Pedagógicas*. Ediciones Antisectarias was converted into the publishing house Editorial Lumen. Under the direction of his brother Carlos, Lumen specialized in religious texts. He was given a chair of pedagogy at the University of Barcelona and wrote several books on the subject as well as on Ramón Llull, the thirteenth-century Mallorcan philosopher. Nevertheless, he remained proud of his previous work and of his connection with Franco, delighted to be asked occasionally for advice on issues such as student unrest. He also maintained his friendship with Franco's chaplain, José María Bulart. Throughout these years, he lived quietly in Barcelona with his widowed mother, his sister María Teresa and her two children. The family's banking wealth had long since been dissipated.

In interviews given in old age, Juan Tusquets tried, in various ways, to dissociate himself from his past. He alleged that it was his sidekick, Joaquim Guiu, who had an obsession with freemasonry, which, he claimed, he did not share.[101] Given the scale and intensity of his publications denouncing the Jewish–masonic–Bolshevik conspiracy, this is clearly Tusquets again being economical with the truth. He denied any participation in the repression, even claiming mendaciously that he had categorically refused to let his lists of names be used by the Francoist authorities. Tusquets tried to give his own anti-masonic work a retrospective respectability by insinuating that it had been commissioned by the much revered liberal Cardinal Francesc Vidal i Barraquer. In fact, the only commission ever given him by Vidal i Barraquer was for his book on Theosophy. Vidal i Barraquer also wrote a prologue for his *Manual de catecisme*. However, he was hardly responsible for Tusquets's subsequent anti-masonic and anti-Semitic campaigns. Indeed, Tusquets's attacks on both Francesc Macià and Niceto Alcalá-Zamora had caused the Cardinal considerable embarrassment.[102]

Despite his accusations against Macià and his virulent attacks on Catalanism during the civil war, Tusquets even claimed, incredibly, 'I always made an effort to do my work without ever renouncing my identity as a Catalan and a Catalanist, whether with Franco or with anyone else.' Even more implausibly, he claimed that, in his reports to Franco during the civil war, he had denounced the Nazi persecution of the Jews after being shocked by the visit made to the concentration camp at Dachau, in 1934, at the invitation of the International Anti-Masonic Association. He said:

> they were camps aimed at killing the Jews through exhaustion. I had gone to Germany with some hope of learning about Hitler and his promises. But I was disillusioned when I saw that it was all paganism, and they were persecuting the Jews. When Franco commissioned me to do a daily résumé of the press, I did so stressing what the Nazis were doing and that the Falange with all its liturgy was just another sect, just like freemasonry.

His memory was surely faulty since, at the time of the visit, the mass detentions of Jews were still four years away. This later description is clearly coloured by what he came to know about Nazi death camps as they operated during the Second World War. When Tusquets visited Dachau in 1934, there is no way he could have known which of the prisoners happened to be Jewish since they were not yet classified as such. Moreover, his claim sits uneasily with his own membership of the Falange and with the fact that he continued to include anti-Semitic propaganda in his lectures and writings and did so with ever greater vehemence as the civil war progressed. In 1939, for instance, he described the swastika as 'this symbol, to be respected at least when it represents the new state of our well-beloved Germany'. In all of his interviews, he boasted of his friendship with Franco, claiming absurdly that he knew him to be an Anglophile, that he was enthusiastically pro-Catalan and that he had dealt with Mussolini and Hitler only out of necessity.[103]

In another instance, it can only be assumed that his memory had deceived him. He claimed that while advising Franco about how he should go about treating Catalonia he had told him that he had made a big mistake in naming General Severiano Martínez Anido as Captain General of the region. He claimed he told the Caudillo that doing so had 'a damaging impact in Catalonia, especially among the workers who were strongly against the appointment'. In response to Tusquets's warning, Franco allegedly said that 'he was thinking about whether it would be possible to remove Martínez Anido, adding "Just think that before doing what I want, I have to burn many individuals." Then he explained why he had made Martínez Anido Captain General of Catalonia.' Leaving aside the sheer improbability of Franco explaining any decision to a junior member of his staff, there are bigger problems with the anecdote. At no point in his life was Martínez Anido ever Captain General of Catalonia. He was both Military and Civil Governor of Barcelona before 1923. During the dictatorship of Primo de Rivera, he was his effective minister of the interior, a post that he also held in Franco's first government. An even bigger flaw in an anecdote about an unlikely conversation supposed to have taken place after the civil war is that Martínez Anido had died in December 1938.[104]

Tusquets was an intelligent and, apparently, deeply religious man. What he absolutely was not was an honest man. His energetic decade-long crusade against the Jews, the freemasons, the left and Catalan and Basque nationalism was built on considerable, albeit misplaced, investigative skills as well as malicious exaggeration and outright mendacity. Its consequences, in terms of lives lost or ruined, is incalculable. In the numerous duplicitous interviews given near the end of his life, he downplayed – not to say expurgated – his role both in fomenting the hatreds that led to the civil war and in facilitating the repression during the war. He passed blame for his campaigns on to his friend Joaquim Guiu and shamelessly denied his anti-Catalanism. There is no way of knowing whether these fabrications were the fruit of remorse for what he did. It is, however, more likely that he was merely trying to safeguard his reputation as a learned holy man.[105]

4

The Poet: José María Pemán

When he died on 9 July 1981, José María Pemán was celebrated by figures of both right and left as a liberal monarchist, a hugely prolific author of more than sixty-five plays, fifteen books of poetry, thirty novels and political works, hundreds of speeches and lectures and frequent columns in the press.[1] Two months before his death, an infirm Pemán was awarded by King Juan Carlos what is regarded as the world's highest chivalric honour, the Order of the Golden Fleece, usually the exclusive preserve of heads of royal families. His benevolent image was enhanced when photographs from the ceremony showed the King crouching down to speak to a seated Pemán.[2] His honours, his vast literary output and, by all accounts, his personal charm obscured the fact that for twenty-five years he was one of the most toxically divisive figures on the extreme right in Spain. Through the period from the mid-1920s to the late 1940s, he was successively a stalwart of the Primo de Rivera dictatorship, a bitter enemy of the democratic Second Republic, an advocate of the extermination of the left during the civil war and an unwavering supporter of the Francoist cause thereafter. His writings and speeches between the mid-1920s and mid-1930s contributed massively to the breakdown of political coexistence that was the prelude to civil war. His virulent propaganda campaigns during the war encouraged and justified the savage repression unleashed by the Francoist forces. It is as a fomenter of hate that this acclaimed literary figure appears in this book.

Pemán was a fervent monarchist whose outpourings were laced with arrant snobbery and relentless anti-Semitism. After 1947, his position evolved somewhat. While his admiration for Franco was lasting, it was tempered from the 1950s as he realized that the

Dictator would never restore the monarchy in the person of the exiled heir to the throne, Don Juan de Borbón. Even so, during the years of the Franco regime, he was considered to be a regime intellectual, if hardly as intimate with the Dictator as he implied in his writings. He managed to transmit his ideas while avoiding outright confrontation with the regime and his columns were very occasionally censored during the 1950s and 1960s.[3] The stark discrepancy between the reality of his past and the benevolent image of his later years was the result of a mendacious recasting of his past record rather than of his convictions. He never reneged on his past in the way that a genuinely regretful Dionisio Ridruejo, the Falangist poet, did. Rather, he simply denied it.[4]

José María Pemán was born in Cadiz on 8 May 1897. His parents were Juan Gualberto Pemán, a prominent deputy of the Conservative Party for El Puerto de Santa María, and María Pemartín, of a wealthy wine-producing family from Jerez. José María's education in the elite Marianista college of San Felipe Neri equipped him with a considerable classical culture and deeply traditionalist right-wing ideas. One of his mother's two brothers was married to Inés Primo de Rivera, the sister of the future Dictator, Miguel. José María's cousin José Pemartín, the son of his other maternal uncle, would be a close ideological collaborator. He inherited land and vineyards in the form of the El Cerro estate in Jerez from his family and established strong links with the local aristocracy when, in 1922, he married María del Carmen Domecq Rivero Núñez de Villavicencio y González, the daughter of the Marquesa viuda de Casa Domecq. This was reflected in his speeches and writings, in his opposition to agrarian reform and in his elitism and snobbery.[5]

He studied law at the University of Seville and followed that with a doctorate on Plato at Madrid University. He practised briefly as a criminal lawyer, but, after being accused of a serious irregularity in 1924, quickly abandoned the profession. In his own memoirs, he attributed the brevity of his legal career to his desire to dedicate himself to literature. His independent income permitted him to devote himself more to poetry. He was a *beato*, a devout and indeed sanctimonious Catholic. He introduced himself to the influential editor of the Catholic daily *El Debate*, Ángel Herrera Oria, the *éminence grise* of political Catholicism in Spain, by sending him copies of his books. In 1909, along with the Jesuit Ángel Ayala, Herrera had founded the ultra-conservative Asociación Católica Nacional de Propagandistas (ACNP), a group of dynamic, high-flying Catholics in the professions. Impressed by Pemán's books and his ostentatious piety, in 1925 Herrera invited him to write for *El Debate* and chose him to be the local secretary of the ACNP in Cadiz. As such, for almost five years, he threw himself into a campaign to ensure that books considered subversive, as listed in the Vatican index, be removed from private libraries. From 1928, he used his authority in the dictatorship's 'single' party, the Unión Patriótica (UP), to employ the police to seize pornographic literature from street kiosks.[6]

Thanks to his relationships with both Miguel Primo de Rivera and Ángel Herrera, Pemán found himself in a position to play an important role nationally as a key mouthpiece of the Unión Patriótica. He claimed later that it was during his propaganda events for the UP that he honed the oratorical skills that secured his fame in the Francoist zone during the civil war. He learned how to manipulate audiences large and small, using different techniques if there were women present.[7] In the province of Cadiz, his importance in the Unión Patriótica cemented his links with the most reactionary local elements, the *cacique* (powerful political boss) of Jerez, Francisco Moreno y Zulueta de Reales, Conde de los Andes, and the *caciques* of Cadiz, Admiral Ramón de Carranza, Marqués de la Villa de Pesadilla, and his son, Ramón de Carranza, Marqués de Soto Hermoso.[8] For Pemán, the nation was bitterly divided between an anti-Spain embracing everything that was heterodox and foreign and an authentic Spain of traditional religious and monarchical values. This was expressed in the mission that he foresaw for the UP: 'the time has come for Spanish society to choose between Jesus and Barabbas.'[9]

The Unión Patriótica never became the party that Pemán longed for and was more a civic organization of the upper and middle classes who used it to manifest support for the regime and so derive the corresponding benefits.[10] In July 1927, Primo made him President of the Cadiz branch of the UP. Its newspaper, *La Información*, became a mouthpiece for Pemán's increasingly authoritarian ideas. As was to be expected, despite the regime's empty promises to combat corruption, he did nothing to challenge the power of Moreno y Zulueta and the Carranza family. Pemán's links with the regime grew ever stronger. In 1927, he was made a member of the newly created corporative, non-elected Asamblea Nacional Consultiva, an ineffective faux parliamentary attempt to legitimize the regime.[11] He became the semi-official ideologue of the regime and composed its handbook, *El hecho y la idea de la Unión Patriótica*. In the book, Pemán devoted many pages to denouncing popular sovereignty and universal suffrage. He also made a sustained attack on the idea that regional languages were any justification for separatism, dismissing the Gallego and Catalan languages as mere dialects and the Basque Euskera as 'a venerable relic'.[12] He edited a series of the Dictator's speeches with the title *El pensamiento de Primo de Rivera*.[13] He was made secretary of the section of the Asamblea Nacional drafting a new constitution. The section's unfinished project aimed to eliminate individual freedom and political parties.[14]

In November 1929, a spectacular banquet, presided over by the Dictator himself, was held to honour Pemán's contribution to the Unión Patriótica. In his speech of thanks, he declared that Spain faced 'a new problem: the Fatherland is under attack in its very foundations from communism, separatism and terrorism. It faces the harsh choice of Fatherland or Soviets, of order or anarchy.' He saw the nation as divided between its internal Communist enemies and its patriotic defenders, united in the Unión Patriótica.[15] Thanks to Pemán, the idea of the 'anti-Spain' was to become central to the justification of civil war against the left and the repression carried out by the military rebels.[16]

Pemán's links with and belief in the political superiority of the aristocracy was consolidated at the beginning of August 1927 when Alfonso XIII made him a knight of the exclusive Orden de Montesa in the Madrid church of La Concepción Real de Calatrava. This deeply racist and reactionary order was open only to those who could prove their aristocratic origins, had a coat of arms, were unsullied by 'vile mechanical or industrial occupations or manual labour, [are] neither Jewish or Moorish nor have Jewish or Moorish blood, nor have any ancestors who profited from usury or commerce'.[17]

During this period, Pemán consolidated his links with extreme right-wing theorists who would be his key collaborators in the efforts to bring down the Republic – Ramiro de Maeztu, Victor Pradera, José Calvo Sotelo and Antonio Goicoechea.[18] As the Dictator's star waned, Pemán became one of his last-ditch supporters, ever more committed to defend his authoritarian and anti-democratic ideas.[19] They grew so close that the last of their frequent lunches together took place on 28 January 1930, the day that Primo resigned.[20] In the weeks after presenting his resignation to Alfonso XIII, Primo convened several meetings with Pemán and his other key collaborators. He talked of mounting another military coup to be led by himself or a younger general. In the event, he could not find the necessary support. Suspecting that he might not succeed, he had urged his followers to create a political party that could carry the banner of his regime's ideas.[21] After Primo de Rivera's death in Paris on 16 March, queues of people gathered outside Pemán's house in Cadiz to offer him their condolences.[22]

In fulfilment of Primo's wishes, a group of his ministers, his son José Antonio and Pemán announced the creation of the Unión Monárquica Nacional. For Pemán, it was a question of creating a vehicle to make political use of those who supported the dictatorship.[23] The UMN's manifesto proclaimed its commitment to continuing the work of the dictatorship, with devotion to his memory and submission to his doctrine.[24] Primo was buried with considerable pomp in Madrid on 3 April. Pemán accompanied the gun carriage that carried his coffin. Inevitably, he would be one of the main orators in 1930, along with José Antonio Primo de Rivera, in the UMN's nationwide propaganda campaign advocating an authoritarian monarchy.[25] Throughout this time, he cultivated his relationship with Alfonso XIII. In late October 1930, when the King visited Cadiz, Pemán was one of the pole-bearers of the canopy held over the monarch as he entered the church of Santo Domingo.[26]

Alongside José Antonio, Pemán was an avid participant in the UMN campaign threatening 'sacred violence' to prevent the coming of a republic. His speeches were provocative and bellicose. He declared on 1 October 1930 that if the Socialists wanted political power they would have to fight for it in the streets and not win it in voting booths. Although short-lived, the UMN was a stepping stone to the Spanish fascism of the 1930s, the monarchy the ceremonial icing on a dictatorial cake. Stressing that 'the masses do not trust political programmes, they long for a leader', he declared that 'It is only for the time being that we should be moderate so as not to divide the monarchist right.'[27] Pemán's speeches provoked considerable hostility from the left. One of them so impressed a young monarchist intellectual, Eugenio Vegas Latapie, that he approached Pemán afterwards. It was the beginning of a close and important friendship.[28] After another in Oviedo in 1930, he was invited to dinner by the Marqués de la Rodriga, whose house, library and Dresden dinner service Pemán described years later with his habitual snobbery. In the early hours of the morning, General Franco arrived and joined in the convivial post-prandial conversation or *tertulia*. Pemán would later make much of this, their first brief meeting.[29]

In December, in the course of the campaign, Pemán denied that the UMN was the same as the Unión Patriótica, claiming that it was an entirely new party. Barely five months earlier, he had advocated that the Unión Patriótica should simply change its name to Unión Monárquica Nacional.[30] Given the heterogeneous nature of Primo's supporters, it was difficult to secure a united list of candidates for the municipal elections of 12 April 1931. As a result of tactical differences with Carranza and the Conde de los Andes, Pemán resigned as President of the provincial branch of the UMN and announced that he was withdrawing from politics. He did not run in the elections.[31]

The victory of the Republican–Socialist coalition in the municipal elections appalled Pemán. He was outraged that a popular vote could usher in the Second Republic and, in one day, defeat what he regarded as immutable principles established over centuries. After the burning of the churches in Madrid on 12 May 1931, he proclaimed 'the end of the world'.[32] Accordingly, he joined Ramiro de Maeztu, Vegas Latapie and other ideologues in trying to set up a journal to propagate authoritarian monarchism and forge links with similar authoritarian movements in Europe. Vegas Latapie was deeply impressed by Action Française. The Marqués de Quintanar, who was an admirer of the right-wing Portuguese group Integralismo Lusitano, was among those who had discussed with Primo the idea of such a journal.[33]

Within hours of the establishment of the Republic, the principal figures of the UMN met in the home of the Conde de Guadalhorce, Rafael Benjumea y Burín, who had been Primo's Minister of Development. Believing that the monarchy had fallen because it had been insufficiently authoritarian, they agreed to found a 'school of modern counterrevolutionary thought'.

Money was donated by the Marqués de Pelayo and other aristo-crats to fund subversive activities against the Republic to be organized by General Luis Orgaz. Part of these funds went to creating the cultural society Acción Española. Its legal political activities would justify conspiracy in preparation for a military coup. The first number of its theoretical journal appeared on 15 December 1931 under the nominal editorship of the Conde de Santibáñez del Río (another of Quintanar's titles).[34] The leaders of Acción Española would constitute the ideological dynamo that linked the moderate authoritarianism of Primo de Rivera to the ruthless violence of Francoism.[35]

Initially, the society was a component part of Ángel Herrera's Acción Nacional, which soon changed its name to Acción Popular. Publicly at least, Pemán made a token acceptance of its legalist tactic and rejected violence. This was contradicted by his advocacy of a national crusade in defence of religion and the Fatherland. This meant a struggle to overthrow the Republic, which he regarded as anti-clerical and subject to noxious foreign influences.[36] Early in 1932, Pemán gave a lecture to the members of the society. His subject was 'the lunacy of democracy' by which 'the masses had rebelled against their rightful position of subjugation and respect for their superiors'. His target was 'the treachery of intellectuals in not prevent-ing this but rather encouraging the desire of the masses for a political voice'. He repeated the lecture in various parts of Spain. In Valencia in April, he directed his criticisms against Unamuno and Ortega y Gasset.[37]

In May 1932, he founded a magazine, *Ellas. Semanario de Mujeres Españolas*, ostensibly aimed at mobilizing the female vote. However, articles on fashion, clothes and recipes merely served as a camouflage for Catholic, fascist, anti-Semitic and misogynistic material that, in another publication, might have fallen foul of the censorship. For the first number, Pemán wrote an article denouncing universal suffrage in which he made the revealing comment: 'the role of the woman is not the active role of conquest but the passive role of being conquered'. Despite his declared distaste for democracy, he accepted, patronizingly, that 'it is necessary to give the Spanish woman clear and superficial lessons about the most fundamental aspects of our great traditional and Spanish ideology and teach her how best to contribute to the diffusion and triumph of that ideology'. Elsewhere, he wrote that 'God's punishment of woman for the original sin was the pain of motherhood and her subjection to the man for him to dominate her'.[38] The magazine frequently published anti-Semitic articles with titles such as 'Socialism, Ally of Judaism', 'Traitors Who Sell their Fatherland', 'Facing the Invasion of the Jews' and 'Socialism, Communism, Judaism'. After several months, since he was allergic to routine administrative work, Pemán relinquished his role as editor of the magazine but remained as a contributor and columnist.[39]

Pemán took no active part in General Sanjurjo's attempted coup d'état of 10 August 1932 but was on its fringes. He attended some of the preparatory meetings and was a friend of one of the key military plotters, Colonel José Enrique Varela. His involvement was suspected by the police but could not be proven. Nevertheless, he fled to Gibraltar, writing years later: 'at a time of severe danger, I took refuge there for a few days'.[40] In the light of the failure of the coup, the leaders of Acción Española intensified their conspiratorial activities. The principal objective was a massive fund-raising effort to ensure that the next coup would be more successful. In a short time, they accumulated 17 million pesetas.[41] Central to the preparation for the next coup was a propaganda effort to denigrate the Republic. It was rendered difficult because much of the right-wing media was banned after the coup. In *Ellas*, which was not affected by the closure, Pemán published numerous extravagant hymns of praise to those involved in the Sanjurjada. He celebrated those who 'heroically gave their lives for Spain on 10 August 1932' and denounced the exile of 145 army officers involved to the town of Villa Cisneros in the Spanish colony of Western Sahara.[42] He took part in the campaign against Catalan autonomy with public speeches and also with articles in *Ellas*. He described Catalonia as 'not so much drunk on separatism as slightly dizzy with it'. He claimed that there were only a few sincere Catalan nationalists and denounced the majority of advocates of independence as cynics who were using nationalism to get jobs in the regional institutions. Accordingly, he called for a powerful Spanish nationalism to combat the Catalan separatists.[43] In *El Debate*, he described the Catalan autonomy statute as 'destructive, catastrophic and unbelievably ugly', the work of 'the decadent masses'.[44]

After the failure of the military coup, Acción Popular split. The more moderate elements became the Confederación Española de Derechas Autónomas. The Acción Española group created a political party, Renovación Española, that was committed to the violent destruction of democracy. As an advocate of anti-parliamentarian monarchy, Pemán called for union with the Carlist Comunión Tradicionalista.[45] He participated, along with Antonio Goicoechea, in a lecture series organized by the Comunión Tradicionalista in the Cinema de la Ópera in Madrid. On 23 February 1933, Vegas Latapie organized a banquet for 400 diners as an act of homage to Pemán in the Ritz Hotel. One of the speakers was Pedro Sainz Rodríguez, who read a fiercely provocative message from José Calvo Sotelo – 'We are at war!' – and expressed his delight that the ex-combatants of the First World War in Italy, Germany, Portugal, Poland and other countries were ready to die in the struggle to put an end to what he called 'the parliamentary scarecrow'. Pemán's speech was a battle cry for the conquest of the state by phalanxes of warriors determined to crush democracy. As part of his campaign to unite the forces of the extreme right, Pemán wrote in the Carlist newspaper *El Siglo Futuro*. His objectives were achieved by the creation of an electoral coalition under the name TYRE (Tradicionalistas y Renovación Española).[46] In March 1933, in an article in *Ellas*, he praised the efforts of his friend José Antonio Primo de Rivera to create a fascist party and extolled the Italian Fascist regime for its values of 'authority, obedience, hierarchy, discipline'.[47] The activities underlined Pemán's ever closer connection with the Acción Española group. He wrote of his delight that, in it, the aristocracy was finally assuming its rightful role in the struggle to overthrow the Republic.[48]

On 27 September 1933, *El Divino Impaciente*, Pemán's dramatic representation of the life of San Francisco Javier, was premiered in Madrid. At the behest of Manuel Herrera Oria, brother of Ángel, he

had set out to write a work that would combat the laic legislation of
the Republic which was perceived on the right as religious persecution. This response to the expulsion of the Jesuits, despite lasting
three hours and being written in verse, enjoyed spectacular success.
For months afterwards, day after day, across Spain there were
hundreds of performances for which there were long ticket queues
that often became anti-Republican demonstrations. There can be
little doubt that the play's impact contributed to the right's success in
the elections of November 1933. Performed in Fascist Italy, the Third
Reich, Ireland and several Latin American countries, and selling
more than 100,000 copies, it made Pemán, already a rich man, a lot
of money.⁴⁹

During the campaign for the November 1933 elections, Pemán
stood as an independent monarchist deputy for Cadiz with the
ultra-reactionary party Acción Popular-Unión Ciudadana y Agraria
which ran in coalition with the CEDA. It defended the interests of
the landowning oligarchy threatened by the Republic's agrarian
reform projects. As well as Pemán, its candidates included both
Ramón de Carranza and José Antonio Primo de Rivera. Its anti-
democratic line was manifest in the headline 'It is necessary to vote
for candidates who will go to parliament to destroy the parliamentary regime'. Pemán was a tireless campaigner with a virulent
rhetoric accusing the Republic of being an atheistic, Marxist regime
determined to destroy Spain. Calling for a return of Spanish greatness through an authoritarian monarchy, one of his slogans was 'Let
us vote so that one day voting will no longer be necessary'. Among
his fellow candidates for the local ultra-right coalition were Ramón
de Carranza, José Antonio Primo de Rivera and two Carlists. In the
Teatro de las Cortes in San Fernando, on 13 November, at a meeting
that he addressed along with Carranza and José Antonio Primo de
Rivera, a group of anarchists opened fire on the front stalls. It is not
clear which of the three prominent right-wing candidates were their
intended targets. A merchant was killed and the wife of Estanislao
Domecq was seriously wounded by four bullets. Pemán was elected
to the Cortes as the candidate of the Unión Ciudadana y Agraria. On
taking up his seat, he announced that he would act as an independent monarchist.⁵⁰

In a revealing comment on the electoral triumph, he declared,
'This is the moment to reflect on the total uselessness of this [demo-
cratic] system.' The system's defect in his eyes was that, despite having
won this time, in the next elections the right could lose.[51] Although,
until the military coup of July 1936, Pemán remained an open enemy
of the Republic and was fiercely critical of both the parliamentary
monarchists and the accidentalism of the CEDA, his activity was
negligible. He made only two speeches, both in the spring of 1934, in
favour of amnesty for the conspirators of the Sanjurjada. He was
inhibited by an inability to improvise or deal with interruptions and
heckling. Two knowledgeable commentators, Dionisio Ridruejo and
Ramón Serrano Suñer, coincided in regarding his speeches as artifi-
cial and lacking in all spontaneity.[52] He was made a member of the
Comisión de Instrucción Pública but failed to attend a single meeting. However, he did take over as President of Acción Española in the
spring of 1934 and was active in pushing for the creation of the
Bloque Nacional, the successor to TYRE, which loosely linked
Renovación Española, the Comunión Tradicionalista and Dr José
María Albiñana's Partido Nacionalista.[53]

In December 1933, Pemán wrote an enthusiastic preface to a
volume of Calvo Sotelo's speeches in which he proclaimed his belief
in the existence of the Jewish–masonic–Bolshevik conspiracy. To
eulogize Calvo, he contrasted him with the Republican intellectuals
who had betrayed the Fatherland, 'those who flirted with Moscow
and with Amsterdam, those who, like adulterous husbands, kept
nocturnal assignations in exotic lodges ... those who melted with
pleasure in the Synagogues of Tetuan.'[54] Amsterdam, being the location of many diamond dealers, was shorthand for Judaism. Pemán's
most substantial political work during late 1934 and early 1935 was a
series of eight long articles that he wrote for *Acción Española*, with
the title 'Cartas a un escéptico en materia de formas de gobierno'
(Letters to a sceptic about forms of government), that were subsequently collected together as a book.[55] The unnamed sceptic to whom
the letters were addressed may be seen as a follower of Pemán's own
patron, Ángel Herrera. Overall, Pemán was attempting to refute
Herrera's notion that forms of government were 'accidental' and that
what was fundamental was their social and political content.

Accordingly, he set out to demolish all arguments in favour of republicanism and to justify hereditary monarchy.[56] He praised monarchy as superior to the republican form of government, which he presented as 'more natural but cruder, more backward, more sinful'. The great contribution of monarchy was 'to overcome the animal nature of mankind and to help fulfil its rational nature'.[57] There was little intellectual substance to arguments like 'the liturgies of republican presidents are like comical parodies of royal ceremony. Escorts, carriages, palaces are natural adjuncts to inherited majesty; but they are irritating vanities in the case of upstart rulers.'[58] He listed among the disadvantages of republicanism the lack of both 'the august impartiality' and 'the prestige of royalty'. Even more feeble was his argument that 'republican governments have to be made up of party politicians and the very sound of that is repugnant'.[59]

Pemán's eulogistic justification of hereditary monarchy presented it as 'an age-old formula, the product of universal wisdom, accepted across the world'. It is, he argued, 'a power received from God for the good of the community'. One of its advantages over a republic, he maintained, was its capacity to control socialism.[60] Both the First and Second Republics were represented as disastrous and criminal regimes characterized by disorder, civil strife and economic ruin.[61] The 'Cartas' dismissed the coming of the Second Republic as the fault of lukewarm monarchists who failed to defend what most mattered. Pemán condemned any elected president as a *cacique* or a politician who had merely reached the peak of their personal ambition as against the hereditary prince who ruled as a duty of service. It was as if he had never heard of Alfonso XIII.[62]

At the rally organized on 22 April 1934 by Gil Robles to pressurize Alcalá-Zamora to approve an amnesty for those involved in the 10 August coup attempt, an anthem was sung to the music of Grieg's *Sigurd Jorsalfar* with lyrics by Pemán. Its belligerent lyrics included the lines 'Onwards, with faith in victory, for the Fatherland and for God, to win or to die.'[63] In the Cortes, Pemán defended Sanjurjo with the bizarre argument that the electoral victory of the right in November 1933 had been 'a vote not just for the amnesty of those punished for their part in the Sanjurjo coup but for the complete and absolute vindication of the 10 August coup'. On 20 May 1934, Pemán spoke at the 1,000-person banquet in the Hotel Palace to welcome back Calvo Sotelo from exile.[64]

Pemán did not stand for re-election to the Cortes in the elections of February 1936, which was hardly surprising given his sparse success as a parliamentary deputy. He did speak on behalf of a friend at several meetings in La Mancha. Having been listened to politely by a Socialist audience, he ended his speech, so he claimed later, with the words 'Perhaps we will never see each other again. Maybe today we are arranging to meet again face to face across trenches or barricades. If that is the case, I assure you now that I will fight you with courage but without hatred.' As events were to show, that was far from the truth.[65]

Inevitably, he was appalled by the victory of the Popular Front. Nevertheless, he played an important role in the preparations for a military uprising. Among the papers of General Varela seized in Barcelona were Pemán's handwritten lists of the government to be established after the rebels were victorious.[66] Similarly, before Calvo Sotelo made the notorious speech in the Cortes, on 16 June, that contributed considerably to the ambience of civil war, he asked Pemán to prepare some notes for his manifesto for the coming military coup.[67] When Calvo Sotelo was murdered on 13 July, Pemán wrote an obituary for *Acción Española* that, owing to the outbreak of war, did not appear until October 1936. In it, he revealed his attitude to the uprising: 'There is nothing to be said. First, because it is prohibited. Secondly, the brutal act itself says it all with its own incomparable eloquence. About that, there is nothing to be said but there is much to be done! And by God and Santiago, it will be done!'[68] Subsequently, Pemán wrote several enthusiastic tributes to Calvo Sotelo. In one of them, he told the outrageous lie that Calvo Sotelo had known nothing about the forthcoming military coup. In the same essay, he also attributed to Margarita Nelken the death threat allegedly hurled at Calvo Sotelo by Dolores Ibárruri (La Pasionaria) on 16 June in the Cortes.[69]

It was typical of the flippancy with which Pemán smeared Republican figures. Not only was the alleged threat not made by Margarita Nelken, neither was it made by Ibárruri. During that notorious Cortes session of 16 June, Calvo Sotelo had expressed support for an uprising, declaring, 'I would consider to be a madman any officer who, faced with his destiny, was not ready to rise for Spain and against anarchy.' The Prime Minister, Santiago Casares Quiroga, replied that, after that provocative statement, he would hold Calvo Sotelo responsible for whatever might happen. The subsequent intervention by Pasionaria was largely an exposé of the manoeuvres of the right to justify a rising. In it, she said, 'And if there are little reactionary generals who, at a given moment, worked up by elements like Señor Calvo Sotelo, can make an uprising against the state, there are also soldiers of the people who can keep them under control.' It was from that comment that the Francoist myth was constructed that Pasionaria had threatened Calvo Sotelo and therefore bore some responsibility for his assassination on 13 July.[70] Accurate detail or even veracity was not a feature of Pemán's writings and speeches. After the relief of the Alcázar de Toledo, he composed a hymn of praise to the 'heroic feat' of the military cadets that he assumed to be the principal defenders of the Alcázar. In fact, they constituted less than 1 per cent of the rebel forces in the fortress, the vast majority of whom were Civil Guards.[71]

His public justification of the coup and the accompanying terror began early. The coup was almost immediately successful in Cadiz and Jerez and the killing began at once. Once it was clear that Jerez was safely in the hands of the rebels, he emerged from his estate, El Cerro de Santiago, and soon became the official voice of the rebels.[72] His public acclaim for the slaughter began on Radio Jerez on 24 July. He spoke of the 'internal enemy of the *patria*', as if the Republicans were troublesome colonial rebels. With apparent satisfaction, he rejoiced in the failure of the military coup because it would have been too easy a way to save Spain, 'like winning the lottery or being brought breakfast in bed with the newspapers'. 'Spanish official life', he declared, 'was too rotten to be remedied without pain. A quick and painless coup was too low a price to pay for the desired treasure, a great and resurgent Spain.' No matter how hard the war might be, he hailed it as both 'necessary' and 'appropriate'. The war, whose purpose was to protect the Virgin from being Russian and Jewish, 'had been sent by God to teach Spaniards a lesson, to permit them to purify themselves, to leave behind their past sins and errors, and to reach the end pure and cleansed'.

The war was being fought against what he called 'hordes of barbarian invaders'. The implicit comparison of the working-class left with the Berber invaders of 711 was emphasized when he declared, 'The war with its flashes of gunfire has opened all our eyes. The notion of alternating political parties has been replaced for ever by the idea of extermination and expulsion, the only valid response to an enemy that is wreaking more destruction in Spain than any ever caused in history by the invasion of a foreign nation.'[73] At the end of July 1937, speaking in Santiago de Compostela, he declared that Spain was fighting to be free of 'international Jewry', not to be the servant of England nor to provide Russia with 'stolen gold and artworks', but to return to 'its destiny as the right hand of God'.[74]

His relish when speaking of the killing was invariably accompanied by obsequious flattery of its protagonists. From the beginning, Queipo de Llano was the object of his most outrageous sycophancy. At the ceremony celebrating the military rebels' adoption of the monarchist flag on 15 August 1936, he was carried away on flights of empty rhetoric about their providential mission. He boasted that 'Twenty centuries of Christian civilization are mobilized behind us'. He bizarrely addressed Queipo as 'el segundo Giralda', the Giralda being the bell tower of the cathedral. He asked him rhetorically, 'In those first twenty-four hours, is it not true that you had something superhuman behind you? Could you not sense on your shoulder, guiding you and urging you on, the girlish face of the Virgen de los Reyes [the patron of Seville]? Yes, the whole affair had the seal of Providence.' He went on to lavish praise on Franco for his serenity, on Queipo for his 'fearlessness' and on Millán Astray's missing arm. He ended by calling on the Virgin to give 'my poor voice, as the jongleur and proclaimer of this crusade right across Spain, the sinews and muscle so that the ¡Arriba España! that comes from the bottom of my heart can push my Fatherland beyond the stars'.[75]

In the aftermath of Queipo's capture of Seville, columns spread out to conquer surrounding towns and villages. To the east, they extended into Cordoba and, to the west, into Huelva. The same task was being accomplished with equal savagery in Cadiz by the column of Pemán's

friend Manuel Mora Figueroa. Pemán justified this on the grounds
that the defeated left must be fully annihilated: 'Since the enemy is in
the house, there no question of the enemy front retreating. Even after
the enemy is defeated and smashed, it is still living among us, fled to
the hills, or hidden, waiting in disguise to ambush us. This demands,
after every step won, a police purge, the garrisoning of the villages.'[76]

The process of capturing villages, particularly those where the left
had been in control for a few days, had the enthusiastic participation
of the younger male members of the landowner families that had
been challenged by the agrarian reform of the Republic. Some joined
the columns moving on Madrid. Others, including friends of Pemán,
such as Ramón de Carranza, created a kind of landowners' cavalry
known as the Policía Montada de Voluntarios. These units were made
up of both the landowners and those of their employees specialized
in horse breeding and training (*caballistas*, *garrochistas*, *rejoneadores*,
domadores de caballos). As if taking part in a sport or hunting expe-
ditions, they carried out a continuous campaign against the left in the
south.[77] Pemán ecstatically applauded the efforts of these members of
his own class, the *señoritos*, and the jollity with which they went
about their bloody business. He wrote of the 'redemption of the
señoritos', no longer just rich playboys but, 'taking up a rifle or riding
a horse into battle, they had become grown-up gentlemen, *señores*'.[78]

Usually wearing the uniform of the Falange, Pemán followed the
columns of Castejón and Yagüe in their deadly advance from Seville
to Madrid. He was chauffeured, both then and indeed for much of
war, in the Rolls-Royce of his cousin José Domecq de la Riva, 'Pepe
Pantera', a famous racing driver.[79] Such was his identification with the
rebel cause that, at the end of August 1936, a less than voluntary
public subscription was organized in Lucena (Cordoba) to pay for
the printing and distribution of 10,000 copies of one of his speeches.
The speech was his paternalistic 'Alocución a los obreros', addressed
to the workers with implausible claims of what the victorious rebels
would do for them. Those workers who had survived the savage
repression in the areas controlled by Queipo de Llano would have
had a different view of what was on offer.[80]

To clinch his position, Pemán had sought an audience in early
August with Franco at the Palacio de Yanduri in Seville to ask permis-

sion 'to visit the battle fronts and have access to the respective military headquarters'. He was already visiting the fronts, but now Franco made him the rebels' official itinerant propagandist. In this, his second meeting with Franco, Pemán was entranced: 'his simplicity and farsightedness are admirable … He seems unaware of his enormous power and of the fact that he is followed with total unanimity.' With carte blanche from Franco to visit the headquarters of the main rebel army units, Pemán could travel freely throughout the conquered territory to ramp up warlike frenzy through his speeches to the troops and also to civilians in rearguard cities. He claimed that Franco even invited him to be one of the first to enter Madrid. Since his troops had just taken Maqueda, Franco confidently expected the capital to fall imminently.[81]

Around this point in September 1936, Pemán had a conversation with the head of the Junta Técnica, General Miguel Cabanellas. In one of his books of memoirs, Pemán refers to him as Virgilio Cabanellas, which was a symptom of his insouciant way with detail. Miguel Cabanellas asked him for help in drafting a decree to forbid the wearing of mourning, particularly by the mothers, widows and fiancées of executed Republicans. He wanted 'to put an end to that sort of living protest and dramatic testimony that, after conquering any town, we see in the squares and on the street corners, those black and silent figures that in reality are a sign of protest as much as of grief'. Pemán allegedly replied, 'I think that too much killing has been, and is still being, done by the Nationalists.' This account was clearly meant to be a testament to his humanitarianism and moderation. However, glimmers of the real Pemán of the time were revealed in his admission that it was not that the killings were unjustified but simply that, in public relations terms, they were too numerous. He spoke of 'that sad, but doubtless necessary, function of the killings to set an example as a punishment and a warning'. Utterly implausible is his claim that, in asking Cabanellas to contemplate reducing the scale of the repression, he invited him to consider what had been written by Bernanos and Hemingway. With characteristic sloppiness, in reconstructing his conversation with Cabanellas he forgot that the original English version of *For Whom the Bell Tolls* was not published until 1940 and was translated into Spanish in Mexico only in 1944. It was not published in Spain until 1968. Furthermore, the original French version of Bernanos's *Les Grands Cimitières sous la lune* was not published until 1938 and not translated into Spanish until 1986, five years after Pemán's death.[82]

As perhaps befitted a pious Catholic of his time, Pemán was homophobic and his prejudices were particularly alert when it came to Azaña.[83] Cipriano Rivas Cherif, Azaña's close friend and brother-in-law, recalled that during the war he, along with the actress Margarita Xirgu and the poet Federico García Lorca, was regularly accused by Pemán of homosexual perversion.[84] Intriguingly, Ramón Ruiz Alonso, the man who arrested Lorca, stated on more than one occasion that the reason for Lorca's death was 'literary rivalry'. Clearly, there were many reasons that accounted for right-wing hostility towards Lorca in Granada.[85] It is highly unlikely that literary rivalry was one of them. Nevertheless, it is difficult not to suspect that Pemán was the poetic rival of Lorca to whom Ruiz Alonso referred.

Pemán himself inadvertently revealed his competitive feelings towards Lorca when he recalled meeting him in a railway station in Madrid in 1934. He described that occasion in a disingenuous article published in 1948, the principal purpose of which was to counteract the negative publicity that the murder was still generating for the regime. To this end, he was at pains to suggest, absurdly, that Lorca's work did not have a political dimension, thereby implying that he was killed for non-political reasons. He could not resist claiming that, on that 1934 occasion, they had discussed the respective impacts of his own *El divino impaciente* and Lorca's *Yerma*. His readers in *ABC* would have known all about the spectacular success of Pemán's play. Accordingly, there was an underhand derogatory edge to his comment that *Yerma* was 'a work with minority appeal'. With barely concealed satisfaction, Pemán claimed that there were hardly any seats filled at each performance of *Yerma* and that its continued presence in the theatre was artificially maintained for political reasons. This undermined his efforts to present an apolitical Lorca but could not conceal the rivalry that might have inspired Ruiz Alonso's remarks.[86] Whatever personal resentment impelled Ruiz Alonso, like Pemán a one-time parliamentary CEDA deputy and devotee of Ángel

Herrera, to insinuate that he was implicated in the murder of Lorca remains a mystery.

Shortly after the murder of Lorca on 18 August became known, the distinguished composer of *The Three-Cornered Hat* Manuel de Falla telephoned Pemán to express his horror. Thirty-three years later, Pemán claimed, in a letter to the Lorca scholar Eduardo Molina Fajardo, that as soon as he had confirmed the death he had immediately left a note at Franco's headquarters in Cáceres stressing the negative impact that the news would have and suggesting an immediate investigation.[87] This account is simply untrue. Altogether more plausible are the memoirs of Eugenio Vegas Latapie. Vegas recounted that Falla had sent Pemán a letter on 18 September expressing his disquiet about the scale of the repression. Assuming that Pemán, like himself a devout Catholic, would be equally appalled, he begged him to use his prestige to try to have the killings stopped. Not long afterwards, on 22 September, Pemán accompanied Vegas Latapie and Eugenio Montes on a mission to see Franco at his headquarters in the Palacio de los Golfines de Arriba in Cáceres. Among several issues that they wanted to discuss was the need to reduce the number of indiscriminate killings in the rebel rearguard. In the event, it was Vegas who raised the issue. Pemán did not speak, incapable of contributing without a prepared text. Franco simply demonstrated a total lack of interest in their concerns.[88]

In his reply to Falla some days later, with a characteristic blend of untruth and exaggeration, Pemán wrote, 'I have exactly the same concerns as you and I have taken some steps in that regard that, with God's will, have been successful in some individual cases. Now, I must speak with some authorities that do me the honour of listening to me, [to suggest] that, if at the beginning it was necessary to act with harsh rigour, now could be the time to open the way to a degree of clemency that might be applied to those who mistakenly went too far.' In fact, his interventions in individual cases were few. Years later, he claimed that, in the meeting with Franco in Cáceres – at which, according to Vegas Latapie, he had not spoken – he had pleaded for clemency for an unnamed person.[89] If indeed Pemán had suggested to Cabanellas that the scale of killing was excessive, that encounter may have been the basis of the claim in his letter to Falla. Certainly, there are few recorded cases of his interventions. It is known that, after appropriate manifestations of repentance, he did intervene on behalf of the poets Manuel Machado and Gerardo Diego.[90] In a later memoir, he repeated his claim to have intervened, ineffectually, in the case of an unnamed friend in Cadiz. As late as 1976, he could still write that 'harsh repression, what is called "exemplary punishment", is part of the painful panoply of the characteristic instruments of a war. I believe that the same result could have been achieved with a lower quota of executions.' Pemán's views on the repression could be deduced from his praise for the Zamacola family, two of whose scions led a notorious gang known as the 'Lions of Rota', guilty of murder and rape in the province of Cadiz.[91]

Over the years, Pemán's account of Lorca's death and of his reaction evolved. In mid-1937, he wrote to the actress Lola Membrives, who had raised the issue with him. Already suspecting her of Republican sympathies, he brushed aside her concerns, writing in schoolmasterly fashion, 'The sad episode of the shooting of Lorca has nothing to do with the great national cause and is something about which the most fervent Nationalist should suspend judgement until the full facts are known.'[92] In early December 1948, he published the article mentioned above, in which, while acknowledging the horror of Lorca's death, he was at pains to say that it had nothing to do with the repression carried out by Franco's forces. Indeed, as always, his principal concern was public opinion because the murder was 'one of the accusations most commonly used in Latin America to criticize the Franco regime.'[93]

After the encounters with Franco and Cabanellas, Pemán returned to Cadiz for a brief stay but was soon on the road to fulfil Franco's mission. He spoke before the microphones of Radio Club Portugués, denouncing the Republicans as Marxists with 'a predilection to cut open women's bellies, the blind instinct of those who have neither God nor Fatherland'. He proclaimed that the Spanish Civil War had to be fought because the work of the Inquisition had been left unfinished.[94] Next, he headed for the Madrid front to link up with the African columns of General Varela that, it was believed in the rebel zone, were about to enter Madrid. He had been commissioned by Franco 'to relate the capture of the Republican capital in a radio broadcast to Spain and the entire world'.[95] He wrote an absurdly lyrical, hubristic article at the Madrid front just as the presumed final push began: 'the Spanish army has one foot inside. The leap is imminent. The cannon knew and so its fire made an almost human cry … Never in the history of the world has a capital city of the size and population of Madrid been captured in war'.[96]

He made dozens of speeches throughout the rebel zone and wrote many articles. In September, in a speech in Cadiz, he played with the conceit that the only good literature in such times could be found in the harangues of warlike generals like Franco, Millán Astray, Yagüe and Queipo de Llano whose eloquence was to be measured in the implementation of their threats. He pursued the imagery by speaking of Yagüe's entry into Badajoz and the subsequent massacre. He recounted with relish how 'the Regulares [Moroccan troops] with knives between their teeth, a flash of silver against the black shadow of their faces, threw themselves into the breach. What greater eloquence could there be!' Praising the bloodshed along the route followed by Yagüe's columns, he likened it to the necessary fertilizer for a future rich harvest. He compared the mission of those columns to the War of Independence of 1808–14, declaring that this one, like its predecessor, had 'as its purpose, the expulsion from Spain of the foreign hordes encamped there'.[97] He put the same thought in more chilling terms in April 1937 in a broadcast on Radio Jerez when he described the war as 'this magnificent struggle to bleed Spain'.[98]

Vegas Latapie commented that all Pemán really wanted to do was range over the battlefields making speeches to the troops, chat with generals in their headquarters, strut around rearguard towns in uniform and visit hospitals to be photographed with the wounded and the nurses.[99] Pemán himself frequently boasted of making speeches 'in churches and in barracks, under the sun and under the stars. I have harangued soldiers before they went into combat and I have cheered up the wounded in front-line hospitals.' In another speech, he embellished this claim: 'I have spoken on country paths and village sidewalks, in town squares and in streets. I have even held forth to a group of soldiers about to go into battle. I have also heard applause in hospitals, where some of the wounded had to clap with just one hand because the other, plucked like a rose, was already on

the blessed altar of the Fatherland.'[100] In late September, finding
himself in Vitoria, he was recognized in the street. A crowd gathered
and, allegedly, begged him for a speech. One of his next stops was
Pamplona. There, to address a crowd from the balcony of Carlist
headquarters, he wore a red beret.[101] On at least one occasion, he
addressed Republican troops by loudspeaker across the lines, decry-
ing their susceptibility to Communist influence. 'How is it possible',
he asked, 'that you have turned against Spain and against the God
before whom your mothers taught you to pray? Why are you serfs of
the red foreigner?'[102]

In his Falangist outfit, he had free access to the headquarters of
Generals Queipo de Llano, Varela, Yagüe, Solchaga and Aranda.[103] He
made speeches at several military ceremonies at which rapidly
trained officers, *alféreces provisionales* (provisional second lieutenants), swore their oath of loyalty to the flag. His hugely successful
play *De ellos es el mundo* was a summary of the civil war as a battle
between evil assassins and saintly Francoists. It included a hymn of
praise to the *alféreces provisionales*. In April 1938, he was rewarded by
being made an honorary *alférez provisional* himself. Thereafter, he
alternated between Falangist and military uniforms in his public
appearances.[104]

In early October 1936, Pemán had been rewarded for his efforts by
being appointed President of the Comisión de Cultura y Enseñanza,
one of the seven sections of the Junta Técnica del Estado created by
Nicolás Franco. Under the overall presidency of General Fidel Dávila,
the other six were Hacienda; Justicia; Industria, Comercio y Abastos;
Agricultura y Trabajo Agrícola; Trabajo and Obras Públicas y
Comunicaciones. The Comisión was the brainchild of Pemán's friend
Eugenio Vegas Latapie, who was determined to put the ideas of
Acción Española into practice. Its principal mission was to crush 'la
anti-España', the idea promulgated by Pemán and others. This meant
purging schools, training colleges (*colegios normales*) and universities
of their liberal and left-wing staff. Pemán and his fellow contributors
to *Acción Española* had fomented the notion that they were responsible for the proliferation of poisonous democratic, Socialist,
Communist, anarchist, anti-clerical and feminist ideas. In particular,
ideas emanating from the work of the great liberal intellectual centre,

the Institución Libre de Enseñanza, were anathema. Vegas Latapie was determined to ensure that one of the primordial missions of the Francoist project would be the eradication of the Republic's educational reforms by means of a national brainwashing, and the Comisión de Cultura y Enseñanza was to be the first step. Its work would be sustained initially by an apparatus of terror and thereafter by means of the total control of the media and the education system.

The project was enthusiastically embraced by Pemán, who had long since denounced intellectuals. Nevertheless, he initially refused the post, citing his horror of any kind of administrative work – 'my total inability to sit at a desk to write anything other than poetry, plays or articles'. He claimed later that military pressure had obliged him to accept. In fact, his reluctance was little to do with any desire to write poetry and plays. He wanted to have a deputy who would free him to continue his visits to the front and his propaganda work there. He finally accepted on the condition that there be a vice-president to undertake the administrative functions. The choice, on General Mola's recommendation, was Enrique Suñer Ordóñez, who substituted for Pemán in most of the weekly meetings with the presidents of the other six commissions. Suñer shared Pemán's obsession with the idea of the Jewish–masonic–Bolshevik conspiracy. By 1970, however, Pemán could be found dissociating himself from the work of the Comisión, forgetting his presidency and claiming that he had only been a member of its board.[105]

Suñer was a zealot thirsting for revenge for perceived slights under the Republic. His schemes were facilitated by the fact that, by early 1937, he was left to run the headquarters of the commission in Burgos. Pemán had his principal residence in Cadiz which, together with his endless jaunts around the battlefronts, gave Suñer considerable freedom. It was during what Vegas Latapie called his 'war tourism' that Pemán, sporting his Falangist blue shirt and his red Carlist beret, made most of his murderous harangues.[106] According to his wife, he barely managed to spend two months at home in any one year of the war.[107]

The scope of the Comisión's ambition was laid out on 10 December 1936. Instructions were sent to local 'committees for the purging of the education system'. Drafted by Vegas Latapie and signed by Pemán, who had not bothered to read it, the text declared that the purge was intended to be both punitive and preventive. There would be no tolerance for 'those who have poisoned public opinion and bear the primary and greatest responsibility for all the crimes and destruction that have alarmed the world and have put most honourable homes in Spain into mourning'. The text declared that those guilty of atrocities and outrages 'are simply the spiritual children of the professors and teachers who, in institutions like the so-called Institución Libre de Enseñanza forged generations of unbelievers and anarchists'.[108]

When he finally read the text, Pemán wrote a revealing letter to Vegas Latapie, who was one of the members of the Comisión and, in the early days, was effectively running it. In his letter, Pemán lamented that 'since this damned circular has made me appear to be the Torquemada of this Inquisition, the tears and supplications of Cadiz, Seville and Cordoba reach me every day'. He implied that, by taking on the responsibility of the Comisión, he was squandering the reputation that he had spent years fabricating.[109] It was as if he could not see that the aims of the Comisión were entirely in accord with his public statements of the previous decade. It was not until 1970 that he felt the need to try to dissociate himself from the project.[110]

Indeed, despite his private protestations to Vegas Latapie of feeling uncomfortable about the work of the Comisión, in public he vehemently justified it. In a speech in Salamanca on 18 March 1937, broadcast on Radio Nacional, he described the war as 'Spain fighting against what is not Spain'. Within this crusade against the anti-Spain, he declared that 'the task of purging the intellectuals was not just a crude cleaning-up job but an exquisitely delicate operation requiring the iron fist to be used in such a way as to save that part of intellectual life deemed worthy of redemption'. He spoke in spine-chilling terms of the rebels' dilemma when confronting 'the purge of human material'. In other words, leaving aside the Jews, freemasons and Marxists who had to be exterminated, the question was whether any members of the liberal intelligentsia deserved redemption. He was in little doubt that most were deserving of the harshest punishment: 'For the crime of high treason constituted by participation in the Jewish–masonic–internationalist pact, all the worse when committed by intellectuals, the New State will be implacable.'

The range of those intellectuals who could be targeted was revealed in a nostalgic rant about the opposition to the Primo de Rivera dictatorship. He could not conceal his resentment of the philosopher Miguel de Unamuno, by implication the sort of intellectual who had had to be purged. He referred to the *Hojas Libres*, the clandestine newssheets produced by Unamuno and other members of the exiled resistance against the Primo de Rivera dictatorship. Sent into Spain from Paris, the *Hojas* exposed the corruption of the regime and thereby outraged Pemán. Speaking as if Primo's regime had not been a dictatorship, he fulminated against 'those *Hojas Libres* that summed up all the vileness of literary salons and all the cowardice of clandestinity'.[111] By this time, Unamuno was dead, having died on 31 December 1936. However, Pemán had an opportunity, before the venerable intellectual's demise, to witness his downfall.

Pemán was a participant in the infamous event at the University of Salamanca at which Unamuno is reported to have made his celebrated statement about the rebel war effort – 'you will win but you will not convince'. Pemán was present in his capacity as President of the Comisión de Cultura y Enseñanza and made the final speech just before the notorious intervention of Millán Astray. It was a long, repetitive, bombastic and empty rehash of the clichés about the crusade against the anti-Spain. He proudly began by describing his propaganda activities, again comparing himself to a medieval travelling minstrel:

Truly, it is difficult in these wartime days in which we live, and even more so for someone like me who is living in its midst, criss-crossing Spain fulfilling the duties of a patriotic jongleur; it is difficult to put the soul and the spirit to one side sufficiently to deal with a subject such as that which needs to be dealt with in this event. But, when all is said and done, to speak at this rearguard event, to speak here in the University of Salamanca, which is a component of the crusade, a place where the final battle will be fought, the battle for thought, for ideas, for the spirit. And to come here to speak of the work of the old Spain is not to leave the firing line and the battle front where, in the last resort, the fight is raging to restore the same eternal values of Spain that we are all going to defend.

His speech inflamed further the toxic atmosphere in the hall.[112] According to a contemporary account in *ABC*, when Millán Astray shouted out 'Muera la inteligencia!' – 'Death to the intelligentsia!' – Pemán tried to correct this public-relations faux pas by exclaiming, 'No, let us not say death to the intelligentsia but rather death to bad intellectuals.'[113] Years later, he denied that he had done so, attributing the correction to Millán Astray himself.[114]

After the event in the university, an 'intimate' banquet was organized in Pemán's honour by the Guardias Cívicos de Salamanca and the Alcalde (Mayor) of the city, Francisco del Valle Marín. The other speakers at the event, with the exception of Unamuno, were also invited to the dinner. As Pemán returned to his hotel, he was halted in the street by Millán Astray, who embraced him. To the delight of the many onlookers for whom Millán was performing, he unhooked his medal for sufferings for the Fatherland and gave it to Pemán. The latter, equally aware of the publicity opportunity, kissed the medal before returning it.[115] As will be seen, Pemán's compulsive sycophancy extended beyond Franco, Queipo de Llano and Millán Astray to Mussolini and Hitler.

Around 16,000 teachers were victims of the Comisión, at best losing their jobs, at worst suffering imprisonment or execution. There are innumerable cases in the state gazette, the *Boletín Oficial del Estado*, of university teachers removed from their positions. The notifications were signed off by Pemán as President of the Comisión de Cultura y Enseñanza.[116] It is difficult to calculate how many teachers were shot as a result of collective summary trials. Some provincial studies indicate that the figure ran into several hundreds. For instance, there were more than forty executions of teachers in León and at least thirty in Burgos and Zaragoza. When Franco created his first government on 1 February 1938, the Comisión was dissolved and incorporated into the newly created Ministry of Education under Pedro Sainz Rodríguez. Although some of the executions occurred before Pemán's appointment, it was under his direction that the purges of teaching staff had been institutionalized; they continued well into the 1940s.[117] In practical terms, Pemán played little part in the day-to-day work of the Comisión. This was left to Suñer, who replaced him as its President in June 1937. In later years, despite claiming that he had only been a member of the Comisión, Pemán would claim the lucrative lifetime pension that came with his role in it, a role that was the equivalent of minister of education.[118]

Whatever he might say in later life, there could be little doubt of Pemán's belief in the work of the Comisión. In early May 1937, in a speech to schoolteachers in Salamanca, Pemán declared, 'Nothing in Spain is laic, or neutral, or indifferent. Everything is either satanic or divinely religious … So, carry into the schools a military sense and even a sense of being a militiaman … Teach them the meaning of the Yoke and the Arrows [the Falange symbol], these beautiful, magnificent symbols that speak of the poised spirit of the New Spain, hard and authoritarian like the yoke yet free and audacious like the arrows.'[119] Later in the year, he attended, in Burgos, a mass meeting of 12,000 Falangist and 9,000 Carlist students which he happily described in his diary as presenting 'a marvellous Hitlerian image'. However, he was distressed that the two groups stood in separate blocks, distinguished by their different uniforms, the Falangists with their blue shirts and the Carlists with their red berets. He lamented not only the lack of unity but also Franco's poor oratory which meant he would never make a fascist leader.[120]

As he carried on his work as a propagandist and with the Comisión, his views were becoming ever more extreme. He published a typically incendiary and racist article in mid-December 1936. In response to 'the short-sighted who whisperingly questioned Franco's use of Moorish mercenaries to save Spain', he claimed comically that 'they were returning to Spain to give thanks to Western civilization and to defend it'. It was part of an elaborate conceit in which the barbarism of the East was confronted by the West, consisting of Spain, Morocco, Portugal and Chile, which, for him, 'as a legitimate Spanish phenomenon, acquired a global dimension'. To that group were to be added Fascist Italy and Nazi Germany, which had recently recognized Franco's Spain. To illustrate the opposing forces of Eastern barbarism, he described the aftermath of a battle: 'one day, beneath a bloody-red sunset, I saw the Casa de Campo on the outskirts of Madrid, littered with Russian, Jewish and Senegalese corpses. The world keeps on turning and history repeats itself; once again aggression from the East, once again barbarians at the gate.' The Jews, he was saying, no longer controlled the Republic from afar but now came to fight within Spain.[121]

It is difficult to believe that those who read Pemán's articles or cheered his speeches could actually have understood all of his rhetorical inventions. The same might be said of Pemán himself. In a speech in San Sebastián on 21 January 1937, he spoke of 'the rebel cause's character of imperial universality' and 'shouted out a slogan about the zealous Hispanic essence of the New Way of Thinking'.[122] His enormous body of work was testimony to his gift of what in Spanish is called 'verbal fluency' but might often have been more accurately rendered as 'verbal diarrhoea'. One critic referred to him as 'an exceptionally clever columnist who knew how to say nothing in a highly charming way'.[123]

In December 1936, he had told the Marqués de Quintanar that he was working on an epic poem about the war. He wrote while accompanying the columns besieging Madrid, reading sections to the officers in the various headquarters and command posts. It would become *Poema de la bestia y el ángel*, another Manichaean interpretation of Spanish politics and society that would be one of the most important anti-Semitic texts produced in Spain. In the words of Herbert Southworth, it was a lyrical transcription of *The Protocols of the Elders of Zion*. Over the next months, Pemán did public readings of the draft text.[124] The extracts were effectively incitements to violence based on the racist devaluation of the enemy that was a constant of Pemán's speeches. In May 1937, he declared on Radio Nacional that the war was being fought against 'a greasy Jewish and masonic Europe'. Alongside adulation for Franco, he justified the violence and destruction: 'The flames of Irún, Guernica, Lequeitia, Malaga or Baena are like the burning of the stubble to leave the land fertilized for the new harvest. We are going to have, my fellow Spaniards, land clean and flattened on which to lay imperial foundation stones.'[125]

Driven by his hunger for political prominence, Pemán was a willing collaborator in the dissolution of his own monarchist groups, Acción Española and Renovación Española and their incorporation into Franco's newly created single party Falange Española Tradicionalista y de las Juntas Ofensivas Nacional-Sindicalistas, a clumsy fusion of the Falange, the Carlists and every other group on the right. Pemán and his cousin Julián Pemartín acted as brokers between the Carlists and the Falange. As he was to do in relation to many aspects of his career at this time, he later reneged on his links with the Falange in a virtuoso display of risible, and indeed contradictory, sophistry. He denied that he had played any part in the unification, claiming rather that he had merely acquiesced in an imposition from above.[126] This, again, is not true. On 13 September 1936, he confided in another cousin, his lifelong collaborator José Pemartín, his conviction that the forces fighting the Republic should unite within the Falange. He recounted that he had told Franco that, in his view, he and his generals should impose unification within the Falange.[127] On 8 May 1937, the secretary of the newly created Junta Política, Captain Ladislao López Bassa, wrote to Pemán as President of Accion Española with an entirely unthreatening invitation for the entity to become part of FET y de las JONS. Without delay, Pemán replied with 'our enthusiastically affirmative response', proclaiming that Acción Española's members would enter the unified single party 'with great joy and pride'.[128] On 16 May, as President of Acción Española, he led a group to Salamanca to offer Franco their unctuous adhesion to the new single party. He was rewarded some months later by being made one of the fifty members of the Consejo Nacional de FET y de las JONS, Franco's copy of Mussolini's Gran Consiglio del Fascismo. He accepted this prestigious honour secure in the knowledge that it would involve him in no work.[129]

In April 1938, the *Poema de la bestia y el ángel* was published in a luxury edition by the journal *Jerarquía*, edited by the Falangist priest Fermín Yzurdiaga.[130] In fact, Pemán despised Yzurdiaga and his followers for taking their fascism too far from Catholic doctrine. In his diary on 18 October 1937, he had denounced them as 'a watery, vague and narcissistic group'.[131] Nevertheless, he was happy to be published by Yzurdiaga. In his text, the civil war between military rebels and the democratic Republic was portrayed as the battle between Satan and God who had chosen Spain to be the last defender of Western civilization against the threat of 'the red and Semitic East'. This epic struggle was related by the Angel of the Apocalypse. Drawing on *The Protocols of the Elders of Zion*, Pemán blamed the Jews and the masonic lodges for all the ills not only of Spain but also of the entire world. Behind the rhetorical mask of science and liberty, on earth the beast took the form of the 'Elder of Zion' the instruments of whose power were the masonic lodge and the synagogue. The purpose of both, according to Pemán, was the annihilation of Catholic Spain. The 'Elder of Zion' cursed both the earth and the Cross. 'The masonic lodge and the synagogue give battle launching their double curse. First, against the earth, which the Jew hates and persecutes because he loves only portable wealth, as befits his wandering existence. Second, against the Cross, the secular hatred of his race'. Pemán 'explains' the Elder's curse of the earth as motivated by jealousy: 'because my rootless wandering people do not possess their own land, I curse the entire earth'.[132]

This alleged double threat was a veiled reference to the Republic's agrarian reform and its disestablishment of the Catholic Church. As a landowner and a pious Catholic, Pemán was resentful of these measures of the Second Republic, which he saw as the instrument of the Jews: 'The treacherous enemy, the serpent that chokes the throat of Spain and squeezes the life from its body, is the Synagogue, the occult power'. The 'Synagogue' was anti-Semitic shorthand for anything to do with the left.[133] Other explicit contemporary references saw him claim that the assassination of Calvo Sotelo had been the work of a cabal of the Jews, the freemasons and multinationals like Shell and ITT allegedly seeking revenge for his confrontation with international Jewish finance in his efforts to nationalize the oil business and telephone network in Spain. He was either unaware of or chose to ignore the fact that Franco's fuel needs were being met on credit by Texaco.[134] Alongside Pemán's anti-Semitism could be seen his misogyny. In his account of the siege of the Alcázar, he wrote of 'the cries of wild beasts from one thousand men drunk with madness and one thousand filthy whores in the frenzy of hungry, loveless sex'.[135]

Throughout 1938 and 1939, Pemán sent copies of his poem to significant figures of the regime and also to Alfonso XIII. After 1945, however, he ceased to mention it and made every effort to erase it from his biography.[136] As early as 1939, he claimed that the anti-Semitism of *Poema de la bestia y el ángel* did not derive from racist hatred.[137] This was undermined by the poem's stereotypical descriptions of the Elders of Zion with 'crows' noses and goats' beards'. He describes the fictional Elders of Zion 'Leaning over the map of Spain, one hundred hooked noses like crows' beaks and one hundred goats' beards, plotting the division of Spain, God's second tunic'.[138] Racial hatred is also exuded in his malicious recreation of one of the visits made by the Socialist deputy Margarita Nelken to the besieged Alcázar of Toledo in August 1936:

> And that evening, silhouetted against a blood-red twilight, a blonde Valkyrie, her hair streaming in the wind, fills the air with rancour: 'On the stones of the Alcázar,' she cries, 'our militiamen will lie with your women.' The bleeding fingernails of her painted hands profane the serene evening and the sweet fields of Toledo replete with golden bees. Accursed and damned be you, Hebrew woman, mother of a bastard child. By name, Margarita! The name of a flower and the spirit of a hyena![139]

There exist photographs of Pemán in 'the sweet fields of Toledo' accompanying Pepe Sáinz Nothnagel, the Jefe Provincial of the Toledo Falange, surveying Republican corpses.[140]

In late May and early June 1938, Pemán and Millán Astray visited Italy together to take part in a huge celebration of Italo-Spanish solidarity. While there, Millán Astray, who fancied that he resembled the Italian poet–adventurer Gabriele D'Annunzio, asked Pemán, 'Is it true that I resemble D'Annunzio?' Although he had never seen D'Annunzio, Pemán replied, 'I have no doubt that your bald pate like a Renaissance dome and your one eye make you rather like him physically.'[141] They were invited to stand on either side of Mussolini as he presided over a gathering of 150,000 Black Shirts. In his speech, Pemán, announced as a representative of 'the new fascist Spain', exulted in the growing dominance of fascism: 'We are en route to the Fascist Peace, heir to the Pax Romana.' He was photographed, alongside Millán, standing rigidly to attention in Falangist uniform, raising his right arm in the fascist salute.[142] So mesmerized was he by the Duce and the discipline of the marching Fascists that, on his return to Spain, he wrote an adoring portrait of the Fascist leader under the title 'Straight from the Horse's Mouth'. Afterwards, through diplo-

matic channels, he asked for a signed photograph of the Duce.[143] His
adoration of the Duce was transmitted in the *Poema de la bestia y el
ángel* where he wrote of 'the Eagle of Rome': 'the gaze of a Caesar,
clear and semi-divine, with a cranium round like a steel helmet and
a prominent lip that challenges Destiny'.[144]

Still bedazzled by his encounter with Mussolini, at a vast rally in
Seville on 18 July 1938 to celebrate the second anniversary of the
military rebellion he opened his lengthy speech by addressing the
audience as 'Comrades of the Falange'. Then he launched into a
fervent justification of the existence of FET y de las JONS that was in
total contradiction to his previous writings on the glories of hereditary monarchy. In the course of his harangue, he praised German
Nazism and Italian Fascism as 'movements twinned with ours'. He
then went on to claim that the single party, 'this fascist formula', was
the only way to unite society with those in power. His recital of
historical precedents for this included the slave societies of Athens
and Sparta. He referred to the Secretary General of FET y de las
JONS as 'our secretary' and praised Queipo de Llano's 'justice', his
'death penalties for those who poison the minds of the workers'. He
ended by proudly calling on his 'comrades one and all' to remember
that he was 'a member of the Consejo Nacional but above all a poet
who loves Spain and wants a glorious future for Spain within the
Falange'.[145]

He was probably unaware of the contradictions in his panegyric,
more a case perhaps of cognitive dissonance than of sheer hypocrisy.
Pemán's erstwhile comrades from Acción Española were already so
irritated by 'his Falangist caprices' that they had begun to distance
themselves from him. However, this speech was so frenzied in its
Falangist enthusiasm that senior monarchists like Eugenio Vegas
Latapie and Jorge Vigón wrote furious letters reprimanding him.
They were particularly annoyed by his metaphor about Franco's
unification of the various forces into FET y de las JONS, in which he
described the Caudillo as a sculptor in wood who, after completing
his work, sweeps up the leftover chippings. If Vigón's letter was ironic,
Vegas Latapie's was a harsh and unrelenting criticism of Pemán for
abandoning the ideals of Acción Española in order to associate with
those who enjoyed the sinecures, prebends and other privileges of the

Falange. There was an implicit accusation of cowardice since, unlike Vegas, Pemán had not fought at the battle front. Vegas's friendship with Pemán remained cordial but was never quite the same again. Vegas's memoirs portray him as a charming egoist, only interested in his own advancement.[146]

In an article published in 1967, referring to one of many photographs of himself in Falangist uniform Pemán declared airily, 'I was never formally a member of any political party or group other than the Unión Patriótica to which I was taken by Miguel Primo de Rivera, who said it was not political.' He dismissed his use of Falangist insignia while a member of the Consejo Nacional as a meaningless formality.[147] He had forgotten the pleasure he used to derive from the pre-eminence that it gave him. On 27 January 1939, for instance, to celebrate the fall of Barcelona, wearing the blue shirt of the Falange and the Carlist red beret, he presided over a huge parade in Cadiz in his capacity as a Consejero Nacional de Falange Española Tradicionalista y de las JONS. In his speech, he crowed that Franco's victories were a humiliation for the democracies.[148] At this time, he was writing articles dismissing Catalan and Basque as minor dialects of Spanish, using the same terminology that he had used during the fiercely anti-Catalan dictatorship of Primo de Rivera.[149]

Inevitably, he wanted it both ways. In his article, he praised Falangism as 'a leaven of enthusiasm and as a call for social justice'. He admitted that a couple of years previously he had taken part in an event in Cadiz at which he had sung the Falangist hymn 'Cara al Sol' while making the fascist stiff-arm salute. Nevertheless, as always with an eye on public relations, given that Spain was at the time trying to gain entry into the European Common Market, he acknowledged that 'it is damaging to the interests of the Fatherland to keep gestures, hymns and uniforms that might be out of date'. The page on which his article appeared also carried, presumably without deliberate irony, an advertisement for a laxative for constipation sufferers.[150]

Not long after the publication of the *Poema de la bestia y el ángel*, Pemán was commissioned by his friend Pedro Sainz Rodríguez, now Minister of Education, to write the official history of Spain for children. Issued in September 1939, with an unctuous dedication to Franco, what he produced was an obligatory text in schools and was thus a highly profitable enterprise. As in his wartime speeches at the front, his central theme was the constant crusade against Spain's enemies. In the first volume, which proceeded from the earliest times to 1504, the enemies of civilization were the Arabs and the Jews. Bizarrely, the two were seen as united. Pemán's contempt for both saw him dismiss the glories of Arab civilization as a superficial varnish masking the savagery and barbarism and depict the Jews as motivated only by their hatred of Spain and of Christianity. 'The Jews in Spain', he claimed, 'were real spies and political conspirators, who lived in a secret alliance with the Moors, as the hope of the Turks ... They were organized in real secret societies based on intrigue and conspiracy in which they prepared horrendous crimes.'[151]

He depicted the Inquisition as a benevolent institution whose great achievement was to cleanse Spain of the Jews. In a feeble effort to distance Spain from the racist policy of the Third Reich, he asserted that the expulsion of the Jews was driven by 'the highest religious and patriotic motives and not by any question of racial hatred'. The key to the reconquest of Spain from Islam was to secure Seville and Cordoba, 'cleansing them of Jews'.[152] In the second volume, the Arabs and Jews were replaced as the most vicious enemies of Spain by Protestantism and freemasonry.[153] Typical was his bigoted account of the complex process whereby the feudal system was dismantled by means of the disentailment of ecclesiastical and aristocratic lands. The liberal Prime Minister Juan de Dios Álvarez Mendizábal, who was of Jewish origins, was frustrated in his hope that the expropriation, and sale, of the lands of the religious orders would both resolve the financial problems created for the crown by the Carlist wars of the 1830s and lay the basis for the future prosperity of Spain by creating a self-sustaining smallholding peasantry. However, the confiscated properties were sold at auction in large blocks which meant that they were far beyond the means of even existing smallholders. For Pemán, Mendizábal was just a Jewish thief engaged in the somewhat contradictory enterprise of enriching the bourgeoisie and carrying out the revolution.[154] The author of this entirely Manichaean interpretation of the history of Spain, and indeed the principal advocate of the idea of the clash between Spain and the anti-Spain, in later life mocked the idea. He insinuated that it derived

from what he called the Republican interpretation of Spanish history
in terms of goodies and baddies.[155]

In late March 1939, Pemán was at the headquarters of General
Solchaga. On the 28th, he accompanied the first of Franco's troops to
enter Madrid and announced the victory to the nation from the
studios of Unión Radio, which had been seized by fifth columnists.
His fanciful account described the chivalrous attitude of the occupying troops towards prisoners of the Republican army and denounced
the pillage by anarchists of the homes of his friends. He claimed that,
within two days, it was back to normal.[156] Many years later, he wrote
a more sugary account of those days, in which, ignoring the repression unleashed on Madrid, he praised what he called the return to
normality.[157] His role in the war was celebrated on 17 July in a massive
ceremony in which the capitals of every province sent him a dedicated parchment illustrated with a famous local landscape or
monument. In a tone of false modesty, his speech summed up what
he had done 'for God and the Fatherland': 'In their service, I ranged
over Spain from north to south, from east to west, I embraced Spain's
earth with the ambition of an anxious bridegroom and on this earth
I gave the war my grain of sand.'[158]

In a book written around this time, Pemán proclaimed his
commitment to fascism. He justified this with the bizarre claim that
the Spanish variant of fascism was a religious phenomenon. However,
that did not inhibit his praise for Hitler and Mussolini.[159] In 1940, he
produced an obsequious portrait of Franco which is still to be found
on the website of the Fundación Nacional Francisco Franco. He
portrayed the providential Caudillo as 'fulfilling the work of God'
and praised his 'absolute and irreproachable austerity'. If ignorance
could excuse this portrait of the corrupt Caudillo, it is difficult to
know how best to explain his gloss on Franco's war effort and the
subsequent repression:

He was able to distribute in exact doses forgiveness, punishment
and instruction ... We will never be able to show adequate gratitude to the Caudillo for the absolute even-handedness and
calmness with which he faced his difficult balancing act. He was
the magnificent, rock-steady surgeon concerned as much with the

anaesthetic as with doing his job. He conquered the red zone as if he were caressing it: saving lives, keeping bombing to a minimum.[160]

The ever forgetful Pemán clearly did not remember his broadcast from Radio Castilla on 8 December in which he described how, from the Cerro de los Ángeles, he had seen flames rising from the rooftops of Madrid: 'Nationalist artillery and aircraft, before taking Madrid, are first purifying it.'[161] Moreover, in this eulogy of Franco and also in his controversial tribute to Calvo Sotelo, he seemed oblivious to the contradictions between his praise for Franco's dictatorship and his advocacy of the hereditary monarchy. The only explanation is that he was sufficiently naive to believe that Franco was merely preparing the way for a restoration.

Astonishingly, Pemán later claimed that he was never excessive in his admiration for Franco.[162] Again, his memory failed him. Around the time that he was writing his eulogy of Franco, the Caudillo was authorizing substantial government funds to pay for the imaginary synthetic gasoline offered to him by an Austrian petty thief and confidence trickster, Albert von Filek. Franco had been convinced that Filek had rejected spectacular international offers for his invention and had presented the idea to the Caudillo simply out of personal devotion. Eventually, after proper tests had been carried out, the scam was exposed and Filek imprisoned.[163] Pemán, however, wrote later of the episode in nonsensical terms: 'I am sure that Franco never believed in the magic gasoline. But it did not suit him to expose the myth lest someone fell into the trap.'[164]

The early triumphs of the Third Reich accentuated the fascist tendencies of the Movimiento, as the Falange Española Tradicionalista y de las JONS was coming to be called. This concerned Pemán only because it seemed to threaten the eventual return of the monarchy. It certainly did not diminish his anti-Semitic enthusiasms. A clash came during the cycle of lectures held in 1940 at the Academia de Jurisprudencia to celebrate the life of Calvo Sotelo. Pemán closed the series on 13 July. In his speech, he attributed the inspiration for the Movimiento to his hero which, by implication, took the glory from José Antonio Primo de Rivera, whom he praised for his lofty social origins, his poetry and his profession as a lawyer.[165] Immediately afterwards, Pemán was congratulated by Miguel Primo de Rivera. On the following day, he took the train to Cadiz. That evening, a Falangist arrived in an official car and gave him an astonishingly aggressive letter from Miguel Primo de Rivera in which he accused him of being 'an enemy of the regime' and of hating José Antonio. He said that, if Pemán denied this, he would be 'adding cowardice to his deceitfulness'. Informed by the porter of Pemán's building that he had gone to Cadiz, Primo de Rivera wrote, 'I regret that this has prevented me acting on my decision to slap you, which I will do the next time that I see you.' The reference to slapping him was a challenge to a duel. Apparently, the letter was written at the behest of Ramón Serrano Suñer, who had taken offence because he believed that the speech diminished the role of his friend José Antonio and the Falange.[166]

Pemán's first reaction was to write to Miguel Primo de Rivera explaining that he had misinterpreted the lecture. However, having drafted an emollient letter on 16 July, he refrained from sending it when he discovered that numerous copies of Primo de Rivera's letter had been circulated within the Francoist establishment. Now highly alarmed and indignant, Pemán consulted his friend General Varela, who was Minister of War. Varela suggested that he go to Madrid and arrange that his seconds in the apparently inevitable duel be their mutual friend the Carlist General Ricardo Rada and the Under-Secretary of the Ministry, General Camilo Alonso Vega, who was a lifelong friend of Franco. Miguel Primo de Rivera named as his seconds two Falangists, the writer Manuel Halcón and Manuel Mora Figueroa, the Civil Governor of Cadiz. The situation was worthy of Viennese operetta since Pemán, his opponent and their four seconds were all friends. Moreover, Pemán had sent the text of his speech to Franco via Jorge Vigón. Franco was hardly likely to share Serrano Suñer's disquiet since Pemán's speech had implicitly proclaimed him king by suggesting that he could be succeeded only by a monarch: 'Today Spain has a single command. She now has a monarchy in the purest sense.' Accordingly, Franco told Alonso Vega to resolve the matter quietly. Halcón, Rada and Alonso Vega easily persuaded the only-too-willing Miguel Primo de Rivera to withdraw his challenge.[167] Nevertheless, for some days afterwards Pemán had police protection at his home in Cadiz. Eventually, friendly letters between the two antagonists restored peace.[168]

Serrano Suñer's role in the affair could be perceived in further consequences for Pemán. On 23 July 1940, the dour Minister of Education, José Ibáñez Martín, had Pemán removed from his post as Director of the Real Academia. For nearly two years, until May 1942, the press was ordered not to give him any publicity and he was prohibited from writing in *ABC*. Serrano Suñer ensured that his membership of the Consejo Nacional of the Falange was not renewed. Pemán responded by going on a lecture tour in Spanish America. (He was eventually restored to the academy in October 1944.)[169] The enmity between Pemán and Serrano Suñer was soon intensified. In the run-up to his fall from power in September 1942, Serrano Suñer was facing intense hostility from senior generals. At a private banquet in honour of a friend who had been awarded an important military decoration, a speech by Camilo Alonso Vega was followed by another by Pemán. Pemán made a veiled reference to what was perceived as Serrano Suñer's excessive power: 'The peace won by a soldier should be administered by that soldier.' The audience of officers and monarchists cheered Pemán loudly. Inevitably, word reached Serrano who persuaded Franco that Pemán had made a subversive speech in favour of an uprising. Needless to say, the subsequent investigation exonerated Pemán.[170]

Six weeks before his death in Rome on 28 February 1941, Alfonso XIII abdicated in favour of his son Juan. Almost immediately Vegas Latapie and Pemán began to work assiduously for the restoration of the monarchy. Vegas wrote to Don Juan on 22 February urging him to appoint a secretary and a council. Among the names that he suggested as its members was that of Pemán. Eventually, Pemán was named head of the Consejo Privado, which included Sainz Rodríguez and Gil Robles among others.[171]

The German invasion of Russia that June delighted Pemán, although after Stalingrad he began to harbour doubts about the Third Reich. Nevertheless, it was not until much later that he began gradually to rewrite the history of his admiration for Hitler. Similarly, although slightly uncomfortable about Franco's failure to restore the monarchy, he was slow to associate with the monarchist opponents of the Caudillo and remained sycophantically loyal to the regime from which he drew his substantial ministerial pension. Things changed with the defeat of the Third Reich in May 1945.[172] He began gradually to establish some distance from the Francoist regime from which he continued to derive considerable benefit. Franco had appointed him in February that year as a *procurador* (unelected deputy) in his pseudo-parliament, the Cortes, which he had fabricated two years before to curry favour with the Allies. One-third of the members were directly nominated by the Generalísimo.

The changing of Pemán's tune was a reflection of Franco's modified policy. His two-faced cynicism matched that of his master. With an eye on the Western Allies, Franco began to place less emphasis on the Falange and slightly more on the regime's deeply conservative variant of Christian Democracy. For foreign consumption, he introduced the conservative Catholic Alberto Martín Artajo as Foreign Minister. Maintaining an iron control over foreign policy himself, Franco used Martín Artajo as the acceptable face of his regime. Artajo told Pemán that he spoke on the telephone for at least one hour every day with Franco and used special earphones to leave his hands free to take notes. Pemán cruelly wrote in his diary, 'Franco dictates international policy and Artajo is the minister-stenographer.'[173]

When Don Juan de Borbón took up residence in the fashionable Portuguese resort of Estoril, near Lisbon, in February 1946, Pemán was one of the 458 signatories of a collective letter of greeting to him known as *el Saluda*. All were prominent figures of Francoist society. Franco was apoplectic with rage, telling his cabinet, 'This is a declaration of war … They must be crushed like worms.' Perceiving the *Saluda* as a masonic conspiracy, he announced that he would put all the signatories in prison without trial. Dissuaded from doing that, he instead went through the list of signatories, listing appropriate punishments ranging from withdrawal of passports to tax inspections or dismissal from their posts. Pemán was not among those punished. His loyalty to Franco was beyond question. Moreover, he wrote a sinuously sycophantic letter to Franco's cabinet secretary and effective deputy, Luis Carrero Blanco, in which he managed to stress that his devotion to Franco was in no way diminished by his commitment to the monarchy. He expressed his 'admiration and affection for the general who won the war and to whom Spain owes so much'. His position could be summed up as 'no Franco without a king; no king without Franco'.[174] Unlike his friends Eugenio Vegas Latapie, Pedro Sainz Rodríguez and the Marqués de Quintanar, he did not go into exile.

After the Second World War, Pemán concentrated on his literary activities as playwright and newspaper columnist. His principal political activity, which falls outside the scope of this chapter, was aimed at the restoration of the monarchy. Everything that he did in that context was carefully framed within a loudly proclaimed loyalty to Franco and his regime. Indeed, those elements of the regime that Franco himself was keen to erase were attributed by Pemán to the Falange, with which he himself had once been so closely identified.[175] He was intelligent enough to see that things were changing and cynical enough to keep his views to his private diary. On 15 December 1946, he had lunch with Martín Artajo, who told him that Franco actually believed in the Falange and treated the Falangist ministers as if they were family. Pemán wrote in his diary, 'My God, if they had told me that Franco had a lover, it would have seemed bad and really surprised me, but this is worse: he has got a "conviction". I always thought he didn't have one because not having one was the key to surviving with the easy, cold agility which underlay his greatest successes – his capacity for calculation, coldness and ingratitude.'[176]

By the early 1950s, he had returned to his habitual – but now grudging – admiration for Franco, writing of the consummate skill with which the Caudillo played the various regime factions against one another.[177] In 1957, he was named President of the Consejo of Don Juan. As he gradually realized that Franco had no intention of naming Don Juan as his successor, there were expressions of frustration, albeit confined to his diary. He wrote on 14 October 1958: 'Franco is driving the automobile of Spain as if it were a heavy lorry, that is to say, with Gallego malice and an infantry general's lack of sophistication.'[178]

In April 1970, at the request of some friends, Josep Benet, Albert Manent, Jordi Pujol and Salvador Casanovas, he wrote a column in *ABC* in defence of the Catalan language. This was in response to an intervention by Adolfo Muñoz Alonso in the debate on educational reform in which he had spoken of the 'virus' of regional languages. Although Muñoz Alonso's offending remark was removed from the record of the sessions, it caused a scandal.[179] Pemán's column was a far cry from the ferocious anti-Catalanism of his articles in the 1930s. It was notable that he seemed to be attacking Muñoz Alonso as a Falangist. His defence of the Catalan language was a symptom of his flexible memory and of his ability to evolve with the times. And, after all, change was in the air.

During that long process whereby Pemán freed himself of his past on the extreme right, he seemed to live by a principle that he had adumbrated in the 1920s. Addressing those who were uncomfortable about abandoning the old monarchist parties to join the Unión Patriótica for fear of being thought turncoats, he had declared, 'I appeal to those Spaniards who are inhibited by the prejudice about "changing one's shirt", when to change one's shirt if it is dirty or ripped by use is logical, hygienic and even good form.'[180] Having held numerous political positions during the 1920s in the Unión Patriótica and the Asamblea Nacional, in the 1930s as a leader of the Unión Monárquica Nacional, as a parliamentary deputy and as President of Acción Española, and during the civil war as a minister in Franco's first government and as a member of the Consejo Nacional of the Falange, it is notable that, in a memoir published in 1976, Pemán could speak of 'my lack of any active political vocation'. It is as if, with the death of Franco, he thought that his own Francoist past was expunged. With an equal lack of self-knowledge – or mendaciousness – he could claim that, in the meeting with Franco that led to his being given the role of itinerant propagandist for the rebels and effectively minister of education, he had been comforted by his conviction 'that Franco knew that I had neither ambition nor even interest in politics'.[181]

Pemán died in Cadiz on 9 July 1981. Over time, his physical appearance had evolved from that of the typically moustachioed Falangist fanatic to something nearer that of an owl-like cleric. To his dying day, he maintained his deep admiration for Franco.[182] Despite the image carefully cultivated in his book about his meetings with the Dictator, the admiration was far from mutual. In Franco's table talk, there are numerous complaints about what he saw as Pemán's malicious tongue and untruths. Having said that, Franco was not given to speaking highly of anyone with the possible exception of Hitler and Mussolini.[183] In recent years, a growing awareness of the dark side of Pemán and his role in the civil war has inspired efforts to remove his name from some of the many streets named after him in towns across Spain. They were deflected in the case of Jerez by renaming the street Poeta José María Pemán.[184]

5

The Messenger: Gonzalo de Aguilera

In a notorious boast, an aristocratic landowner with an estate in the province of Salamanca told foreigners that, on the day that the Spanish Civil War broke out, he had lined up his labourers, selected six of them and shot them as a lesson to the others. A retired cavalry officer, his name was Gonzalo de Aguilera y Munro. His estate, Dehesa del Carrascal de Sanchiricones, was located between Vecinos and Matilla de los Caños, two villages respectively 30 and 35 kilometres to the south-west of Salamanca. The claim that he had committed this extreme atrocity was actually untrue. The archives of the Asociación de Memoria Histórica de Salamanca have no record of any such act. However, there is a grain of truth in the claim.[1]

On 12 August 1936, four agricultural labourers were murdered at an estate in nearby San Pedro de Rozados, Dehesa de Continos, the property of one of Aguilera's friends. The executions were carried out by Francoist soldiers. It is likely that Aguilera approved of and even envied what the owner of Continos had done. Knowing about it, he perhaps fantasized about his involvement and later exaggerated it to stress his identification with the rebel cause.[2] Whatever the basis in fact, the sentiments behind Aguilera's boast were representative of the hatreds that had smouldered in the Spanish countryside over the previous years. Nevertheless, in many letters to his wife during the civil war, Aguilera demonstrated concern for the domestic servants in the Dehesa del Carrascal de Sanchiricones and for the farm workers on his estate. This was linked to a constant preoccupation with the various seasonal tasks involved with the health and saleability of livestock.[3]

The cold and calculated violence of what happened at the Dehesa de Continos reflected an attitude common among the big landowners of the *latifundio* regions of Spain. The violent social conflicts of the period from 1918 to 1921, known as the 'three Bolshevik years' (*trienio bolchevique*), had been crushed by military repression but the consequent hatreds continued to smoulder on both sides. The strikes of the *trienio* had outraged the landlords, who could not forgive the insubordination of labourers (*braceros*) whom they considered to be almost subhuman. Accordingly, the paternalism which had somewhat mitigated the daily brutality of the day labourers' lives came to an abrupt end. The social divisions were hardened after April 1931, when the Second Republic's attempts at agrarian reform saw the landowners flouting legislation governing rural labour and 'locking out' unionized labour either by leaving land uncultivated or simply by refusing to offer work. Workers who were hired were paid starvation wages. The gathering of acorns, normally kept for pigs, or of windfall olives, the watering of beasts and even the gathering of firewood were denounced as 'collective kleptomania.'[4] Hungry peasants caught doing such things were subjected to savage beatings by the Civil Guard or armed estate guards.[5]

After the fall of the Republican–Socialist coalition in the autumn of 1933, the landowners had returned to the semi-feudal relations of dependence that had been the norm before 1931. Consistent infractions of labour legislation led in the summer of 1934 to a national harvest strike being called by the Socialist landworkers' union, the Federación Nacional de Trabajadores de la Tierra. Despite being legal, the strike was fiercely repressed by the Minister of the Interior, Rafael Salazar Alonso, a representative of the landowners of one of the most conflictive provinces, Badajoz. The FNTT had been crippled, union members were harassed by the Civil Guard, and estate security was tightened to prevent hunger being alleviated by poaching or the theft of crops. The south was badly hit by drought in 1935, unemployment rose to more than 40 per cent in some places and beggars thronged the streets of the towns. Living in close proximity, the hungry and the well-to-do rural middle and upper classes regarded each other with fear and resentment. Hatreds were intensified during the right-wing campaign for the elections of February

1936 while natural disaster intensified social tension. After the prolonged drought of 1935, early 1936 brought rainstorms that ruined the olive harvest and damaged wheat and barley crops. Left-wing victory in the elections coincided with even higher unemployment. Labour legislation was reinforced and workers were 'placed' (*alojados*) on uncultivated estates. Landowners were infuriated by signs that peasant submissiveness was at an end. Those that they expected to be servile were now assertively demanding reform. The shift in the balance of power provoked the anger and the fear of the *latifundistas*. Many of them joined, financed or expectantly awaited news of the military plot to overthrow the Republic.[6]

When the civil war began, in *latifundio* areas of the Republican zone many landowners were in serious danger of their lives from the local left. Aguilera's boast, whether or not based on fact, was of a piece with the actions of other landowners who took retaliatory measures in advance. Many landowners joined the uprising, accompanied Franco's columns and played an active role in selecting victims in captured villages for execution.[7] The hatred of the landowners for the rural proletariat found an appropriate instrument in Franco's African columns. Explicit parallels were drawn at the time between the left in mainland Spain and the Rif tribesmen, the 'crimes' of the reds in resisting the military uprising being seen as identical to the 'crimes' of the tribesmen who massacred Spanish troops at Annual in Morocco in 1921. The role of the African columns in 1936 was seen as identical to that of the Regulares and Legionaries who relieved Melilla in 1921.[8] The savagery visited upon the towns conquered by Spanish colonial forces was simply a repetition of what they did when they attacked a Moroccan village.

The attitude of the military rebels towards the left and towards the rural and industrial working class made sense only in terms of the post-colonial mentality. The Africanistas and the landowners viewed the landless peasants and the industrial proletariat as a racially inferior, subject colonial race. When they talked about the left, they did so in pathological terms. It was brilliantly summed up by the correspondent of the *Chicago Daily Tribune*, Edmond Taylor:

The enemy was a complex molecule of a spiritual poison called communism for convenience, but liberalism was the most deadly individual element in it, and the most hated. Introduced into the human organism, this poison acted like a germ virus; not only incurable, but infectious. Certain men known as the Leaders had perversely inoculated themselves with the poison, and like Satan in Catholic mythology, were deliberately trying to spread the infection as widely as they could. As the incarnation of evil these men deserved punishment. Their victims who might have been good Spaniards if they had not had the bad luck to be infected by the Leaders, did not merit punishment properly speaking, but they had to be shot in a humane way because they were incurable and might infect others.[9]

Another journalist, John Whitaker of the *Chicago Daily News*, put it more bluntly: 'The use of the Moors and the wholesale execution of prisoners and civilians were the trump cards of the "best" elements in Spain ... I talked with all varieties of them by the hundreds. If I were to sum up their social philosophy, it would be simple in the extreme – they were outnumbered by the masses; they feared the masses; and they proposed to thin down the numbers of the masses.'[10] Edmond Taylor found that this was a view shared by Captain Gonzalo de Aguilera, the Salamanca landowner who claimed, mendaciously, that he had shot six of his workers: prisoners 'were worth taking because you could question them and it saved ammunition, but not worth keeping, so they were not kept'.[11] This was in the early days of the war. By early 1937, prisoners were kept alive with a view to incorporating many of them into the rebel forces.

This idea might have figured in such crude terms in the private conversations of army officers. In public, however, rebel propagandists thought it more respectable to talk of a 'movement' to put an end to the Jewish–masonic–Bolshevik conspiracy in order to defend Spain, or, to be more precise, a particular and partisan definition of Spain. From this had evolved the idea of a war to the death between Spain and the anti-Spain. A revealing gloss on this notion was given by a prosecutor during a court martial in Seville in late 1937:

Spanish grandeur was at its height in the sixteenth century, when the sun never set on her dominions. Our great century, the century of the mystics, the saints and the artists. The century of the Spanish Empire! Well, do you know how many inhabitants our Fatherland had then when it was truly great? Twelve million! What does it matter if half the population has to disappear if that is what is required for us to reconquer our Empire?[12]

During the march of Franco's troops to Madrid, the chief reporter of the United Press in Europe, Webb Miller, was deeply shaken by the atrocities that he witnessed at Santa Olalla between Talavera and Toledo. In Toledo, after the liberation of the Alcázar, there were pools of blood in the streets and the footprints of those who had tracked through it were evidence of the profusion of summary executions. A Francoist officer explained the policy to him: 'we are fighting an idea. The idea is in the brain, and to kill it we have to kill the man. We must kill everyone who has that "red" idea.'[13] One of the more extreme versions of that theory was expounded by Captain Aguilera who, during the civil war, was a key liaison with the foreign press in the rebel zone.

His ideas were outrageous, but because he expounded them so eloquently, in virtually native English, and without inhibition, journalists found him compellingly quotable. Aguilera was a polo-playing cavalryman and convinced all of the journalists with whom he worked that he was a great all-round sportsman. He was also the eleventh Conde de Alba de Yeltes, a *grande de España* and a major landowner with estates in the provinces of Salamanca and Cáceres. When he told John Whitaker, 'We've got to kill and kill and kill, you understand,' he was merely expressing the views of his commanding officer, General Mola.[14]

Aguilera recounted this biological theory of the origins of the war to Charles Foltz, the correspondent of the Associated Press:

'Sewers!' growled the Count. 'Sewers caused all our troubles. The masses in this country are not like your Americans, nor even like the British. They are slave stock. They are good for nothing but slaves and only when they are used as slaves are they happy. But we,

the decent people, made the mistake of giving them modern hous-
ing in the cities where we have our factories. We put sewers in these
cities, sewers which extend right down to the workers' quarters. Not
content with the work of God, we thus interfere with His Will. The
result is that the slave stock increases. Had we no sewers in Madrid,
Barcelona, and Bilbao, all these Red leaders would have died in
their infancy instead of exciting the rabble and causing good
Spanish blood to flow. When the war is over, we should destroy the
sewers. The perfect birth control for Spain is the birth control God
intended us to have. Sewers are a luxury to be reserved for those
who deserve them, the leaders of Spain, not the slave stock.'

A British journalist who laughed at these bizarre notions was expelled
from Nationalist Spain after Captain Aguilera had denounced him as
'a dangerous Red'.[15]

Aguilera was far from unique. Four officers in charge of the foreign
press figure frequently in the later accounts of correspondents. But
the most frequently named were the head of Franco's press service,
Luis Bolín, and of course Aguilera. Bolín had been made an honorary
captain in the Foreign Legion as a reward for his role in securing
Franco's passage from the Canary Islands to Morocco. Wearing
breeches and high boots, against which he would rap a riding crop,
he strode menacingly among the correspondents with a fierce scowl.
Despite the fact that 'he couldn't fix a bayonet or put a clip into a rifle',
he wore the uniform always and behaved in a boorish manner that
embarrassed the real officers of the corps. According to Sir Percival
Phillips of the *Daily Telegraph*, they despised and detested him: 'They
think he has no right to be strutting about in their uniform.'[16] Bolín,
according to Noel Monks of the *Daily Express*, would spit on piles of
freshly executed Republican prisoners, many of them mere boys,
saying 'Vermin!'[17] He was loathed and feared by the foreign press
corps because of his frequent threats to shoot newspapermen.[18] He
would gain a kind of lasting fame by dint of his arrest and mistreat-
ment of Arthur Koestler shortly after the Nationalist capture of
Malaga in February 1937.[19]

While Arthur Koestler was on death row in a Francoist prison in
Seville, a terrifying experience recounted in his book *Dialogue with*

Death, a major international campaign for his release was launched. Victor Cazalet, the Conservative MP for Chippenham, a prominent member of the pro-Franco Friends of National Spain Committee, wrote to his friend the Marqués Merry del Val enquiring about the situation. Alfonso Merry del Val, one-time Spanish Ambassador to London, replied on 12 April 1937 with a letter replete with untruths which was typical of the attitudes of the Spanish upper classes. Both mendacious regarding Koestler's plight and insensitively oblivious to the fact that Victor Cazalet was an advocate for a Jewish homeland in Palestine, Merry wrote 'Concerning the bolshie Jew Koestler, whose scarlet red activities are of international fame, I can tell you he is well and enjoying the best of health in Seville.' He went on to say: 'the whole fuss kicked up about him is merely a newspaper stunt'.[20]

Of Bolín's other subordinates, one, Major Manuel de Lambarri y Yanguas, was a rather amiable bohemian who, in civilian life, had worked in Paris as an illustrator for the magazine *Vogue*.[21] Another, Captain Ignacio Rosales, held views only slightly more refined than those of Aguilera.[22] According to Virginia Cowles, the American journalist who was writing for the *Daily Telegraph* and the *Sunday Times*, Rosales was a Barcelona millionaire.[23] He explained to his charges 'that the masses cannot be taught; that they need a touch of the whip for they are like dogs and will mind only the whip. There is no understanding in such people, they must be got in hand. Held in hand where they belong.' Like many officers, from Mola downwards, Rosales shared the biological explanation of class conflict in Spain: 'an influx of strains inimical to Spain through the industrial cities of the coast; Spain must cleanse herself of this taint in her bloodstream. She is purifying herself and will rise up from this trial new and strong. The streets of Madrid will run red with blood, but after – after – there will be no unemployment problem.'[24] In fact, 'organic determinism' was a central part of Spanish right-wing thinking from José Ortega y Gasset's *España invertebrada* to Ernesto Giménez Caballero's *Genio de España*. It was central to the mindset of army officers.[25] Aguilera later expounded the idea in virulent terms in his unpublished book 'Cartas a un sobrino' (Letters to a nephew).[26]

Franco himself told the correspondent of the French newspaper *Candide*, in August 1938, that fascism varied according to national characteristics because each nation was an organism and each national fascism its immune system's reaction, 'a defence mechanism, a sign of wanting to live, of not wanting to die, that, at certain times, takes over an entire people'.[27] For Franco, as for Aguilera and Rosales, the logic of this argument was that any individual whose ideas did not fit with their conception of the *patria* was a symptom of a disease and therefore had to be eradicated.

Aguilera repeated his organicist theory to Whitaker:

You know what's wrong with Spain? Modern plumbing! In healthier times – I mean healthier times spiritually, you understand – plague and pestilence used to slaughter the Spanish masses. Held them down to proper proportions, you understand. Now with modern sewage disposal and the like, they multiply too fast. They're like animals, you understand, and you can't expect them not to be infected with the virus of Bolshevism. After all, rats and lice carry the plague. Now I hope you can understand what we mean by the regeneration of Spain.[28]

Whitaker travelled with the senior staff of the African columns that marched on Madrid. His daily conversations with them convinced him that Aguilera was completely representative of their mentality, differing from the majority only in that he spoke perfect English and had no inhibitions about recounting his theories to any journalist that he could back into a corner.

Aguilera would wet his throat with another tumbler of brandy and proceed, to the approving nods and comments of other leading officers of Franco's army. 'It's our program, you understand, to exterminate a third of the male population of Spain. That will clean up the country and rid us of the proletariat. It's sound economically, too. Never have any more unemployment in Spain, you understand. We'll make other changes. For instance, we'll be done with this nonsense of equality for women. I breed horses and animals generally, you understand. I know all about women. There'll be no more nonsense about subjecting a gentleman to court action. If a woman's unfaithful to him, he'll shoot her like a dog. It's disgusting, any interference of a court between a man and a wife.'[29]

The misogyny revealed to Whitaker had clearly festered since its early appearances in his letters to his then lover, Inés Luna. There, he had written of his desire to 'educate you to my taste', declared that 'The wife must be under no influence other than that of her husband' and talked of his need to change her character.[30]

Captain Aguilera was the son of the tenth Conde de Alba de Yeltes, Lieutenant Colonel Agustín María de Aguilera y Gamboa of the Spanish Cavalry, and an English mother named Mary Ada Munro. She was born in Boulogne-sur-Mer in France of relatively humble origins, which, in order not to embarrass Agustín, she later hid behind an invented past as a Scottish aristocrat. When they met, on a train in France, the twenty-nine-year-old Mary was probably a schoolteacher. Gonzalo was born in Madrid on 26 December 1886. At the time, his parents were unmarried. Perhaps in denial of this reality, for the rest of her life Ada Munro would adopt a rigid puritanism. In particular, she had a horror of social scandal and a highly moralistic attitude towards single mothers. She was unable to wed until 1899 because the regent María Cristina would not grant Agustín de Aguilera the permission necessary for a member of the aristocracy, an officer of the royal escort and a courtier to contract matrimony. When they did marry, Agustín lost his title and it was not restored until 1910 by Alfonso XIII. Both Gonzalo and his sister María del Dulce Nombre (known in the family as Nena) were brought up in a home in which English, French and Spanish were spoken equally. In 1909, he wrote to Inés Luna, 'English is the one I speak best and it's odd that, in English, the words come to me easily but I speak Spanish badly when I want to say things well.' It is not known if Gonzalo had a happy childhood since Agustín and Ada were extremely strict parents.[31]

Certainly, aged nine, he was sent to England as a boarder at a recently established Jesuit preparatory school, Wimbledon College. He then followed in the footsteps of his father when, in October 1897, he entered Stonyhurst College, the Jesuit public school in Lancashire, which he attended until July 1904.[32] His school career was singularly undistinguished. Despite his later reputation as a gentleman scholar, he was always in the lower part of his class and he left no mark of achievement in sport.[33] After Stonyhurst, with no possibility of gaining entrance into a British university, he spent some time studying science and philosophy in Bavaria, with comparable lack of success, although he did learn German. During that period, he claimed in his autobiography that he had been much influenced by Kant's *Critique of Pure Reason*. He also acquired a taste for the music of Bach and Wagner. Despite his lack of academic achievement, in addition to his talent as a linguist he had considerable musical skill, had an interest in mechanics and was a voracious reader. He wrote to his lover Inés Luna in December 1909, 'When I was in Germany, I was always going into factories (for pleasure not because my father made me) and I had planned to go into industry.' In the same letter, he spoke of being able to play the guitar. On his return to Spain in 1905, liberated from the Jesuits, Aguilera spent two years in Madrid living the life of a *señorito*, a rich idler and an Anglophile snob imbued with a strong sense of entitlement.[34]

After the death of his father, Aguilera became the eleventh Conde de Alba de Yeltes.[35] He made sure that every journalist in his charge was aware of his aristocratic rank, although for some reason several of them came away with the idea that he was the seventeenth Count. Given that he was prone to compulsive boasting, perhaps he hoped thereby to imply that his title was even older than it was. Similarly, he led his friends in the press corps to believe that he had served with great gallantry in the Moroccan War, fighting at the head of a unit of mounted Regulares, and had distinguished himself by his courage and a recklessness bordering on the suicidal. One admirer described him as 'a hard-bitten ex-cavalryman of what I believe is known as "The Old School".[36] There is no reason to dispute that he saw action or shared to the full the prejudices of his peers. However, in a war in which the rewards for courage and temerity were considerable, as the meteoric career of Francisco Franco showed, his military records show little of significance.

At the unusually late age of twenty-one, Gonzalo de Aguilera was conscripted into the Spanish army in February 1908 as a private in the cavalry. Posted to an army stud farm, he took immediate leave of

absence. In August 1908, thanks to the influence of his father, he was
able to enter the Academia de Caballería in Valladolid as a somewhat
mature student. To the intense annoyance of Don Agustín, he did not
use his intellectual ability and was a lazy student. His letters to Inés
Luna, written from the cavalry academy, indicate his lack of interest
in his studies. Either to avoid class or else to catch up on missed
material, he frequently spent time in the infirmary with a real knee
injury but often with imaginary ailments, abetted by his friendship
with the unit's doctor. Much of his time was spent writing hundreds
of lovesick letters to Inés and just staring at her portraits. He was also
often confined to quarters because of his involvement in student
japes.[37] Nevertheless, he graduated as a second lieutenant (*alférez*) in
June 1911. After a brief period in the Hussars, in February 1912 he
volunteered to serve in Morocco, hoping to flee garrison life in Spain
only to find it again in Africa. In February 1912, Gonzalo was sent to
Melilla where he spent a month on the staff of the Captain General of
the Territory before serving in a number of fighting units. After
seeing action, he was awarded the Cruz Primera Clase del Mérito
Militar in November 1912. He was promoted to first lieutenant on 13
July 1913. His brief quest for adventure and glory ended one month
later when he was posted to the mainland, remaining in Alcalá de
Henares and Madrid. He was able to lead a relatively privileged existence, spending two months' leave in London in the summer of 1914
and taking part in horse trials in Badajoz in 1915. In October 1915,
he was posted to the staff of the Ministry of War.[38]

In June 1916, because of his fluent German, English and French,
he was sent to Berlin where, as a junior military attaché, until
November 1917 he assisted in the Spanish Embassy's work with the
so-called Oficina Pro Captivis protecting the interests of prisoners of
war, inspecting prison camps, organizing prisoner exchanges and
keeping their families informed. This was a humanitarian project
created partly on the initiative of Alfonso XIII, who may well have
recommended Gonzalo de Aguilera for the position.[39] The horrors
that Gonzalo saw on both the Eastern and Western Fronts profoundly
affected him. However, he seems to have internalized his reactions. It
is possible that his already limited enthusiasm for the military life
was diminished. Certainly, on his return to Spain, he sought few

postings away from Madrid. In the late 1940s or early 1950s, he wrote of the German experience in his autobiographical 'letters to a nephew':

> As you know, during the First World War, I was in Germany and I saw up close those mountains of pain and suffering that modern war brings in its wake and which no individual can possibly escape. Those piles of corpses of men, women and children at the side of the frozen roads of Poland, those huge massacres in the West where I could also observe the first victims of poison gas who coughed up thick bronchial mucus. Aix-la-Chapelle in its entirety was a field hospital and on the days of major battles I saw lorries being loaded with arms and legs to be taken for burial. In the rear-guard, I saw the sorrows of families and economic ruin. There I began to cease being a Christian; for it is not possible that a loving and omniscient deity could not find other means to fulfil its ends than through the martyrdom and perdition of its creatures.[40]

This experience may well have brutalized him. Certainly, his enthusiasm for the slaughter of the 'reds' during the Spanish Civil War suggested that it had done nothing to humanize him.

After his return to Spain one month before his thirty-first birthday, he served in mainland posts, in Madrid and Salamanca. It has been suggested that, at some point in his career, he was aide de camp to General Sanjurjo. However, there is no reference to any service with Sanjurjo in his military records.[41] He was not involved in the successful pacification of Morocco in 1925, although he served again briefly in Africa. In December 1926, he was posted to Tetuán where he was involved at the head of a Tabor (battalion) of mounted Regulares patrolling and protecting the roads surrounding the town – which could be the basis of his boasts of courageous exploits.[42] He remained in Morocco until August 1927, after which he passed into the reserve, having been seconded to the Military Household of Alfonso XIII, and consolidated his personal friendship with the King. He would retire from the army in protest at the requirement that officers swear an oath of loyalty to the Republic. He took advantage of the generous voluntary retirement terms of the decrees of 25 and

29 April 1931 promulgated by the newly installed Minister of War, Manuel Azaña.[43]

His return from Germany in November 1917 enabled him to see his lover, the twenty-five-year-old Francisca Magdalena Álvarez Ruiz, whom he had set up in an apartment in Madrid some years earlier. In awe of his father, he had tried to keep their relationship a secret. In the spring of 1916, Magdalena had fallen pregnant and, in December, bore him a son, Gonzalo, out of wedlock. He continued to support her in the Madrid apartment but did not see the nearly one-year-old Gonzalo for the first time until his return from Germany. He did not acknowledge Gonzalo for several years because both his mother and his father heartily disapproved of what they considered the scandalous relationship with Magdalena. Just as he himself had been a partly unwanted child, he never demonstrated any strong feelings of love or affection for his son. He was promoted to captain in July 1919 and was part of the unit that escorted Alfonso XIII on his summer holidays. On 1 December that year, his father died and Gonzalo inherited the title of Conde de Alba de Yeltes and the family estates. Although now free to marry Magdalena, he did not do so until 1935.[44] Indeed, he continued to live the life of a well-heeled bachelor, often spending lengthy periods of leave in Paris and London. He took eighteen months' leave of absence from March 1924 to August 1925, during which time his second son, Agustín, was born.[45] In Salamanca, he became friendly with Diego Martín Veloz, a fiercely reactionary landowner, who had many connections with the military conspirators including Generals Queipo de Llano and Goded. He had been involved in Sanjurjo's attempted coup in August 1932 and, in the spring of 1936, he collaborated with the Salamanca garrison in the preparation of the uprising. When the war began, Martín Veloz, like other landowners of Salamanca, would put enormous energy into recruiting peasants for the rebel forces.[46]

The disdain that Gonzalo showed towards Magdalena, something that would be an intermittent feature of their relationship, was symptomatic of his sense of aristocratic entitlement. Moreover, he was a dedicated womanizer. In this, as a tall, handsome cavalry officer, Gonzalo had had considerable success. On 16 April 1909, he had met in Madrid the already mentioned Inés Luna Terrero, a celebrated beauty from Salamanca. A whirlwind romance began. Inés was extremely rich and, like Gonzalo, spoke English, French and German. She was a progressive feminist who shocked local opinion because she smoked and, instead of riding side-saddle, rode astride wearing trousers.[47] Over the next seven months, he wrote her many letters, of which over 100 have survived. An extraordinary compendium of exaggerated romanticism, arrogant misogyny, ill-temper and duplicity, they are immensely revealing of his character and his desire for solitude. In the first ones, he addressed her formally as *usted*. Within three days of meeting her, he wrote to her with characteristic vehemence, 'Adored Inés … I love you, I love you, I will always love you.' A wild infatuation had possessed him and soon he was mentioning marriage.[48]

Within weeks, however, his tone passed from that of an adoring vassal to one of male superiority, oscillating between addressing her with variants of 'My adored, My beloved, My idolised Inés' and calling her 'My beloved little girl'. Many of his recorded statements, particularly his boasts to war correspondents during the civil war, suggest that Gonzalo needed respectful subservience. The scepticism shown by Inés in surviving annotations that she made to the letters suggested that she would not be able to fulfil that requirement. On a letter of 22 April 1909 in which he claimed that she was making him suffer, she wrote later, in English, 'You jest!!!!!!!!' On one sent on 1 July 1909, she wrote alongside one of his exaggerated declarations of love, 'Puppy love, like water in a basket'. Long after they had split up, she added to a letter in which he had claimed that he would never forget her: 'how times change'. Her suspicions were more than justified. In August, she was devastated when gossip reached her, from her paid companion Luisa, about Gonzalo's infidelity with several women but most seriously with the voluptuous Magdalena Álvarez. He had met Magdalena in a Madrid dance hall in 1908 when he was about to join the Academia de Caballería in Valladolid. She was then a sixteen-year-old who worked ironing clothes.

At first, Gonzalo angrily denied the relationship but soon suggested that Inés would be better off with someone else.[49] At the same time, he made ever more extravagant declarations of love, often in French. He spoke of Inés as 'ma petite fiancée'. Nevertheless,

Inés maintained doubts about his relations with other women, including Luisa, an accusation that he laughed off. 'That Luisa one is talking rot. She only knows me by sight and she won't really even know my name because lots of us have said things to her and even pinched her … The stuff about me having two girlfriends isn't true either. I would have told you. Does Luisa know that you are my girl-friend? If she does know, maybe she's just saying these things to annoy you.'[50]

However, as Inés's suspicions about Magdalena were confirmed, he began to beg forgiveness for hurting her, speaking of his shame and the injustice of his actions. 'I have the firm determination never to displease you again and to be always submissive. I want you to be my queen but always love me.'[51] However, as this did little to dissipate her mistrust, he grovelled more and more, writing, 'I'm thinking of you and what a swine I've been – I'm a contemptible wretch.' He offered 'sincere contrition for the sorrow that I feel for having been such an animal. I am under your dominion and you can do with me anything you want.' In fact, he seems to have let Inés know that he was still in touch with Magdalena, doing so in an aggressive letter that she must have destroyed since it is not among those that she saved. In response to her fury, he squirmed again: 'you are going to be my wife'; 'my infamy provokes such regret and makes me so angry with myself that I can find no peace without trying to show you that, if I hurt you and made you suffer, therein lies my punishment.'[52]

It is difficult to ascertain to whom he was lying – to Inés or to himself. Inés herself seems to have expressed her own doubts. Since he regularly received letters from Magdalena at the academy, his rela-tionship with her was well known to his fellow cadets and therefore impossible to keep secret.[53] To anticipate an almost certain discovery of his infidelity, he clumsily offered to send her two letters that he had received in September from Magdalena, whom he described as 'my old girlfriend'. He claimed that he had not told Inés about them before out of concern that she might think that his relations with Magdalena had any other basis than pity: 'When you read the letter I'm sure that you too will feel sorry for her.' Some days later, he sent Inés one of the letters from Magdalena, claiming implausibly not to be able to find the other. He brushed off its importance, claiming that she had asked him for money because her mother was ill and she herself needed new clothes. He mocked the inelegance and grammatical errors of the letters, referring to her as 'the slut'. He said that he awaited Inés's instructions on how to reply and ended with the words 'I love you with all my soul and I will never more think of anyone but you.'[54]

In fact, the letter from Magdalena forwarded to Inés revealed her to be far from the pathetic creature described by Gonzalo. She upbraided him because his delay in replying to her previous letter had made her anxious that he had fallen from his horse: 'It is stupid of me to worry and upset myself over someone who doesn't deserve it.' He seems not to have read carefully what he was forwarding to Inés. It was clear that it was Magdalena, not her mother, who was ill. She wanted clothes, not to go to the theatre, but in order to look nice for his next visit. Her letter is full of indications that she was in frequent contact with Gonzalo and was his kept lover. She wrote:

> Gonzalo, do me the favour of sending whatever money you can. My skirt is being dyed and I can't collect it and I would like to have it to wear when you come. You will say that I'm being cheeky to ask but you told me to do so when I need to. Write soon by return of post … The days until I next see you seem ever longer. I think only of you from the time I get up until I go to bed and even when I'm sleeping. Goodbye, my love. You know that I love you with all my heart and your Magdalena will be yours alone.[55]

He had responded by sending her enough money to buy a skirt, some blouses and a pair of boots. Having admitted this to Inés, he made out that it was an act of charity to a pauper.

Inés could not have failed to notice the clues to his mendacity in Magdalena's letter and continued to harbour outright suspicion. He responded angrily:

> ¡¡Inés!! What's this all about. Haven't I done what you asked? Don't I say that I will do whatever you think best? Aren't I completely under your thumb? So, on what basis do you write to me as you did this morning? Is there no more affectionate way of expressing

what you want? Do you want us to finish? Is this how you respond to my frankness? Just imagine if I had said nothing and had her living her with me? … either you don't love me or you don't understand me.[56]

This outburst inflamed her suspicions even further and she responded by talking of trying to contact Magdalena via an intermediary. He was furious, accusing Inés of committing a huge indiscretion and an 'atrocity', ostensibly because he claimed that her doing so would damage both of their reputations. 'If anyone found out, what would they think of you? What would they say about me?' It is more likely that he didn't want word of his relationship with Magdalena to reach his parents.[57] Nonetheless, Inés pressed ahead and demanded to see all of Magdalena's letters to him. He responded that he could not do so because they were in Madrid and, in any case, he needed them to exchange for his letters to Magdalena. He wrote imperiously: 'Once again I insist that neither you nor anyone else does anything.'[58]

He was soon begging forgiveness for his bad temper. In an effort to persuade Inés that he had finished with Magdalena, he wrote about her in demeaning terms. 'As I told you in Salamanca, the slut has not written to me. I was sure that you imagined that she and I were more intimate than was the case.' As she remained mistrustful, he ran down Magdalena even more.

> Your letter is just constant suspicion. Do you think I don't love you? Is it because of that other one? How can I send you her letters if I never receive any? You say that I'm weak with her. Not a bit of it! If she was ever interested in me it was because I had her under my thumb, because I answered her letters. I would love you to see my answers. I don't know how to get that one out of your mind. She means nothing to me. I'm not going to see her or write to her ever again and it won't bother me in the least.

He went on to assert that, if he ever got another letter from Magdalena, he would forward it to Inés unopened. Nevertheless, egged on by the whisperings of Luisa, Inés continued to doubt him.[59] Accordingly, he disparaged Magdalena even more: 'As for skirts and boots, there is no danger that I will be doing more charity work. I really got out of my depth doing that.'[60]

The love affair with Inés seems to have hit insuperable obstacles between the Christmas holidays of 1909 and the first weeks of 1910. She seems to have badgered him with her suspicions and demanded that he should prove his love by marrying her. This provoked a crisis in their relationship. It appears that the demand of the exotic, free-thinking Inés for marriage jolted him into a preference for Magdalena who admired and adored him uncritically. He responded by cruelly telling Inés in late January 1910 that his feelings for her had been merely physical passion. He went so far as to suggest that she should part with him 'because things were going too fast and heading for a catastrophe'.[61] To her distraught response, he replied with a brutal sophistry: 'My deception has only the excuse that I wanted to love you and I wanted to see if, with time, I could love you. I do love you but not enough to marry you … For some time, I've been telling you that there was something that prevented total frankness between us and that something was that I didn't love as I would want to love the woman who was to be my wife.' He then asked feebly if they might not remain friends.[62] Over the next five months, along with criticisms of her character, he returned to making impassioned declarations of love combined with repetitions of his determination not to marry her. In heated evocations of their physical relations, he declared, 'You are morally mine because you have desired to be mine.' She accused him of keeping a harem, ended her letters 'with a handshake' and even went so far as to say, in response to news about his knee injury, that she would be delighted if he were crippled. In one letter to him, she signed off 'À bientôt sapillo' (See you soon, little toad).[63]

Nevertheless, their relationship staggered on for some time largely at his initiative. After a lengthy interval in their surviving correspondence, she wrote and broke off with him definitively. He wrote in early 1911 that the formality of her letters shocked him to the extent of leaving him expecting her to address him using the formal *usted*.[64] In desperation, he arranged to get leave for a month in the hope of seeing her in Madrid. She rejected his every attempt to visit her and ordered her coachman not to stop if they passed him in the street. He wrote, 'I have an uncontrollable desire to see you and your not letting me just spurs me on.' He took to standing outside her house all day in the hope of seeing her. Where he wrote, 'You will have seen that I have an Asiatic patience to wait seated or rather standing,' she added a drawing of a stick man. 'Thus', he wrote, 'people will see that you have definitively told me to go to blazes and that you want nothing to do with me.' He went on: 'I want to see you so much but you cannot imagine how much.' At this, she annotated his letter with the words 'you need to control yourself'. He ended with a threat to kill himself: 'Goodbye, cruel Inesilla, let me see you just for a moment some time. If your resentment is deep, my remorse is no less and makes me want to shoot myself outside your window but I'm a coward even in that.' Here she inserted a drawing of a stick man with smoking gun and a comment, 'Ooh, I'm scared,' the word 'liar' and a drawing of a heart with an arrow through it.[65]

Gonzalo made sporadic attempts to get Inés to come back to him. He wrote to her twice when he was stationed in Morocco. In the first letter, he speculated, 'if you were to forgive me …' In the second, he wrote, 'I feel an irresistible desire to kneel before you and rip myself apart and the more I suffered the happier I would be because I would feel as if I had made amends for my faults.'[66] The siege went on well into 1919. He wrote to her every couple of months while serving in Germany during the First World War, hinting at the possibility of their reuniting. In one letter, he wrote, 'There are women to spare here but, given that I have never liked German women, they just annoy me. Moreover, I fancy getting married and I want to return to Spain to do so because I don't have many more years as a young man and I have to make use of them.' In another, he wrote, 'everyone is getting married and you and I will end up dressing saints' statues in a church'. He was worried that someone else might snare her and revealed a degree of jealousy: 'What are you up to? How many lovers have you got?' Apparently aware of his ongoing links with Magdalena, Inés would reply less frequently with non-committal letters. He invited her to travel to Germany or to Switzerland where he could easily see her. Nothing came of his efforts. After he had inherited his father's titles and lands in December 1919, now a cavalry captain he secured a posting in Salamanca. As late as 1922, he was writing embittered letters lamenting her rejection of his overtures.[67]

Inés never married and apparently, for the rest of her life, carried a torch for him. Despite these feelings for Gonzalo, she later had many lovers, including Miguel Primo de Rivera. She met the Dictator at the Madrid racecourse in the spring of 1928 when he was already engaged to Mercedes 'Nini' Castellanos. They were soon lovers, meeting secretly in her suite at the Hotel Palace. At considerable political cost, the Dictator broke off his engagement to Nini in June 1928. He continued to see Inés even during his brief exile in Paris after his fall from power. There was talk of marriage but he died in March 1930 before anything could come of it.[68]

Gonzalo's father had never approved of Inés but he was even more furious about Magdalena, who had eight siblings and was from a social stratum far below that of Gonzalo.[69] Magdalena's father, Ginés Álvarez, was a modest *cochero* (a man who hired out carriages and, later, cars) in the Chamberí district of Madrid and her mother, Julia Ruiz, took in ironing, as, at that stage of her life, did Magdalena. Agustín forbade him to see her, but Gonzalo ignored him. If the relationship caused difficulties for him, it did so even more for Magdalena. As a kept woman, she was cast adrift by her family and social milieu. She was isolated, having to bring up the baby alone, unable to accompany Gonzalo in society and rejected by his family. To make matters even more difficult for her, Gonzalo was still trying to revive the relationship with Inés by means of letters worthy of a lovesick adolescent. In 1924, to the delight of his mother, it seemed that he would propose matrimony to the twenty-two-year-old Livia Falcó y Álvarez de Toledo, the daughter of the Duque de Fernán Núñez. The relationship was brought to an end in the summer of 1925 by the intervention of Magdalena. With the now eight-year-old Gonzalo at her side and pushing a pram containing the recently born Agustín, she confronted Livia in the street. She told her that there were three reasons why she could not marry Gonzalo de Aguilera: the two children and the pistol that she waved in Livia's face, with which she would shoot her if she continued to see him. Gonzalo finally moved in with Magdalena in Madrid in 1930.[70]

Testimony to his snobbery can be seen in Gonzalo's belief that the Álvarez de Toledo family were parvenus since they had not attained aristocratic rank until the fifteenth century, even though the Condado de Alba de Yeltes had not been established until 1659.[71] His snobbery was also revealed in his attitude to the relationship between his sister Nena and his best friend, Colonel Abilio Barbero Saldaña, a brilliant pilot in the Spanish air force. The irony resided in the fact that both Gonzalo's father, who had married below his station, and Gonzalo, who would marry Magdalena, were united in fierce opposition to Nena's marriage to Abilio on the grounds of his social inferiority. They refused to attend their wedding ceremony in January 1929 and resisted all attempts by Nena and Abilio to restore cordial relations. The issue led to Gonzalo finally marrying Magdalena. He realized that, if he died as a bachelor, his title would pass, not to his own sons, but to the children of Nena and Abilio. Accordingly, when Nena and Abilio had their first son in May 1930, he applied successfully for the regulatory royal permission to wed, although he did not do so until April 1935. Despite now living with Magdalena, he still pursued the social life of a bachelor.[72]

Gonzalo's aristocratic prejudices and his deeply conservative social circle guaranteed that he would sympathize totally with the military rebels in 1936. Among his friends were key elements in the conspiracy, such as the autogyro inventor Juan de la Cierva and Luis Bolín, then the London correspondent of *ABC*. Nevertheless, unlike many of his aristocratic and military friends, he had played no part in the conspiracy of whose gestation he must have been aware. He had followed the progress of events during the spring of 1936 with growing concern and, when he heard the news of the assassination of Calvo Sotelo on 13 July, he made the dramatic decision to flee Madrid. He piled Magdalena and their two sons into his car, with minimum luggage, and drove to Salamanca.[73]

His mother, his sister and her husband and two young children remained in Madrid. Unlike Gonzalo, Abilio Barbero had not left the army in protest at Azaña's military reforms and was now a brigadier general and head of a section of the General Staff. As a friend of Mola, he was in danger. As might have been expected, he was arrested and he and his family suffered dreadful privations during the war. Despite the disdain with which Mary Ada Munro had treated Nena and Abilio, they looked after her throughout the conflict. What Gonzalo learned of the suffering in Madrid of his mother, sister and nephews inevitably intensified his visceral hatred of the Republicans.[74]

Having moved into the neglected and dilapidated house at Carrascal de Sanchiricones, and suffering from flu, Aguilera came out of retirement when he heard that war had broken out and volunteered for the Nationalist forces, hoping to serve as a cavalry officer. Despite a shortage of officers, he was surprisingly snubbed by the military authorities in Salamanca. Accordingly, he went to Burgos where, late on 24 July, he was received by General Mola, commander of the Army of the North, whom he knew both from his own service in Morocco and through his brother-in-law Abilio. Mola realized that, with his linguistic skills, Gonzalo would be useful within the rebel propaganda machinery. Accordingly, Gonzalo was informally attached to Mola's General Staff in the Oficina de Prensa y Propaganda, which was being run by Juan Pujol Martínez. Pujol had been editor (director) of the Madrid daily *Informaciones*, which belonged to Juan March. Aguilera was given the task of supervising the movements and the output of the foreign press correspondents – sometimes serving as a guide, at other times as a censor.[75]

One of his first assignments was to accompany a group of reporters from Burgos to Salamanca in order to interview Miguel de Unamuno. They were André Salmon of *Le Petit Parisien*, Hubert 'Red' Knickerbocker of the International News Service and Harold Cardozo of the *Daily Mail*. Permission was granted by the military authorities on the assumption that it would lead to a propaganda coup given Unamuno's ferocious criticisms of the Republic at the time. The three journalists were carefully chosen because of their sympathies for the rebel cause. Aguilera was alarmed when Unamuno declared that he would usually be aligned against the winners, whoever they might be. However, he was delighted overall with the interview since Unamuno had described the rebels' cause as 'the struggle of civilization against barbarism'. At midnight, Aguilera took the trio to dinner at Salamanca's Grand Hotel. At the table, he could not contain the loathing that he felt for Unamuno because of his part in the downfall of the Dictator Miguel Primo de Rivera and King Alfonso XIII.[76]

Within days of his appointment to Mola's staff, he was established in an hotel in Burgos. After that first assignment, he was enthusiastically driving south each day and got involved in the fighting for the passes through the Guadarrama mountains at the Alto de León between the villages of Guadarrama and San Rafael.[77] He was soon shepherding foreign journalists to cover the northern army's advance into the Basque Country. This involved him travelling tirelessly across the northern front, spending the night sometimes in Burgos, sometimes in Valladolid. His delight in this new activity was marred by concern that his house in Madrid might have been looted, by fears for his mother's safety and because he missed Magdalena.[78]

In the course of the civil war, he wrote whenever he could to his wife. It is noteworthy that, after the years in which he had mistreated her, and despite the fact that he would eventually try to kill her, every one of his twenty-four surviving letters is deeply affectionate. Redolent of his letters to Inés twenty-five years earlier, they begin with variants of 'My beloved wife', 'My most beautiful wife' and 'My beloved Minona' (his term of endearment for her). They end with variants of 'Goodbye, love of my life, you know how much I love you', 'you know how much your husband loves you' and 'you know that I am thinking of you always and longing to see you'.[79]

According to Sefton Delmer of the *Daily Express*, he 'spoke the best English of all the officers on Mola's staff'. His English was so good that, according to Harold Cardozo of the *Daily Mail*, he could easily have been taken for an Englishman.[80] This was hardly surprising given that his mother was English and that he had been educated in England, where, incidentally, he had acquired a solid grounding in Latin. On one occasion, his excellent English saved the American correspondent Webb Miller from execution. The Francoist authorities intercepted an abbreviated telegram from the United Press, of which Miller was the European News Manager, asking him to investigate rumours of a plot to assassinate Mola. It was assumed that Miller was involved in such a plot and he was arrested. As he was being led away, he fortunately saw Aguilera and managed to attract his attention by shouting to him. Aguilera looked into Miller's case and was able to clear up the misunderstanding.[81] Rich, aristocratic officers abounded on the rebel side and so were to be found in the press apparatus. At its Burgos headquarters, the fledgling American journalist Frances Davis encountered an officer who spoke Oxford

English as he smacked his boots with a riding crop – almost certainly Aguilera. After explaining to her that the press would be at the orders of the army, he changed the subject and asked if she had the *New Yorker*: 'Dashed amusing publication. If you have any copies to spare bring them in with you when you come, eh? Cheerio.'[82]

Despite Aguilera's formal position as liaison with the press, he lost no opportunity to join in the fighting. John Whitaker, although appalled by his politics, admired his courage: 'Aguilera was one of the bravest men I have ever seen. He was actually happiest under fire and, when I wanted to get to the front, he connived with me on trips of our own, after the propaganda bureau had vetoed them.'[83] He was involved in the Nationalist capture of Irún on 4 September. The entire, and extremely bloody, battle was witnessed by the foreign press corps after he had led them into the town as if they were a unit of the conquering rebel forces.[84] He had also taken part in action in the Guadarrama and Somosierra passes to the north of Madrid as Mola's forces threatened the capital. When Mola's Army of the North finally made contact with Franco's African columns in early September, Aguilera moved south to escort the press corps so that they could cover the attacks on the capital and on Toledo. Along the way, he told the correspondents whom he had led into Irún 'that he would take them into Madrid in the same way when the "slave stock" there had been crushed'.[85] On one occasion during that advance, he and Captain Roland von Strunk, a German military observer, in Spain under the cover of being correspondent of the Nazi *Völkischer Beobachter*, fought off Republican militiamen with rifle fire until they were rescued from a perilous position. They were commended for the number of the enemy that they killed. During the siege of Madrid, Aguilera took part in combat action in the Casa de Campo, Pozuelo, Aravaca and Jarama.[86]

Unlike most press officers, who felt responsible for the safety of the journalists assigned to them, Aguilera operated on the principle that if risks had to be taken to get stories then, so long as they were favourable to the military rebels, he would help the reporters take them. Walking up and down the line of journalists' cars with his swagger stick, Aguilera would organize the trips to the front. He regularly took his charges into the firing line and was 'bombed, machine-gunned and shelled' with them.[87] It was the most frequent complaint of the journalists in the rebel zone that they were expected to publish anodyne communiqués while being kept away from hard news. This was more often the case when the military rebels were doing badly and especially so for journalists regarded as too 'independent'. Even favoured individuals were subjected to humiliating delays while waiting to be issued with passes for visits to the front, during which they would be closely monitored.[88] Accordingly, Aguilera was extremely popular with the right-wing journalists in his charge because he was prepared to take them dangerously near to the front and would use his influence with the censor to help them get their stories passed. Junkets to the front organized by Aguilera were regarded as particularly exciting given his delight at being under fire and his assumption that the journalists shared his addiction to danger.[89] Hubert Knickerbocker of the International News Service thought him 'our best friend of all the White officers ... Captain Aguilera is fifty-two, looks forty, acts thirty, and is the best press officer it has ever been my pleasure to meet, because he really takes us to the news, namely the front.'[90]

Despite his adventurism, Aguilera expected 'his' journalists to toe the line. On 11 September 1936, F. A. Rice, the correspondent of the conservative *Morning Post*, went to Burgos to seek a pass to the front. He was detained and interrogated by Aguilera. He had first met Aguilera on 25 August and had posted a despatch that sought to give a picture of the Stonyhurst old boy that would appeal to his paper's predominantly public school readership. He wrote about Aguilera, without mentioning his name, merely as 'a Spanish captain': 'Tremendously efficient, almost impossibly brisk, a good man, one would imagine, in a tight place; I can see him as a prefect at Stonyhurst, greatly respected and not very popular.' In another piece, sent from France and not therefore subjected to the rebel censorship, Rice had used the phrase 'insurgent frightfulness' in relation to the rebel attack on Irún on 1 September. Aguilera objected to both articles. He accused Rice of divulging his name in the first despatch – which he had not done – and judged his references to him to indicate 'a not wholly respectful attitude'. Rice pointed out to Aguilera that the information that he was an old Stonyhurst boy had been volunteered by himself and was clearly of interest to an English correspondent. Moreover, he had not been given it in confidence. Aguilera alleged that the doubt thrown on his popularity at school twenty years before was damaging and actionable. What Rice referred to later as 'these singularly humourless exchanges' continued when Aguilera expressed outrage at the use of the phrase 'insurgent frightfulness'. He reminded Rice that journalists would 'be seriously dealt with' if they referred to the rebels as 'insurgents' or to the Republicans as 'loyalists' or 'Government troops' instead of 'Reds'. Aguilera gave Rice a stark choice. He could leave Spain or remain under strict oversight, without permission to cross the frontier – which was the only way of filing a story outside the Francoist censorship. 'My messages would be heavily censored and twisted to the insurgent view. Those correspondents who represent journals of policy wholly favourable to the insurgents would have priority in the sending of messages, and as one who hitherto has been admitted to both sides, I had no guarantee when I should be allowed out.' Rice chose to leave. He was searched at Pamplona, his films confiscated and personal letters read, then escorted to the frontier. Rice's newspaper, the *Morning Post*, commented on his expulsion in an editorial: 'It proclaims *urbi et orbi* that any news emanating from Right sources belongs rather to the realm of propaganda than to that of fact.'[91]

In the case of John Whitaker, whom Aguilera had every reason to regard as hostile to the rebel cause, the treatment was altogether more sinister. At first, Aguilera had been sympathetic to him because he had been awarded the Italian Croce di Guerra in Ethiopia. He had taken Whitaker on trips that the rebel propaganda bureau had vetoed. However, having got to know a number of the field commanders of the African columns, Whitaker had started to evade the ministrations of Aguilera and the press staff. He began to visit the front to see things for himself. Aguilera felt that Whitaker was witnessing Francoist methods that he was not meant to. In the early hours of one morning during the march on Madrid, Aguilera turned up at Whitaker's lodgings with a Gestapo agent and threatened to have him shot if he went near the front except on accompanied tours. 'Next time you're unescorted at the front, and under fire, we'll shoot you. We'll say that you were a casualty to enemy action. You understand!'[92] From a Francoist point of view, Aguilera was entirely correct in his instinct that Whitaker was dangerous. His recollections of what he saw in Spain are among the most bloodcurdling, and convincing, accounts of the behaviour of the Army of Africa.

The deeply conservative Cardozo regarded Aguilera as being 'often a good friend to journalists' despite his 'hair-raising' driving.[93] Aguilera had at his disposal a chauffeur named Tomás Santos but insisted on driving himself in a Mercedes that Cardozo described as 'one of the most temperamental cars I have ever seen. It either rushed ahead at some seventy miles an hour, taking corners in hair-raising style, or else it sulked and the whole line of Press cars was reduced to following it at not much faster than a walking pace.'[94] The old Harrovian, prominent Tory and Catholic convert Arnold Lunn found Aguilera's skilful but carefree driving a terrifying yet exhilarating experience, the key to which he thought was a typically Spanish oriental fatalism and indifference to death. Lunn wrote wryly of Aguilera's habit in mountainous country of taking blind corners on the inside even if it meant being on the wrong side of the road:

> It is difficult on any reasonable theory of chances to explain the fact that Aguilera is still alive. Sooner or later, one would think, he would meet his opposite number on a corner, but he has not met him yet. I asked him if he could provide a clue to this problem. 'The fact is', he said gravely, 'that I have a curious kind of sixth sense. Call it clairvoyance or telepathy or what you will. I just know when a car is meeting me round the next bend, and I slow up and get to the other side of the road.' ... Before we parted, I had almost begun to believe in his telepathic claims, for more than once he slowed up and moved over to the right side of the road just in time to avoid a collision with a car round a bend which he might have sensed but could not have seen. And there were more rational grounds for my faith, for his skill was uncanny. I remember one occasion when his clairvoyant talent was not functioning. We were whizzing down a mountain road with a sharp drop to our left. We had cornered, on the wrong side as usual, and as we came round the corner, we met a vast lorry. This failed to disconcert Aguilera who swept out of its way with his usual adroitness. He was,

however, taken completely by surprise by a big trailer attached to
the lorry which swung out as the lorry passed us, and almost
forced us over the edge of the mountain road.[95]

On one occasion while driving Lunn, Aguilera was incensed by a
pedestrian who was too slow in getting out of the way when he blew
the horn of the speeding Mercedes. He simply accelerated towards
the young man, who leapt for safety. 'A fellow did that to me the other
day,' he told Lunn,

> but luckily for him my brakes are good. While he was recovering
> from the shock of being missed by inches, I jumped out, seized
> him by the scruff of the neck and bundled him into the car. The
> village was near the top of the mountain pass, and I drove downhill
> for eight miles while he whimpered beside me. I then turned him
> out of the car and left him to walk home. I bet he sweated before he
> got there. That chap was a typical Iberian. You know your *Don
> Quixote*, don't you? Well, Quixote is the conquering Franco-
> Norman type, tall, fair, blue eyes, and so on. Sancho Panza, on the
> other hand, is a sturdy, thick-set Iberian. There was nothing wrong
> with the Sancho Panzas until the Reds got hold of them, but of
> course they'll never produce leaders.[96]

On another occasion, he had assured several correspondents that he
had shot one of his chauffeurs for running his car off the road. 'He
was a red all the time,' he explained.[97] Like his story of shooting six
farmworkers, it may just have been an example of his tendency to
exaggerate. The combination of the state of the roads and Aguilera's
driving took its toll on the Mercedes. In April 1937, travelling from
Burgos to Vitoria with a French journalist, it skidded in heavy rain
and tumbled 200 metres down a hillside near the hamlet of Castil de
Peones. Both driver and passenger escaped with just bruises. He kept
the car going with looted parts, managing on one occasion to replace
a damaged wheel with one from a car burned out during the bombing of Guernica.[98]

Sefton Delmer, despite being informed by Aguilera that he was
being expelled from rebel Spain, wrote later that he would 'always

have the warmest affection' for him. While in Burgos, he called him 'Aggy' and they remained friends after the war.[99] Aguilera had been embarrassed by having to inform Sefton Delmer that he was under arrest and would be obliged to leave Nationalist Spain. His role in the matter was limited to reading out an order that claimed that Delmer had published information likely to be of use to the enemy and that his despatches were 'calculated to make the Spanish armed forces look ridiculous'. In fact, the pair immediately went off to have a drink together. Moreover, after the Spanish war, they met in London and Aguilera told Delmer that his expulsion had been on German orders. The report used to justify the expulsion had recounted a Republican air raid on Burgos. Delmer had described how a small British plane had inadvertently arrived in the midst of it, attracted the anti-aircraft fire of the Burgos batteries and still managed to land unscathed. The despatch, an amused Aguilera told him over a drink, 'not only encourages the Reds to attack Burgos again. But it makes our ack-ack gunners look inefficient'. Aguilera liked Delmer and confided in him that he did not give a damn what the reporter said about the artillery since he was a cavalryman himself.[100]

In a letter sent from Stockholm, where he was en route to cover the Finnish–Russian war, Delmer wrote, 'of all the press officers, censors and escorts, I ever ran into you were the first, foremost and the one I liked and admired best! I never minded your chucking me out – obviously I was more valuable to your cause reporting the other side rather than yours!!!'[101] More liberal journalists were nauseated by the Count's political attitudes – a mixture of callous cruelty and high-minded snobbery. In addition to his racism and his sexism, Aguilera was convinced that a crucial issue which would influence the outcome of the war was 'the existence and the influence of satanic powers'.[102]

According to the American correspondent Edmond Taylor, Aguilera was 'a cultured man with the mannerisms and tricks of speech of an officer in the Indian army, rich and aristocratic too'. Aguilera had told Taylor that he was the 'descendant of a conquistador and an Indian princess – Montezuma, I believe', another tale that may well have been pure invention.[103] The young American correspondent Frances Davis was fascinated by Aguilera:

He is of an old Spanish family of landowners. His face is thin, colorless; his hair is straw; his light eyes, too, seem to have no color. He wears a white silk scarf in the neck of his tunic, for he is a sensuous man and likes to feel the cool silk; and it is also a badge of his arrogance. He wears boots of very fine, soft leather and carries a little whip. He himself is above all law, discipline and regulation. Educated in England, he is very proud of his clipped Oxford speech, of the facility with which he uses the language. 'I've got the gift of the gab,' he says. 'Right? Eh?'[104]

In the evening, over a drink, Aguilera, in his upper-class English growl, would mesmerize the journalists in his care with his racist interpretation of the war. One dimension of his theory was that:

the war was a conflict between Nordic and Oriental ideologies, the Oriental element, represented by the Reds, naturally, having been introduced into Spain by the Moors, who in the course of time became the slaves of the northern Spaniards and thus begat the proletariat. The proletariat having been converted to Marxism, an Oriental doctrine which was in their blood anyhow, were now trying to conquer Spain for the Orient, and the insurrection was quite literally a second *reconquista* by the Christian Nordics.[105]

Despite his extreme views, as the relationships with Delmer and Knickerbocker imply, most correspondents rather liked Aguilera. An extraordinary indication of this may be seen in a telegram to him from the aristocratic Pablo Merry del Val, who had overall responsibility for foreign correspondents, forwarding a message from the Australian journalist Noel Monks. Monks was one of the reporters who had publicized the bombing of Guernica and was thus loathed by the Francoist authorities. After Guernica, the *Daily Express* had posted him to Madrid for his own safety. There he had looked up Ada Munro and wrote to Merry del Val, 'PLEASE TELL CAPTAIN AQUILERA [sic] I HAVE JUST SEEN HIS MOTHER MADRID STOP SHE SAFE AND WELL SEND [sic] HER LOVE CARED FOR BY BRITISH JOURNALISTS REGARDS NOEL MONKS'.[106]

After he had returned to London, Arnold Lunn remained in touch with Aguilera.[107] He considered him 'not only a soldier but a scholar'. In the Sierra de Gredos, Aguilera said to Lunn, 'The Reds are always ranting about the illiteracy in Spain, but if they'd spend a few months living among the mountains they might begin to understand that the people who can't read are often wiser than the people who can. Wisdom isn't the same thing as education. I have got shepherds on my farms who are immensely wise, perhaps because they read the stars and the fields and perhaps because they don't read newspapers.' There was clearly an element of social discrimination in his views since he also boasted of having a library of 3,000 books that he had read and annotated. He believed it to have been vandalized by the mob in Madrid, a cause of understandable bitterness.[108]

After the civil war, he wrote two books himself. Only the first, on the atom, was published, in 1946. It carried on its frontispiece a note stating that 'Given that the profits, such as they are, of this book are intended to benefit the Little Sisters of the Poor of a certain province, there will be no complimentary copies.'[109] The second, 'Cartas a un sobrino', written in the late 1940s and early 1950s, did not find a publisher. It was an idiosyncratic and autobiographical work in which he developed ostensibly scholarly versions of the ideas with which he had regaled journalists during the war.[110]

An English volunteer on Franco's side, Peter Kemp, also noted that Aguilera was widely read, very knowledgeable about literature, history and science, with a brilliant if eccentric intellect and a command of vituperation that earned him among the foreign correspondents the nickname during the civil war of *el Capitán Veneno* (Captain Poison).[111] He had a long-historical view of why the Western democracies were decadent:

The people in Britain and America are beginning to go Communist the way the French have gone. There's that man Baldwin in England. Doesn't even know he is a red, but the reds control him. And, of course, that man Roosevelt is a howling red. But it goes back further than Baldwin and Roosevelt. It begins with the Encyclopedists in France – the American and French revolutions. The Age of Reason indeed! The Rights of Man! Does a pig have rights? The masses aren't fit to reason and to think. Then you pick up with the liberal Manchester school in England. They are the criminals who made capitalism. You ought to clean up your own houses. If you don't, we Spaniards are going to join the Germans and Italians in conquering you all. The Germans have already promised to help us get back our American colonies which you and your crooked Protestant imperialism robbed us of. And we're going to act pretty soon, you understand.[112]

Shortly after the Francoists conquered Toledo, Aguilera wrote a revealing letter to Magdalena from Cáceres. He complained both of stomach trouble and of not getting enough sleep:

but it was all worthwhile because I entered Toledo on the first day. Then I went in again on two more days. My love, the Alcázar has been extraordinary because, at the end, they were just defending a pile of rubble. There were no wounded among the women and children (about 600) and the only deaths were of two old ladies who were more than seventy. They killed lots of reds there. The walk up to Plaza de Zocodover was with dead bodies all around. In taking the city, we lost only one hundred men, which is nothing. They are desperate and cannot hold out. The road from Talavera to Santa Olalla was full of red corpses – there were more than two thousand among the vines and olive trees. We had to drive at full speed because the stench was appalling. The first few days before they started to bury them were a nightmare.[113]

His delight in the slaughter suggests that most of the things he said to journalists were heartfelt.

After Franco's armies had been halted at Madrid, Aguilera both accompanied journalists and took up arms himself in the various battles around the capital that followed in early 1937. During the rebel effort to close the circle around Madrid, he fought in the battle of Jarama. He also played a dual role throughout the Nationalist campaign against the Basque Country during the spring of 1937. He took part in fighting having attached himself to the Brigadas de Navarra and he also continued to watch over the press corps. He was at the front every day and, on one occasion, had a frightening car accident.[114] During the attack on Bilbao, he entered the city before the bulk of Mola's forces accompanied by some of the more hot-blooded and reckless members of the press corps.[115] Aguilera, his colleague Major Lambarri and a group of journalists including Harold Cardozo of the *Daily Mail* were mobbed by an enthusiastic pro-Nationalist crowd. Cardozo and the other journalists were wearing the red berets of the Carlist militia (the Requeté) and felt embarrassed to have been fêted under false pretences. Major Lambarri merely laughed saying, 'I was kissed by much prettier girls than you.' Cardozo felt that, in contrast, Aguilera was seriously displeased. 'His strict military mind and his personal political tendencies made him view this involuntary association of foreigners in what he looked upon as an occasion for intimate Spanish patriotic rejoicing with rather a jaundiced eye, and he was somewhat sarcastic and biting in his comments.'[116]

In private, however, Aguilera revealed to his wife his delight in the effusive greetings of women in Bilbao. He wrote to Magdalena, 'We are already in Bilbao. And do you know who was the first army officer to enter the city? Your husband. Never in my life have so many women kissed me in so little time. It was overwhelmingly emotional ... I went out on the balcony of the Provincial Council and the crowd fell silent and I improvised a little speech.'[117] He was equally thrilled that his involvement with the correspondents conferred on him a degree of celebrity. He wrote, 'You will get a surprise when you hear the radio speaking about me. Almost all the papers quote me constantly, especially in France. I have more photos that they brought me yesterday and I have been in the cinema newsreels and they have even seen me in London.'[118] It was not the first time that he had boasted of his growing celebrity. 'I have lots of photographs and I'll see if I can send you them. I've appeared in lots of foreign papers and recently they have written about me quite a bit.'[119] He would have been particularly delighted to receive an issue of the weekly *The Sphere* in which his photograph was prominently displayed, since it was a magazine that his English friends read. Syndicated agency reports in the regional press also mentioned him.[120] His pleasure in his presence in the media suggests that his claim to have killed six peasants and his chauffeur, and other exaggerations, revealed his frequent need for attention and were a form of self-affirmation.

Aguilera entered the ruins of Guernica with units of the Brigadas de Navarra. Subsequently, like the entire Francoist press service, he was involved in the cover-up after the bombing of Guernica. This involved the intense monitoring of 'untrustworthy' journalists who tried to get near the ruins of the town and the expulsion of those who wrote unwelcome reports. It also extended to giving strong guidance to sympathetic journalists on how their articles should be written.[121] In this regard, there took place an incident that was to cause him, and his superiors, some embarrassment. This was the arrest of Hubert Knickerbocker during the campaign against the Basque Country in April 1937. Knickerbocker was a journalist who, through his articles in the Hearst press chain, had done much for the Francoist cause.[122] On 28 March 1937, he sent the following telegram to Aguilera: 'Next few days will come over Irun frontier. Would be very grateful if you would help by informing authorities to expedite my entry. Looking forward to seeing you.'[123] If Aguilera intervened, it was to no avail.

On 12 April, Knickerbocker was halted at the frontier when he attempted to cross from France into Spain. This sign of growing intolerance of foreign correspondents on the Francoist side was interpreted by the American Ambassador, Claude Bowers, as meaning that 'there must be something in the present situation that General Franco does not care to have blazoned to the world'.[124] The campaign to conquer the Basque Country certainly had elements, particularly the bombing of undefended towns by the Luftwaffe, that the Francoist authorities would not want witnessed by foreign correspondents. Despite being told that he could not proceed into Spain, Knickerbocker sneaked over the frontier. He was caught, imprisoned and subsequently expelled from Spain. On his return to London, he wrote, 'Denunciation by persons unknown had brought about my arrest.' In a later book, he stated, 'The Gestapo had me arrested and thrown into a death cell in San Sebastián for thirty-six hours, whence I escaped by the determined vocal efforts of my friend and fellow correspondent, Randolph Churchill.'[125]

If indeed Knickerbocker was arrested by the German agents, it is unlikely that the denunciation came from Aguilera; more probably, his arrest was simply part of the security surrounding the activities of the Condor Legion, the German force helping Franco. He may or may not have believed that his plight was Aguilera's fault. Nevertheless, the incident soured his hitherto favourable attitude to the Francoist cause. A few days after his return to London, his newspaper cabled him with the question 'What sort of society would Insurgent General Francisco Franco establish if he won the civil war?' Knickerbocker exacted revenge in a highly effective and devastating fashion. He simply replied to the question, in the *Washington Times* on 10 May 1937, with an account of Aguilera's anti-Semitic, misogynistic, anti-democratic opinions and, in particular, his claim that 'We are going to shoot 50,000 in Madrid. And no matter where Azaña and Largo Caballero (the Premier) and all that crowd try to escape to, we'll catch them and kill every last man, if it takes years of tracking them throughout the world.' Knickerbocker's article was quoted extensively in the US Congress on 12 May 1937. It may be presumed to have been a significant propaganda blow against the Francoists, coming as it did shortly after the bombing of Guernica. Aguilera, rendered as a mythical Captain Sánchez, was quoted as saying, 'It is a race war, not merely a class war. You don't understand because you don't realize that there are two races in Spain – a slave race and a ruler race. Those reds, from President Azaña to the anarchists, are all slaves. It is our duty to put them back into their places – yes, put chains on them again, if you like.' Furious about F. D. Roosevelt's election, he said, 'All you Democrats are just handmaidens of bolshevism. Hitler is the only one who knows a "red" when he sees one.' His most commonly used expression was 'take 'em out and shoot 'em!' He believed that trade unions should be abolished and membership of them be punishable by death. His beliefs on the pernicious effects of education had also been expounded to Knickerbocker: 'We must destroy this spawn of "red" schools which the so-called republic installed to teach the slaves to revolt. It is sufficient for the masses to know just enough reading to understand orders. We must restore the authority of the Church. Slaves need it to teach them to behave.' Aguilera had repeated to Knickerbocker views about women roughly similar to those to which he had treated Whitaker: 'It is damnable that women should vote. Nobody should vote – least of all women.'

The Jews, he believed, were 'an international pest'. He described
liberty as 'a delusion employed by the "reds" to fool the so-called
democrats. In our state, people are going to have the liberty to keep
their mouths shut.'[126] It seems unlikely that Knickerbocker's article in
the *Washington Times* damaged the personal relationship that he had
with Aguilera. In August 1937, Aguilera was planning a visit to
London and wrote to Knickerbocker suggesting that they meet. In a
friendly reply, addressed to 'Captain Aggie', Knickerbocker
announced regretfully that a meeting would not be possible because
he was just off to Shanghai.[127]

In mid-January 1937, the Delegación del Estado para Prensa y
Propaganda had been created, headed by the pro-Nazi and fiercely
anti-Semitic professor Vicente Gay Forner of the University of
Valladolid. However, Aguilera remained with Mola's General Staff
until after the Basque campaign. Mola himself died in a plane crash on
3 June that year. Rumours abounded that the crash had not been an
accident but rather the consequence of sabotage arranged by Franco.
Gonzalo, who was a devotee of Mola, was convinced of this and had
no qualms about expounding his theory to friends and relatives.[128]

With the demise of his patron, Aguilera was transferred, on 19
July, to the Delegación.[129] At around that time, and perhaps because
he resented the loss of freedom implied by this new posting, he
applied to resume active service as a cavalryman. It seems that the
application was unsuccessful.[130] This made little difference to his
readiness to be directly involved at the front. He took part in the
subsequent assault on Santander, again accompanying the Navarrese
Brigades. He actually entered the defeated city on 24 August, joined
by the correspondent of *The Times*, two hours before any other
Nationalist forces. He drove through thousands of Republican militiamen, still armed but utterly paralysed and dejected by the rapidity
of their defeat.[131]

Shortly afterwards, Virginia Cowles found herself in the recently
captured city. Captain Aguilera offered to drive her to León where
she would be nearer Franco's headquarters as he continued with his
attack on Asturias. He still had the pale-yellow Mercedes, on the back
seat of which he kept two large rifles and 'a chauffeur who drove so
badly he was usually encouraged to sleep'. Wearing a cap from which

a blue tassel swung, cavalry boots and spurs, he drove as if riding a racehorse. On roads clogged by refugees and Italian troops, he would drive along cursing at other traffic. He occasionally complained, 'You never see any pretty girls. Any girl who hasn't got a face like a boot can get a ride in an Italian truck.' He gave little sign of being on his best behaviour for a foreign correspondent. If anything, the brutality of his speech was inflamed by the presence of Miss Cowles, an attractive woman who looked a little like Lauren Bacall. On stopping to ask the way and asking someone who turned out to be German, he said afterwards, 'Nice chaps, the Germans, but a bit too serious; they never seem to have any women around, but I suppose they didn't come for that. If they kill enough Reds, we can forgive them anything.'[132]

> 'Blast the Reds!' said Aguilera suddenly. 'Why did they have to put ideas into people's heads? Everyone knows that people are fools and much better off told what to do than trying to run themselves. Hell is too good for the Reds. I'd like to impale every one and see them wriggling on poles like butterflies …' The Captain paused to see what impression his speech had made, but I gave no reply, which seemed to anger him. 'There's only one thing I hate worse than a Red,' he blazed. 'What's that?' 'A sob-sister!'[133]

During the attack on Gijón, Aguilera spotted a long line of men with picks and shovels. 'Red prisoners, captured at Santander,' he told his journalistic charges. 'I hear they built one of the mountain roads in eight days. Not much chance for sleep, eh? That's the way to treat them. If we didn't need roads I would like to borrow a rifle and pick off a couple.'[134] Virginia Cowles asked Major Lambarri if the ordinary soldiers in the Nationalist army knew why they were fighting. Keen to oblige, he amiably picked a young soldier at random and asked him. The boy 'replied "We are fighting the Reds." I asked what he meant by the Reds, and he said, "The people who have been misled by Moscow." Why did he think they had been misled? And he answered: "They are very poor. In Spain it is easy to be misled."' This innocuous answer infuriated Aguilera, who was listening. He rounded on the boy, 'So you think people aren't satisfied?' The terrified boy stammered, 'I didn't say that, Señor,' to which Aguilera replied brutally, 'You said they were poor. It sounds to me as though you are filled with Red ideas yourself.'[135] By now, Captain Aguilera regarded Virginia Cowles as a 'Red' herself in consequence of a passing remark. When he was ranting about the sheer destructiveness of the 'Reds' because they had blown up a bridge, she had observed that perhaps they were simply trying to block the rebel advance. The suggestion that the 'Reds' were motivated by military logic rather than intrinsic evil provoked him to glare at her and snap, 'You talk like a Red.' With a hostile report on her unreliability, he put events in train for her arrest. Fortunately for her, a chain of chance encounters permitted her to get to the French border.[136]

Aguilera's English admirer Peter Kemp wrote after the war, 'Loyal friend, fearless critic and stimulating companion that he was, I sometimes wonder if his qualities really fitted him for the job he was given of interpreting the Nationalist cause to important strangers. For example, he told a distinguished English visitor about shooting six of his farm labourers – "*Pour encourager les autres*, you understand."' Kemp's doubts derived from Aguilera's 'original ideas on the fundamental causes of the Civil War. The principal cause, if I remember rightly, was the introduction of modern drainage. Prior to this, the riff-raff had been killed off by various useful diseases; now they survived and, of course, were above themselves. Another entertaining theory was that the Military rebels should shoot all the bootblacks.' 'My dear fellow,' Aguilera explained to Kemp, 'it only stands to reason! A chap who squats down on his knees to clean your boots at a café or in the street is bound to be a Communist, so why not shoot him right away and be done with it? No need for a trial – his guilt is self-evident in his profession.'[137] After Peter Kemp's memoirs had been published, Aguilera took out a writ against him because of the story about shooting the farm labourers. According to his publishers, Kemp withdrew the story – to little avail, since the book was already out of print. In any case, Aguilera had repeated the story to others, including the correspondent of the French Havas Agency, Jean d'Hospital.[138] Clearly, it never occurred to him that his disquisitions were sufficiently remarkable to find their way into print.

Although Aguilera was uninhibited when talking with journalists, particularly if he thought they were right-wing sympathizers of the Francoist cause, he never forgot his job as a propagandist for that cause. When the rebel armies conquered Asturias, the repression carried out by the Moorish Regulares and the Legion was particularly fierce.[139] It is hardly surprising that Aguilera was anxious to ensure that there be no photographs taken of soldiers carrying umbrellas or pushing bicycles lest it give the impression that they were looting. Nevertheless, he was not above a little looting himself, and 'was heard murmuring that there was something very thrilling and tempting about it, and that after all it was not a bit like ordinary robbery'. When he accompanied the Moroccan troops that entered Barcelona in January 1939, he managed to get into the office of the President of the Generalitat, Lluís Companys, and stole his radio set.[140]

Aguilera told Lunn one day, 'It is the melancholy duty of our generation to act as the ministers of exemplary justice. We can only save Spain from a repetition of these horrors if we impress upon the minds of this generation a fact of supreme importance, the fact that there is a God in heaven and justice on earth.' He took pride in the application of summary 'justice'. He told Lunn, 'We shall win. We are the most merciful. We shoot, but we do not torture.' However, he rather spoiled the impact of his words when he turned to Lunn and remarked in an aside about Charles Foltz, the correspondent who had raised the issue of atrocities: 'There is, of course, one aspect of this business which we can't expect our young friend to understand, the existence and the influence of satanic powers. But my friend Kaid Ali Gaurri,' he looked towards a Moor at the next table, 'he would understand.'[141] Aguilera was wonderfully complacent. On the Moors, he said, 'We are proud to fight side by side with them, and they are proud to fight with us. After the Moroccan War we sent soldiers to govern them, and had no trouble until the Spanish Republic started sending politicians. If that had lasted, we should have lost Morocco.'[142] His view of the Moors of the Regulares and the Legion was not shared by other observers. Edmond Taylor wrote, 'they had carried with them out of Africa a spiritual atmosphere like the stench in the den of a beast of prey, stench of carrion and of the beast'.[143]

John Whitaker regarded Captain Aguilera as merely the mouth-piece for many on the Nationalist side. Indeed, precisely for this reason, Luis Bolín kept a tight rein on the press officers. According to Sir Percival Phillips of the *Daily Telegraph*, the majority of them:

> are young grandees or diplomats, amiable weaklings for the most part, ruled by Bustamente [a pseudonym for Bolín] with a rod of iron. He telephones them at all hours of the day and night, scold-ing, ordering but never advising, and, as a result of this drilling, they never express an opinion, even on the weather, lest some correspondent should cable that such-and-such a view is held 'in G.H.Q.' or 'in well-informed circles' or 'by spokesmen of the *Generalísimo*' … they also keep all officers away from us as care-fully as if we had the plague.[144]

Despite Bolín's efforts, it was not difficult to find many with views similar to those of Aguilera. The theories of the eccentric millionaire, Captain Ignacio Rosales, were like those that Taylor, Knickerbocker, Whitaker and others had heard from Aguilera.

In April 1939, Aguilera retired from the army, still a captain, and returned to his estates and his books. He decided not to go back to the home in Madrid that had been so thoroughly ransacked. He put great effort into finding the several thousand beautifully bound and annotated books of his library, of which he managed to recover around one-third. His main residence was Carrascal de Sanchiricones where initially he devoted considerable energy to building up his agricultural enterprises, particularly cattle, horses and wheat. He wrote detailed, and extremely affectionate, letters to his mother relat-ing the particulars.[145] However, he soon became profoundly disillusioned by the politics of the Spain in which he found himself after the civil war. He was disgusted that Franco showed no intention of restoring the monarchy and favoured the upstarts of the Falange over an aristocracy no longer treated with deference. In personal terms, he had no commercial success as a writer and he was alienated from his two sons, neither of whom followed the path that he would have liked. He seemed not to be a respected figure in what passed for high society in Salamanca. Moreover, as a landowner, despite his initial efforts to modernize his estate, he soon lost interest and money, leaving its administration to Magdalena. He passed much of his time tinkering with electrical and mechanical gadgets, reading widely and experimenting with modern farming. Apart from occasional bursts of bad temper, he treated the staff in the house and the farmworkers with consideration and generosity. He and Magdalena spent long periods away from Sanchiricones, particularly during the winter months, dividing their time between Andalusia, Madrid and the Basque Country. He rarely opened letters; instead he collected them and then burned them all at once.[146]

Gonzalo went with some frequency to visit friends in London. He wrote articles on scientific subjects, especially the atom, for his local Salamanca newspaper, *La Gaceta Regional*. This was facilitated by his friendship with the editor, Francisco Bravo, one of the founders of the Falange.[147] His scientific interests were summarized in his book on the atom. His set of 'Letters to a nephew' ('Cartas a un sobrino') was a remarkably erudite but disorganized mixture of oblique memoirs, history and philosophy written in the late 1940s and early 1950s. The range of reference was staggering, from the *Osservatore Romano* to the reports of the American Psychiatric Association, from Greek myth to Leibniz.[148]

At times self-pitying, the work was riddled with signs that he found the return to civilian life extremely difficult. It began bitterly with the statement that his life had been led in isolated meditation and surrounded by mistrust. Using the royal 'we' in reference to himself, he attributed this to 'the misfortune of usually knowing more than the chorus in which we found ourselves and of always having expressed the disgust or the contempt provoked in us by the half-formed opinions of the daring and crackpots'. He claimed to have been accused of being a rebel and unadaptable. This he thought inevitable since he felt himself to be surrounded by 'hypocrisy, lies, envy and trickery'. He was disgusted with the post-civil-war context, feeling that the moral certainties of the war had been replaced by compromise and the emasculation of 'principios firmes'. In a reference to his retirement from the army in 1931 and his war service, he wrote, 'All my life, I have tried to serve the *patria* freely and without any ulterior motives of seeking prebends or emoluments. Several times, by dint of opposing the prevailing tide and injustice, I have faced serious personal disadvantage and the sadness of not having achieved much.'[149]

The book expanded many of the ideas with which he had regaled the members of the press corps in his charge during the civil war. He was profligate with learned references to Aristotle, Cicero, the fathers of the Church and a host of medieval philosophers, as well as Calvin, Galileo, Spinoza and Descartes. These were interspersed with bizarre statements such as 'by political hygiene, I mean here what the English call wisdom' and 'the word revolution is of essentially satanic significance since the first revolutionary was Lucifer'.[150] He was particularly proud of his readings in English literature, philosophy and history, making ample reference to Shakespeare, Marlowe, Hume, Adam Smith, Gibbon, Buckle, Darwin, J. S. Mill, Bentham and George Bernard Shaw. He made comparisons between the Spanish Inquisition and Soviet communism, linking the Holy Office and the Soviet secret police, the GPU. This did not imply any softening of his views on communism – it remained 'the black cloud from the east' and an 'immense malignant tumour'. The problem was rather the communist elements of early Christianity.[151]

In the midst of a discussion on the relative merits of different races, he wrote of the 'patent superiority' of the white man. In a variant of the racist ideas purveyed to Whitaker and his colleagues, he divided humanity into the 'Nordic–European races' and 'the Afro-Asiatic masses', indicating that 'the centralist state, as its name suggests, is the most appropriate to rule over the destinies of inferior masses'. 'In Africa, with the nervous system peculiar to the black race, in which excitement acquires more or less epileptic forms, it requires only a continual rhythm accompanied by a tambourine or a drum to produce mystical forms of ecstasy, and since they are simplistic people, their mysticism degenerates into sexual lubricity.'[152]

As this suggests, the book reveals an obsession with sex that could be discerned in his letters to Inés Luna. In those, there were frequent references to kissing and heavy petting that were unusually explicit in the social circles inhabited by the couple.[153] Aguilera was particularly interested in proving the 'sexual abnormalities of people inclined to the priesthood' and in establishing that 'Christianity has always attracted women and eunuchs.' He particularly associated religious mysticism with sexual aberration, to be found in 'virgins with menstrual deficiencies' and what he called 'euconoides' (near eunuchs?). Misogyny abounded. He declared that a woman who reached thirty still a virgin becomes a 'bitter spinster who, for the peace of everyone else, is better behind the bars of a cloister'. Echoing his remarks to Whitaker about a man's right to kill his wife, he wrote, 'adultery is a crime whose immediate punishment by the death of the guilty pair at the hands of the outraged husband has always been accepted as the natural law in all societies until the appearance of the symptoms of the decadence of civilization'. He also produced a defence of the chastity belt as a necessary barrier against female promiscuity, on which he blamed the degeneration of the race in terms of the introduction of cancer, sexual perversion, mental instability and abnormal skin pigmentation.[154]

The recurring theme was anti-clericalism: 'in Spain and other Christian countries where the religious orders have exercised a near monopoly of education, the more control they have had of education, the greater has been the material and ethical decadence and the greater the tendency to corruption'.[155] In this regard, he was delighted that a friend had told him that he was 'crazier than Don Quijote' for criticizing the Catholic Church.[156] He came near to justifying the anti-clerical atrocities committed by the left during the civil war: 'As regards the headless multitude which functions entirely on the basis of its instincts, as soon as social restrictions are weakened and riot controls the streets, its sure inclinations lead it to burn churches and kill priests.' This was all part of a demolition of the Francoist glorification of Spanish history. In a savage account of the golden age of Spanish history so dear to Francoist rhetoric, he referred to the iconic figures of Isabel la Católica and Santa Teresa de Ávila as 'butch' (*marimachas*). Even if the incoherence of much of the text had not impeded publication, it is inconceivable that the Francoist censorship would have allowed it.[157]

Gonzalo became a well-known 'character' in Salamanca. He was an assiduous member of a *tertulia* of doctors and academics that used to meet at the Café Novelty in the Plaza Mayor. These included the one-time Falangist and later Rector of the University of Salamanca

Antonio Tovar and the university's Professor of Musicology Padre
José Artero. During the civil war, Artero had been active in the
Servicio de Recuperación de Objetos de Culto that had been seized
by the left, especially by anarchists in Catalonia. His consequent
hatred had led him to make a notorious comment while officiating at
a ceremony held in the cathedral of Tarragona on 21 January 1939.
Artero got so carried away that, during his sermon, he shouted,
'Catalan dogs! You are not worthy of the sun that shines on you!'
Another of his friends was the Falangist Francisco Bravo Martínez,
who was editor of the local newspaper, *La Gaceta Regional*.[158]

Leaving clouds of dust in his wake, wearing a leather helmet and
his cavalry uniform trousers, Aguilera would make his daily journey
to the provincial capital on a motorcycle. In the early 1960s, an
acquaintance described him as follows: 'of distinguished bearing,
impeccably dressed, tall, with a moustache and a hypnotic and
disturbing gaze, he climbed stairs with great difficulty, as a result of a
pulmonary emphysema that made him pant continually and breathe
agonizingly in the midst of great exhaustion'.[159] He was regarded as a
local eccentric, known for the amusing articles and poems that Bravo
Martínez permitted him to publish in *La Gaceta Regional*.[160] All the
bookshops of Salamanca used to keep interesting new titles for him
on the reasonable assumption that he would buy them. To the booksellers and the doctors alike, his erudition seemed bottomless. Apart
from the doctors, he had few real friends. He remained a solitary
figure, just as he had often described himself in his letters to Inés
Luna from the Academia de Caballería.[161] He knew other landowners
but none ever achieved any kind of closeness with him. His conversation was considered fascinating, although his irritability did not
encourage friendship or intimacy of any kind. He spoke often of writing a book about 'a strange personage in Africa'.[162] He could not
reconcile himself to civilian life and, as he got older, became increasingly difficult, abrasive and bad-tempered. He neglected his estates
and his house, both of which became badly run down.

The same acquaintance who had noted Aguilera's distinguished
appearance described a confrontation that Gonzalo had with a tax
official in Salamanca provoked by his failure to open letters from the
tax department. Aguilera alternated threats with an old-fashioned

courtesy. Referring to the pistol that he was carrying, he shouted, 'No one knows what I am capable of doing!' On another occasion, needing to speak to the Alcalde of Matilla de los Caños, Alipio Pérez-Tabernero Sanchón, whom he hated for no obvious reason, he rode into the town hall on horseback. In similar spirit, for declaring on 1 October 1942 in the Hotel Palace in Madrid that he was 'an enemy of the regime', he was obliged to pay a huge fine of 10,000 pesetas (more than the annual salary of an army captain). He avoided a prison sentence thanks only to the intercession of a powerful friend, the Civil Governor of Salamanca. On another occasion, in May 1948, he was hit with another big fine of 25,000 pesetas for failing to declare his wheat production to the Servicio Nacional del Trigo.[163]

Aguilera's public, and rather boastful, anti-Francoism seems to have derived from two linked areas of resentment. On the one hand, he was furious that Franco was making no effort to restore the monarchy and was indeed at loggerheads with the heir to the throne, Don Juan de Borbón. On the other, he felt that Franco had replaced the elegant society of the old aristocracy with a corrupt and grasping set of Falangist parvenus. In 1945, when the newly created state tobacco monopoly known as Tabacalera SA replaced the old Compañía Arrendataria de Tabacos, he was offered the post of provincial representative for Salamanca, a socially prestigious and highly paid sinecure. Instead of accepting what was a reward for his services, he took it as a degrading insult. The regime emissary who came to his estate with the news was greeted with an enraged response: 'I'm telling you and that bastard Franco to get off my land immediately.' In a similarly irascible outburst of wounded pride, in 1959 he severed his membership of his club, the exclusive Gran Peña. When he reached the age of seventy, the club ceased to collect his subscription as it did with all members. He was outraged because he perceived this as a patronizing act of charity. He remained a monarchist and thus a supporter of Don Juan de Borbón. This led to his becoming ever more anti-Francoist. He was invited to, but did not attend, the coming-out (*puesta de largo*) of Don Juan's daughter Margarita in Estoril in 1955.[164]

He developed persecution mania. At some point in 1962, he was visited by the tenants of one of his estates in Cáceres who were concerned by rumours that he was about to grant the tenancy to someone else. They had previously written to him but received no answer. He burst into the salon where they were waiting, slamming the door, then strode quickly from one side of the room to the other, shouting, 'I have not written to you because I don't answer letters from anyone.' When they started to leave, he asked them to stay but kept talking ceaselessly for several hours, jumping from one unconnected subject to another. He would stop only for coughing fits provoked by his emphysema or else to eat a bowl of porridge. He recalled the day, 24 August 1937, when he had entered Santander ahead of the Francoist forces, relating the fear that he felt, only to change his mind, saying, 'No, not fear, I have never been afraid in my life.' In his ramblings, he explained his eccentric theories about religion and about his wife's charitable work. He finally let them go, assuring them of the continuity of their tenancy. They left convinced that they had been in the presence of a total lunatic.[165]

Magdalena was concerned when he began to talk of suicide and refused to allow any decisions to be taken about the running of the estate or even about the maintenance of the house. She became so afraid of his violent rages that in late 1963, for her own protection, she asked her two sons to come and live in the family home in Carrascal de Sanchiricones. The elder, aged forty-seven, Gonzalo de Aguilera Álvarez, was a retired cavalry captain. He had fought in the civil war and been badly wounded. While in hospital, he had fallen in love with Manuela Lodeiro, a nurse at the military hospital in Lugo. In an echo of his own father's reaction to his relationship with the socially inferior Magdalena Álvarez, the Conde had reacted furiously and forbidden them to marry. They did so anyway and settled in Lugo, where they had a daughter, Marianela. The younger son, Agustín de Aguilera Álvarez, also had a difficult relationship with his father. To Gonzalo's fury, in 1951, when he was twenty-five, Agustín had eloped with, and later married, the eighteen-year-old María Ángeles Núñez Ispa. He had become a farmer in Majarromaque near Jerez and lived there with his wife and their two daughters and young son.[166] Knowing only too well the irascibility of their father, and despite the inconvenience for their own families, the two sons agreed to their mother's request and spent as much time as possible in

Sanchiricones watching over their father. It is possible that their arrival provoked feelings of jealousy in Gonzalo because of their close attachment to their mother, whom he perceived as no longer loving him.[167]

After a year, things had not improved. The family reluctantly discussed having Gonzalo declared mentally incapacitated and placing him in psychiatric care. For fear of scandal and with a natural horror of seeing the head of the household declared insane, they hesitated. Discovering what was going on, he was furious and his fits of rage became more distressing. Finally, they put the matter in the hands of a lawyer in Salamanca. Given that Gonzalo now suffered bronchial problems and rarely attended the *tertulia* in the café in the Plaza Mayor, it was possible to fabricate the pretext of a visit of two of his medical friends in order to have him diagnosed. A psychiatrist, Dr José Fermín Prieto Aguirre, accompanied by another doctor, Emilio Firmat Cimiano, concluded that Gonzalo was paranoiac. He became so difficult that his sons rearranged the house to provide him with a separate apartment with his own television and his books. They hid all the many guns and knives which, as an assiduous hunter, he possessed. He believed himself to have been kidnapped and imprisoned by his family. At the beginning of August 1964, he had even written a letter to this effect to the judicial authorities in Salamanca. He had wild fits of rage, shouting threats and insults from his solitary apartment. He would occasionally find weapons and, in mid-August, his sons took a flick knife away from him. The legal process to have him committed, however, was lengthy and tortuous.

Before the arrangements were completed, Gonzalo completely lost his mind. After lunch, at four o'clock on the sultry afternoon of Friday 28 August 1964, his younger son Agustín went into the Conde's room to look for some papers. When his father complained of his feet being sore, Agustín knelt and started to massage them. Bizarrely echoing his beliefs on how to deal with bootblacks, Don Gonzalo began to abuse his son. He pulled out an old revolver that he had managed to hide, a souvenir of his time in Africa, and and without warning shot Agustín. Badly wounded in the chest, Agustín turned and staggered out of the room. His brother Gonzalo, alerted by the sound of the gunfire, ran into the room and the Conde shot him full in the chest and in the arm. Stepping over his elder son's corpse, he then set off in search of Agustín in order to finish him off. He found him lying dead at the door of the kitchen. He then calmly reloaded his revolver. Magdalena, now aged seventy-two, came out of her room. She saw her husband glaring at her while reloading his pistol over the body of his son, and she managed to lock herself in another room as he came after her. Some estate workers, who had come in after hearing the gunshots, stood paralysed, frightened by the sight of Gonzalo waving his revolver threateningly. They managed to call the Civil Guard while Magdalena escaped through a window. When the Guards arrived, they ordered Gonzalo to throw down his gun and come out with his hands in the air. His fury spent, he did so. When one of them asked him about shooting his sons, he replied calmly, 'I killed Agustín because he is not my son and, as for Gonzalo, if I hadn't killed him, he would have killed me.'

After surrendering, still in his pyjamas, he sat outside the house for more than three hours quietly awaiting the arrival of the investigating magistrate from Salamanca. His wife, beside herself with grief and rage, screamed at him, 'Assassin! Murderer!' Until calmed down by the farmworkers, she shouted to the Civil Guards, 'Kill him, he's a savage.' He was arrested and taken to the provincial psychiatric sanatorium of Salamanca where he was detained. He and his Civil Guard escort had been driven to Salamanca in the car in which the reporters of the local newspaper, *La Gaceta Regional*, had arrived at the house. Those journalists who interviewed him recounted that, en route, he chatted amiably to the driver. He spoke about various cars that he had had at different times, about football, about the traffic system established in France and about the poor state of the roads – 'I'm talking just to put what happened out of my mind,' he said. When told that he was being taken to a psychiatric clinic, he remarked that psychiatrists are not usually in their right minds and added, 'I called the ones that visited me village quacks and they got angry with me.'[168] During the months spent in the psychiatric hospital, he entertained himself by loudly insulting the nuns who staffed it.[169] His daughter-in-law, Concepción Lodeiro López, and granddaughter, Marianela de Aguilera Lodeiro, escaped the carnage because they had gone to Lugo to make the arrangements for the girl's wedding. The wife and three children of Agustín were in southern Spain. Although judicial investigations began, Gonzalo never stood trial. He remained in hospital suffering an incurable dementia linked to a deep depression. Ceasing to take the medication prescribed for his pulmonary, circulatory and psychiatric problems, he died in the hospital of cardio-respiratory failure, nearly nine months after his crime, in May 1965. He was survived by his widow Magdalena, who died seven years later, in December 1972.[170]

It would be wrong to assume that Aguilera's earlier rantings were simply the fruit of the extraordinary psychological disturbance that finally emerged in the tragic denouement of this family. There is little doubt that he was utterly typical of others such as Rosales who had been chosen by Mola, or Pemán who had been chosen by both Queipo de Llano and Franco, as appropriate spokesmen for their cause. One officer had told Webb Miller that "'we must kill everyone who has that 'red' idea". Another amiable, attractive, intelligent young insurgent officer told me he had himself executed seventy-one men.'[171] There is even less doubt that Aguilera's views were close to those of Mola, Franco, Queipo de Llano and other senior military rebels. Rather than simply concluding that Aguilera was mad, it would be more fruitful to consider the extent to which his – and their – psychological disturbance derived from a combination of their rigid Catholic upbringing, the internalization of the savagery in which they participated in Morocco and the justifications that they found in the writings of Tusquets, Carlavilla and Pemán.

6

The Killer in the North: Emilio Mola

Emilio Mola Vidal was responsible for the murders of more than 40,000 civilians in the provinces that he controlled during the Spanish Civil War. In death he was honoured with a huge monument and was posthumously given a dukedom by Franco. He was the subject of several adulatory biographies.

He was born on 9 July 1887 in Placetas, in the province of Santa Clara Cuba, where his father, Emilio Mola López, a harsh disciplinarian, a captain in the Civil Guard, was stationed. His mother, Ramona Vidal Caro, was a Cuban of Catalan origin. His father brought him up in an ambience of rigid military discipline. In 1894 the family went to Spain and settled in Girona, where Emilio finished his primary and secondary education. In August 1904, barely seventeen years old, he entered the Academia de Infantería de Toledo as a cadet. There he was imbued with the sense that the defeat by the United States of 1898 had shamed the army, thanks to the treachery of politicians. Along with many fellow students, he acquired a deep hostility to the civilian world which they saw as a fount of vice and corruption in contrast to what they were taught was the decency and honour of the military. In the academy, his seriousness saw him acquire the nickname 'the Prussian'. He graduated as number one in his year (*promoción*).[1] This was reflected in later life in his unpopularity. Guillermo Cabanellas commented, 'he was not the sort of person who was liked. Not even his subordinates liked him much, not just because he imposed a rigid discipline but also because of his coldly distant way of treating people.' His unpopularity has been attributed to obsessive nitpicking, among other vices.[2]

According to José María de Iribarren, the young Catholic lawyer who was his secretary from July to December 1936, 'he was always rough and short in conversation and usually harsh and severe in manner'. This contrasts with his apparent good humour during the civil war. Mola was quite ugly but was able to joke about it with Iribarren. He recounted that, when he was a student in the military academy, a professor had asked him what disguise he had used during the carnival. When Mola replied that he had not used any, the professor replied, 'The truth is you don't need to put a mask on. Your face already looks like a mask.'[3] These contradictions were perceptively summed up by Iribarren: 'This dogmatic man, with his severe expression, harsh eyes and dry lips, is deep down sentimental and, at times, a child.' Iribarren described him as having 'an extraordinary personality, an iron will, an exceptionally domineering character and being shrewdly sharp. Everything in public that was harsh, imperious, inflexible was effusive and good-humoured in private.' Mola recounted that, while Director General of Security, he had played a practical joke on Colonel José Riquelme with a fake bomb. When someone gave him a telescope, he was thrilled, showing it to visitors. He played in his office with a machine gun that someone gave him and rolled a model grenade around the floor. Iribarren saw him as 'a giant with the soul of a child'.[4]

Before he was twenty, Emilio was on active service in Spain's colonial war in Morocco as a lieutenant. Like other Africanistas, he learned a cruel form of warfare in which no prisoners were taken. It was a war in which the only merit was bravery, and in 1909 he was awarded the Medalla Militar. In August 1911, in a quest for rapid promotion, he transferred to the Fuerzas Regulares Indígenas (native regulars), a force of shock troops created two months earlier at the initiative of Lieutenant Colonel Dámaso Berenguer in response to significant defeats in 1909 and 1911. Made up of locally recruited mercenaries, the Regulares were renowned for their brutality. Mola was tolerant of their savagery but utterly rigid in terms of imposing his own authority. Many more qualified officers, such as artillerymen and engineers, believed that the system of battlefield-merit promotions favoured the foolhardy over the professional. Mola was an enthusiast for the merit system and came to loathe its critics, many of whom were Republicans, insinuating that they were cowards.[5]

As an officer in the Regulares, Mola became a protégé of Berenguer. He was wounded in 1912, as a result of which he was promoted to captain *por méritos de guerra*. In February 1914, for bravery at the front, he was promoted to major. He had brief spells in the peninsula, in Barcelona, Santander and Madrid, but soon returned to Morocco where he was heavily involved in combat. In 1921, he was promoted to lieutenant colonel by seniority (*antigüedad*). He led the Regulares of Ceuta in the operations after Annual and was wounded again.[6] In January 1922, in Ceuta, he married the twenty-eight-year-old María de la Consolación Bascón y Franco. Consuelo Bascón was from Seville. He was stationed in Logroño in May 1922 but returned to Africa in August 1924, participating in the landing at Alhucemas that ended the Rif war a year later. He had two further promotions by *méritos de guerra*: in February 1926 he was promoted to colonel, and in October 1927 to brigadier general, and was awarded a second Medalla Militar. He was made military commander of Larache. The merit promotions would be challenged under the Republic.[7]

Dar Akobba, his memoir of his African experiences, written in the months before the outbreak of war in 1936, was awash with descriptions of crushed skulls and billowing intestines. The book suggests that he had been utterly brutalized by his African experiences. For instance, he wrote with relish of the remnants left in a river bed of an enemy *harka* (guerrilla band) that had ambushed a unit of his Regulares that in turn wreaked a savage revenge. The ravaged corpses showed signs of deliberate mutilation. 'Corpses and more corpses in the water, among the stones and the oleanders, buried under the debris of what had been their trenches, all naked or half-naked, with horrible wounds, skulls smashed in, arms and legs separated from the torso, bellies slit open and exposed to the elements, foul intestines of indefinite colour. There was a pronounced smell of butchery.'

Knowing that one way to accelerate promotion was to augment the number of enemy casualties, he called a fellow officer: 'I want you to come because there's often a lot of invention about how many Moors died in an action, so I really want you to see these "stiffs".' He described how 'the soldiers could not repress their enthusiasm on seeing so many dead *harqueños* [Moroccan guerrillas]. There were few who did not smash a cranium with their rifle butts or use machetes to cut out a heart.[8] In addition to basking in bloodshed, Mola's memoir is marked by persistent boasting about his own prowess in a relatively minor operation in the summer of 1924, the defence of Dar Akobba, a well-fortified observation point during the siege of Xauen by the Rif leader Abd el-Krim, prior to the evacuation which began in November.[9] His biographer, Colonel Carlos Blanco Escolá, describes Mola as 'a man marked by bitterness, ambition, awash with hypocrisy, cruel with a liking for the macabre and excessively given to self-worship'.[10]

On 13 February 1930 in the wake of the fall of General Primo de Rivera, Alfonso XIII chose as the Dictator's successor General Dámaso Berenguer, to head a government of transition back to constitutional normality. Mola's distinguished service in the Regulares under Berenguer led to his appointment as Director General of Security. At the time commander of the important Atlantic garrison at Larache, he accepted the post with great reluctance as it interrupted his military career.[11] His acceptance of the post, as a result of personal loyalty to Berenguer, undermined his prior reputation as something of a liberal. As student demonstrations and workers' strikes were becoming ever more common, he threw himself into the main task of repressing political subversion. Until the collapse of the monarchy fourteen months later, Mola devoted himself to crushing labour and student agitation as he had crushed rebellion in Morocco. Francisco Franco's brother Ramón, a celebrated aviator, claimed that Mola treated the Spanish population in the same way as he had the tribesmen of the Rif.[12]

To this end, he created a crack anti-riot squad, physically well trained and well armed. Efficient and hard-working, he became immensely well informed about the doings of the Republican opposition through the Brigada de Investigación Social (BIS), a cadre of secret police agents headed by the deeply reactionary Santiago Martín Báguenas with the sinister Luis Fenoll Malvasía as his deputy. With their assistance, Mola set up an elaborate espionage system devoted to the surveillance of Republicans, especially those in the army and the universities. Undercover policemen successfully infiltrated left-wing groups and then acted as agents provocateurs under the supervision of Fenoll. This same network was still substantially in place in 1936 when Mola used it to help his conspiratorial activities in the preparation of the military uprising.[13]

The tall, bespectacled Mola may have had the air of a monkish scholar but, like other Africanistas, he hated the left for its opposition to the colonial adventure. He was a fervent believer in the Jewish–masonic–Bolshevik *contubernio*.[14] The Socialist Juan Simeón Vidarte was part of a delegation from the Ateneo de Madrid that visited him at this time to plead for the release of some young members of the society who had been arrested for taking part in a demonstration. Mola refused them on the grounds that the men in question were not political prisoners but politicians guilty of common crimes and that all members of the Ateneo were freemasons and therefore under Jewish influence. Recounting the scene years later, Vidarte recalled, 'He was tall, gawky, with authoritarian mannerisms, harsh and hard.'[15] Indeed, the vehemence with which he criticized Ramón Franco was to sour his relations with his brother, General Franco. On 4 November 1930, Ramón escaped from a military prison where he had been confined for pro-Republican declarations. Mola wrote in his memoirs that, in doing so, he behaved 'like a common criminal'. On 15 December Ramón, as part of the frustrated revolutionary effort, stole an aircraft and set off to bomb the royal Palacio de Oriente. He desisted after seeing children playing in the gardens. A pamphlet, apparently emanating from Mola's office, denounced him as 'a bastard [who], apparently drunk on your blood, stole a military aircraft and bombed Madrid with leaflets urging rebellion and the proclamation of the Republic'. It went on to call for Ramón and his fellow rebels to be pursued like rabid dogs. A furious General Franco travelled from Zaragoza where he was head of the Academia General Militar to protest, but Mola denied any responsibility.[16]

Mola overestimated the menace of the minuscule Spanish Communist Party, which he viewed as the instrument of sinister Jewish–masonic machinations. This reflected the credence that he gave to the fevered reports of his agents, in particular those of Martín Báguenas and of the sleazy and obsessive Julián Mauricio Carlavilla del Barrio. Mola himself, like Franco and other generals, was also an assiduous reader of the bulletins and other publications of the Entente Internationale contre la Troisième Internationale, having been given a subscription by General Primo de Rivera. In April 1930, obsessed by the need to crush the perceived Communist threat, he set up the Junta Central contra el Comunismo, made up of representatives of the Ministries of War, the Navy and Justice, together with Lieutenant Colonel José Ungría Jiménez, who in late June 1927 had been appointed secretary of the Centro Español Antibolchevique, the Spanish branch of the Entente. Ungría's job was to disseminate anti-Communist propaganda from the Entente while the surveillance of Communists was entrusted to Mola's newly created Sección de Investigación Comunista within the BIS. Ungría passed information from Mola's network of agents to the Entente in Geneva where it was incorporated into the bulletins sent to Franco and other senior officers.[17] Mola's views on Jews, Communists and freemasons were also coloured by information received from the Paris-based Russkii Obshche-Voinskii Soiuz. Even after he had lost his position, Mola remained in close contact with the ROVS leader Lieutenant General Evgenii Karlovich Miller.[18] At dinner with his staff on 14 August 1936, he declared, 'The Jews hate the idea of nationhood. They are an accumulation of age-old malice, evil intentions and ancient racial resentments.'[19]

Ironically in the context of their later collaboration during the civil war, one of those whom Mola had under surveillance because of his involvement in anti-monarchical machinations was Gonzalo Queipo de Llano. Queipo was head of a military revolutionary committee that had drafted detailed plans for the seizure of key communication centres and military barracks. The Republican conspirators were followed by Mola's agents as they tried to forge links with the anarchist movement and to buy arms.[20] He had several officers arrested including Ramón Franco.[21] The main Republican plot was undermined by the premature uprising by the garrison of the tiny Pyrenean mountain town of Jaca in the north of the province of Huesca. On 12 December 1930, Captains Fermín Galán, Ángel García Hernández and Salvador Sediles jumped the gun three days before the agreed date for the nationwide action and their revolt was put down.[22] Galán and García Hernández, as the two ringleaders, were tried by summary courts martial, on 13 December, and sentenced to death.[23] The defeat of the Jaca rebels was a debilitating reverse for the plotters, provoking the withdrawal of numerous officers. The planned national rebellion nonetheless went ahead on 15 December. Rebel aviators captured the air base at Cuatro Vientos, but they were isolated once the expected general strike had failed to materialize.[24]

Mola's future was blackened by the execution of Galán and García Hernández and also by the student disturbances on 25 March 1931. In the University of Madrid's Faculty of Medicine in the San Carlos building in the Calle Atocha, student demonstrations in support of amnesty for political prisoners were brutally repressed by the Civil Guard. A student and a Civil Guard were killed and a further sixteen people seriously hurt. Mola was blamed for the use of indiscriminate force. His Africanista instincts could be seen in his excuse that 'San Carlos had been turned into the Kasbah [fortress] of the rebellion'.[25]

Three weeks later, on 14 April, the Second Republic was proclaimed. Among the chants of the crowds rejoicing in the streets were demands for the head of Mola. A mob had arrived before his house but militants of the Federación de Juventudes Socialistas prevented them burning it.[26] Convinced that he would be arrested for his pursuit of the Republican opposition, Mola spent a week in hiding in the Toledo estate of an aristocratic acquaintance.[27] Despite his pursuit of Republicans, his disgust at the King's flight ensured that he would have little enthusiasm for a restoration of the monarchy. Moreover, in the view of Serrano Suñer, as Director General of Security 'he saw such things, weaknesses, desertions and cowardice, that perhaps that is why he no longer had any monarchist fervour'.[28]

On 21 April, he gave himself up to the Minister of War, Manuel Azaña. Despite swearing an oath of loyalty to the Republic, a deeply mortified Mola was arrested and imprisoned in what he later called a 'damp and stinking cell' in a military jail. On 22 April he was interrogated by a judge about the events of 25 March. He is thought to have claimed that the order to use the Civil Guard had been given by the Minister of the Interior, the Marqués de Hoyos.[29] He had fallen foul of one of the victims of his time as Director General of Security, Ángel Galarza Gago of the ultra-Jacobin Partido Republicano Radical-Socialista. Made State Prosecutor (Fiscal General del Estado) on 15 April, Galarza brought with him considerable baggage.[30] As a result of his participation in the pro-Republican conspiracy of December 1930, Galarza had been imprisoned and was furious to have been given a longer sentence than his fellow accused. During the struggle against the monarchy, calls for the punishment of the beneficiaries of the old regime had led, in July 1930, to the creation of an informal 'responsibilities commission' in the Madrid Ateneo in the hope of bringing Alfonso XIII and the collaborators of the dictatorship to justice. Six members of the Republic's provisional government – Azaña, Fernando de los Rios, Prieto, Marcelino Domingo, Maura and Alcalá-Zamora – had belonged to the Commission and once in power ensured that its findings were implemented. Allocating responsibility was a popular cause but also a poisoned chalice, splitting the Republican coalition and creating enemies, among whom Mola was prominent.[31]

Galarza ordered that Mola face trial for 'criminal negligence' in the repression of the San Carlos demonstration. Mola was charged and an indictment was prepared but, on 28 April, an unsuccessful legal protest was made against the order on the grounds that he was not responsible for the repression of the demonstration at the Faculty of Medicine. On 1 May, while Mola's trial was pending, the Marqués de Hoyos was questioned. He claimed that, as minister, he had given no detailed instructions beyond the command to prevent disorder. On 3 July, the Tribunal Supremo overturned the order for Mola's imprisonment and he was released.[32] However, after one day of freedom, Galarza, who had been made Director General of Security on 13 May, ordered his rearrest. While awaiting a trial that never happened, Mola remained as number 31 on the list of brigadier generals, but was left without a posting. His outrage was understandable.[33] General Berenguer had already been arrested for various offences but primarily because of his role as Minister of War during the summary trial and execution of Galán and García Hernández. These arrests fed the right-wing perception of the Republic as vindictive.[34] In the eyes of the Africanistas, Mola was a hero of the African war who, as Director General of Security, had merely been doing his job of controlling subversion. Mola would later express his hatred of the Ateneo in a speech in Valladolid in October 1936: 'All we did was flick aside that castle in the air built by the stupid intellectuals of that junkshop, the Ateneo.'[35]

In the summer of 1931, Lerroux and other cabinet ministers protested about Mola's continued imprisonment which Prieto described as 'iniquitous' given that his wife was about to give birth to their fourth child. Azaña arranged on 5 August for his imprisonment to be commuted to house arrest.[36] Unsurprisingly, seeing those whom he had recently pursued now in positions of power, Mola nurtured a rancorous hostility to the Republic and a bitter hatred of Azaña personally, not to mention a resentment of Alfonso XIII whom he regarded as a cowardly deserter. This hostility was intensified by Azaña's military reforms which had led to the examination of his promotions to colonel and brigadier general. Both were considered questionable. Although he did not lose his rank of brigadier general, he slid down the seniority list to the level where he would have been had he been promoted by seniority. However, on 10 August 1932, he was transferred to the Second Reserve, which effectively meant forced retirement. This saw him plummet humiliatingly from his position at the beginning of 1932, of number ten on the list of brigadier generals, to number 240 on the Second Reserve list. The fact that this took place on the day of the failed coup of General Sanjurjo, in which he had not participated, seems to have been a mere coincidence.[37] The justification was a technicality, the application of a decree of 9 March 1932 which established the transfer to the Second Reserve of any general who had spent more than six months without a posting. Mola must have suffered considerable anxiety during the months of waiting in vain for a posting. It has been suggested that this harsh measure by Azaña was a reprisal for the Tribunal Supremo's verdict exonerating Mola from responsibility for the events of March 1931.[38] Perhaps inevitably, in the light of this seemingly malicious decision, Mola, influenced by the paranoid reports received from Carlavilla and the dossiers supplied by the ROVS, was ever more convinced that the coming of the Republic was the work of Jews and freemasons.

During the period following his retirement, Mola developed his hobby of making wooden toys, particularly model ships and soldiers, which he did with some skill. He also wrote, under the pseudonym

W. Hooper, a chess manual. Not being a chess player himself, he based it on other primers and wrote it in three weeks. It was a great success in South America and made him a lot of money.[39] These activities have been used by his hagiographers to imply that he was forced to do so by poverty. In fact, between 22 April 1931 and 10 August 1932 when he was without a posting he received 80 per cent of his general's salary. After 11 August 1932, when he was placed in the Second Reserve, this was reduced to 75 per cent.[40] He would have lost certain bonus payments associated with active service. Nevertheless, he also wrote three successful volumes of memoirs: *Lo que yo supe, Tempestad, calma, intriga y crisis* and *El derrumbamiento de la monarquía*. In late 1931, in the first volume of these memoirs, he wrote that he had been awakened to the threat of freemasonry by a pamphlet received from France. 'When, in fulfilling my duties, I investigated the intervention of the masonic lodges in the political life of Spain, I became aware of the enormous strength at their disposal, not through the lodges themselves but because of the powerful elements that manipulated them from abroad – the Jews.' The right-wing journal *Acción Española* celebrated the appearance of the book with a rapturous nine-page review by Eugenio Vegas Latapie, one of its founders and a fierce advocate of violence against the Republic.[41]

By the time Mola came to write the second volume of his memoirs, *Tempestad, calma, intriga y crisis*, he was more explicit in his attacks on freemasons and Jews. He implied that this was because, in addition to the reports of General Miller, he had now read the anti-masonic works of Father Tusquets and *The Protocols of the Elders of Zion*. Thus Mola wrote that the instability that had led to the establishment of the Republic derived from 'the hatred of a race, transmitted through a cleverly manipulated organization. I refer specifically to the Jews and to freemasonry. That is the basic issue, everything else is minor.' He attributed the Jews' alleged hatred of Spain to three motives: 'the envy produced in them by any people that has a fatherland of its own; our religion for which they feel unquenchable revulsion because they blame it for their dispersion throughout the world; the memory of their expulsion'. He then bizarrely connected these 'motives' to freemasonry: 'These are the three points of the masonic triangle of the Spanish lodges.'[42] Miller continued to send reports to Mola throughout the civil war.[43] Mola seemed to regard the *Protocols* as factually accurate documents.[44]

In December 1933, Mola concluded his bitterly polemical book *El pasado, Azaña y el porvenir*, in which he gave voice to the widespread military animosity towards the Republic in general and towards Azaña in particular. Azaña was, he declared, 'a rabid anti-militarist', 'a cold, sectarian and vain man with baggage more of hatred than of good intentions. From the minute he took over the Ministry of War, he dedicated himself to crushing, nay to pulverizing, the army.'[45] Appalled by what he regarded as the unpatriotic anti-militarism of the left, he attributed it to various causes, mainly to the fact that:

decadent nations are the favourite victims of parasitical international organizations, used in their turn by the Great Powers, taking advantage of the situation in weak nations, which is where such organizations have most success, just as unhealthy organisms are the most fertile breeding ground of the virulent spread of pathological germs. It is significant that all such organizations are manipulated if not actually directed by the Jews.

The organisations that I am talking about constitute the most fearful enemy of the nationalist feelings of peoples.

Once the real objective of these organisations is known, it is hardly surprising that their most intense efforts are directed against the military institutions since they regard them as the stronghold of the nationalist idea. The Jews, the tenacious promoters of these campaigns, don't care about the destruction of a nation, or of ten, or of the entire world, because they, having the exceptional ability to derive benefit from the greatest catastrophes, are merely completing their programme. What has happened in Russia is a relevant example and one that is very much on Hitler's mind. The German Chancellor – a fanatical nationalist – is convinced that his people cannot rise again as long as the Jews and the parasitical organizations that they control or influence remain embedded in the nation. That is why he persecutes them without quarter.[46]

Morose and shy, Mola was not previously noted for his popularity. With this best-seller, he found himself an object of admiration among the most reactionary Africanistas.[47]

In April 1934, the amnesty passed by the government of Alejandro Lerroux permitted Mola to return to the army on active service. In the second half of 1934, he wrote three times to his friend and mentor General Sanjurjo to express his concern that the Radical government was losing its grip on public order. He was not involved in the repression after the events of October in Asturias and Catalonia. Nevertheless, concerned that the left might rise again after its defeat, he wrote again to Sanjurjo, expressing his worries about the left and Catalan separatism.[48] In May 1935, when Gil Robles became Minister of War, he annulled the revisions made by Azaña. Determined to strengthen the repressive power of the government, he appointed Franco Chief of the General Staff and, conscious of his own ignorance in military affairs, left Franco to run the ministry. Franco purged the senior ranks of the army of loyal Republican officers and promoted known opponents of the regime. He named Mola military commander of Melilla in the summer of 1935, and at the end of the year head of all the Spanish forces in Morocco. The use of the African Army in the repression of Asturias had intensified its hostility towards the left. For six months, Mola worked in fertile ground to prepare for the anticipated role of the African Army on the Spanish mainland in an eventual uprising. During this period, he and Franco put a large number of colonels in key positions that would later facilitate the coup of July 1936.[49] In the peninsula too, much was being done by Franco to prepare the later rebel war effort. Fortifications were built overlooking Madrid and there were manoeuvres held against a projected working-class enemy. To the delight of Sanjurjo, Franco secretly brought Mola to Madrid and established him in a secluded office in the Ministry of War to prepare operational plans for the use of the colonial army to crush left-wing unrest.[50]

The immediate impact on Mola of the Popular Front victory in the elections of 16 February 1936 came five days later when the new Minister of War, General Carlos Masquelet, put a number of proposed postings before the cabinet. Among them was that of Franco to be Comandante General of the Canary Islands, of Goded to be Comandante General of the Balearic Islands and of Mola to be Military Governor of Pamplona. The transfer of Mola to Pamplona was the most short-sighted of these postings. The Navarrese capital was the headquarters of the Carlist movement and its militia, the Requeté. Consequently, Mola would find himself in an excellent place from which to make plans for the mainland insurrection.

Mola regarded his transfer not just as a preventative move by the government but also as a personal insult delivered by the hated Manuel Azaña, now Prime Minister. He was particularly outraged because, when he left Ceuta, he was insulted by a crowd of Republican sightseers who came to rejoice at his departure.[51] Moreover, most Africanistas feared that the victory of the Popular Front might lead to their prosecution for the atrocities committed in Asturias as well as to the implementation of Azaña's revision of promotions. No one could feel more vulnerable in this regard than Mola given the publication of his book of virulent insults against Azaña. Before leaving Morocco on 4 March, Mola had passed the leadership of the conspiracy in Morocco to Lieutenant Colonel Juan Yagüe – head of the Legion in Ceuta.[52] He had already written to Sanjurjo on 3 March, expressing his unconditional loyalty and stating that he would not get involved in any coup attempt other than at his orders.[53] En route to Pamplona, he spent eight days in Madrid during which time he participated in the key meeting of generals on 8 March as well as contacting Colonel Valentín Galarza Morante, head of the right-wing conspiratorial organization, the Unión Militar Española, and important civilian figures such as Calvo Sotelo, Juan de la Cierva and Antonio Goicoechea. He also renewed his links with his old subordinates in the police, especially Martín Báguenas, who would be of vital importance in facilitating preparations for the coup.[54]

In Madrid, at the crucial meeting on 8 March, Generals Mola, Franco, Orgaz, Villegas, Fanjul and Varela, despite their shared rhetoric about the need to 'save Spain', were motivated by resentment of the loss of key positions and hatred of the progressive Republic. Those present at the meeting undertook to act if the Popular Front dismantled the Civil Guard or reduced the size of the officer corps, if revolution broke out or if Largo Caballero were asked to form a government. Varela, claiming to speak on behalf of Sanjurjo, declared that all that was necessary was an audacious coup in Madrid. In contrast, the more pessimistic Mola was concerned that the preparations on the mainland were less advanced than those in Africa. Moreover, he argued in favour of a coordinated civilian–military uprising in the provinces.[55]

Despite Mola's misgivings, the others agreed that Varela, supported by Orgaz, should make preparations for a coup on 20 April. However, they were discovered by the security services. Varela was removed from active service and put under house arrest in Cadiz. On the orders of Sanjurjo, the preparatory material for the Varela–Orgaz coup, maps, names and notes, were handed over to Mola. Given his work with the garrisons in Africa, the intelligence network that he controlled through Martín Báguenas and his own Prussian efficiency, he was clearly the man to organize the rising. At the end of May, Sanjurjo formally recognized Mola as Director. He could count on the invaluable collaboration of Galarza, who would be known among the plotters as 'the technician'.[56]

When Mola arrived in Pamplona, he confided in the acting Military Governor, Colonel José Solchaga, his worry that there were many doubters in the army. Among them, he included 'Franquito'. Allegedly, when they met a couple of days later prior to their respective departures to their new postings, Franco had said to him, 'You go first and I will go afterwards.'[57] Mola himself was extremely cautious. Galarza knew that he was being watched by the police and warned Mola that there were government agents within the UME.[58]

Mola's doubts about possible failure were assuaged by the financier Juan March. He would provide invaluable encouragement and financial support to Mola and others.[59] Deeply hostile to the Republic, he was delighted when told of the 8 March meeting of conspiratorial generals but was alarmed to hear of their fears about the risks, particularly in the case of Mola who was alleged to have said, 'For the Fatherland, I am ready to risk my life but not my bread and butter.' March sent him a message, 'You mustn't worry about your family. If anything happens to you, Juan March will look after their needs. Moreover, he guarantees you, up front, one million pesetas.' This permitted Mola to settle his wife and four children in Biarritz.[60]

Leaving aside his personal concerns, Mola was confident of help for the coup from Juan March, together with substantial sums from Calvo Sotelo and Goicoechea and several Navarrese and Basque financiers and industrialists.[61]

The Republican government hoped that removing Mola from Morocco to the small garrison at Pamplona would neutralize him. It was assumed that Mola would have few dealings with the deeply reactionary local Carlists. After all, he had often commented to fellow officers that his grandfather had been killed by Carlists as a liberal.[62] However, he still held the key strands of the plot, with confidence in the most influential officers in Morocco and in his police network. He reached Pamplona on 14 March and, within three days, local officers introduced him to B. Félix Maíz, a thirty-six-year-old local building contractor who was to be his initial liaison with the Carlists. Discovering a shared enthusiasm for *The Protocols of the Elders of Zion* and the works of Juan Tusquets, they hit it off immediately. To Maíz's delight, Mola, who was still receiving paranoiac anti-Communist reports from the ROVS in Paris, told him that 'we confront an enemy that is not Spanish'. Maíz, whose memoirs include lengthy extracts from the *Protocols*, believed that a war to the death was imminent between Christians and the stooges of the Jews, 'the great beast – tightly knit hordes emerging from the swamp of evil'. Maíz viewed the political situation in even more extreme terms: 'all over Spain, there are teams of creatures injected with rabies who are seeking Christian flesh in which to sink their filthy teeth'.[63] Another important local collaborator was Raimundo García y García 'Garcilaso', editor of the *Diario de Navarra* and a Cortes deputy. Like Maíz, he shared the extreme-rightist views of Tusquets. He had met Mola in Morocco. In Africa, he had become friendly with Sanjurjo. In 1936, he was able to use his position as Cortes deputy to facilitate his role as liaison between Sanjurjo and Mola.[64]

The military uprising of 17–18 July 1936 was more carefully planned than any previous coup. The lessons of Sanjurjo's failed attempt of 10 August 1932 had been well learned. Mola aimed at a coordinated seizure of garrisons of all of Spain's fifty provinces and a swift annihilation of the organized working class. Over the next months, he issued a series of secret instructions which laid out the blueprint for the terror to be unleashed by the rebels. Five of these sets of instructions were numbered and there were additional ones specifically for the armed forces and for Morocco. The first, drawn up at the end of April 1936, outlined 'The objective, the methods and the itineraries'. It did not suggest that the motivation for the uprising was religious nor that it was a response to disorder. The justification was the electoral victory of the left and the consequent threat of reforming legislation. The central pillar of success would be ruthless political terror to defeat a numerically superior enemy: 'It will be realized that extreme violence will be required for the swift reduction of the enemy which is strong and well organized. Of course, all leaders of political parties, societies and trade unions not linked to our movement will be imprisoned and exemplary punishment imposed on them in order to strangle any rebellion or strikes.'[65]

For Mola, terror was, first of all, about dismantling any possible resistance on the road to power but also about 'purifying' Spain of the noxious elements of the left. However, it would also be systematic in the areas that he controlled where there was little danger from the left. One of his first decisions was to order the execution of his chauffeur because he suspected him of sympathizing with the Popular Front.[66] The hatred of the Republic that underlay the instructions was expressed virulently in a broadcast of 27 February 1937. He saw the Republic as the instrument with which 'international Jewry and sectarian freemasonry' aimed to destroy Spain. 'The Second Republic was born and, since it was conceived with the sin of treachery, it was born stunted, deformed, bastard; more than a birth, it was an abortion, and as an abortion it was doomed to perish and it perished.'[67]

The second of the secret instructions, dated 25 May, outlined a novel strategy. The focus of previous coup attempts had been Madrid, whence columns would spread out and conquer the rest of Spain. Aware of the difficulties of dominating the capital, Mola's plan was for Madrid to be attacked by columns from cities where he was confident that the coup would succeed such as Burgos, Valladolid, Zaragoza and Valencia. For the southern cities where he had doubts, his plan was to use the African Army. Mola's instructions to the forces in Morocco were extremely violent. On 24 June, he sent one of his most revealing and decisive messages to Yagüe, whom he had left in charge of the conspiracy there, now naming him 'head of all the forces in Morocco … until the arrival of a prestigious general'. It stated that, given his total confidence in Yagüe, he authorized him to carry out the coup as he saw fit although ordering him to act 'with great violence since hesitation can lead only to failure'.[68] Yagüe replied enthusiastically, 'I'm optimistic … The young are in the streets, killing and dying for their ideals. The best, the strongest, the bravest will win and they will rule with authority because they have reached the top with bravery and blood'.[69] Six days after the first set of instructions for Yagüe, there arrived twenty-five more specific ones that would guide Yagüe not only in Morocco but later in mainland Spain. These included orders to use Moroccan mercenaries and the Foreign Legion, to employ the Falange to control public order (which meant a free hand in the repression) and 'to eliminate left-wing elements, Communists, anarchists, trade unionists, freemasons etc.'[70]

In mid-May, the tireless Yagüe sent an emissary, Lieutenant Colonel Seguí, to Pamplona to inform Mola that the Moroccan garrisons were ready to rise.[71] On 25 May, Mola drew up his second set of secret instructions, the strategic plan for regional risings to be followed by concerted attacks on Madrid by columns coming from the provinces.[72] Nevertheless, as a long letter to Sanjurjo on 4 June demonstrates, he was extremely pessimistic because of the evident lack of civilian support for a coup. He wrote that more violence should be generated to create a spiral of terror and left-wing reprisal to create panic on the right.[73] On 1 July, he complained that 'there has been an effort to provoke violence between the two opposing political sectors that we could use as an excuse to proceed but so far – despite the help of some political elements – it has not fully materialized because there are still idiots who believe in coexistence with the representatives of the masses who dominate the Popular Front'.[74]

A key moment was securing the collaboration of General Gonzalo Queipo de Llano on 1 June. Queipo's role as Director General of the border force, the Carabineros, gave him licence to travel all over Spain.[75] Despite the most lukewarm sympathy with the ideology of Carlism, Mola was fully cognizant of his need for its support – what he called 'an important and indispensable national force'. Aware that the regiments at his disposal included many conscripts from Asturias who were likely to be Socialists, he wanted to strengthen their ranks with 1,500 to 2,000 Carlist fanatics.[76]

However, he was concerned that the Carlists' help was offered with unacceptable conditions that 'would make us prisoners of that political sector at the moment of victory'. He was infuriated by the intransigence of the Carlist leader Manuel Fal Conde. Mola was loath to mortgage the future not least because, to secure the collaboration of Miguel Cabanellas, the general in command of Zaragoza, he had to commit to the maintenance of the Republican flag and its anthem, the 'Himno de Riego', and to call constituent elections to decide the future of Spain. Mola desperately needed 12,000 rifles and 1 million cartridges and had to appeal to Cabanellas, who had been a deputy for Jaén in the Cortes and was one of the freemasons that Mola considered to be enemies of Spain.[77] In his secret instruction of 5 June, he stated that, after the victory of the uprising, there would be established a military directory that would not change the Republican regime.[78]

The conspiracy was facilitated by the government's complacency in the face of repeated warnings. The Director General of Security, José Alonso Mallol, worked tirelessly to combat Falangist terrorism and to monitor the activities of hostile officers. In May, he gave Azaña and Casares Quiroga a list of more than 500 conspirators who he believed should be arrested immediately. Fearful of the possible reactions, Azaña and Casares failed to act. Mallol pointed the finger at Mola but nothing was done. Shortly after Casares had been appointed Prime Minister, he dismissed information from the Navarrese Communist Jesús Monzón about the Carlist accumulation of weaponry.[79] Casares's complacency encouraged Mola, who was anyway inclined to be daring and seemed to enjoy the danger, to be more open in his activities.[80] He had a degree of protection provided by his one-time subordinate Santiago Martín Báguenas, who ran the espionage network set up by the conspirators. Although on obligatory leave of absence, Martín Báguenas maintained contact with his colleagues in the Dirección General de Seguridad and provided Mola with fevered, not to say invented, accounts of alleged Soviet activities in Spain. More importantly, he was able to keep Mola informed of any inspections planned for Pamplona, which gave him ample time to conceal any incriminating evidence.[81] Alonso Mallol's deep suspicions about what was being plotted in Pamplona saw him arrive in the city late on 3 June with sixty policemen and a substantial force of Assault Guards from surrounding provinces. The ostensible purpose of the mission was to intercept contraband weapons coming over the frontier but, in reality, it was to dismantle the conspiracy. Since Mola had been warned in advance by Martín Báguenas, Alonso Mallol's men found nothing incriminating.[82] On 15 June, at the monastery of Irache, near Estella in Navarre, Mola held a secret meeting with the commanders of the garrisons of Pamplona, Logroño, Vitoria and San Sebastián. On discovering this, the Mayor of Estella informed the Civil Governor of Navarre, who posted units of Civil Guards around the monastery. When the Governor telephoned Casares Quiroga for further instructions, the Prime Minister indignantly ordered their removal, saying that Mola was a loyal Republican who should be respected by the authorities.[83]

In late June, Mola settled the division of duties among the conspirators. Franco was expected to command the rising in Morocco. Cabanellas would be in charge in Zaragoza, Mola himself in Navarre and Burgos, Saliquet in Valladolid, Villegas in Madrid, González Carrasco in Barcelona, Goded in Valencia. Goded insisted on exchanging cities with González Carrasco.[84] Mola and the other conspirators were reluctant to proceed without Franco despite his dithering. As successively commander of the Legion, Director of the Academia General Militar and Chief of the General Staff, his influence within the officer corps was unique. The coup had little chance of succeeding without the Moroccan army, which was unquestioningly loyal to Franco. As Franco hesitated, Mola became more infuriated. On 8 July, one of the senior conspirators, General Alfredo Kindelán, managed to speak briefly with Franco by telephone and was appalled to learn that he was still not ready to join. Mola was informed two days later.[85] On 12 July, the day that the aircraft due to take him from the Canary Islands to Morocco reached Casablanca, Franco sent a coded message to Kindelán in Madrid for onward transmission to Mola. It read 'geografía poco extensa' and meant that he was refusing to join the rising on the grounds that he thought that the circumstances were insufficiently favourable. Kindelán received the message on 13 July. On the following day, he sent it on to Mola in Pamplona in the hands of a beautiful socialite, Elena Medina Lafuente Garvey, who, along with Consuelo Olagüe and Luisa Beloqui, was one of the conspirators' messengers. Medina had sewn it into the belt of her dress. When he read the message, Mola flew into a rage, furiously hurling the paper to the ground. After he had cooled down, he ordered that the pilot Juan Antonio Ansaldo be found and instructed to take Sanjurjo to Morocco to do the job expected of Franco. The conspirators in Madrid were informed by Mola that Franco was not to be counted on. However, two days later, a further message arrived to say that Franco was with them again.[86]

On 16 July, Mola's immediate superior, General Domingo Batet, head of the military region of Burgos, had a tense meeting with him at the monastery of Irache. He gave Batet his word of honour that he would not get involved in any adventure nor take part in a subversive uprising. When he did rebel and Batet rang him to remonstrate, he claimed that an enterprise to save the Fatherland was neither an adventure nor a subversive uprising. He commented later, 'I lied to Batet on that occasion conscious that my word and my honour mattered less than the interest of Spain.'[87]

Mola was so deeply pessimistic about the uncertainty regarding civilian support for the rising and Franco's participation that he contemplated abandoning the entire project.[88] Both Mola's doubts and his cruelty were revealed in his fifth secret instruction of 20 June which included the following threat: 'It is necessary to warn the timid and the ditherers that those who are not with us are against us and will be treated as enemies. For those comrades who are not comrades, the victorious movement will be ruthless.'[89] It was irresponsible for him to press ahead despite knowing that, without immediate success for the rising, a long and bloody civil war would ensue. On 15 July, during the fiesta of San Fermín, Mola was plunged into despair by news brought to Pamplona by his younger brother Ramón. The thirty-nine-year-old Ramón, an infantry captain in Barcelona, was Emilio's liaison with the plotters there. The Generalitat's security services had uncovered the plans for the rising in Catalonia and a deeply pessimistic Ramón begged his brother to desist. Emilio replied that it was too late and ordered Ramón to return to Barcelona. It was a virtual death sentence. When the coup failed, as Ramón had predicted, he shot himself. This contributed to the further brutalization of Mola. In contrast, he would be unmoved by the fact that the President of the Generalitat, Lluís Companys, saved the life of his father, the eighty-three-year-old retired General of the Civil Guard Emilio Mola López.[90]

He was having to juggle the contradictory requirements of Cabanellas and the Carlists, who wanted to establish a theocratic monarchy, while he was thinking in terms of a republican military dictatorship with a regime that accepted religious freedom. According to José María de Iribarren, the difficulties of securing Carlist support had led Mola to contemplate shooting the Carlist leader Fal Conde and committing suicide himself.[91] He drafted an application to leave the army and he was considering retiring to Cuba.[92] The conflict was resolved partly by the intervention of Sanjurjo, Garcilaso and the Conde de Rodezno. Mola had considerably better relations with the Falange which, having less to offer, was not so exigent.[93] It is difficult to calculate the impact of the news of the murder of Calvo Sotelo on 13 July since Mola was to claim that eight hours earlier he had already issued orders for the Army of Africa to rebel. The assassination decided the participation of many who had been hesitating.[94]

Despite a flood of disturbing news, Casares Quiroga initially failed to see the seriousness of the situation. However, by 9.00 p.m. on 18 July, he had resigned and, in an effort to placate the rebels, Azaña appointed a centrist cabinet under the moderate Republican Diego Martínez Barrio. He made the extraordinary gesture of telephoning Mola at 2 a.m. on 19 July to propose a compromise solution. To avoid a bloody fratricidal struggle, Martínez Barrio was making the humiliating sacrifice of dealing with a mutinous general. The conversation was icily polite but futile. Offered a place in the cabinet, Mola refused on the grounds that it was too late and an accommodation would mean the betrayal of the rank and file of both sides.[95]

Mola's proclamation of martial law in Pamplona earlier on 19 July 1936 declared: 'Re-establishing the principle of authority unavoidably demands that punishments be exemplary and imposed without hesitation or vacillation in terms of both their severity and their speed.'[96] Later on the same day, he addressed a meeting of all of the alcaldes of the province of Pamplona and told them, 'It is necessary to spread terror. We have to create the impression of mastery eliminating without scruples or hesitation all those who do not think as we do. There can be no cowardice. If we vacillate for one moment and fail to proceed with the greatest determination, we will not win. Anyone who helps or hides a Communist or a supporter of the Popular Front will be shot.'[97] One of the first victims was the commander of the Civil Guard in Pamplona, José Rodríguez Medel, whose crime was to have remained loyal to his oath to obey the constituted power. When he refused the invitation to join the rising, Mola told him that he was safe to leave. Allegedly, he said later, 'We have to liquidate that bastard.' Rodríguez Medel was shot shortly afterwards by Civil Guards of his garrison. Three Civil Guards who refused to join the rebellion were also shot.[98] Mola declared to a group of journalists in mid-August that 'My goal is to reconstruct Spain and to punish the miserable murderers who are our adversaries.'[99]

Like his fellow conspirators, Franco and Queipo de Llano, Mola regarded the Spanish proletariat in the same way as they did the Moroccans, as an inferior race that had to be subjugated by sudden, uncompromising violence. The identification of the colonized Moroccans with Spanish workers had been developing in the years of the Republic. At the beginning of the war, Mola declared that 'it is up to us, and only us, the military, to initiate it [the rebellion]. It is our right; it is the national will, because we know exactly the scale of our power.'[100] Military dreams of creating a new Spanish empire had been replaced by the determination to subjugate Spain itself by the same methods as had been used in Morocco.

However, while Franco and Queipo applied in southern Spain the exemplary terror they had learned in North Africa, Mola was in charge of the repression in the significantly different provinces of the north. In Navarre, Álava, the eight provinces of Old Castile, the three of León, the four of Galicia, two-thirds of Zaragoza and virtually all of Cáceres, the coup was successful within hours or days. The excuses used for the slaughter in Andalusia and Badajoz, alleged left-wing atrocities or a threatened Communist take-over, could not be used in those deeply conservative Catholic areas that quickly fell under

Mola's control. Essentially, the 'crime' of those executed was to have voted for the Popular Front, to have challenged their own subordination as workers or as women.[101] Despite minimal left-wing resistance, the repression there, under Mola's overall jurisdiction was carried out by the Carlists, the Falange and other local rightists. It was an indiscriminate festival of blood. In his determination to eliminate 'those who do not think as we do', Mola had had lists compiled by eager collaborators, including Garcilaso. Those to receive 'exemplary punishments' included, as well as trade unionists and members of left-wing parties, nonconformists of all kinds – freemasons, vegetarians, nudists, spiritualists, Esperantists – who would be arrested and, if not murdered, tortured.[102] In the copy of his diary that he gave to his friend José María Azcona, Iribarren wrote that Mola had deleted the sentence 'This war will solve for us the agrarian problem,' a sentiment worthy of Gonzalo Aguilera.[103]

Yet, despite his instructions for exemplary terror, a mere ten days after the uprising he remarked to his secretary, Iribarren, 'Every civil war is terrifying but this one is of truly terrible violence.'[104] A similar glimmer of remorse could be seen in a comment made on 30 August. When Gil Robles visited him in Valladolid and asked him how things were going, Mola put his head in his hands and cried, 'We've got ourselves into a right mess. I'd give anything for this war to be over by the end of the year and to have cost only one hundred thousand lives.'[105]

Having sent Juan Ansaldo to collect Sanjurjo from Portugal, the news of his death when their plane crashed on 20 July, together with the defeats of Fanjul in Madrid and Goded in Barcelona, plunged Mola into despair. His lurches from wild optimism to suicidal pessimism suggest that he was bipolar.[106] Two days after Sanjurjo's fatal accident, Mola moved his headquarters south-west to Burgos, thus freeing himself of the Carlists. In his first speech in Burgos, he had claimed to be in control of all of Spain except for Madrid and Barcelona.[107] He gave triumphalist interviews to several foreign newspapermen. On 23 July, in a conversation punctuated by the sounds of Republicans being shot, he told the American Reynolds Packard and his wife Eleanor, 'You can be sure that the fighting will be over within the next three weeks. I tell you this because if I were not sure that this revolution would succeed quickly and without much bloodshed, I never would have taken part in it.' Packard described him as 'A tall, homely man who peered through tortoise-shell glasses and groped for words to express himself. He struck us as incapable of political hypocrisy.'[108]

The British correspondent of the *Daily Express*, Sefton Delmer, described him as 'a tall, slightly stooping, elderly looking ascetic who, with his short-sighted spectacled eyes, was more my idea of a papal secretary than a general'. 'Optimism personified,' Mola declared. 'We command all Spain, except for Madrid, Barcelona and Bilbao. And we shall take Madrid before the month is out.' He told a French journalist that he was confident of starving Madrid into surrender. Delmer, sympathetic to the rebel cause, recorded:

> Punctually at two o'clock every night I was awakened by volleys of shots. They were the shots fired by Mola's execution squads who night after night dragged their captives from the crowded prison to carry out the summary death sentences passed by the courts martial during the day. And day after day more prisoners – civilians, not soldiers taken in battle – were being brought in to take the places of those killed the night before.[109]

On 24 July, Mola set up a provisional seven-man military directory, the so-called Junta de Defensa Nacional. He announced to his staff that 'as was originally planned, it is in the interests of the new regime that a national government, a Junta de Defensa, be set up. If we do not do it at once, we run the risk that some other group will get in first. Now is not the time for me to say any more about that.' Those remarks indicated that he was already thinking in terms of rivalry with Franco and Queipo.[110] The initial plan had been for a government under the presidency of Sanjurjo. Goicoechea and others from the monarchist Renovación Española group convinced Mola that an exclusively military directory would inhibit political squabbles. It consisted of Generals Mola, Miguel Ponte, Fidel Dávila and Andrés Saliquet and two colonels from the General Staff, Federico Montaner and Fernando Moreno Calderón under the nominal presidency of Miguel Cabanellas, the most senior major general in the rebel camp after the death of Sanjurjo. Mola did not include Franco in the Junta de Defensa until 3 August.[111]

He had been accompanied from Pamplona by the one-time extreme leftist and subsequently Radical deputy for Ciudad Real Joaquín Pérez Madrigal. In a remarkable act of hypocrisy and prescience, this erstwhile member of the group known as the 'wild boars' had appeared in Pamplona on 18 July seeking 'purification and redemption'. After making contact with the Conde de Rodezno and Garcilaso, he managed to insinuate himself on to Mola's staff.[112] He later claimed that he had played a tiny part in the confection of the Junta de Defensa. In his version, Mola had originally contemplated naming as General Severiano Martínez Anido. Pérez Madrigal claims that he persuaded Mola that Martínez Anido's reputation for brutality made Cabanellas a better bet, presenting the fact that he was regarded by his fellow rebels as dangerously liberal as an advantage in terms of the international image of the military rebels. In fact, Mola unilaterally appointed Cabanellas to preside over the Junta ostensibly because of his seniority but in reality because he was anxious to get him away from active command in Zaragoza. Mola himself had visited Zaragoza on 21 July and had been appalled to find Cabanellas exercising restraint in crushing opposition to the rising. Once Cabanellas had been extracted from Zaragoza, Mola charged Pérez Madrigal with keeping him out of the way by taking him on endless propaganda tours of the rebel zone.[113]

It was in the areas of Spain where the military coup met little or no resistance that the real war aims of the rebels were made clear. This meant the annihilation of everything that the Republic signified, whether challenges to the privileges of landowners, industrialists, the Catholic Church and the army or outrage at the Republic's progressive reforms in terms of education and women's rights. The execution of trade unionists, members of left-wing parties, elected municipal officials, Republican functionaries, schoolteachers and freemasons, who had committed no crimes, constituted what has been called 'preventive assassinations'.[114] At an early stage, Mola got in touch with the Jefe Provincial of the Falange in Navarre, José Moreno, to authorize its participation in the butchery. The slogan of the Navarrese Falange was 'Comrade, you are obliged to persecute

Judaism, freemasonry, Marxism and separatism. Burn their books and publications.'[115] When Mola was informed about the atrocities, he is said to have replied, 'Like you, I regret such things but I need the Falange and so I have had to give it some authority.' There could be no doubt that he encouraged the killing.[116]

It was in Navarre, in fact, that Mola had been able to feel totally confident of success. There, one in every ten people who had voted for the Popular Front was murdered, a total of 2,822 men and 35 women.[117] On 19 July, Mola sent a column of 1,800 men under Colonel Francisco García Escámez from Pamplona to Logroño. There they unleashed a massive repression.[118] As Civil Governor of Logroño, Mola appointed an artilleryman, Captain Emilio Bellod Gómez, telling him, 'Be harsh, very harsh,' to which Bellod replied, 'Don't worry, General, that is exactly what I will do.' From 19 July until Bellod was replaced in January 1937, the bulk of the killing took place and the majority of it was extra-judicial. Beatings and torture, imprisonment and death were the fate of leftists. There were women murdered, and the wives of executed leftists had their heads shaved, were forced to drink castor oil and were frequently subjected to rape and other forms of sexual humiliation. In the capital, Logroño, the provincial prison and the municipal cemetery were soon full. By the end of December, there had been nearly 2,000 executions in the province, including more than forty women. In the course of the war, 1 per cent of the total population was executed.[119] A similarly ferocious repression was unleashed on Galicia. Even in comparison with the provinces of Old Castile, the repression throughout Galicia was massively disproportionate to the extremely limited scale of resistance, which might be taken as a symptom of the rebels' awareness of their own illegitimacy.[120] There were more than 4,500 executions in Galicia, including seventy-nine women.[121]

The other provinces soon under Mola's orders experienced the same scale of savagery. One of his closest and most reliable collaborators was Major General Andrés Saliquet Zumeta, who organized the coup and the subsequent repression in Valladolid. Saliquet used Falangist militias to crush left-wing resistance throughout the province. All through the late summer and autumn, anyone who had held a position in a left-wing or liberal party, municipal council or trade union was likely to be seized by Falangists and shot. Exact figures for the scale of the repression in the province of Valladolid are impossible to calculate since many deaths were not recorded. The most recent local study places the total at over 3,000.[122] That Mola was aware of the criminality involved was demonstrated in mid-August when a radio message to the commander of the Civil Guard in Valladolid was intercepted in the Ministry of War in Madrid. En route from Valladolid to Burgos, Mola had been annoyed when his car was delayed while the road was cleared of a large number of corpses. In his message he demanded that future executions take place away from main roads and that the bodies be buried immediately.[123]

In Salamanca and other towns in the province like Ciudad Rodrigo, Ledesma and Béjar, the resistance was swiftly and brutally crushed. Since there had been virtually no violence in Salamanca in the months preceding the military coup, most liberals and leftists made no attempt to flee. Nevertheless, the military organized a witch-hunt of liberals, leftists and trade unionists. Local rightists created a Guardia Cívica, paramilitary units that carried out a virtually uncontrolled repression that degenerated into personal vendettas and naked criminality. Armed Falangist columns swooped on villages and took away those denounced as leftists. After interrogation and torture, some just 'disappeared', while others were transferred to the provincial prison. Many of those imprisoned would die of illnesses contracted in the unhygienic conditions of a prison which had been designed for 100 prisoners but housed over 2,000 during the war, twelve or more to cells intended for one or two men.[124]

On 31 July 1936, from Radio Pamplona, Mola made the first of several radio broadcasts, in all of which he underlined his commitment to merciless continuation of the repression, declaring, 'I could take advantage of our present favourable circumstances to offer the enemy some negotiated settlement; but I do not want to. I want to defeat them to impose my, and your, will upon them and to annihilate them. I want Marxism and the red flag of communism to be remembered in history as a nightmare but as a nightmare that has been washed clean by the blood of patriots.' This linked to the organicist theories of the extreme right. For Mola, bloodshed was a biological necessity.[125] In private, he expressed similar views. On 18

August, speaking with Millán Astray, he said, 'At this point in the war, I have opted for war without quarter. Those who have taken up arms against us, against the army, shoot them. If I saw my father in the enemy ranks, I would shoot him myself.'[126] His boast that he was happy to sign three or four death sentences every day was one of the many revelations in the diary of José María Iribarren that led to an outraged Manuel Arias Paz, the Delegado de Prensa in the Oficina de Prensa y Propaganda, having the book confiscated. In the same conversation, he revealed that, had he not been a soldier, he would have liked to be a surgeon.[127]

On 20 August, Mola moved his headquarters to the Ayuntamiento (city hall) of Valladolid. He would remain there for two months. While his furniture was still being moved in, he went to Salamanca to receive a visit from Yagüe. There was much bragging about the bloodshed in Badajoz. When it was time for Yagüe to leave, a cheering crowd gathered around his convoy of cars. Mola ostentatiously embraced him, saying, 'This is my favourite pupil.'[128]

In mid-December, the philosopher Miguel de Unamuno wrote to his friend Quintín de Torre about Franco and the repression: 'Regarding the Caudillo – I suppose you mean poor General Franco – he controls none of this repression here, this savage rearguard terror. He just lets it happen. The rearguard repression is in the hands of that poisonous and rancorous monster of perversion, General Mola.'[129]

After the deaths of Sanjurjo, Goded and Fanjul, Mola was left as the only general capable of being a future challenger to Franco. Mola and Franco were worlds apart in both political preferences and temperament. Iribarren made a tacit comparison between them: Mola 'was neither cold, imperturbable nor hermetic. He was a man whose face transmitted the impressions of each moment, whose stretched nerves reflected disappointments.' He seemed oblivious to security issues, strolling around Burgos in civilian clothes either alone or with a friend, going into cafés or to the cinema. He made car journeys without an escort. There were no security arrangements at his chaotic headquarters. Virtually anyone could wander in to talk to him.[130] He disregarded not only his own safety but also his image. Mola did not encourage the press, while Franco was giving interviews on a regular basis, mendaciously broadcasting his own importance. In contrast, Mola consistently refused to give interviews to the press, acquiring along the way the nickname 'el general invisible'.[131]

However, as the technical mastermind of the rising, Mola harvested considerable failures. The Moroccan army under Franco's command would soon emerge as the cornerstone of Nationalist victory. Mola's assumption of success in all the major cities except Madrid was the key failure of his planning. Even by his own admission, it was a near impossibility. In mid-June, he told a group of his collaborators in Pamplona, 'there is no chance of winning either in the barracks or the streets'.[132] The defeat of the uprising in Barcelona, Valencia, the Basque Country, Santander and Asturias severely undermined the capacity of the garrisons of Zaragoza, Pamplona, Burgos and Valladolid to send columns towards Madrid. Mola had long since been aware of the lack of enthusiasm among the conscripts of the mainland army. Moreover, somewhat late in the day, he perceived the shortage of weapons and ammunition. By 22 July 1936, he was lamenting to the monarchist José Ignacio Escobar that even the smallest military aid from France to the Madrid government would be enough to tip the balance in favour of the Republic. He reluctantly accepted that he lacked sufficient forces to take Madrid and therefore would be dependent on Franco's African columns.[133] Regarding his deficiencies as a strategist, it is noteworthy that he commented on 15 August that, in his entire career, he had never commanded forces as numerous as those that he had sent to Somosierra.[134]

Both Mola and Franco sent pleas for help to the Third Reich. The difference was that Franco's emissaries were Germans with direct links to the Nazi Party, armed with credible documentation and relatively ambitious requests. Mola's envoy, José Ignacio Escobar, had neither papers nor specific demands other than for 10 million rifle cartridges. He had to seek out old contacts within the conservative German diplomatic corps, which was hostile to any adventurism in Spain. In the eyes of the German authorities, Franco was clearly the leading rebel general while Mola appeared unprofessional and lacking vision. Indeed, Mola himself seemed incapable of thinking beyond the rifle cartridges and what they might cost.[135] On 3 August, he despatched a rather pathetic telegram to Franco: 'I beg you to send a telegram to Agramonte, the Ambassador in Berlin, telling him to inform German political figures that you and I are completely in agreement regarding both military actions and the project for national reconstruction. It is important because there are those there who believe the contrary.'[136]

There is considerable circumstantial evidence to suggest that Franco was deliberately delaying his advance on Madrid because he did not want the capital to fall while the Junta de Defensa, controlled by Mola, still existed. However, at the same time at Franco's headquarters in Morocco, according to his cousin, 'We were paralysed by fear that General Mola's columns would reach Madrid before Franco's and would trample on our plans.' If the capital fell while Franco's columns were still only halfway there, the political triumph would be Mola's. On 11 August, Mola pleaded with Franco to speed up the advance on Madrid: 'Both political and economic factors oblige me to reiterate the need for you to advance on Madrid as soon as possible. The enemy is demoralized – I have documents to prove it – and we must not give them any respite.' Mola was right. The lack of a serious defence of Madrid, before the arrival of Russian aid or the International Brigades, offered a unique opportunity. Franco replied cunningly on the same day: '1) Like you, I have always considered the occupation of Madrid to be the primordial and most urgent problem, and all efforts must be directed towards its solution. 2) At the same time, pockets of resistance must be reduced and the interior of occupied territory be controlled, especially in Andalusia.' In other words, while accepting Mola's accurate assessment of the importance of a rapid advance on Madrid, he was going to be otherwise engaged in the pacification of the south which, obviously, would delay the fall of Madrid. His scheme could be seen when, on the following day, after Yagüe's capture of Mérida, Franco ordered him to divert his advance 62 kilometres to the west to pacify Badajoz, a city of no strategic importance.

Nine days later, on 20 August, a desperate Mola sent a telegram: 'Given the impossibility of advancing on the Madrid front as a result of enemy air superiority, what is your plan for an advance on Madrid? If there is going to be a delay, I will have to concentrate my activity on another front. I urgently need your answer.' Franco replied that his

advance would be slow. On 3 September, an ever more frantic Mola
sent another request to Franco:

> My dear general, I urgently need you to send me one million
> cartridges. I'm also badly short of machine guns. I beg you to send
> me as soon as possible half of those that you have received from
> Germany. The people here are turning against me because they
> think that I'm doing nothing to get them the necessary equipment.
> They're saying that everything goes to you and that you are keep-
> ing the air support for yourself. They're not wrong ... Send the
> materiel that I asked for and that you offered the other day. I can't
> believe that you would abandon me with the excuse that you are
> short of munitions and other key elements.[137]

Mola had failed to anticipate that his forces would be weakened by
the need to send troops to San Sebastián, to Asturias and to Aragon,
or by the length of time it took Franco to get the Army of Africa to
the mainland. Yagüe and his forces had been ready to leave Morocco
for the mainland on 15 July and had three merchant ships ready –
Monte Toro, *Vicente Puchol* and *Antonio Lázaro* – to carry the troops
and their artillery to Spain. Although the Dragon Rapide sent to
collect Franco flew into the Canary Islands that same day, 15 July, he
did not leave until the 18th. By then, the navy was in Republican
hands and controlling the Straits of Gibraltar. Mola wrote in his note-
book, 'The situation that we are suffering is the result of what should
and could have been done but was not done.' There was considerable
bitterness at Mola's headquarters at the time and later as a result of
Franco's delays, with mutterings about his hypocrisy. Certainly, Mola
made it clear that he did not trust Franco but that he put the war
effort ahead of any settling of accounts.[138]

Mola's initial plan for a rapid coup was undermined by the failures
of Fanjul in Madrid and Goded in Barcelona and by Franco's delays
in getting the Army of Africa to the mainland. Mola himself contributed to the failure of the rising in the capital by his delay in sending
columns from Burgos, Pamplona and Valladolid, in order to help the
rebels there. Instead, because of his own and the Carlists' hatred of
Basque nationalism, he weakened the strike on Madrid by dividing

his forces for an assault on Guipúzcoa. His hesitation permitted improvised workers' militias to halt the columns of soldiers, Carlist Requetés and Falangists that he sent against Madrid in the passes through the mountainous territory that guarded the capital, the Somosierra pass in the Sierra to the north and the Alto del León to the north-west. Things were going so badly that he had to resort to lying to his subordinates. Iribarren wrote later of 'his inner torment'. As early as 25 July, he had telegraphed Franco to say that he was contemplating moving all his forces to the north of the Duero basin to wait for Franco's columns. With characteristic firmness and optimism, Franco replied, 'Stand firm, victory certain.'[139] Mola had underestimated the level of popular resistance in Barcelona and Valencia. His failure to extend his network of conspirators in the navy had delayed the arrival in Spain of the African Army. Generally speaking, he seemed to have a relatively limited notion of the utility of aircraft in the conflict to come.

Having organized the uprising, Mola harboured ambitions of acquiring power. This can be seen in the words of the announcer on his mouthpiece Radio Castilla, who, presumably with his permission, presented him in eulogistic terms:

> Spaniards, here you have a man with all the qualities of the great leaders, of those who have the clear intelligence to see, the iron will to fulfil their tasks, and the steady hand and resolute determination to lead a people to victory. General Mola, at the same time as he is head of an army, is also the leader of a nation that is fighting for its very existence, for the authentically Christian and Spanish civilization which is threatened by death at the hands of the anti-Spain of Marxism, separatism and freemasonry.

By 13 September, the same announcer presented him as one of the Caudillos who would bring victory.[140] Maíz comments on the General's irritation before the end of July that Franco's headquarters was spreading the notion that Mola had promised Franco the headship of the movement.[141]

Franco would be the beneficiary of Hitler's decision to send twenty bombers to the rebels. On 29 July, a jubilant Franco had telegraphed

Mola: 'today the first transport aircraft arrives. They will go on arriving at the rate of two per day until we have twenty. I am also expecting six fighters and twenty machine guns.' The telegram ended triumphantly, 'We have the upper hand. ¡Viva España!'[142] On 1 August, it was again Franco reassuring Mola with a telegram reading: 'we will ensure the successful passage of the convoy, crucial to the advance'.[143]

On 31 July, after being told that the French press had suggested that Prieto had been appointed to negotiate with the rebels, Mola exploded: 'Negotiate? Never! This war can end only with the extermination of the enemies of Spain.' Mola told Iribarren that 'A war of this kind has to end with the domination of one side and the total extermination of the defeated. They've killed one of my brothers but they'll pay for it.'[144] In fact, his brother Ramón had committed suicide when he saw that the rising had failed. On 14 August, Mola would be heard saying, 'A year ago, I would have trembled at having to authorize a firing squad. I wouldn't have been able to sleep for the sorrow of it. Now, I can sign three or four every day without batting an eyelid.'[145]

Throughout the spring of 1936, March made financial guarantees to overcome the hesitations of several key generals and keep them in the conspiracy. In March, for the purchase of arms, he also provided Franco and Mola with a credit of £500,000 through the Kleinwort Bank. This was increased to £800,000 in August and to £942,000 in December. In Biarritz that spring, arms purchases were on the agenda of Mola's frequent meetings with March, who typically imposed harsh repayment and interest conditions.[146]

Despite being the dynamo behind the military coup, Mola's position was fatally weakened by the death of Sanjurjo and the failures of Goded in Barcelona and Fanjul in Madrid – for which he was arguably partly to blame because of his delays in sending troops towards Madrid.[147] In addition to his military deficiencies, Mola made some serious political errors in the internal power stakes. His aim for postwar Spain was a republican dictatorship, free of Marxism and freemasonry. He declared to the French press on 24 July, 'Our movement is only republican. The Fatherland can find its noble expression only in a regime freely chosen by the people.'[148] On 1 August, the heir to the Spanish throne, Don Juan de Borbón, arrived in Spain in a chauffeur-driven Bentley. Using the pseudonym 'Juan López', and

wearing a blue overall and red beret and sporting the monarchist flag
on an armband, he set off for the front. Mola, hearing of his plan to
volunteer to fight on the rebel side, on 2 August ordered the Civil
Guard to arrest him. Don Juan was detained in Aranda, then escorted
to the frontier. A furious Mola is alleged to have threatened to have
him shot 'with all the honours appropriate to his elevated rank'. To
behave so abruptly and without consulting his fellow generals
revealed both Mola's lack of subtlety and his anti-monarchist sentiments. On the following day, the founder of the Spanish air force, the
Infante Alfonso de Orleans Borbón, arrived in Burgos from his
French exile and volunteered his services as a pilot. He was sent
packing by the Chief of Mola's General Staff. Both incidents impelled
deeply monarchist officers to transfer their political loyalty to
Franco.[149]

This was consolidated by Franco's astute initiative in Seville on 15
August when he announced that the rebel forces would adopt the
monarchist red–yellow–red flag. Mola was simply not consulted and
his own naivety was soon exposed further. When Franco later
prevented Don Juan volunteering to serve on the battleship Baleares,
he carefully presented an action that was part of his own plans for
absolute power as motivated by both anxiety for his safety and the
need to ensure that the heir to the throne should be 'King of all
Spaniards' and not be compromised by having fought on one side in
the war. According to Iribarren, Mola was furious that Franco was
going back on his word that there would be no change to the flag or
the Republican regime.[150]

By 7 August, Franco had established his headquarters in Seville. At
that stage, there was still little communication between him and
Mola. On or around 12 or 13 August, Mola informed an agent of the
German intelligence services that his forces were desperately short of
aircraft, a whole range of arms and, above all, ammunition and that
he was having difficulty in liaising with Franco. At that stage, the
German agent reported, 'In my opinion, supplies for the northern
group are especially urgent at present, since thus far the southern
group has been supplied exclusively.'[151] Four days later, telephone
contact between Seville and Burgos was established and the two
generals spoke. Apparently oblivious to any eventual political impli-

cations, Mola acceded to Franco's insistence that there should be no duplication of dealings with the Germans, a matter in which he had been more successful. He thus ceded to Franco the overall control of supplies. He seems not to have perceived the importance of the international dimension of the war. His political allies were astounded by his naivety. José Ignacio Escobar asked him if he had therefore agreed on the telephone that the head of the movement be Franco. Mola replied guilelessly, 'We didn't speak about that and nothing has been decided yet. It is an issue which will be resolved when the time comes. Between Franco and me there are neither conflicts nor personal ambitions. We see entirely eye to eye and to leave in his hands this business of the procurement of arms abroad is just a way of avoiding a damaging duplication of effort.' An appalled Escobar argued that this effectively announced to the Germans that Mola was second-in-command. By ceding control of arms supplies, Mola had ensured that Franco would be the dominant figure on the rebel side. Escobar was convinced that Mola had been able to organize the coup, assuming that it would lead to a rapid victory. Now, he saw that Mola was overwhelmed by the scale of the task before him and was therefore ready to defer to Franco.[152] Mola's easygoing attitude to the control of arms supplies was a reflection of the stark differences between him and Franco both in personal ambition and in temperament.

Despite the concerns of his supporters, Mola remained on good terms with Franco.[153] Moreover, he seemed prepared to recognize Franco's superior position in terms of foreign supplies and battle-hardened troops. A lengthy missive on 4 August saw Franco presenting himself as the source of largesse in terms of financial backing and military hardware. He boasted that foreign suppliers made few if any demands for early payment. He could offer to send Mola aircraft.[154] On 16 August, Franco flew to Burgos. Photographs reveal, and Mola could not have failed to notice, the acclaim with which Franco was received by the local population. This suggested that he was already seen as the real leader. After dinner, they spent several hours locked in secret conclave. Although no decision was taken, it was clear to both that the efficient prosecution of the war required a single overall military command.[155] Given Franco's virtual monopoly of contacts with the Germans and Italians and the rapid advance of his African columns, Mola must have realized that the choice of Franco to assume the necessary authority would be virtually inevitable. Franco's staff had already loaded the dice by convincing German military intelligence that the victory in Extremadura had indisputably established him as 'Commander-in-Chief'. Portuguese newspapers and other sections of the international press described him as 'Commander-in-Chief' presumably on the basis of information supplied by his headquarters. The Portuguese Consul in Seville had referred to him as 'the supreme commander of the Spanish army' as early as mid-August.[156] A German agent reported to Admiral Canaris, the head of German military intelligence, in mid-August that 'The victory at Extremadura has outwardly established contact between the northern and the southern group, as well as contact with Lisbon. The Commander-in-Chief is definitely Franco.'[157]

Mola was gradually being forced towards the same view. On 20 August, he sent a pessimistic and deferential message to Franco. Reporting that his own forces were facing difficulties on the Madrid front because of the government's air superiority, he asked about the progress of Franco's own advance on the capital. In the event of Franco's advance being delayed, Mola was essentially asking if he should concentrate his activities on another front. Franco's reply the next day made it clear that he was expecting his advance to be considerably delayed.[158] Mola was thinking of how best to coordinate their efforts in the interests of the war effort rather than of a power struggle. Nevertheless, on the evening of 23 August, a visit from Johannes Eberhard Franz Bernhardt in Valladolid made him aware of the extent to which Franco was consolidating his own position. A German businessman in Morocco, Bernhardt was an active member of the Nazi Party and a friend of Mola. He conveyed the welcome news that an anxiously awaited German shipment of machine guns and ammunition was on its way by train from Lisbon. Mola's delight was severely diminished when Bernhardt said to him, 'I have received orders to tell you that you are receiving all these arms not from Germany but from the hands of General Franco.' Mola went white but was forced to accept that this was the consequence of the fact that General Helmuth Wilberg, head of the inter-service commission

Republican orphans forced to give the fascist salute to Franco murals in a scene from the documentary *To Die in Madrid*, 1965.

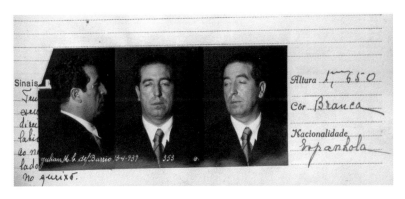

Portuguese police identity file of Mauricio Carlavilla, 13 April 1939.

José María Pemán (right) examines Republican corpses in Toledo with the local
Falangist chief, Pepe Sainz Nothnagel, October 1936.

Pemán harangues a meeting of the Falange with Queipo de Llano seated third from
right, 18 July 1938.

Father Joan Tusquets in Barcelona, portrait printed in AVUI newspaper, 5 November 1993.

Refugees flee towards Madrid as the rebel columns advance from the south, August 1936.

Exhausted refugees, fleeing from Málaga to Almería, rest in a village along the way, 8–9 February 1937.

Aguilera (centre) in Talavera de la Reina with group of foreign correspondents including Kim Philby (second from right), 1936.

Aguilera as a young hussar at the time he was courting Inés Luna.

Portrait of General Emilio Mola.

Mola (leaping) with General Franco
(centre) and General Cavalcanti,
Burgos, 16 August 1936.

Queipo de Llano addresses his troops in Almadén in the province of Ciudad Real, one of the last Republican towns to fall, 27 March 1939.

Mourning women after the purge of the district by Major Castejón in Triana, Sevilla.

Republican Women, the widows of murdered leftists, and young teenage girls with shaved heads forced to make the fascist salute in Montilla, Córdoba, August 1936.

Hitler greets Queipo de Llano in Kessel with returning Condor Legion, 4 June 1939.

Ramón Serrano Suñer,
Franco and Mussolini,
Bordighera, 12 February 1941.

Hitler greets Francoon
on his arrival at Hendaye,
23 October 1940.

appointed by Hitler to coordinate German intervention, had already agreed that Franco would be the conduit for German supplies which were to be sent only when requested by him and to the ports indicated by him.[159]

At the end of August, news reached Mola's headquarters of a letter sent by Franco to Casares Quiroga on 23 June. Of labyrinthine ambiguity, the text both suggested that the army would be loyal if treated properly and insinuated that it was hostile to the Republic. The clear implication was that, if only the Prime Minister would put Franco in charge, the plots could be dismantled. In later years, his apologists presented the letter as either a skilful effort to put Casares off the scent or a last magnanimous peace-making gesture. There is no evidence that the letter was ever received. If it was, Casares failed to take the opportunity to neutralize Franco, either by buying him off or by having him arrested. Mola believed it to be inconceivable that Casares Quiroga received the letter. If he had, Franco would have been relieved of his command immediately. At the time, Mola was furious about the letter because he regarded the text as evidence of Franco's duplicity and potential betrayal of the plans for the uprising.[160]

Given the difficulties faced by Mola in his advance on Madrid, he began instead a campaign to cut off the Basque Country from the French border. He declared that he intended a 'crushing victory' and had no thought of a negotiated peace.[161] Irún and Fuenterrabía were shelled from the sea and attacked daily by German and Italian bombers. The bombers also dropped rebel pamphlets threatening to repeat what had been done in Badajoz. Irún's poorly armed and untrained militia defenders fought bravely but were overwhelmed on 3 September. Thousands of panic-stricken refugees fled over the international bridge from Irún across the River Bidasoa to France. The Basque Country, Santander and Asturias were now isolated from France as well as from the rest of Republican Spain. Rebel forces occupied San Sebastián on Sunday 13 September. Mola issued an ultimatum on 25 September calling for the immediate surrender of Bilbao, threatening an all-out assault by land, sea and air. On 12 October, he declared that he would capture Bilbao within a week.[162]

Despite the coordination between Franco and Mola, first by telegram and later by telephone, the issue of a single command was on the agenda. Mola flew to Cáceres on 29 August to discuss the matter with his fellow general.[163] The rebels consolidated their position throughout August and September as General José Enrique Varela connected Seville, Cordoba, Granada and Cadiz. The speed with which Franco's columns moved northwards and spread out through Andalusia and Extremadura contrasted with Mola's failure to capture new territory. Franco's forces enjoyed the support of the Third Reich and Fascist Italy whereas Mola was left to his fate. It has been suggested that Mola compensated for his paralysis at the battle front by intensifying the repression in the rearguard. In the evening of 15 August, on Burgos's Radio Castilla, he gave carte blanche to all of those involved in the repression, declaring, 'Someone has said that the military movement was prepared by ambitious generals encouraged by certain political parties annoyed by an electoral defeat. That is not true. We have launched the movement, fervently seconded by the honourable working people, to free the Fatherland from anarchy and chaos.' Mola proclaimed his intention to annihilate the enemy, for whom 'death would be insufficient', and that he would contemplate no negotiation. The same message of extermination and surgical removal of those perceived as hostile to the rebels' notion of Spain could be heard in all of his broadcasts.

In that same August broadcast, he laid out his justification for the savagery that he had unleashed: 'My words go out to our enemies, since it is only right and proper that they know what to expect lest, when the time arrives for the settling of scores, they have recourse to the legal principle that "no punishment can be imposed on an offender that was not established before the offence was committed".'

Mola declared that the coup intended to free Spain from the Jewish–masonic–Bolshevik conspiracy – 'the symbolic triangles and compasses of the lodges and the incestuous concubinage of the gold of the soulless capitalists and the apostles of the Internationals' – 'from the chaos of anarchy, chaos which since the rise of the Popular Front has been prepared in detail with the cynical support and the morbid complacency of certain members of the government'. The instruments of this anarchy were 'the clenched fists of the Marxist hordes'. For Mola, the blame for unleashing them lay squarely with one man:

Only a monster with the complex psychological constitution of
Azaña could foment such a catastrophe; a monster who seems
rather the absurd brainchild of a new and fantastic Dr Frankenstein
than the fruit of the love of a woman. When I hear people demanding his head, I think they are being unjust. Azaña should be locked
away, just that, locked away, so that selected brain specialists might
study in him a case of mental degeneration, perhaps the most
interesting to have occurred from the times of primitive man to
the present day.[164]

In his speech on 15 August, he threatened those whom he considered
'the lukewarm' in their support for the rebel cause. This was seen in
his treatment of the 'blandengue' (weakling) General Víctor Carrasco
Amilibia, the military commander of Logroño. A hesitant member of
the conspiracy, Carrasco imposed martial law and arrested the Civil
Governor, the Alcalde and the commander of the Civil Guard.
However, he did not unleash the scale of repression expected by
Mola, who sent Colonel García Escamez to begin the dirty work.
Carrasco was arrested on Mola's orders, imprisoned for three years,
then tried for 'negligence' and expelled from the army.[165]

While the Republic floundered in search of foreign assistance and
its disorganized militias fell back on the capital, the rebels tightened
up their command structure. On 21 September, at an airfield near
Salamanca, the leading rebel generals met to choose a commander-
in-chief both for obvious military reasons and to facilitate ongoing
negotiations for aid from Hitler and Mussolini. Franco had let both
monarchists, through General Alfredo Kindelán, and Falangists, via
Colonel Juan de Yagüe, think that he would further their aims.
Kindelán organized the meeting. Franco was chosen as single
commander despite reluctance on the part of some of his fellow
generals but not, surprisingly, of Mola. Mola stated, 'I believe the
single command to be of such importance that if we haven't named a
generalísimo within a week, I am not going on. I'm saying: that's that.
I'm going.'[166]

This probably reflected Mola's recognition both of the difficulties
faced by his northern forces relative to the spectacular successes of
Franco's Army of Africa and of the fact that he could not match

Franco's contacts with the Germans and Italians. Despite his awareness of Franco's frustrating hesitations about joining the rising,
publicly at least, Mola took his rival's elevation with good grace. As
he got in the car after the meeting, Mola told his adjutants that the
meeting had decided to create the post of *generalísimo*. When asked
if he had been appointed, a puzzled Mola replied, 'Me? Why? Franco.'
Some weeks later, he told a friend that he had put forward Franco's
name: 'he is younger than me, has higher rank, is immensely well
liked and is famous abroad'. Franco was twenty-third in the list of the
twenty-four major generals on active service, Mola four points lower
at number three on the list of brigadier generals.[167] However, according to Maíz, when he returned from Salamanca, Mola was deeply
unhappy at what had transpired. Moreover, he was aware of the
extent to which the Germans were supporting the candidacy of
Franco. Maíz claims that he was determined to challenge Franco but,
when encouraged to do so by his friends, he would always reply, 'First
we take Bilbao, then we'll go to Salamanca.' On 26 November 1936, at
a dinner in Navalcarnero, Franco heard Mola and Varela discussing
whether the post-war future would be republican or monarchist.
Varela suggested that Mola would make a good president of the post-
war republic.[168] In other words, Mola was assuming that the question
of the headship of state was to be decided after the war. When
Solchaga expressed his disquiet at Franco's elevation, Mola replied,
'Just obey and get on with winning the war.' A deeply pessimistic
Solchaga added, 'You know my view, since the good guys are dying,
at the end they'll put us survivors in prison.' Mola consoled him,
saying, 'If I survive, a lot of them are going to have a nasty surprise
because I have kept all the correspondence.'[169]

By the time of the follow-up meeting in Salamanca on 28
September to establish the powers to be exercised by the single
commander, Franco had loaded the dice by a momentous decision at
Maqueda. There, he diverted his troops from an attack on Madrid to
the more politically advantageous project of relieving the besieged
Alcázar of Toledo. Mola was infuriated by Franco's decision because
of what it meant in terms of his chances of capturing Madrid. Yagüe
could have fallen on Madrid while it was undefended. He wrote in
the notes for his future history of the war, 'We are wasting time with

so much acclaim for the Caesar and so much cheering the imperial eagle. Less propaganda.' He was still muttering about it six months later, writing in his diary in March 1937: 'In September Madrid could have fallen and with it everything else. Today everything else has to fall so that Madrid might fall.'[170] Mola and others, who had agreed only to make Franco military Commander-in-Chief, were alarmed by a proposal by Kindelán that the rank of *generalísimo* carry with it the function of Chief of State 'as long as the war lasts'. Mola agreed reluctantly only because he saw no alternative. Neither he nor the monarchist generals who had hoped that the clause opened the way to the restoration of Alfonso XIII anticipated that, having been made head of the government of the Spanish state, Franco would simply arrogate to himself the full powers of a head of state.[171]

In Ávila, shortly afterwards, Mola told the monarchist politician Pedro Sainz Rodríguez that he had pushed Franco's candidacy because of his military abilities and because he was likely to get the most votes. However, he declared that he regarded Franco's leadership as transitory, a provisional situation that would have to be reviewed after the war. His logic derived from the naive view that Franco had military rather than political ambitions and would not oppose such a rethink. He was assuming that he himself would play a major role in moulding the political future after the war.[172] Many years later, Queipo de Llano said to the monarchist Eugenio Vegas Latapie that it would have been disastrous to appoint Mola 'because we would have lost the war'.[173]

Once in total control, at the cost of losing Madrid, Franco reorganized the rebel forces. Queipo de Llano was given command of the Army of the South. Mola was given command of the Army of the North, created by the merging of his troops with the Army of Africa. Because of the delay caused by the diversion to Toledo and the slowing down of the rhythm of operations during the two weeks in which Franco was otherwise occupied consolidating his power, the march on Madrid did not begin again until 12 October. Mola had been given a poisoned chalice. The shambolic and virtually undefended capital that he had urged Franco to attack in mid-August would soon be bolstered by the arrival of Russian tanks and aircraft and the International Brigades.[174] Mola himself was happy to seize the opportunity to make good his own failure to capture Madrid at the beginning of the war. He was interviewed by the Australian correspondent Noel Monks in early October as the siege of Madrid was beginning and told him, 'Just stay here a few days and we will have coffee in the Puerta del Sol.' Monks published the comment and Republican wags set up a table to await him, marked 'Reserved for General Mola'. Rebel optimism was such that radio stations broadcast the news that Mola was preparing to enter Madrid on a white horse.[175]

Monks and other correspondents heard Mola's irresponsible statement that, in addition to the four columns attacking Madrid from outside the city, he had a fifth column inside ready to rise up. It effectively implied that the snipers and others who were trying to undermine the Republic were soldiers. It led to the elimination of right-wing prisoners, especially army officers who had pledged to join their rebel comrades. The repression in Madrid intensified as rebel columns drew nearer and the bombing of the city became more frequent. The name given to the threat by Mola, fifth column, provided a label that would be used to justify the elimination of rebel sympathizers in the capital.[176] Republican politicians started making references to the speech from early October. In popular parlance and political rhetoric, the term 'fifth columnist' came to be used to denote any rebel supporter, real or potential, active or imprisoned. The term was first adopted in early October by the Communist orator Dolores Ibárruri as a device to raise awareness and arouse popular passion. Ibárruri declared:

> That traitor Mola said that he would launch 'four columns' against Madrid, but that only the 'fifth column' would begin the offensive. The 'fifth column' is the one which lurks within Madrid itself and which, despite all measures, continues to move in the darkness. We sense its feline movements; its dull voice is to be heard in rumours, stories and outright panic. This enemy must be crushed immediately while our heroic militia is fighting outside Madrid.[177]

Two days later, at the ceremony at which she was made honorary commander of the Communist 5th Regiment, she repeated her remarks about Mola and the 'the hidden traitors and those who lie in ambush thinking that they can act with impunity. We will show them that they are mistaken.'[178]

Five days later, the Political Commissar of the 5th Regiment, Comandante Carlos Contreras (the pseudonym of the Italian Communist and Russian agent Vittorio Vidali), presented an even more explicit analysis of Mola's remarks as a blueprint for those who would undertake the elimination of the fifth column. 'General Mola has been kind enough to point out to us where the enemy is to be found. Our government, the government of the Popular Front, has already taken a series of measures aimed at cleansing Madrid rapidly and energetically of all those doubtful and suspect elements who could, at a given moment, create difficulties for the defence of our city.'[179]

Contreras's speech confirmed 'fifth column' as the generalized term for rebel supporters who found themselves in the Republican zone.[180] On 21 October, the Juventudes Socialistas Unificadas issued a broad definition of the term which embraced all those who actively or passively supported the rebels. It ended with the declaration that 'the extermination of the "fifth column" will be a huge step in the defence of Madrid'.[181] Thus Mola contributed to the greatest single atrocity in the Republican zone, the murder of 2,500 prisoners at the village of Paracuellos de Jarama, on the outskirts of the capital, carried out by anarchists and Communists in collaboration.[182] Prisoners were assumed to be fifth columnists. In his final post-war report to Stalin, the Bulgarian Stoyan Minev, alias Boris Stepanov, from April 1937 the Comintern's delegate in Spain, wrote proudly that the Communists took note of the implications of Mola's statement and 'in a couple of days carried out the operations necessary for cleansing Madrid of fifth columnists'.[183]

By the end of the month, Mola's forces had taken a ring of small towns and villages near the capital, including Brunete, Móstoles, Fuenlabrada, Villaviciosa de Odón, Alcorcón and Getafe. However, it was too late and, by 22 November, his attack had ground to a halt. The time to take Madrid had been before Franco diverted his forces to Toledo. That felt like a betrayal to Mola, one of many reasons for him to feel an intensifying discomfort with Franco. The Italian Ambassador, Roberto Cantalupo, reported to Rome in mid-March 1937:

> If there was any logic in history, the head of the New Spain could
> have been General Mola, founder of the *movimiento salvador* when
> Franco was still in Morocco whence he should have arrived in July.
> Mola had already fought the first serious battles with the
> Communists of Madrid and organized military resistance. This
> then redounded to the credit of Franco because of a series of
> circumstances of which the most important was the fact that he
> brought with him the best troops ... But between Mola and Franco
> the true politician was, at that time, the former. Calm, tenacious
> and thoughtful, wise in words and in his command of men, seri-
> ously well prepared for public life.

In Cantalupo's view, Mola was holding himself in readiness for a
future power struggle.[184]

Mola was aware that the leaders of both the Falange, Manuel
Hedilla, and of the Carlists, Manuel Fal Conde, felt resentment that
their contribution to the war effort was not being recognized. In late
November 1936, Kindelán, Mola and others were outraged when
Franco promoted his brother, the one-time anarchist Ramón, to lieutenant colonel and made him commander of the air base in Mallorca.
Things soon got worse. As President of the Carlist National War
Junta, Manuel Fal Conde, had infuriated Franco by his efforts since
late October to assert the autonomy of Carlism. Matters came to a
head in December. After it had been decided to grant regular army
rank to militia officers as provisional second lieutenants (*alféreces
provisionales*), Fal Conde, with the permission of Mola, on 8
December set up a separate Real Academia Militar de Requetés to
train Carlist officers. Franco was irate, regarding this as tantamount
to a coup d'état, and contemplated having Fal Conde executed. To
avoid the risk of conflict with the Requetés fighting at the front, he
contented himself with sending him into exile in Portugal. Given
Varela's Carlist sympathies, he shared Mola's disgust. This reached a
peak with the unification of the Falange and the Carlist Comunión
Tradicionalista. There was talk in the Falange, among the Carlists and
between several generals, about a move against Franco. However,
Mola opposed such a move lest it lead to the loss of German and
Italian aid. Nevertheless, when the decree of unification was publi-

cized he remarked that it destroyed both the Falange and the Comunión Tradicionalista. The need to win the war made him ready to swallow his disquiet, but he said to Vigón, 'This will all be sorted. It is only provisional.' Franco was aware of this through informers in Mola's headquarters and in the Falange. It is therefore understandable that it should have been assumed that Franco was behind Mola's fatal accident a few months later and an attempt on his life the night before.[185]

The rebel failure at Guadalajara imposed on Franco a momentous strategic volte-face, long advocated by Mola and the other senior generals. Evidence that the Republic was concentrating its best troops in the centre and neglecting other fronts led him reluctantly to abandon his obsession with Madrid and to destroy the Republic by instalments elsewhere. Even before Guadalajara, Franco's strategy was being questioned at Mola's headquarters, especially by Colonel Juan Vigón Suerodíaz, his shrewd Chief of Staff. Mola's reliance on Vigón was revealed in his comment that he was 'my hands and my feet'. Vigón wrote to Kindelán on 1 March 1937 urging him to persuade Franco to give priority to operations in the north in order to seize the armaments factories and coal, iron and steel reserves of the Basque provinces.[186] Similar pleas were made by General Hugo Sperrle, commander of the Condor Legion, who suggested that coordinated ground–air operations could bring success in the Basque Country.[187] It took three weeks and the disaster at Guadalajara before Franco was persuaded by Sperrle's boasts that the Condor Legion would be decisive. On 23 March, he called Mola to Salamanca and gave him specific orders for 40,000 troops to be massed to attack and take Bilbao.[188]

The Italians were less than impressed with the military capacity of the forces at Mola's disposal. Cantalupo had written to Count Galeazzo Ciano, Mussolini's Foreign Minister, in mid-February: 'The Army of the North gives Mola – who seems intellectually quite superior to Franco – some tens of thousands of men of little military value, of appalling organization and inexperienced, so far at least, in important actions.' Despite Mola's intellectual superiority, Cantalupo had little doubt that Franco was capable of dealing with any challenge from his rival.[189] Mola's operational plan was sent to the Germans on

20 March. On the following day, Colonel Wolfram von Richthofen, the Condor Legion's Chief of Staff, wrote in his diary, 'they expect idiotic things from us but hopefully they can be sorted out'. The arrangements for liaison with Sperrle and Richthofen were hammered out at meetings held on 22, 24 and 26 March involving General Alfredo Kindelán, as head of Franco's air force, General José Solchaga and General José López Pinto as field commanders and the diminutive Juan Vigón as Mola's Chief of Staff. Richthofen was infuriated by Mola's facile optimism that there would be little spirit of resistance in Bilbao because of fears of the Asturian left and that it would all be over in a matter of weeks. If Mola was wrong about Bilbao falling easily, the campaign, Richthofen noted, would be protracted. He explained to his Spanish counterparts the novel strategy of 'close air support', using aircraft for sustained ground attacks to smash the morale of opposing troops and block their lines of retreat.[190] Some days before the assault began, Franco informed Cantalupo that he required overall command of the Italian and German forces: 'He insists tenaciously that he must be entrusted with the supreme command of all the troops in this action and must have the freedom to use the Italian divisions alongside the Spanish ones.'[191] The strategic inadequacy of both Mola and Franco was such that it was not long before both the Germans and the Italians were demanding a greater say in key decisions. On 9 April, Cantalupo reported to Ciano on 'the almost total lack of unity of action between the Generalísimo and Mola and Queipo de Llano'. According to Cantalupo, after approving the operational plans Franco left things to the others, apart from making the occasional vague comment.[192] The German Ambassador Wilhelm Faupel and General Mario Roatta, commander of the Italian volunteer corps, agreed to tell Franco plainly that he must act on German and Italian military advice if he was to receive further help.[193]

Given the inexperience of Mola and Vigón, they were obliged to accept the help and advice of Sperrle and Richthofen who were anxious to practise and develop their new technique. In consequence, with Franco's acquiescence, the Germans had the decisive voice in the campaign. Sperrle wrote in 1939, 'All suggestions made by the Condor Legion for the conduct of the war were accepted gratefully and followed.' While the advance was being planned, Richthofen wrote in his diary on 24 March, 'we are practically in charge of the entire business without any of the responsibility', and, on 28 March, 'I am an omnipotent and effective field commander ... and I have established effective ground–air command.'[194] It was agreed at these meetings that attacks would proceed 'without consideration for the civilian population'.[195] However, Richthofen's frustration with Mola intensified rapidly. At a meeting on 24 March, Mola had difficulty understanding the German's plans. Having declared nearly six months previously that he would capture Bilbao within a week, he now aimed to do so in three weeks. It would take nearly three months. The next day, he ordered an advance for 30 March despite the fact that the necessary artillery would not be ready until the 31st. Richthofen told him that his planes would not take off until that day. A humiliated Mola rang Franco to insult the German flyers, and a disgusted Richthofen commented in his diary, 'Just too idiotic.'[196]

On 31 March, Mola arrived in Vitoria to put the final touches to the offensive that now was to be launched on the following day. To generate mass fear, he issued a threat that was both broadcast and printed in a leaflet dropped on the main towns: 'If your submission is not immediate, I will raze Vizcaya to the ground, beginning with the industries of war. I have ample means to do so.'[197] With a comparable determination to crush enemy morale, he ordered the execution of sixteen prisoners in Vitoria.[198] This act of gratuitous violence was followed by a massive four-day artillery and aircraft bombardment of eastern Vizcaya, in which the small picturesque country town of Durango was destroyed by two bombing attacks by the Italian Aviazione Legionaria which killed over 300 civilians.[199]

On 2 April, Sperrle criticized Mola's facile optimism that the Basques did not want to fight. He went further, demanding to know why Mola had not followed up the initial air assault with the advance expected by the Germans. Sperrle accused Mola of letting retreating Basques regroup because his infantry was timid, his artillery operated only once per day and his men were allowed to stop for lunch. According to Solchaga, Mola aggressively responded that his men were exhausted after forty-eight hours of fighting over difficult terrain.[200] Richthofen heatedly accused him of a lack of energy and feeble leadership. A smirking Vigón silently agreed. Mola responded with ineffectual references to the difficult terrain and to the lack of training of his men. Sperrle threatened that, if Mola's men could not coordinate adequately with the available air forces, the planes would be better taken to another front.

Mola then tried to move the subject away from the deficiencies of his men by demanding that priority be given to the destruction of the industries of Bilbao. When an astounded Richthofen asked how it could make any sense to destroy industries which were about to be captured, Mola replied, 'Spain is totally dominated by the industrial centres of Bilbao and Barcelona. Under such a domination, Spain can never be cleaned up. Spain has got too many industries which only produce discontent.' He added that 'if half of Spain's factories were destroyed by German bombers, the subsequent reconstruction of Spain would be greatly facilitated'. Richthofen listened thunderstruck to Mola's idea that Spain's health required the annihilation of the industrial proletariat, then listed all the reasons why it was madness to destroy a country's industrial base, telling him that 'he had never heard such rubbish'. Nevertheless, Mola told Vigón to issue the order. When Richthofen said that it had to come from a higher authority, Mola himself signed orders for attacks on Basque industrial targets. Sperrle and Richthofen delayed while awaiting clarification from Franco. Franco visited the front on 4 April, ostensibly to witness the triumph, but in fact to resolve the differences between Mola and Sperrle. While there, he seems to have given permission for the partial implementation of the order signed by Mola on 2 April. On 9 April, an air attack took place on the explosives factory of Galdácano.[201]

Following his clashes with Sperrle and Richthofen on 2 April, Mola's advance on Bilbao continued to be held up by stubborn Basque resistance and appalling weather which prevented air attacks. There were clashes between Richthofen and a furious Mola. Richthofen accused him of failing to adjust the movements of his troops to accord with the readiness of the Condor Legion and sent a protest telegram to Franco on 9 April.[202] Some weeks later, the German Ambassador Faupel reported to Berlin that the Bilbao offensive had 'from the very first day suffered from faulty preparation, mistakes of the commanders and wholly insufficient training of the troops'.[203] This was a view shared by the Italian high command. The Italians acknowledged that Mola was possibly inhibited by fear that indiscriminate attacks on civilians might alienate his Carlist supporters.[204] On 20 April, Mola's forces began the second phase of their offensive with German air support. Richthofen's aircraft managed to drop bombs on Mola's troops which led to a fierce clash between the two.[205] Sperrle, Richthofen, Mola and Vigón were sufficiently frustrated by the slowness of the advance to talk on 23 April of reducing Bilbao to 'debris and ash'.[206] On the night of the 25th, Richthofen wrote in his diary, 'units ready for tomorrow'.[207] On the same night, on Mola's instructions, the rebel radio at Salamanca broadcast the following warning to the Basque people: 'Franco is about to deliver a mighty blow against which all resistance is useless. Basques! Surrender now and your lives will be spared.'[208] The mighty morale-destroying blow to which Mola's broadcast referred would fall not on Bilbao but on a smaller but equally significant target, the historic town of Guernica. The authorization for the attack came from Franco rather than from Mola, although both were careful to avoid putting orders in writing.[209]

The subsequent international outrage about Guernica threw up a number of astonishing insights into the mentality of the Francoist high command and, in particular, that of General Mola. According to the US Ambassador, Claude Bowers, the destruction of Guernica was 'in line with Mola's threat to exterminate every town in [the] province unless Bilbao surrenders'.[210] Mola and Vigón were fully aware that Guernica was the ancient capital of the Basque Country and of deep symbolic importance to the Basque people. Even as the Francoist authorities were denying that Guernica had been bombed, a manic Mola repeated on the radio his earlier threat: 'We shall raze Bilbao to the ground and its bare desolate site will remove the British desire to support Basque Bolsheviks against our will. We must destroy the capital of a perverted people, who dares defy the irresistible cause of the national idea.'[211] Mola participated fully in the operation to hide responsibility for the bombing. On 28 April, as Guernica was on the point of being occupied, he ordered that the international press, the Red Cross and all persons unauthorized by the rebel authorities be prevented from entering the town, which was sealed for five days after it had been captured. During that time, the ruins were cleared of evidence of bombing and of corpses.[212] At the beginning of May, the Italian Ambassador in London, Dino Grandi, reported that Mola's threats had provoked considerable disquiet in the press and in Parliament.[213] Years later, Iribarren, having lost his admiration for Mola, recalled the atrocities. In September 1970, talking to his friend José de Arteche about the efforts of Vicente Talón to exonerate Mola over the bombing of Guernica, he said, 'It was Mola's obsession to teach the Basques a lesson they would never forget.' He frequently told Arteche, 'All he thought about was killing.'[214]

Successful though the attack was in strategic terms, it was a disaster in public relations and left Richthofen furious about Mola's most recent failure to advance and take advantage of the opportunity which his aviators had created: 'the town was completely blocked for at least twenty-four hours, it was the ideal precondition for a great success, if only the troops had been thrown in'. In a later report, describing the destruction of Guernica as the most successful of a series of operations aimed at cutting off large numbers of Basque troops east of Bilbao, Richthofen lamented that the slow advance of Mola's forces allowed the Basques to withdraw from the encirclement and regroup safely to the west of Guernica.[215] By late May, Mola's troops had Bilbao surrounded, but he did not live to see how the attacks of the Condor Legion would permit his forces to break through the defensive lines on 12 June. A week later Bilbao fell.

German complaints about Mola's dilatory style are sustained by the analysis of the Basque historian Xavier Irujo. On 29 April, a Francoist radio station claimed that 'one of the most outstanding qualities of General Mola is his decisiveness and speed'. However, the average pace of Mola's advances on the Basque Country throughout the civil war was 0.2 kilometres per day. During the campaign of spring 1937, when he enjoyed German and Italian air support, it had still been only 0.6 kilometres per day.[216]

Franco did not perceive Mola as going too slowly. Serrano Suñer believed that his brother-in-law was actually concerned about the potential impact of a triumph for Mola in the Basque Country. Serrano cites Mola's speeches of 29 January and 28 February 1937 as the basis of Franco's preoccupations. In these, Mola was proposing that Franco's monopoly of power be loosened, allowing him to remain as head of state and Commander-in-Chief of the army but leaving politics in his (Mola's) hands as head of the government. Both Serrano and Maíz see these speeches as evidence of Mola's desire for a more liberal post-war polity than would later be the case under Franco.[217]

Even in the Republican zone and later among the Republican exiles, there was speculation about the possibly sinister reasons behind Mola's death. Juan Simeón Vidarte was ready to see the hand of Franco. He claimed that Franco was jealous because Mola was about to get the glory of capturing Bilbao. Furthermore, he suspected that Mola might have been plotting something with the renegade Falangist leader Manuel Hedilla, who had visited him in Pamplona on 12 July. Vidarte regarded it as suspicious that both the Carlist leader Manuel Fal Conde and Hedilla had been silenced by Franco and assumed that it was motivated by the fact that both men had links to Mola. Although there were many complex reasons for Franco's actions against both, it is certainly the case that there were rumours going around the rebel zone in early 1937 that Mola would form a government and include Hedilla as a minister.[218]

Mola's secretary José María Iribarren kept a diary. With a tiny pencil, on a cigarette packet on his knee, he would note down the dinner-table conversations of Mola and his visitors.[219] In early 1937, he made a selection of his own notes and other documents as the basis of a book. He read parts of the manuscript to Mola, who made some corrections and gave his approval. Mola told him that it would be useful for the memoir about the conspiracy and the uprising that he himself was writing. Iribarren's manuscript was then delivered to his publisher in Zaragoza. The local censorship, manned by two university professors, passed it without change because they knew that it had been approved by Mola. It was published on 3 May and Iribarren sent copies to Franco, Mola and other generals and also to Gil Robles. Mola wrote immediately to thank him and wished him 'the success it deserves'.[220]

Some days later, *La Gaceta Regional* of Salamanca printed a eulogistic review. However, the press chief, Manuel Arias Paz, reacted hysterically. Appointed by Serrano Suñer in April 1937, Arias Paz was a major of the engineers who had created a radio station for Franco. Basically an arrogant bully, he had no qualifications for the job he had been given beyond extreme reactionary views and devotion to Franco. His own literary output consisted merely of some articles about how best to evaluate a second-hand car.[221] He ordered all copies of Iribarren's book to be confiscated from bookshops and destroyed. He had Iribarren himself arrested on 24 May and his hotel rooms searched. Iribarren managed to send a plea for help to Mola, who was in Vitoria overseeing the Basque campaign. Mola ordered his release. Arias Paz obeyed that order but then demanded that Iribarren appear before him at the offices of the Delegación de Prensa y Propaganda in Salamanca. Once there, he subjected him to an aggressive interrogation.

An apoplectic Arias Paz shouted repeatedly that Iribarren should be shot for what he had revealed in his book. The portrayal of Mola and his circle talking constantly of the Moroccan campaigns implied a parallel between the civil war and the colonial war, something damaging for the rebels' image. Similarly alarming to Arias Paz was Iribarren's record of Mola's references to the 'uprising' and the 'conspiracy', which implied that the coup had not been a spontaneous popular movement. He was even more alarmed by the revelations of Mola's comments about the weaknesses and deficiencies of his fellow conspirators and, above all, by the disclosure that, on 16 July the previous year, Mola had given his word of honour to Batet that he would not rebel. The book's reproductions of the coarse references by Mola and his comrades to the repression, especially to executions without trial and to what they planned to do when Madrid fell, were seen as a gift to Republican propaganda.

The book was dedicated to Mola and in the preface it was explained how Mola had amended and then approved the manuscript. This was dismissed out of hand by Arias Paz, who claimed mendaciously that Mola had told him that he had not read the book closely. Iribarren was allowed to leave but was rearrested the next day and he spent several more hours in jail, expecting at any moment to be shot. Arias Paz then appeared and casually mentioned that he had forgotten to inform the police about Mola's order that Iribarren be released. He had similarly forgotten to tell Iribarren that, far from disowning him, Mola had defended him vehemently on the telephone. In contrast, as Iribarren later discovered, many senior officers close to both Mola and Franco had taken offence at the book.[222] After unsuccessful efforts to get a revised and expurgated edition through the censorship, Iribarren was persuaded by Joaquín Arrarás to write an entirely new and eulogistic biography of Mola. 'You have seen Mola in his slippers but, for the public, you have to provide another, heroic and eulogistic, account of the dead general.'[223]

On 2 June, Mola had a blazing row with Franco on the telephone. It is not known what they were talking about, but his adjutant heard him say before he slammed down the receiver, 'I don't understand. No. I repeat. I'm not having that.' He was heard to express his frustration that Franco paid more attention to the Germans than to him and also to mutter about Franco permitting corruption. It has been speculated that Franco had suggested removing Mola as commander of the northern army to deprive him of the glory of conquering Bilbao.[224]

Mola died in a plane crash on 3 June 1937. He set out from Pamplona for Vitoria and thence flew on to Burgos. In the province of Burgos, between the villages of Castil de Peones and Alcocero, the aircraft crashed and everyone on board was killed. Eyewitnesses from the villages who saw the plane just before the crash spoke of it flying with its engines silent. This gave rise to suspicions of sabotage along the lines of sugar being introduced into the fuel tank, something which would account for the motors stalling. That suspicion was fed by the fact that, as Iribarren recounted, on the night before the fatal accident Mola had been the victim of what seemed to be an attempt to ram his car. The official explanation that the aircraft simply hit a hillside in thick fog is undermined by the statements of witnesses who could clearly see the aircraft. The shepherd who first reached the crashed plane commented that he had seen it flying haphazardly as if it had no pilot. The father of the pilot, Ángel Chamorro, was convinced that his son had been murdered.[225] Allegedly, on hearing the news of Mola's death, his widow Consuelo Bascón had exclaimed, 'This is Franco's doing!'[226] It is certainly the case that Franco was deeply annoyed by rumours that Mola wanted to head the government, leaving Franco as military leader, head of state and head of the Falange. Both Franco and Serrano Suñer feared that, on Mola's next visit to Burgos, he would issue a full-scale ultimatum. This would explain the conflictive telephone conversation on the eve of Mola's death.[227]

Franco received the news coldly. His attitude was shared by his staff. In Valladolid the next day, Vegas Latapie bumped into José Antonio de Sangróniz, the head of Franco's diplomatic office. When Vegas expressed his distress, Sangróniz replied, 'All things considered, it's no big deal. A general who dies at the front … it's pretty normal.'[228] In January 1937, Cantalupo had reported to Rome on 'the silent and latent conflict between generals Franco, Mola and Queipo de Llano'.[229] The German Ambassador Faupel reported that Franco 'undoubtedly feels relieved by the death of General Mola. He told me recently: "Mola was a stubborn fellow, and when I gave him directives which differed from his own proposals, he often asked me: 'Don't you trust my leadership any more?'""[230]

One of the first things that Franco did after Mola's fatal accident was order that all of Mola's papers be confiscated. Mola had told Iribarren that he was writing a history of the conspiracy and of the war. This is confirmed by Maíz, who had access to his notebooks and quotes them in his last book. An officer of the General Staff came to Mola's quarters in Vitoria and seized his papers. Maíz claimed that this happened while Mola was still en route to Burgos. It is reasonable to speculate that Franco did not want a version of events to circulate that would expose his dubious contribution to the preparation for the uprising.[231] Franco attended Mola's funeral and showed not the slightest trace of emotion. As the body was brought down the steps of divisional military headquarters, the Generalísimo flung his right arm out energetically in the fascist salute. As he had put weight on in recent months, his uniform split open at the armpit to the suppressed hilarity of some of the onlookers.[232] Years later, apparently unaware of Richthofen's criticisms of Mola's military incompetence, Hitler commented, 'The real tragedy for Spain was the death of Mola; there was the real brain, the real leader. Franco came to the top like Pontius in the Creed.'[233]

The Psychopath in the South:
Gonzalo Queipo de Llano

During the civil war and in its immediate aftermath, Gonzalo Queipo de Llano y Sierra enjoyed limitless adulation. His first biographer discovered 'in his energetic and uncomplicated soul, in his pure yet droll spirit, in his flexibility and bravery, in his complex good looks, the style of a thoroughbred soldier'.[1] For other hagiographers, he was simply 'a noble Spaniard', 'the archetype of the Spanish soldier'.[2] The journalist Enrique Vila dedicated his account of the conquest of Seville to 'General Queipo, gigantic protagonist of the epic of Seville that saved Spain'.[3] None of these toadies would ever outdo the man himself. Although with false humility he would talk of the pain it caused him 'to betray his sincere modesty', he constantly referred to himself as 'the initiator of the movement that saved Spain'.[4] Yet this same paragon was, throughout his life, a chronic malcontent, erratic, unreliable, unstable and volatile, irascible and always ready to resort to violence. Obsessed with his prestige and the symbols thereof in terms of medals and titles, he was a bully, a sneak who informed on his comrades and a sycophant who lavished adulation on his superiors. After he took over Seville, his daily radio broadcasts, an inexhaustible fount of what today is known as 'fake news', spewed forth incitement to murder and rape. Under his jurisdiction, more than 60,000 people were murdered in Andalusia and Extremadura. The contrast between the hagiography and the reality could not be more acute.

Born on 5 February 1875 in Tordesillas on the banks of the River Duero, Gonzalo Queipo de Llano was the fifth son of the town magistrate Gonzalo Queipo de Llano y Sánchez and the rather aristocratic (and immensely proud of it) Mercedes Sierra y Vázquez de Novoa.

The magistrate had gambled away the family's once considerable land holdings. Accordingly, when Gonzalo left school at the age of fourteen, his parents placed their hopes on his becoming a priest. However, he rebelled against the harsh discipline of the seminary just as he had earlier rejected that of his school. The crisis came after only four months when, as a painful punishment for one of his escapades, he was obliged to kneel in prayer on a sack of chickpeas. With three companions, he fled the seminary, pelting with stones the priests who tried to stop them. He hid in the home of an aunt in El Ferrol. His mother was appalled but his father accepted that Gonzalo might be better suited to military life. His ambition was to join a cavalry regiment, but he was too young. As a temporary measure, he joined the regimental band of the artillery in July 1891. Totally devoid of musical ability, his career as a bugler did not prosper. In 1893, his father used his political influence to secure Gonzalo's admission to the Academia de Caballería at Valladolid, where his intellectual mediocrity saw him fail important examinations. What he lacked in intellect, he made up in energy and aggression. That, together with a fortuitous shortage of cavalry officers in the colony of Cuba, ensured his eventual and rather delayed graduation in February 1896.[5]

His career henceforth was characterized by a tendency to uncontrolled violence. En route to Cuba, where he arrived in May 1896, he was mocked by another passenger about his academic failings and responded by punching him in the face. After a heavy drinking session that August, a Cuban acquaintance suggested that they go to a brothel, boasting that he had found a beautiful prostitute there and had set her up as his exclusive lover. It turned out that Queipo, ignorant of her profession, was sleeping with the same woman. Beside himself with fury, Queipo threw the man out of a speeding carriage. Believing that he had killed him, Queipo fled. While he was in hiding, the barracks where he was stationed was attacked by rebels and all his comrades slaughtered. After this astonishing stroke of luck in avoiding the massacre, one of many such strokes in his military career, he was decorated several times and promoted to first lieutenant and then to captain for his rash bravery in various clashes with the Cuban rebels. A combination of temerity, irresponsibility and brutality was also manifest in a hobby which consisted of shooting the bulls required to feed his unit. Another pastime was molesting pedestrians who combated the sun by wearing broad-brimmed straw hats with wide ribbons and by covering their faces with a kind of talc. Assuming them to be Cuban rebels, Queipo would stop them, and forcibly cut the ribbons from their hats and wipe their faces clean. He would beat up those who resisted. To keep him out of trouble, the military authorities repatriated him. Spain's defeat by the United States in 1898 ensured that Queipo would never return to Cuba.[6] It was during his time there that he contracted hepatitis, probably from unclean water. With typically irresponsible bravado, he refused to have it treated lest an admission of illness might diminish his self-image as a man of steely masculinity. The consequent damage to his liver meant that, when finally diagnosed much later, he was advised to eliminate alcohol and fat from his diet. It was advice that he rarely took.[7]

On 5 October 1901, he married Genoveva Martí, a deeply shy and therefore apparently cold young woman. She was mortified to discover that Queipo had failed to request official permission to wed, as a result of which he was confined to barracks for the first month of their marriage. It was not to be a happy union. They would have three daughters, Ernestina (born 1903), Mercedes (1905) and María de la Asunción or Maruja (1907), and a son Gonzalo (1911). However, Queipo was an inveterate womanizer. That, together with his exploits, including several duels, made their coexistence difficult for Genoveva. In later life, ever more withdrawn, she would rarely accompany him to social events. Her place at his side was increasingly taken by their daughter Maruja, on whom he lavished an unhealthy favouritism.[8]

The acquisition of a wife and family did nothing to limit the pleasure he took in physical risk or violence. During training for action in Morocco in May 1908, one of his men was thrown from his horse into an unusually torrential River Henares. Queipo dived in and saved the drowning cavalryman, for which act of bravery he was decorated. In October 1909, his regiment landed in Melilla. After eight years of stultifying barracks life, he was delighted by the opportunity to fight in the recently created Spanish protectorate of Morocco. His stay was short and by 18 December he was back in Spain. From June 1910 to the following March, he was on a mission to Argentina to study horse breeding. On his return to North Africa, he was made director of a stud farm between Larache and Alcazarquivir. In November 1911, he was promoted to major. Over the next few years in Morocco, he took part in actions with his usual rash bravery. His narcissism and ambition reached pathological levels. As he rose slowly through the ranks, his temerity increased alongside his egoism. In July 1913, he led a cavalry charge at Alcazarquivir, engaging with a joyful fury in bloody hand-to-hand combat. He was rewarded in April 1914 with promotion to lieutenant colonel.[9]

For Queipo, as for so many officers, Morocco was a brutalizing experience. His view of the rebellion of the Rif tribesmen was that it should be crushed with overwhelming force. Like many Africanistas, including Francisco Franco, he was bitterly opposed to those who advocated establishing the Spanish presence in Morocco by peaceful means. Nevertheless, Queipo's relations with Franco were always tense. He later claimed that he had been shocked by the younger man's evident pleasure in having savage beatings inflicted on his Moorish soldiers for minor infractions of regulations.[10] In fact, over the years, Franco had harboured many grudges against Queipo dating back to an incident in Africa when, in the presence of other ranks, Queipo had accused him of cowardice.[11] Like other Africanistas, Queipo believed fervently in the army's right to intervene in politics to protect Spain not just from its external enemies but also from those that the generals deemed to be its internal enemies.

Queipo was weighed down with medals for valour but not with the decoration that he most craved, Spain's greatest military honour, the Cruz Laureada de San Fernando.[12] Franco's brother, the aviator Ramón, ridiculed Queipo for the way he exaggerated his triumphs in Morocco and for his obsession with uniforms. Queipo insisted that all officers under his command grew moustaches and humiliated those whose bristles did not meet his satisfaction. He also demanded that they always wore gloves. To mock him, some started to wear them along with their swimming costumes when they went to the beach.[13]

Queipo served in Morocco at a time when the Spanish occupying forces faced major revolts from the indigenous population. The occupiers were vulnerable because they held some important towns but

little of the hinterland. The towns were linked by chains of wooden
blockhouses, garrisoned by platoons of twenty-one men who lived in
appallingly isolated conditions and whose morale was undermined
by the uncertainty of the arrival of water, food and firewood that
were due every few days. The senseless loss of life among Spanish
conscripts saw popular hostility against the colonial adventure intensify and governments become ever more reluctant to sink resources
into the war. This led to a deep division between politicians opting
for a defensive policy of guarding the towns and the Africanista
officers like Queipo anxious to see the full-scale occupation of the
Rif. Among those officers who thought that the answer was the
conquest of the entire territory was the impetuous General Manuel
Fernández Silvestre. He engaged in a reckless campaign in early 1921,
moving swiftly westward from Melilla and occupying inaccessible
and hostile territory. This brought him into conflict with Abd
el-Krim, the aggressive new leader who had begun to unify the
Berber tribes of the Rif. In the third week of July 1921, Abd el-Krim
scored a massive victory over Fernández Silvestre near Melilla.
Beginning at the village of Annual, over a period of three weeks, his
forces inflicted a rout and rolled back the Spanish occupation almost
to Melilla itself. Garrison after garrison was slaughtered. The deficiencies of the poorly fed Spanish forces were brutally exposed.
Provoked by the brutality of the occupiers, the local tribes wreaked
horrific revenge massacres at outposts near Melilla, Dar Drius, Monte
Arruit and Nador. Within a few weeks, 9,000 Spanish soldiers died.[14]
Over the next two years, the territory was gradually clawed back but
the central question was now starkly posed – withdrawal or occupation?

Queipo was promoted to brigadier general in December 1922 and,
four months later, given command of the Ceuta zone. The establishment in September 1923 of the military dictatorship under General
Miguel Primo de Rivera might have given hope to Africanistas like
Queipo. However, it was reported to the Dictator that, on hearing the
news, Queipo had exclaimed, 'They've put Miguel Primo in power!
He'll lead us into anarchy!'[15] Typically, he did not make his concerns
public, refusing to sign a telegram of protest against the new regime
drafted by some fellow officers. In fact, he and Primo shared a friend-

ship going back to a time when Queipo had acted as Primo's second in a duel against the liberal writer Rodrigo Soriano. However, Queipo's inflated ego soon saw the relationship deteriorate. In his memoir of this period, he insinuated that every military reverse in Morocco was simply the consequence of his own views being ignored.[16] His obsession with Spain's 'mission' in Morocco led him to collaborate in January 1924 with several other officers, including Francisco Franco, in establishing the *Revista de Tropas Coloniales*, a mouthpiece for the more aggressive imperialists in the army. In characteristically exaggerated rhetoric, he expressed the widespread Africanista frustration with the politicians whom they blamed for Spain's decline. In a sycophantic hymn of praise to Alfonso XIII, 'our King, pride and hope of the Fatherland', he paid tribute to the Africanistas as 'a group of courageous individuals prepared to risk everything to revive the Spanish spirit'.[17]

By the summer of 1924, the Dictator was talking increasingly of the need to abandon the Moroccan protectorate. The first step was an operation to do away with 400 positions and blockhouses. Evidence of imminent withdrawal provoked the desertion of large numbers of Moroccan mercenaries from the Spanish ranks and encouraged the Rif leader Abd el-Krim to go on the offensive. He attacked in force, cutting the Tangier–Tetuán road, threatening Tetuán itself. The Dictator issued a communiqué on 10 September 1924 announcing the evacuation of the zone. A number of officers, including Franco, allegedly tried to persuade Queipo de Llano to lead a plot to overthrow Primo de Rivera. On 23 September, a column set off from Tetuán to relieve the besieged garrison at Xauen in the mountains. That a subordinate had been given responsibility for the operation infuriated Queipo, who wrote an intemperate letter of protest that led to him being relieved of the Ceuta command. There had already been calls for his dismissal after a tasteless speech to a delegation of Portuguese archaeologists in August 1923. In response, he wrote a series of lengthy letters complaining that he had been mistreated. Xauen was abandoned in November 1924.[18]

Queipo's commitment to the annihilation of Moroccan resistance by unrestrained brutality brought him into conflict with several other senior officers including Primo de Rivera's friends Generals Ricardo

Burguete, José Villalba Riquelme and Alberto Castro Girona, who
advocated more enlightened methods of conquest. They were known
as the *civilistas*. Queipo denounced Riquelme as a cowardly pacifist.
He was alleged to have insulted Castro Girona in similar fashion,
although he vehemently denied doing so. The real motive of his
hostility to Castro Girona was more personal and utterly trivial.
When Queipo succeeded him as military commander in Tetuán,
Castro had continued to use the official chauffeur-driven car and
residence associated with the post. Things got worse as Queipo
became increasingly involved in encouraging opposition to the dictatorship. At first, Primo de Rivera was tolerant, aware that Queipo
usually acted before thinking. As General Leopoldo Saro had told
Queipo in a letter of June 1926, 'you have the misfortune always to
think aloud'.[19] In fact, the thoughts, such as they were, behind
Queipo's opposition to the regime were simply personalized resentments against senior figures whom he believed to have underestimated
his merits. He wrote to the King in 1925 a letter of complaint about
his perceived injustices. The terms in which he wrote were so offensive that it ensured their later mutual hostility.[20]

Inevitably, Queipo was relieved of his command in Tetuán but,
within a year, he had been made Military Governor of the province
of Cordoba. However, that did not prevent him making constant
jibes about the Dictator and his regime that, inevitably, were reported
back to Madrid. For instance, at a dinner given by local landowners,
he repeated a joke circulating in Seville that a recently opened
urinario público (public lavatory), signposted 'UP', was the local
headquarters of Primo de Rivera's political party, the Unión
Patriótica. To avoid the consequences of his scurrilous remarks, he
immediately launched a campaign to ingratiate himself with the
Dictator. He told fellow officers that the accusations against him were
'calumnies, lies and spiteful inventions' and that he supported the
military directory without reservation. However, he was linked with
conspiracies against the dictatorship and was soon removed from his
post.[21] The *civilistas* got their revenge on him when the army's promotion committee, the Junta Clasificadora del Ejército, chaired by
General Burguete, refused to promote him to major general and, in
March 1928, relegated him to the reserve list. The justification was

that he was 'undisciplined, rebellious and inclined to disobey orders'. His immediate response was a verbose letter of complaint and self-justification occupying sixteen closely typed foolscap pages. When his appeal was ignored, he indignantly refused Primo de Rivera's offers of lucrative civilian posts and even spoke of challenging him to a duel.[22]

Allegedly, the King had promised Queipo that he would not sign the document consigning him to the reserve. It was this perceived personal betrayal, combined with the offence to his pride, rather than any patriotic motive that led to him joining the Republican movement to overthrow the monarchy (for which, in 1931, he would be lavishly rewarded). In his letter of June 1926, Leopoldo Saro had urged Queipo to seek reconciliation with Primo. He quoted the Dictator as having said, 'It is a real pity that he is so determined to clash with me, since he is a good man that I used to like a lot.' Queipo's inflated pride prevented his taking this advice. The Dictator wrote to a friend that 'Queipo is his own worst enemy ... Given that I know his character only too well, I had to assume that he would not leave without trying, like Samson, to pull down the pillars of the temple, devoting himself to building up his own reputation and besmirching that of everyone else.' In contrast with this tendency to emulate Samson, while in enforced idleness Queipo devoted himself to setting up a small factory that made bluing (sometimes known as laundry blue or dolly blue). He then wrapped it in twists of paper and spent the mornings going around working-class barrios selling them house to house. He also worked on a book that was published in late 1930. *El general Queipo de Llano perseguido por la dictadura* (General Queipo de Llano Persecuted by the Dictatorship) was a hymn of praise to himself, an egotistical account of his achievements in Morocco and a lamentation for the persecution to which he believed he had been subjected. It was irrefutable testimony to his overweening pride and arrogance.[23]

At the same time, to anyone who would listen, Queipo criticized Primo de Rivera in the most insulting terms. In early February 1930, he heard a rumour that the General's brother, José Primo de Rivera, had referred to him as a boastful lout. He responded with a letter to Primo's brother José in which he declared that he was ready to settle accounts with the Dictator himself. It ended with a challenge – 'no one has dared take me on' – and his address, a clear invitation to a duel. Since José Primo de Rivera was an elderly sick man with no sons, the Dictator's eldest son, José Antonio, took it upon himself to defend the family honour. On 11 February, he went to the home of Queipo, who declined to admit him but suggested that they meet in the Lyon d'Or, the café in the Calle Alcalá where his *tertulia* of friends used to gather. That same evening, José Antonio, his brother Miguel and their cousin Sancho Dávila appeared in the café. José Antonio pulled out the letter and asked Queipo if he was the author. When Queipo replied in the affirmative, José Antonio punched him in the face and knocked him to the floor. The fifty-five-year-old Queipo was quickly on his feet and laying into an assailant nearly thirty years his junior. A brawl ensued and the police were called. Since the victim was a general and the three aggressors were lieutenants in the reserve, the incident fell under military jurisdiction. It ended with José Antonio's dishonourable discharge from the army and Queipo's enduring resentment of him. The long-term consequence was to intensify right-wing suspicions of Queipo de Llano.[24]

In his book, he made a legitimate critique of the scale of corruption under Primo de Rivera's dictatorship. There was an element of projection about his biting criticism of characteristics of Primo that he himself shared in abundance, such as his vanity and his womanizing.[25] Fuming at the humiliation of his failed promotion, Queipo de Llano forgot his hitherto slavish devotion to Alfonso XIII and demonstrated, in Ian Gibson's memorable phrase, his 'transferable loyalty'.[26] He had hoped that the arrival in power of his friend Dámaso Berenguer would lead to the approval of his promotion but it appeared that Alfonso XIII had forbidden it. Queipo denounced Alfonso and the Borbón dynasty as usurpers and later contrasted the monarchy with the Republic, 'the regime that exists in Spain today that, having been voted in by the people, is the truly legitimate one'.[27] Driven by personal resentment rather than political commitment, he became President of the Asociación Militar Republicana. He claimed to be a freemason and described himself as 'unwaveringly republican and a democrat to the end'. A serious Republican officer, Antonio Cordón, did not trust him. He believed that Queipo was conspiring not from conviction but just because he felt slighted by Alfonso XIII.[28] Two decades later, he admitted as much in a letter to General Franco: 'By family tradition and because of my own way of thinking, I was always, I am now and I will die, as a fervent monarchist.'[29]

A future provisional Republican government under the presidency of Niceto Alcalá-Zamora had been negotiated on 17 August 1930 in San Sebastián. To facilitate the transition to a republic, in September, a military revolutionary committee was created from a wide spectrum of the armed services. It was chaired by Queipo who, along with Ramón Franco, elaborated detailed plans for the seizure of key communication centres and military barracks. In fact, the Director General of Security, General Emilio Mola, was aware of the plans and had Queipo and others briefly arrested. When other more committed conspirators visited him in prison, they found him surrounded by friends, drinking wine and thoroughly enjoying the role of victim. They found his rants against the King to be no more than empty boasts.[30] Nevertheless, a fellow conspirator later commented that Queipo had argued in favour of the assassination of Alfonso XIII.[31]

Queipo's relations with Mola were poor after the arrest, and resentment festered because of comments about Queipo in Mola's account of his time as Director General of Security. Mola stated that police vigilance had been relaxed because Queipo had given his word of honour to the Prime Minister, General Berenguer, that he was not involved in the Republican conspiracy:

> I have been seriously criticized because, being aware of the revolutionary activities of General Queipo de Llano, I did not have him under strict surveillance. To this, I must reply that he was being watched until shortly before the coup was launched. One morning, the Prime Minister, after an interview with General Queipo, ordered me to lift the surveillance on him. He said that he had no reason to doubt his sincerity, believing him to be a perfect gentleman, and accepted as true his claim that the reason for his frequent visits to the home of Alcalá-Zamora [the leader of the Republican movement] was simply that Alcalá was producing a preface for a book that he was writing.

When Mola refused to apologize for the insinuation that he was a dishonourable liar, the ever irascible Queipo first contemplated challenging him to a duel but then decided that it would be better to get revenge by publishing a book with his own version of events.[32]

The key to the plot in Madrid was the Cuatro Vientos military airfield. The joint military and civilian Republican 'revolutionary committee' had been assured that the Socialist Unión General de Trabajadores would support a military coup with a strike. The prospects of success were diminished when on 12 December, three days before the agreed date, hoping to spark off a pro-Republican movement in the north-eastern garrisons of Huesca, Zaragoza and Lérida, Captains Fermín Galán, Ángel García Hernández and Salvador Sediles rose in Jaca (Huesca). Galán and García Hernández were shot after summary courts martial on 14 December. Their executions led to the withdrawal from the plot of numerous officers, particularly from the artillery. Although forces under Queipo de Llano and aviators from Cuatro Vientos went ahead the next day, they did so with intense, and fully justified, pessimism. In fact, the entire operation was doomed once the expected general strike in Madrid failed to materialize. The affair ended in a fiasco, albeit one that was later to see the protagonists hailed as heroes.[33]

General Franco sent a letter expressing his outrage about these events to his friend the then Colonel José Enrique Varela. He wrote of his brother Ramón, 'he's beyond redemption, completely mad and has lost all common sense'. Referring to Queipo, he went on, 'The Jaca affair is an abomination, the army is full of hypocrites and cowards, and a hot-headed maniac dragged it down in the filthiest way.'[34] Despite Franco's contempt, Queipo de Llano would be one of the greatest eventual beneficiaries of the Cuatro Vientos incident. This was despite the fact that an important fellow plotter and future head of the Republican air force, Ignacio Hidalgo de Cisneros, believed that the hesitations of Queipo had, along with the absence of the general strike, contributed to the defeat of the revolutionary movement. After an initial success at the airfield, the next step was to neutralize the nearby army garrison of Campamento, but Queipo delayed and lost all possibility of surprise, and the aerodrome was recaptured. Hidalgo de Cisneros described Queipo as 'the typical blustering cavalryman out of novels and the theatre. In uniform, he looked good, he was tall, strong with enormous moustaches and so seemed energetic and decisive.' Queipo and the other principal conspirators fled into exile. With Ramón Franco, Queipo spent several weeks in Portugal before reaching Paris via Belgium on 11 January 1931. En route, the group made a detour to visit the exiled Catalan leader Francesc Macià in Brussels. According to Hidalgo de Cisneros, Queipo de Llano, who was a notorious anti-Catalanist, 'began to reveal his lack of diplomacy or rather his facility to make offensive remarks'. He insulted the venerable Macià, telling him that he despised his nationalist ideas and that he had reluctantly joined the others in the visit only because Macià was also a victim of Primo de Rivera.[35]

Later in Paris in the first months of 1931, with only the most exiguous funds, the group was under close vigilance by the French police. Queipo de Llano caused problems with the virulence of his criticisms of the monarchy and the Catholic Church in his ill-considered interviews. General Burguete later contemptuously described Queipo's performance: 'Always the clown, you behaved while you were abroad as the perpetual buffoon.'[36] To try to control him, the others ensured that someone accompanied him at all times – telling him, to his great satisfaction, that he was too important not to be escorted by a bodyguard. His vanity was piqued because, unlike Ramón Franco, Prieto and the Republican politician Marcelino Domingo, there was no secret police agent following him around. He also exercised his priapic tendencies, spending considerable time and energy trying unsuccessfully to seduce Elena, the beautiful young cashier in the *pension* where they were staying. On one occasion, while socializing with the attractive female dancers and singers in a nightclub, he got into a fight and was arrested. He was distressed when the incident was reported in the French press. Vidarte's wife, Francesca Linares, trying to comfort him, said, 'It's only natural that you are worried, General. Your reputation in Republican circles could suffer.' He replied furiously, 'What the hell do I care about the Republicans! I'm worried about what my wife will say!' When news arrived of the proclamation of the Second Republic on 14 April, the group immediately set off for Spain. On their arrival, they were greeted as heroes at the frontier and, later, in Madrid.[37]

Shortly after the establishment of the provisional government, Queipo was promoted to the rank of major general, a reward for his efforts in the Republican opposition. The promotion was backdated to 31 March 1928, when it had originally been blocked. Unlike most of his future comrades on the rebel side during the civil war, his resentment of officers who had collaborated with the dictatorship led him to applaud the controversial military reforms of Manuel Azaña. He was showered with preferment, being named commander of the Primera División (that is, of the Madrid military region, the equivalent of the old post of captain general), and later given several other significant postings.[38] However, neither his new positions nor his much cosseted moustache were of any avail when he renewed his amorous assault on Elena, who visited Madrid in the spring of 1931.[39] In the context of the latent military hostility to the fledgling Republic, Queipo was regarded as a valuable asset. However, his commitment to the democratic regime had no other basis than his resentment of the King.[40]

He made numerous public declarations of loyalty. As head of the Madrid military division, he took to the streets in an effort to stop the rash of church burnings in May.[41] His sense of his own popularity saw him run, unsuccessfully, as an independent candidate for Salamanca in the general elections of 28 June 1931. To the annoyance of the Catholic leader José María Gil Robles, a rival candidate, he used his official car complete with military chauffeur for his election campaign. Despite this advantage, he received only 13,500 votes, just 4 per cent of those cast.[42] In public, he behaved like a figure from Viennese operetta, seizing every opportunity to wear full-dress uniform complete with his general's sash (fajín). He even appeared at the Madrid Casa del Pueblo thus attired to declare his commitment to the Socialist cause.[43] At the official opening of the newly elected Cortes on 28 July 1931, he rode alongside the President's car on a prancing mare that had previously belonged to the King.[44] Shortly afterwards, at an event at the Casino Militar in Seville – the main club for officers in the city – he referred to the cabinet, presumably inadvertently, as 'His Majesty's government'.[45]

By the summer of 1931, his erratic private statements were making clear the scale of his unreliability. He was heard to say: 'I could be a dictator – there is no one more appropriate – and I could rule for seven or eight years before facing the same fate as Miguel Primo de Rivera.' The Minister of War, Manuel Azaña, received numerous complaints about Queipo's arrogant and authoritarian behaviour towards his subordinates. In May, soon after his nomination as head of the First Military Region, he had set about replacing the senior officers of the Madrid garrison in the most heavy-handed manner, humiliating them in front of their troops. He caused great offence with a speech declaring that the troops need not obey or respect the officers that he had just removed from command of their units. In Bilbao, he claimed that, prior to the establishment of the Republic, 'the army had been no more than a body of lackeys at the service of the house of Borbón'. His words nearly provoked violence from officers present who were furious to hear such words from a notorious turncoat who had once been a favourite of the King. In early July 1931, he had a reporter arrested for writing a critical article about him. Azaña had been obliged to intervene and have the journalist freed, commenting that Queipo seemed to be unaware that he did not have the sweeping powers over civilians enjoyed by captains general under the monarchy.[46]

Queipo did not remain long as head of the First Military Region. On 30 July 1931, he was made Inspector General of the Army. Although he was pleased with this new promotion, he tried to make life impossible for his successor as commander in Madrid, General Rafael Villegas y Montesinos. He cultivated Niceto Alcalá-Zamora, now President of the Republic, by dint of informing on fellow officers who were involved in monarchist conspiracies.[47] On 6 December, courtesy of this burgeoning friendship, he was also made head of the President's military household. Queipo's family began to spend summers with that of Alcalá-Zamora at the presidential summer residence in La Granja. This opened the way to close friendships between their children, especially between Ernestina Queipo de Llano and the President's eldest son Niceto. The pair eventually married on 29 December 1934. Queipo's wife Genoveva remained ever more firmly in the background and his constant companion was his attractive daughter Maruja, now in her mid-twenties.[48]

Meanwhile, Queipo did everything he could to curry favour with Manuel Azaña, now Prime Minister as well as Minister of War. In late 1931, he was a frequent visitor to Azaña's office, carrying tittle-tattle about fellow officers who were conspiring against the Republic, such as Generals Goded, Barrera and Sanjurjo. On 21 September, he even appeared late at night at Azaña's home to make baseless accusations and declare his own commitment to the Republic. Queipo's syco-phantic readiness to inform on his comrades derived from his wish to have Azaña's support for a new bid to be a parliamentary deputy, this time as a candidate of the Radical Party for Valladolid. Azaña's response, that he would be delighted to endorse his candidacy if he had support from the Valladolid branch of the party, was not what Queipo had hoped for. Azaña had little respect for him, commenting in his diary, 'Queipo is a bit simple and short of brains.'[49]

In his post as Inspector General, Queipo was totally inefficient, meddling in issues beyond his jurisdiction, making indiscreet speeches and generally causing problems. Azaña remarked, 'he is utterly frivolous and tactless', and complained about his constant interference: 'He's driving me crazy.' In contrast, Queipo saw himself as a figure of huge national importance, and he was constantly on the lookout for opportunities to make speeches.[50] In December 1931, his inflated sense of his own worth saw him demand the use of a bullet-proof car. He was told that the only such car in government hands was one constructed for General Primo de Rivera. He then browbeat the Under-Secretary of the Ministry of War into having it sent to him. When Azaña found out, he ordered the car returned 'so that he understands what orders mean'.[51] Queipo concluded that his efforts to ingratiate himself with Azaña had been fruitless and, exploiting the proximity provided by his position, in 1932 switched his efforts to clinching his personal relationship with Alcalá-Zamora. He poured poison into receptive ears, telling the President that military plots abounded but that Azaña was too frivolous to take notice. Queipo's scandalmongering brought him closer to Alcalá while contributing to simmering tensions between the Prime Minister and the President. At this time, Queipo's constant affirmations of his loyalty to the Republic and to Alcalá-Zamora did not go unnoticed in the political establishment. Diego Martínez Barrio, deputy leader

of the conservative Republican Radical Party, described his sycophancy towards the President: 'scandalmongering and loquacious,
non-stop, full of his loyalty to the Republic and to Don Niceto, with
whom he sought, and achieved, a family link'.[52]

General Sanjurjo was aware that Queipo had denounced his
conspiratorial activities to Azaña and Alcalá-Zamora. When it briefly
appeared that his military coup of 10 August 1932 had succeeded in
Seville, Sanjurjo apparently exclaimed, 'How I'm going to laugh at
Queipo de Llano,' a reference both to his public protestations of
republicanism and his efforts to undermine the plot. Queipo considered himself a friend of Sanjurjo. When he heard about the remark,
he was nonplussed. Lacking self-awareness, he could not see the
connection between his betrayal of Sanjurjo and Sanjurjo's annoyance.[53] He was so annoyed that, during the official ceremony to pay
tribute to various officers who had played key roles in frustrating
Sanjurjo's coup, Queipo contravened protocol by making a speech
and enthusiastically presented the Alcalde of Seville, Dr José
González Fernández de Labandera, to the crowd.[54] Four years later,
on 10 August 1936, Labandera was executed in Seville on the orders
of Queipo de Llano.[55]

Queipo's growing resentment of Azaña fed on his unrequited
desire to secure a parliamentary seat for himself in the Cortes. It was
manifested maliciously on 7 March 1933 during a heated debate
about Casas Viejas, the small village in Cadiz where an anarchist
revolutionary movement had culminated in the deaths of several
villagers shot by Assault Guards. The officers responsible claimed
falsely that they had been acting under orders. An utterly implausible
story was invented that Azaña had personally given the order 'shoot
them in the belly'. Queipo de Llano, still attempting to insert himself
into the Radical Party, spoke to Rafael Salazar Alonso, a senior
collaborator of the party's leader, Alejandro Lerroux. In the corridors
of the Cortes, in front of witnesses, Queipo told Salazar Alonso about
a letter from a lieutenant in the Guardia de Asalto claiming that he
and others who had signed a declaration that there was no such order
to shoot had done so under duress. This not only contradicted what
Azaña was saying in the Cortes but, coming from Queipo, seemed to
have the presidential imprimatur.

When Azaña found out, with the reluctant agreement of Alcalá-Zamora he obliged Queipo to resign his post, which left him once more in the reserve. Ever the malcontent, Queipo began to talk darkly of taking reprisals against the government. Azaña did not regard his threats as serious:

> People are starting to say of this six-foot-six-inch general that he will do this, that and the other. The Dirección General de Seguridad has reported this to me. I don't believe that he will do anything. What he will doubtless do is churn out nonsense, something he does naturally. No one in the army takes any notice of him. It was his ineptitude that caused one of the most annoying incidents in the early days of the Republic when changes in the command of the Madrid garrison were ordered and he implemented them in a brutal fashion.[56]

After Azaña had left the government, in September 1933, Lerroux rewarded Queipo, appointing him Inspector General of the Carabineros (border guards). The position was a senior one, with substantial financial remuneration, but it did not match Queipo's ambitions.

In May 1935, Gil Robles became Minister of War and appointed Francisco Franco as Chief of the General Staff. Alcalá-Zamora reproached him for the appointment, saying, 'Gil Robles, why on earth do you insist on this appointment when you know that it is opposed by virtually the entire army, starting with the head of my military household, General Queipo de Llano?'[57] It is inconceivable that Franco did not learn of this. Moreover, that same month, Queipo de Llano clashed with Gil Robles over his opposition to a proposed pay rise for the Carabineros. A letter that he wrote to the Minister asking him to influence a Cortes vote on the issue appeared in the press after Queipo distributed its text widely among his comrades. In the wake of the resulting scandal, he was dismissed from his post, although he would be quickly reinstated – a reflection of his close relationship with the President.[58]

Queipo was shocked by the impeachment of Alcalá-Zamora on 7 April 1936 on the grounds of acting unconstitutionally. His response was twofold. He immediately began to seek out another avenue to preferment within the Republic while also beginning to plot against the regime. The target of his machinations was Diego Martínez Barrio, who was now acting President (after the impeachment and before the appointment of Azaña as the new President on 10 May). Fearful of losing his post as Inspector General of the Carabineros, he visited Martínez Barrio in full-dress uniform with all his medals on display. To the amused contempt of Martínez Barrio, he whined about the 'indecent' hostility that he believed many politicians felt towards him, swearing on his medals that he was a 'a man of honour and a Republican from head to foot'. Beside himself with indignation, he told Martínez Barrio that the pain caused him by accusations of disloyalty to the Republic was worse than death. He subsequently wrote, on 23 June, a grovelling letter to Martínez Barrio requesting his intercession to help one of his nephews, Gonzalo Queipo de Llano y Buitrón, secure a job as a municipal judge in Malaga. If this request was successful, the General wrote, his nephew, when he became a judge, would do the bidding of Martínez Barrio.[59]

At the same time as he was swearing loyalty to Martínez Barrio, Queipo was trying to make contact with General Mola about joining the developing anti-Republican military conspiracy. Mola was understandably suspicious given Queipo's reputation as a prominent Republican. There was also personal hostility between them. It will be recalled that, in 1930, as Director General of Security, Mola had spied on Queipo's anti-monarchical activities. Within months, the tables had been turned. Mola was arrested on 21 April 1931 for that earlier surveillance. After four months in the cells, he was released, deeply embittered, on condition of giving Queipo de Llano (then head of the Madrid military region) his word of honour not to flee. If that was not enough to sour their relations, Mola had spoken ill of Queipo in his memoirs of that period and Queipo had retaliated in his book *El movimiento reivindicativo de Cuatro Vientos* with an energetic attack on Mola.[60] All of this explains why Queipo had not been invited to the meeting of dissident officers held in Madrid on 8 March 1936 at which it was decided that the exiled General Sanjurjo should head the proposed coup and that preparations should begin with Mola as overall director and Colonel Valentín Galarza as liaison chief.[61]

Now, in April 1936, when Queipo requested that they meet, Mola was deeply distrustful. As Queipo later admitted to the chronicler of the rebellion, Joaquín Arrarás, Mola, like many other officers, regarded him as a traitor and a Republican. Given his experience of the man and his own instincts as a policeman, he took the precaution of first asking Galarza to investigate Queipo's commitment to the conspiracy. Once he was reassured, he agreed to a meeting.[62] It took place in Pamplona on 12 April, only two days after Queipo's letter to Martínez Barrio. Queipo boasted that he had been using the travel facilities provided by his position as Inspector General of the Carabineros to aid the brewing conspiracy. He had, he claimed, used inspections of various garrisons to ascertain whether their officers would join the rising. A pleasantly surprised Mola asked him to continue exploiting his freedom of movement to estimate support for the conspiracy. Queipo returned on 1 June and Mola invited him to give a talk in the non-commissioned officers' club. He was taken more fully into Mola's confidence when they met again on the following day at the Casa Otamendi, an inn 20 kilometres outside Pamplona. When they convened again on 23 June, Queipo expressed his desire to lead the rising in his native Valladolid. He was less than pleased to be told that this job had already been given to General Andrés Saliquet and that he was expected to lead the rising in Seville. He understandably regarded the revolutionary capital of Andalusia as a poisoned chalice. Nevertheless, he accepted.[63]

Although he achieved success in Seville, he would still be complaining about his exclusion from the rising in Valladolid fifteen years later. He wrote a letter to Franco that was at best a wildly exaggerated, at worst a largely fictional, reconstruction of his own activities in the preparation of the conspiracy. In it, he claimed that he had started to conspire against the Republic shortly after its inception. Even more flagrant was his assertion that his anti-Republican activities were such as to make him the inspiration behind the military coup of 1936. Despite not being invited to the meeting at which Mola was appointed director of the conspiracy, he claimed bizarrely that it was he who had persuaded Mola to act in this capacity: 'I became the initiator of the rebel movement and I managed to convince Mola to take on the job of organizing it.' The remainder of

his letter is an amazing confection of lies, including the claim that
when he first reached Seville he found that 'nothing had been
arranged and ... I personally initiated the uprising and assured its
success'.[64]

This was a blatant untruth, since local rightists in Seville had been
planning a coup since 1931. In July that year, in response to an anarcho-syndicalist strike in Seville, the landowners' clubs, the Círculo de
Labradores and the Unión Comercial, had formed a paramilitary
group known as the Guardia Cívica. It was financed by the most
prominent rightists of the city, Javier Parladé Ybarra, Pedro Parias
González, a retired lieutenant colonel of the cavalry and substantial
landowner, and José García Carranza, a famous bullfighter known as
'Pepe el Algabeño'. Well armed, the Guardia Cívica was led by a brutal
Africanista, Captain Manuel Díaz Criado, known as 'Criadillas'
(Bull's Balls). These extreme rightists violently repressed the strike.
They took prisoners and shot four of them in the Parque de María
Luisa, murders that were the first step towards the creation of the
civilian infrastructure of both the failed military uprising of August
1932, Queipo de Llano's coup and his subsequent regime.[65]

The Sanjurjada in August 1932, despite its failure, would have a
successful legacy thanks to Major José Cuesta Monereo, a General
Staff officer who was adjutant to General Miguel Cabanellas, the
Director of the Civil Guard. Cuesta Monereo accompanied
Cabanellas in his tours of inspection to Seville and was in the city
that August. He was sent there by Cabanellas to act as liaison between
the conspirators and the local Civil Guard. On the morning of 10
August, he had placed himself at the orders of the Civil Governor of
Seville, Eduardo Valera Valverde, whose attitude to the coup was
ambiguous. Cuesta carried messages between Valera and Pedro
Parias and the Guardia Cívica. His role gave him a unique perspec-
tive on the mistakes made and contributed to his planning of the
1936 coup in Seville. The success of working-class forces in 1932
taught him the importance of preventing the workers converging on
the nerve centres of the city, the telephone building, the town hall,
military arsenals and the Gobierno Civil, the office of the province's
civil governor. Cabanellas was dismissed because of his suspected
involvement in the conspiracy, but Cuesta went unpunished.[66]

Despite Queipo's complaints to the contrary, plans were well advanced when he first contacted the local conspirators in April 1936. The problem was that they did not trust him sufficiently to take him into their confidence. His links with Alcalá-Zamora and the preferment that he had received from the Republic ensured their suspicion. In particular, the local Falange was deeply hostile to Queipo, in large part because its leader was José Antonio Primo de Rivera's cousin Sancho Dávila, still seething from the fight in the Lyon d'Or in 1930. Pepe el Algabeño, also a Falangist, mistrusted the new arrival's motives.[67] Queipo needed the recommendation of Lieutenant Colonel Alberto Álvarez-Rementería to his brother Eduardo (a major and President of the Falange's Comité Militar in Seville) in order to meet Major Cuesta Monereo who, aided by Captains Manuel Gutiérrez Flores and Manuel Escribano Aguirre, was the real organizer of the local conspiracy. Cuesta Monereo's meticulous organizational skills were to be the key to the coup's success in Seville.[68]

Queipo's principal aim on this first visit to Seville in April was to see his old friend General José Fernández Villa-Abrille y Calivara, the commander of the Segunda División (the Seville military region) and try to recruit him for the conspiracy. Although Villa-Abrille rejected Queipo's proposal, he failed to denounce his subversion to the authorities. Thereafter, Queipo made little active contribution to the local conspiracy. However, once contact was made with Cuesta Monereo in July, Queipo would be introduced to conspirators from all the local units of the army, ranging from cavalry, artillery and transport to communications. Already, in mid-May, Cuesta had persuaded Major Santiago Garrigós Bernabéu, the second in command of the region's Civil Guard, to join the conspiracy. By the time Queipo made his second and third visits in July, Garrigós had prepared the mutiny of all Civil Guard posts in the province.[69] The fact that there were so many elements involved belied Queipo's later claims to have organized the coup almost single-handed.[70]

Villa-Abrille continued to assure the Republican local and national authorities that there was no subversion afoot within his command. On 7 June, when the Minister of Agriculture Mariano Ruiz-Funes visited Seville, Villa-Abrille and the commanders of all major units swore their loyalty to the government. When the Civil Governor, José María Varela Rendueles, told him that he had had reports of seditious links between the garrison and local civilian extreme rightists, Villa-Abrille denied it categorically. He also failed to inform Varela Rendueles when Queipo made his second visit to Seville in early July.[71] Typically, Queipo de Llano showed his gratitude to his friend by threatening to kill him.[72]

On that second trip, Queipo established himself in the centrally located Hotel Simón. Through the good offices of Eduardo Álvarez Rementería, he was able to meet Cuesta Monereo and officers of the Falange's Comité Militar. General Villa-Abrille, to avoid having to meet Queipo and thus report on the meeting, went to Huelva claiming to be supervising General Staff exercises there. He was accompanied by Captain Gutiérrez Flores, an enthusiastic Falangist conspirator. Cuesta Monereo suggested to Queipo that they both, with Captain Escribano Aguirre, follow Villa-Abrille. While Queipo waited in an inn on the outskirts of Huelva, first Gutiérrez Flores, then Cuesta Monereo and Escribano, tried to persuade Villa-Abrille to meet him. Fearful of being compromised, Villa-Abrille dithered, saying, 'Does it have to be now? Couldn't General Queipo come to my office tomorrow?' Finally, he alarmed both Cuesta Monereo and Queipo when he said that, if he met Queipo, he would be obliged to report the encounter to the government.[73]

On 15 July, Queipo took his wife and youngest daughter Maruja to Malaga, where he thought they would be safe in the home of his married daughter Mercedes. When the rising failed in the city, they took refuge in the Italian Consulate until they could board an Italian steamer and be brought to Seville in August.[74] Queipo himself had barely reached Madrid on 16 July when Galarza instructed him to return to Seville. Despite knowing about Cuesta's meticulous planning, he later described it as a suicide mission. He arrived in Seville at 8.00 a.m. on the following day, took a room at the Hotel Simón, made a formal visit to General Villa-Abrille and then went to the province of Huelva with the excuse of carrying out an inspection at Ayamonte on the River Guadiana, opposite Portugal. In the capital Huelva, however, he received a message from Cuesta Monereo informing him that the rising had started in Morocco and urging him to return to Seville immediately. Astonishingly, he did not cancel the inspection in Ayamonte, motivated presumably by fear of arrest. To this end, he visited the Civil Governor Diego Jiménez Castellanos and assured him of his loyalty to the Republic. Convinced, Jiménez Castellanos informed Varela Rendueles that Queipo had said that, after Ayamonte, he would return to Seville and board a plane to Madrid. There, he said, he would take command of government forces to crush the military coup. Nevertheless, as Queipo was about to leave for Ayamonte, he was again intercepted by Cuesta Monereo's messenger who urged him to return to Seville. Because of his protestations of loyalty, Jiménez Castellanos had instructed the Civil Guard to let him pass en route to the Andalusian capital. Queipo repaid the gesture by having him shot on 5 August.[75]

Queipo's hesitation en route to Ayamonte suggests that he was thinking of fleeing to Portugal. Certainly, he and his hagiographers later explained away his less than heroic behaviour in the first hours of the military coup in highly implausible terms. In his June 1950 letter to Franco, he made the bizarre claim that he had gone to Huelva 'using the pretext of inspecting the border guards lest his presence in Seville provoke suspicions'. His duplicitous meeting with Jiménez Castellanos was presented as a daring and courageous move.[76]

When Queipo de Llano arrived in Seville on the morning of 18 July, the first thing that he did was to visit Villa-Abrille at Divisional Headquarters. Since acknowledgement of this encounter would have undermined his later account of the conflictive meeting at noon of the same day when he arrested his one-time friend, Queipo denied that the earlier meeting had taken place. Indeed, he claimed that the first thing that he did on arrival was to meet Pepe el Algabeño, airily telling him to alert the Falange while he went to eat a steak. In response to his declarations about this in subsequent articles and broadcasts, Cuesta Monereo wrote to him later: 'Your memory about this business is not entirely accurate.'[77] It was, presumably, only after leaving Villa-Abrille's office that he met Pepe el Algabeño. Queipo claimed that, when he returned to General Villa-Abrille's headquarters, he single-handedly arrested him and General Julián López-Viota, together with their ADCs. He claimed that, in order to do so, he had been obliged to punch Villa-Abrille.[78] However, other eyewitnesses testified that Queipo did not punch his friend but rather embraced him and amiably tried to persuade him to join the uprising.[79] According to Cuesta Monereo, Villa-Abrille's failure to denounce Queipo's conspiratorial activities was a crucial element in the rising's success in Seville. Villa-Abrille's reward was that, instead of execution, he suffered 'prisión atenuada' (probably house arrest) with his full general's pay.[80]

Even more heroic were Queipo's accounts of how he single-handedly 'captured' the infantry barracks and its commander Colonel Manuel Allanegui Lusarreta. Allegedly, with complete disregard for his own safety, Queipo went to the barracks with his ADC, Captain César López Guerrero, and Captain Escribano. In this spurious version, when he failed to persuade Colonel Allanegui to join the rebellion, he ordered one of his companions to return to Divisional Headquarters and bring Cuesta Monereo to intercede with Allanegui. He then remained alone, as a voluntary hostage among a throng of loyal Republicans. He claimed that he considered resolving the situation 'with bullets', implying that he was ready to fight the entire infantry regiment on his own.[81] In fact, Queipo was far from alone. There were other infantry officers present who helped him try to convince Allanegui to take over. The situation was resolved when they persuaded Allanegui to accompany them to Divisional Headquarters to consult Villa-Abrille. Unaware that Villa-Abrille was already under arrest, Allanegui agreed and was detained on arrival.[82]

With the most senior Republican officers detained, the success of the coup in Seville was assured. Queipo attributed this to his own daring and brilliance in confronting massive (imaginary) forces ranged against him. On 23 August, he gave an interview to the American newspaperman Hubert Knickerbocker, claiming that his success was the consequence of sheer audacity:

> It was a Red city with tens of thousands of Frente Popular supporters ready to go out in the streets and shoot the military. But General de Llano beat them to it. With only one hundred and eighty soldiers, he knew he could do nothing but die if he took the defensive. So, he put his one hundred and eighty soldiers in cars

and sent them riding about the city, blazing away at the least sign of resistance.[83]

These boasts may have been partially inspired by Queipo's resentment of the fact that, on 24 July, the recently constituted Junta de Defensa Nacional had issued its first decrees on the organization of the rebel forces, which included the appointment of 'Generals Francisco Franco as head of the Army of Morocco and the South of Spain and Emilio Mola as head of the Army of the North'. It burst the bubble of his pride and pleasure in his triumph in Seville. Outranking both Franco and Mola, Queipo was so incensed that he scratched out these lines from the telegram. Until 26 August, his only official post was merely as Inspector General of the Carabineros, although he had assumed the position of head of the Segunda División, in succession to Villa-Abrille. On that day, he was confirmed as head of the Segunda División and made General-in-Chief of the forces operating in Andalusia. Franco was given command of the 'Moroccan forces and the Expeditionary Army'. On 1 October, Queipo's independence as commander of the Army of the South would come to an end with the designation of Franco as Generalísimo and head of state. Henceforth, he would be both Inspector General of the Carabineros and head of the Army of the South but under Franco's overall command.

At the same time, Franco was furious about Queipo's boasts of conquering Seville with a few men when, in fact, he had made considerable use of the first contingents of the Army of Africa that Franco had sent to the mainland.[84] The more Queipo trumpeted his personal heroism, the more he was diminishing the aid received from Franco. Inevitably, the underlying tension between the two escalated. Within a year of the events, Queipo had reduced the alleged number of soldiers at his orders. In a lengthy account, published in early 1938 but written before, he repeated his claim that he had captured the city against overwhelming odds with spontaneous bravery helped only by 130 soldiers and fifteen civilians. In his radio broadcast of 1 February 1938, he made an even wilder exaggeration, declaring that he had taken the city with fourteen or fifteen men. He claimed to one of his hagiographers that he had been opposed by a force of over 100,000 well-armed 'Communists'. In fact, the workers defeated had only eighty rifles between them and little ammunition and were armed, if at all, only with hunting shotguns, ancient pistols and knives.[85]

Far from being an act of spontaneous heroism, the coup had been meticulously planned by Cuesta Monereo and carried out by a force of at least 4,000 men. The great majority of the Seville garrison were involved in the coup, including (among many others) units of artillery, cavalry, communications, transport, the quartermaster corps, sappers and the Civil Guard. This is quite clear even from the lists included in the slavish hymn of praise to Queipo de Llano by the journalist Enrique Vila.[86] This large force seized the nerve centres of the city, the telephone building, the town hall and the Gobierno Civil, after artillery bombardment. Applying what Cuesta Monereo had learned in August 1932, to prevent workers coming from the outlying areas the main access routes into the centre were blocked and indiscriminate terror applied in the working-class neighbourhoods.[87] Interestingly, years later Cuesta Monereo was still attributing the success of the coup in Seville to the 'personal bravery and daring' of Queipo.[88]

Under Queipo's overall supervision, the subsequent crushing of working-class resistance within the city was undertaken by Major Antonio Castejón Espinosa of the Foreign Legion. Rebel historiography minimized the role of the Army of Africa in the bloody suppression of the workers' districts of Triana, La Macarena, San Julián and San Marcos. It was claimed that he did so with just thirty Legionaries that he had brought from Morocco, twenty other Legionaries already in Seville, fifty Carlist Requetés, fifty Falangists and another fifty Civil Guards.[89] Against largely unarmed civilians, these 200 well-armed men would still have been a substantial force. Nevertheless, in a later report to Cuesta Monereo, Captain Gutiérrez Flores revealed that, on 21 July 1936, both the Assault Guard and the already complete V Battalion of the Legion were also involved in the operation.[90] The Falangists came mainly from the Círculo de Labradores, the rich landowners' club. The civilian participation in the rising was organized by the leaders of the Círculo, Ramón de Carranza, Pedro Parias González and Pepe el Algabeño. Queipo de Llano rewarded them by making Carranza Alcalde and Parias Civil

Governor of Seville.[91] On the morning of 19 July, armed rightists led by Carranza employed what he himself described as 'brutal punishment' to crush working-class resistance in the districts around the Gran Plaza, Amate and Ciudad Jardín.[92] Artillery bombardments left houses destroyed. For his final attack on La Macarena, on 22 July, Queipo used aircraft to bomb and strafe the district.[93] The systematic terror left thousands of victims. Nevertheless, Queipo prohibited public mourning, a prohibition incessantly and threateningly repeated in the press and on the radio.[94]

After the immediate conquest of the barrios, a more systematic repression began. Mass killings were carried out under the umbrella of the proclamation of martial law, the Bando de Guerra issued by Queipo de Llano on 18 July but drafted by Cuesta Monereo some days earlier.[95] In every town and province across Western Andalusia, although the wording might vary slightly, the sweeping terms in which the *bando* was drawn up effectively decreed that anyone who opposed the rising would be shot.[96] Those who carried out the killings could then claim that they were 'applying the Bando de Guerra' as if this were a legal procedure. In consequence, with no judicial basis, men were taken out and shot, their bodies left by the roadside either to rot or until the municipal authorities came to collect them. In fact, Queipo de Llano had no authority to issue any such edicts.[97] Cuesta invigilated the process, demanding hundreds of reports from local Civil Guard posts on the repression in each town and village in Andalusia and Extremadura.[98]

On 23 July, Queipo de Llano issued another *bando* which stated baldly that any strike leaders caught would be shot along with an equal number of strikers chosen at the discretion of the military authorities. It declared that anyone who disobeyed his edicts would be shot without trial. On the following day, Queipo issued his Sixth Bando, which would be the basis for indiscriminate repression. It stated that 'on discovering acts of cruelty against individuals in any town or village, the leaders of the local Marxist or Communist organizations will be shot. In the event of them not being found, an equal number of their members, arbitrarily selected, will be shot without this prejudicing the sentences that will later be passed against the guilty ones.'[99] This *bando* was used to justify the execution of large numbers of men, women and children who were innocent of any crimes.

To take charge of the process, Queipo de Llano chose a sadist, the infantry Captain Manuel Díaz Criado, who had commanded the Guardia Cívica responsible for the murders in the Parque de María Luisa. He gave him the title of Delegado Militar Gubernativo de Andalucía y Extremadura, with the power of life and death over the people of the region. On his orders, the working-class districts of Triana and La Macarena were stripped of their male populations. Among hundreds of prisoners taken and herded into the provincial prison were children and old men. Most were quickly taken out and shot without any pretence of judicial procedure. Others were left to rot in the fetid prison ship *Cabo Carvoeiro*.[100] Díaz Criado was a degenerate thug who used his position to satisfy his bloodlust, to enrich himself and to obtain sexual gratification. Queipo was fully aware of the use that Díaz Criado made of his unlimited powers but would hear no complaint against him. That is perhaps not surprising since there were accusations that Queipo himself sexually abused Republican women who came to ask for his help.[101] Finally, in mid-November 1936, Franco himself felt obliged to insist on Díaz Criado's removal. His replacement by the Civil Guard Major Santiago Garrigós Bernabéu brought little relief to the terrorized population.

Queipo and Cuesta took a close interest in the repression in the rest of Seville and the neighbouring provinces. It was carried out partly by Castejón's troops and partly by a mixed column of Falangists, Civil Guards and mounted units financed by local land-owners and led by Ramón de Carranza, the new Alcalde of Seville.[102] Their atrocities were encouraged and celebrated by Queipo in highly effective thrice-daily radio broadcasts that were described by Cuesta Monereo as 'weapons of war'. He regularly included incitements to mass rape and murder and boasts about terror and 'punishment' being inflicted on small towns and villages. In his afternoon broadcast on 23 July, for instance, addressing striking workers, he stated, 'I authorize you to kill like dogs those who put pressure on you and I will take full responsibility for this and you will incur none.'[103] On other occasions, he denied that any killing was done by forces under his command: 'Absolutely nobody can prove that a single person has been murdered in any town anywhere.'[104]

There was a section of his evening broadcast on the same day that the censorship felt was too explicit for reproduction in the press. He declared, 'Our brave Legionaries and Regulares have shown the red cowards and their wives too what it means to be a real man. These Communist and anarchist women deserve it. After all, they have made themselves fair game by practising free love. And now they will at least have known real men, and not queer militiamen. Kicking their legs about and struggling won't save them.' On 31 July, three paragraphs from the report in *La Unión* of his afternoon broadcast were blacked out by the censorship. The censor often made deletions when the speeches contained graphic sexual imagery. At other times, it was because they contained military information. On 1 June 1937 and again in early September, Queipo complained that the censorship had cut part of his speech and demanded that this not happen again.[105] Years later, Cuesta Monereo admitted that what appeared in the press was merely an extract that 'did not include the vulgar and obscene comments or vicious sarcasm and venomous insults that he always threw out'.[106] Given what did get published, it is difficult to imagine the toxic impact of the unexpurgated originals.

Many of Queipo de Llano's speeches were replete with sexual references that, given their largely extemporary nature, cast a revealing light on his psychological state. On 26 July 1936, he declared, 'I tell you to kill like a dog any queer or pervert who criticizes this glorious national movement.'[107] Arthur Koestler interviewed Queipo de Llano at the beginning of September:

For some ten minutes he described in a steady flood of words, which now and then became extremely racy, how the Marxists slit open the stomachs of pregnant women and speared the foetuses; how they had tied two eight-year-old girls on to their father's knees, violated them, poured petrol on them and set them on fire. This went on and on, unceasingly, one story following another – a perfect clinical demonstration in sexual psychopathology. Spittle oozed from the corners of the General's mouth, and there was the same flickering glow in his eyes which I had remarked in them during some passages of his broadcast.

Koestler commented on the broadcasts, 'General Queipo de Llano describes scenes of rape with a coarse relish that is an indirect incitement to a repetition of such scenes.'[108]

Many on the rebel side were disgusted by the obscenity of Queipo's language. Typical examples were his assertions that Dolores Ibárruri, Pasionaria, should be employed as a whore for Republican troops, claiming that, as a young woman, she had been a cheap prostitute in a tavern in Somorrostro.[109] At the end of August 1936, while describing the advance on Talavera, he boasted about the capture of female prisoners and what the Regulares would do to them and made another jibe about Dolores Ibárruri: 'How happy the Regulares are going to be and how jealous Pasionaria will be!'[110] In a similar vein were his denunciations of alarmist rumours as the work of 'effeminates' or 'perverts'.[111] The young Falangists Dionisio Ridruejo and Pedro Gamero del Castillo, the provincial chief of the Falange in Seville, were both distressed by the vulgarity of Queipo's speeches.[112]

Typically repellent was his commentary on an atrocity that he had supervised. On 18 September, the leaders of around 8,000 refugees trapped in the province of Badajoz decided to undertake a forced march towards Republican lines. They divided this desperate human mass into two groups, the first consisting of about 2,000 people, the second of approximately 6,000. The first contingent had a dozen men armed with rifles and about 100 with shotguns, the second about twice as many weapons to protect the young children, women with babes in arms, pregnant women and many old people who made up the bulk of the columns. The first, smaller column reached the Republican zone. The larger, slower column crossed the main road from Seville to Mérida between Monesterio and Fuente de Cantos. Inevitably, the column spread out and broke up into several groups, the aged and those with young families moving much more slowly than others. Queipo de Llano was fully informed of the civilian composition of the columns, their sparse armament and their location. Nevertheless, he attacked them as if they were well-equipped military units. An elaborate ambush was mounted by a force of 500 soldiers, Civil Guards and Falangist and Carlist militia. Many refugees were killed and wounded and more than 2,000 were taken prisoner and brought to Llerena. In his broadcast on 18 September, Queipo de Llano boasted about this gratuitous savagery, describing it as a brilliant victory over what he called 'an enemy force'. He presented the unarmed civilians of the refugee column as militiamen whom he accused of cowardice for being defeated by 500 soldiers. He spoke in sinister terms of the prisoners including many wounded. 'There are also numerous women, some schoolteachers and other educated professionals.' In Llerena, a massacre took place over the next month. Prisoners were machine-gunned each morning in the bullring and many women were raped.[113]

The broadcasts were massively popular in rebel Spain and also for thousands of rightists trapped in the Republican zone. Heard there, they were probably the trigger for bloody acts of reprisal.[114] In fact, as with so many elements of Queipo's reputation, the original idea for the broadcasts came from Cuesta Monereo. He had arranged the seizure of the studios of Unión Radio Sevilla with the cooperation of his friend the retired army Major Antonio Fontán de la Orden, who was director of the radio station. Cuesta also made the necessary technical arrangements with Fontán as well as contributing substantially to the drafting of the scripts.[115]

In graphic examples of what Gamel Woolsey called 'the pornography of violence',[116] Queipo recounted spine-chilling, albeit utterly implausible, atrocities that were more indicative of his own psychopathology than of any reality. He claimed that men were impaled alive on stakes then forced to watch as their wives and daughters 'were first raped before their eyes, then drenched with petrol and burned alive', that priests had their stomachs cut open and filled with quicklime, that women had gasoline-soaked cottonwool inserted into their vaginas and then ignited, that nuns were raped and priests tortured on the streets of Barcelona.[117] A senior official of Queipo's propaganda service, Antonio Bahamonde y Sánchez de Castro, travelled from town to town, vainly seeking evidence of the horrendous atrocities described in the nightly broadcasts. Later, in exile, he wrote that these were figments of Queipo's imagination.[118] An indication of the impact of these obscene inventions could be seen in the memoirs

of the Anglo-American poet and novelist Helen Nicholson, Baroness
de Zglinitzki, who listened every night in Granada to what she called
Queipo's 'bed-time story'.[119] The English zoologist Sir Peter Chalmers
Mitchell listened in Malaga as Queipo de Llano began 'to belch out
his jeers and threats'.[120]

In 1933, in his book about the frustrated revolution of December
1930, Queipo had excoriated those who had shown no clemency
when ordering the executions of Galán and García Hernández.[121] In
his broadcast of 5 August 1936, he demanded that the words 'amnesty
and pardon' be removed from the dictionary. On 30 August, Queipo
declared that the search for Republican criminals would go on for ten
or twenty years. He also claimed that, in the rebel zone, there were no
atrocities. With no sense of irony, he asserted that any killing that was
done according to the *bando* was perfectly legal and that extrajudicial
executions were carried out 'according to the rules set out in the
bando, not for the fun of killing like they did, with the greatest cruelty,
burning people alive, throwing them into wells and dynamiting
them, putting out people's eyes, cutting off women's breasts'.[122] Among
the invented atrocities was the claim that, in the historic town of
Ronda, large numbers of prisoners were killed by being thrown into
the *tajo*, the nearby gorge through which the River Gaudalevín runs,
over 90 metres below.[123] In fact, in Ronda, there was just one case,
that of a man, terrified of being caught by the anarchist committee,
who committed suicide by throwing himself into the *tajo*.[124]

What is known of Queipo de Llano's broadcasts derives from the
following day's press reports together with occasional snippets
recorded by those who heard them. Comparisons, when they are
possible, between the two sources suggest that the texts in the press
were a pale reflection of the ferocity of the original speeches. A
revealing case came about as a result of the rebels' adoption of the
monarchist flag on a baking-hot Sunday, 15 August 1936. It was yet
another occasion on which the latent antipathy between Franco and
Queipo was intensified. Franco had arrived with Millán Astray, but
Queipo had refused to accompany the reception party, saying, 'If
Franco wants to see me, he knows where to find me.' He then arrived
late for the ceremony, where he launched into a rambling speech that,
as it got longer and more complicated, provoked sly smiles from

Franco and Millán Astray. The press refrained from comment on the irony of the man who had helped bring about the Republic insulting its flag and demonstrating unrestrained enthusiasm for the monarchy.[125] A Portuguese journalist described the ceremony beneath a scorching sun: 'Queipo de Llano, the radio general, appears. Seville adores him. His facile and vulgar jokes, his harsh laugh, his noisy eloquence was on everyone's lips.'[126]

On the radio that night, Queipo repeated his earlier eulogies of the monarchist red–yellow–red flag. The following day's press recounted part of his broadcast. However, what was not included was a virulent diatribe against the red–yellow–purple Republican flag. What he said was recorded by the poet and propagandist José María Pemán, who was taking part in the show. Exposing once more his obsessions and perhaps his sexual past, Queipo declared that 'the colour purple, in my youth, called to mind above all the colour of permanganate, the usual remedy for gonorrhoea and other diseases of love-making'. An adjutant was usually on hand to switch off the microphone when Queipo started to talk in explicit sexual terms. The version of the broadcast reported in the press did not include the offending remark, but it is not clear if this was because the adjutant had been quick off the mark or because later censorship had intervened.[127]

Newspaper editors knew better than to print the more outrageous incitements to rape and murder. Indeed, there was concern in rebel headquarters that Queipo's excesses might be damaging to their cause abroad. The radio technicians could often anticipate when Queipo was about to swear or give voice to an obscenity. One of them had the job of trying to cover the vulgarity by making a noise with a sheet of metal.[128] It was not enough. Accordingly, on 7 September the instinctive self-censorship of the press was formalized and reinforced by Cuesta Monereo. Some of his fourteen points were routine, to prevent the publication of sensitive military information or of references to assistance reaching the Republic from abroad or to the contribution of Germany and Italy to the rebel cause. Cuesta specifically ordered that the printed version of the radio broadcasts be expurgated: 'In the broadcast chats by the General, any notion, phrase or insult, even though accurate, and doubtless the result of excessive zeal in the expression of his patriotism, whose publication is not appropriate or advisable, for reasons of discretion that will easily be appreciated by our intelligent journalists, shall be suppressed.' In particular, with regard to Queipo's gloating about the repression, Cuesta's instructions stipulated: 'Regarding repressive measures, care must be taken not to repeat shocking phrases or gruesome terms, stating instead simply that "justice was done", "they got the punishment they deserved", "the law was applied", etc., etc.'[129]

It was widely believed that Queipo was drunk when he made his broadcasts. According to the American Ambassador, 'He talked so much like a man half overseas that the loyalists dubbed him "the drunkard of Seville" and they put on a clever radio skit under the title, punctuating the General's wildest comments with cries of "viva vinos".'[130] Florentín Ara, a professor in Jaca, listened to Unión Radio de Sevilla as one of the best sources of news. He recorded his shame and disgust on hearing Queipo de Llano's broadcasts, writing in his diary, 'I had hoped to hear a leader worthy of the broad nature of the movement; but when I listened to the obscenities, lies and vulgarities of this drunken general who is supposed to have come to reconstruct Spain, as a man and as a Spaniard I felt offended and indignant.'[131]

Gerald Brenan's wife, Gamel Woolsey, wrote in 1939: 'He had a tremendous fascination for us, we could never resist him.' She and Gerald found him simultaneously entertaining and nauseating:

Nothing at all like him can ever have been heard on the air before, and never will again. He really has tremendous personality on the radio, he creates a character which seems combined of ferocity and a sort of boisterous, ferocious good humour. I am told that he does not drink at all, but he has the mellow loose voice and the cheerful wandering manner of the habitual drinker. He talks on for hours always perfectly at ease, sometimes he stumbles over a word and corrects himself with a complete lack of embarrassment, speaks of 'these villainous *Fascistas*' and an agonized voice can be heard behind him correcting him, 'No, no, mi General, Marxistas.' 'What difference does it make' – says the general and sweeps grandly on – 'Yes, you *canalla*, you anarchists of Malaga, you wait until I get there in ten days' time! I'll be sitting in a café in the Calle Larios sipping my beer, and for every sip I take ten of you will fall. I shall

shoot ten of you for every one of ours! (he bellows) if I have to drag
them out of their graves to shoot them!'

Brenan wrote years later:

He was a magnificent broadcaster. His whole personality, cruel,
buffoonish, satirical but wonderfully alive and actual, came
through on the microphone. And this was because he did not
attempt any oratorical effects but simply said what came into his
head. His whisky voice, though we were later told that he did not
drink, added to the effect … he was completely natural and at ease.
Sometimes, for example, he could not read his notes. Then he
would turn to his staff and say, 'I can't read this. Is it five hundred
or five thousand Reds we have killed?' 'Five hundred, *mi general*.'
'Well, never mind. Never mind if this time it's only five hundred.
For we are going to kill five thousand, no five hundred thousand.
Five hundred thousand just to begin with, and then we'll see.' …
His broadcasts were stuffed with scurrilous anecdotes, jokes,
insults, absurdities, all wonderfully alive and vivid but horrifying
when we realised the mass executions that were going on all round
him.[132]

Similarly, the Falangist José Antonio Giménez-Arnau, who used to
listen while in hiding in San Sebastián in 1936, wrote later, 'On some
nights we managed to pick up the voice of Queipo de Llano. How
could we not believe, as the "reds" claim, that he was drunk if I myself
believed it? When I met him much later in Rome and I tell him this,
he howls with laughter because he never touched a drop in his entire
life.'[133]

Given his violent personality, Queipo's excesses probably did not
require alcohol. Moreover, in view of his early history of hepatitis, he
should not have been drinking. That does not mean, however, that he
did not do so. After all, he was also supposed to avoid red meat but
regularly ate steak. Nevertheless, Cuesta Monereo commented long
after Queipo's death that 'It wasn't that he didn't drink but rather that
he shouldn't drink. He had serious liver problems. How often did I, a
teetotaller, take the glass from his hand just as he was about to make

a toast because I knew the harm that it did him?' On the occasion of
the fall of Toledo, without realizing that the microphone was still live,
at the end of his programme he shouted, 'Bring wine for fuck's sake.'[134]
On 25 July, he spoke of sharing with a group of taxi drivers a glass of
wine from the many cases sent him by local producers. The next day,
he said that his reference to the gifts from vineyard owners had
provoked rumours that he and his officers were often drunk and that
he owed his throaty voice to the alcohol that he consumed: 'I would
love it to be the case because I really like wine! But my liver prevents
me trying even a drop.'[135] At a ceremony in March 1938, he declared,
'I would have liked to celebrate this event with a drink with you, but
I am a teetotaller, despite what my enemies say.' His grandson wrote,
'I never saw him drink beyond a small glass of wine at lunch.'[136]

It would appear that the bloodlust expressed in his speeches was
the consequence not of alcohol but rather of his instinctive delight in
cruelty. This was made clear in the methods by which, after securing
his power base in the city of Seville, Queipo gradually dominated all
Western Andalusia. He took a direct supervisory role. For example,
he wrote to General José López Pinto on 4 August urging him to
speed up the process of annihilating the left in Cadiz. That letter to
López Pinto reflected Queipo's awareness that they had reached a key
moment in the repression and needed to be merciless. Many towns
and villages of Cadiz, Huelva, Seville and much of Cordoba and
Granada were under rebel control, but the bulk of their inhabitants
were predominantly Republican, Socialist and anarcho-syndicalist in
their sympathies. To prevent any resistance in the rearguard as his
columns moved north, Queipo ordered that the repression be stepped
up and prisoners be killed. Two days after the letter to López Pinto,
Queipo sent the retired Lieutenant Colonel Eduardo Valera Valverde,
who had been involved in the Sanjurjo coup of 1932, to be Civil
Governor of Cadiz. His instructions were to 'proceed with greater
energy'. In response, from 8 August, Varela Valverde initiated more
systematic executions.[137]

Queipo boasted about his part in the repression in the 'sworn
declaration of services rendered' presented with his application for
the Cruz Laureada de San Fernando. About the operation to occupy
the mining districts in the north of the province of Huelva, he wrote,

'The punishment meted out was terrible. In those operations, the enemy lost more than 4,000 men. As a result, there were no more breaches of the peace.' On 31 July, instructions calling for 'energy in the repression' were issued to the invading columns, signed by Queipo although probably drafted by Cuesta Monereo. 'The enemy' consisted of the 40,000 civilians in the area. There was some sporadic resistance and it is the case that there were eleven right-wing victims in Salvochea (El Campillo). Two weeks later, instructions from Queipo's General Staff made it clear that his columns enjoyed massive superiority of weaponry and expected little by way of resistance.[138] As his broadcasts demonstrated, Queipo observed their progress through the mining districts with pleasure.[139]

The physical terror that was the basis of Queipo's power was accompanied by large-scale economic repression, what Rúben Serém has called the 'Kleptocratic State' – 'the economic equivalent of the military scorched-earth policy adopted by the Army of Africa', with Seville the testing ground for the rest of rebel Spain.[140] It took many forms. Sheer intimidation saw local workers' societies and trade unions 'voluntarily' dissolving themselves and handing over their funds.[141] Donations of gold and silver by the very rich may have been voluntary but intimidation cannot be discounted. Numerous devices were invented to facilitate economic plunder. Obligatory fund-raising, which was effectively organized extortion, had the dual function of financing the war effort and punishing Republicans. From the earliest days of the war, 'subscriptions' were being started for various causes, initially 'for the soldiers' and later to buy aircraft, to support the army, to buy the battle cruiser *España*. Those who refused or were unable to contribute were denounced as 'hostile to the regime'. They were punished with fines for those who could pay and imprisonment or execution for those who could not on the grounds that their inability to pay constituted 'aid to the rebellion'.[142] In his speeches, again without irony, Queipo praised the patriotic spirit of workers who handed over their wages for the subscriptions.[143] On one occasion, he negotiated with a highly dubious businessman a deal for the monopoly of the importation of rice. In return for half of the profits, he granted the concession and threatened to have the man shot if he cheated him.[144]

A share of the 'contributions' regularly ended up in the pockets of the Falangists or Civil Guards sent to collect them.[145] Queipo was personally one of the greatest beneficiaries of the sums collected. On 25 August 1936, a valuable antique swagger stick with a gold handle was bought for him with money raised by a subscription. Ten days later, another raised the money for an album, engraved in gold, containing 37,000 signatures of people expressing their homage.[146] The greatest personal benefit accrued through an elaborate scheme relating to another subscription launched in August 1937 to thank him for saving Seville. It was to be a 'lasting testimony of gratitude to the liberator of Seville but also to guarantee him a comfortable financial position after the war'.[147] In his broadcasts, he constantly declared that he had no need of tributes. However, in his *charla* (chat) on 16 August, referring to 'the subscription being made as a tribute to my person', he let slip the phrase 'because of my own felicitous initiative'. Within four months, he announced that the contributions had reached the astonishing sum of 2,147,291 pesetas. Public statements of the total amount varied, from Queipo's claim on the radio to 2,200,000 pesetas according to *ABC* and even to 2,500,000 pesetas claimed by the Civil Governor, as reported in *La Unión*.[148] In fact, the money raised by the subscription barely reached 100,000 pesetas. Moreover, although both his hagiographers and his son proclaimed that it had been donated mainly by 'humble folk', there was no subscription beyond obligatory deductions from the salaries of municipal and provincial functionaries.[149]

Beyond the modest sum raised from salary deductions, the larger amounts proclaimed by Queipo, the Civil Governor and the press permitted the purchase of a magnificent estate (*cortijo*) called Gambogaz, in 550 hectares of land in the area known as La Cartuja in Camas on the outskirts of Triana.[150] Persisting with the falsehood that the larger sum was the fruit of the subscription, he declared that this patriotic homage allowed him to use the money as he wished. Nevertheless, on 8 December 1937, in response to accusations emanating from the Republican media, he denied that the estate had been bought in order for him to live off its income. He claimed that the purchase of Gambogaz was to carry out agrarian reform.[151] To mask his personal gain, the fiction was fabricated that the money

from the subscription had been used to create a charitable foundation to buy land for war wounded and the poor. He claimed in his
broadcast of 24 December that year that the sole purpose of
Gambogaz 'is to use it for social purposes, to help and improve the
lot of agricultural workers and implement agrarian reform'.[152]

In fact, far from being facilitated by a simple act of popular enthusiasm, the operation was an elaborate swindle. The constant
references to the 'subscription in my honour' were mainly directed at
inflating the notion of his popularity. However, the money raised by
the 'subscription' was far from sufficient for what he wanted. Recent
investigations by descendants of the original owners of the estate and
by a civic organization in Seville, the Plataforma Gambogaz, have
revealed that the bulk of the money to purchase the estate was
provided in the form of a mortgage loan by the Banco de España
which was never paid back. Queipo secured these funds by claiming
that they were for a newly created entity with a social function, the
Fundación Benéfica Social Agraria Gonzalo Queipo de Llano. On 24
December 1937, a notary, Fulgencio Echaíde Aguinaga, acting as a
frontman, had purchased, for 1,300,000 pesetas, 480 hectares of the
Gambogaz estate. The remaining 70 hectares were left in the hands of
the family of the vendor, José Vázquez Rodríguez. Echaíde Aguinaga
then donated the estate to the Fundación. A group of Queipo's
cronies, including Pedro Parias and Ramón de Carranza, made up a
board of trustees under the presidency of the military judge Colonel
Francisco Bohórquez Vecina. It was announced that the purpose of
the foundation was 'to acquire and provide plots of land for those
supporters of the rebel cause of impeccable conduct who had suffered
personally or economically through their participation in the
Crusade'. Over the next few years, the family of Vázquez Rodríguez
was pressured by physical threats from Queipo and Ramón de
Carranza into selling the remaining 70 hectares to the Fundación for
much less than they were worth. In October 1943, the Fundación
Agraria transferred the ownership of the estate to Queipo de Llano.[153]

From 1937 to 1939, Gambogaz housed a concentration camp for
Republican prisoners. On several occasions between 1938 and 1943,
Queipo's estate manager secured what was effectively slave labour to
work the estate. When the prisoners in the camp were insufficiently

skilled, applications for the specialized labour required were regularly made to the Civil Governor of the province, who would in turn send the relevant instructions to the warden of the provincial prison of Seville. This is revealed by the following instruction from the Civil Governor to the warden in May 1939:

> The 'Fundación Queipo de Llano' of the Gambogaz estate needs labourers for the harvest. Since, on other occasions, prisoners have been used for these purposes on the estate in question, please, on my authority, choose from among the said prisoners thirty of good conduct and behaviour who have the necessary skills and experience. The estate manager, Emilio Elena Landa, will take charge of them and they will remain on the estate, as prisoners under my authority.[154]

The accumulated profits from the estate permitted Queipo to buy more land elsewhere in the province.[155] The process followed with Gambogaz had certain similarities to that which allowed Franco to acquire the Pazo de Meirás.[156] The estate became Queipo's personal retreat where, particularly in his final days, he would indulge his interest in horse and cattle breeding.[157]

The scale of Queipo's power created considerable friction with Franco, whom Queipo despised. He was never able to conceal his contempt for a man who was below him in the seniority scale. His tactlessness ensured that his younger comrade was fully aware of this contempt. For instance, on hearing that, by way of disguise, Franco had shaved off his moustache in the course of his journey from the Canary Islands to Morocco, Queipo made a much repeated quip that the moustache was the only thing that Franco ever sacrificed for Spain.[158] The loathing was mutual. Franco always felt uncomfortable when faced with the barely concealed disdain of Queipo, which dated back to their time in Africa.[159] He distrusted Queipo for his betrayal of the monarchy in 1931. In August 1936, they had heated arguments in Seville. While Franco wanted his African columns to drive on to Madrid, Queipo wanted to use the troops from Morocco for a major campaign to spread out from the Seville–Huelva–Cadiz triangle that he controlled in order to conquer all of Andalusia.[160] Franco simply ignored Queipo's aspirations. He had already, on 1 August, ordered a column north to occupy Mérida and deliver 7 million cartridges to the forces of General Mola. The column had set out on Sunday 2 August in trucks provided by Queipo loaded with ammunition from the Seville armaments factory. Queipo seethed for years over Franco's failure to acknowledge this and other crucial assistance.[161]

In mid-August 1936, Queipo demonstrated both his own vengeful personality and his contempt for Franco. He ordered the execution of the two sons of General Ricardo Burguete, Luis and Manuel. His hostility to Burguete dated back to their time in Africa. He hated Luis Burguete because he had denounced him for alleged cowardice in Morocco; and he had never forgiven Ricardo Burguete for his role as President of the Junta Clasificadora del Ejército that in 1928 had refused him promotion to major general. Devastated by grief, Burguete gave vent to his views on Queipo in an article entitled 'Yo acuso' published in the Republican zone. He reviewed Queipo's career in Morocco as a cycle of cowardly and deceitful acts. He called him a 'miserable buffoon, coward and drunkard'. Referring to his broadcasts, he wrote, 'Your antics as an alcohol-soaked hen fit in well with your murderous heart.' Queipo referred to the insults in his broadcast of 17 March, saying merely that they did not bother him.[162]

In a similar act of petty revenge, on 14 August Queipo court-martialled General Miguel Campins, the recently appointed military commander of Granada, for the crime of 'military rebellion'. His actual 'crime' was to have delayed obeying Queipo when he telephoned him at 3.00 in the afternoon of 18 July and ordered him to declare martial law in Granada. He had replied that an act of such gravity needed consideration. He was aware of no disorders that would justify the step. He then delayed two days before declaring martial law. His delay was the consequence of wanting to avoid unnecessary bloodshed in the city.[163] Queipo initially accepted Campins's explanation for the delay then changed his mind and denounced him furiously in his broadcast of 21 July: 'I have to give you an account of the treachery of General Campin [sic] who has played a vile double game, deceiving both the government and me.' He suggested that, if Campins had been an honourable man, he would have committed suicide.[164]

Campins was a close friend of Franco and in the late 1920s had been his second-in-command at the Academia General Militar of Zaragoza. Franco wrote a number of letters to Queipo requesting mercy for Campins. Determined to have Campins shot, Queipo read them, then simply tore them up. Under the presidency of General José López Pinto, an extreme rightist and close collaborator of Queipo, the tribunal sentenced Campins to death. Franco made a last desperate effort to save his friend, sending his cousin Pacón with another letter. Queipo refused to open it, saying, 'I don't want to open any more letters from your general about this irksome business. Tell him that Campins will be shot tomorrow.' Campins was shot by a firing squad of Legionaries on 16 August. Unaware of this, Dolores Roda, Campins's wife, sent a telegram to Queipo begging for news of her husband. Queipo wrote the instruction, 'inform her that her husband died on the 16th of this month'. This message was sent eleven days later to General Cabanellas in Zaragoza for onward transmission to her.[165]

The brutal treatment of Campins was evidence of Queipo's gratuitous cruelty, as were the executions of Jiménez Castellanos and Labandera a few days earlier. His treatment of Campins was partly driven by a desire to humiliate Franco. It was another brick in the wall of their mutual hostility. Franco took his revenge in 1937 by ignoring Queipo's own pleas for mercy for his friend General Domingo Batet, who was condemned to death for opposing the rising in Burgos.[166] Franco was not alone among the high command in despising Queipo for his obscene radio broadcasts. Nevertheless, despite the friction between them and his own ambitions, Queipo had voted for Franco at the historic gathering on 21 September at the recently improvised airfield near Salamanca to choose an overall commander of the rebel forces. Many years later, Queipo de Llano, on criticizing Franco, was asked by the monarchist Eugenio Vegas Latapie why he had voted for him. He replied, 'And who else could we appoint? It couldn't be Cabanellas. He was a convinced Republican and everyone knew that he was a freemason. Nor could we name Mola because we would have lost the war. And my prestige was seriously impaired.' Nonetheless, Queipo made no secret of his dissatisfaction with the decision taken.[167] The next stage of Franco's ascent to supreme power was the further meeting held in Salamanca one week after the first. Before the afternoon session began, Queipo and Mola had returned to their respective headquarters and so were not present when a reluctant agreement was reached to the effect that Franco would be head of the government as well as Generalísimo. In fact, the President of the Junta Técnica del Estado of Burgos, General Miguel Cabanellas, still harboured doubts and decided to sign the decree only late in the night of 28 September after lengthy telephone consultations with Mola and Queipo. According to Cabanellas's son, Queipo said, 'Franco is a swine. I have never liked him and never will. However, we've got to go along with his game until we can block it.'[168] He told Dámaso Gutiérrez Arrese, one of the medical staff in Franco's headquarters, 'Make no mistake. Nothing good will come of this because we have chosen a leader who is an egotist and petty-minded.' There was no shortage of willing confidants to pass on such comments to Franco.[169]

On the same day that Campins was shot, Federico García Lorca was arrested. He was shot two days later. There have been several claims that the order for the poet's death was given by Queipo, either by telephone or, more probably, by radio, to the newly appointed Civil Governor of Granada, the forty-five-year-old Comandante José Valdés Guzmán, an Africanista as well as an early member of the Falange. Valdés had contacted Queipo to check if he could proceed with the execution. At least two acquaintances of Valdés claimed that Queipo responded, 'Give that one coffee with milk, lots of coffee,' a euphemism for 'kill him'.[170]

One of Queipo's granddaughters, the historian Genoveva García Queipo de Llano, disputed allegations of her grandfather's bloodlust on the basis of her personal knowledge of him. Regarding the death of Lorca, she wrote, 'it is most probable that he did not even know who Lorca was nor had even heard about his situation'. It is unlikely that Queipo was unaware beforehand of Lorca's reputation as a famous Republican poet, playwright and champion of the poor. If he did not, it is probable that Valdés would have explained that the poet was a friend of the Socialist leader Fernando de los Ríos and a homosexual. Both facts would have been more than sufficient to explain Queipo's permission for him to be shot.[171] Another of Queipo's granddaughters, Ana Quevedo, has claimed implausibly that, when Queipo heard the news, he was angry about what he saw as a costly political error. Ana was not born until ten years after the death of Lorca and was five years old when Queipo died. Genoveva was one year older. Accordingly, it is unlikely that either girl discussed the case with him and they can only have based their assertions on the word of third parties.[172]

As Generalísimo, Franco had limited Queipo's active role in the war to clinching control of the Second Military Region. However, because of his own failure to take Madrid, Franco accepted Queipo's proposal for a piecemeal advance towards Malaga. A sporadic campaign to mop up the rest of Andalusia had started in mid-December with considerable success.[173] The March on Malaga began on 9 January 1937, under the joint command of the Italian Mario Roatta on land and Queipo, who was installed on the battle cruiser *Canarias*.[174] After sustained bombing raids by Italian aircraft and bombardment by rebel warships, on Monday 8 February a poorly defended Malaga was occupied by columns of rebel and Italian troops.[175] In the preceding months, Queipo had been threatening in broadcasts and in leaflets dropped on the city to inflict bloody revenge for the repression carried out by anarchists during the seven months since the war started.[176] His grisly threats confirmed the spine-chilling tales brought by thousands of refugees about the savagery of the Army of Africa when they entered their pueblos in Cadiz, Seville, Cordoba and Granada. The collapse of Antequera on 12 August and of Ronda on 17 September had seen Malaga flooded by desperate and hungry women, children and old people.[177]

Despite the ease of his victory, Queipo showed no mercy. Hundreds of Republicans were shot.[178] Before the occupiers began the executions, tens of thousands of terrified refugees fled via the only possible escape route, the 175 kilometres along the coast road to Almería. Their flight was spontaneous and they had no military protection. In his broadcast on 8 February, Queipo recounted with delight that 'great masses of fugitives headed out of Malaga towards Motril and our aircraft came to help them run by bombing them and setting fire to their trucks'. The scale of the repression inside the fallen city explained why they were ready to run the gauntlet. Within the city itself nearly 4,000 Republicans were shot in the first week alone and the killings continued on a large scale for months. Along the roughly surfaced road, littered with corpses and the wounded, terrified people trudged without food or water.[179]

It has been calculated that there were more than 100,000 on the road, some with nothing, others carrying kitchen utensils and bedding. It is impossible to calculate the death toll but it seems to have been over 3,000.[180] In his broadcasts, Queipo denied that he had attacked the refugees and blamed their flight on Republican propaganda.[181] However, in the self-aggrandizing account in his application for the Laureada, he boasted that 500 Republicans had been 'pursued mercilessly and all killed'. The refugees who blocked the road out of Malaga were shelled from the sea by the warships *Cervera* and *Baleares*, bombed from the air and then machine-gunned by the pursuing Italian units. Discussing the reasons why Queipo had engaged in this gratuitous slaughter in Seville and other captured cities, Gerald Brenan declared, 'Not that he can have disliked doing so for he was a natural sadist and the executions went on without pause for months after his position was safe'.[182]

In addition to his bloodlust, both anti-Semitism and admiration for Hitler were regular features of his speeches. One of the most extreme was his broadcast on 4 September 1936. In somewhat contradictory terms, he referred to 'a race as cowardly as the Hebrew' before going on to outline the ambitious plans of the Jews for world domination. 'In these critical moments, the Jews are also fighting in Spain and their role in the struggle is not because they care about democracy and freedom, it is because their objective is on a rather greater scale. They are fighting for Judaism against Christianity, in the belief that the moment has come for Judaism to impose their domination of the world.' Confusing the various forces on the Republican side, he claimed that 'freemasons, anarchists, Socialists, etc., etc., united with Judaism are just the tentacles of the same beast'. They were tools in what he claimed was the 'struggle of the Jewish race, using all means, to dominate the entire globe'. The initials USSR (URSS in Spanish) did not stand for 'the Union of Soviet Socialist Republics' but for 'the Rabbinical Union of the Elders of Zion' (Unión Rabínica de los Sabios de Sión).[183]

Queipo often claimed that the governments of the democracies were puppets of the Jews and sought to insult Republican politicians by alleging that they were of Jewish origin. On 15 October 1936, alongside a hymn of praise for Hitler, he declared that 'without a shadow of doubt, the Jews have endangered the foundations of our civilization'. In February 1937, he reaffirmed his belief in the authenticity of *The Protocols of the Elders of Zion*. On 8 March, praising Islamic hostility to Judaism, he referred to 'that race that propagates communism, hoards gold and aspires to subjugate the world and make all peoples as despicable as itself'. Two months later, in May, he declared that the wealth of the United States was in Jewish hands and returned to the notion of Jewish world domination.

On 10 September, he denounced Soviet Russia as the first link in what he saw as the chain of Jewish world domination. It was thus but a short step to adulation of the Third Reich: 'I have always believed in the great talent of Hitler and his collaborators. They demonstrated this by first expelling from Germany that treacherous, cowardly and accursed race that, having gained control of all the gold in the world, thanks to the stupidity of the Christians, now wants to take over the world with the help of Prieto, De los Ríos and other brutes in their pay'.[184] In October 1938, he represented Franco at a ceremony in Cadiz to say farewell to Italian troops who were being repatriated. In his speech to the departing forces, he thanked them for their idealism in coming to Spain 'to fight the wretches on Moscow's payroll who wanted to destroy their Fatherland and deliver it defenceless into slavery under foul Judaism'. He paid tribute to Mussolini for his aid in a war 'that we are fighting, not so much against the Spanish reds as against miserable Judaism that had no qualms about allying with the forces of Moscow'.[185]

Queipo had an anti-Semitic rationalization for his actions in Seville: 'Bolshevism had chosen Seville as a target for its horrors, which shame civilized society. Atheists, Jews, freemasons, reds in general, all allied themselves against our Fatherland'.[186] Queipo imposed a fine of 138,000 pesetas on the tiny Jewish community of Seville. He also gave the local Falange free rein to attack and pillage their homes and businesses.[187] His views were disseminated by the Falange, which distributed apocalyptic leaflets: 'You were horrified witnesses to the catastrophe planned by the assassins at the service of Moscow. Spain was at the mercy of the Asiatic spirit of Russia. Jewry, freemasonry, Marxism are the three obstacles to our salvation. We breathed a pestilent air of the sewers, of a disease-ridden cesspool, infected by malign debris of vileness and destruction, which has now been purified by joyful winds of justice.'[188]

Queipo had wanted his victory at Malaga to be the first step in a triumphal march through Eastern Andalusia. However, Franco was obsessed with Madrid and had no desire to give away triumphs to Queipo de Llano. Accordingly, he prohibited further eastwards advance, to the lifelong chagrin of Queipo.[189] Deeply resentful, Queipo realized that his capacity to challenge Franco was constantly diminishing.[190] Nonetheless, having conquered large areas of Andalusia, he was building his own autonomous power base for a future challenge to Franco. A symbolic indication of the rivalry was Queipo's creation, in emulation of Franco's ceremonial Moorish Guard, of a unit of twenty mounted Regulares as his own escort.[191] In Franco's eyes, Queipo remained a problem if not a serious threat.

Franco was sufficiently worried about the signs of Queipo's political ambitions to send his brother Nicolás to Seville in an unsuccessful attempt to cut Queipo's links with the local oligarchy. The growing tension was the subject of a report by the Italian Ambassador, Roberto Cantalupo, to Ciano on 1 March 1937:

Particularly since the occupation of Malaga, General Queipo de Llano has initiated a personal policy that is perfectly obvious not only in his inane daily radio speeches that delight the masses and win him an easy popularity. It is visible too in actions that clearly aspire to be a policy of government throughout the region of Seville. It is a policy based on manoeuvres among the parties and control of vast economic interests. It aims to create a base from which he would eventually be able to move easily to higher, probably more central, positions, and certainly against Franco. All this is well known to the extent that the Generalísimo's brother went privately to Seville to undermine Queipo de Llano's scheme by cutting him off from key capitalist elements. However, Franco's inability to control Queipo de Llano and to contain him in a disci-

plined fashion within the limits permitted to a general with
command of troops inevitably provokes criticism, comment and
pessimistic conclusions regarding his abilities as a politician. His
language and his approach remain weak and impersonal.[192]

It would not be until 30 January 1938, when Franco created his first
regular cabinet, that Queipo's marginalization was complete. The rule
of the Junta Técnica del Estado of Burgos was formally brought to an
end without Queipo even being consulted. On the same day, he was
forbidden to continue with his radio speeches. His last speech was
broadcast on 1 February. To protect his reputation in Seville, he made
an implausible speech in which he stated that the decision to stop the
broadcasts was his alone, a fraudulent claim that was repeated years
later by Cuesta Monereo. At the same time, he claimed that Franco
had offered him the Ministry of Agriculture but he had refused.[193]

The creation of Franco's cabinet heralded the end of Queipo's independent fief in the south. Queipo had never reconciled himself to
Franco's dominance. In turn, Franco was determined to break
Queipo's power as viceroy of Seville. Serrano Suñer became Minister
of the Interior and the dominant figure. To begin the process of
diminishing Queipo's power, in February 1938 Serrano Suñer
promoted his protégé Pedro Gamero del Castillo, the provincial chief
of the Falange in Seville, to Civil Governor of the entire province. To
Queipo's outrage, in October Gamero dismissed Ramón de Carranza
as Alcalde. Queipo immediately flew to Burgos to demand that the
decision be reversed. When, despite Queipo's physical threats,
Serrano Suñer refused, the friction between them became intense.[194]

Moreover, Queipo loathed Serrano Suñer and was regarded in
some circles as a possible leader of military opposition to the Falange.
In May 1939, Franco received a letter from Colonel Juan Beigbeder,
the High Commissioner in Spanish Morocco, informing him that
Queipo was planning a visit to Morocco. Cuesta Monereo, now a
lieutenant colonel, had been making soundings on behalf of Queipo
for the creation of a military directory to replace Franco and to
neutralize the power of the Falange.[195] In a gesture of self-aggrandize-
ment, when the German Condor Legion had returned to Germany,
Queipo, without Franco's permission, had flown ahead in order to be

in Berlin to greet them.[196] Franco was intensely annoyed but he did not act immediately. He and Serrano Suñer were biding their time.

However, Queipo provided Franco with the excuse for more decisive action when he went too far with an act of public disrespect. With his daughter Maruja at his side as usual, he made a provocative speech on 18 July, the day on which Franco was celebrating his victory. Among other provocations, he expressed his outrage that Franco had granted the military decoration of the Cruz Laureada de San Fernando to Valladolid but not to Seville, his own power base. He claimed that he had never wanted the medal for himself, an outright lie. His annoyance was understandable given the role played by Seville in the 1936 rising and the fact that Valladolid was a centre of Falangist strength. He assumed that the honour given to Valladolid was a humiliation devised by Serrano Suñer. His reference to the frail Serrano was unmistakable: 'The way things are going, ragdolls with bellies stuffed with sawdust or fragile figures made of clay will be turned into heroes.' Among the many untruths in his speech, he claimed that Mola had told him that he had been about to flee to France until he heard Queipo speaking on Radio Sevilla. Queipo also boasted that he had really wanted to lead the uprising in Madrid and that, if he had been allowed to do so, the outcome there would have been different. He infuriated Franco by recalling that he had been given power by the military and then only provisionally.[197]

The accumulation of personal insults and the public criticism of the power of Serrano Suñer stung Franco into taking action. He lured Queipo to Burgos on the pretext of calling him for 'consultations'. He simultaneously sent General Andrés Saliquet to take over his functions in Seville. Queipo had never forgiven Saliquet for being chosen in his stead as leader of the rising in Valladolid. It was a carefully calculated humiliation by Franco in revenge for a long list of slights suffered at the hands of the sneering Queipo. In a bitter meeting, the Generalísimo brandished a thick file of copies of Queipo's speeches and letters replete with insulting remarks about him. Allegedly, some of these letters had been supplied by Cuesta Monereo who, with Queipo's end in sight, was presumably securing his own position.[198] On 20 July, Queipo was dismissed as Captain General of the Second Military Region (Franco had reinstated the old rank) and posted to 'the service of other ministries'. He was confined in Burgos in the modest Hotel María Isabel, which was surrounded by a police cordon that, he later claimed, had orders to shoot to kill if he tried to leave.

His alarm was visible in an interview that he gave to the American journalist Reynolds Packard. In this, he trotted out the official version that, at a cordial meeting, he had been delighted to accept the offer by his friend Franco of an appointment abroad.[199] Talk of sending him to Buenos Aires came to nothing. Instead, it was decided to send him to head a non-existent Spanish military mission in Rome, where he would be under Fascist observation.[200] Serrano had told Mussolini's Foreign Minister, Count Galeazzo Ciano, that he regarded Queipo as 'loco'. When the proposal reached Rome on 27 July, Ciano commented, 'a clever move to put an end to the current gossip, to free himself of Queipo de Llano and, at the same time, to keep him under control'.[201] General Gastone Gambara, the head of the Italian Military Mission in Spain, reported to Ciano that Serrano Suñer had told him that Queipo was an 'incorrigible traitor'.[202]

During his last days before leaving for Italy, Queipo was escorted by General Antonio Sagardía Ramos, the Inspector General of the national police. So close was Sagardía's attention that Queipo called him 'my babysitter'. Queipo used his remaining time in Spain to make a kind of farewell tour of Andalusia, although he had been forbidden to go to Seville. Rumours were spreading within the army that there was going to be a rebellion in local garrisons in favour of Queipo and so troops were confined to barracks for some days.[203] In his report to the Minister of War, General Varela, Sagardía noted that the Civil Governor of Cordoba, Eduardo Valera Valverde, had told him of Queipo's dismay that news of his demotion had not led to an uprising in Andalusia. In anticipation of a coup, he had ordered Valera Valverde to ignore any instructions from Franco's headquarters that contradicted his own decrees. Sagardía also reported on corrupt activities by Queipo that recalled the subterfuges used in the purchase of Gambogaz. Sagardía stated that Queipo had flouted Francoist legislation in order to protect the properties in Priego de Córdoba of Alcalá-Zamora and his friends. He had collected rents on their behalf and sent the proceeds to Alcalá-Zamora in Paris. He further revealed that, thanks to Queipo's protection, huge profits were being made at the tannery belonging to Queipo's son-in-law, Calixto García Martín, the husband of Mercedes.[204]

Prevented from returning to Seville to arrange his household and collect his belongings, Queipo was obliged to await his family and luggage at Alcalá de Guadaira. On 16 August, he left for Rome together with his daughter Maruja and two adjutants, César López Guerrero and Julián Quevedo. His wife Genoveva refused to accompany him and remained in Seville. After a further delay in Barcelona, on 21 August the party reached Rome, where it was made clear that he had no particular mission. His exile was to be a gilded confinement in Rome, a gigantic and beautiful prison where he was kept under constant police observation. He used the time to start to write self-congratulatory memoirs and long letters of complaint to those he considered had slighted him. Even though it is not the practice of those who write an autobiography to speak ill of their subject, the scale of untruth and exaggeration in what has survived of the letters and memoirs produced by Queipo is breathtaking.[205]

Queipo allowed Pedro Sainz Rodríguez to read his draft memoirs in Rome. 'I remember that he spoke about Franco with real passion. It was a diatribe against him. It retold all the insulting anecdotes that were current among Franco's enemies, and, usually, when he appeared in the narrative, he called him "fat-arsed Francine". He recounted incidents from Franco's life in Africa, emphasizing the icy cruelty and pleasure with which he would watch the punishment beatings meted out to Regulares.'[206]

The ease of Franco's victory over Queipo was surprising even for such a master at controlling his domestic rivals. Along with his consequent resentment of Franco, Queipo's enmity towards Serrano Suñer increased commensurately. Every perceived indignity and discourtesy, such as police vigilance or the time taken by Mussolini to grant him an audience, he attributed to Serrano Suñer as much as to Franco. In fact, when he was finally received by the Duce, he complained about the delay. Mussolini responded by showing him a letter from Franco describing Queipo as 'a dangerous anti-fascist'. At the end of the audience, Queipo was presented with a red leather document folder containing a signed photograph of the Duce. On the way back to his hotel, he ordered his adjutant Julián Quevedo to tear it up.[207] On 1 October 1940, when Serrano Suñer, now Foreign Minister, arrived in Rome for a meeting with Ciano, Queipo was obliged to be part of the Embassy contingent to greet him. With typical childishness, he refused to shake hands or speak to him and declined to attend the official lunch at the Italian Foreign Ministry. Ciano made numerous complaints about Queipo's behaviour in Rome, which he described as 'characterized by constant and unrestrained insults and outrageous remarks directed against the Generalísimo and Head of State, the Minister of the Army, against myself and against the government in general'. To explain how someone on an official mission could talk in such a way, Serrano Suñer told Ciano that Queipo was 'a bandit and a beast'.[208]

The resentment against Serrano Suñer that began in 1938 when, as Minister of the Interior, he broke Queipo's power as the independent lord of Seville, festered over the years. When Serrano published his book on Spain's role in the Second World War, he did not go into detail about the Spanish Civil War. Queipo was furious that Serrano referred only to his 'golpe audaz' (daring coup) in Seville in July 1936. Then when Queipo read Serrano's remarks to Ciano in the published version of the Italian Minister's diary, he gave vent to his grudges in two furious and deeply offensive letters.[209] In response to the first, Serrano Suñer replied in measured terms and declined to match Queipo's aggressively insulting tone. On 24 October 1948, in justification of his language, Queipo responded with typical lack of restraint: 'When we speak about snakes, usually we do so with indifference and repugnance. However, if we actually see one in front of us, we instinctively feel the desire to crush it. So, it is just as well that this dialogue between us has taken place in writing because, if I had found you in my presence, instinct would have impelled me to try to crush you.'[210]

During his time in Italy, Queipo's relationship with his daughter Maruja, now in her early thirties, long since more than paternal, became possessively suffocating. He refused to leave the hotel for any official or social functions unless she accompanied him and he deliberately frightened away any men who showed an interest in her. One of these would-be suitors was the fifty-five-year-old Julián Quevedo, a widower. He showered Maruja with attention and gifts and gradually his feelings were reciprocated. Apart from one brief visit to Rome, Queipo's wife remained in Seville. Already uneasy about the nature of her husband's relationship with their daughter, Genoveva was delighted by the growing affection between Maruja and Julián Quevedo. Not entirely disinterestedly, she commented on it to the General who had hitherto not noticed the burgeoning relationship. He reacted with jealous fury and became even more obsessive in his efforts to ensure that Maruja was never alone with Julián. This intensified Genoveva's existing suspicions. When Maruja decided to marry Julián without his permission, Queipo flew into an uncontrollable rage and disinherited her. Her mother then gave vent to her suspicions and asked Maruja if his opposition to the marriage 'was to do with motives that went beyond paternal love'. She then asked her daughter if Queipo had ever taken liberties with her. When Maruja refused to answer, her mother drew an understandable and distressing conclusion.[211]

Alongside his resentments of Franco, Serrano and even of Julián Quevedo, Queipo found space for his grudges against the exiled Alfonso XIII, whom he never forgave for what he regarded as the King's betrayal in 1928. Although they were guests in the same hotel in Rome, Queipo rudely refused to accept his invitation to talk about their past differences, sending a message to the effect that he had no desire to listen to his excuses. He even failed to greet the King when they coincided in the hall or in the lift. When Alfonso XIII died on 28 February 1941, Queipo went to sign the condolence book. An aristocratic lady, waiting in line, said, 'General, His Majesty forgave everyone before he died.' Taking this as a reference to his betrayal of the King in 1931, he barked back, 'To forgive, Madame, it is not necessary to die. Do you really think that, if I had not forgiven him, I would be here today?' In fact, rather than sorrow at the King's death, his purpose in appearing in full-dress uniform to give his condolences was to flout orders from Franco, who was reluctant for there to be any official mourning for the King.[212]

Partly because of his intense jealousy of Maruja, Queipo decided to disobey Franco's explicit orders and returned to Spain in June 1942. He hoped to have more control of her movements in the family home. Even back in Seville and living with his wife, his obsession with Maruja grew and he put intense pressure on her to break off her relationship with Julián Quevedo. When they eventually married in Madrid at the beginning of July 1946, no other member of the family attended the ceremony and Queipo prevented her collecting her belongings from the family home. She spent the night before the wedding at the residence of a friend. Queipo sent some nuns to her fiancé's home to search it, believing that they would find her there *in flagrante*. To the nuns' embarrassment, they found Quevedo alone.[213]

In 1939, when Roatta's assistant Lieutenant Colonel Emilio Faldella had published an account of the campaign, Queipo wrote him a furious letter complaining that his book had diminished his role in the campaign.[214] According to a secret police report filed in March 1942, Queipo was reluctant to return to Rome because of the backlash from his ongoing polemic with Faldella. He had written a circular letter to all the garrison colonels of the Italian army stating that 'Faldella was a cheap liar and that he, as a general and a Spaniard, refuted publicly the effrontery of the said colonel.' He continued to correspond heatedly with Faldella.[215]

Queipo went to considerable efforts between 1939 and 1942 to secure the Cruz Laureada de San Fernando. After his initial application of 29 June 1939 had gone unresolved for eleven months, he wrote a letter of complaint to Franco about the delay. In it, and in the attached account of his services, he cited as his principal merits his capture of Seville and the conquest of the provinces of Huelva, Cadiz and Malaga and of most of Jaén, Granada and Badajoz, where he attributed the success of the repression to 'my personal action'. He also claimed that the military coup of 1936 was prepared at his initiative: 'I was the initiator of the movement of salvation.' He wrote that, after visiting garrisons all over Spain, 'I came to the conclusion that it would be better for General Mola to take over.' He alleged that what had decided Mola to go ahead was his offer to secure the collaboration of General Miguel Cabanellas. He further claimed that it was agreed that he would lead the uprising in Valladolid and that news of this provoked wild enthusiasm among rightists in the city. In the event, the rising in Valladolid was put in the hands of General Saliquet and Queipo was sent to Seville. There, he claimed, once again conveniently forgetting Cuesta Monereo's meticulous planning, there was nothing organized and there was no reliable section of the garrison. He reprised his much rehearsed account of how he took the city by dint of his own daring and a tiny group of soldiers. He went on to assert that many garrisons had joined the rising in response to his first radio broadcasts. Most astonishing of all, he alleged that 'control of Seville was the most crucial event of the war, without which it would have been impossible to sustain the war effort, let alone win the war'. He reminded Franco that he had twice promised to award him the medal, once in the autumn of 1936 in Burgos and again in 1938 when he relieved him of command of the Army of the South.[216] Before responding to the application, Franco demonstrated his malice towards Queipo. On 15 March 1940, he awarded both Queipo and his hated rival Saliquet the Medalla Militar as if their contribution to the rebel victory had been equal. The arguments in favour of the award were similar to those used by Franco to grant himself the Laureada. The decree was signed by Varela as Minister of War, an act later described by Queipo as a 'punishable crime'. His fury derived from the fact that Saliquet was given the credit for the operation in Badajoz to capture the Valle de la Serena which Queipo claimed was his alone. He was further offended by the fact that Varela described his part in the operation as merely that of providing assistance to Saliquet. Since he was in Rome at the time, Queipo was unable to attend the spectacular ceremony at which Franco bestowed the medal on Saliquet alone. Queipo's simmering resentment was intensified when his application for the Laureada was rejected in May 1941.[217]

In his memoirs, Queipo made the remarkable statement, 'I served the Generalísimo with a loyalty unequalled by anyone.'[218] Clearly, Franco did not see things in that way. In 1942, he twice further humiliated Queipo. His status of 'at the service of other ministries' was rescinded and he was left without a posting. In July 1942, when the Francoist Cortes was created in order to give a liberal veneer to the dictatorship, Queipo was one of the very few senior generals not given a seat as a *procurador*, along with other critics of Franco, Kindelán, Yagüe and Varela.[219] Queipo was finally awarded the Gran Cruz Laureada in February 1944, after having requested it repeatedly. The award reflected the fact that Franco was trying to bolster his position, with monarchist opposition growing within the high command and the Allies pressuring him to break his ties with the Third Reich. A huge crowd gathered in Seville's Plaza de España on 8 May to witness the ceremony at which Franco pinned the medal on him. A spectacular military parade was organized.[220]

On 1 April 1950, already seriously ill, Queipo learned that Franco had given him the title of Marqués de Queipo de Llano. He was disappointed partly because he aspired to a dukedom, but he was principally outraged that Saliquet was also ennobled at the same level. His anger smouldered and eventually he sent an irate letter to Franco in which he wrote, 'it is disagreeable for me to say that, yet again, I have been put on the same level as General Saliquet whom I would never describe to my grandchildren as a model of civic or military virtue worthy of emulation'. He described Saliquet's triumph in Valladolid as easy by comparison with his own in Seville and referred to his own military exploits as 'brilliant'.

In a largely mendacious account of his merits, Queipo, who had done so much to bring about the Republic in 1931, wrote:

I was never an anti-monarchist, even though I became an irreconcilable enemy of King Alfonso. I felt for him such affection and attachment that I was always ready to lay down my life for him, but he repaid my attachment and loyalty with the cruellest mockery. After that, I no longer had any reason to be loyal. And so I swore that, though once I would have risked my life to defend him, henceforth I would risk it to drag him from the throne ... I frantically attempted to establish contacts with many types of individuals until I finally achieved my goals [the establishment of the Republic] ... shortly afterwards [following the electoral victory of the Popular Front] I began to conspire against the Republic with a view to restoring the Monarchy.[221]

In 1954, Franco remarked to his cousin Pacón, 'I could see at every turn that he was irked by my being in command and resented having to obey me.'[222] Queipo died on 9 March 1951. Franco did not deign to attend the funeral, sending in his place the Minister of the Army, Fidel Dávila. The man who had presided over the murder of tens of thousands of Andalusians was buried dressed as a 'repented sinner' of the Confraternity of the Virgin of the Macarena. A liar, a cheat, a murderer, there is no reason to suspect that he repented of any of his actions.[223]

8

The Never-Ending War against the *Contubernio*

The success of the fictional Jewish–masonic–Bolshevik conspiracy in both justifying and generating enthusiasm for the rebel war effort is indisputable. It might be thought that the need for lies about the Jews was over. However, as is often the way with mendacity, it generates the need for more. That is not to say that the propagandists of the 'conspiracy' did not sincerely believe in its existence. Indeed, in the aftermath of the civil war, believing himself to be part of an unstoppable international fascist tide, Franco gave free rein to his conviction of the toxic threat posed by Jews and freemasons. His anti-Semitic rhetoric was echoed by senior military comrades. At the farewell banquet for the Condor Legion in May 1939, General Alfredo Kindelán declared, 'We fearlessly faced the enemies of our faith and of our civilization. We fought against Communism, international freemasonry and the Jews, and we defeated them with the help of the Almighty and the Virgin Mary.'[1]

Fourteen months later, on the fourth anniversary of the military coup, Franco addressed the high command of the army, navy and air force. He compared the war against the Republic to the reconquest of Spain from Islam. He likened the regime that came out of their victory to the state built by the Catholic monarchs, Ferdinand and Isabel. He rejected the values of the liberal monarchy and evoked the glories of their golden century: 'We have not shed the blood of our dead to return to the decadent past, to the sad liberalism that lost us Cuba and the Philippines. Their blood was spilt to build a nation and create an empire.' He cited the achievements of Ferdinand and Isabel as lighting the way to the imperial glories that he planned. They, he claimed, 'found a Spain divided and defeated, miserable, mean and selfish'. Their first objective was to forge a nation by uniting the two parts of Spain, Aragon and Castile. Central to this enterprise was 'the expulsion of the Jews, significant simply as a racist act, like those in vogue today, to prevent the achievement of unity being undermined by a foreign race, whose people were slaves to materialist ends'.[2]

Similar sentiments were trotted out in late December 1940, at the offering ceremony for the Apostle Santiago. The Civil Governor of La Coruña, Colonel Emilio de Aspe Baamonde, represented Franco and read out his speech. He made the prayer to the Apostle: 'O Santiago, after we freed the Fatherland from the Jewish yoke with the blood of our dead, and determined to create a new and perfect order, do not let the seeds of the dark powers of the sect flower again and plunge us once more into the darkness of iniquity.'[3] It would not be until the tide of Axis success began to recede that Franco confronted the need to lie about his anti-Semitism. Similarly, it would not be until he needed the assistance of the United States that he felt the need to conceal his obsession with freemasonry.

The flood of lies about the Jewish–masonic–Bolshevik plot continued well into the Second World War and beyond. This was especially the case during the Franco regime's slavish collaboration with the Third Reich. The German Embassy in Madrid distributed millions of leaflets and hundreds of thousands of anti-Semitic pamphlets and pumped considerable subsidies into a willing Spanish press – something that could not have happened without official approval. The Falangist media apparatus was especially open to the blandishments of Hans Josef Lazar, the sinister Press Secretary of the German Embassy, a man whose virulent anti-Semitism was almost certainly aimed at obscuring his own Jewish origins. A brilliant propagandist with a staff of 432, he devoted the bulk of a very substantial budget to bribery. He supplied the willing Falangist beneficiaries with Nazi propaganda material that they then printed as factually correct news. Lazar's success was not confined to the Falange. The Carlists and monarchists who had swallowed the myth of the Jewish–masonic–Bolshevik conspiracy, including Franco himself, did not need German bribes to go on believing. Among many, many others, newspapers such as *ABC* and *Informaciones* continued to peddle the myth.[4]

The Francoist effort to prove that anti-Semitism had not been central to regime propaganda began before the end of the world war. The denials hinged on claims about the Franco regime's efforts on behalf of Jewish refugees. There is no doubt that a significant number of Jewish lives were saved as they fled from Nazi terror through Spain. Between 20,000 and 35,000 Jewish refugees passed through Spain, some clandestinely and others 'legally', albeit grudgingly, allowed transit but not residence.[5] The operative words are 'through' and 'grudgingly'. Refugees who managed to enter Spain without onward visas were kept in overcrowded, unhygienic prison camps. Jewish relief organizations were banned in Spain and therefore were prevented from giving humanitarian aid to the refugees. In June 1941, the Ministry of Foreign Affairs under Serrano Suñer informed Spanish consuls in Greece and the Balkans that the government did not recognize local Sephardic Jews as Spanish citizens and that they could not be afforded consular protection. The regime allowed the Gestapo to seize German Jewish, and other, refugees and take them back to the Third Reich.[6] The fact that many Jews survived, by getting into Spain, has been the basis of the self-congratulatory myth that Franco's attitude towards the Jews was benevolent.[7] After 1945, his regime made a great effort to propagate both that myth and the even bigger one that Franco himself had secretly supported the Western Allies in the war by means of a neutrality heroically maintained against overwhelming odds. In a speech in 1946, he claimed that he had saved Britain from defeat in the Second World War.[8] Franco was the principal protagonist of his regime's efforts to reinvent the past. In a widely reproduced interview with the ultra-right-wing North American politician Merwin K. Hart in San Sebastián on 18 August 1947, he told the outrageous lie that 'Having been requested to give shelter to many thousands of Jewish children, Spain offered model installations to receive them, guaranteeing them religious freedom under the tutelage of those doctors of their faith that wished to accompany them. Although international intrigues prevented this, to the serious detriment of so many unfortunate creatures, the noble and tolerant position of Spain could not be clearer.'[9] On 7 June 1950, Franco stated, in an interview with the *Daily Mirror*, that in Spain's Moroccan protectorate and other colonial possessions Jews enjoyed total freedom of religion as well as the help and protection of the Spanish authorities.[10]

This effort was intensified in the autumn of 1949 when the regime published in French, English and Spanish a long pamphlet, *España y los judíos*, in reply to a speech made before the General Assembly of the United Nations at Lake Success by the Ambassador of Israel, Abba Eban.[11] On 16 May that year, speaking against a proposal from several Latin American nations in favour of the re-establishment of diplomatic relations with Spain, Ambassador Eban said:

> We do not for a moment assert that the Spanish regime had any direct part in that policy of extermination; but we do assert that it was an active and sympathetic ally of the regime that was responsible and thus contributed to the effectiveness of the Alliance as a whole ... For us, the central and inescapable point is the association of this regime with that Nazi–Fascist alliance which corroded the moral foundations of civilized life and inflicted upon the human race its most terrible and devastating ordeal. Of that coalition, the only surviving expression is the Spanish regime which welcomed, accepted, congratulated and upheld the prospect of Nazi supremacy in Europe and the world.'[12]

To rebut Eban's words, the fifty pages of the pamphlet claimed that Spain had saved thousands of Jews from France, French Morocco, Hungary, Bulgaria, Romania and Greece and contrasted Franco's alleged benevolence towards the Jews with the supposed indifference of Great Britain.[13] It asserted that Spain had acted not out of opportunism but from 'sympathy and friendship towards a persecuted race, with which Spaniards feel themselves to be united by links of blood and of culture'.[14] This was barefaced hypocrisy in the light of the many justifications made by prominent collaborators of Franco of the Inquisition's aim of purifying Spanish blood by eliminating Jewish and Moorish admixture. The pamphlet did not mention the efforts made by the regime to prevent Jewish refugees remaining in Spain. Moreover, the text revealed the latent anti-Semitism of the regime, affirming that the expulsion of the Jews in 1492 had been the only way to guarantee the survival of the Spanish nation.[15] In fact, fundamental to Francoist policy was the assumption that the 1492 expulsion of the Jews remained in force.[16]

As Ambassador Eban stressed, an explanation was required for how the supposedly humanitarian attitude of Franco had been possible in the context of his regime's virulent anti-Semitic rhetoric and his strategic help for the Third Reich. That assistance was proffered while Hitler's Germany carried out genocide against the Jews and ceased only once it was apparent that the Reich was going to lose the war. Eban cited the fact that Franco himself and other important figures of his regime had expressed their approval for the anti-Semitic measures of the Third Reich.

From the outbreak of the Second World War until the end of 1942, the Franco dictatorship had not allowed Jewish refugees to settle in Spain, even if they held Spanish passports. Both those who entered Spain illegally during the first years of the war and those whose onward transit arrangements failed were imprisoned in the concentration camp of Miranda de Ebro, 85 kilometres north-east of Burgos. Some were turned back at the frontier.[17] Ironically, it was the belief, shared by Franco and his friend and adviser Luis Carrero Blanco, that the Jews controlled the politics and the economy of the United States and Great Britain that led, after 1943, to the opportunistic decision to improve the treatment of Jewish refugees. After the fall of Mussolini, Franco was obliged to countenance the possibility that, if Hitler lost the war, his regime would need the friendship and goodwill of the Anglo-Saxon powers. Accordingly, it was as an insurance policy that he began to contemplate the idea of currying favour with the international Jewish community. Concerned about the regime's image in the foreign press, which Franco believed to be under Jewish control, he accepted suggestions from his advisers that it was time to improve relations with the World Jewish Congress. The first step would be the creation of the myth of Spain's rescue of Jewish refugees. In fact, despite the post-war rhetoric about this, the regime's fundamental policy towards Jewish refugees differed little from its attitude from 1936 to 1945.

At the end of the civil war, the synagogue in Barcelona had been looted and then barred and bolted. Jewish refugees were held at the French border and prevented from entering Spain.[18] On 14 June

1940, Franco seized the opportunity provided by the German conquest of France to occupy Tangier. The consequent attacks on Jewish refugees in Tangier were praised by the Falangist wireless station at Valladolid, which described the victims as 'Anglophile and Francophile scum' and expressed regret that Hitler had not 'exterminated the lot'. Terrified Jews, fearing the worst, fled the area.[19] In his interminable end-of-the-year speech broadcast on 31 December 1939, a striking anti-Semitic declaration was buried in the rhetoric about the victors' implacable justice and questionable statistics about the economy. In an approbatory reference to the race laws in the Third Reich, he said:

> Now you will understand the motives that have impelled some nations to combat, and to block the activities of, those races marked by the stigma of greed and self-interest. They have had to do so because the dominance in their societies of these races is a cause of concern because it endangers the achievement of their historic destiny. By the grace of God and the clear foresight of the Catholic Kings, we were freed many centuries ago from such a heavy burden. However, we cannot remain indifferent to this new flowering of avaricious egoists, so hungry for worldly wealth that they would rather sacrifice their children than abandon their corrupt interests.

As well as being published in the press at the time, the complete text was widely circulated in pamphlet form.[20] Needless to say, Franco's most anti-Semitic declarations were eliminated from later collections of his speeches.

A constant spur to Franco's anti-Semitism was the advice of the naval Captain Luis Carrero Blanco, with whom he maintained close links from their first meeting in 1925 until the latter's assassination in 1973. In a strategic plan drawn up for Franco in early August 1938 on the role of the navy in the Mediterranean, Carrero had written that the war was 'a life or death struggle in which the very existence of Christian civilization was at stake'. The report pleased Franco so much that Carrero was promoted to be the effective Chief of Staff of the fleet.[21] At the end of the civil war, Carrero wrote his reflections on the rebellion of below-deck crews in July 1936. He described the Republic as 'the bridgehead of communism and communism on its own is nothing, but with freemasonry, democracy and plutocracy, it is a tool of Judaism.' This was the language of Father Tusquets and can only have ingratiated Carrero further with Franco.[22]

On 7 May 1941, Franco named Carrero Under-Secretary of the Presidency, in other words, his cabinet secretary. In practical terms, he had become Franco's political chief of staff. His brief was 'to prepare for the Caudillo the material on which his decisions would be based, draft the consequent orders or instructions and oversee their implementation'. His hand can be seen in many of Franco's speeches. The ideas that he would bring to Franco's table could be seen from a book that he was writing at the time:

> Spain, paladin of the faith in Christ, finds herself once again combating the real enemy: Judaism. It is one more phase of the centuries-old secular struggle that shakes the world. The world, even though it does not seem so, experiences endless conflicts that, despite their different origins, essentially amount to religious war. It is the struggle of Christianity against Judaism. A war to the death, as must be the struggle between Good and Evil, between truth and lies, between the light and the darkness.

Carrero added that the Jews, in their war against Christianity,

> had used the Reformation, the ideas of the Encyclopaedia, liberalism, left-wing atheism, freemasonry, Marxism, communism, all as landmines to blow up the impregnable fortress of Catholic Christianity. With extraordinary cunning, the Jews have always attacked the idea of the Fatherland, using simultaneously, in a seeming paradox, the weapons of separatism, internationalism, capitalism, materialism, atheism. The means change but the end is always the same. To destroy, to annihilate, to besmirch Christian civilization in order to erect on its ruins the utopian Zionist empire of the chosen people.[23]

In mid-December 1941, at a time when Franco was still enthused by German successes in Russia, Carrero drew up a report drafted in militant terms. Here he wrote: 'The Anglo-Saxon–Soviet alliance that has been established because of a personal initiative by Roosevelt, at the service of the masonic lodges and the Jews, is really the front line of Judaic power. This can be seen in the hoisting of the flags of the entire complex of the democracies, freemasonry, liberalism, plutocracy and communism. These are the classic weapons used by Judaism to provoke a catastrophic situation aimed at provoking the collapse of Christian Civilization.' Carrero believed that if Spain were to enter the war it had to be on the side of the Axis because, he wrote, 'the Axis is fighting today against everything that constitutes the anti-Spain'.[24]

As the German offensive against Russia faltered, Carrero's confidence in the Third Reich's invincibility was somewhat shaken. The Anglo-American landings in North Africa on 8 November 1942 (Operation Torch) were inevitably a further cause for concern. Nevertheless, he remained convinced of ultimate German victory. This was clear in a report that he drafted for Franco on 11 November. In this, he reiterated what Franco already believed: that 'Spain has a clear will to intervene alongside the Axis because it is fighting against our natural enemies, that complex of democracies, freemasonry, liberalism, plutocracy and communism, the weapons with which Jewish Power seeks to annihilate Christian civilization whose defence is our universal destiny.' By 18 December, the combination of Allied successes in North Africa and the Russian counterattack that would lead to victory at Stalingrad inclined Carrero to urge caution on Franco. He still argued that the cause of the war was 'the fundamental Jewish plan to annihilate Europe as the means to reduce Christian civilization to ruins'.[25]

On 29 May 1942, Franco had given a speech to the Sección Femenina of the Falange at the Castilla de la Mota in Medina del Campo in the province of Valladolid. At this iconic building associated with Isabel de Castilla, the Catholic queen who had expelled the Jews 450 years earlier, Franco echoed, in his encomium to her, the ideas of Vallejo Nágera. His praise for Isabel again centred on her achievement of 'racial unity', because 'when the Jews betrayed Spain they were expelled' and because she finally 'created a revolutionary policy, a totalitarian and racist policy'. The implicit comparison with the racial policy of the Third Reich suggested that he took pride in what he saw as the Germans simply following the example of Isabel.[26]

Franco often revealed his conviction that the Jewish–masonic–Bolshevik conspiracy really existed. He believed that the Jews were the allies of both American capitalism and Russian Bolshevism. In April 1943, he sent Pope Pius XII a document which he claimed he had received from an utterly trustworthy source, and which he maintained was the text of a letter from Roosevelt to Stalin. He alleged that it was proof of 'international freemasonry and Judaism ordering their followers to carry out a programme of hatred against our Catholic civilization'.[27] The Vatican was not convinced. A few weeks later, on 4 May in Huelva, Franco denounced 'the monstrous activities of propaganda organizations in the service of capitalism, of Judaism, sowing ideas and spreading them for idiots and the less able to repeat'.[28]

There was little to distinguish the religion-based anti-Semitism of the Francoist right from the racism of the Third Reich. This was demonstrated in several ways. Already, Franco's friend Antonio Vallejo Nágera was a devotee of eugenic theories. The similarity of the regime's Jewish policy to that of Nazi Germany could be seen in the rejection by the then Minister of Foreign Affairs, the Conde de Jordana, of a proposal in January 1939 that 150,000 Romanian Catholics of Jewish origin be allowed to settle in Spain. Despite the fact that these largely prosperous individuals were likely to bring considerable financial resources to Spain, the regime's Minister in Romania, Pedro de Prat y Soutzo, revealed in a report to the Foreign Ministry his opinion that 'the baptismal waters' would not 'greatly change the mentality and the race' of these Jews and that their arrival in Spain 'would be similar to that of a plague of parasites'.[29]

On 11 May 1939, Franco's government in Burgos had published an order regarding 'Regulations for the crossing of Spanish frontiers, and application form for authorization to enter Spain'. The order included a list of the categories of persons who were to be refused a passport or a visa, including those 'who had a marked Jewish character, Jews (except those notable for their special friendship for Spain and proven loyalty to the Movimiento Nacional) and also freemasons'. The order did not specify how 'a marked Jewish character' was to be identified by the consuls to whom application was made other, presumably, than by appearance.[30] On the identity papers and residence permits of Jews the word *Judío* was stamped in red ink. One of the few surviving personal dossiers from 1944, of a Jewess from Barcelona, María Sinaí León, specified that she had no known political affiliation but 'It is to be supposed that she poses the dangers associated with the Jewish race to which she belongs.' Another, from as late as 1957, reported on an individual considered 'dangerous because of his Israelite origins'. Elsewhere in the same dossier, this individual was denounced as an enemy of the 'national cause' for 'racial reasons'.[31]

Then, in early June 1939, as Minister of the Interior and effective head of the Falange, Ramón Serrano Suñer took part in the events in Rome to celebrate the return home of the Italian troops who had fought for Franco. In the course of reaffirming the newly victorious Franco's solidarity with the Axis, he declared that Judaism was the enemy of the New Spain.[32] Subsequently, as Minister of Foreign Affairs, he opposed the entry into Spain of Jewish converts to Catholicism. This was hardly surprising given the enthusiasm with which much of the rebel press had welcomed German and Italian anti-Semitic legislation.

December 1939 saw the publication of the seventh edition of one of the most commercially successful Spanish translations of the *Protocols*, that by the Duque de la Victoria. It was hailed in *ABC* as 'a prophetic revelation of the evils that Spaniards in particular have had to suffer'. The print runs of this edition and of another, produced with the labour of defeated Republican prisoners that appeared soon afterwards, were soon sold out.[33] Around this time, another virulently anti-Semitic tract was published. The author was the fanatical ultra-rightist policeman Juan Segura Nieto, who had helped Tusquets produce and distribute the bulletin supporting the military conspirators in Barcelona, the *Cuadernos de Información*. Like Tusquets, Segura Nieto was a member of the España Club. Now, having passed the three years of the civil war in hiding in Barcelona and mourning the death of his equally militant sister, he vented his bitterness in his ¡*Alerta!* ... *Francmasonería y Judaísmo*. The revival of interest in the

Protocols seems to have been inspired by the regime's propaganda services.[34]

Anti-Semitic publications were encouraged by the regime. Serrano Suñer's protégé Ángel Alcázar de Velasco wrote, with his master's approval, 'communism is a doctrine at the service of Judaism … We Spaniards have still not taken on board the havoc being wreaked by this sect with its grim, silent, sinister work. It is enough to skim *The Protocols of the Elders of Zion* or the agreements of the Jewish Congress held in Basle in 1897 to see the ambitions and objectives of Judaism.' He claimed that the Jews were destroying Christian values by using their control of the press, the cinema and the world of fashion to foster degenerate ideas.[35] Even a more liberal, indeed later revered, Falangist leader, Dionisio Ridruejo, was not immune to anti-Semitism. As a volunteer in the Spanish Blue Division, while passing through Poland en route for Russia in late August 1941 his unit encountered a column of prisoners. He wrote, 'many wear the hateful armband with the star of Zion. Here, we can feel sorry for these poor helpless people despite the repulsion – not to say atavistic hatred – that is produced in us by "the chosen race".'[36]

Numerous reports about German atrocities in Eastern Europe crossed Franco's desk, emanating from officers of the Blue Division, from a delegation of doctors and from diplomats.[37] On 5 March 1943, the Spanish Ambassador in Berlin, Ginés Vidal, wrote as follows to Jordana:

On Friday 26 and Saturday 27 February, a series of raids were carried out in Berlin and other cities across Germany to expel the remaining Jews still resident in the Reich … I assume that by now they will have all been deported to regions in Eastern Europe. According to rumours that you will have heard, which are naturally impossible to substantiate, these, and prior, operations are 'deportations' only in name. They are actually the transfers in appalling conditions to places where they can be easily eliminated regardless of sex or age.[38]

Despite his knowledge of the Holocaust, Franco permitted the pres-
entation of a ferocious anti-Semitism – both racist and religious – to
Spanish public opinion through the tightly controlled official media
of his regime, both that of the Catholic Church and that of the
Falange. There can be little doubt that, like Franco and the diplomatic
representatives of the regime, newspaper editors and their foreign
correspondents were aware of the persecution to which the Jews were
being subjected across continental Europe by the German occupiers.[39] Professor Alfonso Lazo located in the daily press ninety-eight
articles about anti-Jewish persecution carried out by the Germans.
Thirty-three were merely descriptive while sixty-five were enthusiastically sympathetic. There was no example of atrocities against the
Jews being criticized. The measures favourably reported, such as the
expulsions of Jewish communities and the imposition of forced
labour in several European countries, were justified in terms of being
directed at 'dangerous elements'. Many Falangist and Catholic magazines also were replete with anti-Semitic propaganda.[40]

Even if journalists did not relate horrifying details of the extermination camps, language frequently used to describe Jews, such as
'foul and diseased', suggested both knowledge and ample approval of
extermination policies. Regarding legislation in Vichy France to
remove social parasites, a Spanish correspondent commented, 'when
it comes to parasites, there is no one to beat individuals of Jewish
origins'. Germany's victory over France in 1940 was hailed as opening
the way to 'the dissolution of Judaism'. The declarations of Himmler
regarding 'the elimination of anti-social elements' coincided with
repetitions in the press and in Franco's speeches that the Jews were
anti-social elements. After all, Franco's own definition of the Jews as
elements of 'social perturbation and danger' leaves little doubt as to
the anti-Semitism of his regime.[41]

On 5 May 1941, in response to an alleged danger posed by Spain's
Hebrew population, the Dirección General de Seguridad initiated the
process of building an archive with the names of all the Jews resident
in Spain. The then Director General was another protégé of the
Minister of the Interior, the fervently pro-Nazi José Finat Escrivá de
Romaní, the Conde de Mayalde. 'Circular no. 11' was sent to every
civil governor requesting individual reports on 'the Spanish and

foreign Israelites resident in the province', indicating their 'personal and politico-social affiliations, means of support, commercial activities, level of danger, police record'.

The preamble to the circular emphasized:

> the need to know exactly and in detail the persons and places that, at any given moment, could be an obstacle to or a means of opposing the postulates of the New State, [and required] that particular attention be paid to the Jews resident in our Fatherland, collecting, in the required way, such details and background information as are necessary, in each and every case, to determine their ideology and means of action both within and outside Spanish territory.

The document went on to specify that 'the persons who are the object of the measure with which I am entrusting you will be principally those of Spanish origin with Sephardic names, given that, by dint of their assimilation in our Society and the similarity of their temperament with ours, they have greater probabilities of hiding their origins and even of going unnoticed without our having any possibility of restricting the impact of their subversive intrigues'.[42] This initiative had been preceded in December 1939 by the collection of information on Jews living in Barcelona by the then Civil Governor, Wenceslao González Oliveros, a committed admirer of Nazi racist policies. As the flow of refugees from German-occupied Europe increased, so entry into Spain was more tightly controlled.[43]

There had been arrests of Jews since the end of 1940.[44] It has been suggested that the purpose of the census that was being assembled on the basis of the answers provided by the civil governors was to facilitate the deportation of the Jews in the event of Spain entering the world war on the side of the Axis. Shortly after Serrano Suñer became Minister of Foreign Affairs on 20 May 1942, the Conde de Mayalde was sent to Berlin as Spanish Ambassador. It is possible, although there is no documentary proof, merely suspicion, that the Conde de Mayalde handed the list to Himmler, in order to ingratiate himself.[45] This is entirely plausible since there had been close collaboration between the Francoist police and the Gestapo since 1937. Moreover, as has been seen, Father Juan Tusquets had long since been feverishly elaborating lists of presumed Jews and freemasons. At the suggestion of Franco himself, his headquarters (Cuartel General) had created the Sección Judeo-Masónica of the military intelligence service, the Servicio de Información Militar, under the joint direction of Father Tusquets and Major Antonio Palau.[46]

After the fall of Serrano Suñer in September 1942, Operation Torch one month later and the subsequent Axis reverses in North Africa, the regime's press was ordered to temper its pro-German enthusiasm. Nevertheless, in April 1943, the Falange obliged the entire Spanish media to publish a statement that linked the Francoist efforts in the civil war with the efforts of the Germans in the Second World War: 'The Spanish war, like today's war, was a civil war in both the European and universal sense; it was a war between fascism and anti-fascism. On one side Jews, freemasons, democrats, liberals, Communists and anarchists; on the other side Spain, Italy and Germany. On a much larger scale, that situation is being repeated today.'[47]

José María Doussinague, the pro-German Director General of Foreign Policy in the Ministry of Foreign Affairs, had long believed that the only interest to Spain of Sephardic Jews was their wealth.[48] In early January 1943, he sent instructions to Spanish diplomats to avoid offering any undertaking to save Jews with Spanish passports and to prevent any link being made between Sephardic Jews and Spanish nationality. Regarding Sephardic Jews in the country to which they were appointed, consuls were to make it their principal concern to prevent the Germans seizing the wealth and property of those Jews which, the instruction stated, 'was to a certain extent part of Spain's national patrimony'. Three weeks later, the German Embassy in Madrid informed the Spanish government that, from 31 March 1943, the Third Reich was going to end the 'special treatment' that had hitherto been extended to Spanish Jews resident in France, Belgium, the Netherlands and other occupied territories. Henceforth, they would be arrested and deported along with Jews of other nationalities. Berlin recommended that the Spanish government repatriate its Jewish nationals by that date.

Doussinague wrote a note to the Conde de Jordana, Serrano Suñer's replacement as Minister of Foreign Affairs, in which he said that this posed the following 'serious dilemma'. If Spain allowed Sephardic Jews to be exposed to German laws, 'We run the risk of an intensification of the international hostility against us, especially in America, where we will be accused of being assassins and accomplices of murderers.' The text of his note revealed that he was fully aware of what was being done to the Jews by the Germans and furthermore that he did not oppose it. He wrote that 'it is unacceptable to contemplate the solution of bringing them to Spain where their race, their wealth, their Anglophilia and their freemasonry would turn them into agents of all kinds of intrigues'.

The two possible solutions proposed by Doussinague were either that they be repatriated to their country of birth in the Balkans or that they be allowed to pass through Spanish territory en route to any other country that had given them an entry visa. Accepted by Jordana and Franco, Spanish policy towards its Jewish citizens was based on these suggestions of Doussinague. In line with his first recommendation, in February he ordered Ginés Vidal, the Spanish Ambassador in Berlin, to secure entry visas to Greece, Turkey or any other country for the Spanish Jews. However, it soon became clear that other countries would not take Spanish Jews whom Spain itself would not accept. With some reluctance, two months later, he amended his position. At the suggestion of Vidal, a number of Jews – not to exceed 250 at any one time – would be allowed to remain in Spain until they could make successful applications for visas.

Doussinague proposed this on the grounds that, if Spain did not offer some form of protection to the Jews, 'it would have an extremely damaging impact' on the country's international reputation. Nevertheless, the policy adopted by Jordana was more stringent: 'the entry of Jews into Spain would be allowed only when they had an absolute written guarantee that they were in transit and would be permitted to stay for very few days. Otherwise, we simply cannot permit this because we must not intensify our existing problems with this far-reaching new departure.' In this regard, Jordana wrote to the Minister of War, General Carlos Asensio Cabanillas, on 28 December 1943:

The problem is that the several hundred Jews with Spanish nationality who are in Europe right now are either in concentration
camps or bound for them. We cannot let them settle in Spain
because it is not in our interests and the Caudillo will not allow it.
Nor can we abandon them to their present plight and ignore the
fact that they are Spanish citizens because this could provoke a
press campaign against us overseas, particularly in the United
States, and result in serious international difficulties. Accordingly,
we have considered bringing them in groups of around one
hundred, more or less. Only after one group leaves Spain – going
through the country like light goes through glass, without a trace
– do we allow in the next group, which in turn would be moved on
to allow the next lot to come. Using this mechanism, it will be clear
that, under no circumstances, will we allow the Jews to settle in
Spain.

Moreover, in Jordana's proposals, Jewish candidates for entry to Spain
would have to provide full documentation to prove the citizenship of
themselves and their families, a condition which considerably
reduced the numbers of those eligible. When this was discussed in
cabinet, Jordana assured the Minister of the Interior, Blas Pérez, that
the strictest police control would be imposed on these Jews during
their transit through Spain. At least one Spanish diplomat wrote to
Doussinague to protest that this policy was condemning many
Spanish Jews to death.[49]

On 7 April 1943, Churchill had lunch with Franco's Ambassador
in London, the Duque de Alba, and raised the issue of the closure of
the Spanish frontier to Jewish refugees and escaped prisoners of war.
In no uncertain terms, the Prime Minister told Alba 'that if his
Government went to the length of preventing those unfortunate
people seeking safety from the horrors of Nazi domination, and if
they went farther and committed the offence of actually handing
them back to the German authorities, that was a thing that would
never be forgotten and would poison the relations between the
Spanish and British peoples'. Churchill's account of the meeting was
forwarded to the British Ambassador in Madrid, Sir Samuel Hoare,
who, like Alba himself, reported it to Jordana.[50]

The American Ambassador in Madrid, Carlton Hayes, reiterated to both Franco and Jordana what Doussinague had said about the damage being done to Spanish prestige in Allied countries by the regime's Jewish policy. Franco was especially concerned about his image in the foreign press, which he was convinced was under the control of the Jewish–masonic–Bolshevik alliance. Accordingly, in November 1943, he finally accepted the suggestions of Jordana, Javier Martínez de Bedoya and his own brother Nicolás that the moment had come to improve relations with the World Jewish Congress as the first step towards the construction of the myth of his efforts on behalf of the Jewish refugees. If there is any possibility that Franco and his ministers and functionaries did not know exactly how the anti-Semitic measures of the Third Reich were implemented in the gas chambers of the Nazi camps, there is little reason to suppose that they would have disapproved. Carlton Hayes, who was otherwise sympathetic to Franco, believed that the Caudillo's new policy towards the Jews was elaborated exclusively in terms of its propaganda value.[51]

In April 1944, the Chargé d'Affaires of the Spanish Legation in Budapest, Miguel Ángel de Muguiro, informed Madrid that the Hungarian government had sent hundreds of thousands of Jews to the German camps in Poland. At the same time, the government in Madrid was receiving many petitions from Jewish organizations in Morocco requesting that hundreds of Jewish children from Eastern Europe be saved by bringing them to Tangiers. It is therefore evident that Franco's government was fully informed about the slaughter of the Jews by the Nazis. In May 1944, Muguiro was replaced as Chargé d'Affaires by a young Catholic diplomat, Ángel Sanz Briz. He was horrified when he learned, in meetings with diplomats from other neutral countries, that the number of Hungarian Jews sent to the camps was nearly half a million. Subsequently, documents written by two prisoners, Rudolf Vrba and Alfred Wetzler, who had managed to escape from the extermination camp at Auschwitz came into his possession. They outlined what had happened in 1943 to 45,000 Jews from Salonica who had been sent to Auschwitz. Sanz Briz forwarded the documents directly to Franco, expressing his horror that the trains that went to German camps were carrying women, children and old people.

Finally, as a result of requests sent to Madrid, from both London and Washington, Sanz Briz received Franco's reluctant authorization to repatriate a limited number of Jews as long as they were of Spanish origin. The Hungarian government gave permission for Sanz Briz to issue 200 Jews with passports. In fact, Sanz Briz issued hundreds of passports and letters of protection certifying the Sephardic origins of 2,000 Jews. By the simple device of stamping the visas and certificates with numbers lower than 200, he managed to deceive the Hungarian administration, which given the scale of instability in the country was already overwhelmed. He rented several buildings on which he had placed notices reading 'Annexe of the Spanish Legation. Extraterritorial Building'. When the Red Army was nearing Budapest, Sanz Briz was withdrawn and his efforts were continued by Giorgio Perlasca, an Italian employee of the Legation.[52]

Sanz Briz was not the only Spanish diplomat to save Jewish lives. It has been estimated that Julio Palencia Álvarez-Tubau, the Spanish Minister Plenipotentiary in Sofia, saved around 600 Jews, for which he was declared persona non grata by the Bulgarian authorities. An attaché in the Spanish Embassy in Berlin, José Ruiz Santaella, made heroic efforts to save Jewish lives. The Ambassador in Bucharest, José Rojas Moreno, managed to save numerous Jews between 1941 and 1943 by the device of having official-looking signs placed on their homes stating 'Here reside Spanish citizens'. Sebastián de Romero Radigales, the Consul in Athens, despite the dogged opposition of Doussinague at the Ministry of Foreign Affairs, and at considerable risk to himself, managed to save more than 350 Sephardic Jews from Salonica from death in the German camp of Bergen-Belsen in Hanover. The Ministry had had ample opportunity to prevent their deportation to Bergen-Belsen but had done nothing. It took the desperate intervention of Romero Radigales to secure their release and transfer to Spain. The Consul General in Paris, Bernardo Rolland de Miota, against the decided opposition of the pro-Nazi Spanish Ambassador, Félix de Lequerica, took personal risks in order to facilitate the journey to Spanish Morocco of around 2,000 Jews. The activities of all of these diplomats were carried out without the permission of the Spanish Ministry of Foreign Affairs.[53] This further underlined the fact that his insurance policy of ingratiating himself with the international Jewish community, adopted at the suggestion of his advisers, had not inclined him to express any opposition to German atrocities against the Jews.

The regime's controlled press announced Hitler's death as if he had died heroically in combat. It was insinuated that the horrors of the German extermination camps were the consequence of the chaos of defeat. Franco's efforts to project the idea that he had saved the lives of many Jews ignored the fact that his regime did everything possible to prevent Sephardic Jews settling in Spain after the Second World War. In July and December 1945, his government issued two decrees stating that those Jews who had not received Spanish citizenship under the decree of the dictatorship of General Miguel Primo de Rivera in December 1924 or who were not listed in the citizens register could not be considered as Spanish nationals. The Madrid government stated that it would facilitate the repatriation to their countries of origin of any Jews who held Spanish citizenship. The purpose of both decrees was to prevent Sephardic Jews who had previously lived elsewhere entering and settling in Spain.[54] After the Second World War, Franco's *éminence grise*, Carrero Blanco, made a series of radio broadcasts using the pseudonym 'Juan de la Cosa'. In these, between November 1945 and October 1946, he denounced the ongoing Nuremberg trials as 'vengeful' and 'criminal'.[55]

The efforts of Jordana and Martínez Bedoya to ingratiate the regime with world Jewry and the publication of the pamphlet *España y los judíos* revealed the scale of Franco's concern about what he saw as the immense power of the Jews in America, Britain and elsewhere. Accordingly, although his anti-Semitic utterances continued after the defeat of the Third Reich, they were made behind the mask of a pseudonym. He continued to make frequent references to materialist sects and masonic conspiracies which suggest that his belief in the Jewish–masonic–Bolshevik conspiracy had survived the defeat of the Axis.[56] Nearly two years after the death of Hitler, Franco, the self-proclaimed saviour of the Jews, was writing a series of fifty anti-Semitic and anti-masonic articles in the Falangist daily *Arriba*, using the pseudonym 'Jakim Boor'. The first appeared on 14 December 1946, just two days after a plenary session of the General Assembly of the United Nations had excluded Spain from all its dependent bodies;

called on the Security Council to study measures to be adopted if, within a reasonable time, Spain still had a government lacking popular consent; and called on all member nations to withdraw their ambassadors.

In his article, Franco blamed the hostility of the United Nations on the perfidy of both freemasons and Jews. Claiming that the staff of the organization was made up of freemasons, he declared that:

> This explains the lukewarm, effectively complicit, response to the monstrous crimes and persecutions suffered by the Catholic Church in Europe. Freemasonry, like Judaism, hates the Catholic religion. Dominating as they do the international assemblies and their member governments, why would they condemn, or take measures against, what deep down pleases them? What a difference between the hypocritical and feeble condemnations of this that flash across the agencies, the press and the airwaves that they control and their outrage, when a handful of Jews were the target of German racism, that impelled them to go to war.

Franco's dismissal of the Shoah as merely 'a handful of Jews falling foul of race laws' revealed an indifference to, if not approval of, the slaughter of millions of Jews. It is hardly surprising, given that he saw the murder of tens of thousands of his own citizens as the application of justice.[57]

Article after article revealed his essential hostility towards 'a people embedded in the society in which they live, that sees in freemasonry the ideal field for the machinations to which they have been dragged by an inferiority complex and resentment about the diaspora, they are the Jews of the world, the army of speculators accustomed to breaking or skirting the law, who ally with freemasons, in order to feel powerful'.[58]

In 1952 the articles were collected and published as a book, *Masonería*, still under cover of the pseudonym. Franco's authorship was eventually acknowledged in 1982 when the institution devoted to safeguarding his memory, the Fundación Nacional Francisco Franco, published a facsimile edition of the book.[59] At the time he wrote the articles, Franco was under the illusion that the use of the pseudonym Jakim Boor would allow him to unleash his anti-Semitism and hatred of freemasonry without diplomatic consequences. To compound the fraud, it was officially announced that he had received 'Mr Jakin Boor [sic]' in an audience.[60] The subterfuge was of little avail. The fact that these articles were published in *Arriba*, the official daily of the Falange, was interpreted in the *New York Times* as signifying official sanction at the highest level for the views expressed therein. The White House received thousands of telegrams of protest. Washington was fully aware that the articles were the work of Franco.[61] When finally alerted to the damage that these diatribes were doing to Spain's international position, he introduced some feeble arguments into an article in mid-July 1950, in an effort to prove that he was not anti-Semitic. The context in which he put forward his claims completely undermined them.

Franco referred to *The Protocols of the Elders of Zion* as if it were a serious historical document which had 'exposed the Talmudic doctrines and their conspiracy to seize the levers of power in society'. However, he claimed that, by fomenting anti-Semitism, the *Protocols* had drawn attention away from freemasonry. 'That everything Spanish, for the simple fact of being Spanish and Catholic, is equally detested by freemasonry and Judaism is self-evident. But Judaism does not mean the Hebrew people but rather that conspiratorial Jewish minority that uses freemasonry as one of its instruments.'

He went on to contradict himself with a revealing justification for the expulsion of the Jews in 1492. 'The expulsion of the Jews from Spain had no racial, nor even religious, character given the Jews had lost this character and turned themselves, during the fifteenth century, into a fanatical and murky sect of non-believers, lacking any religious bases, that driven by a deep malice against Catholics conspired against them with treacherous hypocrisy.' The examples that he gave of this malice included the sacrifice and crucifixion of children by Jews. Accordingly, wrote Franco, the move to expel the Jews was not religious in motivation but merely aimed at 'the extirpation of some degenerate, conspiratorial, criminal secret sects, which, if they were not yet freemasonry, were the prelude to what it would become.' In this demented account, the expulsion did not put an end to the danger posed by 'Jewish secret societies'.[62] It seems that

Franco was unaware that, after the expulsion of the Jews in 1492, the *estatutos de limpiezas* (statutes of blood purity) had been enacted to prevent anyone with Jewish blood from occupying high office.[63]

It has been speculated that, in composing his articles, Franco and Luis Carrero Blanco worked together as co-authors on the basis of drafts commissioned from the restless eccentric, not to say deranged, Ernesto Giménez Caballero, who fancied himself as the Spanish D'Annunzio.[64] Once a surrealist and a founder of Spanish fascism, he had also been briefly an idolater of Azaña, who regarded his writings as lunatic and stupid.[65] The flamboyant Giménez Caballero was a fantasist who jumped frivolously from one idea to another, leaving a trail of rapidly produced books and pamphlets. He managed to become part of the circle of sycophants surrounding Franco through his work in the press and propaganda section of the improvised rebel government in Salamanca. The unit had been placed under the erratic leadership of General José Millán Astray in early October 1936. When Giménez Caballero turned up in November looking for work and claiming to bear a message from Mussolini, he managed to get an interview with Franco himself. Having read his *Genio de España*, Franco was keen to make use of him in the propaganda operation being built up by Millán Astray.[66]

It is a significant comment on the ambience of the Francoist establishment that, in his quest for preferment, Giménez Caballero, once a key member of the philo-Sephardic movement that had celebrated Spain's Jewish heritage, found it convenient to intensify the anti-Semitic tone of his own writings. This was partly a reflection of the fact that his philo-Sephardism had had an imperialist dimension and partly a response to the suspicions of fellow members of the Falange that both his physical appearance and his interest in the Sephardic Jews of Salonica and Morocco meant that he was a Jew himself.[67] In his articles, he argued, in terms similar to those used by Pemán, that all Jews and freemasons were the allies of the Republican government and Russia. He went so far as to advocate using the auto-da-fé 'to purify' Spain from the Jews who had infiltrated the country.[68] An enthusiast for 'Latin fascism', he had been initially hostile to Nazism, which he saw as a pagan phenomenon as against Italy's Christian Fascism. Indeed, he had argued, in the 1932 version of his frequently republished panegyric of fascist mysticism *Genio de España*, that whereas Nazi anti-Semitism was racist, the Spanish variant was entirely religious. Nevertheless, even then he justified Nazi racism on the grounds that 'the *nature of Israel* is also essentially racist, based on the continuity of blood, on "jus sanguinis" [rights of blood]. The Jews are the Hitlerians of the East.' By 1939, he was brushing aside the idea of there being any Spanish anti-Semitic racism with a bizarre assertion. He claimed that the expulsion of the Jews in 1492 was not about racial purification but about the beginning of racial pluralism. 'We are', he declared, 'a people that sires new breeds but is never racist.' The term *raceador* is usually applied to stallions put out to stud in order to improve a breed. He claimed that this breeding achievement was because Spain is a 'fertile and spirited country. We are procreators, stallions, Don Juans, magnificent, virile people-creating studs.' As late as the seventh edition of 1971, these assertions remained in print.[69] It is possible that the later anti-Semitism was his response to Falangist accusations that he was a Jew.

Giménez Caballero's remarks about virility, breeding and Don Juanism and his efforts to curry favour with Franco were a reflection of the fact that he was driven in equal measure by his libido and his ambition. Sexual imagery abounded in his erotico-fascist writing. In a 1937 newspaper article, he wrote of Franco, 'He does not have a sabre. All that can be seen in his jacket pocket is a little black and silver baton. This is his symbol of command, his magic wand. His truncheon, his incomparable phallus.'[70] Although Franco's thirst for adulation seemed unquenchable, it is difficult to see how the dour Gallego could have swallowed such nonsense. Giménez Caballero's lifelong efforts to ingratiate himself with Franco could hardly have been more sycophantic or indeed prurient. He gave many adulatory speeches but outdid himself in his little book *España y Franco*:[71]

We have seen Franco in the early hours of the morning, in the midst of heat or of snow, his soul and his nerves stretched to breaking point, leaning over the battle plan or the map of Spain, operating on the living body of Spain with the urgency and tragedy of a surgeon who operates on his own daughter, on his own mother, on his own beloved wife. We have seen Franco's tears fall on the body of this mother, of this wife, of this daughter, while over his hands runs the blood and the pain of the sacred body in its death-rattle.[72]

Giménez Caballero's ambition and sexual obsession were to the fore in an outlandish episode in late 1941. In September in Berlin, Hitler had met Pilar Primo de Rivera, daughter of the Dictator Miguel and sister of the founder of the Falange, José Antonio. This led to fevered speculation by Giménez Caballero, who was present. He hatched a grotesque plan to mate her with the Führer. This erotic fantasy was meant to ensure Spain a leading position in the new fascist world order which he expected to come from Hitler's victory in the world war. In tune with his idea that the mission of Spain was to sire new races, he now cherished the idea of establishing a new dynasty that would guarantee the perpetuation of the new order, blending Teutonic efficiency with Mediterranean sensuality. The opportunity to float the scheme came in October at a conference in Weimar chaired by the Nazi Minister of Propaganda and Popular Enlightenment, Joseph Goebbels. He had already ingratiated himself with Goebbels by making the crazed offer to get the Jesuits to become propagandists for Hitler. At a cocktail party for the delegates, Giménez Caballero shared with Magda Goebbels his ideas for Latinizing Hitler. Thereafter, he returned to Madrid where he informed Franco and went on to Rome where he informed contacts in the Vatican of his scheme 'to catholicize Hitler'. Back in Berlin on 23 December 1941, he was invited to dinner at the home of Goebbels, who was called away leaving Giménez Caballero with Magda. In the course of a steamy encounter with the statuesque Frau Goebbels, he repeated his idea for securing the future of the world. She disabused him of it by confiding that the Führer's wounds during the First World War prevented his participation in any reproductive enterprise.[73]

On his return to Madrid, Giménez Caballero informed Franco of the fate of his self-appointed mission. The Caudillo's reaction is not recorded, although Giménez Caballero claimed that 'he understood'. Giménez Caballero also took it upon himself to speak with the Papal Nuncio and other ecclesiastical contacts.[74] When Franco was composing the articles published under the name Jakim Boor, Giménez Caballero was in close contact with him. He telephoned Franco on 4 December 1947 to congratulate him on his fifty-fifth birthday. He followed this up the next day with a grovelling request for an audience: 'having predicted since 1932 that Your Excellency would be the natural King of Spain and having contributed moreover to making that come true with my efforts and my pen, I believe I have more right than perhaps anyone else in our country to offer you my predictions about the immediate future'.[75]

The articles to which Giménez Caballero and Carrero Blanco contributed were fervently anti-Semitic but, despite their undermining his quest for good relations with the United States, which he believed to be the puppet of international Jewry and freemasonry, Franco went ahead with the sequence of articles.[76] The intensification of Franco's anti-Semitism in the late 1940s reflected his anger at the opposition of the State of Israel to the re-establishment of diplomatic relations with Spain, an opposition openly manifested in the speech of Abba Eban. There can be no doubt that the publication of the pamphlet *España y los judíos* enjoyed his full support. Despite this propaganda initiative, it was clear from his articles that his belief in the Jewish–masonic–Bolshevik conspiracy was as strong as ever. He wrote:

The Judaic nature of freemasonry can be seen in its literature and its rites. The problem of whether freemasonry is an especially Jewish work or an instrument used by Judaism from the nineteenth century onwards is not important as far as we are concerned. The fact is that they work together hand in hand and the Jews tend to hold important positions in many of their lodges. But as freemasonry has managed to control most of their members, the same cannot be said for Judaism; the Hebrew is first and foremost a Jew rather than a mason and subordinates all the interests of the order to his Jewish beliefs and passion, despite holding important positions within freemasonry. This justifies the fact that the traditional atheism that in Catholic countries freemasonry drags along with it joins forces with the atavistic hatred that the Jew has felt towards the true religion since the coming of Christ, his death and his resurrection. This feeds his fighting spirit and his wish to destroy the existing order.[77]

The appointment of Cardinal Angelo Roncalli as Pope John XXIII initiated a liberalization within the Catholic Church which rendered obsolete Franco's anti-Semitic and anti-masonic defence of an antiquated concept of Catholicism. Thanks to the liberal ecumenism of Pope John XXIII, the Catholic Church relaxed its enmity towards Judaism. This led to the creation in October 1961 of the educational society Amistad Judeo-Cristiana. Its representatives made many complaints to Manuel Fraga Iribarne, Franco's Minister of Information and Tourism from 1962 to 1969, about the scale of anti-Semitic items appearing in the press and on radio and television. He appeared sympathetic, but there is no evidence that he took any action. Indeed, his attitude towards the Jews was revealed after he had been dismissed by Franco. For many centuries, the Catholic Church included in the Good Friday liturgy a prayer *pro perfidis judæis*, for the conversion of the 'treacherous Jews' who were accused of the murder of Jesus Christ. After Holy Week 1959, Pope John XXIII had eliminated the prayer. In 1971, Fraga Iribarne gave the homily in the Cathedral of Zamora on Good Friday. In a passage on the circumstances of the crucifixion of Jesus Christ after he had been accused of sedition, Fraga declared: 'the terrible lesson of Holy Week must be reassessed and reassimilated. The Jews preferred injustice to disorder, stagnation to hope and miracles, egoism to charity. They have still not expiated the blood that fell on them and their children. Money, as always, was the great temptation. Judas betrayed for thirty pieces of silver.' He continued, 'Of course, Jews and Romans were wrong, Jerusalem and Israel would be destroyed.' Despite the positive achievements of the Amistad Judeo-Cristiana, anti-Semitism continued to dominate sections of the Church.[78]

The survival and official toleration of anti-Semitism in the course of the Franco dictatorship could be seen in the fact that the regime's rigid censorship permitted the publication, along with other anti-Semitic works, of twelve editions of *The Protocols of the Elders of Zion*.[79] When Luis Carrero Blanco was assassinated by ETA terrorists on 20 December 1973, he was reported to be carrying with him handwritten draft notes of his political testimony which he planned to read to the council of ministers. This deeply reactionary document was allegedly inspired by the *Protocols*. A copy of the book was found on his bedside table and it was apparently the last thing that he read before his death.[80]

Anti-Semitism was a key part of the legacy of the Franco dictatorship. In 1979, the *Protocols* were still being quoted as documentary evidence of the evil machinations of Jews and freemasons. As Tusquets had done before him with regard to the Second Republic, César Casanova González-Mateo used the *Protocols* as a guide to the democratic transition in the mid-1970s. According to his publisher, Alberto Vassallo de Mumbert, Casanova's *Manual de urgencia sobre el Sionismo en España* revealed how 'the programme set out in *The Protocols of the Elders of Zion* is being meticulously implemented in our Fatherland'. In a reference to Franco's last public speech, Vassallo issued a stark warning:

> Reader. Franco was right when he warned Spaniards about the Jewish–masonic conspiracy in cahoots with international Marxism. And since we Spaniards lent a deaf ear and hid our heads under our wings, now we have them threatening us from every street corner, distorting our thinking through the press, the radio, the television and the theatre and organizing an assault on power to destroy all the moral and material values that have constituted the great patrimony of the Spanish people as the paladin and the reserve of the values of the West.[81]

Casanova himself accused the then Prime Minister, Adolfo Suárez, of being so liberal as to be a lackey of the Zionists. He wrote, 'How revealing are *The Protocols of Zion* with regard to the current situation in Spain. They are like pages torn from today's press! And yet they are neither more nor less than quotations from *The Jewish–Masonic Peril. The Protocols of the Elders of Zion* … The Zionist mission has been achieved by President Suárez.'[82] His vehement anti-Semitism was apparent throughout: 'The old and historic Sanhedrin has managed to perpetuate itself as a secret society throughout the centuries with unchanging doctrines, methods and goals. It was based for many years in London until, drawn by the smell of money, it moved to New York. From there it directs and controls all the movements of capital, revolutions, arms sales, wars, pornography and other ways of destroying or degrading peoples.' He praised Franco and Carrero Blanco for their efforts to defend Spain against the threat of 'the mission imposed by the Elders of Zion to dominate the world'. In much the same way that the works of Carlavilla, Tusquets and Pemán set out to undermine the Second Republic, Casanova Gonzalez-Mateo's *Manual de urgencia* argued that the Jewish–masonic–Bolshevik conspiracy had brought about the transition to democracy in Spain in order to destroy Catholicism.[83]

Anti-Semitic discourse remained pervasive long after the death of Franco. Its most spectacular commercial success was the enormous and fantastical treatise by Fernando Sánchez Dragó, *Gárgoris y Habidis. Una historia mágica de España*, first published in 1979. Among its many curious notions about the relationship between Spain and the Jews can be found a bizarre thesis that the Jews themselves were responsible for the Holocaust.[84] In 1981, Cecilio Calleja wrote in the Catholic daily *Ya*, 'The number-one enemy of Spain and of the Church is freemasonry. This has been stated by the Church, by Mauricio Carlavilla, Vicente de la Fuente, Francisco de Luis, General Francisco Franco, Eduardo Comín Colomer, Juan de la Cosa [the pseudonym of Carrero Blanco], Ricardo de la Cierva, and it is all confirmed by *The Protocols of the Elders of Zion*.'[85]

The blood libel about the alleged ritual sacrifice of a child by Jews in 1489 in the village of La Guardia in Toledo is still to be found on the website of the Archdiocese of Madrid.[86] On Saturday 13 February 2021, a rally was held in Madrid's Almudena cemetery next to the monument to the Blue Division to commemorate the Spanish volunteers who died fighting with the Germans in Russia. Flags bearing Nazi symbols and placards carrying anti-Semitic slogans were on display. According to press reports, one of the leading demonstrators, Isabel M. Peralta, made a speech in which she said, 'It is our supreme obligation to fight for Spain and fight for a Europe that is weak and has been brought down by the enemy. An enemy that is always the same, albeit with different masks: the Jew. Because there is no greater truth than that the Jew is to blame. The Jew is to blame and the

División Azul fought for that reason. Communism is a Jewish invention.'[87] Peralta has been linked with extreme rightist groups that have attacked immigrants. Speaking at another event, she denounced young immigrants as 'carriers of disease' and as 'foreign filth that come to rape, to threaten, to steal, to mug and to disturb the peace'. On Twitter, she declared: 'I am clearly right. It is only too obvious what the consequences are of pointing out that Zionism and certain strata of that race are the people that control the world.'[88]

Thus, the lies survive.

Notes

Chapter 1: Fake News and Civil War

1. Jorge Villarín, *Guerra contra el judaísmo en España. Crónicas del frente* (Cadiz: Establecimientos Cerón, 1937).

2. Haim Avni, *Spain, the Jews, and Franco* (Philadelphia: The Jewish Publication Society of America, 1982) pp. 43–5; Isidro González, *Los judíos y la segunda República, 1931–1939* (Madrid: Alianza Editorial, 2004) pp. 151–68, 199–210, 259–66; *Jewish Chronicle*, 31 March 1933, 2 November 1934.

3. Juan Tusquets, *La Francmasonería, crimen de lesa patria* (Burgos: Ediciones Antisectarias, 1936) p. 51.

4. Juan Tusquets, *Masones y pacifistas* (Burgos: Ediciones Antisectarias, 1939) p. 262.

5. Isabelle Rohr, *The Spanish Right and the Jews, 1898–1945: Antisemitism and Opportunism* (Brighton: Sussex Academic Press, 2007) p. 4.

6. Pedro Carlos González Cuevas, *Acción Española. Teología política y nacionalismo autoritario en España (1913–1936)* (Madrid: Editorial Tecnos, 1998) pp. 148–55.

7. Juan Tusquets, *Orígenes de la revolución española* (Barcelona: Editorial Vilamala, 1932).

8. Anon., *Los peligros judeo-masónicos. Los protocolos de los Sabios de Sión* (Madrid: Fax, 1932).

9. Juan Tusquets et al., *Los poderes ocultos de España. Los Protocolos y su aplicación a España – Infiltraciones masónicas en el catalanismo – ¿El señor Macià es masón?* (Barcelona: Editorial Vilamala, 1932). The translation was by Alfonso Jaraix.

10. Enrique Herrera Oria, *Los cautivos de Vizcaya. Memorias del P. Enrique Herrera Oria, S.J., preso durante cuatro meses y medio en la cárcel de Bilbao y condenado a ocho años y un día de prisión* (Bilbao: Aldus S.A., 1938) pp. 12–13; Anon., *Protocolos de los Sabios de Sión* (Valladolid: Libertad/Afrodisio Aguado, 1934); Onésimo Redondo, 'El autor y el precursor de los Protocolos' and 'El precursor de los Protocolos', *Libertad*, Nos. 55 and 57, 27 June, 11 July 1932, reproduced in *Obras completas. Edición cronológica II* (Madrid: Publicaciones Españolas, 1955) pp. 201–4, 223–6.

11. Tusquets et al., *Los poderes ocultos de España*; Gonzalo Álvarez Chillida, *El antisemitismo en España. La imagen del judío (1812–2002)* (Madrid: Marcial Pons, 2002) pp. 302–3, 496–7.

12. Ramiro Ledesma Ramos, 'La ruta de Alemania', *JONS*, no. 1, May 1933, in *Escritos políticos, 1935–1936* (Madrid: Herederos de

Ramiro Ledesma Ramos, 1988)
pp. 67–70; Ramiro Ledesma Ramos,
¿Fascismo en España?, 2nd edn
(Barcelona: Ediciones Ariel, 1968)
p. 302.

13. *Jewish Chronicle*, 7 December 1934;
Arriba, 18 April, 2 May 1935;
Álvarez Chillida, *El antisemitismo*,
pp. 342–3; José Antonio Primo de
Rivera, *Obras*, 4th edn (Madrid:
Sección Feminina de FET y de las
JONS, 1966) p. 192.

14. Sancho Dávila and Julián Pemartín,
*Hacia la historia de la Falange.
Primera contribución de Sevilla*
(Jerez: Jerez Industrial, 1938)
pp. 24–7.

15. *Acción Española*, no. 10, 1 May
1932, p. 422.

16. *Ibid.*, pp. 434–8; Mgr Ernest Jouin,
*Le Péril judéo-maçonnique: Les
'Protocols' des Sages de Sion* (Paris:
Revue Internationale des Sociétés
Secrètes, 1932).

17. Julián Cortés Cavanillas, *La caída
de Alfonso XIII. Causas y episodios
de una revolución*, 7th edn (Madrid:
Librería de San Martín, 1933)
pp. 25, 33–4.

18. Dr F. Murillo, 'El mejoramiento de
la raza, base del engrandecimiento
de Alemania', *Acción Española*, no.
44, 1 January 1934, pp. 780–93,
especially pp. 782–3; Wenceslao
González Olivero, 'Algunas notas
sobre el momento científico de la
doctrina racista', *Acción Española*,
no. 52, 1 May 1934, pp. 329–37,
especially pp. 335–6, and *Acción
Española*, no. 53, 16 May 1934,
pp. 417–28.

19. Herbert R. Southworth, *Conspiracy
and the Spanish Civil War: The
Brainwashing of Francisco Franco*
(London: Routledge, 2002)
pp. 166–7.

20. Francisco Franco Bahamonde,
'Apuntes' personales sobre la
República y la guerra civil* (Madrid:

Fundación Nacional Francisco
Franco, 1987) pp. 7–9; Federico
Grau, 'Psicopatología de un
dictador: entrevista a Carlos Castilla
del Pino', *El Viejo Topo*, Extra No. 1,
1977, pp. 18–22.

21. Pilar Jaraiz Franco, *Historia de una
disidencia* (Barcelona: Editorial
Planeta, 1981) pp. 58–60.

22. José Antonio Ferrer Benimeli,
'Franco contra la masonería',
Historia 16, year II, no. 15, July
1977, pp. 43–4.

23. George Hills, *Franco, the Man and
his Nation* (New York: Macmillan,
1967) p. 157; Luis Suárez
Fernández, *Francisco Franco y su
tiempo*, 8 vols (Madrid: Fundación
Nacional Francisco Franco, 1984) I,
pp. 197–8.

24. Brian Crozier, *Franco: A
Biographical History* (London: Eyre
& Spottiswoode, 1967) pp. 92–3;
Southworth, *Conspiracy*, pp. 130,
167.

25. José Antonio Ferrer Benimeli,
Masonería española contemporánea,
2 vols (Madrid: Siglo XXI, 1980) II,
pp. 168–70; Francisco Franco
Salgado-Araujo, *Mis conversaciones
privadas con Franco* (Barcelona:
Editorial Planeta, 1976) p. 152.

26. Fernando García Lahiguera, *Ramón
Serrano Suñer. Un documento para
la historia* (Barcelona: Argos
Vergara, 1983) p. 41; Heleno Saña,
*El franquismo sin mitos.
Conversaciones con Serrano Suñer*
(Barcelona: Grijalbo, 1982) p. 42;
Ramón Garriga, *La Señora de El
Pardo* (Barcelona: Editorial Planeta,
1979) pp. 57–9.

27. Francisco de Luis, *La masonería
contra España* (Burgos: Imprenta
Aldecoa, 1935) p. 153.

28. Tusquets, *Orígenes*, pp. 30–44,
137–42; De Luis, *La masonería
contra España*, pp. 6, 99–102,
158–60, 191; Martin Blinkhorn,

Carlism and Crisis in Spain, 1931–1939 (Cambridge: Cambridge University Press, 1975) pp. 46, 179; Álvarez Chillida, *El antisemitismo*, pp. 181, 334–8.

29. *El Debate*, 22 August 1933.

30. *El Debate*, 17 October 1933.

31. *El Debate*, 24 September 1933.

32. Álvarez Chillida, *El antisemitismo*, p. 336.

33. *El Debate*, 17 October 1933.

34. *El Socialista*, 17 October 1933. Gil Robles's visit to Germany had not gone unnoticed (see *ibid.*, 14 October 1933). For the gloss by De los Ríos, see *ibid.*, 21 October 1933).

35. *CEDA*, 31 October 1933.

36. *Jewish Chronicle*, 23 March 1934, pp. 47–9.

37. *El Debate*, 21, 22, 24 April 1934; *El Socialista*, 22, 24 April 1934; José Monge Bernal, *Acción Popular (estudios de biología política)* (Madrid: Imp. Sáez Hermanos, 1936) pp. 258–61; Henry Buckley, *Life and Death of the Spanish Republic: A Witness to the Spanish Civil War* (London: I. B. Tauris, 2013) pp. 126–7.

38. *El Debate*, 21, 28 May 1935; *Arriba*, 13 June 1935 (which graphically illustrated its report of the Uclés meeting with a photograph of pigs jostling for swill); *JAP*, 14 March, 27 April, 1 June 1935.

39. Franco to the Secretary of the Entente, 16 May 1934, reproduced in *Documentos inéditos para la historia del Generalísimo Franco*, vols I, 2-I, 2-II, III, IV (Madrid: Fundación Nacional Francisco Franco, 1992–4) pp. 11–12; Hills, *Franco*, p. 193.

40. Southworth, *Conspiracy*, pp. 162–3; Suárez Fernández, *Franco*, I, pp. 268–9.

41. Franco Bahamonde, *'Apuntes' personales*, pp. 11–12.

42. *Documentos inéditos*, I, p. 12.

43. Southworth, *Conspiracy*, pp. 179–83; *Documentos inéditos*, I, pp. 13–23.

44. *Documentos inéditos*, I, pp. 11–23.

45. Hills, *Franco*, p. 207; Franco Bahamonde, *'Apuntes' personales*, p. 23.

46. Paul Preston, *Franco: A Biography* (London: HarperCollins, 1993) pp. 115–19; Crozier, *Franco*, p. 174; Suárez Fernández, *Franco*, II, p. 30 n. 38.

47. *JAP*, 28 December 1935.

48. Fernando Montero Pérez-Hinojosa, '"Gracia y Justicia". Un semanario antimasónico en la lucha contra la segunda república española', in José Antonio Ferrer Benimeli (ed.), *La masonería en la historia de España* (Zaragoza: Diputación General de Aragón, 1989) pp. 385–408; Álvarez Chillida, *El antisemitismo*, p. 338.

49. *Gracia y Justicia*, 7, 21 December 1935, 4 January 1936; José Antonio Ferrer Benimeli, *El contubernio judeo-masónico-comunista* (Madrid: Istmo, 1982) pp. 279–81.

50. Álvarez Chillida, *El antisemitismo*, pp. 295–6, 312–18; Javier Domínguez Arribas, *El enemigo judeo-masónico en la propaganda franquista (1936–1945)* (Madrid: Marcial Pons Historia, 2009) pp. 161–2.

51. Marta Simó Sánchez, 'La memoria de l'Holocaust a l'Estat Espanyol. Des d'una perspectiva sociològia i una perspectiva històrica', doctoral thesis, Universitat Autònoma de Barcelona, 2018, pp. 208–9.

52. José García Rodríguez, *La organización ilegal y clandestina. Unión Militar Española (UME). Azote de la II República española* (Madrid: Autor, 2014) pp. 33, 139–45.

53. *ABC* (Seville), 24 July 1936.

54. Luis Castro, *'Yo daré las consignas'. La prensa y la propaganda en el*

primer franquismo (Madrid: Marcial Pons, 2020) pp. 57–60, 106.

55. *ABC* (Seville), 20 December 1936.

56. Rohr, *The Spanish Right and the Jews*, p. 5.

57. *Ibid.*, pp. 73, 75, 79–80; Álvarez Chillida, *El antisemitismo*, pp. 369–72.

58. *Jewish Chronicle*, 19 February 1937.

59. *Jewish Chronicle*, 19 March 1937.

60. *Jewish Chronicle*, 24 September, 8 October 1937, 30 September 1938.

61. Cardenal Isidro Gomá, *Por Dios y por España, 1936–1939* (Barcelona: Editorial Casulleras, 1940) pp. 310–14.

62. *ABC* (Madrid), 29 September 1939; Francisco Franco Bahamonde, *Palabras del Caudillo 19 abril 1937–7 diciembre 1942* (Madrid: Ediciones de la Vicesecretaría de Educación Popular, 1943) p. 145.

63. Tusquets, *Orígenes*. On his relations with Franco, see interview with Lluís Bonada, 'Joan Tusquets', *Avui*, 28 February 1990, and Antoni Mora, 'Joan Tusquets, en els 90 anys d'un home d'estudi i de combat', Institut d'Estudis Tarraconenses Ramón Berenguer IV, *Anuari 1990–1991 de la Societat d'Estudis d'Història Eclesiàstica Moderna i Contemporània de Catalunya* (Tarragona: Diputació de Tarragona, 1992) pp. 237–9.

64. María Luisa Aisa Rodríguez, *El Cardenal Gomá y la guerra de España. Aspectos de la gestión pública del Primado, 1936–1939* (Madrid: Consejo Superior de Investigaciones Científicas, 1981) pp. 241–2.

65. Gomá, *Por Dios y por España*, pp. 465–7; Giuliana Di Febo, *Ritos de guerra y de victoria en la España franquista*, 2nd edn (Valencia: Publicacions de la Universitat de València, 2012) p. 51.

66. Manuel Álvaro Dueñas, 'Por ministerio de la ley y voluntad del Caudillo'. La Jurisdicción Especial de Responsabilidades Políticas (1939–1945) (Madrid: Centro de Estudios Políticos y Constitucionales, 2006) pp. 125–6; Enrique Suñer, *Los intelectuales y la tragedia española*, 2nd edn (San Sebastián: Editorial Española, 1938) pp. 143–53.

67. Suñer, *Los intelectuales*, p. 81.

68. *Ibid.*, pp. 5–6, 166–7, 171.

69. *Ibid.*, pp. 166–7.

70. *Ibid.*, p. 35.

71. *Ibid.*, p. 171.

72. Diego Catalán, *El archivo del romancero. Historia documentada de un siglo de historia*, 2 vols (Madrid: Fundación Ramón Menéndez Pidal, 2001).

73. Antonio Vallejo Nágera, *Higiene de la Raza. La asexualización de los psicópatas* (Madrid: Ediciones Medicina, 1934).

74. Carlos Castilla del Pino, *Pretérito imperfecto. Autobiografía (1922–1949)* (Barcelona: Tusquets, 1997) p. 301.

75. Antonio Vallejo Nágera, *Eugenesia de la hispanidad y regeneración de la raza española* (Burgos: Talleres Gráficos El Noticiero, 1937) p. 114; Antonio Vallejo Nágera, *Divagaciones intranscendentes* (Valladolid: Talleres Tipográficos Cuesta, 1938) pp. 15–18.

76. Antonio Nadal Sánchez, 'Experiencias psíquicas sobre mujeres marxistas malagueñas', in *Las mujeres y la guerra civil española* (Madrid: Ministerio de Cultura, 1991) pp. 340–50; Michael Richards, 'Morality and Biology in the Spanish Civil War: Psychiatrists, Revolution and Women Prisoners in Málaga', *Contemporary European History*, vol. 10, no. 3, 2001, pp. 395–421; Javier Rodrigo, *Cautivos. Campos de concentración*

en la España franquista, 1936–1947 (Barcelona: Editorial Crítica, 2005) pp. 141–6; Carl Geiser, *Prisoners of the Good Fight: Americans against Franco Fascism* (Westport, Connecticut: Lawrence Hill, 1986) p. 154; Antonio Vallejo Nágera, *La locura y la guerra. Psicopatología de la guerra española* (Valladolid: Librería Santarén, 1939) pp. 222–3; Antonio Vallejo and Eduardo Martínez, 'Psiquismo del Fanatismo Marxista. Investigaciones Psicológicas en Marxistas Femeninos Delincuentes', *Revista Española de Medicina y Cirugía de Guerra*, no. 9, 1939, pp. 398–413; Ricard Vinyes, *Irredentas. Las presas políticas y sus hijos en las cárceles franquistas* (Madrid: Ediciones Temas de Hoy, 2002) pp. 62–70.

77. Vinyes, *Irredentas*, pp. 49–57.

78. Jacques Maritain, *Los rebeldes españoles no hacen una guerra santa* (Valencia: Ediciones Españolas, 1937) p. 2.

79. Jacques Maritain, 'Préface', Alfred Mendizábal, *Aux origines d'une tragédie: la politique espagnole de 1923 à 1936* (Paris: Desclée de Brouwer, 1937) pp. 24–31.

80. Ramón Serrano Suñer, *Siete discursos* (Bilbao: Ediciones Fe, 1938) pp. 53–7.

81. *ABC* (Seville), 21 June 1938.

82. Herbert R. Southworth, *El mito de la cruzada de Franco*, ed. Paul Preston (Barcelona: Random House Mondadori, 2008) pp. 296–306; Tusquets, *Masones y pacifistas*, pp. 99–116.

83. Carlos Fernández Santander, *Antología de 40 años (1936–1975)* (Sada-A Coruña: Ediciós do Castro, 1983) p. 56.

84. José Pemartín, *Qué es 'lo nuevo' … Consideraciones sobre el momento español presente*, 3rd edn (Madrid: Espasa Calpe, 1940) p. 17.

85. *Ibid.*, pp. 322–33.

86. Anon. (Herbert R. Southworth), *Franco's 'Mein Kampf': The Fascist State in Rebel Spain: An Official Blueprint* (New York: The Spanish Information Bureau, 1939) pp. 3, 5, 6.

87. Rohr, *The Spanish Right and the Jews*, pp. 92–4.

88. *Ibid.*, pp. 84–9; Álvarez Chillida, *El antisemitismo*, pp. 366–8; Michael Richards, *A Time of Silence: Civil War and the Culture of Repression in Franco's Spain, 1936–1945* (Cambridge: Cambridge University Press, 1998) p. 57; *Jewish Chronicle*, 7, 21 August, 4 September 1936, 26 February 1937.

89. *La Ciudad y los Campos*, no. 263, 30 January 1937; no. 264, 6 February 1937; no. 265, 13 February 1937; no. 266, 20 February 1937; no. 268, 6 March 1937; no. 269, 13 March 1937; no. 270, 20 March 1937, quoted Sid Lowe, *Catholicism, War and the Foundation of Francoism: The Juventud de Acción Popular in Spain, 1931–1939* (Brighton: Sussex Academic Press/Cañada Blanch, 2010) pp. 201, 247.

90. *ABC* (Madrid), 20 May 1939; Franco Bahamonde, *Palabras del Caudillo 19 abril 1937–7 diciembre 1942*, pp. 101–2.

91. *ABC* (Madrid), 19 July 1939; Giuliana Di Febo, *La santa de la raza. Un culto barroco en la España franquista (1937–1962)* (Barcelona: Icaria Editorial, 1988) p. 59.

Chapter 2: The Policeman: Mauricio Carlavilla

1. Mauricio Carlavilla, *Anti-España 1959. Autores, cómplices y encubridores del comunismo* (Madrid: Editorial Nos, 1959) p. 69.

2. Eladio Romero García, *Julian Mauricio Carlavilla del Barrio. El policía franquista que destapó la*

conspiración mundial (Almería: Círculo Rojo, 2018) pp. 15–17.

3. Carta de solicitud para las oposiciones a agente de policía, Melilla, 25 October 1920; Expediente 1736, Expediente personal de Julián Mauricio Carlavilla del Barrio, Archivo General del Ministerio de Interior; Carlavilla, *Anti-España 1959*, p. 347.

4. Expediente 1736, Carlavilla, doc. 8, 3 June 1922 (Carta del Gobernador de Valencia pidiendo traslado de Carlavilla, 6 June 1922).

5. Eduardo González Calleja, *El máuser y el sufragio. Orden público, subversión y violencia política en la crisis de la Restauración (1917–1931)* (Madrid: Consejo Superior de Investigaciones Científicas, 1999) p. 53.

6. Ángel Smith, *Anarchism, Revolution and Reaction: Catalan Labour and the Crisis of the Spanish State, 1898–1923* (New York: Berghahn Books, 2007) pp. 347–50; Abel Paz, *Durruti en la revolución española* (Madrid: Fundación Anselmo Lorenzo, 1996) pp. 94–106; Ricardo Sanz, *El sindicalismo y la política. Los 'Solidarios' y 'Nosotros'* (Toulouse: Autor & Imprimerie Dulaurier, 1966) pp. 103–18.

7. Expediente 1736, Carlavilla, doc. 11, 17 March 1923 (destinado a Segovia), doc. 13, 22 March 1923 (destinado a Bilbao), doc. 15, 19 April 1923 (llega a Bilbao), doc. 238, 4 March 1947 (solicitud de licencia de uso de armas), doc. 272, 30 January 1940 (expediente disciplinario).

8. Mauricio Karl (pseudonym of Mauricio Carlavilla del Barrio), *Asesinos de España. Marxismo, anarquismo, masonería. Compendio* (Madrid: Imp. Sáez Hermanos, 1936) pp. 134–9. Henceforth Karl, *Compendio*.

9. Carlavilla's account of his activities in Bilbao is found in Indalecio Prieto, *Yo y Moscú*, Prólogo, comentarios y notas de Mauricio Carlavilla (Madrid: Editorial Nos, 1960) pp. 429–38. Prieto's account of the assassination attempt is found in Indalecio Prieto, *Entresijos de la guerra de España (Intrigas de nazis, fascistas y comunistas)* (Buenos Aires: Editorial Bases, 1954) pp. 75–7.

10. Expediente 1736, Carlavilla, doc. 31, 1 December 1924 (Felicitación a funcionarios en la contención de revueltas y la represión de anarquistas y comunistas).

11. Expediente 1736, Carlavilla, doc. 18, 2 October 1923 (enviado de Bilbao a Madrid), doc. 23, 8 October 1923 (asume destino en Madrid), doc. 37, 19 October 1925 (destinado a Morocco), doc. 40, 4 November 1925 (llega a Tetuán), doc. 42, 25 January 1926 (investigaciones en Bilbao); Eduardo Connolly, 'Mauricio Carlavilla: el encanto de la conspiración', *HIBRIS. Revista de Bibliofilia* (Alcoy), no. 23, September–October 2004, pp. 4–5.

12. *ABC*, 11 April 1927.

13. Expediente 1736, Carlavilla, doc. 46, 28 March 1927 (Marques de Magaz a Pedro Bazán, Director General de Seguridad).

14. Expediente 1736, Carlavilla, doc. 43, 15 December 1926 (cese de Carlavilla), doc. 43 bis, 30 November 1926 (informe de la Alta Comisaría de España en Marruecos), doc. 44, 21 January 1927 (solicitud de destino), doc. 44 bis, 14 March 1927 (Bazán, petición de detalles), doc. 45, 14 March 1927 (informe de la Alta Comisaría), doc. 47, 27 June 1927 (le dan plaza en Madrid), doc. 47 bis, 21 July 1928

(petición de pagos desestimada), doc. 52, 14 March 1928 (petición de pagos).

15. Expediente 1736, Carlavilla, doc. 49, 16 January 1928 (pasa a 1ª Brigada de la División de Ferrocarriles), doc. 53, 4 December 1928, doc. 55, 5 February 1929 (una felicitación).

16. *El Imparcial*, 9 October 1928; *La Voz*, 10 October 1928.

17. *La Voz*, 31 January 1929.

18. Carlavilla, *Anti-España 1959*, pp. 431–3.

19. *Ibid.*, p. 434.

20. Karl, *Compendio*, pp. 62–8, 76–81.

21. Carlavilla gave his own account of this in *ibid.*, pp. 82–9; Mauricio Karl (pseudonym of Mauricio Carlavilla del Barrio), *El enemigo. Marxismo, anarquismo, masonería*, 4th edn (Santiago de Chile: Ediciones Ercilla, 1937) pp. 92–9. For an account debunking Carlavilla's version, see Juan-Simeón Vidarte, *No queríamos al Rey. Testimonio de un socialista español* (Barcelona: Grijalbo, 1977) pp. 256–9. On Primo's marriage plans, see *Estampa*, 24 April 1928; *ABC*, 24, 28 May; 1, 9 June 1928.

22. Carlavilla, *Anti-España 1959*, p. 434.

23. *ABC*, 27 December 1930.

24. Enrique Castro Delgado, *Hombres made in Moscú* (Barcelona: Luis de Caralt, 1965) pp. 62–5.

25. Expediente 1736, Carlavilla, doc. 67, 6 January 1931 (pasa a la división de investigación social), doc. 272, 1 February 1940 (expediente de depuración); González Calleja, *El máuser y el sufragio*, p. 565.

26. Emilio Mola Vidal, *Obras completas* (Valladolid: Librería Santarén, 1940) pp. 624, 757–8. Carlavilla, *Anti-España 1959*, pp. 18, 434–8.

27. Mauricio Karl (pseudonym of Mauricio Carlavilla del Barrio), *Sodomitas* (Madrid: Editorial Nos, 1956) pp. 136–61.

28. Carlavilla, *Anti-España 1959*, p. 439.

29. Mauricio Karl (pseudonym of Mauricio Carlavilla del Barrio), *El comunismo en España. 5 años en el partido, su organización y sus misterios* (Madrid: Imp. Sáez Hermanos, 1931) pp. 5–8, 439; Karl, *El enemigo*, p. 11.

30. *Mundo Gráfico*, 1 June 1932; *ABC*, 15 March 1932, p. 15.

31. *ABC*, 17 April 1932.

32. *Heraldo de Madrid*, 25 February 1932.

33. *La Época*, 3 March 1932.

34. *Ahora*, 30 November 1932; *ABC*, 7 December 1933; Carlavilla, *Anti-España 1959*, p. 27.

35. *Acción Española*, no. 10, 1 May 1932, pp. 439–41.

36. Expediente 1736, Carlavilla, doc. 129, 27 September 1935 (separación del Cuerpo de Investigación y Vigilancia), doc. 272, 1 February 1940 (expediente de depuración).

37. *Ahora*, 19, 25 September, 20 November 1931, 30 November 1933; Alejandro Lerroux, *La pequeña historia. Apuntes para la historia grande vividos y redactados por el autor* (Buenos Aires: Editorial Cimera, 1945) p. 436.

38. Expediente 1736, Carlavilla, doc. 272, 1 February 1940 (expediente de depuración); Carlavilla, *Anti-España 1959*, pp. 26–7; Juan Antonio Ansaldo, ¿Para qué? de Alfonso XIII a Juan III (Buenos Aires: Editorial Vasca-Ekin, 1951) p. 50.

39. *ABC*, 21 June 1935 (Jefe Superior de la Policía de Madrid), 11 July 1935 (comisario jefe del Cuerpo de Vigilancia), 17 August 1935, 11 November 1935 (Jefe Superior de la Policía de Barcelona), 27 November 1935 (Delegado General de Orden Público). Cf. José María Miguélez Rueda, 'Transformaciones y

cambios en la policía española
durante la II República', *Espacio,
Tiempo y Forma. Serie V, Historia
Contemporánea*, vol. 10, 1997,
p. 219; Manuel Tuñón de Lara, *La
España del siglo XX*, 2nd edn (Paris:
Librería Española, 1973) pp. 275,
362, 381; *Ahora*, 1, 7 August 1935;
Lerroux, *La pequeña historia*,
pp. 434–7, 579–80.

40. On Carlavilla and his writings, see
Herbert R. Southworth, *Antifalange.
Estudio crítico de 'Falange en la
guerra de España' de Maximiano
García Venero* (Paris: Ediciones
Ruedo Ibérico, 1967) p. 175;
Herbert R. Southworth, *Conspiracy
and the Spanish Civil War: The
Brainwashing of Francisco Franco*
(London: Routledge, 2002) pp. 207,
212–13; Gonzalo Álvarez Chillida,
*El antisemitismo en España. La
imagen del judío (1812–2002)*
(Madrid: Marcial Pons, 2002)
pp. 320–1. According to Ricardo de
la Cierva, *Bibliografía sobre la
guerra de España (1936–1939) y sus
antecedentes* (Barcelona: Ariel,
1968) pp. 115, 140, 365, his name
was Mauricio Carlavilla de la Vega.
However, one of his later books,
published when he no longer felt
the need for a pseudonym, is signed
'Mauricio Carlavilla del Barrio
"Mauricio Karl"' (*Sodomitas*).

41. Karl, *El enemigo*, pp. 24–31, 171;
Karl, *Compendio*, pp. 20–6, 35–45,
177, 196–207.

42. Karl, *Compendio*, p. 154.

43. *Ibid.*, pp. 70–5; *ABC*, 5 July 1934, 21
August 1934.

44. Letter from 'Mauricio Karl', *La
Época*, 19 September 1934; *El Siglo
Futuro*, 20 September 1934.

45. Expediente 1736, Carlavilla, doc.
118; *ABC*, 24 September 1934
(destinado a la Oficina de
Información y Enlace de la
Dirección General de Seguridad).

46. *Ahora*, 3 May 1936; *El Sol*, 3 May
1936; *Claridad*, 4 May 1936.
Carlavilla's presence in Asturias on
the staff of Doval was noted in the
devastating report on the atrocities
by Félix Gordón Ordás, reproduced
in Margarita Nelken, *Por qué
hicimos la revolución* (Barcelona/
Paris/New York: Ediciones Sociales
Internacionales, 1936) p. 183.

47. Karl, *Compendio*, p. 321.

48. *Declaración del testigo Juan Aguasca
Bonmati a la Causa General*,
Archivo Histórico Nacional,
FC-Causa General, 1630, exp. 1,
p. 15.

49. Expediente 1736, Carlavilla, doc.
272, 1 February 1940 (expediente de
depuración). On the financing of
the additional copies, see *Claridad*,
16 May 1936.

50. Karl, *Compendio*, p. 397.

51. *La Nación*, 4 October 1935; *La
Época*, 10 October 1935; Romero
García, *Carlavilla*, pp. 72–3.

52. Karl, *Compendio*, pp. 21–4 (Los
judíos en España), 85–9, 320–1
(free copies to army). On Cambó,
pp. 74–5; Julio Rodríguez Puértolas,
Literatura fascista española, 2 vols
(Madrid: Ediciones Akal, 1986,
1987) I, p. 309; Maximiano García
Venero, *Falange en la guerra civil de
España. La unificación y Hedilla*
(Paris: Ruedo Ibérico, 1967) p. 309.

53. *El Siglo Futuro*, 25 January, 2, 4
March 1936.

54. Álvaro de Albornoz, 'El orden
público', *La Libertad*, 5 July 1935;
'Mauricio Karl replica al ex ministro
Albornoz', *El Siglo Futuro*, 27 July
1935; Karl, *Compendio*, p. 330. The
quotation about Casares: Karl, *El
enemigo*, p. 119.

55. Karl, *El enemigo*, pp. 108–11.

56. *La Voz*, 28 February 1935; *La Época*,
5 March 1935.

57. Felipe Ximénez de Sandoval, *José
Antonio (Biografía apasionada)*,

Prólogo de Ramón Serrano Suñer (Barcelona: Editorial Juventud, 1941) pp. 70–1.

58. Expediente 1736, Carlavilla, doc. 129, 27 September 1935 (separación del Cuerpo de Investigación y Vigilancia), doc. 272, 1 February 1940 (expediente de depuración); *ABC*, 6 May 1936; *Ahora*, 6 May 1936; *Claridad*, 5 May 1936; *El Socialista*, 6 May 1936; Juan-Simeón Vidarte, *Todos fuimos culpables* (Mexico City: Fondo de Cultura Económica, 1973) p. 111.

59. Expediente 1736, Carlavilla, doc. 138, 23 January 1936 (recurso contencioso-administrativo en el Tribunal Supremo); *ABC*, 24 October 1935.

60. Eduardo González Calleja, *Contrarrevolucionarios. Radicalización violenta de las derechas durante la segunda República, 1931–1936* (Madrid: Alianza Editorial, 2011) pp. 97, 114–15, 118; Antonio Cacho Zabalza, *La Unión Militar Española* (Alicante: Egasa, 1940) pp. 13–18; Stanley G. Payne, *Politics and the Military in Modern Spain* (Stanford, California: Stanford University Press, 1967) pp. 293–4, 301–11. Payne's account is heavily influenced by his interviews with Pardo Reina.

61. Expediente 1736, Carlavilla, doc. 272, 1 February 1940 (expediente de depuración); *ABC*, 3 May 1936; *Ahora*, 3 May 1936; *Claridad*, 2, 16 May 1936; *El Socialista*, 3 May 1936.

62. Expediente 1736, Carlavilla, doc. 272, 1 February 1940 (expediente de depuración); *Claridad*, 4 May 1936; José María García Márquez, *La 'Semana sangrienta' de julio de 1931 en Sevilla. Entre la historia y la manipulación* (Seville: Aconcagua, 2019) p. 127; Juan Ortiz Villalba, *Sevilla 1936. Del golpe militar a la*

guerra civil (Seville: Diputación Provincial, 1997) pp. 158–9; Edmundo Barbero, *El infierno azul (Seis meses en el feudo de Queipo)* (Madrid: Talleres del SUIG (CNT), 1937) p. 39.

63. *Claridad*, 2, 4 May 1936; *ABC*, 3, 7 May 1936; *Ahora* 3, 6, 7 May 1936; *El Sol*, 3 May 1936; Expediente 1736, doc. 272, 1 February 1940 (expediente de depuración); Romero García, *Carlavilla*, pp. 78–80.

64. Archivo Histórico Nacional, Sumario 167/1936, FC-AUDIENCIA T MADRID CRIMINAL, 76, exp. 17.

65. *ABC*, 3 May 1936; Payne, *Politics and the Military*, p. 504.

66. Expediente 1736, Carlavilla, doc. 272 (expediente de depuración), 1 February 1940; *Claridad*, 4 May 1936.

67. Julian Zugazagoitia, *Guerra y vicisitudes de los españoles*, 2 vols, 2nd edn (Paris: Librería Española, 1968) I, p. 99; Julio Gil Pecharromán, *José Antonio Primo de Rivera. Retrato de un visionario* (Madrid: Temas de Hoy, 1996) p. 507.

68. Joan Maria Thomàs, *El gran golpe. El 'Caso Hedilla' o cómo Franco se quedó con Falange* (Barcelona: Editorial Debate, 2014) pp. 368–9; Zugazagoitia, *Guerra y vicisitudes*, I, pp. 176–7, 261–2. See Largo Calvo's account in Ascensión Hernández de León-Portilla, *España desde México. Vida y testimonio de transterrados* (Madrid: Algaba, 2004) pp. 221–39, especially pp. 231–2; his letter to his father, 20 September 1936; Bernardo Gil Mugarza, *España en llamas, 1936* (Barcelona: Ediciones Acervo, 1968) pp. 231–2.

69. Expediente 1736, Carlavilla, doc. 272, 1 February 1940 (expediente de depuración); Thomàs, *El gran golpe,*

pp. 34–5; Ximénez de Sandoval, *José Antonio*, p. 585; Maximiano García Venero, *Falange en la guerra civil de España. La unificación y Hedilla* (Paris: Ruedo Ibérico, 1967) pp. 309, 343; Connolly, 'Mauricio Carlavilla', p. 6.

70. *F.E.*, 1 October 1936.

71. Francisco Franco Bahamonde, *Textos de doctrina política. Palabras y escritos de 1945 a 1950* (Madrid: Publicaciones Españolas, 1951) pp. 334–5; Paul Preston, *El Cid and the Masonic Super-State: Franco, the Western Powers and the Cold War* (London: London School of Economics, 1993) *passim*.

72. Karl, *Compendio*, pp. 65, 89, 259, 296–7, 391.

73. Expediente, 1736 Carlavilla, doc. 238, 6 March 1947 (Informe sobre la carrera de Carlavilla); Archivo General de la Policía, Archivo Bajas, expediente 1.376, doc. 144, 19 September 1939, doc. 168, 5 October 1940, quoted by José Luis Rodríguez Jiménez, 'Carlavilla, un personaje al servicio de las teorías conspirativas judeo-masónico-comunistas y de la conspiración contra la Segunda República Española', in José Antonio Ferrer Benimeli (ed.), *La masonería española. Represión y exilios* (proceedings of XII Symposium Internacional de Historia de la Masonería Española) (Zaragoza: Gobierno de Aragón, 2010) pp. 871–85; Romero García, *Carlavilla*, pp. 90–2. On these financial operations, see Eusebio Medina García, 'Contrabando en la frontera de Portugal. Orígenes, estructuras, conflicto y cambio social', doctoral thesis, Universidad Complutense de Madrid, 2001, especially p. 242.

74. Arquivo Nacional, Torre di Tombo, Lisbon, PIDE, Serviços Centrais, Registo Geral de Presos, liv. 57, registo nº. 11232 (Carlavilla), 59, registo nº. 11645 (Velez).

75. Expediente 1736, Carlavilla, doc. 272, 1 February 1940 (expediente de depuración).

76. Josep Cruanyes, *Els papers de Salamanca. L'espoliació del patrimoni documental de Catalunya* (Barcelona: Edicions 62, 2003) pp. 15–16, 42–56; José Luis Rodríguez Jiménez, 'Una aproximación al trasfondo ideológico de la represión. Teoría de la conspiración y policía política franquista', in Jaume Sobrequés, Carme Molinero and Margarida Sala (eds), *Els camps de concentració i el mon penitenciari a Espanya durant la guerra civil i el franquisme* (Barcelona: Museu de'Historia de Catalunya/Editorial Crítica, 2003) pp. 416–20; Paul Preston, *The Spanish Holocaust: Inquisition and Extermination in Twentieth-Century Spain* (London: Harper Press, 2012) pp. 486–9; Álvarez Chillida, *El antisemitismo*, p. 394.

77. Expediente 1736, Carlavilla, doc. 159, 9 March 1940 (Tribunal Supremo, recurso), doc. 160, 9 May 1940 (anulación de la separación de 1935), doc. 161, 16 May 1940 (reconocido como anticomunista y antimasón), doc. 162, 16 May 1940 (agente de 1ª clase con antigüedad hasta 1 April 1937), doc. 169, 21 November 1940 (petición de abono de haberes desde que fue separado por la República).

78. Rodríguez Jiménez, 'Una aproximación al trasfondo ideológico de la represión. Teoría de la conspiración y policía política franquista', pp. 416–19.

79. Karl, *Sodomitas*, pp. 58–61.

80. Expediente 1736, Carlavilla, doc. 172, 2 March 1941 (solicitud de excedencia), doc. 180, 8 May 1941

(cesa en el cargo por 'excedente voluntario'), doc. 186, 30 July 1941 (solicitud de reingreso en la plantilla de Madrid y destinado, 13 August 1941 a Palma de Mallorca), doc. 197, 31 December 1941 (nombrado inspector de segunda clase), doc. 198, 19 January 1942, doc. 204, 27 April 1942, doc. 206, 5 May 1942, doc. 210, 19 June 1942, doc. 218, 5 August 1942, doc. 221, 20 August 1942 (asuntos médicos), doc. 228, 22 September 1942 (solicita excedencia voluntaria), doc. 229, 9 October 1942 (concedida).

81. Archivo General de la Policía, Archivo Bajas, expediente 1.376, doc. sin numeración, cited by Rodríguez Jiménez, 'Carlavilla, un personaje', pp. 884–5; Romero García, *Carlavilla*, p. 183.

82. *Informaciones*, 16, 18 September 1936; Eduard Masjuan Bracons, 'Eduardo Barriobero y Herrán i la justícia revolucionària a la Barcelona de 1936', Segon Congrés Recerques, *Enfrontaments civils. Postguerres i reconstruccions*, 2 vols (Lleida: Associació Recerques y Pagés Editors, 2002) II, pp. 1024–35.

83. *El Imparcial*, 9 October 1928; *La Voz*, 10 October 1928; Francisco Horacio, 'La Policía del mundo contra los ladrones internacionales', *Estampa* (Madrid), 27 August 1932, no. 242, pp. 7–11.

84. Expediente 1736, Carlavilla, doc. 238, 13 December 1947 (solicitud), doc. 242, 12 January 1948 (ingreso); Connolly, 'Mauricio Carlavilla', p. 5.

85. Expediente 1736, Carlavilla, doc. 244, 9 December 1952 (reingreso al cuerpo), doc. 248, 30 December 1952 (traslado a Madrid), doc. 256, 6 October 1953 (ascenso a Comisario de 1ª clase), doc. 277, 13 February 1957 (jubilación).

86. Connolly, 'Mauricio Carlavilla', p. 14.

87. *ABC*, 10 October 1956.

88. Sidney Warburg, *El dinero de Hitler*, Prólogo y ampliaciones históricas de Mauricio Carlavilla, 'Mauricio Karl' (Madrid: Editorial Nos, 1955) p. 284. The advertisement in *ABC*, 9 November 1956.

89. Karl, *Sodomitas*, pp. 10, 13–19, 58–66, 103–8, 137, 192–5, 223–62.

90. Mauricio Carlavilla, *Satanismo* (Madrid: Editorial Nos, 1957) pp. 28–34, 60, 112–13. For a survey of his publishing ventures, see Romero García, *Carlavilla*, pp. 136–48.

91. *ABC*, 9 November 1956.

92. W. G. Krivitsky, *I Was Stalin's Agent* (London: Hamish Hamilton, 1939) and W. G. Krivitsky, *In Stalin's Secret Service* (New York: Harper & Row, 1939).

93. Boris Volodarsky, *Stalin's Agent: The Life and Death of Alexander Orlov* (Oxford: Oxford University Press, 2013) pp. 54–6, 73–4.

94. Valentín González, 'El Campesino', *Yo escogí la esclavitud*, Prólogo de Mauricio Carlavilla 'Mauricio Karl' (n.p., n.d.). On the gestation of the book, Herbert Rutledge Southworth, '"The Grand Camouflage": Julián Gorkín, Burnett Bolloten and the Spanish Civil War', in Paul Preston and Ann L. Mackenzie (eds), *The Republic Besieged: Civil War in Spain, 1936–1939* (Edinburgh: Edinburgh University Press, 1996) pp. 262–72; Burnett Bolloten, *The Spanish Civil War: Revolution and Counterrevolution* (Hemel Hempstead: Harvester Wheatsheaf, 1991) p. 810.

95. *ABC*, 14, 24 November, 3 December 1953.

96. Jesús Hernández, *Yo fui un ministro de Stalin* (Mexico City: Editorial

América, 1953); Jesús Hernández, *Yo, ministro de Stalin en España*, Prólogo y notas de Mauricio Carlavilla (Madrid: Editorial Nos, 1954) pp. 5–35; Fernando Hernández Sánchez, *Comunistas sin partido. Jesús Hernández, Ministro en la guerra civil, disidente en el exilio* (Madrid: Editorial Raíces, 2007) pp. 13–14, 30–1.

97. Indalecio Prieto, *Yo y Moscú*, Prólogo, comentarios y notas de Mauricio Carlavilla (Madrid: Editorial Nos, 1960) pp. 37–8; Indalecio Prieto, *Cómo y por qué salí del Ministerio de Defensa Nacional. Intrigas de los rusos en España (Texto taquigráfico del informe pronunciado el 9 de agosto de 1938 ante el Comité Nacional del Partido Socialista Obrero Español)* (Mexico City: Impresos y Papeles, S. de R.L., 1940).

98. Francisco Largo Caballero, *Mis recuerdos. Cartas a un amigo*, Prólogo y notas de Enrique de Francisco (Mexico City: Ediciones Unidas, 1954); Francisco Largo Caballero, *Correspondencia secreta*, Prólogo y notas de Mauricio Carlavilla (Madrid: Editorial Nos, 1961); Julio Aróstegui, *Largo Caballero. El tesón y la quimera* (Barcelona: Editorial Debate, 2013) pp. 28, 728.

99. Mauricio Carlavilla, *El Rey. Radiografía del reinado de Alfonso XIII* (Madrid: Editorial Nos, 1956) pp. 98–9.

100. *Ibíd.*, pp. 17–18, 119–24, 306–7, 468–9; Karl, *Compendio*, pp. 56–9.

101. Carlavilla, *El Rey*, pp. 25–31, 59–60, 76, 95–7, 222, 233.

102. Mauricio Carlavilla, *Borbones masones desde Fernando VII a Alfonso XIII* (Barcelona: Acervo, 1967).

103. There is a full, and highly perceptive, analysis of the book in Romero García, *Carlavilla*, pp. 150–8.

104. Carlavilla, *Anti-España 1959*, pp. 376–7.

105. Discurso a las Cortes, 14 May 1946, Franco, *Textos de doctrina política*, pp. 31–59, especially pp. 40–2.

106. Discurso a los abades benedictinos, Francisco Franco Bahamonde, *Franco ha dicho. Primer apéndice (contiene de 1º enero 1947 a 1º abril 1949)* (Madrid: Ediciones Voz, 1949) pp. 75–6.

107. Discurso al Frente de Juventudes, 28 March 1950, Franco, *Textos de doctrina política*, pp. 191–5.

108. Carlavilla, *Anti-España 1959*, pp. 44–6.

109. Serge Nilus, *Protocolos de los sábios de Sión* (Madrid: Editorial Nos, 1963); Connolly, 'Mauricio Carlavilla', pp. 14–15; Aurelio Sallairai, *Protocolos de los sábios de Sión y la subversión mundial* (Buenos Aires: n.p., 1972) pp. 13–14.

110. Pilar Jaraiz Franco, *Historia de una disidencia* (Barcelona: Editorial Planeta, 1981) p. 191; Francisco Franco Salgado-Araujo, *Mis conversaciones privadas con Franco* (Barcelona: Editorial Planeta, 1976) pp. 366, 381–2; Franco, 'Notas mecanografiadas sobre masonería', doc. 45, leg. 246, no. 4, *Manuscritos de Franco*, Fundación Francisco Franco, Madrid.

111. Connolly, 'Mauricio Carlavilla', pp. 6, 11; *En torno al XIX Congreso del Partido Comunista de la U.R.S.S.* (Presidencia del Gobierno. Dirección General de Marruecos y Colonias. Boletin de Información, Especial, 1953); *Beria* (Presidencia del Gobierno. Dirección General de Marruecos y Colonias. Boletin de Informacion, Especial, 1953).

112. Mauricio Karl (pseudonym of Mauricio Carlavilla del Barrio),

Moscú hoy (Barcelona: A.H.R., 1955).

113. Carlavilla, *Anti-España 1959*, pp. 18–20.

114. Recounted to the author by Herbert Southworth after he had interviewed Carlavilla.

115. Connolly, 'Mauricio Carlavilla', pp. 5–7; testimony to the author of Herbert Southworth who visited Carlavilla in the early 1970s; Xavier Casals Messeguer, *Neonazis en España. De las audiciones wagnerianas a los skinheads (1966–1995)* (Barcelona: Grijalbo-Mondadori, 1995) pp. 49, 50, 65, 291; Xavier Casals Messeguer, *La tentación neofascista en España* (Barcelona: Plaza y Janés, 1998) pp. 34, 76.

116. *ABC*, 25 June 1982; *El País*, 26 June 1982.

Chapter 3: The Priest: Father Juan Tusquets

1. On Tusquets's life, see the interviews with Antoni Mora, 'Joan Tusquets, en els 90 anys d'un home d'estudi i de combat', Institut d'Estudis Tarraconenses Ramón Berenguer IV, *Anuari 1990–1991 de la Societat d'Estudis d'Història Eclesiàstica Moderna i Contemporània de Catalunya* (Tarragona: Diputació de Tarragona, 1992) pp. 231–42; Joan Subirà, *Capellans en temps de Franco* (Barcelona: Editorial Mediterrània, 1996) pp. 15–37; and Lluís Bonada, *Avui*, 28 February 1990.

2. Pare Miquel d'Esplugues, 'Pròleg', in Joan Tusquets, *El teosofisme*, vol. 3 (Tremp: Llibreria Central, 1927) p. 21.

3. Juan Tusquets, *Masones y pacifistas* (Burgos: Ediciones Antisectarias, 1939) p. 87.

4. Tusquets, *El teosofisme*, p. 217.

5. Mora, 'Joan Tusquets', p. 234; José Antonio Ferrer Benimeli, *El contubernio judeo-masónico-comunista. Del satanismo al escándolo de la P-2* (Madrid: Ediciones Istmo, 1982) pp. 191–7; Jordi Canal, 'Las campañas antisectarias de Juan Tusquets (1927–1939): Una aproximación a los orígenes del contubernio judeo-masónico-comunista en España', in José Antonio Ferrer Benimeli (ed.), *La masonería en la España del siglo XX*, 2 vols (Toledo: Universidad de Castilla-La Mancha, 1996) pp. 1193–1214; Javier Domínguez Arribas, *El enemigo judeo-masónico en la propaganda franquista (1936–1945)* (Madrid: Marcial Pons Historia, 2009) pp. 237–42.

6. On Tusquets's accusations against Macià, see Juan Tusquets, *Orígenes de la revolución española* (Barcelona: Editorial Vilamala, 1932) pp. 147–51; Tusquets, *Masones y pacifistas*, pp. 103–5; Hilari Raguer, *La Unió Democràtica de Catalunya i el seu temps (1931–1939)* (Barcelona: Publicacions de l'Abadia de Montserrat, 1976) pp. 279–80.

7. *El Correo Catalán*, 3 March 1932; Vidal i Barraquer to Tedeschini, 15 March 1932; Arxiu Vidal i Barraquer, *Esglesia i Estat durant la Segona República espanyola, 1931/1936*, 4 vols in 8 parts (Monestir de Montserrat: Publicacions de l'Abadia de Montserrat, 1971–90) II, pp. 386, 637–8, III, p. 935.

8. On the burglary, see Mora, 'Joan Tusquets', pp. 234–5; Subirà, *Capellans*, pp. 22–3; on steaming open the letters, author's conversation with Albert Manent.

9. Subirà, *Capellans*, p. 37.

10. *La Vanguardia*, 19 February 1932; Tusquets, *Orígenes*, p. 3.

11. Montserrat, 'Pórtico', Tusquets, *Orígenes*, p. 7.
12. Tusquets, *Orígenes*, pp. 51–4, 68–71, 122–5, 207–15.
13. *Ibid.*, p. 13.
14. *Ibid.*, pp. 35–6, 39–40.
15. *Ibid.*, pp. 12–13.
16. Letter from the Grand Lodge of the North-East of Spain, Barcelona, 19 February 1932, highlighting the threat posed by Tusquets's book and referring to the open letter, Archivo Histórico Nacional, secc. Masonería, leg. 792, exp. 11.
17. Ramón Díaz, *La verdad de la francmasonería. Réplica al libro del Pbro. Tusquets* (Barcelona: Librería Española, 1932).
18. Publicity leaflet for Matías Usero Torrente, *Mi respuesta al P. Tusquets* (La Coruña: Imp. Moret, 1934); letter from the lodge of El Ferrol, 1 March 1934, praising Dr Usero's initiative and urging masons to distribute copies, Archivo Histórico Nacional, secc. Masonería, leg. 792, exp. 11.
19. For Tusquets's account, see Mora, 'Joan Tusquets', p. 235; Subirà, *Capellans*, p. 16. I am indebted to Dr Chris Ealham for his observations on the alleged incident.
20. Tusquets, *Orígenes*, pp. 101, 137–8. Alcalá-Zamora wrote in protest to Archbishop Vidal i Barraquer, 26 March 1932, Arxiu Vidal i Barraquer, *Esglesia i Estat*, II, pp. 644–6.
21. *El Correo Catalán*, 28 February 1932; *La Vanguardia*, 24 February, 3 March 1932.
22. Juan Tusquets et al., *Los poderes ocultos de España. Los Protocolos y su aplicación a España – Infiltraciones masónicas en el catalanismo – ¿El señor Macià es masón?* (Barcelona: Editorial Vilamala, 1932).
23. 'Fabio', 'Estudio crítico de los Protocolos', in *ibid.*, pp. 7–34.
24. Jesús Lizárraga, 'Aplicación a España de los Protocolos', in Tusquets et al., *Los poderes ocultos*, pp. 35–46.
25. Esther Tusquets Guillén, *Habíamos ganado la guerra* (Barcelona: Editorial Bruguera, 2007) pp. 62–6.
26. *Las Sectas*, vol. 14, in René Llanas de Niubó, *El Judaísmo* (Barcelona: Editorial Vilamala, 1935) p. 163; *La Vanguardia*, 20 May 1932; *El Siglo Futuro*, 3 April 1933; *ABC*, 5 April 1933.
27. Canal, 'Las campañas antisectarias de Juan Tusquets', p. 1213.
28. Subirà, *Capellans*, pp. 24–5; Mora, 'Joan Tusquets', p. 236.
29. 'Hitler ante el problema judaico', *Las Sectas*, vol. 10, in Juan Tusquets et al., *La dictadura masónica en España y en el mundo* (Barcelona: Editorial Vilamala, 1934) pp. 98–113.
30. Juan Tusquets, 'Intervención de la masonería en la crisis política actual', in Juan Tusquets et al., *Secretos de la política española* (Barcelona: Editorial Vilamala, 1934) pp. 7–15.
31. Joaquín Guiu, 'Muerte cristiana de Don Francisco Macià', in Tusquets et al., *Secretos*, pp. 16–19.
32. 'Desmintiendo una patraña a propósito de Rizal', in Tusquets et al., *Secretos*, pp. 20–172.
33. 'Relación de los talleres dependientes del Grande Oriente Español', in Tusquets et al., *Secretos*, pp. 173–82.
34. Ignasi Riera, *Los catalanes de Franco* (Barcelona: Plaza y Janés, 1998) pp. 126–7.
35. Declaración de Carolina Barderi Solé a la Causa General, Provincia de Barcelona, 21 May 1942, Archivo Histórico Nacional (Pieza segunda de Barcelona. Del Alzamiento Nacional. Antecedentes, Ejército Rojo y Liberación), FC-Causa

General, leg. 1630, exp. 1, p. 485; Declaración del testigo Firmo Casanova y de Vallés a la Causa General, Provincia de Barcelona, 8 June 1942, Archivo Histórico Nacional (Pieza segunda de Barcelona. Del Alzamiento Nacional. Antecedentes, Ejército Rojo y Liberación), FC-Causa General, leg. 1630, exp. 1, p. 507; José Fernando Mota Muñoz, '"Precursores de la unificación": el España Club y el voluntariado español, una experiencia unitaria de la extrema derecha barcelonesa (1935–1936)', *Historia y Política*, 28, 2012, pp. 284, 300; Carlos Píriz González, 'En campo enemigo: la Quinta Columna en la Guerra Civil española (c. 1936–1941)', doctoral thesis, Universidad de Salamanca, 2019, pp. 105–6.

36. Declaración del testigo Juan Aguasca Bonmati a la Causa General, 2 December 1940, Archivo Histórico Nacional (Pieza segunda de Barcelona. Del Alzamiento Nacional. Antecedentes, Ejército Rojo y Liberación), FC-Causa General, leg. 1630, exp. 1, pp. 9–25; Declaración del testigo Renato Llanas de Niubó a la Causa General, 17 March 1942, Archivo Histórico Nacional (Pieza segunda de Barcelona. Del Alzamiento Nacional. Antecedentes, Ejército Rojo y Liberación), FC-Causa General, leg. 1630, exp. 1, pp. 437–8.

37. Ramón Serrano Suñer, 'Prólogo', Tusquets, *Masones y pacifistas*, p. 7.

38. Declaración del testigo Juan Segura Nieto a la Causa General, 5 May 1941, Archivo Histórico Nacional, (Pieza segunda de Barcelona. Del Alzamiento Nacional. Antecedentes, Ejército Rojo y Liberación), FC-Causa General, leg. 1630, exp. 1, pp. 165–6.

39. Tusquets, *Orígenes*, pp. 51–7, 95–6, 122–6, 170, 177, 207–15. On the compilation of lists, see Declaración de Firmo Casanova y de Vallés a la Causa General, pp. 506–8.

40. Maria Thomas, 'The Front Line of Albion's Perfidy. Inputs into the Making of British Policy towards Spain: The Racism and Snobbery of Norman King', *International Journal of Iberian Studies*, vol. 20, no. 2, 2007, pp. 105–27; Josep Puigsech Farràs, 'Lecturas e interpretaciones del ciclo huelguístico en Cataluña. El consulado británico en Barcelona, 1931–1933', *Historia Contemporánea*, Vol.70, 2022, pp. 787–819.

41. Declaración del testigo Bartolomé Gali Colli a la Causa General, Provincia de Barcelona, 28 October 1941, Archivo Histórico Nacional (Pieza segunda de Barcelona. Del Alzamiento Nacional. Antecedentes, Ejército Rojo y Liberación), FC-Causa General, leg. 1630, exp. 1, pp. 307–13.

42. Declaración de Carolina Barderi Solé a la Causa General, pp. 484–6; Declaración del testigo Ramón Tubau Coma a la Causa General, Provincia de Barcelona, 2 June 1942, Archivo Histórico Nacional (Pieza segunda de Barcelona. Del Alzamiento Nacional. Antecedentes, Ejército Rojo y Liberación), FC-Causa General, leg. 1630, exp. 1, pp. 495–9.

43. Declaración de Ramón Tubau Coma, pp. 495–6.

44. Jordi Albertí, *El silencí de les campanes. De l'anticlericalisme del segle XIX a la persecució religiosa durant la guerra civil a Catalunya* (Barcelona: Proa, 2007) p. 337; Josep M. Solé i Sabaté and Joan Villarroya i Font, *La repressió a la reraguardia de Catalunya (1936–1939)*, 2 vols (Barcelona:

Publicacions de l'Abadia de Montserrat, 1989) II, p. 536.

45. Declaración de Firmo Casanova, pp. 507–8; Declaración de Carolina Barderi Solé, Causa General, p. 485; Declaración de Ramón Tubau Coma, pp. 498–9.

46. Tusquets, *Masones y pacifistas*, pp. 99–100.

47. Mora, 'Joan Tusquets', p. 237; Riera, *Los catalanes de Franco*, pp. 126–7, 274; Canal, 'Las campañas antisectarias de Juan Tusquets', pp. 1207–8.

48. Albert Manent i Segimon, *De 1936 a 1975. Estudis sobre la guerra civil i el franquisme* (Barcelona: Publicacions de l'Abadia de Montserrat, 1999) pp. 88–9; Subirà, *Capellans*, pp. 25–7; Mora, 'Joan Tusquets', pp. 236–7.

49. Archivo Gomá, *Documentos de la guerra civil*, vol. 1: *Julio–diciembre 1936*, ed. José Andrés-Gallego and Antón M. Pazos (Madrid: Consejo Superior de Investigaciones Científicas, 2001) pp. 216–20, 488; *Documentos de la guerra civil*, vol. 3: *Febrero de 1937* (Madrid: Consejo Superior de Investigaciones Científicas, 2002) pp. 55–6, 217–18; *Documentos de la guerra civil*, vol. 4: *Marzo de 1937* (Madrid: Consejo Superior de Investigaciones Científicas, 2002) pp. 212–13.

50. Antonio Pérez de Olaguer, *Lágrimas y sonrisas* (Burgos: Ediciones Antisectarias, 1938) pp. 107–11, 127–31.

51. As he put it himself, 'La meva popularitat va a repercutir entre el militars i la gent que preparava el cop d'Estat. De manera que quan aconsegueixo fugir a l'Espanya nacional, sóc rebut amb entusiasme' ('My popularity registered with the army officers and civilians who were preparing the coup d'état. So much so that when I managed to flee to nationalist Spain, I was received

with enthusiasm'). Interviews with Mora, 'Joan Tusquets', p. 237 and Bonada, *Avui*, 28 February 1990.

52. Expediente 1736, Expediente personal de Julián Mauricio Carlavilla del Barrio, Archivo General del Ministerio de Interior, doc. 238, 4 March 1947, doc. 272; Maximiano García Venero, *Falange en la guerra de España. La Unificación y Hedilla* (Paris: Ruedo Ibérico, 1967) pp. 309, 343.

53. Canal, 'Las campañas antisectarias de Juan Tusquets', pp. 1208–9.

54. Juan Tusquets, *Masones y pacifistas*, p. 257.

55. Tusquets, 'Escrito sobre la Instrucción religiosa en la enseñanza oficial', 20 October 1936, Archivo Gomá, *Documentos* 1, pp. 216–17; Gomá to Tusquets, 15 February 1937, Archivo Gomá, *Documentos* 3, pp. 217–18; Tusquets's interviews with Lluís Bonada, *Avui*, 28 February 1990; with Subirà, *Capellans*, pp. 15–16; Ramón Garriga, *La Señora de El Pardo* (Barcelona: Editorial Planeta, 1979) p. 182; Archivo Gomá, *Documentos* 1, p. 336.

56. Subirà, *Capellans*, p. 32.

57. Pérez de Olaguer, *Lágrimas y sonrisas*, pp. 67–8.

58. On Tusquets's role in the SIM, see Domínguez Arribas, *El enemigo judeo-masónico*, pp. 248–50. In the autumn of 1938, Tusquets referred to 'mi buen amigo el comandante Palau' in a letter to Gomá, José Andrés-Gallego, *¿Fascismo o Estado católico? Ideología, religión y censura en la España de Franco, 1937–1941* (Madrid: Ediciones Encuentro, 1997) p. 176. He also admitted his familiarity with the material collected by the SIM, Tusquets, *Masones y pacifistas*, p. 218.

59. Testimony of Ramón Serrano Suñer to the author; García Venero,

Falange, p. 343; Ramón Garriga, *El Cardenal Segura y el Nacional-Catolicismo* (Barcelona: Editorial Planeta, 1977) p. 200; Subirà, *Capellans*, p. 32; José Antonio Ferrer Benimeli, *El contubernio judeo-masónico-comunista*, pp. 191–7; Canal, 'Las campañas antisectarias de Juan Tusquets', pp. 1207–8.

60. Gomá to Pacelli, 8 April 1937, Archivo Gomá, *Documentos de la guerra civil*, vol. 5: *Abril–Mayo de 1937*, ed. José Andrés-Gallego and Antón M. Pazos (Madrid: Consejo Superior de Investigaciones Científicas, 2003) pp. 81–3.

61. Tusquets, *Masones y pacifistas*, p. 258.

62. Subirà, *Capellans*, p. 32; Tusquets to Gomá, 17 February 1937, Archivo Gomá, *Documentos de la guerra civil* 3, pp. 247–8; Hilari Raguer, *La pólvora y el incienso. La Iglesia católica y la guerra civil española (1936–1939)* (Barcelona: Ediciones Península, 2001) pp. 207–8; Joan Maria Thomàs, *Falange, guerra civil, franquisme. F.E.T. y de las J.O.N.S. de Barcelona en els primers anys de règim franquista* (Barcelona: Publicacions de l'Abadia de Montserrat, 1992) p. 465.

63. Subirà, *Capellans*, p. 32.

64. Eduardo Connolly de Pernas, 'El padre Tusquets: olvidando el pasado', *Hibris*, no. 35, 2006, pp. 19–35; Domínguez Arribas, *El enemigo judeo-masónico*, pp. 524–5.

65. Josep Massot i Muntaner, *Església i societat a la Catalunya contemporània* (Barcelona: Publicacions de l'Abadia de Montserrat, 2003) pp. 459–60; Ana Martínez Rus, 'La represión cultural: libros destruidos, bibliotecas depuradas y lecturas vigiladas', in Julio Arostegui (ed.),

Franco. La represión como sistema (Barcelona: Flor del Viento, 2012) pp. 402–3.

66. 'La revolución española y sus fuerzas ocultas. Los Judios'; 'Espiritu demagógico de Israel', *Domingo* (San Sebastián), 14, 21 March 1937, quoted by Josep Benet, *L'intent franquista de genocidi cultural contra Catalunya* (Barcelona: Publicacions de l'Abadia de Montserrat, 1995) p. 115; Borja de Riquer, 'Els catalans de Burgos', *Arreu* (Barcelona), no. 5, November 1976; Domínguez Arribas, *El enemigo judeo-masónico*, pp. 268–70.

67. Domínguez Arribas, *El enemigo judeo-masónico*, pp. 260–2, 266–7; Ramón Serrano Suñer, 'Prólogo', Tusquets, *Masones y pacifistas*, pp. 5–10.

68. Domínguez Arribas, *El enemigo judeo-masónico*, p. 242.

69. *Ibid.*, p. 243.

70. Antonio Pérez de Olaguer, 'La masonería y el doctor Tusquets', *La Unión* (Seville), 21 November 1936, p. 16; Pérez de Olaguer, *Lágrimas y sonrisas*, pp. 109–11.

71. Antonio Ruiz Vilaplana, *Doy fe … un año de actuación en la España nacionalista* (Paris: Éditions Imprimerie Coopérative Étoile, n.d. [1938]) pp. 193–5; Tusquets, *Masones y pacifistas*, p. 99.

72. Juan Tusquets, *La Francmasonería, crimen de lesa patria* (Burgos: Ediciones Antisectarias, 1936) pp. 3–4, 7–8, 13, 19, 23–9, 41–5.

73. Juan Tusquets, *Masonería y separatismo* (Burgos: Ediciones Antisectarias, 1937) p. 8.

74. *Ibid.*, pp. 20–1; Tusquets, *Masonería y pacifismo*, p. 183.

75. Tusquets, *Masonería y separatismo*, pp. 35–47, 62–6; Massot, *Església i societat*, p. 460; Tusquets, *Masones y pacifistas*, 104–6.

76. Borja de Riquer i Permanyer, 'Joan Ventosa i Calvell, l'home de la Lliga Catalana a Burgos. Les relacions dels catalanistes conservadors amb els militars rebels durant la Guerra Civil', *Segle XX. Revista Catalana d'Història*, no. 5, 2021, pp. 37–61.

77. I am indebted to Dr Francesc Borja de Riquer who gave me a copy of the letter, the original of which derives from the Fons Borràs, of the Biblioteca de Catalunya.

78. Juan José Morales Ruiz, *El discurso antimasónico en la guerra civil española, 1936–1939* (Zaragoza: Diputación General de Aragón, 2001) pp. 335–7; Dominguez Arribas, *El enemigo judeo-masónico*, p. 244.

79. Ruiz Vilaplana, *Doy fe*, pp. 193–5.

80. Josep Cruanyes, *Els papers de Salamanca. L'espoliació del patrimoni documental de Catalunya* (Barcelona: Edicions 62, 2003) pp. 42–7; Santiago López García and Severiano Delgado Cruz, 'Víctimas y Nuevo Estado, 1936–1940', in Ricardo Robledo (ed.), *Historia de Salamanca*, vol. V: *Siglo Veinte* (Salamanca: Centro de Estudios Salmantinos, 2001) p. 263.

81. Jaime del Burgo, *Conspiración y guerra civil* (Madrid: Editorial Alfaguara, 1970) pp. 260, 552, 631, 703–6; Ramón Serrano Suñer, *Entre el silencio y la propaganda, la historia como fue. Memorias* (Barcelona: Editorial Planeta, 1977) p. 34; Pedro Sainz Rodríguez, *Testimonio y recuerdos* (Barcelona: Editorial Planeta, 1978) pp. 329–30.

82. Cruanyes, *Els papers*, pp. 15–16, 47–56; López García and Severiano Delgado Cruz, 'Víctimas y Nuevo Estado', p. 264.

83. Ulibarri to Tusquets, 10, 17 May, Tusquets to Ulibarri, 11, 18 May, Ulibarri to Jefe Provincial de Falange de Toledo, 28 June 1938, Archivo General de la Guerra Civil, Masonería A, 792/11. See also Domínguez Arribas, *El enemigo judeo-masónico*, pp. 250–6; Cruanyes, *Els papers*, pp. 234–5.

84. Tusquets, *Masones y pacifistas*, p. 100.

85. *Ibid.*, pp. 45, 48–9.

86. *Ibid.*, pp. 19, 21–2, 87–92.

87. *Ibid.*, pp. 87–90, 224–5.

88. *Ibid.*, pp. 94–8, 120.

89. Martínez Rus, 'La represión cultural', pp. 377–82.

90. Cruanyes, *Els papers*, pp. 29–36, 218–35; Domínguez Arribas, *El enemigo judeo-masónico*, pp. 252–3.

91. Sainz Rodríguez, *Testimonio y recuerdos*, p. 387.

92. Herbert R. Southworth, *El mito de la cruzada de Franco*, ed. Paul Preston (Barcelona: Random House Mondadori, 2008) pp. 108–12; Ramón Serrano Suñer, *Siete discursos* (Bilbao: Ediciones Fe, 1938) pp. 54–7; Raguer, *La pólvora y el incienso*, pp. 285–7; Tusquets, *Masones y pacifistas*, pp. 100–1.

93. Borja de Riquer i Permanyer, *L'últim Cambó (1936–1947). La dreta catalanista davant la guerra civil i el franquisme* (Barcelona: Eumo Editorial, 1996) p. 122.

94. Hilari Raguer, *Escrits dispersos d'història* (Barcelona: Institut d'Estudis Catalans, 2018) pp. 188–9; Andrés-Gallego, *¿Fascismo o Estado católico?*, pp. 134, 161; Archivo Gomá, *Documentos de la guerra civil*, vol. 9: *Enero–marzo de 1938* (Madrid: Consejo Superior de Investigaciones Científicas, 2006) pp. 302–3, 309–10, 374.

95. Mora, 'Joan Tusquets', p. 239.

96. Tusquets, *Masones y pacifistas*, p. 257; Mora, 'Joan Tusquets', pp. 238–9; Riera, *Los catalanes de Franco*, p. 127; Canal, 'Las campañas antisectarias de Juan Tusquets', pp. 1208–9.

97. Stohrer to Wilhelmstrasse, 19 October 1938, *Documents on German Foreign Policy*, Series D, vol. III (London: HMSO, 1951) pp. 772–3; Raguer, *La Unió Democràtica*, p. 463; Tusquets, *Masones y pacifistas*, pp. 188–90.

98. Mora, 'Joan Tusquets', pp. 238–9; Riera, *Los catalanes de Franco*, p. 127; Canal, 'Las campañas antisectarias de Juan Tusquets', pp. 1208–9.

99. Interviews with Bonada, *Avui*, 28 February 1990, with Mora, 'Joan Tusquets', p. 239, with Subirà, *Capellans*, p. 36.

100. Borja de Riquer, 'Els catalans de Burgos', *Arreu* (Barcelona), no. 5, 22–28 November 1976, p. 46; María Luisa Rodríguez Aisa, *El Cardenal Gomá y la guerra de España. Aspectos de la gestión pública del Primado, 1936–1939* (Madrid: Consejo Superior de Investigaciones Científicas, 1981) pp. 186–8, 496–514; Domínguez Arribas, *El enemigo judeo-masónico*, pp. 279–81.

101. Tusquets Guillén, *Habíamos ganado la guerra*, pp. 153–6, 158–61; Mora, 'Joan Tusquets', p. 234.

102. Arxiu Vidal i Barraquer, *Esglesia i Estat*, II, pp. 386, 638, 644–6, III, p. 935; Subirà, *Capellans*, p. 21.

103. Subirà, *Capellans*, pp. 31–2; Tusquets, *Masones y pacifistas*, p. 274.

104. Subirà, *Capellans*, p. 25 (Dachau), 30–1 (Franco), 32–3 (Catalanism); interview with Bonada, *Avui*, 28 February 1990; interview with Mora, 'Joan Tusquets', p. 234; with Canal, 'Las campañas antisectarias de Juan Tusquets', p. 1213.

105. On his success in this regard, see Ramona Valls and Conrad Vilanou, 'Joan Tusquets (1901–1998). Intel·lectual i pensador comparatista', *Revista Catalana de Teología*, vol. XXVII, no. 1 (2002) pp. 107–22.

Chapter 4: The Poet: José María Pemán

1. José Manuel Caballero Bonald, 'A propósito de un caballero', and José María de Areilza, 'Un gran señor jerezano', both in *El País*, 21 July 1981. See also Alberto Reig Tapia, *La Cruzada de 1936. Mitos y memoria* (Madrid: Alianza Editorial, 2006) pp. 244–6.

2. *El País*, 20 May 1981.

3. Javier Tusell and Gonzalo Álvarez Chillida, *Pemán. Un trayecto intelectual desde la extrema derecha hasta la democracia* (Barcelona: Editorial Planeta, 1998) p. 8.

4. Reig Tapia, *La Cruzada de 1936*, pp. 236–87.

5. José María Pemán, *Apuntes autobiográficos. Confesión general y otros* (Madrid: Edibesa, 1998) pp. 23–5, 40–2; Gonzalo Álvarez Chillida, *José María Pemán. Pensamiento y trayectoria de un monárquico (1897–1941)* (Cadiz: Universidad de Cádiz Servicio de Publicaciones, 1996) pp. 17–18, 189–90.

6. *ABC* (Madrid), 28 January 1925; Álvarez Chillida, *Pemán. Pensamiento y trayectoria*, p. 21.

7. Pemán, *Apuntes autobiográficos*, pp. 52–3, 65.

8. Eduardo Ortega y Gasset, *España encadenada. La verdad sobre la dictadura* (Paris: Juan Dura, 1925) pp. 295–8; Álvarez Chillida, *Pemán. Pensamiento y trayectoria*, pp. 22–9.

9. José María Pemán, *El hecho y la idea de la Unión Patriótica* (Madrid: Imprenta Artística Sáez Hermanos, 1929) pp. 28–9, 105, 308–9; Alejandro Quiroga, *Making Spaniards: Primo de Rivera and the Nationalization of the Masses, 1923–1930* (London: Palgrave Macmillan, 2007) pp. 58–60; Julio Gil

Pecharromán, *Conservadores subversivos. La derecha autoritaria alfonsina (1913–1936)* (Madrid: Eudema, 1994) pp. 49–53.

10. Quiroga, *Making Spaniards*, pp. 165–71.

11. Alfonso Bullón de Mendoza y Gómez de Valugera, *José Calvo Sotelo* (Barcelona: Ariel, 2004) pp. 215–16.

12. Pemán, *El hecho y la idea*, pp. 235–55, 390–4.

13. José María Pemán, Prólogo, *El Pensamiento de Primo de Rivera. Sus notas, artículos y discursos* (Madrid: Ediciones de la Junta de Propaganda Patriótica y Ciudadana, 1929).

14. Tusell and Álvarez Chillida, *Pemán*, pp. 19–21.

15. *Unión Monárquica*, 15 November 1929, pp. 28–30.

16. Pemán, *El hecho y la idea*, pp. 253–5.

17. *ABC* (Madrid), 2 August 1927.

18. José María Pemán, *Mis almuerzos con gente importante* (Barcelona: Dopesa, 1970) pp. 89–90; Bullón de Mendoza, *Calvo Sotelo*, p. 228.

19. Pemán, *El hecho y la idea*, pp. 110–11.

20. Pemán, *Mis almuerzos*, pp. 41–55.

21. Eduardo Aunós, *Primo de Rivera. Soldado y gobernante* (Madrid: Editorial Alhambra, 1944) pp. 219–25.

22. *ABC* (Seville), 18 March 1930.

23. José María Pemán, *Obras completas*, vol. V: *Doctrina y oratoria* (Madrid: Escelicer, 1953) pp. 173–6.

24. Eugenio Vegas Latapie, *Escritos políticos* (Madrid: Cultura Española, 1940) p. 8; speech by Quintanar in the Ritz Hotel, Madrid, 24 April 1932, *Acción Española*, no. 10, 1 May 1932; Paul Preston, 'Alfonsist Monarchism and the Coming of the Spanish Civil War', *Journal of Contemporary History*, vol. 7, nos.

3/4, 1972, p. 90; José Calvo Sotelo, *Mis servicios al estado. Seis años de gestión. Apuntes para la historia* (Madrid: Imprenta Clásica Española, 1931) pp. 370–3; Gil Pecharromán, *Conservadores subversivos*, pp. 67–74.

25. Álvarez Chillida, *Pemán. Pensamiento y trayectoria*, pp. 34–5.

26. *ABC* (Seville), 31 October 1930.

27. Shlomo Ben Ami, 'The Forerunners of Spanish Fascism: Unión Patriótica and Unión Monárquica', *European Studies Review*, vol. 9, no. 1, 1979, pp. 49–79, esp. pp. 61–3.

28. Shlomo Ben Ami, *The Origins of the Second Republic in Spain* (Oxford: Oxford University Press, 1978) pp. 183–5; Eugenio Vegas Latapie, *Memorias políticas. El suicido de la monarquía y la segunda República* (Barcelona: Editorial Planeta, 1983) pp. 89–90; Álvarez Chillida, *Pemán. Pensamiento y trayectoria*, pp. 36–9.

29. José María Pemán, *Mis encuentros con Franco* (Barcelona: Dopesa, 1976) pp. 11–20.

30. *ABC* (Madrid), 5 July, 9 December 1930.

31. *ABC* (Seville), 8 March 1931; Diego Caro Cancela, *La Segunda República en Cádiz. Elecciones y partidos políticos* (Cádiz: Diputación Provincial de Cádiz, 1987) pp. 59–61; Álvarez Chillida, *Pemán. Pensamiento y trayectoria*, pp. 40–8; Bullón de Mendoza, *Calvo Sotelo*, pp. 250–5, 266, 270, 274–5.

32. Pemán, *Doctrina*, p. 196.

33. Preston, 'Alfonsist Monarchism', pp. 90–1; Vegas Latapie, *Memorias políticas*, pp. 88–9, 121–6.

34. Eugenio Vegas Latapie, *El pensamiento político de Calvo Sotelo* (Madrid: Cultura Española, 1941) pp. 88–92; Pemán, *Doctrina*, pp. 265–6; Vegas Latapie, *Escritos políticos*, pp. 9–12; Eugenio Vegas Latapie, *La frustración en la*

Victoria. Memorias políticas, 1938–1942 (Madrid: Editorial Actas, 1995) pp. 239–40; 'Maeztu y Acción Española', *ABC* (Madrid), 2 November 1952.

35. Raúl Morodo, *Orígenes ideológicos del franquismo. Acción Española* (Madrid: Alianza Editorial, 1985) pp. 31–9.

36. Álvarez Chillida, *Pemán. Pensamiento y trayectoria*, pp. 55–9.

37. *ABC* (Madrid), 20 February, 19 April 1932; *Acción Española*, no. 6, 1 March 1932.

38. *Ellas. Semanario de Mujeres Españolas*, no. 1, 29 May 1932, p. 5.

39. 'El socialismo, aliado del judaísmo', *Ellas*, no. 47, 16 April; 'Traidores que venden a su patria. Ante la invasión de los judíos', no. 53, 28 May; 'Socialismo, comunismo, judaísmo', no. 58, 2 July 1933; Álvarez Chillida, *Pemán. Pensamiento y trayectoria*, pp. 64, 351.

40. Vegas Latapie, *Memorias políticas*, pp. 136, 144–6; José María Pemán, 'Carta a mi amigo de Gibraltar', *ABC* (Madrid), 13 January 1959; José María Pemán, *Un soldado en la historia. Vida del capitán general Varela* (Cadiz: Escelicer, 1954) pp. 109–22; Gil Pecharromán, *Conservadores subversivos*, pp. 108–13; Pedro Carlos González Cuevas, *Acción Española. Teología política y nacionalismo autoritario en España (1913–1936)* (Madrid: Editorial Tecnos, 1998) pp. 164–72.

41. González Cuevas, *Acción Española*, pp. 172–5.

42. *Ellas. Semanario de Mujeres Españolas*, no. 18, 25 September, pp. 1–2, 8–9, no. 24, 6 November, pp. 1–2, 10, no. 26, 20 November, pp. 1–2, no. 29, 11 December 1932, pp. 2–3.

43. *Ellas. Semanario de Mujeres Españolas*, no. 6, 3 July, p. 1, no. 8, 17 July 1932, p. 1.

44. Pemán, *Doctrina*, pp. 206–8.

45. *ABC* (Madrid), 12, 24 January 1933.

46. *ABC* (Madrid), 24 February 1933; Martin Blinkhorn, *Carlism and Crisis in Spain, 1931–1939* (Cambridge: Cambridge University Press, 1975) pp. 108–11; Joaquín Arrarás, *Historia de la segunda República española* [henceforth *HSRE*], 4 vols (Madrid: Editora Nacional, 1956–68) II, pp. 154–63; Gil Pecharromán, *Conservadores subversivos*, pp. 130–1.

47. *Ellas. Semanario de Mujeres Españolas*, no. 42, 12 March 1933; Blinkhorn, *Carlism*, pp. 156–9.

48. *Acción Española*, no. 37, 16 September 1933, p. 83.

49. Arrarás, *HSRE*, II, p. 264; Vegas Latapie, *Memorias políticas*, pp. 185–6; Álvarez Chillida, *Pemán. Pensamiento y trayectoria*, pp. 65–8.

50. *ABC* (Madrid), 14, 21 November, 15 December 1933; *Blanco y Negro*, 19 November 1933; Pemán, *Apuntes autobiográficos*, pp. 65–6; Gil Pecharromán, *Conservadores subversivos*, p. 144; Caro Cancela, *La segunda República en Cádiz*, pp. 134, 151–2, 161–4, 173–80, 186; Arrarás, *HSRE*, II, p. 280.

51. José María Pemán, 'Situación de paso, no de turno', *Acción Española*, no. 43, 16 December 1933, p. 669.

52. Dionisio Ridruejo, *Casi unas memorias* (Barcelona: Editorial Planeta, 1976) pp. 202–3; Ramón Serrano Suñer, *Entre el silencio y la propaganda, la historia como fue. Memorias* (Barcelona: Editorial Planeta, 1977) pp. 85–6.

53. Álvarez Chillida, *Pemán. Pensamiento y trayectoria*, pp. 71–6; Gil Pecharromán, *Conservadores subversivos*, pp. 197–208.

54. 'Hay que conquistar el Estado', José Calvo Sotelo, *La voz de un perseguido*, vol. 1 (Madrid: Librería de San Martín, 1933) pp. 313–17;

Pemán, 'Prólogo', José Calvo Sotelo, *La voz de un perseguido*, vol. 2 (Madrid: Librería de San Martín, 1934) pp. xi–xv; Bullón de Mendoza, *Calvo Sotelo*, pp. 348–50.

55. José María Pemán, 'Cartas a un escéptico en materia de formas de gobierno', *Acción Española*, no. 58–9, 1 August, pp. 385–93; no. 62–3, 1 October, pp. 25–33; no. 64–5, 1 November, pp. 231–40; no. 66–7, 1 December 1934, pp. 470–9; no. 70, 1 February, pp. 233–45; no. 72–3, March, pp. 417–27; no. 74, 1 April, pp. 22–35; no. 75, May 1935, pp. 275–94; Vegas Latapie, *Memorias políticas*, p. 229.

56. 'Cartas', I, *Acción Española*, no. 58–9, 1 August 1934, pp. 386–7, 391.

57. 'Cartas', II, *Acción Española*, no. 62–3, 1 October 1934, p. 28; 'Cartas', III, *Acción Española*, no. 64–5, 1 November 1934, p. 233.

58. 'Cartas', IV, *Acción Española*, no. 66–7, 1 December 1934, p. 477.

59. 'Cartas', V, *Acción Española*, no. 70, 1 February 1935, pp. 237–8, 243.

60. 'Cartas', VI, *Acción Española*, no. 72–3, March 1935, pp. 417, 421, 427.

61. 'Cartas', VII, *Acción Española*, no. 74, April 1935, pp. 22–3, 34–5.

62. 'Cartas', VIII, *Acción Española*, no. 75, May 1935, pp. 287–8.

63. Arrarás, *HSRE*, II, pp. 361–3.

64. Pemán, *Apuntes autobiográficos*, pp. 68–71; Arrarás, *HSRE*, II, pp. 391, 410.

65. Pemán, *Apuntes autobiográficos*, p. 66.

66. *ABC* (Madrid), 31 July 1936; Pemán, *Varela*, pp. 140–3; Arrarás, *HSRE*, IV, pp. 350–1.

67. José María Pemán, 'Calvo Sotelo, precursor del movimiento nacional', in *La vida y la obra de José Calvo Sotelo. Homenaje de la Real Academia de Jurisprudencia y Legislación a su presidente perpetuo José Calvo Sotelo que ofrendó su vida por Dios y por España el 13 de Julio de 1936* (Madrid: Imprenta de Galo Sáez, 1942) pp. 258–9 (of 255–72).

68. *ABC* (Seville), 23 October 1936.

69. The mistake is in Pemán, *Mis almuerzos*, pp. 89–92.

70. *Diario de las sesiones de Cortes, Congreso de los Diputados, comenzaron el 16 de marzo de 1936*, 4 vols (Madrid: Sucesores de Rivadeneyra, 1936) 16 June 1936. For a blatant statement of the alleged threat, see Luis Suárez Fernández, *Francisco Franco y su tiempo*, 8 vols (Madrid: Fundación Nacional Francisco Franco, 1984) II, p. 36.

71. *ABC* (Seville), 29 September 1936.

72. Pemán, *Doctrina*, pp. 1723–4.

73. José María Pemán, *Arengas y crónicas de guerra* (Cadiz: Establecimientos Cerón, 1937) pp. 11–13.

74. *ABC* (Seville), 28 July 1936. He repeated the ideas in speeches on Radio Jerez on 12 August and on Radio Club Portugués on 29 August, *Ideal* (Granada), 13, 30 August 1936.

75. *ABC* (Seville), 16 August 1936; a slightly different versión in Pemán, *Arengas*, pp. 17–24.

76. Pemán, 'La hora del deber', *ABC* (Seville), 19 August 1936.

77. Paul Preston, *The Spanish Holocaust: Inquisition and Extermination in Twentieth-Century Spain* (London: Harper Press, 2012) Chapter 5.

78. *ABC* (Seville), 30 October 1936.

79. Eugenio Vegas Latapie, *Los caminos del desengaño. Memorias políticas 2, 1936–1938* (Madrid: Editorial Tebas, 1987) p. 69; *Diario de Jerez*, 20 March 2011; Vegas Latapie, *La frustración*, p. 45.

80. Arcángel Bedmar González, *República, guerra y represión. Lucena, 1931–1939*, 2nd edn (Lucena: Ayuntamiento de Lucena, 2010) p. 143; *Ideal* (Granada), 26 August 1936; Pemán, *Arengas*, pp. 25–33.

81. Pemán, *Mis encuentros con Franco*, pp. 47–56, 89.

82. Pemán, *Mis almuerzos*, pp. 152–3; Georges Bernanos, *Les Grands Cimitières sous la lune* (Paris: Plon, 1938).

83. *ABC* (Seville), 21 December 1937.

84. Ian Gibson, *El asesinato de García Lorca* (Barcelona: Ediciones B, 2018) pp. 255–6.

85. Marta Osorio, *Miedo, olvido y fantasía. Agustín Penón. Crónica de su investigación sobre Federico García Lorca (1955–1956)* (Granada: Editorial Comares, 2001) pp. 668–9; Ian Gibson, *El hombre que detuvo a García Lorca. Ramón Ruiz Alonso y la muerte del poeta* (Madrid: Aguilar, 2007) p. 174; Eduardo Molina Fajardo, *Los últimos días de García Lorca* (Barcelona: Plaza y Janés, 1983) pp. 192–5; Gabriel Pozo, *Lorca, el último paseo. Laves para entender el asesinato del poeta* (Granada: Almed, 2009) pp. 138–9.

86. Pemán, 'García Lorca', *ABC* (Madrid), 12 December 1948; Álvarez Chillida, *Pemán. Pensamiento y trayectoria*, p. 89.

87. Pemán to Molina Fajardo, 24 April 1969, in Molina Fajardo, *Los últimos días*, pp. 387–8.

88. Vegas Latapie, *Los caminos*, pp. 71–5; Federico Sopeña, *Vida y obra de Manuel de Falla* (Madrid: Turner, 1988) pp. 195–7; Gonzalo Redondo, *Historia de la Iglesia en España, 1931–1939*, vol. II: *La guerra civil (1936–1939)* (Madrid: Ediciones Rialp, 1993) II, p. 158. Pemán, *Mis encuentros con Franco*,

p. 126 on his need to prepare his conversations.

89. Álvarez Chillida, *Pemán. Pensamiento y trayectoria*, pp. 86–7, 99–100; Pemán, *Mis encuentros con Franco*, pp. 98–100.

90. Álvarez Chillida, *Pemán. Pensamiento y trayectoria*, pp. 387–8.

91. Pemán, *Mis encuentros con Franco*, pp. 142–5. On the 'Leones de Rota', see Fernando Romero Romero, 'Víctimas de la represión en la Sierra de Cádiz durante la guerra civil (1936–1939)', *Almajar* (Villamartín), no. 2, 2005, pp. 209–40; Fernando Romero Romero, 'Falangistas, héroes y matones. Fernando Zamacola y los Leones de Rota', *Cuadernos para el Diálogo*, no. 33, September 2008, pp. 32–8; Carlos Castillo del Pino, *Casa del Olivo. Autobiografía (1949–2003)* (Barcelona: Tusquets, 2004) pp. 372–3.

92. Arcadi Espada, 'José María Pemán y su redentora', *El Mundo*, 22 November 2015.

93. *ABC* (Madrid), 5 December 1948.

94. Pemán, *Arengas*, pp. 36–8; Reig Tapia, *La Cruzada de 1936*, pp. 118–19, 197–8.

95. *ABC* (Seville), 23, 24 October 1936.

96. *ABC* (Seville), 6 November 1936.

97. *ABC* (Seville), 9 September 1936.

98. Pemán, *Arengas*, p. 71.

99. Vegas Latapie, *Los caminos*, pp. 74, 92, 184.

100. *ABC* (Seville), 9 January, 6 July, 2 November 1937.

101. Jorge Villarín, *Guerra en España contra el judaísmo bolchevique* (Cadiz: Establecimientos Cerón, 1937) pp. 30–3.

102. *ABC* (Seville), 12 March 1937; Pemán, *Apuntes autobiográficos*, p. 104.

103. *ABC* (Seville), 16 October, 7 November 1936, 18, 31 July 1937;

Pemán, *Doctrina*, p. 1725; José María Pemán, *De la entrada en Madrid, historia de tres días (27, 28 y 29 de marzo)* (Cadiz: Ediciones 'Verba', 1939) p. 6.

104. *ABC* (Seville), 8 March (premiere of *De ellos es el mundo*), 16 January, 17 April, 14 July, 10 September 1938; *Boletín Oficial del Estado*, 21 April 1938.

105. Vegas Latapie, *Los caminos*, pp. 92–4, 98–102; Redondo, *Historia de la Iglesia*, pp. 145–51; Álvarez Chillida, *Pemán. Pensamiento y trayectoria*, pp. 89–90; Pemán, *Mis almuerzos*, p. 13.

106. Pemán, *Doctrina*, pp. 1731–2; José Ignacio Escobar, *Así empezó* (Madrid: G. del Toro, 1974) pp. 169–73; Jaume Claret Miranda, *El atroz desmoche. La destrucción de la Universidad española por el franquismo, 1936–1945)* (Barcelona: Editorial Crítica, 2006) pp. 36–7; Redondo, *Historia de la Iglesia*, II, pp. 147–9; Francisco Serrat Bonastre, *Salamanca, 1936. Memorias del primer 'ministro' de Asuntos Exteriores de Franco* (Barcelona: Editorial Crítica, 2014) p. 56; Alicia Alted Vigil, *Política del Nuevo Estado sobre el patrimonio cultural y la educación durante la guerra civil española* (Madrid: Dirección General de Bellas Artes y Archivos, 1984) p. 32.

107. *ABC* (Madrid), 2 June 1946.

108. Boletín Oficial del Estado, 10 December 1936; Vegas Latapie, *Los caminos*, p. 104; Redondo, *Historia de la Iglesia*, II, p. 149; Francisco Morente Valero, 'La depuración franquista del magisterio público. Un estado de la cuestión', *Hispania*, vol. 61, no. 208, 2001, p. 671.

109. Vegas Latapie, *Los caminos*, pp. 104–5; Francisco Morente Valero, *La depuración del magisterio nacional (1936–1943). La escuela y*

el *Estado Nuevo* (Valladolid: Ámbito Alarife, 1997) pp. 102, 222.

110. Claret Miranda, *El atroz desmoche*, pp. 36, 40, 63–4; Morente Valero, *La depuración del magisterio*, pp. 226–8; Tusell and Álvarez Chillida, *Pemán*, pp. 49–53.

111. *ABC* (Seville), 19 March 1937.

112. *El Adelanto de Salamanca*, 13 October 1936; *ABC* (Seville), 13 October 1936; Luciano González Egido, *Agonizar en Salamanca. Unamuno julio–diciembre 1936* (Madrid: Alianza Editorial, 1986) p. 135.

113. *ABC* (Madrid), 27 January 1937; Severiano Delgado Cruz, *Arqueología de un mito. El acto del 12 de octubre de 1936 en el Paraninfo de la Universidad de Salamanca* (Madrid: Silex, 2019) pp. 203–7; Luis Moure Mariño, *La generación del 36. Memorias de Salamanca y Burgos* (Sada-A Coruña: Ediciós do Castro, 1989) pp. 75–83; Carlos Rojas, *¡Muera la inteligencia! ¡Viva la muerte! Salamanca, 1936. Unamuno y Millán Astray frente a frente* (Barcelona: Editorial Planeta, 1995) p. 138. It is not the case, as is suggested by Francisco Vigueras Roldán, *Los 'paseados' con Lorca. El maestro cojo y los banderilleros* (Seville: Comunicación Social, 2007) p. 105, that Pemán's remark was made in relation to the murder of Federico García Lorca.

114. José María Pemán, 'La verdad de aquel día', ABC (Madrid), 26 November 1962.

115. *ABC* (Seville), 14 October 1936; Moure Mariño, *La generación del 36*, p. 82.

116. See, for example, Boletín Oficial del Estado, 28 October, 21 November 1936.

117. Morente Valero, *La depuración del magisterio*, pp. 200–1; Wenceslao

Álvarez Oblanca, *La represión de postguerra en León. Depuración de la enseñanza (1936–1943)* (León: Santiago García Editor, 1986) p. 122; J. Crespo Redondo et al., *Purga de maestros en la guerra civil. La depuración del magisterio nacional en la provincia de Burgos* (Valladolid: Ámbito Alarife, 1987) p. 74; Julián Casanova, 'Rebelión y revolución', in Santos Juliá (ed.), *Víctimas de la guerra civil* (Madrid: Temas de Hoy, 1999) p. 95.

118. Vegas Latapie, *Los caminos*, p. 106.
119. *ABC* (Seville), 4 May 1937.
120. Tusell, *Franco en la guerra civil*, pp. 150–1.
121. *ABC* (Seville), 16 December 1936.
122. *ABC* (Seville), 22 January 1937.
123. Álvarez Chillida, *Pemán. Pensamiento y trayectoria*, p. 12.
124. *ABC* (Seville), 13 December 1936, 1, 2, 5 January 1937; Herbert R. Southworth, *El mito de la cruzada de Franco*, ed. Paul Preston (Barcelona: Random House Mondadori, 2008) p. 257.
125. Pemán, *Arengas*, pp. 87, 94–5.
126. Pemán, 'Historia de mi camisa y mi vejez', *ABC* (Madrid), 3 January 1967.
127. Vegas Latapie, *Los caminos*, pp. 69–70.
128. Aniceto de Castro Albarrán, *Guerra santa. El sentido católico del movimiento nacional español* (Burgos: Editorial Española, 1938) pp. 138–9; Vegas Latapie, *Los caminos*, pp. 254–7; Maximiano García Venero, *Historia de la unificación (Falange y Requeté en 1937)* (Madrid: Agesa, 1970) p. 216.
129. Blinkhorn, *Carlism*, p. 285; Tusell and Álvarez Chillida, *Pemán*, pp. 59–60.
130. José María Pemán, *Poema de la bestia y el ángel* (Zaragoza: Ediciones Jerarquía, 1938). The references here are to the post-war

edition of August 1939, *Poema de la bestia y el ángel* (Madrid: Ediciones Españolas, 1939).
131. Tusell, *Franco en la guerra civil*, p. 166.
132. Pemán, *Poema*, pp. 29, 47, 49.
133. *Ibid.*, p. 98; Gonzalo Álvarez Chillida, *El antisemitismo en España. La imagen del judío (1812–2002)* (Madrid: Marcial Pons, 2002) pp. 358–9; Michael Seidman, *The Victorious Counterrevolution: The Nationalist Effort in the Spanish Civil War* (Madison: University of Wisconsin Press, 2011) pp. 194, 207.
134. Pemán, *Poema*, p. 67.
135. *Ibid.*, p. 114.
136. Tusell and Álvarez Chillida, *Pemán*, pp. 58, 263.
137. José María Pemán, *La historia de España contada con sencillez*, 2 vols (Cadiz: Establecimientos Cerón y Librería Cervantes, 1939) I, pp. 225–6; Tusell and Álvarez Chillida, *Pemán*, pp. 57–8.
138. Pemán, *Poema*, pp. 69, 71. The idea of Spain as 'la piel de toro' (a bull's skin) derives from an observation of the Greek geographer Strabo.
139. Pemán, *Poema*, p. 118.
140. See, for example, Gumersindo Montes Agudo, *Pepe Sainz. Una vida en la Falange* (Barcelona: Ediciones Pal-las de Horta, 1939) p. 93.
141. Pemán, *Mis almuerzos*, p. 138.
142. *ABC* (Seville), 5, 11 June 1938.
143. A photograph of Pemán and Millán Astray presiding over the rally, *ABC* (Seville), 4 June, 'Esto os traigo de la fuente misma', 7 June 1938. On the signed portrait, Álvarez Chillida, *Pemán. Pensamiento y trayectoria*, p. 112.
144. Pemán, *Poema*, p. 92.
145. *ABC* (Seville), 20 July 1938.
146. Vegas Latapie, *La frustración*, pp. 61–75, 97–8, 139–40; Tusell, *Franco en la guerra civil*, p. 285.

147. Pemán, 'Historia de mi camisa y mi vejez', *ABC* (Madrid), 3 January 1967.

148. *ABC* (Seville), 27 January 1939; see the photograph of Pemán, in Falangist uniform, Pemán, *Mis encuentros con Franco*, p. 247.

149. Álvarez Chillida, *Pemán. Pensamiento y trayectoria*, pp. 391–2.

150. Pemán, 'Historia de mi camisa y mi vejez', *ABC* (Madrid), 3 January 1967.

151. Pemán, *La historia de España*, I, pp. 68–73, 100–1, 184, 225–6.

152. *Ibid.*, pp. 212, 224–9.

153. *Ibid.*, II, pp. 84, 113, 144–9, 160–1, 193, 206.

154. *Ibid.*, pp. 168–70.

155. Pemán, *Mis encuentros con Franco*, pp. 47–8.

156. Pemán, *De la entrada en Madrid*, pp. 5–7, 15, 22, 24.

157. Pemán, *Mis almuerzos*, pp. 179–83.

158. *ABC* (Seville), 2 April, 16, 18 July 1939.

159. José María Pemán, *Crónicas de antes y después del diluvio* (Valladolid: Imprenta Castellana, 1939) pp. 146, 149, 216, 227, 230–1.

160. José María Pemán, 'Semblanza del Caudillo Franco', *Ejército*, no. 1, 1940.

161. *ABC* (Madrid), 10 December 1936.

162. Pemán, *Mis encuentros con Franco*, p. 108.

163. On the petrol scam, see *La Voz de Galicia*, 8 February 1940; *La Vanguardia Española*, 21 January, 8 February 1940; Charles Foltz Jr, *The Masquerade in Spain* (Boston: Houghton Mifflin, 1948) pp. 258–60; Juan Antonio Ansaldo, *¿Para qué …? de Alfonso XIII a Juan III* (Buenos Aires: Editorial Vasca-Ekin, 1951) pp. 254–6; José Larraz, *Memorias* (Madrid: Real Academia de Ciencias Morales y Políticas, 2006) pp. 248–9; Ignacio

Martínez de Pisón, *Filek. El estafador que engañó a Franco* (Barcelona: Seix Barral, 2018) pp. 141–99.

164. Pemán, *Mis encuentros con Franco*, p. 104.

165. José María Pemán, 'Calvo Sotelo, Precursor del Movimiento Nacional', in Academia de Jurisprudencia, *La vida y la obra de José Calvo Sotelo, Homenaje*, pp. 255–72.

166. Miguel Primo de Rivera to Pemán, 14 July 1940, reprinted in Vegas Latapie, *La frustración*, Letter of 14 July 1940, pp. 207–11.

167. Pemán, 'Calvo Sotelo, Precursor', pp. 269–70; Manuel Halcón, 'Pemán, su impavidez', *ABC* (Seville), 3 November 1967; Pemán, *Mis almuerzos*, pp. 237–47; Vegas Latapie, *Los caminos*, p. 282; Pemán, *Mis encuentros con Franco*, pp. 111–13, 123, 131, 133.

168. Pemán, *Apuntes autobiográficos*, pp. 126–31; letters between Pemán and Primo de Rivera are reprinted in Vegas Latapie, *La frustración*, pp. 212–13.

169. Vegas Latapie, *La frustración*, pp. 213–14; Álvarez Chillida, *Pemán. Pensamiento y trayectoria*, pp. 124–6.

170. Vegas Latapie, *La frustración*, pp. 260–3.

171. *Ibid.*, pp. 226–7, 394; Luis María Anson, *Don Juan* (Barcelona: Plaza y Janés, 1994) p. 325.

172. Tusell and Álvarez Chillida, *Pemán*, pp. 73–6, 82–5.

173. Javier Tusell, *Franco y los católicos. La política interior española entre 1945 y 1957* (Madrid: Alianza Editorial, 1984) p. 118.

174. Xavier Tusell, *La oposición democrática al franquismo, 1939–1962* (Barcelona: Editorial Planeta, 1977) pp. 112–16; Tusell and Álvarez Chillida, *Pemán*, pp. 85–8.

175. Anson, *Don Juan*, pp. 42–5, 59–68, 224, 325–6, 339–54, 375–6, 391–4; José María Toquero, *Franco y Don Juan. La oposición monárquica al franquismo* (Barcelona: Plaza y Janés/Cambio 16, 1989) pp. 252–435; Pedro Sainz Rodríguez, *Un reinado en la sombra* (Barcelona: Editorial Planeta, 1981) pp. 79–80, 83–5, 101–2; Tusell and Álvarez Chillida, *Pemán*, pp. 88–96, 107–12, 126–34.

176. Tusell, *Franco y los católicos*, pp. 111–12.

177. *Ibid.*, p. 331.

178. Tusell and Álvarez Chillida, *Pemán*, p. 135.

179. 'El catalan. Un vaso de agua clara', *ABC* (Madrid), 17 April 1970; Josep Andreu i Abelló, '1970: la campaña en defensa del catalán', *El País*, 16 June 1976.

180. *Unión Monárquica*, 15 November 1929, p. 30.

181. Pemán, *Mis encuentros con Franco*, pp. 43, 47–8; Reig Tapia, *La Cruzada de 1936*, pp. 252–3.

182. Anson, *Don Juan*, p. 60.

183. Francisco Franco Salgado-Araujo, *Mis conversaciones privadas con Franco* (Barcelona: Editorial Planeta, 1976) pp. 208, 335, 356, 477–8, 490–1.

184. Cristóbal Orellana and José García Cabrera, 'Calle José María Pemán, en Jerez, como si tal cosa', *La Voz del Sur*, 20 December 2020.

Chapter 5: The Messenger: Gonzalo de Aguiler

1. Peter Kemp, *Mine Were of Trouble* (London: Cassell, 1957) p. 50; Luis Arias González, *Gonzalo de Aguilera Munro, XI Conde de Alba de Yeltes (1886–1965). Vidas y radicalismo de un hidalgo heterodoxo* (Salamanca: Ediciones Universidad de Salamanca, 2013) pp. 128–9.

2. I am indebted to Ricardo Robledo, who drew my attention to the events in the Dehesa de Continos and provided me with information from the Asociación de Memoria Histórica de Salamanca. See also *La Crónica de Salamanca*, 4 October 2015.

3. Aguilera to Magdalena, 5 August and 2 October 1936, CAY, 1, 96, 2 and 5; Arias González, *Gonzalo de Aguilera*, pp. 139–40.

4. *La Mañana* (Jaen), 16 January 1934.

5. *La Mañana* (Jaen), 1 October 1932, 21, 27 January, 3, 18 February, 5 April 1933; *El Adelanto* (Salamanca), 19 October 1932; *Región* (Cáceres), 24 February 1933; *El Obrero de la Tierra*, 14 January, 4 March 1933, 6, 13, 20 January, 17 February 1934; *El Socialista*, 21 January, 20 April, 1 July 1933. See also Paul Preston, *The Coming of the Spanish Civil War: Reform, Reaction and Revolution in the Second Spanish Republic, 1931–1936*, 2nd edn (London: Routledge, 1994) pp. 101–2, 111, 134–5, 140, 148–9, 184–5.

6. Preston, *The Coming of the Spanish Civil War*, pp. 147–53, 245, 259–60; Paul Preston, 'The Agrarian War in the South', in Paul Preston (ed.), *Revolution and War in Spain, 1931–1939* (London: Methuen, 1984) pp. 159–81.

7. Alfonso Lazo, *Retrato de fascismo rural en Sevilla* (Seville: Universidad de Sevilla, 1998) pp. 11–14.

8. Manuel Sánchez del Arco, *El sur de España en la reconquista de Madrid (diario de operaciones glosado por un testigo)*, 2nd edn (Seville: Editorial Sevillana, 1937) pp. 18–20.

9. Edmond Taylor, 'Assignment in Hell', in Frank C. Hanighen (ed.), *Nothing but Danger* (New York: National Travel Club, 1939) p. 65.

10. John Whitaker, 'Prelude to World War. A Witness from Spain', *Foreign Affairs*, vol. 21, no. 1, October 1942–July 1943, p. 107.
11. Taylor, 'Assignment in Hell', pp. 64–5.
12. Francisco Gonzálbez Ruiz, *Yo he creído en Franco. Proceso de una gran desilusión (Dos meses en la cárcel de Sevilla)* (Paris: Imprimerie Coopérative Étoile, 1937) p. 147.
13. Webb Miller, *I Found No Peace* (London: The Book Club, 1937) p. 344.
14. Whitaker, 'Prelude to World War', p. 107.
15. Charles Foltz Jr, *The Masquerade in Spain* (Boston: Houghton Mifflin, 1948) p. 116.
16. Francis McCullagh, *In Franco's Spain* (London: Burns, Oates & Washbourne, 1937) pp. 104–7.
17. Noel Monks, *Eyewitness* (London: Frederick Muller, 1955) p. 73.
18. McCullagh, *In Franco's Spain*, pp. 104–29; Arthur Koestler, *Spanish Testament* (London: Victor Gollancz, 1937) p. 220; Monks, *Eyewitness*, pp. 80–2.
19. Koestler, *Spanish Testament*, pp. 223–31; Arthur Koestler, *The Invisible Writing*, 2nd edn (London: Hutchinson, 1969) pp. 413–20, 427; Sir Peter Chalmers Mitchell, *My House in Málaga* (London: Faber & Faber, 1938) pp. 269–89; Luis Bolín, *Spain: The Vital Years* (Philadelphia: J. B. Lippincott, 1967) pp. 247–9.
20. Marqués Merry del Val to Victor Cazalet, 12 April 1937, Victor Cazalet papers, MS 917/1/4/13, Eton College Archives, reproduced by permission of the Provost and Fellows of Eton College.
21. Virginia Cowles, *Looking for Trouble* (London: Hamish Hamilton, 1941) pp. 90–4; Harold G. Cardozo, *The March of a Nation: My Year of Spain's Civil War* (London: The Right Book Club, 1937) p. 301.
22. Although he is mentioned by several correspondents, only Virginia Cowles seemed to know his Christian name, which she gave as Ignacio: Cowles, *Looking for Trouble*, p. 70. He does not figure in the *Anuario Militar 1936*, pp. 323, 399. It is possible that the Rosales who acted as a press officer had taken retirement on full pay under the Azaña reforms of 1931 or, like Bolín, simply been given the honorary rank of captain.
23. Cowles, *Looking for Trouble*, p. 70.
24. Frances Davis, *My Shadow in the Sun* (New York: Carrick & Evans, 1940) p. 136.
25. Michael Richards, *A Time of Silence: Civil War and the Culture of Repression in Franco's Spain, 1936–1945* (Cambridge: Cambridge University Press, 1998) p. 18; Juan Carlos Losada Malvárez, *Ideología del Ejército franquista, 1939–1959* (Madrid: Ediciones Istmo, 1990) pp. 28–30.
26. Gonzalo de Aguilera, Conde de Alba de Yeltes, *Cartas a un sobrino* (n.p., n.d.) pp. 72–84.
27. Francisco Franco Bahamonde, *Palabras del Caudillo 19 abril 1937–31 diciembre 1938* (Barcelona: Ediciones Fe, 1939) p. 261.
28. Whitaker, 'Prelude to World War', p. 108.
29. *Ibid.*, p. 108.
30. Aguilera to Inés Luna, 30 November 1909, 9 February, 6 June 1910, Archivo Histórico Provincial de Salamanca, Fondo Luna Terrero, Ines Luna-Gonzalo de Aguilera, Correspondencia 1909 (henceforth AHPS, FLT).
31. Aguilera to Inés Luna, 19 November 1909, AHPS, FLT; Arias González, *Gonzalo de Aguilera*, pp. 32–41.
32. Letter from Father F. J. Turner SJ, Stonyhurst College Archivist, to the author, 19 May 1999; Arnold Lunn,

Spanish Rehearsal (London: Hutchinson, 1937) p. 70.

33. Letter from Father Turner to the author.

34. Aguilera, *Cartas a un sobrino*, p. 28; Arias González, *Gonzalo de Aguilera*, pp. 47–55; Aguilera to Inés Luna, 13 December 1909, AHPS, FLT.

35. Juan Ximénez Embún and Angel González Palencia, *Catálogo alfabético de los documentos referentes a títulos del Reino y Grandezas de España conservados en la sección de Consejos Suprimidos* (Madrid: Patronato Nacional de Archivos Históricos, 1951) pp. 36–7, 51; J. Atienza, *Nobiliario español. Diccionario heráldico de apellidos españoles y títulos nobiliarios*, 3rd edn (Madrid: Aguilar, 1959) p. 790. Curiously, Gonzalo referred to himself variously as sixteenth and seventeenth count.

36. Kemp, *Mine Were of Trouble*, p. 49; Lunn, *Spanish Rehearsal*, pp. 42, 50.

37. Aguilera to Inés Luna, 5, 20, 22 May, 3 June, 19 June, 28, 30 September, 18 October, 4, 28 November, 8, 12 December 1909, 21 January, 12, 19 February 1910, AHPS, FLT.

38. Hoja de servicios de Gonzalo Aguilera y Munro, Archivo General Militar de Segovia (AGMS, secc. 1ª, leg. A–407). The information on his father's attitude based on the testimony to the author, 30 July 1999, of the Cronista de la Ciudad de Salamanca, Dr Salvador Llopis Llopis. See also Arias González, *Gonzalo de Aguilera*, pp. 55–68.

39. Arias González, *Gonzalo de Aguilera*, pp. 70–5.

40. Aguilera, *Cartas a un sobrino*, p. 101.

41. *La Gaceta Regional*, 30 August 1964.

42. Hoja de servicios de Gonzalo Aguilera y Munro, Archivo General Militar de Segovia; *Archivo General Militar de Segovia: índice de expedientes personales* (Madrid: Ediciones Hidalguía, 1959) I, p. 57.

43. Ministerio de la Guerra, Sección Personal, 21 November 1932, leg. 416, Gonzalo Aguilera Munro, Archivo General Militar de Segovia. On the military reforms, see Michael Alpert, *La reforma militar de Azaña (1931–1933)* (Madrid: Siglo XXI, 1982) pp. 133–49.

44. Interview, 30 July 1999, with Dr Salvador Llopis Llopis. Inés Luna died in Barcelona in 1953.

45. Arias González, *Gonzalo de Aguilera*, p. 6.

46. On Martín Veloz, see Javier Infante, 'Sables y naipes: Diego Martín Veloz (1875–1938). De cómo un matón de casino se convirtió en caudillo rural', in Ricardo Robledo (ed.), *Esta salvaje pesadilla. Salamanca en la guerra civil española* (Barcelona: Editorial Crítica, 2007) pp. 264–79, 425, 428; José Venegas, *Andanzas y recuerdos de España* (Montevideo: Feria del Libro, 1943) pp. 74–85; Indalecio Prieto, *De mi vida. Recuerdos, estampas, siluetas, sombras …*, 2 vols (Mexico City: Ediciones Oasis, 1965) pp. 181–92; L. Santiago Díez Cano and Pedro Carasa Soto, 'Caciques, dinero y favores. La restauración en Salamanca', in Ricardo Robledo (ed.), *Historia de Salamanca*, vol. V: *Siglo Veinte* (Salamanca: Centro de Estudios Salmantinos, 2001) pp. 143–4.

47. Aguilera to Inés Luna, 19 April 1909, AHPS, FLT; Salvador Llopis Llopis, *La prócer dama doña Inés Luna Terrero, sus predecesores y familiares cercanos* (Salamanca: Autor, 2000) pp. 221–6.

48. Aguilera to Inés Luna, 22 April, 1 July 1909, AHPS, FLT.

49. Aguilera to Inés Luna, 24 August, 7 September 1909, AHPS, FLT; Llopis Llopis, *La prócer dama*, p. 227.

50. Aguilera to Inés Luna, 9, 11, 12, 14, 18, 19 September 1909, AHPS, FLT.

51. Aguilera to Inés Luna, 30 September 1909, AHPS, FLT.

52. Aguilera to Inés Luna, 3, 6, 8 October 1909, AHPS, FLT.

53. Llopis Llopis, *La prócer dama*, p. 233.

54. Aguilera to Inés Luna, 16, 20 October 1909, AHPS, FLT.

55. Copy of letter provided by Salvador Llopis Llopis. See also Llopis Llopis, *La prócer dama*, pp. 233–4.

56. Aguilera to Inés Luna, 23 October 1909, AHPS, FLT.

57. Aguilera to Inés Luna, 26 October 1909, AHPS, FLT.

58. Aguilera to Inés Luna, 26, 27 October 1909, AHPS, FLT.

59. Aguilera to Inés Luna, 6, 10, 14, 30 November 1909, AHPS, FLT.

60. Aguilera to Inés Luna, 12 December 1909, AHPS, FLT.

61. Aguilera to Inés Luna, 22 January 1910, AHPS, FLT.

62. Aguilera to Inés Luna, 26 January 1910, AHPS, FLT.

63. Aguilera to Inés Luna, 9, 15 February, 4, 5 March, 16, 24 June 1910, Inés Luna to Aguilera, 5 March 1910, AHPS, FLT; Llopis Llopis, *La prócer dama*, p. 237.

64. Aguilera to Inés Luna, 8 February 1911, AHPS, FLT.

65. Aguilera to Inés Luna, 24 March 1911, AHPS, FLT; Llopis Llopis, *La prócer dama*, pp. 237–8.

66. Aguilera to Inés Luna, 7 May, 13 June 1913, AHPS, FLT.

67. Llopis Llopis, *La prócer dama*, pp. 250–4. Salvador Llopis Llopis had access to the later part of the correspondence between Gonzalo and Inés. For whatever reason, they are not in the Inés Luna collection in the Archivo Histórico Provincial de Salamanca.

68. Paul Preston, *A People Betrayed: A History of Corruption, Political Incompetence and Social Division in Modern Spain, 1874–2018* (London: William Collins, 2020) pp. 206, 210.

69. Llopis Llopis, *La prócer dama*, pp. 228–9.

70. Llopis Llopis testimony, 30 July 1999. On Magdalena and her family, see Arias González, *Gonzalo de Aguilera*, pp. 79–91. On Inés, 'De burguesa excéntrica a amante de Primo de Rivera', *El País*, 19 April 2008. On the wealth of her family, see Ricardo Robledo and Santiago Diez Cano, 'La derrota del rentista. Historia económica y política del caso de Luna Terrero (1855–1955)', in S. De Dios and Eugenia Torijano (eds), *Escritos de Historia. Estudios en homenaje al Prof. Javier Infante* (Salamanca: Ediciones Universidad de Salamanca, 2019) pp. 147–70.

71. Aguilera, *Cartas a un sobrino*, p. 167.

72. Arias González, *Gonzalo de Aguilera*, pp. 106–11.

73. Juan de la Cierva to Aguilera, 3 October 1935 (Archivo de la Universidad de Salamanca, Conde de Alba de Yeltes – henceforth AUSA, CAY – 1, 24); Bolín to Aguilera, 28 January 1937 (AUSA, CAY, 1, 80); Arias González, *Gonzalo de Aguilera*, pp. 123–40.

74. Arias González, *Gonzalo de Aguilera*, pp. 124–6; Estado Mayor Central, *Anuario Militar de España 1936* (Madrid: Ministerio de la Guerra, 1936) p. 151.

75. Aguilera to Ada Munro, 19 July 1936, AUSA, CAY, 1, 101, 1; Informe sobre el Capitán de Caballería retirado, D. Gonzalo de Aguilera Munro, 2 December 1937, Ministerio de la Guerra, Sección Personal, leg. 416, Gonzalo Aguilera Munro, Archivo General Militar de Segovia (henceforth Informe GAM, leg. 416, AGMS).

76. Severiano Delgado Cruz, *Arqueología de un mito. El acto del 12 de octubre de 1936 en el Paraninfo de la Universidad de Salamanca* (Madrid: Silex, 2019) pp. 69–79; André Salmon, *Souvenirs sans fin* (Paris: Gallimard, 1955) pp. 17–22.

77. Aguilera to Magdalena, 30 July, 5 August 1936, AUSA, CAY, 1, 96, 1 and 2.

78. Aguilera to Magdalena, 13, 16 September 1936, AUSA, CAY, 1, 96, 3 and 4.

79. For example, Aguilera to Magdalena, 16 September 1936, 4, 17 May 1937, AUSA, CAY, 1, 96, 4, 12, 16.

80. Sefton Delmer, *Trail Sinister: An Autobiography* (London: Secker & Warburg, 1961) p. 277; Cardozo, *The March of a Nation*, p. 63.

81. Miller, *I Found No Peace*, pp. 326–7.

82. Davis, *My Shadow*, pp. 98–9.

83. John T. Whitaker, *We Cannot Escape History* (New York: Macmillan, 1943) p. 109.

84. Informe GAM, leg. 416, AGMS; Cardozo, *The March of a Nation*, pp. 78–87. On the battle for Irún see Hugh Thomas, *The Spanish Civil War*, 3rd edn (London: Hamish Hamilton, 1977) pp. 377–9; Coronel José Manuel Martínez Bande, *Nueve meses de guerra en el norte* (Madrid: Editorial San Martín, 1980) pp. 82–4.

85. Geoffrey Cox, *Defence of Madrid* (London: Victor Gollancz, 1937) p. 19.

86. Informe GAM, leg. 416, AGMS. Lunn, *Spanish Rehearsal*, p. 42, recounts a similar incident in which Aguilera's companion was 'a French journalist'. It is entirely possible that the anecdote was about the experience with Strunk but was distorted in being relayed by either Aguilera or Lunn.

87. Frances Davis, *A Fearful Innocence*, (Kent, Ohio: Kent State University Press, 1981) pp. 151–3; H. R. Knickerbocker, *The Siege of the Alcazar* (London: Hutchinson, n.d. [1937]) p. 136; Cardozo, *The March of a Nation*, pp. 284–6; Miller, *I Found No Peace*, p. 322.

88. Davis, *My Shadow*, pp. 130–1, 165, 171. Francis McCullagh, *In Franco's Spain* (London: Burns, Oates & Washbourne, 1937) pp. 111–12, Cardozo, *The March of a Nation*, pp. 220–1.

89. Taylor, 'Assignment in Hell', pp. 64, 67; Miller, *I Found No Peace*, p. 322; Whitaker, 'Prelude to World War', pp. 108–9.

90. Knickerbocker, *The Siege of the Alcazar*, p. 136.

91. *Foreign Journalists under Franco's Terror* (London: United Editorial, 1937) pp. 26–30. Cf. Herbert R. Southworth, *Guernica! Guernica!: A Study of Journalism, Diplomacy, Propaganda, and History* (Berkeley: University of California Press, 1977) pp. 52, 420 n. 62.

92. Whitaker, 'Prelude to World War', p. 109.

93. Cardozo, *The March of a Nation*, pp. 63, 285–6. Cardozo was addressed as 'Major' by the other journalists.

94. See safe conduct issued Salamanca, 23 November 1936, Informe GAM, leg. 416, AGMS; Cardozo, *The March of a Nation*, p. 286.

95. Lunn, *Spanish Rehearsal*, pp. 50–5.

96. *Ibid.*, pp. 46, 62.

97. Whitaker, *We Cannot Escape History*, p. 115.

98. Aguilera to Magdalena, 15 April, 5 May 1937, AUSA, CAY, 1, 96, 10 and 13.

99. Delmer, *Trail Sinister*, p. 278.

100. *Ibid.*, pp. 277–8.

101. Delmer to Aguilera, 8 March, AUSA, CAY, 1, 82. The letter carries

no year. However, since Delmer writes at length about Constancia de la Mora's book *In Place of Splendor: The Autobiography of a Spanish Woman* (New York: Harcourt, Brace, 1939), it is almost certainly 1940.

102. Lunn, *Spanish Rehearsal*, p. 46.

103. Taylor, 'Assignment in Hell', p. 64.

104. Davis, *A Fearful Innocence* , p. 158.

105. Taylor, 'Assignment in Hell', p. 64.

106. Merry del Val to Aguilera, AUSA, CAY, 1, 88, 2. The telegram is undated but Monks was in Madrid only during May, June and July 1937. Monks, *Eyewitness*, pp. 100–6.

107. Lunn to Aguilera, 19 April, 7 September 1937, AUSA, CAY, 1, 86.

108. Lunn, *Spanish Rehearsal*, pp. 70, 75.

109. Gonzalo de Aguilera, Conde de Alba de Yeltes, *El átomo. Sus componentes, energía y medio* (Madrid: Talleres M. Rollán, 1946).

110. Aguilera, *Cartas a un sobrino*. The book was poorly typeset, presumably at Aguilera's own expense, but not published. The copy in the Biblioteca Nacional in Madrid contains the later addition of several typescript pages, pasted in, presumably by Aguilera himself.

111. Kemp, *Mine Were of Trouble*, p. 50.

112. Whitaker, 'Prelude to World War', p. 108; Whitaker, *We Cannot Escape History*, pp. 108–10.

113. Aguilera to Magdalena, 2 October 1936, AUSA, CAY, 1, 96, 5.

114. Aguilera to Magdalena, 15, 23 April, 10 May 1937, AUSA, CAY, 1, 96, 10, 11, 15.

115. Aguilera to Magdalena, 22 June 1937, AUSA, CAY, 1, 96, 18.

116. Informe GAM, leg. 416, AGMS; Cardozo, *The March of a Nation*, pp. 286–301. In civilian life, Lambarri was a designer for *Vogue*, Reynolds and Eleanor Packard, *Balcony Empire : Fascist Italy at War* (New York: Oxford University Press, 1942) p. 54.

117. Aguilera to Magdalena, 22 June 1937, AUSA, CAY, 1, 96, 18.

118. Aguilera to Magdalena, 17 May 1937, AUSA, CAY, 1, 96, 16.

119. Aguilera to Magdalena, 4 May 1937, AUSA, CAY, 1, 96, 12.

120. *The Sphere*, 14 November, p. 265, 12 December 1936, pp. 16–17. *Belfast Telegraph* and *Yorkshire Evening Post*, 9 November 1936.

121. Southworth, *Guernica! Guernica!*, pp. 64–7, 334–5, 337.

122. *Foreign Journalists*, p. 7.

123. Knickerbocker to Aguilera, 28 March 1937, AUSA, CAY, 1, 84.

124. Bowers to Hull, 12 April 1937, *Foreign Relations of the United States 1937*, vol. I (Washington, DC: United States Government Printing Office, 1954) pp. 279–80.

125. Southworth, *Guernica! Guernica!*, pp. 51–2, 419 n. 59.

126. *Ibid.*, pp. 52, 419–20 n. 60.

127. Knickerbocker to Aguilera, 22 August 1937, AUSA, CAY, 1, 84.

128. Arias González, *Gonzalo de Aguilera*, p. 128.

129. Informe GAM, leg. 416, AGMS.

130. Borrador de la solicitud de reingreso en la escala activa del ejército de Gonzalo Aguilera y Munro, AUSA, CAY, 2, 3.

131. Informe GAM, leg. 416, AGMS; Kemp, *Mine Were of Trouble*, pp. 99–101; General Sagardía, *Del Alto Ebro a las Fuentes del Llobregat. Treinta y dos meses de guerra de la 62 División* (Madrid: Editora Nacional, 1940) p. 106.

132. Cowles, *Looking for Trouble*, pp. 86–7.

133. *Ibid.*, p. 90.

134. *Ibid.*, p. 92.

135. *Ibid.*, p. 93.

136. *Ibid.*, pp. 95–9.

137. Kemp, *Mine Were of Trouble*, p. 50.

138. Letter from Cassell & Co. to Herbert R. Southworth, 27 March 1968, and interview of Southworth

with d'Hospital, 14 September 1968; Southworth, *Guernica! Guernica!*, p. 418 nn. 47, 48.

139. Juan Antonio Sacaluga, *La resistencia socialista en Asturias, 1937–1962* (Madrid: Editorial Pablo Iglesias, 1986) pp. 5–6.

140. Cecil Gerahty, *The Road to Madrid* (London: Hutchinson, 1937) p. 35; Arias González, *Gonzalo de Aguilera*, p. 156.

141. Lunn, *Spanish Rehearsal*, pp. 44–6.

142. *Ibid.*, p. 66.

143. Taylor, 'Assignment in Hell', p. 68.

144. McCullagh, *In Franco's Spain*, p. 112.

145. Aguilera to Ada Munro, 18 June, 1, 9 August, 10, 22 September 1939, 8 November 1940, AUSA, CAY, 1, 101.

146. Arias González, *Gonzalo de Aguilera*, pp. 182–99.

147. Bravo to Aguilera, 9 July 1945, 3 February 1946, Aguilera to Bravo, 2 December 1945, AUSA, CAY, 1, 15.

148. They are undated but there are internal references to the international press which make it clear that he was writing until at least 1953, Aguilera, *Cartas a un sobrino*, pp. 110, 123, note to p. 126.

149. *Ibid.*, pp. 1–2.

150. *Ibid.*, p. 6.

151. *Ibid.*, pp. 32, 71, 97.

152. *Ibid.*, pp. 66–8, 114.

153. Aguilera to Inés Luna, 9 September, 19, 20 November, 4, 13 and undated fragment December 1909, AHPS, FLT.

154. Aguilera, *Cartas a un sobrino*, pp. 82–3, 88–9, 92–6.

155. *Ibid.*, p. 91.

156. *Ibid.* The work is informed by anti-clericalism throughout, but see esp. pp. 78–87 and an asterisked note on p. 218.

157. *Ibid.*, pp. 151–76.

158. Arias González, *Gonzalo de Aguilera*, pp. 216–19; Hilari Raguer, *La pólvora y el incienso. La Iglesia y la guerra civil española* (Barcelona: Ediciones Península, 2001) p. 375.

159. Arias González, *Gonzalo de Aguilera*, p. 11.

160. A survey of his contributions to *La Gaceta Regional*, Arias González, *Gonzalo de Aguilera*, pp. 227–31.

161. Aguilera to Inés Luna, 9 September 1909, 8 February 2011, AHPS, FLT; Arturo Ezquerro, 'Captain Aguilera and Filicide: A Group-Analytic Commentary', *Contexts. Group Analytic Society International*, no. 88, Summer 2020, pp. 1–16. See also a fuller account, Arturo Ezquerro, 'Captain Aguilera and Filicide: An Attachment-Based Exploration', *ATTACHMENT: New Directions in Psychotherapy and Relational Psychoanalysis*, vol. 15, December 2021, pp. 279–97.

162. *El Caso*, 5 September 1964.

163. *Ibid.*; Arias González, *Gonzalo de Aguilera*, pp. 209–12.

164. Arias González, *Gonzalo de Aguilera*, pp. 213–16.

165. *Ibid.*, pp. 255–6.

166. *Ibid.*, pp. 207–8.

167. Ezquerro, 'Captain Aguilera and Filicide', p. 11.

168. Informe GAM, leg. 416, AGMS; *El Adelanto* (Salamanca), 29, 30 August, 1 September 1964; *El Caso*, 5 September 1964; *La Gaceta Regional*, 30 August, 1 September 1964; *ABC*, 24 August 1964; Arias González, *Gonzalo de Aguilera*, pp. 258–67.

169. Testimony to the author, 30 July 1999, of the Cronista de la Ciudad de Salamanca, Dr Salvador Llopis Llopis, biographer of Inés Luna Terrero.

170. Interview of Mariano Sanz González with the Director of the Hospital, Dr Desiderio López, 27 October 1999; Arias González, *Gonzalo de Aguilera*, p. 268.

171. Miller, *I Found No Peace*, p. 344.

Chapter 6: The Killer in the North: Emilio Mola

1. Jorge Vigón, *General Mola (el conspirador)* (Barcelona: Editorial AHR, 1957) pp. 15–18; José María Iribarren, *Mola. Datos para una biografía y para la historia del alzamiento nacional* (Zaragoza: Librería General, 1938) pp. 159–64.

2. On his personality, see Guillermo Cabanellas, *La guerra de los mil días. Nacimiento, vida y muerte de la II República española*, 2 vols (Buenos Aires: Grijalbo, 1973) I, p. 303; Carlos Blanco Escolá, *General Mola. El ególatra que provocó la guerra civil* (Madrid: La Esfera de los Libros, 2002) pp. 29–30.

3. José María Iribarren, *Con el general Mola. Escenas y aspectos inéditos de la guerra civil* (Zaragoza: Librería General, 1937) pp. 352–3.

4. *Ibid.*, pp. 129, 191; Iribarren, *Mola. Datos*, pp. 9–10, 150, 178, 243–4, 277–8.

5. Gustau Nerín, *La guerra que vino de África* (Barcelona: Editorial Crítica, 2005) pp. 26–8, 42; Emilio Mola Vidal, *Obras completas* (Valladolid: Librería Santarén, 1940) pp. 971, 1002; José María Gil Robles, *No fue posible la paz* (Barcelona: Ariel, 1968) pp. 728–35.

6. Ino Bernard, *Mola mártir de España* (Granada: Librería Prieto, 1938) pp. 27–8; Vigón, *Mola*, pp. 22–30.

7. Vigón, *Mola*, pp. 33–6.

8. Mola, *Obras*, pp. 195–201.

9. *Ibid.*, pp. 102, 129–30, 137 ('Todo se esperaba de mi acometividad e inteligencia!'), 228 (Larache 'era modelo de disciplina, instrucción y espíritu' which he attributed to 'un jefe enérgico').

10. Blanco Escolá, *General Mola*, p. 51.

11. Vigón, *Mola*, pp. 12–13.

12. Comandante Franco [Ramón], *Madrid bajo las bombas* (Madrid: Zeus S.A. Editorial, 1931) p. 102;

Blanco Escolá, *General Mola*, pp. 61–4.

13. Mola, *Obras*, pp. 297–8; Eduardo González Calleja, *El máuser y el sufragio. Orden público, subversión y violencia política en la crisis de la Restauración (1917–1931)* (Madrid: Consejo Superior de Investigaciones Científicas, 1999) pp. 221, 286–9, 509–11; Blanco Escolá, *General Mola*, pp. 79–81, 187–8.

14. Mola, *Obras*, pp. 240–51, 259–60, 276–7; González Calleja, *El máuser*, pp. 509–11; Juan-Simeón Vidarte, *No queríamos al Rey. Testimonio de un socialista español* (Barcelona: Grijalbo, 1977) pp. 289–90.

15. Juan-Simeón Vidarte, *Todos fuimos culpables* (Mexico City: Fondo de Cultura Económica, 1973) p. 701.

16. Mola, *Obras*, pp. 454–5, 548–9; Franco, *Madrid bajo las bombas*, pp. 171–2; Ramón Garriga, *Ramón Franco, el hermano maldito* (Barcelona: Editorial Planeta, 1978) pp. 186–93, 201–4; Blanco Escolá, *General Mola*, pp. 188–9.

17. Herbert R. Southworth, *El lavado de cerebro de Francisco Franco. Conspiración y guerra civil* (Barcelona: Editorial Crítica, 2000) p. 235; Mola, *Obras*, pp. 308–12; Eduardo González Calleja and Fernando del Rey Reguillo, *La defensa armada contra la revolución. Una historia de las guardias cívicas en la España del siglo XX* (Madrid: Consejo Superior de Investigaciones Científicas, 1995) pp. 226–32.

18. Vigón, *Mola*, pp. 57–8, 63–4; B. Félix Maíz, *Mola, aquel hombre* (Barcelona: Editorial Planeta, 1976) pp. 25–8, 43–4, 84–6, 238; Paul Robinson, *The White Russian Army in Exile, 1920–1941* (Oxford: Clarendon Press, 2002) pp. 174–7, 208–10, 224–5, 236.

19. Iribarren, *Con el general Mola*, p. 242.

20. Mola, *Obras*, pp. 349, 394–5, 408–12, 435; Franco, *Madrid bajo las bombas*, pp. 87, 104–14; Ramón Garriga, *Ramón Franco, el hermano maldito*, pp. 173–8, 182–9; Carmen Díaz, *Mi vida con Ramón Franco* (Barcelona: Editorial Planeta, 1981) pp. 94–153; Gonzalo Queipo de Llano, *El movimiento reivindicativo de Cuatro Vientos* (Madrid: Tipógrafía Yagües, 1933) pp. 54–5, 63–4.

21. Mola, *Obras*, pp. 417–21, 429–35, 471–82, 495–6.

22. José María Azpíroz Pascual and Fernando Elboj Broto, *La sublevación de Jaca* (Zaragoza: Guara Editorial, 1984) pp. 33–40, 81–7; Graco Marsá, *La sublevación de Jaca. Relato de un rebelde*, 2nd edn (Madrid: Zeus S.A. Editorial, 1931) pp. 57–81, 159–89; Mola, *Obras*, pp. 471–5.

23. Ángel Ossorio y Gallardo, *Mis memorias* (Buenos Aires: Losada, 1946) pp. 161–3; Henry Buckley, *Life and Death of the Spanish Republic: A Witness to the Spanish Civil War* (London: Hamish Hamilton, 1940) pp. 29–30; Azpíroz and Elboj, *La sublevación*, pp. 109–17; Julio Alvarez del Vayo, *The Last Optimist* (London: Putnam, 1950) pp. 197–8; Manuel de Burgos y Mazo, *De la República a …?* (Madrid: Javier Morata, 1931) pp. 83–4.

24. Mola, *Obras*, pp. 447, 543; Largo Caballero, *Mis recuerdos*, pp. 111–13; *Diario de sesiones de las Cortes, Congreso de los Diputados. Comenzaron el 8 de diciembre de 1933*, 18 vols (Madrid: Sucesores de Rivadeneyra, 1935) 11 April 1934.

25. Mola, *Obras*, pp. 763–90; Vidarte, *No queríamos al Rey*, pp. 368–70.

26. *Renovación*, 20 April, 10 May 1931; Iribarren, *Mola. Datos*, p. 34; Juan-

Simeón Vidarte, *Las Cortes Constituyentes de 1931–1933* (Barcelona: Grijalbo, 1976) p. 22.

27. Vigón, *Mola*, p. 75.

28. Ramón Serrano Suñer, *Entre el silencio y la propaganda, la historia como fue. Memorias* (Madrid: Editorial Planeta, 1977) p. 214.

29. Emilio Mola Vidal, Hoja de Servicios, Archivo General Militar de Segovia, 1ª3422M, EXP. 0., pp. 53–4; *ABC*, 23 April 1931; Estado Mayor Central, *Anuario Militar de España 1931* (Madrid: Ministerio de Guerra, 1931) p. 224; Mola, *Obras*, pp. 879–80; Iribarren, *Mola. Datos*, pp. 39–40; Manuel Azaña, *Obras completas*, 4 vols (Mexico City: Ediciones Oasis, 1966–8) I, p. 64.

30. *Gaceta de Madrid*, 16 April 1931; Fernando Jesús Hernández Ruiz, 'Angel Galarza Gago (1892–1966), Ministro de Gobernación de la Segunda República Española, del republicanismo radical socialista al socialismo y al exilio', *Revista Europea de Historia de las Ideas Políticas y de las Instituciones Públicas*, no. 9, 2015, pp. 369–94.

31. Vigón, *Mola*, pp. 75–6; Carolyn P. Boyd, 'Responsibilities and the Second Spanish Republic 1931–6', *European History Quarterly*, vol. 14, 1984, pp. 151–82.

32. *ABC*, 29 April, 2 May, 4 July 1931.

33. *Gaceta de Madrid*, 14 May 1931; Mola, Hoja de Servicios, pp. 53–4; *ABC*, 4 July 1931; Estado Mayor Central, *Anuario Militar de España 1931*, p. 224; Mola, *Obras*, pp. 879–80; Iribarren, *Mola. Datos*, pp. 39–40; Azaña, *Obras completas*, I, p. 64.

34. Alfonso Bullón de Mendoza y Gómez de Valugera, *José Calvo Sotelo* (Barcelona: Ariel, 2004) p. 282; Blanco Escolá, *General Mola*, pp. 126–7; Mola, *Obras*, pp. 879–80;

Iribarren, *Mola. Datos*, pp. 39–40; Azaña, *Obras completas*, I, p. 64.

35. Jesús María Palomares Ibáñez, *La guerra civil en la ciudad de Valladolid. Entusiasmo y represión en la 'capital del alzamiento'* (Valladolid: Ayuntamiento de Valladolid, 2001) p. 54.

36. Azaña, *Obras completas*, IV, diary entries, 5, 6 April 1931, pp. 64, 67; Mola, Hoja de Servicios, p. 54.

37. Estado Mayor Central, *Anuario Militar de España 1932* (Madrid: Ministerio de Guerra, 1932) p. 181; *Anuario Militar de España 1933* (Madrid: Ministerio de Guerra, 1933) p. 392; Vigón, *Mola*, pp. 79–80; Iribarren, *Mola. Datos*, pp. 39–40, 180; on Azaña's reforms, see Blanco Escolá, *General Mola*, pp. 115–25; Gabriel Cardona, 'Mola, el general que pudo mandar', *La Aventura de la Historia*, no. 41, p. 46.

38. I am indebted to Fernando Puell for drawing my attention to the decision of the Tribunal Supremo and the decree of 9 March 1932, *Gaceta de Madrid*, 11 March 1932, p. 1767.

39. W. Hooper, *Manual práctico de ajedrez* (Madrid: Librería Bergua, 1933); Iribarren, *Con el general Mola*, p. 292; Iribarren, *Mola. Datos*, pp. 177, 180–1.

40. Decreto No. 61, *Diario Oficial del Ministerio de la Guerra*, 11 March 1932.

41. *Lo que yo supe. Memorias de mi paso por la Dirección General de Seguridad*, written in 1931 but not published until January 1933: Mola, *Obras*, p. 347. Vegas Latapie's review in *Acción Española*, no. 31, 16 June 1933.

42. Mola, *Obras*, pp. 574–5.

43. B. Félix Maíz, *Mola frente a Franco. Guerra y muerte del General Mola* (Pamplona: Laocoonte, 2007) pp. 251–4, 344–5.

44. Iribarren, *Mola. Datos*, p. 186.

45. Mola, *Obras*, pp. 1045–6.

46. *Ibid.*, pp. 1047, 1096, 1101, 1166–7.

47. Blanco Escolá, *General Mola*, pp. 12–13.

48. Mola to Sanjurjo, 12 August, 9 December 1934, quoted in Fernando del Rey, 'Percepciones contrarrevolucionarias. Octubre de 1934 en el epistolario del general Sanjurjo', *Revista de Estudios Políticos (nueva época)*, no. 159, January–March 2013, pp. 85, 102; Mola to Sanjurjo, 12 August, 10 September, 9 December 1934, quoted in Enrique Sacanell Ruiz de Apodaca, *El general Sanjurjo. Héroe y víctima. El militar que pudo evitar la dictadura franquista* (Madrid: La Esfera de los Libros, 2004) pp. 143, 152, 156–7.

49. Maíz, *Mola*, pp. 24–5; Gabriel Cardona, *El poder militar en la España contemporánea hasta la Guerra Civil.* (Madrid: Siglo XXI de España Editores, 1983) p. 224; Francisco Franco Bahamonde, *'Apuntes' personales sobre la República y la guerra civil* (Madrid: Fundación Francisco Franco, 1987) p. 15.

50. Gil Robles, *No fue posible*, pp. 234–62; Carlos Martínez de Campos, *Ayer 1931–1953* (Madrid: Instituto de Estudios Políticos, 1970) p. 32; Iribarren, *Mola. Datos*, p. 44; B. Félix Maíz, *Alzamiento en España. De un diario de la conspiración*, 2nd edn (Pamplona: Editorial Gómez, 1952) pp. 32–3; Eduardo González Calleja, *Contrarrevolucionarios. Radicalización violenta de las derechas durante la Segunda República, 1931–1936* (Madrid: Alianza Editorial, 2011) pp. 290–6; Ricardo de la Cierva, *Francisco Franco. Un siglo de España*, 2 vols

(Madrid: Editora Nacional, 1973) pp. 392–8.

51. Iribarren, *Con el general Mola*, p. 29.

52. Blanco Escolá, *General Mola*, pp. 214–18, 269–71.

53. Fernando del Rey, 'Los papeles de un conspirador. Documentos para la historia de las tramas golpistas de 1936', *Dimensioni e problemi della ricerca storica*, no. 2, 2018, pp. 130–5.

54. Maíz, *Mola*, pp. 62–5, 92, 199, 205; Bullón de Mendoza, *Calvo Sotelo*, p. 659; Cardona, *El poder militar*, pp. 233–4; Blanco Escolá, *General Mola*, p. 220.

55. Gil Robles, *No fue posible*, pp. 719–20; Joaquín Arrarás, *Historia de la Cruzada española*, 8 vols (Madrid: Ediciones Españolas, 1939–43) II, p. 467; Franco, *'Apuntes' personales*, pp. 33–4; Iribarren, *Mola. Datos*, pp. 45–6; Iribarren, *Con el general Mola*, pp. 14–15; Varela to Sanjurjo, undated March 1936, Sacanell, *Sanjurjo*, pp. 30–2.

56. Del Rey, 'Los papeles de un conspirador', pp. 137–46; José María Pemán, *Un soldado en la historia. Vida del Capitán General Varela* (Cadiz: Escelicer, 1954) pp. 140–8; Federico Martínez Roda, *Varela. El general antifascista de Franco* (Madrid: La Esfera de los Libros, 2012) pp. 121–4; José Solchaga, 'Memorias', *Historia*, no. 16, 2000, pp. 22–36; Jaime Ignacio del Burgo, 'Introducción', Maíz, *Mola frente a Franco*, pp. 92–3; Sacanell, *Sanjurjo*, pp. 188–9, 200, 212, 216; Vigón, *Mola*, p. 92.

57. Maíz, *Mola frente a Franco*, p. 514.

58. Cabanellas, *La guerra*, I, p. 334; Maíz, *Mola*, p. 202.

59. On March's direct contacts with the generals, see Nerín, *La guerra*, pp. 132–3.

60. Arturo Dixon, *Señor Monopolio. La asombrosa vida de Juan March* (Barcelona: Editorial Planeta, 1985) p. 134; Luis Romero, *Tres días de julio (18, 19 y 20 de 1936)*, 2nd edn (Barcelona: Ariel, 1968) p. 20; Bernardo Díaz Nosty, *La irresistible ascensión de Juan March* (Madrid: Sedmay Ediciones, 1977) pp. 303–7; Ramón Garriga, *Juan March y su tiempo* (Barcelona: Editorial Planeta, 1976) pp. 373–6.

61. José Ángel Sánchez Asiaín, *La financiación de la guerra civil española. Una aproximación histórica* (Barcelona: Editorial Crítica, 2012) pp. 118–25, 1143–7; Maíz, *Mola*, pp. 230–5.

62. José Martín Blázquez, *I Helped to Build an Army: Civil War Memoirs of a Spanish Staff Officer* (London: Secker & Warburg, 1939) p. 85.

63. Maíz, *Alzamiento*, pp. 23–8, 52–6, 61–3, 67, 82–6, 110, 142–4, 162, 317–29.

64. Rafael García Serrano, *La gran esperanza* (Barcelona: Editorial Planeta, 1983) pp. 202–5; Maíz, *Mola*, pp. 188, 192, 236; Miguel Sánchez-Ostiz, *El Escarmiento* (Pamplona: Pamiela, 2013) pp. 54–5, 135–7.

65. Juan de Iturralde, *La guerra de Franco, los vascos y la Iglesia*, 2 vols (San Sebastián: Publicaciones del Clero Vasco, 1978) I, p. 48; Fernando Puell de la Villa, 'La trama militar de la conspiración', in Francisco Sánchez Pérez (ed.), *Los mitos del 18 de julio* (Barcelona: Editorial Crítica, 2013) pp. 71–7. All of Mola's instructions, except the second one directed to Yagüe, in Sánchez Pérez (ed.), *Los mitos*, pp. 341–67.

66. Cabanellas, *La guerra*, II, p. 845.

67. Mola, *Obras*, pp. 1192, 1195–6.

68. Mola, 'Directivas para Marruecos', in Sánchez Pérez (ed.), *Los mitos*, pp. 364–5.

69. Luis E. Togores, *Yagüe. El General Falangista de Franco* (Madrid: La Esfera de los Libros, 2010) pp. 193–4; Francisco Alía Miranda, *Julio de 1936. Conspiración y alzamiento contra la Segunda República* (Barcelona: Editorial Crítica, 2011) p. 105.

70. Reproduced in Mohammad Ibn Azzuz Hakim, *La actitud de los moros ante el alzamiento. Marruecos, 1936* (Malaga: Editorial Algazara, 1997) pp. 100–2.

71. Iribarren, *Mola. Datos*, pp. 52, 58–62; Juan José Calleja, *Un corazón al rojo* (Barcelona: Editorial Juventud, 1963) pp. 75–7.

72. Iribarren, *Mola. Datos*, p. 53; Vigón, *Mola*, pp. 91–2; Sánchez Pérez (ed.), *Los mitos*, pp. 343–8.

73. Del Rey, 'Los papeles de un conspirador', pp. 146–50; Gabriel Cardona, *Historia militar de una guerra civil. Estrategias y tácticas de la guerra de España* (Barcelona: Flor del Viento, 2006) pp. 38–42; Blanco Escolá, *General Mola*, pp. 247–8; Ángel Viñas, *¿Quién quiso la guerra civil? Historia de una conspiración* (Barcelona: Editorial Crítica, 2019) pp. 183–6.

74. Sánchez Pérez (ed.), *Los mitos*, p. 366.

75. Vigón, *Mola*, p. 95; Sacanell, *Sanjurjo*, pp. 204–5, 216–18.

76. Blanco Escolá, *General Mola*, pp. 246–7; Sánchez-Ostiz, *El Escarmiento*, p. 204; García Serrano, *La gran esperanza*, p. 178.

77. Cabanellas, *La guerra*, I, pp. 314–16, 351–2; Vigón, *Mola*, pp. 104–5; Maíz, *Mola*, pp. 131–3, 143–55, 193–4, 228–9.

78. Puell, 'La trama militar', pp. 358–9; Viñas, *¿Quién quiso la guerra civil?*, pp. 189–90; Iturralde, *La guerra de* Franco, I, p. 354; Sánchez-Ostiz, *El Escarmiento*, p. 154.

79. Pedro Luis Angosto, *José Alonso Mallol. El hombre que pudo evitar la guerra* (Alicante: Instituto de Cultura Juan Gil-Albert, 2010) pp. 199, 212–14; Dolores Ibárruri, *El único camino* (Madrid: Editorial Castalia, 1992) p. 349; Enrique Líster, *Nuestra guerra* (Paris: Colección Ebro, 1966) pp. 30–1.

80. Iribarren, *Mola. Datos*, p. 71.

81. Maíz, *Alzamiento*, pp. 61–2, 67, 73–5; Viñas, *¿Quién quiso la guerra civil?*, p. 55; Juan Antonio Ansaldo, *¿Para qué …? de Alfonso XIII a Juan III* (Buenos Aires: Editorial Vasca-Ekin, 1951) pp. 47–50; Eugenio Vegas Latapie, *Memorias políticas. El suicidio de la monarquía y la segunda República* (Barcelona: Editorial Planeta, 1983) pp. 158, 162; Julio Gil Pecharromán, *Conservadores subversivos. La derecha autoritaria alfonsina (1913–1936)* (Madrid: Eudema, 1994) pp. 264, 269; Vigón, *Mola*, p. 54.

82. Maíz, *Alzamiento*, pp. 201–5; Maíz, *Mola*, pp. 214–19; González Calleja, *Contrarrevolucionarios*, p. 349; Vigón, *Mola*, pp. 93–4; Iribarren, *Mola. Datos*, pp. 55–6.

83. Mariano Ansó, *Yo fui ministro de Negrín* (Barcelona: Editorial Planeta, 1976) pp. 122–3; Carlos Fernández Santander, *Casares Quiroga, una pasión republicana* (Sada-A Coruña: Ediciós do Castro, 2000) pp. 235–40; Cabanellas, *Guerra*, I, pp. 356, 376–80.

84. Iribarren, *Con el general Mola*, p. 17; *Mola. Datos*, p. 65.

85. 'Prólogo', Alfredo Kindelán Duany, *Mis cuadernos de guerra*, 2nd edn (Barcelona: Editorial Planeta, 1982) p. 42.

86. Alfredo Kindelán, *La verdad de mis relaciones con Franco* (Barcelona: Editorial Planeta, 1981) pp. 173–4;

Maíz, *Alzamiento*, pp. 276–8; Vegas Latapie, *Memorias*, p. 276; Serrano Suñer, *Memorias*, pp. 120–1. On Elena Medina, Consuelo Olagüe and Luisa Beloqui, see Vigón, *Mola*, p. 110; José Antonio Vaca de Osma, *La larga guerra de Francisco Franco* (Madrid: Ediciones RIALP, 1991) pp. 110–11; Iribarren, *Mola. Datos*, p. 73; Ansó, *Yo fui ministro de Negrín*, p. 124; Iribarren, *Con el general Mola*, pp. 39, 42; Luis Romero, *Por qué y cómo mataron a Calvo Sotelo* (Barcelona: Editorial Planeta, 1982) pp. 238, 247–8, 264.

87. Hilari Raguer, *El general Batet. Franco contra Batet. Crónica de una venganza* (Barcelona: Ediciones Península, 1996) pp. 220–5; Maíz, *Alzamiento*, pp. 238–40, 247–52; Iribarren, *Con el general Mola*, pp. 50–3, 180–4; Vigón, *Mola*, p. 109; Maíz, *Mola*, pp. 256–9, 302–4; Iribarren, *Mola. Datos*, pp. 90–5.

88. Vigón, *Mola*, p. 100; Emilio Estéban Infantes, *General Sanjurjo (Un laureado en el Penal del Dueso)* (Barcelona: Editorial AHR, 1958) pp. 254–5; Jorge Fernández-Coppel, *General Gavilán. De enlace del general Mola a jefe de la Casa Militar de Franco* (Madrid: La Esfera de los Libros, 2005) p. 51; Maíz, *Mola*, pp. 223–4; Franco, *'Apuntes' personales*, p. 34.

89. Puell, 'La trama militar', p. 361.

90. Iribarren, *Con el general Mola*, pp. 54–5; Maíz, *Alzamiento*, pp. 231–2; Raguer, *Batet*, p. 227.

91. Cabanellas, *La guerra*, I, p. 353; Maíz, *Alzamiento*, pp. 150–1; Antonio Lizarza Iribarren, *Memorias de la conspiración*, 4th edn (Pamplona: Editorial Gómez, 1969) pp. 105–10; Mola's suicidal despair in a manuscript note added by Iribarren to his *Con el general Mola*, p. 53, and in a letter to a friend written by Iribarren in 1965, quoted by Eugenio Vegas Latapie, *Los caminos del desengaño. Memorias políticas 2, 1936–1938* (Madrid: Ediciones Giner, 1987) pp. 416, 515. Iribarren's letter, Vicente Cacho Viu, 'Los escritos de José María Iribarren', *Cuadernos de Historia Moderna y Contemporánea* (Madrid), vol. 5, 1984, pp. 241–2. See also Franco, *'Apuntes' personales*, p. 37.

92. Estéban Infantes, *General Sanjurjo*, pp. 254–5.

93. Iturralde, *La guerra de Franco*, I, pp. 98–104, 121–4; Maíz, *Mola*, p. 259.

94. Viñas, *¿Quién quiso la guerra civil?*, pp. 398–9; Lizarza, *Memorias*, pp. 113–24, 133–9; Manuel Fal Conde, 'Aportación de Gil Robles al alzamiento', *ABC* (Seville), 30 April 1968; Vigón, *Mola*, pp. 101, 107; Cabanellas, *La guerra*, I, pp. 351–3; Gil Robles, *No fue posible*, pp. 728–33; Maíz, *Mola*, pp. 271, 279.

95. Diego Martínez Barrio, *Memorias* (Barcelona: Editorial Planeta, 1983) pp. 358–64; Iturralde, *La guerra de Franco*, I, pp. 168–9; Maíz, *Alzamiento*, p. 304; Iribarren, *Con el general Mola*, pp. 65–6.

96. Mola, *Obras*, p. 1173.

97. Iturralde, *La guerra de Franco*, I, p. 433. See also Hugh Thomas, *The Spanish Civil War*, 3rd edn (London: Hamish Hamilton, 1977) p. 260.

98. Galo Vierge, *Los culpables. Pamplona 1936* (Pamplona: Pamiela, 2009) pp. 66–7; Iribarren, *Mola, Datos*, pp. 99–103; Iribarren, *Con el general Mola*, pp. 56–60; Sánchez-Ostiz, *El Escarmiento*, pp. 181–96.

99. *Le Temps*, 16 August 1936.

100. Julio González Soto, *Esbozo de una síntesis del ideario de Mola en*

relación con el Movimiento Nacional (Burgos: Hijos de Santiago Rodríguez Editores, 1937) p. 53.

101. Fernando Mikelarena Peña, 'La intensidad de la limpieza política franquista en 1936 en la Ribera de Navarra', *Hispania Nova. Revista de Historia Contemporánea*, no. 9, 2009, p. 5; Iturralde, *La guerra de Franco*, I, pp. 447–54.

102. Sánchez-Ostiz, *El Escarmiento*, pp. 54–5, 66, 136–7, 204–5, 261–2, 277–8.

103. Manuscript note, Iribarren, *Con el general Mola*, p. 191.

104. Iribarren, *Con el general Mola*, p. 155.

105. Gil Robles, *No fue posible*, p. 721 n. 62.

106. Iribarren, *Con el general Mola*, pp. 73–6; Cabanellas, *Guerra*, I, p. 631.

107. Iturralde, *La guerra de Franco*, I, pp. 393–4.

108. Reynolds and Eleanor Packard, *Balcony Empire: Fascist Italy at War* (New York: Oxford University Press, 1942) pp. 44–5.

109. *Le Matin*, 24 July 1936; Sefton Delmer, *Trail Sinister: An Autobiography* (London: Secker & Warburg, 1961) pp. 273–4.

110. Antonio Ruiz Vilaplana, *Doy fe … un año de actuación en la España nacionalista* (Paris: Éditions Imprimerie Coopérative Étoile, n.d. [1938]) pp. 56–7.

111. Maíz, *Alzamiento*, pp. 307–11; *Foreign Relations of the United States 1936*, vol. II (Washington, DC: United States Government Printing Office, 1954), p. 449; *ABC* (Seville), 26 July 1936; Iribarren, *Con el general Mola*, pp. 106–7, 122; Vegas Latapie, *Los caminos*, pp. 32–3; Vidarte, *Todos fuimos culpables*, p. 702.

112. Joaquín Pérez Madrigal, *Pérez (vida y trabajo de uno)* (Madrid: Instituto Editorial Reus, 1955) pp. 137–40; Iribarren, *Con el general Mola*, pp. 194–5; Sánchez-Ostiz, *El Escarmiento*, pp. 179–81.

113. Cabanellas, *La guerra*, I, pp. 632–3; Pérez Madrigal, *Pérez*, pp. 149–64. This is confirmed in a 1944 manuscript note added by Iribarren to the copy of *Con el general Mola*, p. 105, given to his friend José María Azcona; Arrarás, *Cruzada*, III, p. 513, IV, p. 218.

114. Josep Fontana, 'Julio de 1936', *Público*, 29 June 2010.

115. García Serrano, *La gran esperanza*, pp. 153–60.

116. Iturralde, *La guerra de Franco*, I, pp. 438–40.

117. Altaffaylla, *Navarra. De la esperanza al terror*, 8th edn (Tafalla: Altaffaylla, 2004) pp. 718–19; Mikelarena Peña, 'La intensidad de la limpieza política', p. 5.

118. Arrarás, *Cruzada*, III, pp. 498–504; Jesús Vicente Aguirre González, *Aquí nunca pasó nada. La Rioja 1936* (Logroño: Editorial Ochoa, 2007) pp. 55, 63, 66–7, 74, 111–13.

119. Patricio Escobal, *Las sacas (Memorias)* (Sada-A Coruña: Edicios do Castro, 2005) pp. 83–6; Antonio Hernández García, *La represión en La Rioja durante la guerra civil*, 3 vols (Logroño: Autor, 1982) I, pp. 47–60, II, pp. 23–130, 141–73, III, pp. 57–63, 101–37; María Cristina Rivero Noval, *La ruptura de la paz civil. Represión en la Rioja (1936–1939)* (Logroño: Instituto de Estudios Riojanos, 1992) pp. 67–79; Carlos Gil Andrés, *Lejos del frente. La guerra civil en la Rioja alta* (Barcelona: Editorial Crítica, 2006) pp. 107, 212–20, 252; Aguirre González, *Aquí nunca pasó nada*, pp. 966–70.

120. Ramón Villares, 'Galicia mártir', in Jesús de Juana and Julio Prada (eds), *Lo que han hecho en Galicia*.

Violencia política, represión y exilio (1936–1939) (Barcelona: Editorial Crítica, 2007) p. viii; Antonio Miguez Macho, *Xenocidio e represión franquista en Galicia. A violencia de retagarda en Galicia na Guerra Civil (1936–1939)* (Santiago de Compostela: Edicións Lóstrego, 2009) pp. 54–9.

121. Carlos Fernández Santander, *Alzamiento y guerra civil en Galicia (1936–1939)*, 2 vols (Sada-A Coruña: Edicós do Castro, 2000) I, pp. 13, 85–101. The most reliable, and regularly updated, figures for the repression from Lourenzo Fernández Prieto et al., *Vítimas da represión en Galicia (1936–1939)* (Santiago de Compostela: Universidade de Santiago/Xunta de Galicia, 2009) pp. 11–23. Regarding Lugo, higher figures have been presented by María Jesús Souto Blanco, 'Golpe de Estado y represión franquista en la provincia de Lugo', in De Juana and Prada (eds), *Lo que han hecho en Galicia*, pp. 90–6.

122. Enrique Berzal de la Rosa (ed.), *Testimonio de voces olvidadas*, 2 vols (León: Fundación 27 de marzo, 2007) I, p. 18, II, pp. 178–9; Ignacio Martín Jiménez, *La guerra civil en Valladolid (1936–1939). Amaneceres ensangrentados* (Valladolid: Ámbito Ediciones, 2000) pp. 199–208; Palomares Ibáñez, *Valladolid*, pp. 145–7. The names of the women shot figure in the lists on pp. 161–85.

123. Martín Blázquez, *I Helped to Build an Army*, pp. 163–4.

124. Arrarás, *Cruzada*, III, pp. 430–1; Santiago López García and Severiano Delgado Cruz, 'Que no se olvide el castigo: la represión en Salamanca durante la guerra civil', in Ricardo Robledo (ed.), *Esta salvaje pesadilla. Salamanca en la guerra civil española* (Barcelona: Editorial Crítica, 2007) pp. 106–7, 110–17.

125. González Soto, *Esbozo*, p. 31.

126. Iribarren, *Con el general Mola*, p. 282.

127. *Ibid.*, p. 245; Iribarren, *Mola. Datos*, p. 177.

128. Iribarren, *Con el general Mola*, pp. 297–301; Iribarren, *Mola. Datos*, pp. 211–12; Palomares Ibañez, *Valladolid*, p. 54.

129. Miguel de Unamuno, *El resentimiento trágico de la vida. Notas sobre la revolución y guerra civil españolas* (Madrid: Alianza Editorial, 1991) p. 57.

130. Iribarren, *Mola. Datos*, pp. 11, 67–70; Iribarren, *Con el general Mola*, pp. 164–5, 243.

131. Iribarren, *Mola. Datos*, pp. 148–9.

132. Maíz, *Mola*, p. 185.

133. José Ignacio Escobar, *Así empezó* (Madrid: G. del Toro, 1974) pp. 55–8; Vigón, *Mola*, pp. 204–5.

134. Iribarren, *Con el general Mola*, pp. 249–50.

135. Ángel Viñas, *Franco, Hitler y el estallido de la guerra civil. Antecedentes y consecuencias* (Madrid: Alianza Editorial, 2001) pp. 305–8; Escobar, *Así empezó*, pp. 94–118.

136. Viñas, *Franco, Hitler*, p. 428.

137. Francisco Franco Salgado-Araujo, *Mi vida junto a Franco* (Barcelona: Editorial Planeta, 1977) pp. 173, 349–54; José Manuel Martínez Bande, 'Del alzamiento a la guerra civil verano de 1936: Correspondencia Franco/Mola', *Historia y Vida*, no. 93, 1975, pp. 23–9; Carlos Blanco Escolá, *La incompetencia militar de Franco* (Madrid: Alianza Editorial, 2000) pp. 246–55; Cardona, *Historia militar*, pp. 78–82.

138. Maíz, *Mola frente a Franco*, pp. 156–7, 164–73, 182–3, 364.

139. Iribarren, *Mola. Datos*, pp. 130–3; Vigón, *Mola*, pp. 91–2; Maíz, *Mola frente a Franco*, pp. 220–3; Iturralde, *La guerra de Franco*, II, pp. 113–14, 118–19; Franco, 'Apuntes' personales, p. 40; Martínez Bande, 'Correspondencia Franco/Mola', p. 22.

140. Gonzalo Soto, *Esbozo*, pp. 10–17.

141. Maíz, *Mola frente a Franco*, pp. 245–6.

142. Martínez Bande, 'Correspondencia Franco/Mola', p. 21; Suárez Fernández, *Franco*, II, p. 79; Iribarren, *Con el general Mola*, p. 157, cites the telegram arriving on 29 July.

143. Iribarren, *Mola. Datos*, p. 149; Martínez Bande, 'Correspondencia Franco/Mola', p. 21.

144. Iribarren, *Con el general Mola*, pp. 168–9, 222–3.

145. *Ibid.*, pp. 94, 245.

146. Jehanne Wake, *Kleinwort Benson: The History of Two Families in Banking* (New York: Oxford University Press, 1997) pp. 250–4; Sánchez Asiaín, *La financiación de la guerra civil española*, pp. 119–20, 180–5, 199–204.

147. Cardona, *Historia militar*, pp. 38–40.

148. *Le Matin*, 24 July 1936; Nerín, *La guerra*, pp. 149–50.

149. Vegas Latapie, *Los caminos*, pp. 36–42, 292; Francisco Bonmati de Codecido, *El Príncipe Don Juan de España* (Valladolid: Librería Santarén, 1938) pp. 224–37; José María Toquero, *Don Juan de Borbón, el Rey padre* (Barcelona: Plaza y Janés/Cambio 16, 1992) pp. 87–9; Iribarren, *Mola. Datos*, pp. 166–7; Cabanellas, *Guerra*, I, pp. 636–7.

150. José María Pemán, *Mis encuentros con Franco* (Barcelona: Dopesa, 1976) pp. 188–93; Iribarren, *Con el general Mola*, p. 254, manuscript note in Azcona's copy.

151. Seydel to Canaris, 15 August 1936, *Documents on German Foreign Policy* (henceforth *DGFP*), Series D, Vol. III (London: HMSO, 1951), p. 40.

152. Escobar, *Así empezó*, pp. 119–24.

153. Guillermo Cabanellas, *Cuatro generales*, 2 vols (Barcelona: Editorial Planeta, 1977) II, p. 327.

154. Martínez Bande, 'Correspondencia Franco/Mola', p. 22.

155. Franco Salgado-Araujo, *Mi vida*, pp. 189–90; Iribarren, *Con el general Mola*, pp. 262–4.

156. *Dez anos de política externa (1936–1947) a naçaõ portuguesa e a segunda guerra mundial* (Lisbon: Imprensa Nacional de Lisboa, 1964) III, p. 156; *The Times*, 11, 17 August 1936.

157. Seydel to Canaris, 16 August 1937, *DGFP*, D, III, pp. 42–3.

158. Martínez Bande, 'Correspondencia Franco/Mola', pp. 23–4.

159. Angel Viñas, 'Los espías nazis entran en la guerra civil', in Ángel Viñas, *Guerra, dinero, dictadura. Ayuda fascista y autarquía en la España de Franco* (Barcelona: Editorial Crítica, 1984) pp. 50, 57–8.

160. *Gaceta de Tenerife*, 26 August 1936; Maíz, *Mola frente a Franco*, pp. 274–6.

161. *L'Oeuvre*, 17 August 1936.

162. *The Times*, 29, 31 August, 1, 2, 4, 5 September 1936; José Manuel Martínez Bande, *Nueve meses de guerra en el norte* (Madrid: Editorial San Martín, 1980) pp. 64–86; Xabier Irujo, *Gernika 26 de abril de 1937* (Barcelona: Editorial Crítica, 2017) p. 67.

163. Iribarren, *Con el general Mola*, p. 320; Suárez Fernández, *Franco*, II, p. 97.

164. Pemán, *Mis encuentros con Franco*, p. 48.

165. Iribarren, *Con el general Mola*, pp. 78, 88–9; Aguirre González,

Aquí nunca pasó nada, pp. 65–7; Rivero Noval, *La ruptura de la paz civil*, pp. 50–1.

166. Paul Preston, *Franco: A Biography* (London: HarperCollins, 1993) pp. 173–9; Kindelán, *Mis cuadernos*, pp. 103–5; Ramón Garriga, *Nicolás Franco, el hermano brujo* (Barcelona: Editorial Planeta, 1980) pp. 97–104; Cabanellas, *La guerra*, II, pp. 196, 305–6; Iribarren, *Mola. Datos*, pp. 232–3.

167. Estado Mayor Central, *Anuario Militar de España año 1936* (Madrid: Ministerio de la Guerra, 1936) p. 150.

168. Iribarren, *Mola. Datos*, pp. 232–3; Del Burgo, 'Introducción', Maíz, *Mola frente a Franco*, pp. 129–31, 288–90, 309, 321–3.

169. Solchaga, 'Memorias', p. 26.

170. Sacanell, *Sanjurjo*, p. 157; Maíz, *Mola frente a Franco*, pp. 261–5, 276–84, 393–4.

171. Ramón Garriga, *La España de Franco. De la División Azul al pacto con los Estados Unidos (1943 a 1951)* (Puebla, Mexico: Editorial José M. Cajica Jr, 1971) p. 73; Serrano Suñer, *Memorias*, p. 163; *ABC* (Seville), 30 September 1936; *The Times*, 2 October 1936.

172. Pedro Sainz Rodríguez, *Testimonio y recuerdos* (Barcelona: Editorial Planeta, 1978), pp. 248–9.

173. Vegas Latapie, *Los caminos*, p. 87.

174. Maíz, *Mola frente a Franco*, pp. 324–5.

175. Geoffrey Cox, *Defence of Madrid* (London: Victor Gollancz, 1937) p. 19; Noel Monks, *Eyewitness* (London: Frederick Muller, 1955) pp. 71–2.

176. Javier Cervera Gil, *Madrid en guerra. La ciudad clandestina 1936–1939*, 2nd edn (Madrid: Alianza Editorial, 2006) pp. 145–6; Cox, *Defence of Madrid*, p. 39; Monks, *Eyewitness*, p. 71. According to Carlos Contreras,

Milicia Popular, 10 October 1936, Mola's press conference took place a few days earlier.

177. *Mundo Obrero*, 3 October 1936.

178. *Mundo Obrero*, 5 October 1936.

179. Carlos Contreras, 'En defensa de Madrid. La quinta columna', *Milicia Popular*, 10 October 1936.

180. *El Liberal*, 10, 16 October 1936.

181. *Heraldo de Madrid*, 21 October 1936.

182. Paul Preston, *The Spanish Holocaust: Inquisition and Extermination in Twentieth-Century Spain* (London: Harper Press, 2012) pp. 341–75.

183. Stoyán Mínev (Stepanov), *Las causas de la derrota de la República española*, ed. Ángel L. Encinas Moral (Madrid: Miraguano Ediciones, 2003) pp. 93, 111–12.

184. Roberto Cantalupo, *Fu la Spagna. Ambasciata presso Franco. Febbraio-Aprile 1937* (Milan: Mondadori, 1948) pp. 120–1.

185. Maíz, *Mola frente a Franco*, pp. 334–9, 347–50, 372, 394–5, 402–12, 418–19, 431–3, 503–4, 517–18; Jaime del Burgo, *Conspiración y guerra civil* (Madrid: Editorial Alfaguara, 1970) pp. 687–92; Faupel to Wilhelmstrasse, 14 April 1937, *DGFP*, D, III, p. 268; Martin Blinkhorn, *Carlism and Crisis in Spain, 1931–1939* (Cambridge: Cambridge University Press, 1975) pp. 273–5; Iturralde, *La guerra de Franco*, II, pp. 60–2.

186. Maíz, *Mola frente a Franco*, p. 374–5, 383–5, 426; Kindelán, *Mis cuadernos*, pp. 120–3; Vigón, *Mola*, pp. 303–4; José María de Areilza, *Así los he visto* (Barcelona: Editorial Planeta, 1974) p. 132.

187. Franco Salgado-Araujo, *Mi vida*, p. 225.

188. Kindelán, *Mis cuadernos*, pp. 119–20; José Manuel Martínez

Bande, *Vizcaya* (Madrid: Editorial San Martín, 1971) pp. 13–17; Klaus A. Maier, *Guernica 26.4.1937. Die deutsche Intervention in Spanien und der 'Fall Guernica'* (Freiburg: Rombach, 1975) pp. 44–5; Vigón, *Mola*, p. 311; Angel Viñas, 'La responsibilidad de la destrucción de Guernica', in Viñas, *Guerra, dinero, dictadura*, p. 99.

189. Cantalupo to Ciano, 17 February 1937, *I documenti diplomatici italiani* (henceforth *DDI*), 8ª serie, vol. VI (Rome: Libreria dello Stato, 1997) pp. 222–3.

190. Wolfram von Richthofen, 'Spanien-Tagebuch', diary entries for 20, 24, 25, 26 March 1937, reproduced in Maier, *Guernica*, pp. 77–81.

191. Cantalupo, *Fu la Spagna*, pp. 223–4.

192. Cantalupo to Ciano, 9 April 1937, *DDI*, 8ª serie, vol. VI, p. 546.

193. Faupel to Wilhelmstrasse, 21 April 1937, *DGFP*, D, III, pp. 274–5.

194. Richthofen, 'Spanien-Tagebuch', diary entries for 24, 28 March 1937, pp. 79, 82.

195. In 1939, work began on an official Luftwaffe history of the Condor Legion in the Basque Country, Kriegswissenschaftlichen Abteilung der Luftwaffe, Arbeitsgruppe Spanienkrieg, *Die Kämpfe im Norden*. The first draft, Bundesarchiv, Militärarchiv, Freiburg, Akt II L 14/2, p. 29, is uninhibitedly revealing. A later draft of March 1940 was toned down, *Die Kämpfe im Norden*, Bundesarchiv, Militärarchiv, Freiburg, Akt II L 14/3. For instance, it omitted the reference to the attack taking place without consideration for the civilian population. See Herbert R. Southworth, *Guernica! Guernica!: A Study of Journalism, Diplomacy, Propaganda and History* (Berkeley: University of California Press, 1977)

pp. 276, 478 n. 205. I am grateful to Ana Teresa Núñez Monasterio of the Museo de la Paz de Gernika who made both of these documents available to me.

196. Richthofen, 'Spanien-Tagebuch', diary entry for 25 March 1937, pp. 79–80; Maier, *Guernica*, pp. 45–6; Viñas, 'La responsibilidad', pp. 99–102.

197. G. L. Steer, *The Tree of Guernica: A Field Study of Modern War* (London: Faber & Faber, 1938) p. 159; Marisol Martínez and David Mendaza (eds), *La guerra en Araba. El levantamiento militar en Bizkaia*, vol. III of Iñaki Egaña, Marisol Martínez and David Mendaza (eds), *1936 Guerra civil en Euskal Herria* (Pamplona: Aralar Liburuak, 1999) p. 211; Manuel Aznar, *Historia militar de la guerra de España (1936–1939)* (Madrid: Ediciones Idea, 1940) p. 398.

198. Javier Ugarte, 'Represión como instrumento de acción política del Nuevo Estado (Álava, 1936–1939)', *Historia Contemporánea*, no. 35, 2007, p. 259.

199. Jon Irazabal Agirre, *Durango 31 de marzo de 1937* (Abadiño: Gerediaga Elkartea, 2001) pp. 68–84, 96–102; Steer, *Guernica*, pp. 160–70; Southworth, *Guernica!*, pp. 368–9.

200. Solchaga, 'Memorias', p. 28.

201. Maier, *Guernica*, pp. 9–52; Richthofen, 'Spanien-Tagebuch', diary entries for 2, 5 April 1937, pp. 86–7, 90; *Die Kämpfe im Norden*, version 1, pp. 38–9, 46–7; *Die Kämpfe im Norden*, version 2, pp. 57–61; Viñas, 'La responsibilidad', pp. 102–4; Martínez Bande, *Vizcaya*, p. 84.

202. Richthofen, 'Spanien-Tagebuch', diary entry for 9 April 1937, p. 94.

203. Faupel to Wilhelmstrasse, 1 May 1937, *DGFP*, D, III, p. 278.

204. Irujo, *Gernika 26 de abril*, p. 84.

205. Richthofen, 'Spanien-Tagebuch', diary entry for 20 April 1937, p. 99.

206. Richthofen, 'Spanien-Tagebuch', diary entry for 23 April 1937, p. 101.

207. Richthofen, 'Spanien-Tagebuch', diary entry for 25 April 1937, pp. 101–3.

208. Gordon Thomas and Max Morgan-Witts, *The Day Guernica Died* (London: Hodder & Stoughton, 1975) pp. 144, 296; Claude Bowers, *My Mission to Spain* (London: Victor Gollancz, 1954) p. 343.

209. Richthofen, 'Spanien-Tagebuch', diary entry for 26 April 1937, pp. 103–4; Irujo, *Gernika 26 de abril*, pp. 93–6, 105–7.

210. Bowers to Hull, 30 April 1937, *Foreign Relations of the United States 1937*, vol. I (Washington, DC: United States Government Printing Office, 1954) p. 290.

211. *Daily Herald*, 27, 28, 29 April 1937.

212. Irujo, *Gernika 26 de abril*, pp. 109–10, 190–1, 206.

213. *DDI*, 8ª serie, vol. VI, p. 539.

214. José de Arteche, *Un vasco en la posguerra (1906–1971)* (Bilbao: La Gran Enciclopedia Vasca, 1977) pp. 198, 222, 237; Sánchez-Ostiz, *El Escarmiento*, pp. 117–18, 325–6.

215. Richthofen, 'Spanien-Tagebuch', diary entries for 27 and 30 April 1937, pp. 106, 109, and Annex 11, p. 149; Maier, *Guernica*, p. 66; Southworth, *Guernica!*, pp. 276–7.

216. Irujo, *Gernika 26 de abril*, p. 77.

217. Mola, *Obras*, pp. 1185–96; Serrano Suñer, *Memorias*, pp. 211–13; Maíz, *Mola frente a Franco*, pp. 356, 396–402, 420–1; Cacho Viu, 'Iribarren', pp. 249–50.

218. Vegas Latapie, *Los caminos*, p. 194; Maíz, *Alzamiento*, pp. 258–9; Vidarte, *Todos fuimos culpables*, pp. 700–2.

219. Iribarren, *Con el general Mola*, p. 294; Iribarren, *Mola. Datos*, pp. 193–4.

220. Iribarren, *Mola. Datos*, 277–8. There is a detailed account of the process in handwritten notes by Iribarren, prepared in May 1944, for his friend José María Azcona, pp. 1–8. I am grateful to Xabier Irujo for giving me a copy of those notes. Henceforth 'Notas para Azcona'.

221. On the mediocrity of Arias Paz, see Eugenio Vegas Latapie, *La frustración en la Victoria. Memorias políticas, 1938–1942* (Madrid: Editorial Actas, 1995) pp. 69–70.

222. 'Notas para Azcona', pp. 9–25; Vegas Latapie, *Los caminos*, pp. 185, 239–45; Cacho Viu, 'Iribarren', pp. 243–8; Ricardo Ollaquindia, 'Un libro de José María Iribarren condenado por la censura', *Príncipe de Viana* (Pamplona), year no. 64, no. 229, 2003, pp. 471–84.

223. 'Notas para Azcona', pp. 26–36.

224. Maíz, *Mola frente a Franco*, pp. 544–9.

225. Iribarren, *Mola. Datos*, pp. 283–4; José Antonio Silva, *Cómo asesinar con un avión* (Barcelona: Editorial Planeta, 1981) pp. 81–90; Maíz, *Mola frente a Franco*, pp. 552–3, 568–75; Federico Bravo Morata, *Franco y los muertos providenciales* (Madrid: Editorial Fenicia, 1979) pp. 149–81; Blanco Escolá, *General Mola*, pp. 339–40; Vegas Latapie, *Los caminos*, pp. 296–8.

226. Del Burgo, 'Introducción', Maíz, *Mola frente a Franco*, p. 144.

227. Testimony of Ramón Serrano Suñer to the author, 21 November 1990; Heleno Saña, *El franquismo sin mitos. Conversaciones con Serrano Suñer* (Barcelona; Grijalbo, 1982) pp. 94–5; Ignacio Merino, *Serrano Suñer. Conciencia y poder* (Madrid: Algaba Ediciones, 2004) pp. 238–9.

228. Vegas Latapie, *Los caminos*, pp. 291–2.

229. Cantalupo to Ciano, 17 February 1937, *DDI*, 8ª serie, vol. VI, pp. 221–2.

230. Maíz, *Mola frente a Franco*, pp. 503–18, 541–55; Faupel to Wilhelmstrasse, 9 July 1937, *DGFP*, D, III, p. 410.

231. Sacanell, *Sanjurjo*, p. 156; Del Burgo, 'Introducción', Maíz, *Mola frente a Franco*, pp. 553, 560–2; Viñas, *¿Quién quiso la guerra civil?*, pp. 180, 357–8, 361–2.

232. Ruiz Vilaplana, *Doy fe*, pp. 121–2.

233. Adolf Hitler, *Hitler's Table Talk, 1941–1944* (London: Weidenfeld & Nicolson, 1953) p. 608.

Chapter 7: The Psychopath in the South: Gonzalo Queipo de Llano

1. Luis de Armiñán, *Excmo. Sr. General Don Gonzalo Queipo de Llano y Sierra Jefe del Ejército del Sur* (Ávila: Imprenta Católica, 1937) p. 3.

2. Antonio Olmedo Delgado and José Cuesta Monereo, *General Queipo de Llano (aventura y audacia)* (Barcelona: Editorial AHR, 1958) p. 7. See, more recently, Nicolás Salas, *Quién fue Gonzalo Queipo de Llano y Sierra, 1875–1951* (Seville: Abec Editores, 2012) pp. 11–14, 423–32.

3. Guzmán de Alfarache (pseudonym of Enrique Vila), *¡18 de julio! Historia del alzamiento glorioso de Seville* (Seville: Editorial F.E., 1937) p. 7.

4. Jorge Fernández-Coppel (ed.), *Queipo de Llano. Memorias de la guerra civil* (Madrid: La Esfera de los Libros, 2008) pp. 113, 141, 147.

5. Ana Quevedo y Queipo de Llano, *Queipo de Llano. Gloria e infortunio de un general* (Barcelona: Editorial Planeta, 2001) pp. 34–40; Olmedo and Cuesta, *Queipo*, pp. 10–13, 32.

6. Quevedo, *Queipo de Llano*, pp. 41–52, 56–9; Olmedo and Cuesta, *Queipo*, pp. 19–27; Archivo General Militar de Segovia, 'Hoja de Servicios de Gonzalo Queipo de Llano Sierra', pp. 9–11.

7. Quevedo, *Queipo de Llano*, pp. 52–3.

8. *Ibid.*, pp. 66–78.

9. Olmedo and Cuesta, *Queipo*, pp. 36–50; Quevedo, *Queipo de Llano*, pp. 87–97; Archivo General Militar de Segovia, 'Hoja de servicios de Gonzalo Queipo de Llano y Sierra', pp. 16–21.

10. Pedro Sainz Rodríguez, *Testimonio y recuerdos* (Barcelona: Editorial Planeta, 1978) p. 272.

11. Quevedo, *Queipo de Llano*, p. 467; Guillermo Cabanellas, *Cuatro generales*, 2 vols (Barcelona: Editorial Planeta, 1977) II, p. 443; Manuel Barrios, *El último virrey Queipo de Llano*, 3rd edn (Seville: J. Rodríguez Castillejo, 1990) p. 194.

12. Olmedo and Cuesta, *Queipo*, pp. 45–50.

13. Ignacio Hidalgo de Cisneros, *Cambio de rumbo (Memorias)*, 2 vols (Bucharest: Colección Ebro, 1964) II, pp. 15–16.

14. David Woolman, *Rebels in the Rif: Abd el Krim and the Rif Rebellion* (Stanford, California: Stanford University Press, 1969) pp. 83–95.

15. Francisco Hernández Mir, *La dictadura ante la historia. Un crimen de lesa patria* (Madrid: Compañía Ibero-Americana de Publicaciones, 1930) p. 97.

16. Gonzalo Queipo de Llano, *El general Queipo de Llano perseguido por la dictadura* (Madrid, Javier Morato, 1930) pp. 41–3, 68–72, 77–81, 101–3, 131–3.

17. Gonzalo Queipo de Llano, 'Nuestro Propósito', in *Revista de Tropas Coloniales* (Tetuán), year 1, no. 1, January 1924.

18. Queipo de Llano, *El general Queipo de Llano perseguido*, pp. 104–35; Ricardo de la Cierva, *Francisco Franco. Un siglo de España*, 2 vols (Madrid: Editora Nacional, 1973) I, pp. 245–6; Woolman, *Rebels*, p. 138; Guillermo Cabanellas, *La guerra de los mil días. Nacimiento, vida y muerte de la II República española*, 2 vols (Buenos Aires: Grijalbo, 1973) I, pp. 140–1. The letters can be seen in the file on Queipo de Llano in the Archivo General Militar de Segovia.

19. Queipo de Llano, *El general Queipo de Llano perseguido*, pp. 41–3, 68–72, 77–81, 201; Olmedo and Cuesta, *Queipo*, pp. 74–5; Gustau Nerín, *La guerra que vino de África* (Barcelona: Editorial Crítica, 2005) pp. 48–9.

20. Cabanellas, *Cuatro generales*, I, p. 121.

21. Queipo de Llano, *El general Queipo de Llano perseguido*, pp. 157–61, 207–18; Nerín, *La guerra*, pp. 95–6.

22. Queipo to Presidente de la Junta Clasificadora, Archivo General Militar de Segovia, Expediente Queipo de Llano, 28; Queipo de Llano, *El general Queipo de Llano perseguido*, pp. 221–9; Nerín, *La guerra*, p. 49.

23. Cabanellas, *Cuatro generales*, I, pp. 132–3; Olmedo and Cuesta, *Queipo*, pp. 67–72.

24. Queipo de Llano, *El general Queipo de Llano perseguido*, pp. 15–17; Quevedo, *Queipo de Llano*, pp. 240–3; Miguel Primo de Rivera y Urquijo, *Papeles póstumos de José Antonio* (Barcelona: Plaza y Janés, 1996) pp. 24, 26–7, 51; Ian Gibson, *En busca de José Antonio* (Barcelona: Editorial Planeta, 1980) pp. 192–6; Joan Maria Thomàs, *José Antonio. Realidad y mito* (Barcelona: Editorial Debate, 2017) pp. 92–5; Julio Gil Pecharromán, *José Antonio Primo de Rivera. Retrato de un visionario* (Madrid: Temas de Hoy, 1996) pp. 98–9, 142–3; Manuel Azaña, *Obras completas*, 4 vols (Mexico City: Ediciones Oasis, 1966–8) IV, p. 410.

25. Queipo de Llano, *El general Queipo de Llano perseguido*, pp. 24–5.

26. Ian Gibson, *Queipo de Llano. Sevilla, verano de 1936* (Barcelona: Grijalbo, 1986) p. 19.

27. Gonzalo Queipo de Llano, *El movimiento reivindicativo de Cuatro Vientos* (Madrid: Tipógrafía Yagües, 1933) pp. 32, 51.

28. Antonio Cordón, *Trayectoria (Recuerdos de un artillero)* (Seville: Espuela de Plata, 2008) pp. 334–5; Carlos Blanco Escolá, *General Mola. El ególatra que provocó la guerra civil* (Madrid: La Esfera de los Libros, 2002) p. 248.

29. Queipo de Llano to Franco, 18 June 1950, Francisco Franco Salgado-Araujo, *Mi vida junto a Franco* (Barcelona: Editorial Planeta, 1977) pp. 390–2; Archivo Natalio Rivas, Real Academia de la Historia, leg. II-8923; José María Gil Robles, *No fue posible la paz* (Barcelona: Ariel, 1968) pp. 722–6.

30. Emilio Mola Vidal, *Obras completas* (Valladolid: Librería Santarén, 1940) pp. 333–4, 347–50, 394, 434–5, 1038–41; Cordón, *Trayectoria*, pp. 336–7; Queipo de Llano, *El movimiento reivindicativo*, pp. 54–5, 63–4.

31. Juan-Simeón Vidarte, *No queríamos al Rey. Testimonio de un socialista español* (Barcelona: Grijalbo, 1977) pp. 256–9.

32. Emilio Mola Vidal, *Tempestad, calma, intriga y crisis. Memorias de mi paso por la Dirección General de Seguridad* (Madrid: Librería Bergua, 1932) p. 76; Quevedo, *Queipo de Llano*, pp. 252–9, 284–5, 301–2.

33. Graco Marsá, *La sublevación de Jaca. Relato de un rebelde* 2nd edn (Madrid: Zeus S.A. Editorial, 1931) *passim*; José María Azpíroz Pascual and Fernando Elboj Broto, *La sublevación de Jaca* (Zaragoza: Guara Editorial, 1984) pp. 27–36, 109–117; Comandante [Ramón] Franco, *Madrid bajo las bombas* (Madrid: Zeus S.A. Editorial, 1931) pp. 164–74; Queipo de Llano, *El movimiento reivindicativo*, pp. 91–113, 121–8. On the reasons for lack of a strike, see Shlomo Ben Ami, *The Origins of the Second Republic in Spain* (Oxford: Oxford University Press, 1978) pp. 149–50.

34. Franco to Varela, 27 December 1930, Archivo Varela, Cádiz, Expediente Personal Queipo de Llano, Carpeta 148, pp. 75–7.

35. Hidalgo de Cisneros, *Cambio de rumbo*, I, pp. 216–23, 230; Franco, *Madrid bajo las bombas*, pp. 193–203, 223, 229; Nerín, *La guerra*, pp. 86, 202.

36. 'El General Burguete acusa', *ABC* (Madrid), 16 March 1937; Diego Martínez Barrio, *Memorias* (Barcelona: Editorial Planeta, 1983) p. 18.

37. Hidalgo de Cisneros, *Cambio de rumbo*, I, pp. 237–9, 243–6; Vidarte, *No queríamos al Rey*, p. 343; Quevedo, *Queipo de Llano*, pp. 310–11.

38. Azaña, *Obras completas*, IV, pp. 71–2.

39. Hidalgo de Cisneros, *Cambio de rumbo*, II, pp. 15–16.

40. Olmedo and Cuesta, *Queipo*, pp. 73, 79–80.

41. Quevedo, *Queipo de Llano*, pp. 313–17.

42. Gil Robles, *No fue posible*, pp. 39–40; Quevedo, *Queipo de Llano*, p. 319.

43. 'El General Burguete acusa', *ABC* (Madrid), 16 March 1937.

44. Azaña, *Obras completas*, IV, pp. 15, 28–9.

45. Olmedo and Cuesta, *Queipo*, pp. 72–3.

46. Azaña, *Obras completas*, IV, pp. 10–11, 13, 15, 499; Coronel Segismundo Casado, *Así cayó Madrid. Último episodio de la guerra civil española* (Madrid: Guadiana de Publicaciones, 1968) p. 32; Olmedo and Cuesta, *Queipo*, pp. 79–81; Gabriel Cardona, *El poder militar en la España contemporánea hasta la guerra civil* (Madrid: Siglo XXI, 1983) pp. 156–7; Gibson, *Queipo de Llano*, pp. 32–3.

47. Azaña, *Obras completas*, IV, pp. 50, 117–18; Martínez Barrio, *Memorias*, pp. 138–9.

48. *ABC*, 8 December 1931; Azaña, *Obras completas*, IV, p. 263; Quevedo, *Queipo de Llano*, pp. 320–5.

49. Azaña, *Obras completas*, IV, pp. 120, 139, 261.

50. *Ibid.*, pp. 126, 139, 212–13, 304.

51. *Ibid.*, pp. 277–8.

52. *Ibid.*, pp. 301, 376; Martínez Barrio, *Memorias*, pp. 138–9.

53. Manuel Azaña, *Diarios, 1932–1933. 'Los cuadernos robados'* (Barcelona: Grijalbo-Mondadori, 1997) p. 37.

54. Joaquín Arrarás, *Historia de la segunda República española*, 4 vols (Madrid: Editora Nacional, 1956–68) I, pp. 522–3.

55. Juan Ortiz Villalba, *Sevilla 1936. Del golpe militar a la guerra civil* (Seville: Diputación Provincial, 1998) p. 281.

56. *ABC*, 8, 9 March 1933; Azaña, *Obras completas*, IV, pp. 462, 465–6, 498–9; Niceto Alcalá-Zamora, *Memorias* (Barcelona: Editorial Planeta, 1977) p. 235; Quevedo, *Queipo de Llano*, pp. 327–8; Blanco Escolá, *General Mola*, pp. 157–8.

57. Gil Robles, *No fue posible*, p. 235.

58. *ABC*, 9, 10, 11 May 1934; Quevedo, *Queipo de Llano*, pp. 329–36.

58. Martínez Barrio, *Memorias*, p. 322.

60. Mola, *Obras*, pp. 879–80; Iribarren, *Mola*, pp. 39–40; Azaña, *Obras completas*, IV, p. 67.

61. Gil Robles, *No fue posible*, pp. 719–20; Joaquín Arrarás, *Historia de la Cruzada española*, 8 vols (Madrid: Ediciones Españolas, 1939–43) II, p. 467; Francisco Franco Bahamonde, *'Apuntes' personales sobre la República y la guerra civil* (Madrid: Fundación Francisco Franco, 1987) p. 33; B. Féliz Maíz, *Alzamiento en España. De un diario de la conspiración*, 2nd edn (Pamplona: Editorial Gómez, 1952) pp. 50–1; José María Iribarren, *Mola. Datos para una biografía y para la historia del alzamiento nacional* (Zaragoza: Librería General, 1938) pp. 45–6; José María Iribarren, *Con el general Mola* (Zaragoza: Librería General, 1937) pp. 14–15; Felipe Bertrán Güell, *Preparación y desarrollo del alzamiento nacional* (Valladolid: Librería Santarén, 1939) p. 116.

62. Arrarás, *Historia de la segunda República*, IV, p. 345; General Jorge Vigón, *General Mola (el conspirador)* (Barcelona: Editorial AHR, 1957) p. 95; Blanco Escolá, *General Mola*, p. 249.

63. Queipo de Llano to Franco, 18 June 1950, Franco Salgado-Araujo, *Mi vida*, pp. 390–2; Quevedo, *Queipo de Llano*, pp. 348–9; B. Félix Maíz, *Mola, aquel hombre* (Barcelona: Editorial Planeta, 1976) pp. 78–81, 106, 133–5, 199–201, 225–8; Olmedo and Cuesta, *Queipo*, pp. 84–6; Cardona, *El poder militar*, pp. 234, 243.

64. Queipo de Llano to Franco, 18 June 1950, Franco Salgado-Araujo, *Mi vida*, pp. 390–2; Gil Robles, *No fue posible*, pp. 722–4, 726–7.

65. José María García Márquez, *La 'Semana sangrienta' de julio de 1931 en Sevilla. Entre la historia y la manipulación* (Seville: Aconcagua, 2019) pp. 83–5.

66. José Manuel Macarro Vera, *La utopía revolucionaria. Seville en la segunda República* (Seville: Monte de Piedad y Caja de Ahorros, 1985) pp. 253, 264; Leandro Álvarez Rey, *La derecha en la II República. Sevilla, 1931–1936* (Seville: Universidad de Sevilla/ Ayuntamiento de Sevilla, 1993) pp. 251–8.

67. Ronald Fraser, *Blood of Spain: The Experience of Civil War, 1936–1939* (London: Allen Lane, 1979) p. 50.

68. Alfarache, *¡18 de julio!*, pp. 41–2; Manuel Sánchez del Arco, *El sur de España en la reconquista de Madrid (diario de operaciones glosado por un testigo)*, 2nd edn (Seville: Editorial Sevillana, 1937) p. 27; Olmedo and Cuesta, *Queipo*, p. 88; Francisco Espinosa Maestre, *La justicia de Queipo. (Violencia selectiva y terror fascista en la II División en 1936) Sevilla, Huelva, Cádiz, Córdoba, Málaga y Badajoz*, 2nd edn (Barcelona: Editorial Crítica, 2005) pp. 30–1; Luis Bolín, *Spain: The Vital Years* (Philadelphia: J. B. Lippincott, 1967) p. 183; Fernández-Coppel, *Queipo de Llano. Memorias*, pp. 118–19.

69. Espinosa Maestre, *La justicia de Queipo*, pp. 30–33; Alfarache, *¡18 de julio!*, pp. 141–2.

70. Alfarache, *¡18 de julio!*, p. 42; Olmedo and Cuesta, *Queipo*, pp. 86–8.

71. José María Varela Rendueles, *Rebelión en Seville. Memorias de su Gobernador rebelde* (Seville: Ayuntamiento, 1982) pp. 76–80.

72. General Queipo de Llano, 'Cómo dominamos a Sevilla', in *Estampas de la guerra*, vol. V: *Frentes de*

Andalucía y Extremadura (San Sebastián: Editora Nacional, 1938) p. 29.

73. Fernández-Coppel, *Queipo de Llano. Memorias*, p. 25; Alfarache, *¡18 de julio!*, pp. 43–8; Olmedo and Cuesta, *Queipo*, p. 89.

74. Quevedo, *Queipo de Llano*, pp. 351–2, 372, 399–401.

75. Ortiz Villalba, *Sevilla 1936*, pp. 78–9; Fernández-Coppel, *Queipo de Llano. Memorias*, pp. 34–6; Alfarache, *¡18 de julio!*, p. 49; Olmedo and Cuesta, *Queipo*, pp. 94–5, 100–1; Varela Rendueles, *Rebelión en Seville*, p. 105; Espinosa Maestre, *La justicia de Queipo*, pp. 109–14.

76. Archivo Natalio Rivas, Real Academia de la Historia, leg. II-8923; Olmedo and Cuesta, *Queipo*, pp. 100–1; Armiñán, *Queipo de Llano*, pp. 17–18.

77. Alfarache, *¡18 de julio!*, p. 62; Fernández-Coppel, *Queipo de Llano. Memorias*, p. 38.

78. Queipo de Llano, 'Cómo dominamos a Sevilla', pp. 28–30; *ABC* (Seville), 18 July 1937; *La Unión* (Seville), 18 July 1937; *El Correo de Andalucía* (Seville), 18 July 1937.

79. Archivo del Tribunal Militar Territorial Segundo (Seville), SUM 239/1938, quoted by Rúben Serém, *A Laboratory of Terror, Conspiracy, Coup d'état and Civil War in Seville, 1936–1939. History and Myth in Francoist Spain* (Brighton: Sussex Academic Press, 2017) pp. 69–70.

80. Olmedo and Cuesta, *Queipo*, p. 118; Cabanellas, *La guerra de los mil días*, I, p. 395; Barrios, *El último virrey*, p. 87.

81. Queipo de Llano, 'Cómo dominamos a Sevilla', pp. 30–1; Guzmán de Alfarache, *¡18 de julio!*, p. 66; Olmedo and Cuesta, *Queipo*, pp. 103–10.

82. Archivo del Tribunal Militar Territorial Segundo (Seville), 243/1938, quoted by Serém, *A Laboratory of Terror*, pp. 5, 8, 11, 68–71; Espinosa Maestre, *La justicia de Queipo*, pp. 29–33.

83. H. R. Knickerbocker, *The Siege of the Alcazar: A War-Log of the Spanish Revolution* (London: Hutchinson, n.d. [1937]) pp. 27–9.

84. Francisco Espinosa Maestre, *La columna de la muerte. El avance del ejército franquista de Sevilla a Badajoz* (Barcelona: Editorial Crítica, 2003) pp. 1–2; Queipo, *Hoja de Servicios*, pp. 32–3.

85. Queipo de Llano, 'Cómo dominamos a Sevilla', pp. 28–35; *ABC*, 2 February 1938. Similar versions of the same myth can be found in Olmedo and Cuesta, *Queipo*, and Arrarás, *Cruzada*, III, p. 174; Armiñán, *Queipo de Llano*, p. 28. There is an updated version of the myth by Nicolás Salas, *Sevilla fue la clave. República, Alzamiento, Guerra Civil (1931–39)*, 2 vols (Seville: Editorial Castillejo, 1992). For accounts that cast doubt on Queipo de Llano's heroism, see Barrios, *El último virrey*, pp. 50–2, 58–63 and Ortiz Villalba, *Sevilla 1936*, pp. 127–8. The myth of Queipo de Llano's epic deed is deftly dismantled by Espinosa Maestre, *La justicia de Queipo*, pp. 45–56. See also Hugh Thomas, *The Spanish Civil War*, 3rd edn (London: Hamish Hamilton, 1977) pp. 210–12.

86. Espinosa Maestre, *La justicia de Queipo*, pp. 51–53. Vila published his lists in his pseudonymous Alfarache, *¡18 de julio!*, pp. 72–88, 110–15, 130–7, 153–60, 223–69. See also Barrios, *El último virrey*, pp. 88–91, who claims that the rebels had 6,000 men.

87. Sánchez del Arco, *El sur de España*, pp. 27–35; Alfarache, *¡18 de julio!*,

pp. 91–110; Francisco Espinosa
Maestre, *Guerra y represión en el sur
de España* (Valencia: Publicacions
de la Universitat de València, 2012)
pp. 133–69.

88. *ABC*, 31 March 1964.

89. Sánchez del Arco, *El sur de España*,
pp. 17–20, 31; Cándido Ortiz de
Villajos, *De Sevilla a Madrid, ruta
libertadora de la columna Castejón*
(Granada: Librería Prieto, 1937)
p. 27.

90. Informe Gutiérrez Flores, 11
October 1940, Archivo General
Militar (Madrid), Zona Nacional,
armario 18, leg. 35, carpeta 23. I am
grateful to Rúben Sérem for bringing
this document to my attention.

91. Queipo de Llano, 'Cómo
dominamos a Sevilla', pp. 32–3.

92. Rafael de Medina Vilallonga, Duque
de Medinaceli, *Tiempo pasado*
(Seville: Gráfica Sevillena, 1971)
pp. 39–40; Ortiz Villalba, *Sevilla
1936*, pp. 116–17.

93. *El Correo de Andalucía* (Seville), 22
July 1936.

94. Edmundo Barbero, *El infierno azul
(Seis meses en el feudo de Queipo)*
(Madrid: Talleres del SUIG (CNT),
1937) pp. 25–8.

95. Undated letter from Cuesta
Monereo to Queipo de Llano,
Fernández-Coppel, *Queipo de
Llano. Memorias*, p. 42 n. 19.

96. Julio de Ramón-Laca, *Bajo la férula
de Queipo. Cómo fue gobernada
Andalucía* (Seville: Imprenta
Comercial del Diario FE, 1939)
pp. 15–18.

97. Joaquín Gil Honduvilla, *Justicia en
guerra. Bando de guerra y
jurisdicción militar en el Bajo
Guadalquivir* (Seville: Ayuntamiento
de Seville Patronato del Real
Alcázar, 2007) pp. 82–3, 100–5.

98. Servicio Histórico Militar, Madrid,
Zona Nacional, armario 18, leg. 35,
carpeta 22.

99. *ABC*, 24 July 1936; Ramón-Laca,
Bajo la férula, pp. 27–9.

100. Espinosa Maestre, *La justicia de
Queipo*, pp. 251–6.

101. Juan Manuel Baquero, *Que fuera mi
tierra. Anuario 2015* (Seville: Extra!
Comunicación/Dirección General
de Memoria Democrática,
Consejería de Cultura, Junta de
Andalucía, 2016) p. 90.

102. For a survey of the repression under
Queipo's jurisdiction, see Paul
Preston, *The Spanish Holocaust:
Inquisition and Extermination in
Twentieth-Century Spain* (London:
Harper Press, 2012), Chapter 5.

103. *ABC*, 23 July 1936; *La Unión*, 23
July 1936; Gibson, *Queipo de Llano*,
p. 165.

104. *La Unión*, 30 August 1936.

105. *ABC*, 23 July, 16 August, 25 October
1936, 1, 26 June, 5 September, 22
December 1937; *La Unión*, 23, 31
July 1936; Arthur Koestler, *Spanish
Testament* (London: Victor
Gollancz, 1937) p. 31.

106. José Cuesta Monereo, *Una figura
para la historia. El general Queipo
de Llano. Primer locutor de radio en
la Guerra de Liberacion* (Seville:
Jefatura Provincial del Movimiento
de Seville, 1969) p. 31.

107. *ABC*, 26 July 1936.

108. Koestler, *Spanish Testament*, pp. 34,
84–8.

109. *La Unión*, 23 July, 26 October 1936;
ABC, 1 October 1936, 15 November
1937.

110. Cabanellas, *La guerra de los mil
días*, I, pp. 399–401; *ABC*, 30
August 1936; Gibson, *Queipo de
Llano*, p. 431.

111. *La Unión*, 25 July; *ABC*, 26 July, 29
August 1936.

112. Dionisio Ridruejo, *Casi unas
memorias* (Barcelona: Editorial
Planeta, 1976) pp. 150, 212.

113. Francisco Espinosa and José María
Lama, 'La columna de los ocho mil',

Revista de Fiestas de Reina
(Badajoz), August 2001; Espinosa
Maestre, *La columna de la muerte*,
pp. 195-9; José María Lama, *Una
biografía frente al olvido. José
González Barrero, Alcalde de Zafra
en la segunda República* (Badajoz:
Diputación de Badajoz, 2000)
pp. 128-30; Cayetano Ibarra, *La
otra mitad de la historia que nos
contaron. Fuente de Cantos,
República y guerra, 1931-1939*
(Badajoz: Diputación de Badajoz,
2005) pp. 281-93; Ángel
Hernández García, 'La columna de
los ocho mil: una tragedia olvidada',
Revista de Fiestas de Reina, no. 7,
August 2005, pp. 103-8; Ángel
Olmedo Alonso, *Llerena 1936.
Fuentes orales para la recuperación
de la memoria histórica* (Badajoz:
Diputación de Badajoz, 2010)
pp. 168-82; *ABC* (Seville), 19
September 1936.

114. Carlos G. Mauriño Longoria,
Memorias (Ronda: Familia del
autor, n.d. [1937]) pp. 34, 37-8, 42,
48, 54, 64, 68, 74, 80, 92, 98, 103;
Lawrence Dundas, *Behind the
Spanish Mask* (London: Robert
Hale, 1943) pp. 61-8; Gerald
Brenan, *Personal Record, 1920-1972*
(London: Jonathan Cape, 1974)
p. 298.

115. Barrios, *El último virrey*, pp. 78-81,
98-9, 145-7; Gibson, *Queipo de
Llano*, pp. 71-2; Cuesta, *Una figura*,
pp. 26-7; Salas, *Quién fue Gonzalo
Queipo de Llano*, pp. 305-12.

116. Gamel Woolsey, *Death's Other
Kingdom* (London: Longmans,
Green, 1939) p. 126.

117. *ABC*, 16 August 1936; *La Unión*, 11,
13 August 1936; Gibson, *Queipo de
Llano*, pp. 118-19, 330, 343, 356-7.

118. Antonio Bahamonde y Sánchez de
Castro, *Un año con Queipo*
(Barcelona: Ediciones Españolas,
n.d. [1938]) pp. 140-2.

119. Helen Nicholson, *Death in the
Morning* (London: Lovat Dickson,
1937) pp. 27, 72-4, 81-2; Judith
Keene, *Fighting for Franco:
International Volunteers in
Nationalist Spain during the Spanish
Civil War, 1936-1939* (London:
Leicester University Press, 2001)
pp. 249-52.

120. Sir Peter Chalmers Mitchell, *My
House in Málaga* (London: Faber &
Faber, 1938) p. 110.

121. Queipo de Llano, *El movimiento
reivindicativo*, pp. 43-4.

122. *ABC*, 5 August 1936; *La Unión*, 31
August 1936.

123. *La Unión*, 19 August 1936; Gibson,
Queipo de Llano, p. 370.

124. Mauriño Longoria, *Memorias*,
pp. 73, 82.

125. *ABC*, 16 August 1936; Gibson,
Queipo de Llano, pp. 96-100;
Bahamonde, *Un año con Queipo*,
pp. 34-6.

126. José Augusto, *Jornal de um
correspondente da guerra em
Espanha* (Lisbon: Empresa Nacional
de Publicidade, 1936) pp. 39-41.

127. José María Pemán, *Mis almuerzos
con gente importante* (Barcelona:
Dopesa, 1970) pp. 157-8. For the
expurgated version, see *ABC*, 16
August 1936.

128. Gibson, *Queipo de Llano*, pp. 82, 84,
456.

129. Archivo General Militar (Madrid),
armario 18, leg. 6, carpeta 5.

130. Claude G. Bowers, *My Mission to
Spain* (London: Gollancz, 1954)
p. 335. Bowers's transcription is
somewhat faulty. Queipo probably
said in correct Spanish 'viva el vino'.

131. Esteban C. Gómez Gómez, *El eco de
las descargas. Adiós a la esperanza
republicana* (Barcelona: Escega,
2002) p. 135.

132. Brenan, *Personal Record*,
pp. 296-300; Woolsey, *Death's Other
Kingdom*, pp. 34-5.

133. J. A. Giménez Arnau, *Memorias de memoria. Descifre vuecencia personalmente* (Barcelona: Ediciones Destino, 1978) p. 70.

134. Cuesta, *Una figura*, pp. 11, 25, 27.

135. *ABC*, 25 July 1936; *La Unión*, 26 July 1936.

136. *ABC*, 30 March 1938; José Alcalá-Zamora y Queipo de Llano, 'Prólogo', Fernández-Coppel, *Queipo de Llano. Memorias*, p. xv.

137. Espinosa Maestre, *La justicia de Queipo*, pp. 259–60; Eduardo Domínguez Lobato, *Cien capítulos de retaguardia (alrededor de un diario)* (Madrid: G. del Toro, 1973) pp. 79–81.

138. Queipo al Ministerio del Ejército, 29 June 1939; Declaración jurada de los servicios prestados del general Queipo de Llano; Queipo a Franco 31 May 1940, Queipo de Llano y Sierra, Gonzalo, Sección 1ª, leg. Q-13, Archivo General Militar de Segovia. On these operations, see P. Bernabé Copado, SJ, *Con la columna Redondo. Combates y conquistas. Crónica de guerra* (Seville: Imprenta de la Gavidia, 1937) pp. 41–60, 68–85; Francisco Espinosa Maestre, *La guerra civil en Huelva*, 4th edn (Huelva: Diputación Provincial, 2005) pp. 174–254.

139. *ABC*, 16 August 1936; Gibson, *Queipo de Llano*, pp. 382, 408, 418, 424, 426.

140. Ramón-Laca, *Bajo la férula*, pp. 36–7; Serém, *A Laboratory of Terror*, pp. 156–65.

141. *ABC*, 24 July (taxi drivers), 30 July (firefighters) 1936; Serém, *A Laboratory of Terror*, p. 153.

142. *La Unión*, 23, 24 July 1936; Bahamonde, *Un año con Queipo*, pp. 78–88.

143. *La Unión*, 26 July 1936, 11 February, 27 May 1937; *ABC*, 10 August, 5 September, 23 October, 16 November 1936.

144. Antonio Ruiz Vilaplana, *Doy fe … un año de actuación en la España nacionalista* (Paris: Éditions Imprimerie Coopérative Étoile, n.d. [1938]) pp. 127–9.

145. Espinosa Maestre, *La columna de la muerte*, p. 487 n. 363.

146. *ABC*, 25 August, 5 September 1936, 17 August 1937.

147. Olmedo and Cuesta, *Queipo*, pp. 335–8.

148. *ABC*, 17 August, 22 September, 26 December 1937, 18 February 1938; *La Unión*, 28 December 1937.

149. Eva Saiz, 'La ley amenaza el cortijo de Queipo de Llano en Sevilla', *El País*, 25 September 2020; Olmedo and Cuesta, *Queipo*, p. 335; Gonzalo Queipo de Llano, 'Queipo de Llano y La Corta de la Cartuja', *El País*, 15 July 1976.

150. José Villa Rodríguez, 'Andalucía en la segunda República. Tiempo de Frente Popular (febrero–julio 1936)', doctoral thesis, Universidad de Sevilla, 2020, pp. 599–601.

151. *ABC*, 9 December 1937.

152. *ABC*, 24, 25 December 1937; *La Unión*, 18, 22 September 1937.

153. *ABC*, 18 February 1938; Juan Miguel Baquero, 'Así logró Queipo el cortijo Gambogaz: dinero del Banco de España y una fundación para comprar la finca "en diferido"', *elDiario.es*, 22 March 2021; Saiz, 'La ley amenaza'. On the unpaid mortgage, see Bonifacio Canibaño, 'Queipo dejó sin pagar una hipoteca de 750.000 pesetas al comprar Gambogaz', *Diario de Sevilla*, 10 May 2022.

154. I am grateful to José María García Márquez for the information about the concentration camp and for the letter quoted, from the Gobierno Civil de la Provincia de Sevilla to the Director de Prisión Provincial de Sevilla, 17 May 1939. From the file of one of the prisoners in question,

exp. 41003, Juan Fernández Mazón, Archivo Histórico Provincial de Sevilla (AHPSE), Fondo Prisión Provincial, exp. 26130 0007.

155. Juan Manuel Baquero, 'Investigaciones históricas demuestran que la finca sevillana de Queipo de Llano usó esclavos del franquismo', elDiario.es, 1 November 2018; Villa Rodríguez, Andalucía, pp. 599–601.

156. Carlos Babío Urkidi and Manuel Pérez Lorenzo, Meirás. Un pazo, un caudillo, un espolio (A Coruña: Fundación Galiza Sempre, 2017) pp. 57–85, 121–47, 162–83, 223–67.

157. Quevedo, Queipo de Llano, pp. 496–8.

158. Cabanellas, La guerra de los mil días, I, p. 657.

159. Eugenio Vegas Latapie, Los caminos del desengaño. Memorias políticas 2, 1936–1938 (Madrid: Editorial Tebas, 1987) p. 71.

160. Franco Salgado-Araujo, Mi vida, p. 180; Cabanellas, La guerra de los mil días, I, pp. 642–3.

161. See his speech on 18 July 1939, ABC, 19 July 1939; Quevedo, Queipo de Llano, pp. 416–18.

162. 'El General Burguete acusa', ABC (Madrid), 16 March 1937; La Unión, 18 March 1937.

163. Campins, diary entries 1 July–14 August 1936, reproduced in Manuel Turón Yebra, 'El General Miguel Campins y su época (1880–1936)', doctoral thesis, Universidad Complutense de Madrid, 2002, pp. 720–36; letter Campins to Dolores Roda, 21 July 1936, pp. 737–40; letter Campins to General Orgaz, undated, pp. 744–7.

164. La Unión, 22 July 1936; ABC, 22 July 1936.

165. Archivo General Militar de Segovia, Expediente de General Campins, 2ª División Orgánica, Estado Mayor; Dolores Roda de Campins to Queipo de Llano, 16 August 1936; Turón Yebra, 'Campins', pp. 522–49; ABC, 15, 18 August 1936; Franco Salgado-Araujo, Mi vida, pp. 185–8, 348–53; Gibson, Queipo de Llano, pp. 101–5.

166. Gibson, Queipo de Llano, pp. 104–5; Cabanellas, La guerra de los mil días, II, pp. 872–3.

167. Vegas Latapie, Los caminos, pp. 86–7; Sainz Rodríguez, Testimonio y recuerdos, p. 272.

168. Cabanellas, La guerra de los mil días, I, pp. 654–5.

169. Ramón Serrano Suñer, Entre el silencio y la propaganda, la historia como fue. Memorias (Barcelona: Editorial Planeta, 1977) pp. 215–16; Quevedo, Queipo de Llano, p. 465.

170. Ian Gibson, El asesinato de García Lorca (Barcelona: Ediciones B, 2018) pp. 200–2, 237–9; Eduardo Molina Fajardo, Los últimos días de García Lorca (Barcelona: Plaza y Janés, 1983) pp. 49–50, 95, 192–4, 252; Ian Gibson (ed.), Agustín Penón. Diario de una búsqueda lorquiana (1955–56) (Barcelona: Plaza y Janés, 1990) pp. 77–8, 219.

171. Genoveva García Queipo de Llano, 'Un Queipo de Llano incomprensible', ABC (Madrid), 13 June 1986.

172. Quevedo, Queipo de Llano, pp. 397–8.

173. José Manuel Martínez Bande, La campaña de Andalucía, 2nd edn (Madrid: Editorial San Martín, 1986) pp. 153–65. Queipo's own account in 'Servicios de Campaña', appended to 'Declaración de Servicios Prestados', Queipo de Llano y Sierra, Gonzalo, secc. 1ª, leg. Q-13, Archivo General Militar de Segovia.

174. Emilio Faldella, Venti mesi di guerra in Spagna (Florence: Le Monnier, 1939) pp. 233–5.

175. Martínez Bande, La campaña de Andalucía, pp. 169–210.

176. *ABC* (Seville), 23 August, 3
    September, 10, 22 November 1936;
    Edward Norton, *Muerte en Málaga.*
    Testimonio de un americano sobre la
    guerra civil española (Malaga:
    Universidad de Málaga, 2004)
    pp. 170–87, 193–208, 225–42; Juan
    Antonio Ramos Hitos, *Guerra civil*
    en Málaga, 1936–1937. Revisión
    Histórica, 2nd edn (Malaga:
    Editorial Algazara, 2004)
    pp. 217–35, 244–72, 283–5; Ángel
    Gollonet Megías and José Morales
    López, *Sangre y fuego*. Málaga
    (Granada: Librería Prieto, 1937); G.
    Gómez Bajuelo, *Málaga bajo el*
    dominio rojo (Cadiz:
    Establecimientos Cerón, 1937)
    pp. 81–4; Padre Tomás López,
    Treinta semanas en poder de los
    rojos en Málaga de julio a febrero
    (Seville: Imprenta de San Antonio,
    1938) pp. 61–6, 93–101; Francisco
    García Alonso, *Flores del heroísmo*
    (Seville: Imprenta de la Gavidia,
    1939) pp. 76–9, 90–103, 129–36.

177. Encarnación Barranquero Texeira
    and Lucía Prieto Borrego, *Población*
    y guerra civil en Málaga. Caída,
    éxodo y refugio (Malaga: Centro de
    Ediciones de la Diputación de
    Málaga, 2007) pp. 21–99;
    Encarnación Barranquero Texeira,
    Málaga entre la guerra y la
    posguerra. El franquismo (Malaga:
    Editorial Arguval, 1994) p. 202;
    Bahamonde, *Un año con Queipo*,
    pp. 125–9.

178. Bahamonde, *Un año con Queipo*,
    pp. 132–5.

179. *ABC*, 9, 10 February 1937; *La*
    Unión, 10 February 1937;
    Barranquero and Prieto, *Población y*
    guerra civil, pp. 180–209.

180. Dr Norman Bethune, *The Crime on*
    the Road Malaga-Almeria (n.p.:
    Publicaciones Iberia, 1937) pp. 8–9;
    T. C. Worsley, *Behind the Battle*
    (London: Robert Hale, 1939)

    pp. 185–8, 197–201; *The Times*, 17,
    24 February, 3 March 1937.

181. *ABC*, 24 February 1937; *La Union*,
    25 February 1937; Martínez Bande,
    La campaña de Andalucía,
    pp. 210–11.

182. Brenan, *Personal Record*, p. 298.

183. *El Progreso* (Lugo), 5 September
    1936.

184. *ABC*, 15 October, 13 December
    1936, 13 January, 7 February, 7
    March, 15 April, 21, 22 May, 22
    June, 4, 21 July, 5 September, 26, 31
    December 1937, 14 January 1938;
    La Unión, 8, 9 March, 11 September
    1937.

185. *ABC* (Seville), 16 October 1938;
    Proa (León), 16 October 1938; *Azul*
    (Cordoba), 16 October 1938; *El*
    Adelanto (Salamanca), 16 October
    1938.

186. *El Correo de Andalucía* (Seville), 18
    July 1937.

187. Antonio Marquina Barrio and
    Gloria Inés Ospina, *España y los*
    judíos en el siglo XX (Madrid:
    Espasa Calpe, 1987) pp. 131–2.

188. Quoted Serém, *A Laboratory of*
    Terror, pp. 142–3.

189. Cabanellas, *La guerra de los mil*
    días, II, pp. 718–19.

190. Cantalupo to Ciano, 17 February
    1937, Archivio Storico del Ministero
    degli Affari Esteri, Spagna Fondo di
    Guerra, 287/137, b.38.

191. Nerín, *La guerra*, p. 234.

192. Cantalupo to Ciano, 1 March 1937,
    XV, Archivio Storico del Ministero
    degli Affari Esteri, Ufficio Spagna
    b.10.

193. *ABC*, 1, 6, 10 February, 30 June
    1938; Vegas Latapie, *Los caminos*,
    pp. 121–2; Quevedo, *Queipo de*
    Llano, pp. 443–7; Serrano Suñer,
    Memorias, p. 218; Cuesta, *Una*
    figura, p. 33.

194. *ABC*, 17 February, 1 November
    1938; Serrano Suñer, *Memorias*,
    pp. 216–18; Francisco Franco

Salgado-Araujo, *Mis conversaciones privadas con Franco* (Barcelona: Editorial Planeta, 1976) p. 70.

195. Beigbeder to Franco, 11 May 1939, *Documentos inéditos para la historia del Generalísimo Franco*, vols I, 2-I, 2-II, III, IV (Madrid: Fundación Nacional Francisco Franco, 1992–4) I, pp. 412–13; Franco Salgado-Araujo, *Mis conversaciones*, p. 327; Luis Suárez Fernández, *Francisco Franco y su tiempo*, 8 vols (Madrid: Fundación Nacional Francisco Franco, 1984) II, pp. 422–3.

196. Ramón Garriga, *La España de Franco. Las relaciones con Hitler*, 2nd edn (Puebla, Mexico: Editorial José M. Cajica Jr, 1970) p. 64.

197. *ABC*, 19 July 1939; Garriga, *Las relaciones con Hitler*, pp. 64–5.

198. Cabanellas, *Cuatro generales*, II, pp. 438–9, 443; Carlos Fernández Santander, *Tensiones militares durante el franquismo* (Barcelona: Plaza y Janés, 1985) pp. 16–21.

199. Reynolds Packard, 'Franco y yo actuamos estrechamente dice Queipo', *Tiempo* (Bogotá), 26 July 1939.

200. Cabanellas, *Cuatro generales*, II, pp. 438–9; Xavier Tusell and Genoveva García Queipo de Llano, *Franco y Mussolini. La política española durante la segunda guerra mundial* (Barcelona: Editorial Planeta, 1985) pp. 41–2.

201. Galeazzo Ciano, diary entries, 23, 27 July 1939, *Diario 1937–1943*, ed. Renzo De Felice (Milano: Rizzoli, 1980) pp. 322–3.

202. Gambara to Ciano, 9 August 1939, *I documenti diplomatici italiani*, 8ª serie, vol. XII (Rome: Libreria dello Stato, 1952) p. 607.

203. Gabriel Cardona, *El gigante descalzo. El ejército de Franco* (Madrid: Aguilar, 2003) pp. 157, 174; Quevedo, *Queipo de Llano*, pp. 469–71.

204. Minutes of meeting between Sagardía and Varela, 19 August 1939, Archivo Varela, Cadiz, Expediente Queipo de Llano, 0071–0072.

205. Fernández-Coppel, *Queipo de Llano. Memorias*, pp. 321–36; Quevedo, *Queipo de Llano*, pp. 465–71; *The Times*, 22, 25, 26 July 1939.

206. Sainz Rodríguez, *Testimonio y recuerdos*, pp. 271–2; Fernández-Coppel, *Queipo de Llano. Memorias*, is replete with criticism of Franco, pp. 136–44, 149–59.

207. Quevedo, *Queipo de Llano*, pp. 472–9, 486–8.

208. Ciano, diary entry, 1 October 1940, *Diario 1937–1943*, p. 468; Serrano Suñer to Queipo, 6 October 1948, Archivo Natalio Rivas, Real Academia de la Historia (Madrid), leg. II – 8923.

209. Ramón Serrano Suñer, *Entre Hendaya y Gibraltar* (Madrid: Ediciones y Publicaciones Españolas, 1947) p. 18; Serrano Suñer, *Memorias*, pp. 218–19.

210. Queipo de Llano to Serrano Suñer, 24 October 1948, Archivo Natalio Rivas, Real Academia de la Historia (Madrid), leg. II – 8923.

211. Quevedo, *Queipo de Llano*, pp. 479, 489–91, 506–13.

212. Queipo to Franco, 18 June 1950, Franco Salgado-Araujo, *Mi vida*, pp. 390–2; Gabriel Cardona, *Franco y sus generales. La manicura del tigre* (Madrid: Ediciones Temas de Hoy, 2001) p. 50; Giménez Arnau, *Memorias de memoria*, p. 127; Quevedo, *Queipo de Llano*, pp. 480–2.

213. Quevedo, *Queipo de Llano*, pp. 491–8, 503, 510–12.

214. Queipo de Llano to Faldella, 30 November 1939, in *ibid.*, pp. 405–15.

215. Dirección General de Seguridad, Grupo de Información de Madrid, 'Sobre el General Queipo de Llano',

4 March 1942; 'Comentarios de los Ayudantes del General Queipo de Llano', 6 March 1942; Jefatura Superior de la Policía de Madrid, 'Sobre estancia del General Queipo de Llano en esta Capital', 7 March 1942, Expediente Queipo de Llano y Sierra, Gonzalo, secc. 1ª, leg. Q-13, 3, Archivo General Militar de Segovia.

216. Queipo al Ministerio del Ejército, 29 June 1939; Declaración jurada de los servicios prestados del general Queipo de Llano, in Queipo de Llano y Sierra, Gonzalo, secc. 1ª, leg. Q-13, Archivo General Militar de Segovia.

217. Queipo to Franco, 18 June 1950, Franco Salgado-Araujo, *Mi vida*, pp. 390–2; *ABC*, 2 April 1940.

218. Cardona, *La manicura*, p. 56; Fernández-Coppel, *Queipo de Llano. Memorias*, pp. 318–19, 325.

219. Queipo, *Hoja de Servicios*, p. 31; Cardona, *La manicura*, pp. 80–1, 95–6, 99.

220. *ABC*, 9 May 1944; Serrano Suñer, *Memorias*, pp. 219–20; Paul Preston, *Franco: A Biography* (London: HarperCollins, 1993) pp. 511–14; Cardona, *La manicura*, p. 109.

221. Queipo, *Hoja de Servicios*, p. 34; Queipo de Llano to Franco, 18 June 1950, Archivo Natalio Rivas, Real Academia de la Historia (Madrid), leg. II – 8923.

222. Franco Salgado-Araujo, *Mis conversaciones*, p. 64.

223. *ABC*, 10, 11 March 1951; Quevedo, *Queipo de Llano*, pp. 13–27, 516–22.

Chapter 8: The Never-ending War against the *Contubernio*

1. *ABC*, 13 May 1939.

2. *ABC*, 18 July 1940.

3. *ABC*, 31 December 1940.

4. *Jewish Chronicle*, 26 April, 28 June 1940; *The Times*, 6 January 1943; Ramón Garriga, *La España de Franco. Las relaciones con Hitler*, 2nd edn (Puebla, Mexico: Editorial José M. Cajica Jr, 1970) pp. 86–93; Manuel Ros Agudo, *La guerra secreta de Franco 1939–1945* (Barcelona: Editorial Crítica, 2002) pp. 274–7; Sir Samuel Hoare, *Ambassador on Special Mission* (London: Collins, 1946) pp. 54–5, 103–4; Gonzalo Álvarez Chillida, *El antisemitismo en España. La imagen del judío (1812–2002)* (Madrid: Marcial Pons, 2002) pp. 381–4; Javier Terrón Montero, *La prensa de España durante el régimen de Franco* (Madrid: Centro de Investigaciones Sociologicas, 1981) pp. 41–54; Mercedes Peñalba-Sotorrío, 'Beyond the War: Nazi Propaganda Aims in Spain during the Second World War', *Journal of Contemporary History*, vol. 54, no. 4, 2019, pp. 902–26; Ingrid Schulze Schneider, 'La propaganda alemana en España 1942–1944', *Espacio, Tiempo y Forma. Serie V, Historia contemporánea*, no. 7, 1994, pp. 371–86; Ingrid Schulze Schneider, 'Éxitos y fracasos de la propaganda alemana en España: 1939–1944', *Mélanges de la Casa de Velázquez*, no. 31, 1995, pp. 197–218.

5. Bernd Rother, *Franco y el Holocausto* (Madrid: Marcial Pons, 2005) p. 158; José Antonio Lisbona Martín, *Más allá del deber. La respuesta humanitaria del Servicio Exterior frente al Holocausto* (Madrid: Ministerio de Asuntos Exteriores y de Cooperación, 2015) pp. 40–1.

6. *Jewish Chronicle*, 25 April 1940, 13 June 1941, 16 January, 24 July 1942.

7. Rother, *Franco y el Holocausto*, pp. 405–10.

8. Discurso a las Cortes, 14 May 1946, Francisco Franco Bahamonde, *Textos de doctrina política. Palabras*

y escritos de 1945 a 1950 (Madrid: Publicaciones Españolas, 1951) pp. 31–59, esp. pp. 40–2, 55.

9. Franco, *Textos de doctrina política*, pp. 245–58.

10. Francisco Franco Bahamonde, *Franco ha dicho. Segundo apéndice* (Madrid: Ediciones Voz, 1951) p. 79.

11. *España y los judíos* (Madrid: Oficina de Información Diplomática, 1949). The French translation and a commentary in Luciano Casali and Lola Harana, *L'oportunisme de Franco. Un informe sobre la qüestió jueva (1949)* (Catarroja/Barcelona: Editorial Afers/Centre d'Estudis Històrics Internacionals, 2013).

12. *Foreign Relations of the United States 1949*, vol. IV (Washington, DC: United States Government Printing Office, 1975) IV, pp. 742–3; Raanan Rein, *In the Shadow of the Holocaust and the Inquisition: Israel's Relations with Francoist Spain* (London: Routledge, 1997) pp. 35–41.

13. *España y los judíos*, pp. 29, 43, 47; Isabelle Rohr, *The Spanish Right and the Jews, 1898–1945: Antisemitism and Opportunism* (Brighton: Sussex Academic Press, 2007) pp. 1–2. Even shortly before the death of Franco in 1975, the ideas of the pamphlet were being propagated in Spain: Federico Ysart, *España y los judíos en la segunda guerra mundial* (Barcelona: Dopesa, 1973).

14. *España y los judíos*, p. 9.

15. *Ibid.*, pp. 16, 29.

16. Álvarez Chillida, *El antisemitismo*, p. 413.

17. Rohr, *The Spanish Right and the Jews*, pp. 2–3.

18. *Jewish Chronicle*, 14, 26 April, 21 June, 5 July 1940.

19. Matthieu Séguéla, *Pétain–Franco: les secrets d'une alliance* (Paris: Albin Michel, 1992) pp. 80–1; *Jewish Chronicle*, 8 November 1940.

20. *ABC*, 2 January 1940; *Mensaje del Caudillo a los españoles: discurso pronunciado por S.E. el Jefe del Estado la noche del 31 de diciembre de 1939* (Madrid: n.p., n.d. [1940]).

21. Javier Tusell, *Carrero. La eminencia gris del régimen de Franco* (Madrid: Temas de Hoy, 1993) pp. 30–1.

22. Carrero Blanco, 'La revolución comunista en la Marina', quoted *ibid.*, pp. 32–3.

23. Luis Carrero Blanco, *España y el mar* (Madrid: Editora Nacional, 1941) pp. 9–10.

24. Tusell, *Carrero*, pp. 45–52, 60–3.

25. *Ibid.*, pp. 83–7.

26. *Arriba*, 30 May 1942; Francisco Franco Bahamonde, *Palabras del Caudillo 19 abril 1937–7 diciembre 1942* (Madrid: Editora Nacional, 1943) p. 213.

27. Quoted in Xavier Tusell and Genoveva García Queipo de Llano, *Franco y Mussolini. La política española durante la segunda guerra mundial* (Barcelona: Editorial Planeta, 1985) p. 185.

28. *ABC*, 5 May 1943. Much more sophisticated and subtle is the reconstruction by Javier Domínguez Arribas, *El enemigo judeo-masónico en la propaganda franquista (1936–1945)* (Madrid: Marcial Pons Historia, 2009) pp. 84–93.

29. Rohr, *The Spanish Right and the Jews*, pp. 90–1.

30. 'Normas para el paso de las fronteras españolas y modelo de solicitud de autorización para entrar en España', *Información de Equipo Nizkor*: http://www.derechos.org/nizkor/espana/doc/franco9.html, 13 December 2012; 'El bisabuelo de Alberto Ruiz Gallardón, José Rojas Moreno, cómplice del holocausto', *Información de Equipo Nizkor*, http://www.derechos.org/nizkor/espana/doc/hoenigsfeld6.html, 26

December 2012; Rother, *Franco y el Holocausto*, pp. 131–3.

31. Garzón, 'España y los judíos', pp. 20–1.

32. *Arriba*, 7, 10, 11, 14 June 1939; *ABC* (Madrid), 10, 11, 14, 15 June 1939.

33. *ABC* (Madrid), 17 December 1939; Monseñor Jouin, *Los peligros judeo-masónicos. Los protocolos de los Sabios de Sión* (Madrid: Ediciones FAX, 1939); Serguei A. Nilus, *Los protocolos de los sabios de Sión* (Madrid: Imprenta de los Talleres Penitenciarios de Alcalá de Henares, 1940); Álvarez Chillida, *El antisemitismo en España*, p. 496.

34. Archivo Histórico Nacional (Pieza segunda de Barcelona. Del Alzamiento Nacional. Antecedentes, Ejército Rojo y Liberación), FC-Causa General, leg. 1630, exp. 1, Declaración de Juan Segura Nieto, pp. 163–6; Juan Segura Nieto, *¡Alerta! ... Francmasonería y Judaísmo* (Barcelona: Felipe González Rojas, 1940) pp. 7–11, 32–4, 40–9; José Fernando Mota Muñoz, '"Precursores de la unificación": el España Club y el voluntariado español, una experiencia unitaria de la extrema derecha barcelonesa (1935–1936)', *Historia y Política*, 28, 2012, pp. 273–303.

35. Ángel Alcázar de Velasco, *Serrano Suñer en la Falange* (Madrid/Barcelona: Patria, 1941) pp. 28–32.

36. Dionisio Ridruejo, *Los cuadernos de Rusia* (Barcelona: Editorial Planeta, 1978) p. 40.

37. 'Informe secreto sobre el trato a los judíos en Polonia', December 1941, *Documentos inéditos para la historia del Generalísimo Franco*, vols I, 2-I, 2-II, III, IV (Madrid: Fundación Nacional Francisco Franco, 1992–4) II–2, pp. 404–8; 'Informes de la DGS', 28 April, 20 August 1942,

Documentos inéditos, III, pp. 346, 571–2.

38. Vidal to Jordana (5 March 1943), Ministerio de Asuntos Exteriores, R1177-1, quoted by Emilio Sáenz-Francés San Baldomero, 'La deportación en 1943 de la comunidad sefardita de Salónica', *APORTES: Revista de historia contemporánea*, vol. XXVI, no. 77, 2011, pp. 44–5.

39. Rother, *Franco y el Holocausto*, pp. 125–9.

40. Alfonso Lazo, *La Iglesia, la Falange y el fascismo (un estudio sobre la prensa española de postguerra)* (Seville: Universidad de Sevilla, 1995), pp. 188–96; Rother, *Franco y el Holocausto*, pp. 68–77, 125–9.

41. Lazo, *La Iglesia, la Falange y el fascismo*, pp. 187–90.

42. Jacobo Israel Garzón, 'España y los judíos (1939–1945). Una visión general', in Jacobo Israel Garzón and Alejandro Baer, *España y el Holocausto (1939–1945). Historia y testimonios* (Madrid: Ebraica Ediciones, 2007) pp. 18–23.

43. Rohr, *The Spanish Right and the Jews*, pp. 102–3, 106–10.

44. Pilar Vera, 'La huida silenciosa', *Diario de Cádiz*, 30 August 2009; Javier Dale, 'El éxodo de un judío catalán', *La Vanguardia*, 26 March 2010.

45. Jorge M. Reverte, 'La lista de Franco para el Holocausto', *El País*, 20 June 2010.

46. On the measures against Jews and freemasons during the civil war, see Paul Preston, *The Spanish Holocaust: Inquisition and Extermination in Twentieth-Century Spain* (London: Harper Press, 2012) pp. 486–7.

47. Lazo, *La Iglesia, la Falange y el fascismo*, pp. 283–4.

48. Rohr, *The Spanish Right and the Jews*, pp. 30–2, 124; Haim Avni,

Spain, the Jews and Franco
(Philadelphia: The Jewish
Publication Society of America,
1982) pp. 130–5.

49. Javier Tusell, *Franco, España y la II
guerra mundial. Entre el Eje y la
neutralidad* (Madrid: Temas de
Hoy, 1995) pp. 585–9; Eduardo
Martín de Pozuelo, *El franquismo,
cómplice del Holocausto* (Barcelona:
La Vanguardia, 2012) pp. 39–40;
Danielle Rozenberg, *La España
contemporánea y la cuestión judía*
(Madrid: Marcial Pons, 2010)
p. 232; Lisbona Martín, *Más allá
del deber*, pp. 41–5; Rohr, *The
Spanish Right and the Jews*,
pp. 123–47.

50. Martin Gilbert, *Road to Victory:
Winston S. Churchill, 1941–1945*
(London: Heinemann, 1986)
pp. 377–8.

51. Rohr, *The Spanish Right and the
Jews*, pp. 144–6; Javier Martínez
Bedoya, *Memorias desde mi aldea*
(Valladolid: Ambito Ediciones,
1996) pp. 224–32.

52. Rother, *Franco y el Holocausto*,
pp. 128–9, 408–9; Antonio
Marquina Barrio and Gloria Inés
Ospina, *España y los judíos en el
siglo XX* (Madrid: Espasa Calpe,
1987) pp. 212–22; Diego Carcedo,
*Un español frente al Holocausto. Así
salvó Ángel Sanz Briz 5.000 judíos*
(Madrid: Temas de Hoy, 2000)
pp. 199–268; Rohr, *The Spanish
Right and the Jews*, pp. 149–52; Juan
Diego Quesada, 'Franco lo Supo –
Excelencia, esto ocurre en
Auschwitz', *El País*, 21 March 2010.

53. 'Testimony of Isaac Revah, on the
action of the Spanish Consul in
Athens in 1943, Sebastian de
Romero Radigales', *eSepharad*,
https://esefarad.com/?p=35916;
'Diplomáticos españoles y el
holocausto' (Madrid: Ministerio de
Asuntos Exteriores, 2013); Sáenz-

Francés, 'La deportación en 1943 de
la comunidad sefardita de Salónica',
pp. 45–53.

54. Rohr, *The Spanish Right and the
Jews*, p. 153; Álvarez Chillida, *El
antisemitismo*, pp. 414–17.

55. Álvarez Chillida, *El antisemitismo*,
p. 416; Juan de la Cosa (pseudonym
of Luis Carrero Blanco), *Las
tribulaciones de Don Prudencio.
Comentarios de un español*
(Valencia: Semana Gráfica, 1947).
Quotations from the reissued
edition, published under his own
name, Luis Carrero Blanco, *Las
tribulaciones de Don Prudencio.
Diplomacia subterranea.
Comentarios de un español* (Madrid:
Fuerza Nueva, 1973) pp. 163, 170,
183, 334–9.

56. See the references to Franco's
speeches in the chapter on Mauricio
Carlavilla.

57. *Arriba*, 16 July 1949; Jakim Boor
(pseudonym of Francisco
Franco Bahamonde), *Masonería*
(Madrid: Gráficas Valera, 1952)
pp. 65–6.

58. *Arriba*, 11 December 1949; Boor,
Masonería, p. 96.

59. Francisco Franco Bahamonde (J.
Boor), *Masonería* (Madrid:
Fundación Nacional Francisco
Franco, 1982).

60. Rogelio Baón, *La cara humana de
un Caudillo* (Madrid: Editorial San
Martín, 1975) p. 99.

61. Luis Suárez Fernández, *Francisco
Franco y su tiempo*, 8 vols (Madrid:
Fundación Nacional Francisco
Franco, 1984) IV, p. 431–3.

62. *Arriba*, 16 July 1950; Boor,
Masonería, pp. 220–4. For a less
critical, not to say benevolent,
interpretation of Franco's anti-
Semitic outbursts, see Andrée
Bachoud, *Franco* (Barcelona:
Editorial Crítica, 2000)
pp. 232–6.

63. Rohr, *The Spanish Right and the Jews*, p. 5.

64. José Antonio Ferrer Benimeli, *El contubernio judeo-masónico-comunista*, p. 315.

65. Herbert R. Southworth, *Antifalange. Estudio crítico de 'Falange en la guerra de España: la unificación y Hedilla' de Maximiano García Venero* (Paris: Ruedo Ibérico, 1967) pp. 63–70; Manuel Azaña, *Obras completas*, 4 vols (Mexico City: Ediciones Oasis, 1966–8) IV, pp. 229, 421.

66. Ernesto Giménez Caballero, *Memorias de un dictador* (Barcelona: Editorial Planeta, 1979) pp. 88–90.

67. Southworth, *Antifalange*, pp. 32–4; Rohr, *The Spanish Right and the Jews*, pp. 28–30; Andrés Trapiello, *Las armas y las letras. Literatura y guerra civil (1936–1939)*, 3rd edn (Barcelona: Destino, 2010) pp. 63–5.

68. Rohr, *The Spanish Right and the Jews*, pp. 73, 82.

69. Ernesto Giménez Caballero, *Genio de España. Exaltaciones a una resurrección nacional. Y del mundo*, 4th edn (Barcelona: Ediciones Jerarquía, 1939) pp. 110–13; 7th edn (Madrid: Doncel, 1971) pp. 105–9.

70. *La Gaceta Regional* (Salamanca), 25 April 1937, quoted in Carlos Fernández Santander, *Antología de 40 años (1936–1975)* (Sada-A Coruña: Ediciós do Castro, 1983) p. 38.

71. Eugenio Vegas Latapie, *Los caminos del desengaño. Memorias políticas 2, 1936–1938* (Madrid: Ediciones Giner, 1987) pp. 249, 259.

72. Ernesto Giménez Caballero, *España y Franco* (Cegama: Ediciones 'Los Combatientes', 1938) pp. 30–1.

73. Giménez Caballero, *Memorias*, pp. 148–52. On Jesuits: Garriga, *La España de Franco*, pp. 314–15.

74. Giménez Caballero, *Memorias*, p. 154.

75. Giménez Caballero to Franco, 5 December 1947, reproduced by Jesús Palacios, *Las cartas de Franco. La correspondencia desconocida que marcó el destino de España* (Madrid: La Esfera de Los Libros, 2005) pp. 251–2.

76. Ramón Garriga, *El general Yagüe* (Barcelona: Editorial Planeta, 1985) pp. 268–9.

77. Boor, *Masonería*, pp. 96, 140–1; Álvarez Chillida, *El antisemitismo*, pp. 396–401; Domínguez Arribas, *El enemigo judeo-masónico*, pp. 93–7.

78. Álvarez Chillida, *El antisemitismo*, pp. 445–52; Manuel Fraga Iribarne, *Pregón de Semana Santa 1971* (Zamora: Junta Pro-Semana Santa, 1971) [p. 7]; Javier de la Puerta, 'Fraga y los Judíos: Semana Santa en Zamora (1971)', *Diario del Aire*, 18 April 2013.

79. Samuel Hadas, 'Un legado para la transición: Israel', in Raanan Rein (ed.), *España e Israel. Veinte años después* (Madrid: Fundación Tres Culturas del Mediterráneo, 2007) p. 47.

80. Javier Tusell, 'El día en que voló Carrero Blanco', *El País*, 14 December 1998; Ferrer Benimeli, *El contubernio*, pp. 327–8.

81. Alberto Vassallo de Mumbert, 'Introducción del Editor', César Casanova Gonzalez-Mateo, *Manual de urgencia sobre el Sionismo en España. Los innumerables perjuros de nuestra patria* (Madrid: Vassallo de Mumbert, 1979) pp. 9–10.

82. Casanova Gonzalez-Mateo, *Manual de urgencia*, pp. 159–60.

83. *Ibid.*, pp. 72–3, 90–4, 98–101.

84. Álvarez Chillida, *El antisemitismo*, pp. 474–81; Fernando Sánchez Dragó, *Gárgoris y Habidis. Una*

historia mágica de España
(Barcelona: Editorial Planeta, 2001).

85. *Ya*, 19 July 1981, quoted by
Benimeli, *El contubernio*, p. 135.

86. https://oracionyliturgia.
archimadrid.org/2015/09/25/el–

santo–nino–de–la–guardia–
martir–%E2%80%A0–
1489–3–3–2–2/.

87. *El Pais*, 16 February 2021; *The
Times*, 18 February 2021.

88. *20 Minutos*, 16 February 2021.

Bibliography

Archival Sources
Archivo General Militar de Segovia:
   Expediente de General Campins
   Expediente Gonzalo Aguilera Munro
   Expediente Queipo de Llano y Sierra, Gonzalo
   Hoja de Servicios de Emilio Mola Vidal
   Hoja de Servicios de Gonzalo Aguilera y Munro
   Hoja de Servicios de Gonzalo Queipo de Llano Sierra
Archivo Natalio Rivas, Real Academia de la Historia
Archivo Varela, Cadiz
Archivo Histórico Nacional
Archivo Histórico Provincial de Salamanca, Fondo Luna Terrero
Archivo de la Universidad de Salamanca, Fondo Conde de Alba de
   Yeltes
Archivio Storico del Ministero Affari Esteri, Spagna Fondo di
   Guerra, 287/137, b.38.
Ufficio Spagna
Arquivo Nacional, Torre do Tombo, Lisbon, PIDE, Serviços
   Centrais, Registro Geral de Presos
Archivo General del Ministerio de Interior

Published Primary Sources
Archivo General Militar de Segovia: índice de expedientes personales
   (Madrid: Ediciones Hidalguía, 1959)
Archivo Gomá, *Documentos de la guerra civil*, 13 vols, ed. José
   Andrés-Gallego and Antón M. Pazos (Madrid: Consejo Superior
   de Investigaciones Científicas, 2001–7)

Boletín Oficial del Estado

Dez anos de política externa (1936–1947) a naçaõ portuguesa e a segunda guerra mundial III (Lisbon: Imprensa Nacional de Lisboa, 1964)

Diario de sesiones de las Cortes Constituyentes de la República española. Comenzaron el 14 de julio de 1931, 25 vols (Madrid: Sucesores de Rivadeneyra, 1933)

Diario de las sesiones de Cortes, Congreso de los Diputados. Comenzaron el 8 de diciembre de 1933, 18 vols (Madrid: Sucesores de Rivadeneyra, 1935)

Diario de las sesiones de Cortes, Congreso de los Diputados. Comenzaron el 16 de marzo de 1936, 4 vols (Madrid: Sucesores de Rivadeneyra, 1936)

Documentos inéditos para la historia del Generalísimo Franco, vols I, 2-I, 2-II, III, IV (Madrid: Fundación Nacional Francisco Franco, 1992–4)

Documents on German Foreign Policy, Series D, vol. III (London: HMSO, 1951)

Estado Mayor Central, *Anuario Militar de España 1931* (Madrid: Ministerio de Guerra, 1931)

Estado Mayor Central, *Anuario Militar de España 1932* (Madrid: Ministerio de Guerra, 1932)

Estado Mayor Central, *Anuario Militar de España 1933* (Madrid: Ministerio de Guerra, 1933)

Estado Mayor Central, *Anuario Militar de España 1936* (Madrid: Ministerio de la Guerra, 1936)

Foreign Relations of the United States 1936, vol. II (Washington, DC: United States Government Printing Office, 1954)

Foreign Relations of the United States 1937, vol. I (Washington, DC: United States Government Printing Office, 1954)

Foreign Relations of the United States 1949, vol. IV (Washington, DC: United States Government Printing Office, 1975)

I documenti diplomatici italiani, 8ª serie, vol. VI (Rome: Libreria dello Stato, 1997)

I documenti diplomatici italiani, 8ª serie, vol. XII (Rome: Libreria dello Stato, 1952)

Newspapers and Journals

ABC (Madrid)
ABC (Seville)
Acción Española
Ahora
Arriba
Avui
Azul (Córdoba)
Belfast Telegraph
Blanco y Negro
CEDA
Claridad
Daily Herald
Diario de Cádiz
Diario de Jerez
Diario del Aire
Diario Oficial del Ministerio de la Guerra
El Adelanto (Salamanca)
El Caso
El Correo Catalán
El Correo de Andalucía (Seville)
El Debate
elDiario.es
El Imparcial
El Liberal
El Mundo
El Obrero de la Tierra
El País
El Progreso (Lugo)
El Siglo Futuro
El Socialista
El Sol
Ellas. Semanario de Mujeres Españolas
Estampa
F.E.
Gaceta de Madrid
Gaceta de Tenerife

Gracia y Justicia
Heraldo de Madrid
Ideal (Granada)
Informaciones
JAP
Jewish Chronicle
La Ciudad y los Campos
La Crónica de Salamanca
La Época
La Gaceta Regional (Salamanca)
La Libertad
La Mañana
La Nación
La Unión (Seville)
La Vanguardia
La Voz (Madrid)
La Voz de Galicia
La Voz del Sur
Le Matin
Le Temps
L'Oeuvre
Milicia Popular
Mundo Gráfico
Mundo Obrero
Región (Cáceres)
Sphere
The Times
Tiempo (Bogotá)
Unión Monárquica
20 Minutos
Ya
Yorkshire Evening Post

Theoretical Works, Diaries and Memoirs by Protagonists

Aguilera, Gonzalo de, Conde de Alba de Yeltes, *Cartas a un sobrino* (n.p., n.d.)

Aguilera, Gonzalo de, Conde de Alba de Yeltes, *El átomo. Sus componentes, energía y medio* (Madrid: Talleres M. Rollán, 1946)

Anon., *Los peligros judeo-masónicos. Los protocolos de los Sabios de Sión* (Madrid: Fax, 1932)

Anon., *Protocolos de los Sabios de Sión* (Valladolid: Libertad/ Afrodisio Aguado, 1934)

Azaña, Manuel, *Diarios, 1932–1933. 'Los cuadernos robados'* (Barcelona: Grijalbo-Mondadori, 1997)

Azaña, Manuel, *Obras completas*, 4 vols (Mexico City: Ediciones Oasis, 1966–8)

Boor, Jakim (pseudonym of Francisco Franco Bahamonde), *Masonería* (Madrid: Gráficas Valera, 1952)

Cantalupo, Roberto, *Fu la Spagna. Ambasciata presso Franco. Febbraio–Aprile 1937* (Milan: Mondadori, 1948)

Carlavilla, Mauricio, *Anti-España 1959. Autores, cómplices y encubridores del comunismo* (Madrid: Editorial Nos, 1959)

Carlavilla, Mauricio, *Borbones masones desde Fernando VII a Alfonso XIII* (Barcelona: Acervo, 1967)

Carlavilla, Mauricio, *El Rey. Radiografía del reinado de Alfonso XIII* (Madrid: Editorial Nos, 1956)

Carlavilla, Mauricio, *Satanismo* (Madrid: Editorial Nos, 1957)

Carrero Blanco, Luis, *España y el mar* (Madrid: Editora Nacional, 1941)

Carrero Blanco, Luis, *Las tribulaciones de Don Prudencio. Diplomacia subterranea. Comentarios de un español* (Madrid: Fuerza Nueva, 1973)

Casanova Gonzalez-Mateo, César, *Manual de urgencia sobre el Sionismo en España. Los innumerables perjuros de nuestra patria* (Madrid: Vassallo de Mumbert, 1979)

De la Cosa, Juan (pseudonym of Luis Carrero Blanco), *Las tribulaciones de Don Prudencio. Comentarios de un español* (Valencia: Semana Gráfica, 1947)

Faldella, Emilio, *Venti mesi di guerra in Spagna* (Florence: Le Monnier, 1939)

Franco Bahamonde, Francisco, *Franco ha dicho. Primer apéndice (contiene de 1º enero 1947 a 1º abril 1949)* (Madrid: Ediciones Voz, 1949)

Franco Bahamonde, Francisco, *Franco ha dicho. Segundo apéndice* (Madrid: Ediciones Voz, 1951)

Franco Bahamonde, Francisco (originally published under pseudonym Jakim Boor), *Masonería* (Madrid: Fundación Nacional Francisco Franco, 1982)

Franco Bahamonde, Francisco, *Manuscritos de Franco* (Madrid: Fundación Francisco Franco, 1986)

Franco Bahamonde, Francisco, *Mensaje del Caudillo a los españoles. Discurso pronunciado por S.E. el Jefe del Estado la noche del 31 de diciembre de 1939* (Madrid: n.p., n.d. [1940])

Franco Bahamonde, Francisco, *Palabras del Caudillo 19 abril 1937–7 diciembre 1942* (Madrid: Ediciones de la Vicesecretaría de Educación Popular, 1943)

Franco Bahamonde, Francisco, *Palabras del Caudillo 19 abril 1937–31 diciembre 1938* (Barcelona: Ediciones Fe, 1939)

Franco Bahamonde, Francisco, *Textos de doctrina política. Palabras y escritos de 1945 a 1950* (Madrid: Publicaciones Españolas, 1951)

Franco Bahamonde, Francisco. *'Apuntes' personales sobre la República y la guerra civil* (Madrid: Fundación Nacional Francisco Franco, 1987)

Giménez Caballero, Ernesto, *España y Franco* (Cegama: Ediciones 'Los Combatientes', 1938)

Giménez Caballero, Ernesto, *Genio de España. Exaltaciones a una resurrección nacional. Y del mundo*, 4th edn (Barcelona: Ediciones Jerarquía, 1939), 7th edn (Madrid: Doncel, 1971)

Giménez Caballero, Ernesto, *Memorias de un dictador* (Barcelona: Editorial Planeta, 1979)

Jouin, Mgr Ernest, *Le Péril judéo-maçonnique: Les 'Protocols' des Sages de Sion* (Paris: Revue Internationale des Sociétés Secrètes, 1932)

Jouin, Monseñor, *Los peligros judeo-masónicos. Los protocolos de los Sabios de Sión* (Madrid: Ediciones FAX, 1939)

Karl, Mauricio (pseudonym of Mauricio Carlavilla del Barrio), *Sodomitas* (Madrid: Editorial Nos, 1956)

Karl, Mauricio (pseudonym of Mauricio Carlavilla del Barrio),
  *Asesinos de España. Marxismo, anarquismo, masonería.
  Compendio* (Madrid: Imp. Sáez Hermanos, 1936)

Karl, Mauricio (pseudonym of Mauricio Carlavilla del Barrio), *El
  comunismo en España. 5 años en el partido, su organización y sus
  misterios* (Madrid: Imp. Sáez Hermanos, 1931)

Karl, Mauricio (pseudonym of Mauricio Carlavilla del Barrio), *El
  enemigo. Marxismo, anarquismo, masonería*, 4th edn (Santiago de
  Chile: Ediciones Ercilla, 1937)

Karl, Mauricio (pseudonym of Mauricio Carlavilla del Barrio),
  Moscú hoy (Barcelona: A.H.R., 1955)

Llanas de Niubó, René, *El Judaísmo* (Barcelona: Editorial Vilamala,
  1935)

Luis, Francisco de, *La masonería contra España* (Burgos: Imprenta
  Aldecoa, 1935)

Mola Vidal, Emilio, *Obras completas* (Valladolid: Librería Santarén,
  1940)

Mola Vidal, Emilio, *Tempestad, calma, intriga y crisis. Memorias de
  mi paso por la Dirección General de Seguridad* (Madrid: Librería
  Bergua, 1932)

Pemartín, José, *Qué es 'lo nuevo' … Consideraciones sobre el
  momento español presente*, 3rd edn (Madrid: Espasa Calpe, 1940)

Pemán, José María, *Apuntes autobiográficos. Confesión general y
  otros* (Madrid: Edibesa, 1998)

Pemán, José María, *Arengas y crónicas de guerra* (Cadiz:
  Establecimientos Cerón, 1937)

Pemán, José María, *Crónicas de antes y después del diluvio*
  (Valladolid: Imprenta Castellana, 1939)

Pemán, José María, *De la entrada en Madrid, historia de tres días
  (27, 28 y 29 de marzo)* (Cadiz: Ediciones 'Verba', 1939)

Pemán, José María, *El hecho y la idea de la Unión Patriótica*
  (Madrid: Imprenta Artística Sáez Hermanos, 1929)

Pemán, José María, 'Prólogo', *El Pensamiento de Primo de Rivera.
  Sus notas, artículos y discursos* (Madrid: Ediciones de la Junta de
  Propaganda Patriótica y Ciudadana, 1929)

Pemán, José María, *La historia de España contada con sencillez*, 2
  vols (Cadiz: Establecimientos Cerón y Librería Cervantes, 1939)

Pemán, José María, *Mis almuerzos con gente importante* (Barcelona: Dopesa, 1970)

Pemán, José María, *Mis encuentros con Franco* (Barcelona: Dopesa, 1976)

Pemán, José María, *Obras completas*, vol. V: *Doctrina y oratoria* (Madrid: Escelicer, 1953)

Pemán, José María, *Poema de la bestia y el ángel* (Madrid: Ediciones Españolas, 1939)

Pemán, José María, 'Semblanza del Caudillo Franco', *Ejército*, no. 1, 1940

Pemán, José María, *Un soldado en la historia. Vida del capitán general Varela* (Cadiz: Escelicer, 1954)

Queipo de Llano, General, 'Cómo dominamos a Sevilla', in *Estampas de la guerra*, vol. V: *Frentes de Andalucía y Extremadura* (San Sebastián: Editora Nacional, 1938)

Queipo de Llano, Gonzalo, *El general Queipo de Llano perseguido por la dictadura* (Madrid: Javier Morato, 1930)

Queipo de Llano, Gonzalo, *El movimiento reivindicativo de Cuatro Vientos* (Madrid: Tipógrafía Yagües, 1933)

Queipo de Llano, Gonzalo, 'Nuestro Propósito', *Revista de Tropas Coloniales* (Tetuán), year 1, no. 1, January 1924

Redondo, Onésimo, *Obras completas. Edición cronológica II* (Madrid: Publicaciones Españolas, 1955)

Richthofen, Wolfram von, 'Spanien-Tagebuch', reproduced in Klaus A. Maier, *Guernica 26.4.1937. Die deutsche Intervention in Spanien und der 'Fall Guernica'* (Freiburg: Verlag Rombach, 1975)

Ridruejo, Dionisio, *Casi unas memorias* (Barcelona: Editorial Planeta, 1976)

Ridruejo, Dionisio, *Los cuadernos de Rusia* (Barcelona: Editorial Planeta, 1978)

Sallairai, Aurelio, *Protocolos de los sábios de Sión y la subversión mundial* (Buenos Aires: n.p., 1972)

Serrano Suñer, Ramón, *Entre el silencio y la propaganda, la historia como fue. Memorias* (Barcelona: Editorial Planeta, 1977)

Serrano Suñer, Ramón, *Entre Hendaya y Gibraltar* (Madrid: Ediciones y Publicaciones Españolas, 1947)

Serrano Suñer, Ramón, *Siete discursos* (Bilbao: Ediciones Fe, 1938)

Suñer, Enrique, *Los intelectuales y la tragedia española*, 2nd edn (San Sebastián: Editorial Española, 1938)

Tusquets, Joan, *El teosofisme*, vol. 3 (Tremp: Llibreria Central, 1927)

Tusquets, Juan, *La Francmasonería, crimen de lesa patria* (Burgos: Ediciones Antisectarias, 1936)

Tusquets, Juan, *Masonería y separatismo* (Burgos: Ediciones Antisectarias, 1937)

Tusquets, Juan, *Masones y pacifistas* (Burgos: Ediciones Antisectarias, 1939)

Tusquets, Juan, *Orígenes de la revolución española* (Barcelona: Editorial Vilamala, 1932)

Tusquets, Juan, et al., *La dictadura masónica en España y en el mundo* (Barcelona: Editorial Vilamala, 1934)

Tusquets, Juan, et al., *Los poderes ocultos de España. Los Protocolos y su aplicación a España – Infiltraciones masónicas en el catalanismo – ¿El señor Macià es masón?* (Barcelona: Editorial Vilamala, 1932)

Tusquets, Juan, et al., *Secretos de la política española* (Barcelona: Editorial Vilamala, 1934)

Vallejo Nágera, Antonio, *Divagaciones intranscendentes* (Valladolid: Talleres Tipográficos 'Cuesta', 1938)

Vallejo Nágera, Antonio, *Eugenesia de la hispanidad y regeneración de la raza española* (Burgos: Talleres Gráficos El Noticiero, 1937)

Vallejo Nágera, Antonio, *Higiene de la Raza. La asexualización de los psicópatas* (Madrid: Ediciones Medicina, 1934)

Vallejo Nágera, Antonio, *La locura y la guerra. Psicopatología de la guerra española* (Valladolid: Librería Santarén, 1939)

Vallejo Nágera, Antonio and Martínez, Eduardo M., 'Psiquismo del Fanatismo Marxista. Investigaciones Psicológicas en Marxistas Femeninos Delincuentes', *Revista Española de Medicina y Cirugía de Guerra*, no. 9, 1939

Other Books and Articles

Aguirre González, Jesús Vicente, *Aquí nunca pasó nada. La Rioja 1936* (Logroño: Editorial Ochoa, 2007)

Albertí, Jordi, *El silencí de les campanes. De l'anticlericalisme del segle XIX a la persecució religiosa durant la guerra civil a Catalunya* (Barcelona: Proa, 2007)

Alcalá-Zamora, Niceto, *Memorias* (Barcelona: Editorial Planeta, 1977)

Alcázar de Velasco, Ángel, *Serrano Suñer en la Falange* (Madrid/ Barcelona: Patria, 1941)

Alfarache, Guzmán de (pseudonym of Enrique Vila), *¡18 de julio! Historia del alzamiento glorioso de Seville* (Seville: Editorial F.E., 1937)

Alía Miranda, Francisco, *Julio de 1936. Conspiración y alzamiento contra la Segunda República* (Barcelona: Editorial Crítica, 2011)

Alpert, Michael, *La reforma militar de Azaña (1931–1933)* (Madrid: Siglo XXI, 1982)

Altaffaylla, *Navarra. De la esperanza al terror*, 8th edn (Tafalla: Altaffaylla, 2004)

Alted Vigil, Alicia, *Política del Nuevo Estado sobre el patrimonio cultural y la educación durante la guerra civil española* (Madrid: Dirección General de Bellas Artes y Archivos, 1984)

Álvarez Chillida, Gonzalo, *El antisemitismo en España. La imagen del judío (1812–2002)* (Madrid: Marcial Pons, 2002)

Álvarez Chillida, Gonzalo, *José María Pemán. Pensamiento y trayectoria de un monárquico (1897–1941)* (Cadiz: Universidad de Cádiz Servicio de Publicaciones, 1996)

Alvarez del Vayo, Julio, *The Last Optimist* (London: Putnam, 1950)

Álvarez Oblanca, Wenceslao, *La represión de postguerra en León. Depuración de la enseñanza (1936–1943)* (León: Santiago García Editor, 1986)

Álvarez Rey, Leandro, *La derecha en la II República. Sevilla, 1931–1936* (Seville: Universidad de Sevilla/Ayuntamiento de Sevilla, 1993)

Álvaro Dueñas, Manuel, *'Por ministerio de la ley y voluntad del Caudillo'. La Jurisdicción Especial de Responsabilidades Políticas (1939–1945)* (Madrid: Centro de Estudios Políticos y Constitucionales, 2006)

Andrés-Gallego, José, *¿Fascismo o Estado católico? Ideología, religión y censura en la España de Franco, 1937–1941* (Madrid: Ediciones Encuentro, 1997)

Angosto, Pedro Luis, *José Alonso Mallol. El hombre que pudo evitar la guerra* (Alicante: Instituto de Cultura Juan Gil-Albert, 2010)

Anon. (Herbert R. Southworth), *Franco's 'Mein Kampf': The Fascist State in Rebel Spain: An Official Blueprint* (New York: The Spanish Information Bureau, 1939)

Ansaldo, Juan Antonio, *¿Para qué? de Alfonso XIII a Juan III* (Buenos Aires: Editorial Vasca-Ekin, 1951)

Ansó, Mariano, *Yo fui ministro de Negrín* (Barcelona: Editorial Planeta, 1976)

Anson, Luis María, *Don Juan* (Barcelona: Plaza y Janés, 1994)

Areilza, José María de, *Así los he visto* (Barcelona: Editorial Planeta, 1974)

Arias González, Luis, *Gonzalo de Aguilera Munro, XI Conde de Alba de Yeltes (1886–1965). Vidas y radicalismo de un hidalgo heterodoxo* (Salamanca: Ediciones Universidad de Salamanca, 2013)

Armiñán, Luis de, *Excmo. Sr. General Don Gonzalo Queipo de Llano y Sierra Jefe del Ejército del Sur* (Ávila: Imprenta Católica, 1937)

Aróstegui, Julio, *Largo Caballero. El tesón y la quimera* (Barcelona: Editorial Debate, 2013)

Arrarás, Joaquín, *Historia de la Cruzada española*, 8 vols (Madrid: Ediciones Españolas, 1939–43)

Arrarás, Joaquín, *Historia de la segunda República española*, 4 vols (Madrid: Editora Nacional, 1956–68)

Arteche, José de, *Un vasco en la posguerra (1906–1971)* (Bilbao: La Gran Enciclopedia Vasca, 1977)

Arxiu Vidal i Barraquer, *Esglesia i Estat durant la Segona República espanyola, 1931/1936*, 4 vols in 8 parts (Monestir de Montserrat: Publicacions de l'Abadia de Montserrat, 1971–90)

Atienza, J., *Nobiliario español. Diccionario heráldico de apellidos españoles y títulos nobiliarios*, 3rd edn (Madrid: Aguilar, 1959)

Augusto, José, *Jornal de um correspondente da guerra em Espanha* (Lisbon: Empresa Nacional de Publicidade, 1936)

Aunós, Eduardo, *Primo de Rivera. Soldado y gobernante* (Madrid: Editorial Alhambra, 1944)

Avni, Haim, *Spain, the Jews, and Franco* (Philadelphia: The Jewish Publication Society of America, 1982)

Aznar, Manuel, *Historia militar de la guerra de España (1936–1939)* (Madrid: Ediciones Idea, 1940)

Azpíroz Pascual, José María and Elboj Broto, Fernando, *La sublevación de Jaca* (Zaragoza: Guara Editorial, 1984)

Azzuz Hakim, Mohammad Ibn, *La actitud de los moros ante el alzamiento. Marruecos, 1936* (Malaga: Editorial Algazara, 1997)

Babío Urkidi, Carlos and Pérez Lorenzo, Manuel, *Meirás. Un pazo, un caudillo, un espolio* (A Coruña: Fundación Galiza Sempre, 2017)

Bachoud, Andrée, *Franco* (Barcelona: Editorial Crítica, 2000)

Bahamonde y Sánchez de Castro, Antonio, *Un año con Queipo* (Barcelona: Ediciones Españolas, n.d. [1938])

Baón, Rogelio, *La cara humana de un Caudillo* (Madrid: Editorial San Martín, 1975)

Baquero, Juan Manuel, *Que fuera mi tierra. Anuario 2015* (Sevilla: Extra! Comunicación/Dirección General de Memoria Democrática, Consejería de Cultura, Junta de Andalucía, 2016)

Barbero, Edmundo, *El infierno azul (Seis meses en el feudo de Queipo)* (Madrid: Talleres del SUIG (CNT), 1937)

Barranquero Texeira, Encarnación, *Málaga entre la guerra y la posguerra. El franquismo* (Malaga: Editorial Arguval, 1994)

Barranquero Texeira, Encarnación and Prieto Borrego, Lucía, *Población y guerra civil en Málaga. Caída, éxodo y refugio* (Malaga: Centro de Ediciones de la Diputación de Málaga, 2007)

Barrios, Manuel, *El último virrey Queipo de Llano*, 3rd edn (Seville: J. Rodríguez Castillejo, 1990)

Bedmar González, Arcángel, *República, guerra y represión. Lucena, 1931–1939*, 2nd edn (Lucena: Ayuntamiento de Lucena, 2010)

Ben Ami, Shlomo, 'The Forerunners of Spanish Fascism: Unión Patriótica and Unión Monárquica', *European Studies Review*, vol. 9, no. 1, 1979

Ben Ami, Shlomo, *The Origins of the Second Republic in Spain* (Oxford: Oxford University Press, 1978)

Benet, Josep, *L'intent franquista de genocidi cultural contra Catalunya* (Barcelona: Publicacions de l'Abadia de Montserrat, 1995)

Bernanos, Georges, *Les Grands Cimitières sous la lune* (Paris: Plon, 1938)

Bernard, Ino, *Mola mártir de España* (Granada: Librería Prieto, 1938)

Bertrán Güell, Felipe, *Preparación y desarrollo del alzamiento nacional* (Valladolid: Librería Santarén, 1939)

Berzal de la Rosa, Enrique (ed.), *Testimonio de voces olvidadas*, 2 vols (León: Fundación 27 de marzo, 2007)

Bethune, Dr Norman, *The Crime on the Road Malaga–Almeria* (n.p.: Publicaciones Iberia, 1937)

Blanco Escolá, Carlos, *General Mola. Elególatra que provocó la guerra civil* (Madrid: La Esfera de los Libros, 2002)

Blanco Escolá, Carlos, *La incompetencia militar de Franco* (Madrid: Alianza Editorial, 2000)

Blinkhorn, Martin, *Carlism and Crisis in Spain, 1931–1939* (Cambridge: Cambridge University Press, 1975)

Bolín, Luis, *Spain: The Vital Years* (Philadelphia: J. B. Lippincott, 1967)

Bolloten, Burnett, *The Spanish Civil War: Revolution and Counterrevolution* (Hemel Hempstead: Harvester Wheatsheaf, 1991)

Bonmati de Codecido, Francisco, *El Príncipe Don Juan de España* (Valladolid: Librería Santarén, 1938)

Bowers, Claude, *My Mission to Spain* (London: Victor Gollancz, 1954)

Boyd, Carolyn P., 'Responsibilities and the Second Spanish Republic 1931–6', *European History Quarterly*, vol. 14, 1984

Bravo Morata, Federico, *Franco y los muertos providenciales* (Madrid: Editorial Fenicia, 1979)

Brenan, Gerald, *Personal Record, 1920–1972* (London: Jonathan Cape, 1974)

Buckley, Henry, *Life and Death of the Spanish Republic: A Witness to the Spanish Civil War* (London: I. B. Tauris, 2013)

Bullón de Mendoza y Gómez de Valugera, Alfonso, *José Calvo Sotelo* (Barcelona: Ariel, 2004)

Burgo, Jaime del, *Conspiración y guerra civil* (Madrid: Editorial Alfaguara, 1970)

Burgos y Mazo, Manuel de, *De la República a …?* (Madrid: Javier Morata, 1931)

Cabanellas, Guillermo, *Cuatro generales*, 2 vols (Barcelona: Editorial Planeta, 1977)

Cabanellas, Guillermo, *La guerra de los mil días. Nacimiento, vida y muerte de la II República española*, 2 vols (Buenos Aires: Grijalbo, 1973)

Cacho Viu, Vicente, 'Los escritos de José María Iribarren', *Cuadernos de Historia Moderna y Contemporánea*, vol. 5, 1984

Cacho Zabalza, Antonio, *La Unión Militar Española* (Alicante: Egasa, 1940)

Calleja, Juan José, *Un corazón al rojo* (Barcelona: Editorial Juventud, 1963)

Calvo Sotelo, José, *La voz de un perseguido*, 2 vols (Madrid: Librería de San Martín, 1933–4)

Calvo Sotelo, José, *Mis servicios al estado. Seis años de gestión. Apuntes para la historia* (Madrid: Imprenta Clásica Española, 1931)

Canal, Jordi, 'Las campañas antisectarias de Juan Tusquets (1927–1939). Una aproximación a los orígenes del contubernio judeo-masónico-comunista en España', in José Antonio Ferrer Benimeli (ed.), *La masonería en la España del siglo XX*, 2 vols (Toledo: Universidad de Castilla-La Mancha, 1996)

Carcedo, Diego, *Un español frente al Holocausto. Así salvó Ángel Sanz Briz 5.000 judíos* (Madrid: Temas de Hoy, 2000)

Cardona, Gabriel, *El gigante descalzo. El ejército de Franco* (Madrid: Aguilar, 2003)

Cardona, Gabriel, *El poder militar en la España contemporánea hasta la guerra civil* (Madrid: Siglo XXI, 1983)

Cardona, Gabriel, *Franco y sus generales. La manicura del tigre* (Madrid: Ediciones Temas de Hoy, 2001)

Cardona, Gabriel, *Historia militar de una guerra civil. Estrategias y tácticas de la guerra de España* (Barcelona: Flor del Viento, 2006)

Cardona, Gabriel, 'Mola, el general que pudo mandar', *La Aventura de la Historia*, no. 41, 2002

Cardozo, Harold G., *The March of a Nation: My Year of Spain's Civil War* (London: The Right Book Club, 1937)

Caro Cancela, Diego, *La Segunda República en Cádiz. Elecciones y partidos políticos* (Cadiz: Diputación Provincial de Cádiz, 1987)

Casado, Coronel Segismundo, *Así cayó Madrid. Último episodio de la guerra civil española* (Madrid: Guadiana de Publicaciones, 1968)

Casali, Luciano and Harana, Lola, *L'oportunisme de Franco. Un informe sobre la qüestió jueva (1949)* (Catarroja/Barcelona: Editorial Afers/Centre d'Estudis Històrics Internacionals, 2013)

Casals Messeguer, Xavier, *La tentación neofascista en España* (Barcelona: Plaza y Janés, 1998)

Casals Messeguer, Xavier, *Neonazis en España. De las audiciones wagnerianas a los skinheads (1966–1995)* (Barcelona: Grijalbo-Mondadori, 1995)

Castilla del Pino, Carlos, *Casa del Olivo. Autobiografía (1949–2003)* (Barcelona: Tusquets, 2004)

Castilla del Pino, Carlos, *Pretérito imperfecto. Autobiografía (1922–1949)* (Barcelona: Tusquets, 1997)

Castro Albarrán, Aniceto de, *Guerra santa. El sentido católico del movimiento nacional español* (Burgos: Editorial Española, 1938)

Castro Delgado, Enrique, *Hombres made in Moscú* (Barcelona: Luis de Caralt, 1965)

Castro, Luis, *'Yo daré las consignas'. La prensa y la propaganda en el primer franquismo* (Madrid: Marcial Pons, 2020)

Catalán, Diego, *El archivo del romancero. Historia documentada de un siglo de historia*, 2 vols (Madrid: Fundación Ramón Menéndez Pidal, 2001)

Cervera Gil, Javier, *Madrid en guerra. La ciudad clandestina, 1936–39*, 2nd edn (Madrid: Alianza Editorial, 2006)

Chalmers Mitchell, Sir Peter, *My House in Málaga* (London: Faber & Faber, 1938)

Ciano, Galeazzo, *Diario 1937–43*, ed. Renzo De Felice (Milano: Rizzoli, 1980)

Claret Miranda, Jaume, *El atroz desmoche. La destrucción de la Universidad española por el franquismo, 1936–45* (Barcelona: Editorial Crítica, 2006)

Connolly de Pernas, Eduardo, 'El padre Tusquets: olvidando el pasado', *Hibris*, no. 35, 2006

Connolly de Pernas, Eduardo, 'Mauricio Carlavilla: el encanto de la conspiración', *HIBRIS. Revista de Bibliofilia* (Alcoy), no. 23, September–October 2004

Copado, P. Bernabé, SJ, *Con la columna Redondo. Combates y conquistas. Crónica de guerra* (Seville: Imprenta de la Gavidia, 1937)

Cordón, Antonio, *Trayectoria (Recuerdos de un artillero)* (Seville: Espuela de Plata, 2008)

Cortés Cavanillas, Julián, *La caída de Alfonso XIII. Causas y episodios de una revolución*, 7th edn (Madrid: Librería de San Martín, 1933)

Cowles, Virginia, *Looking for Trouble* (London: Hamish Hamilton, 1941)

Cox, Geoffrey, *Defence of Madrid* (London: Victor Gollancz, 1937)

Crozier, Brian, *Franco: A Biographical History* (London, Eyre & Spottiswoode, 1967)

Cruanyes, Josep, *Els papers de Salamanca. L'espoliació del patrimoni documental de Catalunya* (Barcelona: Edicions 62, 2003)

Cuesta Monereo, José, *Una figura para la historia. El general Queipo de Llano. Primer locutor de radio en la Guerra de Liberacion* (Seville: Jefatura Provincial del Movimiento de Seville, 1969)

Dávila, Sancho and Pemartín, Julián, *Hacia la historia de la Falange. Primera contribución de Sevilla* (Jerez: Jerez Industrial, 1938)

Davis, Frances, *A Fearful Innocence* (Kent, Ohio: Kent State University Press, 1981)

Davis, Frances, *My Shadow in the Sun* (New York: Carrick & Evans, 1940)

De Juana, Jesús and Prada, Julio (eds), *Lo que han hecho en Galicia. Violencia política, represión y exilio (1936–1939)* (Barcelona: Editorial Crítica, 2007)

De la Cierva, Ricardo, *Bibliografía sobre la guerra de España (1936–1939) y sus antecedentes* (Barcelona: Ariel, 1968)

De la Cierva, Ricardo, *Francisco Franco. Un siglo de España*, 2 vols (Madrid: Editora Nacional, 1973)

De la Puerta, Javier, 'Fraga y los Judíos: Semana Santa en Zamora (1971)', *Diario del Aire*, 18 April 2013

Del Rey, Fernando, 'Los papeles de un conspirador. Documentos para la historia de las tramas golpistas de 1936', *Dimensioni e problemi della ricerca storica*, no. 2, 2018

Del Rey, Fernando, 'Percepciones contrarrevolucionarias. Octubre de 1934 en el epistolario del general Sanjurjo', *Revista de Estudios Políticos (nueva época)*, no. 159, January–March 2013

Delgado Cruz, Severiano, *Arqueología de un mito. El acto del 12 de octubre de 1936 en el Paraninfo de la Universidad de Salamanca* (Madrid: Silex, 2019)

Delmer, Sefton, *Trail Sinister: An Autobiography* (London: Secker & Warburg, 1961)

Di Febo, Giuliana, *La santa de la raza. Un culto barroco en la España franquista (1937–1962)* (Barcelona: Icaria Editorial, 1988)

Di Febo, Giuliana, *Ritos de guerra y de victoria en la España franquista*, 2nd edn (Valencia: Publicacions de la Universitat de València, 2012)

Díaz, Carmen, *Mi vida con Ramón Franco* (Barcelona: Editorial Planeta, 1981)

Díaz, Ramón, *La verdad de la francmasonería. Réplica al libro del Pbro. Tusquets* (Barcelona: Librería Española, 1932)

Díaz Nosty, Bernardo, *La irresistible ascensión de Juan March* (Madrid: Sedmay Ediciones, 1977)

Díez Cano, Santiago and Carasa Soto, Pedro, 'Caciques, dinero y favores. La restauración en Salamanca', in Ricardo Robledo (ed.), *Historia de Salamanca*, vol. V: *Siglo Veinte* (Salamanca: Centro de Estudios Salmantinos, 2001)

Diplomáticos españoles y el holocausto (Madrid: Ministerio de Asuntos Exteriores, 2013)

Dixon, Arturo, *Señor Monopolio. La asombrosa vida de Juan March* (Barcelona: Editorial Planeta, 1985)

Domínguez Arribas, Javier, *El enemigo judeo-masónico en la propaganda franquista (1936–1945)* (Madrid: Marcial Pons Historia, 2009)

Domínguez Lobato, Eduardo, *Cien capítulos de retaguardia (alrededor de un diario)* (Madrid: G. del Toro, 1973)

Dundas, Lawrence, *Behind the Spanish Mask* (London: Robert Hale, 1943)

Escobal, Patricio, *Las sacas (Memorias)* (Sada-A Coruña: Edicios do Castro, 2005)

Escobar, José Ignacio, *Así empezó* (Madrid: G. del Toro, 1974)

España y los judíos (Madrid: Oficina de Información Diplomática, 1949)

Espinosa Maestre, Francisco, *Guerra y represión en el sur de España* (Valencia: Publicacions de la Universitat de València, 2012)

Espinosa Maestre, Francisco, *La columna de la muerte. El avance del ejército franquista de Sevilla a Badajoz* (Barcelona: Editorial Crítica, 2003)

Espinosa Maestre, Francisco, *La guerra civil en Huelva*, 4th edn (Huelva: Diputación Provincial, 2005)

Espinosa Maestre, Francisco, *La justicia de Queipo. (Violencia selectiva y terror fascista en la II División en 1936) Sevilla, Huelva, Cádiz, Córdoba, Málaga y Badajoz*, 2nd edn (Barcelona: Editorial Crítica, 2005)

Espinosa, Francisco and Lama, José María, 'La columna de los ocho mil', *Revista de Fiestas de Reina* (Badajoz), August 2001

Estéban Infantes, Emilio, *General Sanjurjo (Un laureado en el Penal del Dueso)* (Barcelona: Editorial AHR, 1958)

Ezquerro, Arturo, 'Captain Aguilera and Filicide: A Group-Analytic Commentary', *Contexts. Group Analytic Society International*, no. 88, Summer 2020

Ezquerro, Arturo, 'Captain Aguilera and Filicide: An Attachment-Based Exploration', *ATTACHMENT: New Directions in Psychotherapy and Relational Psychoanalysis*, vol. 15, December 2021

Fernández-Coppel, Jorge, *General Gavilán. De enlace del general Mola a jefe de la Casa Militar de Franco* (Madrid: La Esfera de los Libros, 2005)

Fernández-Coppel, Jorge (ed.), *Queipo de Llano. Memorias de la guerra civil* (Madrid: La Esfera de los Libros, 2008)

Fernández Prieto, Lourenzo, et al., *Vítimas da represión en Galicia (1936–1939)* (Santiago de Compostela: Universidade de Santiago/ Xunta de Galicia, 2009)

Fernández Santander, Carlos, *Alzamiento y guerra civil en Galicia (1936–1939)*, 2 vols (Sada-A Coruña: Ediciós do Castro, 2000)

Fernández Santander, Carlos, *Antología de 40 años (1936–1975)* (Sada-A Coruña: Ediciós do Castro, 1983)

Fernández Santander, Carlos, *Casares Quiroga, una pasión republicana* (Sada-A Coruña: Ediciós do Castro, 2000)

Fernández Santander, Carlos, *Tensiones militares durante el franquismo* (Barcelona: Plaza y Janés, 1985)

Ferrer Benimeli, José Antonio, *El contubernio judeo-masónico-comunista. Del satanismo al escándalo de la P-2* (Madrid: Istmo, 1982)

Ferrer Benimeli, José Antonio, 'Franco contra la masonería', *Historia 16*, year II, no. 15, July 1977

Ferrer Benimeli, José Antonio (ed.), *La masonería en la historia de España* (Zaragoza: Diputación General de Aragón, 1989)

Ferrer Benimeli, José Antonio (ed.), *La masonería española. Represión y exilios*, Proceedings of XII Symposium Internacional de Historia de la Masonería Española (Zaragoza: Gobierno de Aragón, 2010)

Ferrer Benimeli, José Antonio, *Masonería española contemporánea*, 2 vols (Madrid: Siglo XXI, 1980)

Foltz, Charles, Jr, *The Masquerade in Spain* (Boston: Houghton Mifflin, 1948)

Foreign Journalists under Franco's Terror (London: United Editorial, 1937)

Fraga Iribarne, Manuel, *Pregón de Semana Santa 1971* (Zamora: Junta Pro-Semana Santa, 1971)

Franco, Comandante [Ramón], *Madrid bajo las bombas* (Madrid: Zeus S.A. Editorial, 1931)

Franco Salgado-Araujo, Francisco, *Mis conversaciones privadas con Franco* (Barcelona: Editorial Planeta, 1976)

Franco Salgado-Araujo, Francisco, *Mi vida junto a Franco* (Barcelona: Editorial Planeta, 1977)

Fraser, Ronald, *Blood of Spain: The Experience of Civil War, 1936–1939* (London: Allen Lane, 1979)

García Alonso, Francisco, *Flores del heroismo* (Seville: Imprenta de la Gavidia, 1939)

García Lahiguera, Fernando, *Ramón Serrano Suñer. Un documento para la historia* (Barcelona: Argos Vergara, 1983)

García Márquez, José María, *La 'Semana sangrienta' de julio de 1931 en Sevilla. Entre la historia y la manipulación* (Seville: Aconcagua, 2019)

García Rodríguez, José, *La organización ilegal y clandestina. Unión Militar Española (UME). Azote de la II República española* (Madrid: Autor, 2014)

García Serrano, Rafael, *La gran esperanza* (Barcelona: Editorial Planeta, 1983)

García Venero, Maximiano, *Falange en la guerra civil de España. La unificación y Hedilla* (Paris: Ruedo Ibérico, 1967)

García Venero, Maximiano, *Historia de la unificación (Falange y Requeté en 1937)* (Madrid: Agesa, 1970)

Garriga, Ramón, *El Cardenal Segura y el Nacional-Catolicismo* (Barcelona: Editorial Planeta, 1977)

Garriga, Ramón, *El general Yagüe* (Barcelona: Editorial Planeta, 1985)

Garriga, Ramón, *Juan March y su tiempo* (Barcelona: Editorial Planeta, 1976)

Garriga, Ramón, *La España de Franco. De la División Azul al pacto con los Estados Unidos (1943 a 1951)* (Puebla, Mexico: Editorial José M. Cajica Jr, 1971)

Garriga, Ramón, *La España de Franco. Las relaciones con Hitler*, 2nd edn (Puebla, Mexico: Editorial José M. Cajica Jr, 1970)

Garriga, Ramón, *La Señora de El Pardo* (Barcelona: Editorial Planeta, 1979)

Garriga, Ramón, *Nicolás Franco, el hermano brujo* (Barcelona: Editorial Planeta, 1980)

Garriga, Ramón, *Ramón Franco, el hermano maldito* (Barcelona: Editorial Planeta, 1978)

Geiser, Carl, *Prisoners of the Good Fight: Americans against Franco Fascism* (Westport, Connecticut: Lawrence Hill, 1986)

Gerahty, Cecil, *The Road to Madrid* (London: Hutchinson, 1937)

Gibson, Ian (ed.), *Agustín Penón. Diario de una búsqueda lorquiana (1955–56)* (Barcelona: Plaza y Janés, 1990)

Gibson, Ian, *El asesinato de García Lorca* (Barcelona: Ediciones B, 2018)

Gibson, Ian, *El hombre que detuvo a García Lorca. Ramón Ruiz Alonso y la muerte del poeta* (Madrid: Aguilar, 2007)

Gibson, Ian, *En busca de José Antonio* (Barcelona: Editorial Planeta, 1980)

Gibson, Ian, *Queipo de Llano. Sevilla, verano de 1936* (Barcelona: Grijalbo, 1986)

Gil Andrés, Carlos, *Lejos del frente. La guerra civil en la Rioja alta* (Barcelona: Editorial Crítica, 2006)

Gil Honduvilla, Joaquín, *Justicia en guerra. Bando de guerra y jurisdicción militar en el Bajo Guadalquivir* (Seville: Ayuntamiento de Seville Patronato del Real Alcázar, 2007)

Gil Mugarza, Bernardo, *España en llamas, 1936* (Barcelona: Ediciones Acervo, 1968)

Gil Pecharromán, Julio, *Conservadores subversivos. La derecha autoritaria alfonsina (1913–1936)* (Madrid: Eudema, 1994)

Gil Pecharromán, Julio, *José Antonio Primo de Rivera. Retrato de un visionario* (Madrid: Temas de Hoy, 1996)

Gil Robles, José María, *No fue posible la paz* (Barcelona: Ariel, 1968)

Gilbert, Martin, *Road to Victory: Winston S. Churchill, 1941–1945* (London: Heinemann, 1986)

Giménez Arnau, J. A., *Memorias de memoria. Descifre vuecencia personalmente* (Barcelona: Ediciones Destino, 1978)

Gollonet Megías, Ángel and Morales López, José, *Sangre y fuego. Málaga* (Granada: Librería Prieto, 1937)

Gomá, Cardenal Isidro, *Por Dios y por España, 1936–1939* (Barcelona: Editorial Casulleras, 1940)

Gómez Bajuelo, G., *Málaga bajo el dominio rojo* (Cadiz: Establecimientos Cerón, 1937)

Gómez Gómez, Estéban C., *El eco de las descargas. Adiós a la esperanza republicana* (Barcelona: Escega, 2002)

Gonzálbez Ruiz, Francisco, *Yo he creído en Franco. Proceso de una gran desilusión (Dos meses en la cárcel de Sevilla)* (Paris: Imprimerie Coopérative Étoile, 1937)

González, Isidro, *Los judíos y la segunda República, 1931–1939* (Madrid: Alianza Editorial, 2004)

González, Valentín, 'El Campesino', *Yo escogí la esclavitud*, Prólogo de Mauricio Carlavilla (n.p., n.d.)

González Calleja, Eduardo, *Contrarrevolucionarios. Radicalización violenta de las derechas durante la segunda República, 1931–1936* (Madrid: Alianza Editorial, 2011)

González Calleja, Eduardo, *El máuser y el sufragio. Orden público, subversión y violencia política en la crisis de la Restauración (1917–1931)* (Madrid: Consejo Superior de Investigaciones Científicas, 1999)

González Calleja, Eduardo and Del Rey Reguillo, Fernando, *La defensa armada contra la revolución. Una historia de las guardias cívicas en la España del siglo XX* (Madrid: Consejo Superior de Investigaciones Científicas, 1995)

González Cuevas, Pedro Carlos, *Acción Española. Teología política y nacionalismo autoritario en España (1913–1936)* (Madrid: Editorial Tecnos, 1998)

González Egido, Luciano, *Agonizar en Salamanca. Unamuno julio-diciembre 1936* (Madrid: Alianza Editorial, 1986)

González Soto, Julio, *Esbozo de una síntesis del ideario de Mola en relación con el Movimiento Nacional* (Burgos: Hijos de Santiago Rodríguez Editores, 1937)

Grau, Federico, 'Psicopatología de un dictador: entrevista a Carlos Castilla del Pino', *El Viejo Topo*, Extra No. 1, 1977

Hernández, Jesús, *Yo fui un ministro de Stalin* (Mexico City: Editorial América, 1953)

Hernández, Jesús, *Yo, ministro de Stalin en España*, Prólogo y notas de Mauricio Carlavilla (Madrid: Editorial Nos, 1954)

Hernández de León-Portilla, Ascensión, *España desde México. Vida y testimonio de transterrados* (Madrid: Algaba, 2004)

Hernández García, Ángel, 'La columna de los ocho mil: una tragedia olvidada', *Revista de Fiestas de Reina*, no. 7, August 2005

Hernández García, Antonio, *La represión en La Rioja durante la guerra civil*, 3 vols (Logroño: Autor, 1982)

Hernández Mir, Francisco, *La dictadura ante la historia. Un crimen de lesa patria* (Madrid: Compañía Ibero-Americana de Publicaciones, 1930)

Hernández Ruiz, Fernando Jesús, 'Ángel Galarza Gago (1892–1966), Ministro de Gobernación de la Segunda República Española, del republicanismo radical socialista al socialismo y al exilio', *Revista Europea de Historia de las Ideas Políticas y de las Instituciones Públicas*, no. 9, 2015

Hernández Sánchez, Fernando, *Comunistas sin partido. Jesús Hernández, Ministro en la guerra civil, disidente en el exilio* (Madrid: Editorial Raíces, 2007)

Herrera Oria, Enrique, *Los cautivos de Vizcaya. Memorias del P. Enrique Herrera Oria, S.J., preso durante cuatro meses y medio en la cárcel de Bilbao y condenado a ocho años y un día de prisión* (Bilbao: Aldus S.A., 1938)

Hidalgo de Cisneros, Ignacio, *Cambio de rumbo (Memorias)*, 2 vols (Bucharest: Colección Ebro, 1964)

Hills, George, *Franco, the Man and his Nation* (New York: Macmillan, 1967)

Hitler, Adolf, *Hitler's Table Talk, 1941–1944* (London: Weidenfeld & Nicolson, 1953)

Hoare, Sir Samuel, *Ambassador on Special Mission* (London: Collins, 1946)

Ibarra, Cayetano, *La otra mitad de la historia que nos contaron. Fuente de Cantos, República y guerra, 1931–1939* (Badajoz: Diputación de Badajoz, 2005)

Ibárruri, Dolores, *El único camino* (Madrid: Editorial Castalia, 1992)

Infante, Javier, 'Sables y naipes: Diego Martín Veloz (1875–1938). De cómo un matón de casino se convirtió en caudillo rural', in Ricardo Robledo (ed.), *Esta salvaje pesadilla. Salamanca en la guerra civil española* (Barcelona: Editorial Crítica, 2007)

Irazabal Agirre, Jon, *Durango 31 de marzo de 1937* (Abadiño: Gerediaga Elkartea, 2001)

Iribarren, José María, *Con el general Mola. Escenas y aspectos inéditos de la guerra civil* (Zaragoza: Librería General, 1937)

Iribarren, José María, *Mola. Datos para una biografía y para la historia del alzamiento nacional* (Zaragoza: Librería General, 1938)

Irujo, Xabier, *Gernika 26 de abril de 1937* (Barcelona: Editorial Crítica, 2017)

Israel Garzón, Jacobo, 'España y los judíos (1939–1945). Una visión general', in Jacobo Israel Garzón and Alejandro Baer (eds), *España y el Holocausto (1939–1945). Historia y testimonios* (Madrid: Ebraica Ediciones, 2007)

Iturralde, Juan de, *La guerra de Franco, los vascos y la Iglesia*, 2 vols (San Sebastián: Publicaciones del Clero Vasco, 1978)

Jaraiz Franco, Pilar, *Historia de una disidencia* (Barcelona: Editorial Planeta, 1981)

Juliá, Santos (ed.), *Víctimas de la guerra civil* (Madrid: Temas de Hoy, 1999)

Keene, Judith, *Fighting for Franco: International Volunteers in Nationalist Spain during the Spanish Civil War, 1936–1939* (London: Leicester University Press, 2001)

Kemp, Peter, *Mine Were of Trouble* (London: Cassell, 1957)

Kindelán, Alfredo, *La verdad de mis relaciones con Franco* (Barcelona: Editorial Planeta, 1981)

Kindelán Duany, Alfredo, *Mis cuadernos de guerra*, 2nd edn (Barcelona: Editorial Planeta, 1982)

Knickerbocker, H. R., *The Siege of the Alcazar* (London: Hutchinson, n.d. [1937])

Koestler, Arthur, *The Invisible Writing*, 2nd edn (London: Hutchinson, 1969)

Koestler, Arthur, *Spanish Testament* (London: Victor Gollancz, 1937)

Kriegswissenschaftlichen Abteilung der Luftwaffe, Arbeitsgruppe Spanienkrieg, 'Die Kämpfe im Norden' (Bundesarchiv, Militärarchiv, Freiburg, Akt II L 14/2)

Krivitsky, W. G., *I Was Stalin's Agent* (London: Hamish Hamilton, 1939)

Krivitsky, W. G., *In Stalin's Secret Service* (New York: Harper & Row, 1939)

La vida y la obra de José Calvo Sotelo. Homenaje de la Real Academia de Jurisprudencia y Legislación a su presidente perpetuo José Calvo Sotelo que ofrendó su vida por Dios y por España el 13 de Julio de 1936 (Madrid: Imprenta de Galo Sáez, 1942)

Largo Caballero, Francisco, *Correspondencia secreta*, Prólogo y notas de Mauricio Carlavilla (Madrid: Editorial Nos, 1961)

Largo Caballero, Francisco, *Mis recuerdos. Cartas a un amigo*, Prólogo y notas de Enrique de Francisco (Mexico City: Ediciones Unidas, 1954)

Larraz, José, *Memorias* (Madrid: Real Academia de Ciencias Morales y Políticas, 2006)

Martínez de Pisón, Ignacio, *Filek. El estafador que engañó a Franco* (Barcelona: Seix Barral, 2018)

Lazo, Alfonso, *La Iglesia, la Falange y el fascismo (un estudio sobre la prensa española de postguerra)* (Seville: Universidad de Sevilla, 1995)

Lazo, Alfonso, *Retrato de fascismo rural en Sevilla* (Seville: Universidad de Sevilla, 1998)

Ledesma Ramos, Ramiro, *Escritos políticos, 1935–1936* (Madrid: Herederos de Ramiro Ledesma Ramos, 1988)

Ledesma Ramos, Ramiro, *¿Fascismo en España?*, 2nd edn (Barcelona: Ediciones Ariel, 1968)

Lerroux, Alejandro, *La pequeña historia. Apuntes para la historia grande vividos y redactados por el autor* (Buenos Aires: Editorial Cimera, 1945)

Lisbona Martín, José Antonio, *Más allá del deber. La respuesta humanitaria del Servicio Exterior frente al Holocausto* (Madrid: Ministerio de Asuntos Exteriores y de Cooperación, 2015)

Líster, Enrique, *Nuestra guerra* (Paris: Colección Ebro, 1966)

Lizarza Iribarren, Antonio, *Memorias de la conspiración*, 4th edn (Pamplona: Editorial Gómez, 1969)

Llopis Llopis, Salvador, *La prócer dama doña Inés Luna Terrero, sus predecesores y familiares cercanos* (Salamanca: Autor, 2000)

López, Padre Tomás, *Treinta semanas en poder de los rojos en Málaga de julio a febrero* (Seville: Imprenta de San Antonio, 1938)

López García, Santiago and Delgado Cruz, Severiano, 'Víctimas y Nuevo Estado, 1936–1940', in Ricardo Robledo (ed.), *Historia de Salamanca*, vol. V: *Siglo Veinte* (Salamanca: Centro de Estudios Salmantinos, 2001)

Losada Malvárez, Juan Carlos, *Ideología del Ejército Franquista, 1939–1959* (Madrid: Ediciones Istmo, 1990)

Lowe, Sid, *Catholicism, War and the Foundation of Francoism: The Juventud de Acción Popular in Spain, 1931–1939* (Brighton: Sussex Academic Press/Cañada Blanch, 2010)

Lunn, Arnold, *Spanish Rehearsal* (London: Hutchinson, 1937)

Macarro Vera, José Manuel, *La utopía revolucionaria. Sevilla en la segunda República* (Seville: Monte de Piedad y Caja de Ahorros, 1985)

McCullagh, Francis, *In Franco's Spain* (London: Burns, Oates & Washbourne, 1937)

Maier, Klaus A., *Guernica 26.4.1937. Die deutsche Intervention in Spanien und der 'Fall Guernica'* (Freiburg: Rombach, 1975)

Maíz, B. Félix, *Alzamiento en España. De un diario de la conspiración*, 2nd edn (Pamplona: Editorial Gómez, 1952)

Maíz, B. Félix, *Mola frente a Franco. Guerra y muerte del General Mola* (Pamplona: Laocoonte, 2007)

Maíz, B. Félix, *Mola, aquel hombre* (Barcelona: Editorial Planeta, 1976)

Manent i Segimon, Albert, *De 1936 a 1975. Estudis sobre la guerra civil i el franquisme* (Barcelona: Publicacions de l'Abadia de Montserrat, 1999)

María Lama, José, *Una biografía frente al olvido. José González Barrero, Alcalde de Zafra en la segunda República* (Badajoz: Diputación de Badajoz, 2000)

Maritain, Jacques, *Los rebeldes españoles no hacen una guerra santa* (Valencia: Ediciones Españolas, 1937)

Marquina Barrio, Antonio and Inés Ospina, Gloria, *España y los judíos en el siglo XX* (Madrid: Espasa Calpe, 1987)

Marsá, Graco, *La sublevación de Jaca. Relato de un rebelde*, 2nd edn (Madrid: Zeus S.A. Editorial, 1931)

Martín Blázquez, José, *I Helped to Build an Army: Civil War Memoirs of a Spanish Staff Officer* (London: Secker & Warburg, 1939)

Martín de Pozuelo, Eduardo, *El franquismo, cómplice del Holocausto* (Barcelona: La Vanguardia, 2012)

Martín Jiménez, Ignacio, *La guerra civil en Valladolid (1936–1939). Amaneceres ensangrentados* (Valladolid: Ámbito Ediciones, 2000)

Martínez Bande, José Manuel, 'Del alzamiento a la guerra civil verano de 1936: Correspondencia Franco/Mola', *Historia y Vida*, no. 93, 1975

Martínez Bande, José Manuel, *La campaña de Andalucía*, 2nd edn (Madrid: Editorial San Martín, 1986)

Martínez Bande, José Manuel, *Nueve meses de guerra en el norte* (Madrid: Editorial San Martín, 1980)

Martínez Bande, José Manuel, *Vizcaya* (Madrid: Editorial San Martín, 1971)

Martínez Barrio, Diego, *Memorias* (Barcelona: Editorial Planeta, 1983)

Martínez Bedoya, Javier, *Memorias desde mi aldea* (Valladolid: Ambito Ediciones, 1996)

Martínez de Campos, Carlos, *Ayer 1931–53* (Madrid: Instituto de Estudios Políticos, 1970)

Martínez, Marisol and Mendaza, David (eds), *La guerra en Araba. El levantamiento militar en Bizkai*, vol. III of Iñaki Egaña, Marisol Martínez and David Mendaza (eds), *1936 Guerra civil en Euskal Herria* (Pamplona: Aralar Liburuak, 1999)

Martínez Roda, Federico, *Varela. El general antifascista de Franco* (Madrid: La Esfera de los Libros, 2012)

Martínez Rus, Ana, 'La represión cultural: libros destruidos, bibliotecas depuradas y lecturas vigiladas', in Julio Arostegui (ed.), *Franco. La represión como sistema* (Barcelona: Flor del Viento, 2012)

Masjuan Bracons, Eduard, 'Eduardo Barriobero y Herrán i la justícia revolucionària a la Barcelona de 1936', Segon Congrés Recerques, *Enfrontaments civils. Postguerres i reconstruccions*, 2 vols (Lleida: Associació Recerques y Pagés Editors, 2002)

Massot i Muntaner, Josep, *Església i societat a la Catalunya contemporània* (Barcelona: Publicacions de l'Abadia de Montserrat, 2003)

Mauriño Longoria, Carlos G., *Memorias* (Ronda: Familia del autor, n.d. [1937])

Medina García, Eusebio, 'Contrabando en la frontera de Portugal. Orígenes, estructuras, conflicto y cambio social', doctoral thesis, Universidad Complutense de Madrid, 2001

Medina Vilallonga, Rafael de, Duque de Medinaceli, *Tiempo pasado* (Seville: Gráfica Sevillena, 1971)

Mendizábal, Alfred, *Aux origines d'une tragédie: la politique espagnole de 1923 à 1936* (Paris: Desclée de Brouwer, 1937)

Merino, Ignacio, *Serrano Suñer. Conciencia y poder* (Madrid: Algaba Ediciones, 2004)

Miguélez Rueda, José María, 'Transformaciones y cambios en la policía española durante la II República', *Espacio, Tiempo y Forma. Serie V, Historia Contemporánea*, vol. 10, 1997

Miguez Macho, Antonio, *Xenocidio e represión franquista en Galicia.*
  A violencia de retagarda en Galicia na Guerra Civil (1936–1939)
  (Santiago de Compostela: Editions Lóstrego, 2009)
Mikelarena Peña, Fernando, 'La intensidad de la limpieza política
  franquista en 1936 en la Ribera de Navarra', *Hispania Nova.*
  Revista de Historia Contemporánea, no. 9, 2009
Miller, Webb, *I Found No Peace* (London: The Book Club, 1937)
Mínev Stoyán (Stepanov), *Las causas de la derrota de la República*
  española, ed. Ángel L. Encinas Moral (Madrid: Miraguano
  Ediciones, 2003)
Molina Fajardo, Eduardo, *Los últimos días de García Lorca*
  (Barcelona: Plaza y Janés, 1983)
Monge Bernal, José, *Acción Popular (estudios de biología política)*
  (Madrid: Imp. Sáez Hermanos, 1936)
Monks, Noel, *Eyewitness* (London: Frederick Muller, 1955)
Montero Pérez-Hinojosa, Fernando, '"Gracia y Justicia". Un
  semanario antimasónico en la lucha contra la segunda república
  española', in José Antonio Ferrer Benimeli (ed.), *La masonería en*
  la historia de España (Zaragoza: Diputación General de Aragón,
  1989)
Montes Agudo, Gumersindo, *Pepe Sainz. Una vida en la Falange*
  (Barcelona: Ediciones Pal-las de Horta, 1939)
Mora, Antoni, 'Joan Tusquets, en els 90 anys d'un home d'estudi i de
  combat', Institut d'Estudis Tarraconenses Ramón Berenguer IV,
  Anuari 1990–1991 de la Societat d'Estudis d'Història Eclesiàstica
  Moderna i Contemporània de Catalunya (Tarragona: Diputació
  de Tarragona, 1992)
Mora, Constancia de la, *In Place of Splendor: The Autobiography of a*
  Spanish Woman (New York: Harcourt, Brace, 1939)
Morales Ruiz, Juan José, *El discurso antimasónico en la guerra civil*
  española, 1936–1939 (Zaragoza: Diputación General de Aragón,
  2001)
Morente Valero, Francisco, *La depuración del magisterio nacional*
  (1936–1943). La escuela y el Estado Nuevo (Valladolid: Ámbito
  Alarife, 1997)
Morente Valero, Francisco, 'La depuración franquista del magisterio
  público. Un estado de la cuestión', *Hispania*, vol. 61, no. 208, 2001

Morodo, Raúl, *Orígenes ideológicos del franquismo. Acción Española* (Madrid: Alianza Editorial, 1985)

Mota Muñoz, José Fernando, '"Precursores de la unificación": el España Club y el voluntariado español, una experiencia unitaria de la extrema derecha barcelonesa (1935–1936)', *Historia y Política*, 28, 2012

Moure Mariño, Luis, *La generación del 36. Memorias de Salamanca y Burgos* (Sada-A Coruña: Ediciós do Castro, 1989)

Nadal Sánchez, Antonio, 'Experiencias psíquicas sobre mujeres marxistas malagueñas', in *Las mujeres y la guerra civil española* (Madrid: Ministerio de Cultura, 1991)

Nelken, Margarita, *Por qué hicimos la revolución* (Barcelona/Paris/New York: Ediciones Sociales Internacionales, 1936)

Nerín, Gustau, *La guerra que vino de África* (Barcelona: Editorial Crítica, 2005)

Nicholson, Helen, *Death in the Morning* (London: Lovat Dickson, 1937)

Nilus, Serge, *Protocolos de los sábios de Sión* (Madrid: Editorial Nos, 1963)

Nilus, Serguei A., *Los protocolos de los sabios de Sión* (Madrid: Imprenta de los Talleres Penitenciarios de Alcalá de Henares, 1940)

Norton, Edward, *Muerte en Málaga. Testimonio de un americano sobre la guerra civil española* (Malaga: Universidad de Málaga, 2004)

Ollaquindia, Ricardo, 'Un libro de José María Iribarren condenado por la censura', *Príncipe de Viana* (Pamplona), year no. 64, no. 229, 2003

Olmedo Alonso, Ángel, *Llerena 1936. Fuentes orales para la recuperación de la memoria histórica* (Badajoz: Diputación de Badajoz, 2010)

Olmedo Delgado, Antonio and Cuesta Monereo, José, *General Queipo de Llano (aventura y audacia)* (Barcelona: Editorial AHR, 1958)

Ortega y Gasset, Eduardo, *España encadenada. La verdad sobre la dictadura* (Paris: Juan Dura, 1925)

Ortiz de Villajos, Cándido, *De Sevilla a Madrid, ruta libertadora de la columna Castejón* (Granada: Librería Prieto, 1937)

Ortiz Villalba, Juan, *Sevilla 1936. Del golpe militar a la guerra civil* (Seville: Diputación Provincial, 1998)

Osorio, Marta, *Miedo, olvido y fantasía. Agustín Penón. Crónica de su investigación sobre Federico García Lorca (1955–1956)* (Granada: Editorial Comares, 2001)

Ossorio y Gallardo, Ángel, *Mis memorias* (Buenos Aires: Losada, 1946)

Packard, Reynolds and Eleanor, *Balcony Empire: Fascist Italy at War* (New York: Oxford University Press, 1942)

Palacios, Jesús, *Las cartas de Franco. La correspondencia desconocida que marcó el destino de España* (Madrid: La Esfera de Los Libros, 2005)

Palomares Ibáñez, Jesús María, *La guerra civil en la ciudad de Valladolid. Entusiasmo y represión en la 'capital del alzamiento'* (Valladolid: Ayuntamiento de Valladolid, 2001)

Payne, Stanley G., *Politics and the Military in Modern Spain* (Stanford, California: Stanford University Press, 1967)

Paz, Abel, *Durruti en la revolución española* (Madrid: Fundación Anselmo Lorenzo, 1996)

Peñalba-Sotorrío, Mercedes, 'Beyond the War: Nazi Propaganda Aims in Spain during the Second World War', *Journal of Contemporary History*, vol. 54, no. 4, 2019

Pérez de Olaguer, Antonio, *Lágrimas y sonrisas* (Burgos: Ediciones Antisectarias, 1938)

Pérez Madrigal, Joaquín, *Pérez (vida y trabajo de uno)* (Madrid: Instituto Editorial Reus, 1955)

Píriz González, Carlos, 'En campo enemigo: la Quinta Columna en la Guerra Civil española (c. 1936–1941)', doctoral thesis, Universidad de Salamanca, 2019

Pozo, Gabriel, *Lorca, el último paseo. Laves para entender el asesinato del poeta* (Granada: Almed, 2009)

Preston, Paul, 'The Agrarian War in the South', in Paul Preston (ed.), *Revolution and War in Spain, 1931–1939* (London: Methuen, 1984)

Preston, Paul, 'Alfonsist Monarchism and the Coming of the Spanish Civil War', *Journal of Contemporary History*, vol. 7, nos. 3/4, 1972

Preston, Paul, *The Coming of the Spanish Civil War: Reform, Reaction and Revolution in the Second Spanish Republic, 1931–1936*, 2nd edn (London: Routledge, 1994)

Preston, Paul, *El Cid and the Masonic Super-State: Franco, the Western Powers and the Cold War* (London: London School of Economics, 1993)

Preston, Paul, *Franco: A Biography* (London: HarperCollins, 1993)

Preston, Paul, *A People Betrayed: A History of Corruption, Political Incompetence and Social Division in Modern Spain, 1874–2018* (London: William Collins, 2020)

Preston, Paul, *The Spanish Holocaust: Inquisition and Extermination in Twentieth-Century Spain* (London: Harper Press, 2012)

Prieto, Indalecio, *Cómo y por qué salí del Ministerio de Defensa Nacional. Intrigas de los rusos en España (Texto taquigráfico del informe pronunciado el 9 de agosto de 1938 ante el Comité Nacional del Partido Socialista Obrero Español)* (Mexico City: Impresos y Papeles, S. de R.L., 1940)

Prieto, Indalecio, *De mi vida. Recuerdos, estampas, siluetas, sombras …*, 2 vols (Mexico City: Ediciones Oasis, 1965)

Prieto, Indalecio, *Entresijos de la guerra de España (Intrigas de nazis, fascistas y comunistas)* (Buenos Aires: Editorial Bases, 1954)

Prieto, Indalecio, *Yo y Moscú*, Prólogo, comentarios y notas de Mauricio Carlavilla (Madrid: Editorial Nos, 1960)

Primo de Rivera y Urquijo, Miguel, *Papeles póstumos de José Antonio* (Barcelona: Plaza y Janés, 1996)

Primo de Rivera, José Antonio, *Obras*, 4th edn (Madrid: Sección Feminina de FET y de las JONS, 1966)

Puell de la Villa, Fernando, 'La trama militar de la conspiración', in Francisco Sánchez Pérez (ed.), *Los mitos del 18 de julio* (Barcelona: Editorial Crítica, 2013)

Quevedo y Queipo de Llano, Ana, *Queipo de Llano. Gloria e infortunio de un general* (Barcelona: Editorial Planeta, 2001)

Quiroga, Alejandro, *Making Spaniards: Primo de Rivera and the Nationalization of the Masses, 1923–1930* (London: Palgrave Macmillan, 2007)

Raguer, Hilari, *El general Batet. Franco contra Batet. Crónica de una venganza* (Barcelona: Ediciones Península, 1996)

Raguer, Hilari, *Escrits dispersos d'història* (Barcelona: Institut d'Estudis Catalans, 2018)

Raguer, Hilari, *La pólvora y el incienso. La Iglesia católica y la guerra civil española (1936–1939)* (Barcelona: Ediciones Península, 2001)

Raguer, Hilari, *La Unió Democràtica de Catalunya i el seu temps (1931–1939)* (Barcelona: Publicaciones de l'Abadia de Montserrat, 1976)

Ramón-Laca, Julio de, *Bajo la férula de Queipo. Cómo fue gobernada Andalucía* (Seville: Imprenta Comercial del Diario FE, 1939)

Ramos Hitos, Juan Antonio, *Guerra civil en Málaga, 1936–1937. Revisión Histórica*, 2nd edn (Malaga: Editorial Algazara, 2004)

Redondo, Gonzalo, *Historia de la Iglesia en España, 1931–1939*, 2 vols (Madrid: Ediciones Rialp, 1993)

Redondo, J. Crespo, et al., *Purga de maestros en la guerra civil. La depuración del magisterio nacional en la provincia de Burgos* (Valladolid: Ámbito Alarife, 1987)

Reig Tapia, Alberto, *La Cruzada de 1936. Mitos y memoria* (Madrid: Alianza Editorial, 2006)

Rein, Raanan (ed.), *España e Israel. Veinte años después* (Madrid: Fundación Tres Culturas del Mediterráneo, 2007)

Rein, Raanan, *In the Shadow of the Holocaust and the Inquisition: Israel's Relations with Francoist Spain* (London: Routledge, 1997)

Richards, Michael, 'Morality and Biology in the Spanish Civil War: Psychiatrists, Revolution and Women Prisoners in Málaga', *Contemporary European History*, vol. 10, no. 3, 2001

Richards, Michael, *A Time of Silence: Civil War and the Culture of Repression in Franco's Spain, 1936–1945* (Cambridge: Cambridge University Press, 1998)

Riera, Ignasi, *Los catalanes de Franco* (Barcelona: Plaza y Janés, 1998)

Riquer i Permanyer, Borja de, 'Els catalans de Burgos', *Arreu* (Barcelona), no. 5, November 1976

Riquer i Permanyer, Borja de, 'Joan Ventosa i Calvell, l'home de la Lliga Catalana a Burgos. Les relacions dels catalanistes conservadors amb els militars rebels durant la Guerra Civil', *Segle XX. Revista Catalana d'Història*, no. 5, 2021

Riquer i Permanyer, Borja de, *L'últim Cambó (1936–1947). La dreta catalanista davant la guerra civil i el franquisme* (Barcelona: Eumo Editorial, 1996)

Rivero Noval, María Cristina, *La ruptura de la paz civil. Represión en la Rioja (1936–1939)* (Logroño: Instituto de Estudios Riojanos, 1992)

Robinson, Paul, *The White Russian Army in Exile, 1920–1941* (Oxford: Clarendon Press, 2002)

Robledo, Ricardo and Diez Cano, Santiago, 'La derrota del rentista. Historia económica y política del caso de Luna Terrero (1855–1955)', in S. De Dios and Eugenia Torijano (eds), *Escritos de Historia. Estudios en homenaje al Prof. Javier Infante* (Salamanca: Ediciones Universidad de Salamanca, 2019)

Rodrigo, Javier, *Cautivos. Campos de concentración en la España franquista, 1936–1947* (Barcelona: Editorial Crítica, 2005)

Rodríguez Aisa, María Luisa, *El Cardenal Gomá y la guerra de España. Aspectos de la gestión pública del Primado, 1936–1939* (Madrid: Consejo Superior de Investigaciones Científicas, 1981)

Rodríguez Jiménez, José Luis, 'Una aproximación al trasfondo ideológico de la represión. Teoría de la conspiración y policía política franquista', in Jaume Sobrequés, Carme Molinero and Margarida Sala (eds), *Els camps de concentració i el mon penitenciari a Espanya durant la guerra civil i el franquisme* (Barcelona: Museu de'Historia de Catalunya/Editorial Crítica, 2003)

Rodríguez Puértolas, Julio, *Literatura fascista española*, 2 vols (Madrid: Ediciones Akal, 1986–7)

Rohr, Isabelle, *The Spanish Right and the Jews, 1898–1945: Antisemitism and Opportunism* (Brighton: Sussex Academic Press, 2007)

Rojas, Carlos, *¡Muera la inteligencia!¡Viva la muerte! Salamanca, 1936. Unamuno y Millán Astray frente a frente* (Barcelona: Editorial Planeta, 1995)

Romero, Luis, *Por qué y cómo mataron a Calvo Sotelo* (Barcelona: Editorial Planeta, 1982)

Romero, Luis, *Tres días de julio (18, 19 y 20 de 1936)*, 2nd edn (Barcelona: Ariel, 1968)

Romero García, Eladio, *Julian Mauricio Carlavilla del Barrio. El policía franquista que destapó la conspiración mundial* (Almería: Círculo Rojo, 2018)

Romero Romero, Fernando, 'Falangistas, héroes y matones. Fernando Zamacola y los Leones de Rota', *Cuadernos para el Diálogo*, no. 33, September 2008

Romero Romero, Fernando, 'Víctimas de la represión en la Sierra de Cádiz durante la guerra civil (1936–1939)', *Almajar* (Villamartín), no. 2, 2005

Ros Agudo, Manuel, *La guerra secreta de Franco, 1939–1945* (Barcelona: Editorial Crítica, 2002)

Rother, Bernd, *Franco y el Holocausto* (Madrid: Marcial Pons, 2005)

Rozenberg, Danielle, *La España contemporánea y la cuestión judía* (Madrid: Marcial Pons, 2010)

Ruiz Vilaplana, Antonio, *Doy fe … un año de actuación en la España nacionalista* (Paris: Éditions Imprimerie Coopérative Étoile, n.d. [1938])

Sacaluga, Juan Antonio, *La resistencia socialista en Asturias, 1937–1962* (Madrid: Editorial Pablo Iglesias, 1986)

Sacanell Ruiz de Apodaca, Enrique, *El general Sanjurjo. Héroe y víctima. El militar que pudo evitar la dictadura franquista* (Madrid: La Esfera de los Libros, 2004)

Sáenz-Francés San Baldomero, Emilio, 'La deportación en 1943 de la comunidad sefardita de Salónica', *APORTES: Revista de historia contemporánea*, vol. XXVI, no. 77, 2011

Sagardía, General, *Del Alto Ebro a las Fuentes del Llobregat. Treinta y dos meses de guerra de la 62 División* (Madrid: Editora Nacional, 1940)

Sainz Rodríguez, Pedro, *Testimonio y recuerdos* (Barcelona: Editorial Planeta, 1978)

Sainz Rodríguez, Pedro, *Un reinado en la sombra* (Barcelona: Editorial Planeta, 1981)

Salas, Nicolás, *Quién fue Gonzalo Queipo de Llano y Sierra, 1875–1951* (Seville: Abec Editores, 2012)

Salas, Nicolás, *Sevilla fue la clave. República, Alzamiento, Guerra Civil (1931–39)*, 2 vols (Seville: Editorial Castillejo, 1992)

Sallairai, Aurelio, *Protocolos de los sábios de Sión y la subversión mundial* (Buenos Aires: n.p., 1972)

Salmon, André, *Souvenirs sans fin* (Paris: Gallimard, 1955)

Sánchez Asiaín, José Ángel, *La financiación de la guerra civil española. Una aproximación histórica* (Barcelona: Editorial Crítica, 2012)

Sánchez del Arco, Manuel, *El sur de España en la reconquista de Madrid (diario de operaciones glosado por un testigo)*, 2nd edn (Seville: Editorial Sevillana, 1937)

Sánchez Dragó, Fernando, *Gárgoris y Habidis. Una historia mágica de España* (Barcelona: Editorial Planeta, 2001)

Sánchez-Ostiz, Miguel, *El Escarmiento* (Pamplona: Pamiela, 2013)

Saña, Heleno, *El franquismo sin mitos. Conversaciones con Serrano Suñer* (Barcelona: Grijalbo, 1982)

Sanz, Ricardo, *El sindicalismo y la política. Los 'Solidarios' y 'Nosotros'* (Toulouse: Autor & Imprimerie Dulaurier, 1966)

Schulze Schneider, Ingrid, 'Éxitos y fracasos de la propaganda alemana en España: 1939–1944', *Mélanges de la Casa de Velázquez*, no. 31, 1995

Schulze Schneider, Ingrid, 'La propaganda alemana en España, 1942–1944', *Espacio, Tiempo y Forma. Serie V, Historia Contemporánea*, no. 7, 1994

Séguéla, Matthieu, *Pétain–Franco: les secrets d'une alliance* (Paris: Albin Michel, 1992)

Segura Nieto, Juan, *¡Alerta! … Francmasonería y Judaísmo* (Barcelona: Felipe González Rojas, 1940)

Seidman, Michael, *The Victorious Counterrevolution: The Nationalist Effort in the Spanish Civil War* (Madison: University of Wisconsin Press, 2011)

Serém, Rúben, *A Laboratory of Terror, Conspiracy, Coup d'état and Civil War in Seville, 1936–1939: History and Myth in Francoist Spain* (Brighton: Sussex Academic Press, 2017)

Serrat Bonastre, Francisco, *Salamanca, 1936. Memorias del primer 'ministro' de Asuntos Exteriores de Franco* (Barcelona: Editorial Crítica, 2014)

Silva, José Antonio, *Cómo asesinar con un avión* (Barcelona: Editorial Planeta, 1981)

Simó Sánchez, Marta, 'La memoria de l'Holocaust a l'Estat Espanyol.
    Des d'una perspectiva sociòlogia i una perspectiva històrica',
    doctoral thesis, Universitat Autònoma de Barcelona, 2018

Smith, Ángel, *Anarchism, Revolution and Reaction: Catalan Labor
    and the Crisis of the Spanish State, 1898–1923* (New York:
    Berghahn Books, 2007)

Solchaga, José, 'Memorias', *Historia*, no. 16, 2000

Solé i Sabaté, Josep M. and Villarroya i Font, Joan, *La repressió a la
    reraguardia de Catalunya (1936–1939)*, 2 vols (Barcelona:
    Publicacions de l'Abadia de Montserrat, 1989)

Sopeña, Federico, *Vida y obra de Manuel de Falla* (Madrid: Turner,
    1988)

Southworth, Herbert R., *Antifalange. Estudio crítico de 'Falange en
    la guerra de España' de Maximiano García Venero* (Paris:
    Ediciones Ruedo Ibérico, 1967)

Southworth, Herbert R., *Conspiracy and the Spanish Civil War: The
    Brainwashing of Francisco Franco* (London: Routledge, 2002)

Southworth, Herbert R., *El lavado de cerebro de Francisco Franco.
    Conspiración y guerra civil* (Barcelona: Editorial Crítica, 2000)

Southworth, Herbert R., *El mito de la cruzada de Franco*, ed. Paul
    Preston (Barcelona: Random House Mondadori, 2008)

Southworth, Herbert Rutledge, '"The Grand Camouflage": Julián
    Gorkín, Burnett Bolloten and the Spanish Civil War', in Paul
    Preston and Ann L. Mackenzie (eds), *The Republic Besieged: Civil
    War in Spain, 1936–1939* (Edinburgh: Edinburgh University
    Press, 1996)

Southworth, Herbert R., *Guernica! Guernica!: A Study of Journalism,
    Diplomacy, Propaganda, and History* (Berkeley: University of
    California Press, 1977)

Steer, G. L., *The Tree of Guernica: A Field Study of Modern War*
    (London, 1938)

Suárez Fernández, Luis, *Francisco Franco y su tiempo*, 8 vols
    (Madrid: Fundación Nacional Francisco Franco, 1984)

Subirà, Joan, *Capellans en temps de Franco* (Barcelona: Editorial
    Mediterrània, 1996)

Taylor, Edmond, 'Assignment in Hell', in Frank C. Hanighen (ed.),
    Nothing but Danger (New York: National Travel Club, 1939)

Terrón Montero, Javier, *La prensa de España durante el régimen de Franco* (Madrid: Centro de Investigaciones Sociologicas, 1981)

Thomas, Gordon and Morgan-Witts, Max, *The Day Guernica Died* (London: Hodder & Stoughton, 1975)

Thomas, Hugh, *The Spanish Civil War*, 3rd edn (London: Hamish Hamilton, 1977)

Thomàs, Joan Maria, *El gran golpe. El 'Caso Hedilla' o cómo Franco se quedó con Falange* (Barcelona: Editorial Debate, 2014)

Thomàs, Joan Maria, *Falange, guerra civil, franquisme. F.E.T. y de las J.O.N.S. de Barcelona en els primers anys de règim franquista* (Barcelona: Publicacions de l'Abadia de Montserrat, 1992)

Thomàs, Joan Maria, *José Antonio. Realidad y mito* (Barcelona: Editorial Debate, 2017)

Thomas, Maria, 'The Front Line of Albion's Perfidy: Inputs into the Making of British Policy towards Spain: The Racism and Snobbery of Norman King', *International Journal of Iberian Studies*, vol. 20, no. 2, 2007

Togores, Luis E., *Yagüe. El General Falangista de Franco* (Madrid: La Esfera de los Libros, 2010)

Toquero, José María, *Don Juan de Borbón, el Rey padre* (Barcelona: Plaza y Janés/Cambio 16, 1992)

Toquero, José María, *Franco y Don Juan. La oposición monárquica al franquismo* (Barcelona: Plaza y Janés/Cambio 16, 1989)

Trapiello, Andrés, *Las armas y las letras. Literatura y guerra civil (1936–1939)*, 3rd edn (Barcelona: Destino, 2010)

Tuñón de Lara, Manuel, *La España del siglo XX*, 2nd edn (Paris: Librería Española, 1973)

Turón Yebra, Manuel, 'El General Miguel Campins y su época (1880–1936)', doctoral thesis, Universidad Complutense de Madrid, 2002

Tusell, Javier, *Carrero. La eminencia gris del régimen de Franco* (Madrid: Temas de Hoy, 1993)

Tusell, Javier, *Franco en la guerra civil. Una biografía política* (Barcelona: Tusquets Editores, 1992)

Tusell, Javier, *Franco y los católicos. La política interior española entre 1945 y 1957* (Madrid: Alianza Editorial, 1984)

Tusell, Javier, *Franco, España y la II guerra mundial. Entre el Eje y la neutralidad* (Madrid: Temas de Hoy, 1995)

Tusell, Javier and Álvarez Chillida, Gonzalo, *Pemán. Un trayecto intelectual desde la extrema derecha hasta la democracia* (Barcelona: Editorial Planeta, 1998)

Tusell, Xavier, *La oposición democrática al franquismo, 1939–1962* (Barcelona: Editorial Planeta, 1977)

Tusell, Xavier and García Queipo de Llano, Genoveva, *Franco y Mussolini. La política española durante la segunda guerra mundial* (Barcelona: Editorial Planeta, 1985)

Tusquets Guillén, Esther, *Habíamos ganado la guerra* (Barcelona: Editorial Bruguera, 2007)

Ugarte, Javier, 'Represión como instrumento de acción política del Nuevo Estado (Álava, 1936–1939)', *Historia Contemporánea*, no. 35, 2007

Unamuno, Miguel de, *El resentimiento trágico de la vida. Notas sobre la revolución y guerra civil españolas* (Madrid: Alianza Editorial, 1991)

Vaca de Osma, José Antonio, *La larga guerra de Francisco Franco* (Madrid: Ediciones RIALP, 1991)

Valls, Ramona and Vilanou, Conrad, 'Joan Tusquets (1901–1998). Intellectual i pensador comparatista', *Revista Catalana de Teología*, vol. XXVII, no. 1, 2002

Varela Rendueles, José María, *Rebelión en Sevilla. Memorias de su Gobernador rebelde* (Seville: Ayuntamiento, 1982)

Vegas Latapie, Eugenio, *El pensamiento político de Calvo Sotelo* (Madrid: Cultura Española, 1941)

Vegas Latapie, Eugenio, *Escritos políticos* (Madrid: Cultura Española, 1940)

Vegas Latapie, Eugenio, *La frustración en la Victoria. Memorias políticas, 1938–1942* (Madrid: Editorial Actas, 1995)

Vegas Latapie, Eugenio, *Los caminos del desengaño. Memorias políticas 2, 1936–1938* (Madrid: Editorial Tebas, 1987)

Vegas Latapie, Eugenio, *Memorias políticas. El suicidio de la monarquía y la segunda República* (Barcelona: Editorial Planeta, 1983)

Venegas, José, *Andanzas y recuerdos de España* (Montevideo: Feria del Libro, 1943)

Vidarte, Juan-Simeón, *Las Cortes Constituyentes de 1931–1933* (Barcelona: Grijalbo, 1976)

Vidarte, Juan-Simeón, *No queríamos al Rey. Testimonio de un socialista español* (Barcelona: Grijalbo, 1977)

Vidarte, Juan-Simeón, *Todos fuimos culpables* (Mexico City: Fondo de Cultura Económica, 1973)

Vierge, Galo, *Los culpables. Pamplona 1936* (Pamplona: Pamiela, 2009)

Vigón, Jorge, *General Mola (el conspirador)* (Barcelona: Editorial AHR, 1957)

Vigueras Roldán, Francisco, *Los 'paseados' con Lorca. El maestro cojo y los banderilleros* (Seville: Comunicación Social, 2007)

Villa Rodríguez, José, 'Andalucía en la segunda República. Tiempo de Frente Popular (febrero–julio 1936)', doctoral thesis, Universidad de Sevilla, 2020

Villarín, Jorge, *Guerra en España contra el judaísmo bolchevique* (Cadiz: Establecimientos Cerón, 1937)

Vinyes, Ricard, *Irredentas. Las presas políticas y sus hijos en las cárceles franquistas* (Madrid: Ediciones Temas de Hoy, 2002)

Viñas, Ángel, *Franco, Hitler y el estallido de la guerra civil. Antecedentes y consecuencias* (Madrid: Alianza Editorial, 2001)

Viñas, Ángel, *Guerra, dinero, dictadura. Ayuda fascista y autarquía en la España de Franco* (Barcelona: Editorial Crítica, 1984)

Viñas, Ángel, *¿Quién quiso la guerra civil? Historia de una conspiración* (Barcelona: Editorial Crítica, 2019)

Volodarsky, Boris, *Stalin's Agent: The Life and Death of Alexander Orlov* (Oxford: Oxford University Press, 2013)

Wake, Jehanne, *Kleinwort Benson: The History of Two Families in Banking* (New York: Oxford University Press, 1997)

Warburg, Sidney, *El dinero de Hitler*, Prólogo y ampliaciones históricas de Mauricio Carlavilla, 'Mauricio Karl' (Madrid: Editorial Nos, 1955)

Whitaker, John, 'Prelude to World War. A Witness from Spain', *Foreign Affairs*, vol. 21, no. 1, October 1942–July 1943

Whitaker, John T., *We Cannot Escape History* (New York: Macmillan, 1943)

Woolman, David, *Rebels in the Rif: Abd el Krim and the Rif Rebellion* (Stanford, California: Stanford University Press, 1969)

Woolsey, Gamel, *Death's Other Kingdom* (London: Longmans, Green, 1939)

Worsley, T. C., *Behind the Battle* (London: Robert Hale, 1939)

Ximénez de Sandoval, Felipe, *José Antonio (Biografía apasionada)*, Prólogo de Ramón Serrano Suñer (Barcelona: Editorial Juventud, 1941)

Ximénez Embún, Juan and González Palencia, Angel, *Catálogo alfabético de los documentos referentes a títulos del Reino y Grandezas de España conservados en la sección de Consejos Suprimidos* (Madrid: Patronato Nacional de Archivos Históricos, 1951)

Ysart, Federico, *España y los judios en la segunda guerra mundial* (Barcelona: Dopesa, 1973)

Zugazagoitia, Julian, *Guerra y vicisitudes de los españoles*, 2 vols, 2nd edn (Paris: Librería Española, 1968)

Acknowledgements

Trapped in London by the pandemic during the writing of this book, I am in debt to the internet wizardry of Estanislao Sánchez Méndez and Stephen Rainbird, to the labours of Claudio Calles in the archives of Salamanca and to the generosity of Xabier Irujo for access to the papers of José María Iribarren.

Discussions with friends and colleagues have clarified my thought on numerous aspects of the book. Nearly half a century ago, Herbert Southworth alerted me to the toxic writings of Mauricio Carlavilla and the extraordinary career of Gonzalo de Aguilera. More recently, the insights of the clinical psychologist Dr Teresa Miguel Martínez and the psychiatrist Dr Arturo Ezquerro have greatly enriched my understanding of Aguilera. A correspondence initiated more than fifteen years ago with Eduardo Connolly de Pernas about the publications of both Carlavilla and Joan Tusquets has helped in the development of my views on both. Chris Ealham, and the late Josep Massot i Muntaner and Albert Manent helped me disentangle the untruths told by Father Tusquets in later life in order to obscure his less than Christian activities. Severiano Delgado Cruz and Luis Castro illuminated the role of José María Pemán in the persecution of the teaching profession. Ricardo Robledo's unique knowledge of the Salamanca landed class provided invaluable context to my chapter on Gonzalo de Aguilera. I am indebted to Emilio Majuelo and Miguel Sánchez-Ostiz for insight into the repression in Navarre while Mola conducted the war in the north. Rúben Sérem, Francisco Espinosa Maestre and José María García Márquez have regularly come to my aid with regard to Queipo's role in the repression in Seville and throughout Andalusia and Extremadura. Juan Miguel

Baquero and José Villa Rodríguez have helped me to understand the murky world of Queipo de Llanos's property dealings.

I am indebted to my friends Kathryn Phillips-Miles, Simon Deefholts, Linda Palfreeman and Lala Isla for their kindness in reading the text, weeding out stylistic infelicities and helping with translations of the more fanciful and recondite prose and poetry of José María Pemán and Ernesto Giménez Caballero. Yet again, I am delighted to be able to thank Peter James whose meticulous copy-editing invariably enhances my books.

List of Illustrations

Index